P9-DYZ-633

ON BECOMING Cuban

ON BECOMING Cuban

IDENTITY, NATIONALITY, AND CULTURE

Louis A. Pérez Jr.

The University of North Carolina Press   *Chapel Hill & London*

Set in Minion and Eagle types by Keystone Typesetting, Inc.

Manufactured in the United States of America

The paper in this book meets the guidelines for permanence and
durability of the Committee on Production Guidelines for Book
Longevity of the Council on Library Resources.

This book was published with the assistance of the H. Eugene and
Lillian Youngs Lehman Fund of the University of North Carolina
Press. A complete list of books published with the assistance of the
Lehman Fund appears at the end of the book.

Library of Congress Cataloging-in-Publication Data
Pérez, Louis A., 1943–
On becoming Cuban : identity, nationality, and culture / by
Louis A. Pérez, Jr.
    p. cm.
Includes bibliographical references and index.
ISBN 0-8078-2487-9 (cloth: alk. paper)
1. Cuba—Civilization—American influences. 2. Nationalism—Cuba—
History. 3. Cuba—Relations—United States. 4. United States—
Relations—Cuba. I. Title.
F1760.P47   1999
972.91—dc21   98-42664
                  CIP

04   03   02   01   00   6   5   4   3   2

For D M W

CONTENTS

ILLUSTRATIONS

ACKNOWLEDGMENTS

This book has been in the making for nearly ten years, started and stopped, repeatedly, in large part because it has involved a research commitment of daunting dimensions, one made all but impossible by other commitments, both professional and personal. It has sometimes been difficult to conceptualize and complete, for how it has ended was not how it began. In the process of research and writing, it changed constantly, its scope widened, its focus sharpened. Matters of organization and structure presented their own problems. The study moves generally, if unevenly, in chronological fashion. Sometimes the logic of the argument transcends the chronology; occasionally, it is the other way around. There is also repetition, and this, too, is central to the processes examined by this book, for the circumstances did indeed implicate Cubans in what Antonio Benítez Rojo has called *la isla que se repite*.

In recent years, opportunities have presented themselves with sufficient frequency and time to allow me to undertake major portions of the travel and research required, but most of all to finish the writing. The scope of my imaginings for this book no doubt all but guarantees that its goals will not be fully achieved, except perhaps by implication; it is hoped that such signposts will point the way to further investigation.

In this pursuit, many people have helped in many ways. I have been the beneficiary of exemplary generosity and support. Much has been obtained through the kindness of individuals, Cubans and North Americans, who lived through some of the years under study and gave unstintingly of their time and memories in personal interviews, telephone conversations, and extensive exchanges of correspondence. Many of them shared with me their personal archives, private letters, diaries, unpublished manuscripts, and journals. I especially appreciate the numerous responses I received from a *New York Times* "Author's Query" published in 1991, asking to hear from U.S. citizens who lived in Cuba between 1945 and 1959. I am particularly grateful to William H. Dorsey, Ann Hutchison, James C. Manning, Virginia Schofield, Ira Sherman, Richard A. Smith, and J. Bruce Swigert.

I have benefited enormously from the insight and accumulated wisdom of various others who study Cuba. They have had many divergent things to say about the ideas that follow, and it is inconceivable that this book would have taken its present form without their counsel and comments. There were hours and hours of animated conversations and spirited exchanges, long monologues and even longer dialogues, filled with the exhilaration and exasperation of scholarly disputation; ideas were challenged, defended, and modified; some arguments were confirmed and others contradicted; propositions were disputed, some of them disappearing permanently, some dropped but reappearing later in more cautiously constructed phrasings—all heady stuff and all reminders of the passion that ideas often generate.

I extend my profound gratitude to friends and colleagues who, during my work in Cuba in the very difficult times of the past decade, unfailingly extended me the warmest generosity and kindness. They shared private research materials as well as the findings of their own investigations. They provided me with the benefit of their own vast store of knowledge and erudition, for which I remain permanently in their debt. None of this can be adequately repaid, of course—it can only be acknowledged. I am especially indebted to Oscar Zanetti, Jorge Ibarra, Alejandro García, Manuel Moreno Fraginals, Hernán Pérez Concepción, Teresita Yglesia Martínez, Diana Abad, Carmen Barcia, Olga Cabrera, Carlos del Toro, Lohania Aruca, Elena Alavez, Ana Núñez Machín, Francisco Pérez Guzmán, Carmen Almodóvar, Enrique Collazo, Olga Portuondo Zúñiga, Eduardo Torres-Cuevas, José Cantón Navarro, and the late Ramón de Armas.

A particularly heartfelt acknowledgment is due Marel García and Fidel Requeijo, who, year after year while this research was in progress, provided me with the hospitality of their home and their friendship. In more ways than I can recount, more often than I can remember, they were always there: *resolviendo* and *inventando*. Their support of this project has been indispensable.

My work in Cuba would not have succeeded without the help of the administration and staff of the Archivo Nacional, the Biblioteca Nacional José Martí, the Centro de Estudios Martianos, the archival offices of *Bohemia* magazine, the University of Havana, the Instituto de Literatura y Lingüística, the Archivo Histórico Provincial de Matanzas, and especially the Instituto de Historia in Havana. Amparo Hernández Denis at the Instituto provided courteous assistance during the final phase of my research. Special gratitude is owed to Manuel López, director of the Instituto de Historia, for the constancy of his hospitality and support. I would be remiss if I did not single out Sergia Martínez, previously at the Instituto de Historia, for all the years of aid and encouragement, sometimes under difficult circumstances, and without which little else would have been possible.

I benefited greatly from the expertise of staff at many research centers in the United States, principally the National Archives, the Library of Congress, the Smithsonian Institution, the New York Public Library, the Special Collections Division of the University of Florida Library, the New-York Historical Society, the Butler Library of Columbia University, the Perkins Library of Duke University, the Archives and Manuscript Department of the McKeldin Library of the

University of Maryland at College Park, the Wilson Library of the University of North Carolina at Chapel Hill, the Special Collections Department of the Emory University Library, the Joyner Library of East Carolina University, the Friends Historical Collection at Guilford College, and the World Division of the United Methodist Church Archives in New York.

I cannot fully express my appreciation to the staff members of the University of South Florida Library who, during the early years of the project, helped me in ways large and small. Gayle G. Penner, Karen L. Roth, and Pamela S. Tucker never failed. And within the Inter-Library Loan Department, I owe an enormous debt to Mary Kay Hartung and Margaret M. Doherty, and especially to the wonderful, competent staff of Sharon Epps, Pamela See, and Eric Stewart. Research support from the National Endowment for the Humanities Travel to Collection grant and the American Council of Learned Societies Grant-in-Aid was vital in completing the research.

I owe an equally large debt to friends and colleagues who read all or portions of one or another draft of the manuscript and who listened patiently—and critically—to formulations and ideas in various stages of development, most notably Susan Fernández, John Flaherty, and Lars Schoultz. A special acknowledgment of gratitude is for Rebecca J. Scott, who gave the full manuscript a thorough and thoughtful reading. Luis Martínez-Fernández provided many helpful suggestions on the final draft. I am also grateful to Ada Ferrer, John M. Kirk, Gary R. Mormino, Thomas G. Paterson, Catherine M. Skwiot, Marsha Weissman, and James P. Woodard for generously making available to me information and materials obtained in the course of their own work.

That this book was completed in this century is in no small way the result of the invaluable assistance I received in preparing countless drafts and redrafts during the nearly five years of writing. I am indebted to Denise Marks for her help during the early drafts and to Rosalie Radcliffe for her vital support in the finalization of the manuscript. Most of all, I cannot fully express my appreciation to Carole L. Rennick for her support during all the years this manuscript was being prepared. She worked with—and through—early (and often nearly impossible) drafts from the beginning, again and again, always with patience and perseverance. Her collaboration was vital for the completion of this book.

I am also grateful to Elaine Maisner of the University of North Carolina Press for her support through the final phase of preparing the manuscript for publication. That the book has taken the form that it has is in no small way due to her sustained efforts in behalf of this project.

These are moments, further, to reflect on the growing up of my daughters Amara and Maya while this book was in process. Although they are out in the world now, they are never far from my thoughts. There are moments when I miss their childhood, but I am more than adequately compensated by my enjoyment of their adulthood.

Lastly, a special acknowledgment of appreciation to Deborah M. Weissman, who participated in so many different ways in this project. One could hardly ask for more.

Chapel Hill, North Carolina   L A P
September 1998

ON BECOMING Cuban

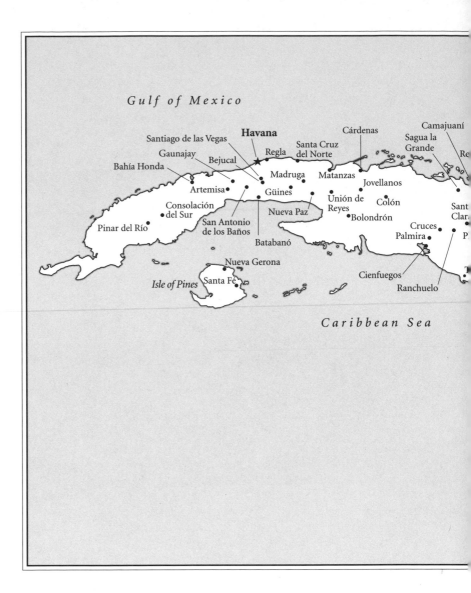

Gulf of Mexico

Camajuaní

Cárdenas

Sagua la
Grande

Re

Havana

Santiago de las Vegas

Santa Cruz
del Norte

Gaunajay

Regla

Bejucal

Bahía Honda

Madruga

Matanzas

Jovellanos

Artemisa

Güines

Unión de
Reyes

Colón

Sant
Clar

Consolación
del Sur

Nueva Paz

Bolondrón

Pinar del Río

San Antonio
de los Baños

Cruces

Palmira

P

Batabanó

Nueva Gerona

Cienfuegos

Ranchuelo

Isle of Pines

Santa Fé

Caribbean Sea

Atlantic Ocean

ibarién

án

• Morón

Spíritus

• Ciego De Avila

icaro

Nuevitas •

Puerto Padre

• Camagüey

Gibara

• Vertientes

Banes

• Martí

Victoria de
las Tunas

Holguín

Antilla

Sagua de Tánamo

Mayarí •

Alto Cedro

Manzanillo •

Bayamo •

Baracoa

Palma Soriano

San Luis •

El Caney

• Guantánamo

Santiago
de Cuba

Daiquirí

Caimanera

INTRODUCTION

This is a study of the Cuban–North American connection, not in the form of these relations, but as a relationship: its multiple and multifaceted aspects examined as one vast, interrelated constellation of factors and forces. The particular focus of the book is the Cuban encounter with the United States and the ways that this encounter influenced the context in which Cuban identity and nationality acquired recognizable forms. What Cubans derived from this experience shaped how they came to understand their relations with North Americans, no less than the relations among themselves. Attention is given to the diverse circumstances under which Cubans sustained contact with North Americans and came to know them, how that familiarity contributed to the assumptions by which Cubans presumed to understand the world, how North American ways revealed themselves, and how those revelations shaped the people Cubans became.

There has always been a temptation to address these issues separately, in monographic form: a study of, for example, Protestant missionaries, or tourism, or baseball and boxing, or music or popular culture, or the influence of motion pictures. But such an approach seemed incapable of yielding the desired outcome: namely, to understand the context and complexity of these linkages as a totality, as a system, and to see how connections worked together, like the strands of a web. In this study the individual strands of the web are examined but the web is left intact, thereby providing some understanding of the relationship of the parts to the whole. The objective is to examine the relationship between, for example, baseball and national identity, Protestant missionaries and revolution, North American motion pictures and television and the shaping of Cuban standards of self-presentation—how, in short, these and other factors contributed to arranging the terms by which nationality in Cuba assumed a distinctive form.

The experience under study spans approximately one hundred years, from the beginning of the 1850s to the end of the 1950s. This was a century of transformation, one that included a protracted struggle against Spanish colonial rule during which period the salient facets of what it meant to be Cuban were set in place. The early republican decades in Cuba coincided with far-reaching changes in the United States; indeed, it is almost impossible to understand postcolonial Cuba without appreciating the multiple ways in which North American developments insinuated themselves into Cuban life. The ascendancy of a consumer culture in the United States, the expansion and export of Hollywood films, advances in transportation and telecommunication systems, to cite some of the more obvious developments, had direct implications for Cuba. The island's struggle against dictatorship during the 1950s raised troubling questions about some of the most fundamental assumptions of daily life, which in turn contributed to what must be seen as a crisis of nationality after 1959.

The antecedents of the Cuban-U.S. relationship reached deeply into the nineteenth century, among Cubans who were searching for ways to give expression to nationality and who found in the United States much to choose from. The encounter occurred in ordinary, everyday fashion and involved hundreds of thousands of people throughout the century, at a time when the assumptions and aspirations that gave discernible meaning to national identity were developing.

Cubans and North Americans came to know each other well, through frequent and close contact, sometimes in pursuit of common objectives, but just as often in defense of conflicting interests. They populated each other's worlds, where they presented a familiar presence and early developed the type of familiarity often reserved for a people of the same nation—which meant, too, that they were susceptible to the influence of the other. They thus began to imitate each other, to borrow from each other, to become somewhat like each other.

Contact between Cubans and North Americans was neither uniform nor unilateral. It assumed many forms, and these forms changed over time. It moved in both directions, often repeatedly back and forth, transformed and transforming. In the course of a century the exchange was a force of enormous vitality, possessing its own logic and the capacity to drive cultural trends, influence social change, and shape political outcomes.

The two cultures converged on each other, interacting and merging, and fused in dynamic adaptation and accommodation. Cubans and North Americans occupied a place in each other's imagination and in their respective fantasies about each other. They intruded on one another as the national character of each was in the process of formation, which is to say that they entered each other's national consciousness and henceforth the character of each would retain permanent traces of this encounter.

The nineteenth century was a decisive time in the formation of Cuban nationality. These were years of a vast emigration to the United States, during which many of the principal arbiters of nationality settled in the North. The emigration included Cubans of all classes and ages, men and women, black and white, over three successive generations. Almost everyone of subsequent importance and influence, the many men and women who contributed to the meaning of nationality in the republic, possessed direct and firsthand living experience in the United States.

Much in the Cuban sense of future and of place in that future was shaped by or otherwise derived from the encounter with the North. The dominant facets of national consciousness were in formation, influenced by growing familiarity with a larger world in which North American usages insinuated themselves into émigré sensibilities. The experience was vital, for it enabled a great many Cubans to become familiar with the modern world, out of which alternative ideological systems and moral hierarchies passed directly into what was then being assembled as Cuban. Process created memory, and some of the central sources of nationhood were derived from experience in the North.

Change in Cuba always seemed to involve the United States as cause or effect, as a source or a means of change, or both. The well-being of many people, specifically as it related to economic development and prosperity, which also implies social peace and political order, was increasingly linked to the United States: entry to its markets, access to its products, use of its capital, application of its technology. At some point late in the nineteenth century, it became all but impossible for Cubans to contemplate their future, especially their future well-being, without pausing first to reflect on their relationship to North Americans.

North American influence was less a linear or unilateral imposition than a complex process of negotiation by which many of its most central propositions were embraced by Cubans as affirmations of progress that offered the promise of a better life. They more than adequately prepared the way for the subsequent arrival of North Americans as bearers of more of the same truths after the U.S. intervention in 1898. Many of the values that subsequently gave meaning to Cuban lives, collectively and individually, were of North American origin.

Throughout the nineteenth century Cubans appropriated and adapted as a means of national identity, principally to develop alternative forms to Spanish colonial claims, often consciously engaged in a process of self-definition as a means of self-determination. Cuban use of North American ways began first as an attempt to negotiate the terms of encounter with a wider world. Much in this transformation involved Cubans in the appropriation of North American forms, adapting them to their own needs, reshaping them in their own image, as imaginative—and, it should be added, effective—devices of national ascendancy. They were conscious of breaking with the colonial past and understood, too, that the point at which the break occurred represented a great divide that had to be crossed; this necessarily meant crossing new thresholds of consciousness of selfhood and nationhood.

The development of consciousness of "Cuban" was not a simple political formulation, of course. It had deeper meanings and larger associations with implications that transcended the pursuit of a free Cuba for Cubans. Also involved was a search for new ways to articulate power, which implied the need to devise different possibilities through which to envisage a new future. This endeavor found its dominant expression in an affirmation of modernity, progress, and above all civilization, much of which derived its main characteristics from North American sources.

In the nineteenth century U.S. forms expanded across the island. Important facets of daily life and ordinary social relations in Cuba were influenced by ways and things North American, often with Cuban acknowledgment and acquiescence, for these forms had become one of the primary means by which Cubans arrived at self-definition. Long before the U.S. intervention in 1898, many Cubans had already developed a familiarity with and an affinity for North American ways.

It is all but impossible to discuss the movement toward ways North American in any terms other than cultural: culture as environment, as context, as process— culture not simply as something that was possessed but culture as a condition that formed and informed the assumptions of daily life. These structures possessed, and indeed were defined by, the capacity to dominate, legitimize, and validate, but most of all they served as agents for integration into the larger normative systems from which they originated.

The idea of culture is used in this study to suggest generally the accumulated stock of values, understandings, and practices Cubans employed to live and maintain themselves, specifically the system of ideas about the nature of the world that served to define boundaries and condition behaviors, inform belief systems, and shape identities. In the pages that follow, attention is given especially to culture as the context within which Cubans assigned value to their actions and meaning to their experiences, the frame of reference by which they made sense of their daily lives. It is also meant to suggest those circumstances that fostered common action and uniform thought, the aggregate of public representations and private ruminations, which, in turn, shaped the social environment in which Cubans arrived at some understanding of what they could sustain as rational expectations and reasonable aspirations. This was a complex process, for it set into place standards by which to assess the capacity of social structures to meet commonly held expectations and aspirations. In the end, it functioned as the means by which identity was formed and fostered through coherence obtained by more or less consistent and generally shared points of view and moral renderings of self.

Central to this discussion is the proposition of national identity not as a fixed and immutable construct but rather as cultural artifact, as contested—and contesting—representations often filled with contradictions and incoherences, almost always in flux. This national identity constantly adjusts to and reconciles perceptions of reality with changing needs, and vice versa, with its own particular history, specifically a way to experience the meaning of inclusion of previously disparate constituencies within the notion of nationality. It is, as it were, a work in progress, in a state of continual development. This is identity as historically contingent, as both national expression and individual construction, possessing multiple forms, often simultaneously, sometimes successively; it is always changing with changing times: open not fixed, more a process than a product. In this sense, culture exists as a system of representation, signifying the practices and institutions from which nationality is derived and acted out.

The power of North American forms was registered early. This is not to suggest that the elements with which Cubans assembled the terms of national identity did not bear discernible moral and material influences from other sources. On the contrary, to be Cuban necessarily implied an amalgamation of diverse national, racial, and ethnic elements, principal among which was Europe, obviously Spain and to a lesser degree France and Italy, as well as Africa and to a lesser degree China. All of these elements exercised in varying degrees— at different times, among different sectors of the population—some influence in shaping the terms by which national identity was transacted. These circumstances were further mediated by notions of gender, class, religion, and age, and gave deeper complexity to the formulation of national identity.

These were sources and structures by which nationality formed, the ways through which identity itself became generally identifiable, through more or less shared values, particularly as they contributed to the definition of a distinct people with common interests. Culture as an aggregate of meanings and values created a coherent and shared sense of reality and often defined the social process by which Cubans were incorporated into the various aspects of their everyday life and through which they were linked to the proposition of nation.

This study has a number of methodological implications, for access to the aforementioned realms must be sought at the intersection of culture and consciousness, an approximation of the motives that guided the behaviors of Cubans, of the awareness that informed them, the constraints that limited them, the hopes that inspired them. They must be sought, too, in those areas of ambivalence and ambiguity between race and nationality, in the energies deployed across gender boundaries, in the persisting contradictions between culture and class, in areas where psychological representation and social reality overlap, and in the tensions between the desire to accommodate and the determination to resist.

Some relationships were clearly discernible and immediately suggested themselves as promising avenues of inquiry. The U.S. presence assumed many forms, and the character of that presence changed over time according to circumstances. It was most obviously economic and political, but it was most decisively cultural, whereby the influence of North American institutions, ideas, values, and norms took hold not through compulsion or coercion but by way of assent and acquiescence. At any given time during the final decades of the nineteenth century, but especially in the first half of the twentieth century, vast numbers of Cubans participated willingly in the very structures by which North American hegemony was exercised and experienced. It is the central proposition of this book that Cuban participation was indispensable to the success of U.S. hegemony and that Cubans bore some responsibility for their own domination, although it must be emphasized that few at the time would have remotely construed their condition as one of "subjugation."

Cubans early mastered the skills to negotiate their encounter with the North, which meant that they developed an extraordinary—but not unlimited—capacity to accommodate North American cultural forms in their midst. Cubans themselves introduced baseball to the island in the nineteenth century. Some of the most noteworthy Protestant inroads were registered by Cuban missionaries. These phenomena became even more pronounced in the twentieth century. Cuba was a country in which many citizens knew something about big-league baseball and professional boxing. Cubans participated eagerly in North American consumer culture and developed loyalties to U.S. brand names. They were unabashedly devoted to Hollywood, its movies and movie stars. In remote country stores it was common for rural consumers to have direct access to canned foods and ready-made clothing, as well as tools and farm equipment, manufactured in the United States, not as instruments of oppression, but as material goods eagerly adopted to improve daily life.

North Americans, in turn, in varying degrees throughout the twentieth century, appropriated and adapted elements of things Cuban in response to cultural transformations and commodity imperatives. Such negotiations took place in both Cuba and the United States, often as a result of tourism, typically by way of popular culture, most notably in the areas of music and dance. The resonance of U.S. hegemony was such, however, that Cubans often reappropriated North American representations of "Cuban" as a strategy calculated to accommodate North American market forms.

North American hegemony was experienced mainly as a cultural inflection: culture served to condition the moral order in which power was exercised and encountered and, in the end, the way power was registered and resisted. The vitality of North American forms was derived from their capacity to shape consciousness, to remake people by redefining the common assumptions of their everyday life.

These were not efforts devised explicitly to control Cubans. On the contrary, they were many of the same ways by which North Americans themselves were formed. And therein lay the power of things and ways North American. Due in part to historical circumstances and in part to geography, Cubans happened to have been among the first people outside the United States to come under the influence of North American material culture.

The success of U.S. hegemony in Cuba was less a function of political control and military domination than a cultural condition in which meaning and purpose were derived from North American normative systems. U.S. influence expanded from within, usually in noncoercive forms, just as often introduced by Cubans themselves as by North Americans. U.S. culture spread rapidly across the island and emerged as one of the most accessible means by which to aspire to well-being and thus was a powerful motivator in the acceptance of new social norms and new cognitive categories. This was the principal way that Cubans entered the postcolonial order, the circumstances under which social institutions were formed and moral hierarchies established, the means by which many citizens arranged the terms of their familiarity with the world at large.

This is not to minimize the role of coercion and violence in defense of the status quo. U.S. armed intervention occurred periodically. Political intermeddling was constant. Nor were these methods of social control and political domination unimportant. Economic control and political power served to obtain some measure of Cuban acquiescence, and could—and did—act as powerful forces to secure Cuban emulation of what was increasingly becoming known as the "American way of life."

But for all the prominence traditionally accorded to the application of force as a method of domination, it was in the end of secondary importance. It was certainly of comparatively lesser consequence and a far more problematical means of obtaining acquiescence to North American interests. On the contrary, force was often counterproductive to the maintenance of the consensual context necessary to sustain U.S. hegemony. Coercion—the open and explicit use of, or threat to use, force and violence—often aroused strong nationalist reactions, immediately and thereafter, and in the process could call into question any Cuban affinity for things North American. An ordinary and otherwise commonplace preference for North American clothing fashions, for example, or the utterance of a North American phrase, like a simple "okay," or a mannerism, like chewing gum, could arouse suspicion, create doubt about one's allegiance, or, in the most extreme circumstances, result in exclusion of or heap discredit on the defenders of North American ways. In certain situations it could jeopardize the very social structures on which U.S. hegemony depended. Such was the case after 1959 and must be considered as central to events immediately following the triumph of the Cuban revolution.

North American influences became a factor in Cuban identity at the time of national formation. They metabolized from within during the routine negotiations of daily life and served as the principal elements by which Cubans arranged their individual lives, assembled their world, and gave meaning to both. Patterns of socialization, modalities of public communication and language, canons of style and self-representation, religion and recreation, no less than dress and demeanor, tastes and toys, were swayed—often decisively—by North American practices and conventions. That these were not usually perceived as instruments of hegemony made them no less central to the workings of systems of domination. Many of these forms were introduced by Cubans, voluntarily and without duress, often joyfully, with exuberance and expectation, as part of everyday, commonplace existence, sometimes with the best of intentions, and almost always in the belief that this approach promised a better life. Such circumstances did not make an affinity for things North American any less real or any less effective as an agent of social control. North American ways, in the end, could not have been imposed from the outside without Cubans on the inside willing and even eager to transform themselves.

That many U.S. practices and products subsequently served as the source of North American domination does not diminish the authenticity of the Cuban intent. It is important to stress that these forms could be transfigured again, for they were constantly in flux and always retained the capacity to provoke national mobilization. Precisely because so many Cubans accepted these truths, from which they devised assumptions and developed aspirations as the ordinary and unremarkable course of their lives, North American ways served to transport them across thresholds that people of few other countries could have even imagined.

Adaptive responses began early. Cubans observed North American ways both at close range and from afar, as colleagues and employees, in social clubs and classrooms, in professional associations and civic organizations, as visitors abroad and hosts at home, through magazines and motion pictures. Responses in the cities differed from those in the countryside, and differences in time—between what was possible at the end of the nineteenth century and the opportunities available in the mid-twentieth century. But it was not simply a matter of appropriation and adaptation. The situation was far more complex. Out of the Cuban encounter with the North, in part as result, in part as reaction, developed new frames of reference, new hierarchies of values, new systems of norms. Because this process was continuous and commonplace, it could not avoid ambivalence and antagonism. It often called into question the means by which Cubans experienced cultural authenticity; it raised doubts about the adequacy—to saying nothing of the authority—of Cuban institutions to articulate and advance national interests.

This was a process that concerned Cubans of all classes, men and women, black and white, young and old, in the city and in the countryside. So thoroughly had North American forms penetrated the structural order of daily life that it was often almost impossible to make a sharp distinction between what was properly "Cuban" and what was "North American." In the end, to challenge "North American," as after the Cuban revolution of 1959, was to challenge what it meant to be "Cuban."

These relationships endured in varying degrees over the course of a century, often in ways that ceased to be apprehended at all. They operated as a system possessed of its own logic. Because that system lacked organization does not mean that it was without order. The power of North American forms resided expressly in their capacity to assume the appearance of normal and ordinary, the ease with which their major elements could be appropriated, and the degree to which these elements influenced the standards to which Cuban men and women aspired to achieve self-definition and self-worth. It is not clear that Cubans fully discerned the sources of their own formation. What is apparent, however, is that U.S. forms penetrated so deeply through habitual usage and became so much a part of everyday life as to be indistinguishable from what passed as commonplace, but most of all for what passed as Cuban.

As the scope and sway of North American hegemony expanded, so did Cuban doubt and disappointment. The boundaries of hegemonic structures rarely came together neatly with complete coherence and congruence. The lines of domination and subordination often converged and overlapped, but just as frequently they diverged and counteracted. They produced contradiction and conflict, ambiguity and ambivalence, creating in the process social space and theoretical alternatives often not possible under any other circumstances.

The North American presence and the Cuban response represented less a clash of abstract social forces than a long and complicated struggle of ordinary people, with common if conflicting interests, human beings with limited resources who often acted out of only partially coherent motives. There were few real heroes or villains among the men and women who participated in these cultural transactions, from which they derived their normative orientations and ideological bearings. Rather, they were mostly trying to get by, accepting reality largely as they found it, choosing to adapt and accommodate rather than to change or challenge. They were, in the end, formed by the community in which they participated in unremarkable fashion. They acquiesced to the everyday, commonplace assumptions of the world as they found it, in the conviction that compliance to prevailing norms would deliver the material bounty, the economic security, and the personal well-being that were the central promises on which North American market culture rested.

This was a complex process, to be sure, teeming with paradoxes and inconsistencies, and though signs abounded everywhere, they were not always apparent. The power of U.S. hegemony was embedded in cultural forms that served as the principal means by which the North American presence was legitimized. It just happened that these forms also served as the means by which North American influences were contested and otherwise diminished or eliminated altogether. They were often the same methods that Cubans employed to articulate nationality. It was perhaps, in the end, a measure of the vitality of North American structures and the creative power of adaptation that these were often the basis on which Cubans chose to challenge the United States.

It is not altogether clear when the grip of North American normative systems, with their derivative emphasis on market culture and consumption, loosened their hold sufficiently to allow Cubans to reexamine the assumptions on which their appeal was based. The process seems to have been well advanced by the

1950s, as North American market culture was increasingly revealing itself to be incapable of meeting Cuban aspirations. The gap between expectations and experience was expanding. This was a lengthy process that unfolded gradually, one that without the political crisis after 1952 might well have persisted for decades if not indefinitely, institutionalized in political competition and cultural transactions, primarily as creative tensions in art, music, fashion, literature, and lifestyles. It was present in those realms of partial recognition, of inchoate awareness and vague perceptions, in the space of human experience where people detect malaise and sense that things are not quite right, but are unable to order them in narrative description or articulate the source of their misgivings; or where they see that things are obviously wrong simply by looking around but are unable to say exactly why, or what should be done and how. It was at that point that Cubans were most susceptible to change. Although they were uncertain that it was exactly the change they wanted, it seemed coherent and compelling, and they went along.

This uncertainty contributed to the undermining of Cuban institutions from within. The military coup by Fulgencio Batista in March 1952 created a context of political illegitimacy that soon raised corollary questions about the moral foundations of institutions of public authority that governed daily life and the authenticity of democratic values. With only limited opportunities to deploy political remedies in response to the deepening social and economic distress of the 1950s, many Cubans resorted to creative deployment of cultural forms to express discontent, which in turn contributed simultaneously to a generalized and deepening crisis, for the authenticity of national structures was found wanting and called into question. Cultural change suggested possibility and expanded the sphere of dissent. Culture thus became a way to develop imaginary strategies to change real conditions, largely as a substitute for the political, but in fact possessed of the capacity to summon alternative visions of the function of the political.

The circumstances under which Cubans plunged into euphoric celebration of revolutionary experimentation in 1959 were found less in propositions than in dispositions. This was a triumph more of will than rationality and in its own way was a replaying of a logic peculiarly Cuban, with antecedents in the nineteenth century: that the potential and the promise of nationality—of being Cuban—was within reach if only the "weight" of North American hegemony could be lifted.

A relationship spanning many decades, involving many generations, came to a climax in an enormously complex denouement in 1959. It is clear now that even the leading actors in those developments, on both sides, did not fully comprehend the complexity of the forces that drove the policies and the politics of the time. The most contentious issues of 1959 had roots that ran deep and wide, encompassing every aspect of the human condition, and were themselves a product of a familiarity from which presumptions were easy to make but difficult to act upon. Well before the revolution in January 1959, many Cubans had come to doubt the assumptions that long had given meaning and purpose to their lives. They had subscribed to those assumptions in good faith, only to discover that they were no longer capable of meeting their needs.

I

BINDING FAMILIARITIES

Every young man's ambition seems to be to go North.
—Samuel Hazard, *With Pen and Pencil*, 1871

We Cubans have come here in search of personal freedom, in return for which we brought with us capital, talent, honest labor and morality. We imported with us the great industry of cigar making and have built up large and prosperous cities, Key West, Ybor City and West Tampa. The first of these a poor uninhabited island and the others lonesome, uncultivated pine lands were soon converted into large and prosperous cities which is due to the constant, productive labor of the law-abiding, liberal handed Cuban people whom [*sic*] never . . . called for alms on the American people. But who instead has contributed more millions of dollars to the United States treasure annually than any other single industry in the whole entire country . . . enriching the business community and being less trouble to the courts of justice of the country than any other foreign people and even the natives themselves.
—M. A. Montejo, Letter to Editor, *Tampa Morning Tribune*, September 12, 1896

The Cuban, as traveler and observer, has visited all parts of the world in search of new ways to introduce into his country, to improve and perfect its industries, to make his life more comfortable.
—Enrique José Varona, 1896

Resemblance [between Cuba and the United States] has been increased by the proximity and frequency of intercourse between the two countries, by an identity of social institutions and aspirations, and by the large number of Cuban youth educated there. . . . The ideas and manner of thought with which they return to the island, are more American than Spanish, and these are continually extended by their influence and their example.
—John S. Thrasher, 1851

Havana will soon become as much American as New Orleans.
—Anthony Trollope, *The West Indies and the Spanish Main*, 1862

The connections began early—almost at the beginning, in fact: first as frontiers of the same empire, later as colonies of rival empires. But imperial rivalries intruded little, if at all, on colonial realities. New World requirements—not Old World regulations—served to shape much of the course and character of contact. Both economies adjusted to the participation of the other, and in the process developed vital linkages on which the well-being of each depended. Cubans and North Americans discovered early that colonists even of rival empires often had more in common with one another than they did with the authorities who governed them. They developed needs that each was uniquely qualified to meet, or perhaps it was the other way around: they developed those needs precisely because they could be so well met by the other. Proximity and accessibility promoted affinity, which joined them in a relationship that was simultaneously reciprocal and inexorable. Geography made these connections possible and convenient; circumstances made them practical and necessary.

SOURCES OF THE BEGINNING

Trade was one important link and early established the basis on which familiarity developed and contact increased. Access to North American markets made the expansion of Cuban sugar production possible and profitable, and the decision to pursue economic development through sugar exports quickly assumed a logic of its own, driven by expansion and more expansion: expanded cultivation, expanded production, expanded exports in pursuit of expanding markets.

But it was not simply a matter of producing more sugar, more efficiently, more profitably. Cuban success was very much derived from a strategy of specialization: production for export at the expense of production for consumption, increasingly to the exclusion of other products, eventually to the exclusion of other markets. It was more cost effective to rely on food imports for internal consumption than sacrifice sugar exports for external markets. That the United States could meet these needs, as well as provide Cuba with necessary industrial and manufactured supplies, from comparatively short distances, in relatively short periods of time, and at reasonably low transportation costs, gave Cuban development its distinctive and definitive characteristics.

The capacity of the United States to provide Cuba with the means with which to expand was at least as important as markets in which to expand. Sugar planters were soon alert to the possibilities of innovation and industrial progress; they were especially receptive to the use of new technologies to improve efficiency and increase production. Producers were direct beneficiaries of North American industrial development, and, indeed, the transfer of technology became a normal part of the stock in trade between Cuba and the United States. The logic of the connection was as compelling as it was self-evident. Reduced travel time and lower transportation costs meant that spare parts, repairs, and replacement pieces for North American machinery could be obtained faster and cheaper than for European equipment.[1]

Technological innovation reached Cuba early and easily, often the instant it became available in the United States. New technology arrived in surges and in succession, often with unexpected results but always with effect. Innovation and renovation became the imperatives driving production, the means, too, by which Cuba was integrated into advanced industrial modes of the North.

Access to technology from the United States served to shape all facets of Cuban economic activity: production strategies no less than transportation systems, commercial relations as well as consumption patterns. Steam power was introduced as early as 1819 and immediately transformed sugar production through improved efficiency and increased exports. Coastwise steamship service arrived in the same year, when entrepreneur Juan O'Farrill bought the *Neptuno* in New Orleans and inaugurated weekly passenger and cargo service between Havana and Matanzas, only a decade after the first commercial use of steamships in the North. Additional steamships were subsequently purchased in the United States, and by 1842 a total of six vessels operated along both coasts of Cuba. Scheduled steamship service with the United States commenced in 1836 and by midcentury linked Havana directly with New York, Philadelphia, Baltimore, Mobile, New Orleans, and Key West.[2]

The railroad arrived during the 1830s and subsequently entered the key sugar zones of Matanzas–Unión de Reyes, Puerto Príncipe–Nuevitas, Cienfuegos–Santa Clara, Cárdenas-Colón, Remedios-Caibarién, Matanzas-Jovellanos, Casilda-Trinidad, and Havana-Matanzas. In all, more than six hundred miles of railroad extended across the island by midcentury, west to east, along both coasts, linking the major sugar districts in the interior with export points on the coast. By the 1890s Cuba claimed the highest ratio of railroad lines to total load mass of all Latin America: 24.6 kilometers of rail for every 1,000 kilometers of national territory.[3]

The telegraph was introduced by Samuel A. Kennedy of New York in 1851, only five years after the completion of the first successful system in the United States. Havana was linked with Bejucal, Güines, and Cárdenas; lines were subsequently extended to Batabanó and Matanzas. Within fifteen years, the Cuban telegraph system connected twenty cities and towns, reaching as far east as Santiago de Cuba. By the late 1850s telegraph service was handling nearly 50,000 messages annually. In 1859 Cuba was linked by boat with the telegraph terminus in Cedar Key, Florida. Submarine cable connected Havana directly with Key West in 1867, only one year after the completion of the North Atlantic cable.[4]

As a result of these developments, production modes, transportation systems, and communication networks expanded around goods and services originating from the North and gave decisive form to the ways in which both economies were forging structural unity. Steam-powered machinery was manufactured by Merrick and Sons of Philadelphia, the Novelty Iron Works of New York, Isaac and Seth Adams of Boston, and the West Point Foundry. Locomotives were built by Porter and Company and Baldwin Locomotive Works of Philadelphia, Schenectady Locomotive Works, and Boston Locomotive Works. Freight cars and passenger coaches were purchased from Davenport and Company of Cambridgeport, New Haven Car Company, Harlan and Holingsworth of Wilmington, and Eaton and Gilbert of Troy. The International Ocean Telegraph Company of New York operated the cable system.

These developments had implications of other kinds. North American machinery required the expertise of trained personnel to install, operate, and service the new equipment. Coastwise steamship service was maintained by North American crews. Railroads were constructed under the supervision of U.S. engineers and operated by U.S. conductors and crews. Poet William Cullen Bryant was not the first foreigner to marvel at traveling in Cuba "by railway, in a car built at Newark, drawn by an engine made in New York, and worked by an American engineer."[5] North Americans provided continuing maintenance of locomotives, rolling stock, track, roadbed, and stations. All through the 1850s, thousands of U.S. workers—mainly engineers, mechanics, and foremen—traveled annually to Cuba to work on the railroads.[6]

Technicians and machinists (*maquinistas*) also arrived to operate and maintain the steam-powered machinery on the sugar estates. "American steam-engines are fast taking the place of animal power," Maturin M. Ballou observed in 1854, "and more or less are monthly exported for this purpose from New York, Philadelphia and Boston. This creates a demand for engineers and machinists, for whom the Cubans are also dependent upon this country." Visiting Cuba several years later, Richard Dana met a North American engineer employed on a Matanzas sugar estate, "one of a numerous class, whom the sugar culture brings annually to Cuba," he noted. "They leave home in the autumn, engage themselves for the sugar season, put the machinery in order, work it for the four or five months of its operation, clean and put it in order for lying by, and return to the United States in the spring. They must be machinists, as well as engineers; for all the repairs and contrivances, so necessary in a remote place, fall upon them."[7]

North Americans integrated themselves at all levels of the Cuban economy. They owned and operated sugar estates, coffee plantations, tobacco farms, and cattle ranches. Visiting Cuba in 1856, George Williams was surprised to find "quite a number of planters from the United States residing here."[8] Increasingly, too, North Americans expanded into other sectors of the economy. U.S. geologists, engineers, and surveyors operated the mines around which developed thriving boomtowns in Pinar del Río, Daiquirí, El Caney, and Santiago de Cuba.[9] In Regla, the great depot of molasses trade, the foundry vital to the maintenance of molasses tanks was constructed and operated by the North American firm Van DeWater and Company.

U.S. mercantile houses, retailers, and shipping agents spread across the island, becoming a ubiquitous presence in almost all port cities along both coasts, east to west (see Appendix Table 1.1). They provided foodstuffs and manufactured goods, extended credit arrangements, and accepted in return sugar and molasses as payment. As transmitters of innovation and material progress, they were one of the principal mediums through which new industrial technologies, production strategies, and equipment entered Cuba.

North American merchants served as channels through which capital subsidized the movement of Cuban exports to U.S. markets and thereby helped finance local production. Merchants summoned into existence new financial structures, insurance systems, shipping agencies, freight handlers, and a host of enterprises specializing in the financing and transportation as well as marketing and distribution of exports and imports. They were conversant with production specifications, price levels, and marketing trends at a time when few other sources of such information were available. "The prosperity of the island has derived no small advantage from those numerous American establishments," asserted English writer Richard Madden in 1849. He continued:

> Improved modes of agriculture, of fabrication, of conveyance, were introduced by the Americans. . . . The substitution in Cuba of the old grinding-mill, rudely constructed of wood, by steam-engine machinery, is also chiefly due to the Americans. To them, therefore, Cuba is indebted for the various improvements in the fabrication of sugar, and modes of conveyance of the produce of its plantation, which enable the proprietors to compete so successfully with those of the English colonies. Cuba, ever since I knew it, has been slowly but steadily becoming Americanised.[10]

As the volume of trade increased, so did maritime traffic. "Vessels are constantly arriving and departing, for the commerce of this place is immense," Margaret Morton Quincy observed in Havana as early as 1828. At midcentury the Cuban trade accounted for as many U.S. merchant vessels as were engaged in the total trade with England and France: 1,702 in 1850 and 2,088 in 1856; only trade with Canada and England exceeded the total tonnage of U.S. trade with Cuba. Hundreds of merchant vessels crowded into Havana harbor; many more lighters swarmed around the port, moving cargo and passengers from ship to shore and back again. The view was breathtaking. Richard Dana marveled at the sight: "What a world of shipping! The masts make a belt of dense forest along the edge of the city, all the ships lying head into the street, like horses at their mangers; while the vessels at anchor nearby choke up the passage ways to the deeper bays beyond."[11]

The number of permanent North American residents swelled throughout the nineteenth century. Between 1846 and 1862 the U.S.-born population of Cuba almost doubled: from 1,260 to nearly 2,500.[12] They settled mostly in the capital—

"Havana is crowded with *Americanos*," George W. Williams commented in 1855—and across the northern coast, as far east as the mining regions of Oriente province. John Glenville Taylor noted that the "district of Holguin, of which Gibara is the port of entry, can boast of more English-speaking society than many other foreign places, of equal size and note." Richard Madden was astonished to discover that "some districts on the northern shores of the island, in the vicinity, especially, of Cárdenas and Matanzas, have more the character of American than Spanish settlements." This presence had become more pronounced ten years later, when R. G. Gibbes visited the province: "Matanzas being mainly settled by citizens from the United States, our language is more common there than in any other Cuban city, and the customs of the place are more Americanized." Cárdenas, in particular, was filled with North Americans and in such numbers that by midcentury it was commonly described as an "American city." "Cárdenas contains about 5000 inhabitants and quite a number of these are Americans," wrote Joseph Dimock in 1859. "I noticed among the clerks and correspondents a great many Yankees. . . . A great number of Americans have come out here with the intention of locating. . . . Cárdenas harbor is full of vessels of which more than half are American, and one sees so many Yankees in the streets that it seems quite homelike here."[13]

Spanish authorities were less cheerful about the growing U.S. presence in Cuba. As early as 1838, Governor General Miguel Tacón was troubled by the increasing number of foreign mining enterprises in Oriente province, warning that it "appears impossible . . . to prevent the miners from introducing Methodist sects and doctrines, that could cause insubordination among the slaves and introduce into our midst confusion and disorder." A decade later, concerned officials in both Cuba and Spain urged that North American acquisition of property on the island be restricted. Three successive governor generals noted the pernicious effects of the North American presence. "The colonies of the Americans on the island increase from day to day," Conde de Alcoy reported in 1849, "as can be seen in the increase registered in Sagua la Grande, Cienfuegos, Matanzas, Cárdenas, etc. Daily the Americans purchase extensive territories and under their auspices Cárdenas is being reborn into a new city." Two years later José G. de la Concha sounded a similar alarm, but with greater urgency and sobriety. The island "has been inundated with foreigners," he argued, "principally from the American Union," who "without doubt [are] the most prejudicial, not only because it appears so natural that they participate in the spirit of expansion . . . that characterizes their country and their democratic tendencies, but also because they are distributed mostly in the countryside, working on the sugar mills and railroads as maquinistas, they disseminate their subversive doctrines everywhere." North Americans had "expanded fully across the island," de la Concha declared, "with far-reaching and baneful consequences." Some of these consequences were apparent even as he wrote. "The English-language has spread among the natives (*naturales*)," remarked Valentín Cañedo shortly thereafter, "not only among the youth of both sexes in the cities and large towns, but even among men well beyond school age."[14]

The island also attracted a large floating population of North Americans. They arrived year-round, for business and for pleasure, travelers in transit, workers under contract, tourists on holiday—mostly to escape the rigors of northern winters and for rest and respite. Many, like former presidents Ulysses S. Grant and Grover Cleveland, traveled for reasons of health and convalescence, to take the warm baths of Güines, San Diego de los Baños, and Madruga. Chemist Richard McCulloh found Güines "a place much frequented by strangers, and particularly by consumptive invalids from the United States." Julia Ward Howe divided the guests in her Havana hotel into "two classes": "invalids and men of business."[15]

Cuba entered the North American imagination as the "tropics," which is to say, as the opposite of what the United States was, specifically what it was not. This was travel less to a place than to a time, to a past in which to pursue undistracted pleasure, in which to linger delighted with the promise of recuperation and rejuvenation—indeed, the island gave a new meaning to recreation and, if not to life eternal, certainly to life anew. To be in Cuba was to be transported back to a simpler time, less rushed and more contemplative. "The scene of things here," Sophia Peabody Hawthorne confided to her diary in 1835, "has all along reminded me of those times described in English novels—when the lords & ladies bright are all in the country & doing every sort of delightful thing for amusement—& there is an abundance of beauty & grace & wit & merriment & music & riding & looking at pictures & drawing, etc etc."[16]

Few travelers to Cuba failed to evoke the image of an earlier time, in fact, the beginning of time, which, of course, was to transcend temporal dimensions and imply another place altogether. "Almost could I have fancied," Charles Rosenberg wrote during a visit to Matanzas, "that I had entered unawares upon that Garden of Paradise, whence our first parents had been driven at the will of their offended Maker." Fredrika Bremer proclaimed Cuba to be the "outer court of Paradise," where the "forms and colors of the vegetation seem to typify a transition from earthly life to a freer and a loftier sphere of beauty." Amelia Murray could not understand why Cuba "made me feel dreamy, as I had never felt before," and Eliza McHatton-Ripley called Havana a "bit of a fairy land." George Williams wrote: "It has awakened new life, love and joy in my soul. . . . No wonder it is considered a paradise!" Cuba was "the Paradise of the earth," exulted Edward Tailer. Silvia Sunshine termed the island a "modern Eden," and John Abbott concluded that "God formed it apparently for a terrestrial paradise."[17]

North American tourists arrived by the thousands. At midcentury about five thousand vacationers and visitors traveled from the United States to Havana annually—"a very large proportion of whom are gentlemen and ladies of the highest respectability," noted the U.S. consul in 1860—and several thousand more entered the island by way of provincial ports.[18]

A vast transient traffic passed through Cuba yearly. The California gold rush placed the island directly on the Isthmian route to and from the west coast. During the sugar harvest North American merchant vessels crowded into Cuban ports, for weeks and months at a time, and crews numbering in the tens of thousands passed their idle time ashore in pursuit of diversion and entertainment. In the 1880s an estimated 32,000 U.S. seamen visited Havana annually.[19]

Something of a tourist industry developed to meet the needs of travelers from the United States. One North American family owned and operated a successful horse and carriage rental business in Havana. Physician Robert Morrell owned an estate near Havana where he pursued a lucrative medical practice that catered to invalid tourists, hosting such notable New Englanders as Oliver Prescott, the Reverend Abiel Abbott, and Sophia Peabody Hawthorne. North Americans also bought and operated a network of hotels and boardinghouses that extended along both coasts, in almost all the major port cities, and bore such names as the Planter's Hotel, Hewitt House, American Hotel, Mansion House, Washington Hotel, Ensor House, and Havana House. Many local merchants recognized the business potential of North American travel. In 1859 Joseph Dimock observed that many Havana stores had posted "English spoken here" signs.[20]

The U.S. presence created needs of other kinds, and more North Americans arrived to meet them. Bars, brothels, and bistros, operated by North Americans principally for North Americans, expanded along both coasts. They became familiar features of the bay streets of the port cities; around these streets there developed a nether world into which North Americans of almost every social type descended. Each year hundreds of railroad laborers, construction workers, and merchant crew members crowded the streets of Havana, many abandoned and without the means to return home—described graphically if unsympathetically by the U.S. consul as "destitute . . . broken down in health, scarcely able to walk, without money, and unable to speak the language of the country . . . crippled, sick, ragged, hungry, weeping." The brothels of Havana were filled with North American women, many hired directly from the United States, others stranded in Cuba without resources or a job, some newly widowed, others recently unemployed. Ellen N. King from New London, Connecticut, obtained work in a Havana brothel after she was dismissed as a governess from a Cienfuegos estate. Actress Adah Isaacs Menken was abandoned by her lover in Havana in 1853; penniless, she turned to prostitution to earn her passage back to the United States.[21]

Drifters and deserters, fugitives and escaped convicts, North Americans with reason for flight, selected Cuba as the destination of choice. Scores of seamen deserted there. In 1860 Tammany Hall boss Isaac Fowler absconded with $150,000 to Havana. When William R. Tweed escaped from a New York prison in 1876, he made straight for Santiago de Cuba. Many Confederate officers, politicians, and planters fled to Cuba after Appomattox, including Generals John C. Breckenridge, Robert A. Toombs, Birkett Fry, John B. Magruder, Jubal A. Early, Commodore John N. Maffitt, and former Louisiana governor Thomas Overton Moore.[22]

In short, North Americans were conspicuous, and their presence rarely passed unnoticed by visitors to the island. Edward Robert Sullivan wrote at midcentury of the "Americans, particularly those returning from California, [who] used to swagger into the *cafés* and restaurants, where they drank raw brandy and devoured pounds of ice, as if for a wager." British historian James Anthony Froude found his hotel "full to overflowing" with North American tourists: "The dining saloon rang with American voices in their shrillest tones. Every table was occupied by groups of them, nor was there a sound in the room of any language but theirs."[23]

Services of other kinds developed to meet the needs of this population. Physicians and dentists from the United States established practices in the North American communities.[24] Many married into local creole families and remained permanently. North American residents soon established their own hospital on finding Cuban hospital facilities unsatisfactory—"in every respect inferior to similar private and local institutions in our own country," complained the U.S. consul.[25] Eventually, the U.S. colony also acquired its own cemetery.

DEFINING DIFFERENCES

For much of the nineteenth century Cuba was in transition. Market-induced change was always at work and always working to change everything else. Expectations altered, as did the ways that Cubans defined their needs and defended their interests. Change produced circumstances that called into question even the most ordinary assumptions of colonial relationships, which increasingly lost credibility—all of which created a readiness for more change or suggested the need for faster change.

Many changes could be quantified in a variety of ways. Increased sugar production was weighed and its value calculated. Rising land values were assessed. Expanding trade revenues were tallied in the form of customs duties, sales taxes, and import fees.

But change could also be invisible or unmeasurable: some of the most momentous shifts in Cuba did not become apparent until many years later. Nevertheless, change was always at work—inexorably, relentlessly governing the lives of vast numbers of people. Technology, transportation, and communications transformed social relations, not just by rearranging the demography of stratification but by remaking all the cultural and material elements of what passed for modernity.

Greater familiarity with the United States contributed to this process. The North American presence served both as a source of change and a measure of change and increasingly assumed structural form inside Cuba. Not all of this change was new, of course; much of it was actually derived from Cuban sources. The requirements of sugar production had already created an environment in which efficiency and planning were central to continued economic development. Cubans shared with North Americans some basic values, including performance, organization, and instrumental rationality, all of which more than adequately lent themselves to North American production methods. Manuel Moreno Fraginals was correct to call attention to the entrepreneurial spirit of the creole bourgeoisie, which regarded the old titled aristocracy and landed nobility with resentment and repugnance. "Nor are they wanting in enterprise," William Hulbert wrote of creoles in 1854. "Cuba, in the matter of railways, may compare favorably with many of the American States, and the railways are the result of Creole energy and enterprise. The Creole planters are indefatigable in their efforts to improve their estates, and to develop the resources of their magnificent island."[26] It is arguable that this was the first creole ruling class whose authority was based not on titles but on achievements. This leadership produced new paradigms of entrepreneurial mobilization and demonstrated through organized and concerted action the capacity to change its world.

What was different at midcentury was that adjustment to market forces necessarily involved new attitudes and methods, a process that extended in many directions concurrently and in varying degrees affected all of Cuba. Part of this involved greater familiarity with, increased use of, and inevitable accommodation to business techniques and commercial practices of the North. This created new opportunities for increased contact with the United States and new ways of introducing Cubans to North American normative structures.

Change also produced discontent and disaffection. Most immediately, change exposed the contradictions of colonialism and set in relief the numerous ways that continued economic development could no longer be contained within existing colonial structures. On all counts, and all at once, Spanish colonialism was straining to accommodate to changes driving the Cuban economy—and revealing itself incapable of doing so. Spain could not furnish adequate shipping to handle Cuban foreign trade or provide suitable markets for Cuban exports. Nor could it supply the capital to finance expansion or the technology to modernize production.

The implications were unambiguous. The importance of Spain to the Cuban economy was diminishing, in almost every sphere, and with far-reaching consequences. Production advances and industrial innovation had transformed key sectors of the colonial economy. Development had been swift, in some instances spectacular. Production increased dramatically, as did exports from and imports to Cuba. Linkages with world markets had enabled Cuba to benefit early and directly from the rapid changes in capitalist production modes, many of which did not reach Spain until years later. Steam-powered machinery was commonplace in Cuba before it was known in Spain. So were steamships. It was not until 1848 that the first railroad operated in Spain. The electric telegraph did not arrive until 1869. Cuba had achieved a level of modernity that far surpassed Spain's, emphasizing the gap between the Cuban potential and Spanish limitations. Spain could not provide Cuba with what it did not itself possess.

Spanish authorities were not entirely unresponsive to Cuban needs and indeed periodically were forthcoming. But it was clear that to yield to Cuban needs encouraged new demands, often in exponential proportion, and that to accede to Cuban requests on every occasion was necessarily to acquiesce to the transformation of the economy in ways that threatened to exclude Spain and facilitate Cuban integration into the North American system. To have met all of Cuba's needs at the speed and to the extent that it demanded would have forced Spain to dismantle the very structures that linked the colony with the metropolis.

In any case Spain had different needs, and, in the end, it was Spanish needs that colonialism was intended to serve. Access to colonial revenues, mainly in the form of taxes, tariffs, and duties, was the time-honored prerogative of empire and one that Spain availed itself of freely and frequently. That Spanish colonial policies increased the cost of production, lowered profits, and raised the cost of living, all at the expense of Cuban well-being, seemed to matter little, if at all. Enrique José Varona spoke for producers and consumers alike when in 1895 he denounced Spanish taxes and tariffs. "Still," he insisted, "if Spain were a country with flourishing industry, one that produced the principal articles that Cuba needed for its consumption and needed for the support and development of its own industry, the damage, although always large, would have been less. But it is a well-known fact that the backwardness of Spanish industries has made it impossible for Spain to provide Cuba with the products it required for its development."[27]

These conditions propelled Cubans in new directions, ones that inevitably challenged the rationale of colonialism. It was not only that change had created new needs. This was part of it, of course. But the problem was deeper. Cuba had developed needs that were fundamentally incompatible with existing colonial structures. Development had added new importance to specialized knowledge and information as the basis for devising rational economic policies and making informed political decisions, much of which lay beyond the ordinary reach of Spanish bureaucrats, if indeed they cared to make rational decisions in behalf of Cuban interests at all. In fact, the colonial government lacked a bureaucracy sufficiently trained to mediate the needs of the colony with the requirements of the metropolis, a deficiency made all the more egregious as economic development increasingly required the support of specialized functions of the state.

Change was also driven by newly discerned contradictions, derived in large measure from alternative value systems with which Cubans had acquired familiarity and according to which they had developed expectations of economic expansion and collective well-being. Cubans understood the necessity to accommodate North American structures, for the development of a highly specialized export economy had derived definitive form primarily from North American market requirements. They recognized, too, the need to master northern methods and practices, with which they increasingly came in contact and on which their well-being depended. These were, in part, facets of a larger transition that, once having commenced, revived old issues of dissatisfaction and created new sources of discontent.

New conditions also facilitated—and often necessitated—expanded contact between Cuba and North America. Both economies closed in on one another and progressively shut out Spain. These needs were symptomatic of changing conditions as well as the source of additional change. The two developments were related, of course, but they were also expressions of Spain's decreasing role and at the same time acted to curtail Spanish participation even further. Cubans were participating in new kinds of business enterprises and experimenting with new production modes, adopting modern industrial technology and developing new transportation systems, expanding into new markets and employing new credit structures. All the while they increased their consumption of U.S. products, consumer goods no less than foodstuffs, manufactured goods and industrial equipment, sundries and staples, all of which, in turn, fostered new tastes and new habits, created preferences for new styles, and produced new modalities of consumption.

The North American presence served as a powerful force for change, not all at once or only in one way, but over time and in many different ways. Because the manner in which these influences worked was rarely apparent immediately and because their consequences were unforeseen, they were accepted as commonplace and thus became a part of everyday life. North American methods were shown to be capable of meeting Cuban needs and improving Cuban lives. Adopted readily and unreservedly, they served increasingly as the means by which Cubans crossed cultural thresholds and made a place for themselves in a changing environment.

Contact with North Americans in Cuba was one source of change. The presence of thousands of maquinistas, for example, was a telling influence. At least as important as their role in servicing the industrial infrastructure was their effect on local working-class culture and labor organization. As early as 1851, John Thrasher could write about the "great contrast observed in the state of mechanic arts" in Cuba and Spain and the "much greater advance of the former in the adoption of mechanical appliances to labor." Thrasher was among the first to discern the impact of "machinists, carpenters, coopers, masons, carriage makers, smiths, etc.," noting: "The trades in their shops, the manner of labor, tools, and style of work in Cuba, resembles ours much more than they do those of Spain, or of Spanish America, and have given to [Cuban] civilization a resemblance to that of the Anglo-American, not found elsewhere out of the United States."[28]

North American mercantile agencies served as another means of gaining access to North American methods. Mercantile houses routinely hired employees locally, generally relatives of clients and customers. The protagonist in Ricardo Núñez de Villavicencio's autobiographical novel *Aventuras emocionantes* (1929) was employed as an office boy (*muchacho de oficina*), "transcribing correspondence, going to the post office, depositing and withdrawing money from the banks, and undertaking all types of errands." Cuban employees often worked their way north to serve apprenticeships at company headquarters in New Orleans, Philadelphia, New York, and Boston. Cuban attorneys frequently joined North American law practices to learn U.S. law and legal procedures.[29]

These relationships contributed to the transformation of Cuban social structures and were themselves the source of strategies by which the creole bourgeoisie promoted its interests and increased its influence. An important sector of the creole middle class originated from these relationships. Producers and property owners used their connections with North American merchants to advance the careers of family members. The correspondence files of some of the large trading companies' archives are thick with letters from Cuban clients requesting employment for relatives and seeking assistance in placing sons in U.S. boarding schools and colleges. "The *hacendados*," observed the Count of Mirasol in 1850, "seeing the advantages that trade brings to foreigners, and seeking to maintain contacts with foreigners, commit their sons to careers in commerce and send them to those countries to study."[30]

Linkages with the United States expanded throughout the nineteenth century. Cubans traveled north with increasing frequency, whereas during the same period their visits to Spain declined. Ease of access partly explained this shift. Distance was also a factor: 20 days by ship from Havana to Cádiz, but 5 days to New York, 2 days to New Orleans, and 6 hours to Key West.

Travel north was related to more than convenience, however. It was itself a reflection of relationships in transition: cause-and-effect associations in a constant dynamic interplay, acting on each other in decisive ways, revealing the possibilities of one relationship and exposing the limitations of the other. The interaction suggested new opportunities, produced new needs, and, inevitably, created new demands. All were related, for much in this experience assumed the form of cognitive assessments of the colonial condition, a process that had to do with the realization that changing needs could not be reasonably accommodated within colonial structures.

Some travel to the United States was for pleasure. Emilio Núñez and María Dolores Portuondo were among the many Cuban newlyweds to honeymoon at Niagara Falls. Many sought relief from the tropical summers long associated with epidemics and pestilence. The trips of the creole bourgeoisie often con-

A view of the Cuban émigré neighborhood in Ybor City, Tampa, ca. 1890s.
(Courtesy of Special Collections, Library, University of South Florida)

sisted of annual pilgrimages to the resort regions of upstate New York to avail
themselves of mineral baths at Saratoga Springs, Sharon Springs, and Niagara
Falls. The ailing wealthy went north for respite and medical reasons; planter
Pedro Diego, for example, visited Saratoga Springs in the summer of 1850 to
recover his health. Planter Eugenio Coffigny complained to a friend of unre-
lieved constipation, for which he hoped "the waters of Saratoga would restore
me fully to health."[31] These vacations—*veranear en el Norte*, as they became
known—became an integral part of the social orbit of the creole bourgeoisie.

Cubans also traveled to the United States to conduct business: to buy and to
sell, to invest, to bank, to borrow. They integrated themselves directly into the
North American economy. Merchants established trading companies in U.S.
cities: Domingo Goicuría and Pedro Santacilla in New Orleans, Carlos Recio in
Key West, Enrique Luis Fritot in Jacksonville, Ernesto Malibrán and Demetrio
Castillo Duany in New York. Many invested in the United States. Some of the
most prominent representatives of the creole bourgeoisie, including Fernando
Diago, Juan Pedro Baró, Tomás Terry, Carlos Drake, and members of the Yznaga
family, owned portfolios thick with North American stocks, securities, and
bonds. By the early 1890s, an estimated $25 million from Cuba were on deposit
in U.S. banks. Others journeyed north to incorporate their companies under
U.S. laws and then returned to invest in Cuba, a strategy designed to secure U.S.

Liceo Cubano, constructed in 1893 by Los Caballeros de la Luz, Ybor City, Tampa. (Courtesy of Special Collections, Library, University of South Florida)

protection against seizure and expropriation. The Cárdenas City Water Works Company and the Cárdenas Ice Company were incorporated in New York by Cuban investors.[32]

Cubans also conducted a variety of business activities in the United States. J. M. Casanova operated the Philipsbury (PA) Water Company. Alberto V. de Goicuría was a successful stockbroker in New York. Rafael E. de los Reyes established a coal business in New Orleans, engaged in real estate development (Delos Realty Company), and subsequently organized the Acme Industrial Life Insurance and Sick Benefit Association (1892) and the Globe Accident and Casualty Company (1894). Nowhere perhaps was the Cuban impact in manufacturing more spectacular than in the cigar industry. Scores of factories opened, first in Key West during the 1860s and 1870s and later in Tampa, Ocala, and Jacksonville during the 1880s; they eventually spread to New Orleans, Philadelphia, Wilmington, and New York.[33]

Sánchez and Haya Cigar Factory, Tampa, 1898. (Courtesy of Special Collections, Library, University of South Florida)

Now Cubans were introducing industry and innovation into the United States, assembling the material and human resources to promote economic and technological development. Cigar production transformed the local economy of a score of communities across Florida. More than 170 factories were operating in Key West by the late 1880s, employing approximately 7,500 workers. Key West grew from a population of less than 700 residents in 1840 to more than 18,000 by 1890 as the value of its cigar manufactures soared from $20 million in 1882 to $100 million in 1892.[34] Additional factories were established in Ocala, Jacksonville, Pensacola, St. Augustine, and other cities. The combined value of the 150 factories in Tampa surpassed $17 million; the labor force, consisting of more than 10,000 workers, received an average weekly wage of $200,000, or 75 percent of the city's total payroll.

Cuban manufacturers were responsible for various other improvements in Key West. Francisco Marrero developed commercial and residential property. Eduardo Hidalgo Gato organized the Key West Street Car Association, which established the first trolley system in the area. Most local banks were set up by Cubans. The most prominent, the Bank of Key West, was owned by Hidalgo

Martínez Ybor Cigar Factory, Tampa, ca. early 1890s.
(Courtesy of Special Collections, Library, University of South Florida)

Gato. Cubans organized the first municipal fire department and introduced gas lighting. "In fact," the U.S. consul in Havana, Ramon Williams, acknowledged in 1892, "Key West has been built up by Cubans. . . . The people here look upon Florida as so much a part of their own country that very often they come here and say 'I want to go to the Key,' just as in Baltimore they would say, 'I am going over to Washington.' "[35]

Cubans also traveled north for their education. Some of this, of course, had to do with accessibility—the proximity of the United States and the efficiency of Cuban-U.S. transportation.

But there were other reasons to study in the North. Few deficiencies of the colonial regime rankled creole sensibilities more than the deplorable condition of education. Simply in terms of numbers—the number of teachers and the number of schools for the number of students—the educational system was unable to meet even the minimum needs of the school-age population. "We have been left without schools, without books, without teachers, and without students," protested Manuel Valdés Rodríguez in 1891.[36] Education was in a wretched state, suffering equally from neglect, mismanagement and malfeasance, inadequate instruction, and insufficient funding.

These were only some of the most obvious deficiencies of colonial education and only part of the problem. More to the point, colonial education had ceased to meet Cuban needs. The specialization of the economy had reached the stage where social diversity was derived from production and distribution, access to which was increasingly possible only by mastery of new information and new skills. The colonial university and *colegio* curricula, with their traditional emphasis on law, philosophy, and letters, under the direction of Catholic religious orders, did not admit change easily—if at all.

Cuban needs had changed, and the colonial curricula had not. New fields of learning, new bodies of knowledge, and especially technical training, science programs, and courses in business law and commerce, all of which were directly related to the forces transforming Cuba, were not readily available on the island. This meant that the knowledge and skills Cubans required to make the transition and guarantee a place for themselves in a rapidly changing economic environment could only be obtained abroad.

Few failed to understand the significance of modern technology and economic organization. Cubans were not slow to decipher the implications of new social divisions of labor, new professions, and new technologies. "The instruction we need most—technological and industrial—does not exist in Cuba," complained Enrique José Varona. "The careers and professions that modern civilization requires most urgently are not studied in Cuba. In order to be a surveyor, an electrician, an industrial engineer, a mechanical engineer, a construction engineer, a mining engineer, the Cuban must go abroad." The future of an entire generation was in the balance, insisted Arturo Rosell. "If we can not get our youth out of here for education abroad, what fate awaits us?" Their "aptitudes will atrophy," Rosell warned, their "aspirations will be crushed."[37]

Cubans traveled north to study by the thousands, mostly the children of the creole bourgeoisie and sons and daughters of the expanding middle classes. The choices seemed unlimited: primary and secondary schools, both public and private, undergraduate education, Catholic schools and boarding schools for daughters, business and commercial colleges for sons, polytechnic institutes, professional and graduate training, medical schools, dental programs, law schools. Planters in particular took measure of the changing technologies that were transforming sugar production and sent their sons north to learn new techniques and modern methods. The two oldest sons of Matanzas planter Ricardo Ponce de León studied mechanical engineering in New York. Luis E. Muñoz del Monte graduated from Rensselaer Polytechnic in 1888, then returned to Matanzas to work in the family mill, Las Cañas. Rafael Sánchez Aballí, who years later would serve as secretary of communications in the government of Gerardo Machado, completed his engineering studies at Columbia University in

1893 before managing the family's Santa Lucía sugar estate in Gibara. Melchor Gastón Rosell received a civil engineering degree from Columbia and returned to the family estate, Dolores, in Matanzas. Rafael Gutiérrez Fernández studied mechanical engineering and later worked in sugar mills in Guantánamo, Manzanillo, and Bayamo. After taking courses in civil and mechanical engineering in New York, José Alejandro Huau was employed by the Matanzas Railroad Company. During the middle decades of the nineteenth century, about two thousand young men enrolled annually in U.S. schools.[38] Families reluctant to send younger children alone to the United States brought North American instructors to Cuba, principally tutors and governesses.

Some of the most prominent representatives of the creole bourgeoisie received their education in the United States. Francisco de Frías (Count of Pozos Dulces) attended school in Baltimore from age ten to sixteen. Others included Francisco Aguilera, Cristobal Madán, Gaspar Betancourt Cisneros, Ricardo del Monte, and Pedro Yznaga. Many pursued undergraduate study in the United States; others attended business colleges and commercial schools. Scores obtained professional training in North America.[39]

For many, the experience in the United States was decisive. "Almost all of the new generation," observed Nicolás Tanco Armero as early as 1861, "go to the country of Washington for their education, and there take in new customs that they are unable to abandon upon their return to the island." Many Cubans spent their formative years in North America, at precisely the time when U.S. classrooms assumed the explicit role of "Americanizing" a growing immigrant population. Indeed, the schooling of immigrant children was made obligatory by the passage of compulsory attendance laws between the 1860s and 1890s. Schools served as "an instrument of Americanization," writes Gerald Gutek, a means of "learning a new language and a new way of life," and an "agent for both cultural unification and transmission of the society." Diverse émigré customs and ideologies would give way to a "deliberate attempt to 'Americanize' the immigrants as quickly and completely as possible" and "inculcate the immigrant children with certain 'American' attitudes and values."[40]

A North American education provided access to new knowledge, new technologies, and new skills and all but guaranteed a successful transition to the postcolonial order, one that Cubans themselves had an important part in creating and one that they were uniquely prepared to fit into. An education abroad, of course, confirmed elite status, but the drama that was unfolding almost imperceptibly in the final decades of the century was more complex. A large number of parents made a coherent assessment of the times in which they lived; they recognized the portents of a vastly changed society for which they sought to prepare their children. No doubt they contributed to actualizing that future and may have even hastened its arrival. But these decisions were themselves a reflection of a time of transition. Assuming that most parents sought to act in the best interest of their children, the decision to educate them in the North was itself a powerful indication of the character of the Cuban transformation.

Education in the United States early assumed a logic of its own. Cubans learned English, acquired new knowledge, and developed new skills, all of which served them well and at the same time confirmed in the popular imagination the importance of North American education to collective well-being and individual mobility. Education offered new possibilities, not the least of which involved mediating from one side or the other the encounter between Cuba and North America. Men and women of all classes, black and white, regarded a North American education as the means to a better life. Aurelia Castillo de González attributed the freedom enjoyed by North American women to their access to a "complete education." Among the reasons that Captain Benigno Ortiz, a man of color and humble origins, gave for joining the Liberation Army in 1895 was to realize the "ambition of his life": to send his two sons to the United States—"even as far as Jacksonville"—to be educated.[41]

Cubans educated in the United States not only attained status, but also, and more important, they were prepared for change. They came to understand the affinity between the cultural idea of self-development and the real social movement toward economic development. Perhaps no other single connection so challenged the premises on which Spanish colonialism rested.

Many educated Cubans returned home changed and bearing change. What could possibly be the outcome of raising the expectations of Cubans to the level of a free people? Gaspar Betancourt Cisneros worried from New York in 1849. He pondered the implications of a relative's decision to educate his sons in the United States: "Will one have labored like my fatuous relative who has brought his three sons to be educated here, to have their first impressions blossom among the books, in a democratic republic, only to take the boys back to live among slaves and in a colonial monarchy? What does he want? To place them in conflict with their own father? To make them live against their ideas and sentiments?"[42]

Cubans educated in the United States did, in fact, develop a partiality for things North American, persuaded that progress and prosperity could be best obtained through North American ways. Their memory of the past and their expectations of the future derived from prevailing North American notions of history and destiny. Many learned reverence for institutions that were not their own and disdain for those that were. This was the first generation of Cubans of any significant number to have acquired an education outside the island, an experience by which they remained permanently distinguished. They gave intellectual form to these stirrings during the 1880s and early 1890s through such publications as La Nueva Era, El Progreso, La Joven Cuba, La Juventud Liberal, and La Juventud Cubana; they were indeed young, and they attached political significance to their youth, as harbingers of change and messengers of modernity.

Cubans returned to the island not only with new knowledge and skills, but also as advocates of progress, with a new sense of purpose and new expectations, committed to introducing new ideas by means and toward ends acquired in the North. They adapted and adjusted and improved upon. Their encounter with the North contributed to the formation of a new consciousness. Old values were henceforth relative, to be sorted out and arranged alongside new values, and subject to evaluation. They took to new methods and learned new techniques, which implied, of course, a new hierarchy of values and new sensibilities, attitudes, and standards, all of which added to their discontent with old ways. In Nicolás Heredia's novel *Leonela* (1893), John Valdespina returns to Cuba in 1866—he had departed as "Juan"—as chief engineer for Smithson Brothers of New York on a railroad construction project. He exudes Yankee confidence—"arrogance," insists one character—and in response to residents of the town of Jarabacoa who doubted the feasibility of the proposed railway, Valdespina responds, "The word 'impossible,' my dear sirs, has been erased from the dictionary of modern civilization," adding:

> This is a virgin country, a rich and fertile land that in order to produce marvels needs only the creative impulse of science and work. I bring the magic wand, the irresistible force, the initiative and the perseverance of the people of the North who make flowers grow from rocks and construct palaces in the desert. That God give me only five years of life and this sterile plain will be a garden, that shack a factory, and the miserable little village will be a city of modern appearance, with hotels, statuary, fountains, schools and hospitals. The road will be lined with beautiful cottages. . . . And since industry and wealth are themselves a source of transformation in the moral order of the universe, these people will be different from what they are today.[43]

Education in the North obliged Cubans to contemplate a new order, thereby increasing their dissatisfaction with the old one. The acquisition of new knowledge, the raised status of other ways of thinking and alternative possibilities, and vindication of values in a world reinterpreted made reintegration into colonial structures difficult, often impossible. In the end, these Cubans were transformed into dissenters from doing things in old ways once better ways became available.

Colonial authorities understood the significance of this development. In 1843 the Ministry of State condemned North American education for "undermining the spirit of nationality" whereby Cubans acquired "habits pernicious to the constituted government." Ten years later Governor General José G. de la Concha sounded an alarm over creole families "sending [their children] to foreign schools, and especially to those in the neighboring American Union, and with grave damage to ties of family and nationality, and with no less harm to [their] country they generally come back with new habits, ideas, and dangerous affectations." They "return to the homes of their parents with tendencies contrary to the institutions that govern us"—indeed, "frankly subversive ideas"—"and disseminate among their relatives, friends and neighbors the insidious doctrines they learned abroad." The absence of adequate educational facilities, de la Concha complained, especially the lack of "programs directly relevant to industry," was forcing Cubans to study abroad, where "they received an education inconsistent with the sentiments of nationality and devoted to the formation of men for societies governed by institutions completely different from those of their country."[44]

Cubans had other reasons to travel north, especially after 1868. In fact, this was not so much travel as it was migration. These were unsettled times in Cuba, when change often arrived in disruptive forms with destructive consequences. These were years of colonial insurrection and war, of economic dislocation and depression, of personal insecurity, of want and discontent, of doubt and despair. Hard times arrived in successive cycles, endless cycles it seemed on occasion, and each cycle set in motion a new wave of emigration with such frequency that it created the appearance of one long, continuous migration.

Cubans were in flight, not for the first time, to be sure, but never before had they fled in such large numbers. Between the 1860s and the 1890s, in the course of three wars, tens of thousands of Cubans emigrated north, an exodus that assumed the proportions of a diaspora. In 1892 a Senate Committee on Immigration estimated that between 50,000 and 100,000 persons traveled annually between Cuba and the United States. During the latter third of the nineteenth century, hundreds of thousands of Cubans moved constantly back and forth between the island and the U.S. mainland to vacation, work, live, and plot revolution.[45]

This population included Cubans seeking to escape past adversity and future uncertainty. The displaced and the dispossessed arrived continuously, together with the unemployed and the unemployable, black and white, young and old, men, women, and children of all social classes, sometimes as entire families but just as often as shattered households. They reconstituted themselves into new communities all along the Gulf coast and up the eastern seaboard. The émigré communities in Florida assumed a conspicuous presence. "He who passes along Seventh Avenue or 14th Street," Carlos Trelles wrote of Tampa in 1897, "would not believe that he is in the United States, for such is the large number of Cubans that one meets and the many business establishments of all kinds that one sees in which all signs are only in Spanish."[46]

The experience of exile (*destierro*) was decisive to the ways Cubans arrived at nationality and identity. Destierro implied uprooting—in its infinitive form, *desterrar*: to remove earth from the roots—to expose, to make vulnerable. But it also suggested adaptation as a means of survival, of borrowing as a means of becoming. The deployment of migratory energies propelled vast numbers across boundaries to chart new territories and explore new possibilities, but mostly to survive change and change to survive. Destierro implied distance from the old and proximity to the new, an occasion to decipher meaning and determine purpose, a time of transition from past to future. Exile was an occasion to discard the old and adopt the new, to leave behind old identities and assume new ones: often to acquire new mannerisms, new religion, new self-representations. Cubans of the emigration could often be identified by their names. Like John Valdespina of Heredia's novel, there were many others: Henry Lincoln de Zayas, Jorge Washington Boudet, Jorge Washington Alfaya, Charles Hernández, Frank Agramonte, Joseph Trelles.

For many, emigration provided an opportunity to acquire new citizenship. Naturalization was part of a larger strategy, less to obtain legal rights in the United States than to secure civil liberties in Cuba. For numerous Cubans, the purpose of travel north was to meet residency requirements for U.S. citizenship and then return to Cuba. Naturalization afforded the basis to claim protection from the U.S. government in a political environment noteworthy for the absence of civil rights. Indeed, U.S. citizenship redefined the legal relationship between the Cuban people and Spanish authorities. Existing treaty arrangements and international law entitled naturalized citizens of the United States rights that were in almost every instance superior to the guarantees available to Cubans under Spanish law. For planters and property owners, U.S. citizenship promised protection against government seizure and provided the legal basis on which to obtain reparations for damages and losses. Some of the most prominent representatives of the creole bourgeoisie became U.S. citizens, including Leonardo del Monte, Cristobal Madán, Antonio Bachiller y Morales, Félix Govín, José Antonio Yznaga, Gaspar A. Betancourt, Andrés Terry, and José María Mora. For Cubans involved in antigovernment activities, U.S. citizenship was often the only guarantee of due process and protection from arbitrary treatment. Arrests of U.S. citizens immediately transformed an otherwise routine internal matter into an international affair. The lives of many captured insurgents were spared by virtue of holding U.S. citizenship. José María Ortega was arrested in 1869 for complicity in insurrection but was released after a formal protest by the U.S. Department of State. When Rafael Fernández de Velasco was arrested and charged with the clandestine transportation of arms in 1880, the U.S. consul communicated immediately with the governor general to insist that Fernández "be set free or accorded a speedy trial."[47]

The exact number of Cubans who obtained U.S. citizenship during the nineteenth century is incalculable but must be presumed to have approached the tens of thousands. Children born to naturalized citizens also acquired U.S. citizenship, and consular registries contain the names of hundreds of minors. Estimates of qualified electors for the 1876 presidential election included 12,000 Cuban-born residents. Thousands of others resided in Cuba. An 1881 consular survey of North American citizens residing in Havana registered a total of 2,492 citizens, of whom 1,502 were born in Cuba. A year later consul Adam Badeau wrote of another "several thousand" naturalized U.S. citizens. The U.S. vice consul in Cienfuegos reported "thousands of them" returning to the island at the end of the Ten Years War.[48]

Naturalization was also a way to create space inside Cuba, a way to defend nationality by affirming what Cubans were not—they were not Spaniards—and a way to draw distinctions between Cuban and Spanish. In 1873 Francisco de Frías (Count of Pozos Dulces) extolled the rights of U.S. citizens in the Havana monthly *Revista Cubana*; he invited the obvious inferences by stressing what Cubans did not have, including "freedom of association, freedom of industry and work, freedom of education, political freedom, unlimited freedom of the press, and respect for all religious denominations." Cubans, too, could claim these rights, Frías suggested: "All the civil and political privileges enjoyed by U.S. citizens can also be obtained by naturalization. . . . The foreigner has a right to the security of his person, his home, his private papers and effects against all illegal search and seizure. . . . All children of foreign parents born on the soil of the United States, even if not citizens, by virtue of birth are entitled to all the privileges of American citizenship."[49] U.S. citizenship promised parity; it was a means to advance the claim of a Cuban nationality, even if in the form of U.S. citizenship. This was also a way to introduce notions of justice, due process, and civil liberties, based primarily on North American legal forms, into the formulation of Cuban nationality, rights that Cubans claimed as their own, and henceforth served as the standard by which to measure the performance of government. In still one more way Cubans became implicated in a world that was not entirely their own, if only as a means to make a world of their own; it was another way that elements of a borrowed nationality were integrated with a new nationality.

MEANINGS IN TRANSITION

Throughout the nineteenth century Cubans went to the United States by the tens of thousands, as tourists and travelers, vacationers and visitors, for education and employment, to escape political repression and plot colonial revolution. They represented a broad population: planters, merchants, manufacturers, workers, and members of the middle class, including attorneys, engineers, physicians, dentists, journalists, teachers, publishers, writers, and students. Among them were intellectuals José Antonio Saco and Rafael María Mendive; journalists Carmela Nieto de Herrera, Víctor Muñoz, Enrique Piñeyro, Julio Villoldo, Rafael Serra, and Raimundo Cabrera; labor leaders Carlos Baliño and Diego Vicente Tejera; historian Pedro José Guiteras; painter Leopoldo Romañach; poets Miguel Teurbe Tolón and Bonifacio Byrne; and novelists Cirilo Villaverde, Miguel de Carrión, Carlos Loveira, and Luis Rodríguez Embil.

Cubans integrated themselves at all levels of North American society. They attended school, obtained jobs, set up households, and raised families in communities across the United States. They established medical and dental practices

Hotel de La Habana, 1889, the first hotel constructed in Ybor City, Tampa. (Courtesy of Special Collections, Library, University of South Florida)

and opened law offices. They engaged in all types of commercial activities. Many operated small business enterprises and retail stores. They adapted to North American ways of doing business, used local newspapers to advertise their goods and services, and learned that good business meant prompt service and competitive pricing. In local advertisements Antonio López, who owned the United States Laundry in Key West, assured prospective customers of "promptness in delivery and moderation in price [that] will prove satisfactory to all."[50] Luis M. Arredondo, who graduated from Manhattan College in 1882, subsequently worked as an interpreter for various New York hotels. The number of Cuban-owned hotels and boardinghouses increased throughout the nineteenth century; many served as the point of entry for newly arrived émigrés.[51]

Cubans bought countless retail stores, cafés and restaurants, pharmacies, barbershops, and *bodegas* (general stores). In New York, Manuel García Cuervo owned the Bodega Cubana and sold products of Cuba and *sanwiches* of all types. Julián Moreno was proprietor of the Restaurant Cubano, where "the food is Cuban, it's good, and moderately priced." Emiliano Pérez operated the barbershop in the lobby of Central Hotel. José Guillermo Díaz, who identified himself as an "ex-professor of the Faculty of Pharmacy at the University of Havana," operated the Columbia Pharmacy on Lexington and Eighty-seven Street. Echemendía and Company was a Cuban-owned publishing house. Néstor Ponce de

Valdés Brothers General Store, owned by Julián, Carlos, and Juan Valdés, Tampa, 1897. (Courtesy of Special Collections, Library, University of South Florida)

León and Ignacio Mora owned bookstores. *Patria*'s roster of Cuban advertisers in New York between 1892 and 1895 listed forty cigar manufacturers, thirty-five physicians, twenty-five merchants, twenty attorneys, fifteen music teachers, six dentists, five bodegas, four restaurants, three drugstores, and two colegios.[52] In Key West, Gabriel Ayala owned the Nuevo Siglo grocery store, J. Avelino Delgado operated the Singer Sewing Machine agency, and D. Báez and Company managed a popular dry goods store. In Tampa, the Valdés Brothers operated a successful dry goods establishment. Manuel Moreno de la Torre, proprietor of El Bazar Americano, sold shoes, hats, and "Cuban style clothing"; Manuel Viñas's La María bakery sold "Cuban and American style bread." Marcos I. Sánchez operated a real estate office, Francisco Ysern was the proprietor of the Salón Central liquor store, and Antonio Salazar managed El Central restaurant.

Cubans were appointed to government positions and elected to political office at the municipal, state, and federal levels. In Key West, Alejandro Mendoza, Enrique Esquinaldo, Rogelio Gómez, and Juan María Reyes served as justices of the peace; Alfredo Reynoso was chief of police, and Juan Busto, Delio Cobo, Marcos Mesa, Juan Carbonell, Manuel Varela, and José Valdés were members of the city council. Isaac Carrillo received a federal appointment as southern district attorney, and Carlos Manuel de Céspedes and Manuel Govín were installed as officers in the U.S. customhouse in Key West. Céspedes subsequently won the mayoral seat in Key West, and Govín served as postmaster of Jacksonville. José Alejandro Huau was elected to four terms on the Jacksonville city council. Celestino Cañizares became mayor of Ocala. Manuel Moreno, Manuel Patricio Delgado, José Gonzalo Pompés, and Fernando Figueredo Socarrás were sent to the Florida legislature. Figueredo Socarrás, a Rensselaer graduate, served as superintendent of schools in Hillsborough County and mayor of West Tampa. The first West Tampa city council included Vidal Cruz, S. Fleitas, Martín Herrera, J. D. Silva, and R. Someillán. In 1874 Aniceto G. Menocal was appointed chief engineer in the U.S. Navy and supervised all canal surveys in Panama and Nicaragua. He later designed the naval gun plant in Washington, D.C., and helped establish the naval base in the Philippines before retiring with the rank of commander. Joaquín Castillo Duany held a commission in the U.S. Navy and was assigned as surgeon to the 1881 Polar expedition. José Primelles Agramonte, who in 1887 graduated from Columbia University with a degree in civil engineering, obtained employment with the New York City Streets Department. Juan Guiteras served a tour of duty as a physician in the U.S. Army and subsequently joined the staff of the Marine Hospital Service. Charles Hernández was raised in Brockton, Massachusetts, where he attended public school, worked for the Brockton Electric Light Works, and served nearly a decade in the Massachusetts National Guard. Sotero E. Escarza graduated in civil engineering from Rensselaer in 1894 and for the next five years worked in the Pennsylvania Railroad Division of Bridges. José Agustín Quintero received a law degree from Harvard in 1849 and settled in New Orleans, where he was a member of the editorial staff of the *Picayune*. During the Civil War he served in the Confederate diplomatic corps in Latin America.

Still others fully integrated themselves into North American society, acquiring new identities and new careers, and went back to Cuba as representatives of U.S. interests. Pedro Bustillo graduated from the New York Business College, obtained U.S. citizenship, and returned to Havana in 1883 as the general agent of the Equitable Life Assurance Society. Another Business College graduate, Felipe Estrada, directed the Departamento Hispano Americano of the New York Life Insurance Company, also in Havana. Hipólito Dumois from Santiago de Cuba was educated at St. John's College in New York before taking a job with the American Ore Dressing Company copper mines in Oriente. Joaquín Chalons earned an engineering degree in North America, then returned to work for the Steel Ore Company in Santiago de Cuba. Esteban Duque Estrada graduated from the Stevens Institute of Technology in Hoboken, New Jersey, and in 1883 joined the Bethlehem Iron Company to supervise railroad construction in Santiago de Cuba. In Heredia's *Leonela*, John Valdespina studied engineering at William Penn College in Pennsylvania before returning to Cuba as chief engineer on the railroad construction project for Smithson Brothers.

Cubans found employment as educators and taught a generation of North Americans in a variety of fields. Luis A. Baralt Peoli and Antonio Franchi taught Spanish at Columbia University. Others included Mariano Cubí y Soler (Louisiana State University), Calixto Guiteras (Girard College), and Luis Felipe Mantilla (New York University). Federico Edelman Pinto served on the New York Board of Education and taught evening classes at DeWitt Clinton High School. Professors of medicine included Carlos J. Finlay (Columbia) and Juan Guiteras (University of Pennsylvania Medical School). Manuel González Echeverría was a professor of mental diseases at the State University of New York and founded the first asylum for epileptics and the mentally ill in the state. Gonzalo Núñez advertised his services as "professor of piano." Pianist Pablo Desvernine emigrated to New York in 1869 and taught piano to young adults, the most famous of whom was Edward MacDowell. Juan de Valera, the son of a sugar planter, earned a living teaching piano in New York, where he met and married Irish immigrant Catherine Coll. He died shortly after the birth of their son Eduardo, and Catherine returned to Ireland; she then gave the boy's name its Gaelic form: Eamon.

Some Cubans established private schools. In 1885 Tomás Estrada Palma founded a college preparatory school, Instituto Estrada Palma, in Central Valley, New York. Eduardo Pla directed an elementary school in Sussex County, New Jersey. Also in New York, Carlos de la Torre established El Progreso elementary school, Demetrio Castillo Duany opened a business school, Inocencio Casanova organized the Instituto Casanova, and N. A. Carbó and J. R. Parras operated the Academia de Idiomas. In Tampa, Cirilo Pouble founded the Academia Pouble.

A generation of Cuban musicians and performers spent their most productive years in the United States. In 1875 pianist Ignacio Cervantes, a student of Louis Gottschalk, arrived in New York, where his recitals earned him critical acclaim. Shortly after emigrating to New York in 1889, soprano Ana Aguardo was appointed soloist at the San Francisco Xavier Church. Opera singer Rosalía Díaz de Herrera performed on the Philadelphia and Washington stage under the professional name of Rosalía Chalía. Flutist Guillermo M. Tomás developed a following in New York during the 1880s and 1890s. Concert pianist Emilio Agramonte established the New York School of Opera and Oratory in 1893 and served as director of the Eight O'Clock Musical Club and conductor of the Gounod Choral Society of New Haven.

The emigration served as the crucible of nation, for many vital elements of Cuban nationality were forged and acquired definitive form in North America. Some of the most important leaders of independence emerged from this community. Martín Morúa Delgado, Enrique José Varona, Rafael Serra, Manuel Sanguily, Diego Vicente Tejera, Francisco Vicente Aguilera, and José Morales Lemus all lived in the United States. Néstor Ponce de León resided in New York for thirty years before returning to the island in 1899. José Martí lived most of his adult life in the North. The principal leaders of the Cuban Revolutionary Party (PRC), Tomás Estrada Palma and Gonzalo de Quesada, were U.S. citizens and longtime residents of New York. Quesada received a law degree from Columbia.

Some of the most prominent military chieftains of the Liberation Army also emerged from this community. General Francisco Carrillo, commander of the Fourth Army Corps, and Colonel Julio Sanguily were U.S. citizens. General Pedro Betancourt, commander of the Matanzas division, was a U.S. citizen and a graduate of the University of Pennsylvania Medical School. Chief of Expeditions General Emilio Núñez, a naturalized U.S. citizen, and General Carlos García Velez both graduated from Penn in dentistry. General José Ramón Villalón, who served on the staff of Antonio Maceo, received an engineering degree from Lehigh University. General Eugenio Sánchez Argamonte (Fordham) was chief of the medical corps. General Carlos Roloff, a naturalized U.S. citizen, had previously worked for Bishop and Company in Caibarién. Colonel José Miguel Tarafa (New York Business College) was chief of staff for General Javier Vega of the Third Army Corps of Oriente. General Carlos María de Rojas (Harvard) served on the staff of General José María Rodriguez. The staff of General Calixto García was especially well represented with alumni of U.S. schools, including Chief of Staff General Mario G. Menocal (Cornell), Colonel Juan Miguel Portuondo Tamayo (Columbia), and Major Luis Rodolfo Miranda (Packard Business College).

Destierro was a transformative experience. For Cubans absorbed with matters of *patria*, the United States provided an environment in which the evolving discourse on nation was offered up freely at public forums among a vast number of participants. The proliferation of Cuban publications in exile—pamphlets, periodicals, and books, but mostly newspapers—was nothing less than extraordinary. Scores of newspapers, which appeared in almost every émigré community, were devoted primarily to the proposition of Cuba Libre in all of its ideological representations and programmatic manifestations. This was a free and frankly opposition press, defying—if from a distance—Spanish censorship and openly committed to overthrowing Spanish rule. (See Appendix Table 1.2.)

A mass readership emerged within émigré communities, and what concerned it most was the ongoing debate on nation. Some newspapers, most notably *Patria*, *El Yara*, and *El Avisador Cubano*, enjoyed national circulation. Many that were smuggled into Cuba were read daily by *lectores* (readers) to thousands of workers on hundreds of cigar factory floors.

The émigré press contributed to consciousness of nationality by creating open fields of exchange and expanding the modes of communication. These were local newspapers, to be sure, a source of local news and advertisements. But local news was also news of the nation and fostered community out of neighborhood, constituency out of community, and nationality out of constituency. This was a long-standing process of integration and inclusion, a narrative on nation that engaged Cubans of all social classes, men and women, black and white, conducted openly and in public.

The press contributed directly to a unified and informed constituency. Much of the exchange took place in editorials, letters to the editor, petitions, and public meetings—almost all of which would have been inconceivable inside Cuba. In expatriate communities from New Orleans to New York, the text of émigré newspapers resonated with renderings of nation. These were important conduits of the competing versions of patria debated in countless meeting halls and back rooms, on front porches and sidewalks, at factories and in homes, in barbershops and bodegas, in cafés and restaurants, and at hundreds of political clubs and patriotic *juntas*.

These were decisive developments, for the very process by which national identity formed was in large measure by way of discourse sustained outside Cuba by huge numbers of people who were daily subjected to North American influences, large and small, and who in the ordinary course of events drew on their environment to advance the cause of Cuba Libre. The circumstance of exile thus had a major impact on the elements used to define and defend patria. That these forms could themselves affect the character of identity was not readily apparent at the time, but increasingly the methods used to create nation also shaped the content of nationality.

The development of the émigré press was very much a product of this condition. Newspapers were in transition in the United States, as technological innovations reduced production costs and increased circulation. Improvements in communications by telegraph, cable, and telephone, as well as advances in transportation by road, rail, and sea, made for efficient collection of news and rapid distribution of newspapers. The cylinder presses that replaced the manually powered flatbed presses of the 1850s further reduced costs and increased efficiency. During the 1860s inexpensive newsprint made from wood pulp supplanted costly rag paper. These were the years, too, of the cheap penny press, popular urban-based newspapers focusing on social and economic issues, directed at specific readerships, and on which the émigré press was modeled.[53] Timing and circumstances made a network of émigré newspapers possible, allowing Cubans to publish at low cost for mass distribution at cheap prices.

That political dissidents could emigrate to the United States and enjoy comparative freedom of action all but guaranteed that much of the opposition to Spain would move to the North. The United States soon became the principal base from which to organize and sustain rebellion. The political leadership of almost all separatist uprisings between 1868 and 1898 was headquartered in New York. Indeed, often it was actually easier for Cubans in the western end of the island to join an insurrection in the eastern end by traveling north. The narrator of Raimundo Cabrera's partly autobiographical novel *Sombras que pasan* (1916) recalled the Ten Years War: "To conspire in Havana in 1870 and 1871 was a dangerous activity and all but absolutely impossible. More than an armed camp, the capital was a prison. On each street corner, a sentry post of armed guards; the cafés and grocery stores were under the surveillance of Volunteers; in every door way, a guard, an armed gate-keeper. In the homes, every Cuban man with a policeman near by. Three Cubans could not get together on a street corner or on the plazas without arousing suspicions."[54] Gustavo Robreño's historical novel *La acera del Louvre* (1925) similarly recalled the days when many Cubans "traveled abroad on the pretense of vacation or business" as a way to reach the rebellion. The "strict vigilance exercised by colonial authorities in the capital," Robreño remembered, "made it impossible for *habaneros* to join the insurrection and it was absolutely indispensable to go abroad, to return as members of an expedition."[55]

Much in Cuban political culture thus developed around the use of the United States as a surrogate site of opposition from which to plot conspiracies and plan for war, to raise funds and organize resistance, to publish opposition newspapers, and to establish hundreds of revolutionary clubs, patriotic juntas, and political associations. Inevitably, in the search for allies and assistance, Cubans involved North Americans in their affairs. And this also became a permanent feature of the Cuban practice of politics.

The circumstance of exile produced new ways to articulate discontent and to assemble power. Such mobilization for change, frankly subversive and revolutionary, could not have developed inside Cuba in the same way. Previous challenges to Spanish rule had originated from clandestine plots organized by small groups of conspirators, limited largely to representatives of creole elites.

The exile experience opened the discourse on nation to the participation of thousands of Cubans, for the discursive process itself functioned as a means of mobilization. The political base of the *independentista* constituency broadened, acquiring greater social diversity and ideological range, and eventually assumed the proportions of a populist mass-based movement. The incorporation of new social groupings guaranteed that the final rendering of patria, the one that would serve as the call to action, addressed the concerns of a vast and heterogeneous constituency. It was in exile that definition of national community broadened and the meaning of patria was transformed, the point at which a moral imperative insinuated itself into the final representation of patria. Nation was subsequently conceived in programmatic terms as national identity expanded to incorporate an explicit ideological content to free Cuba. These were not altogether new tendencies, of course. Much in these formulations had antecedents earlier in the nineteenth century. What was different after 1868, however, was a matter of degree, and eventually the difference in degree was sufficiently great to create a distinction in kind.

During the North American exile the meaning of national community expanded to include the working class, the poor—in the formulation of José Martí, *los humildes* and *los pobres de la tierra*. Martí understood the importance of

José Martí with Cuban cigar workers in front of the Martínez Ybor Cigar Factory, Ybor City, Tampa, 1892. (Courtesy of Centro de Estudios Martianos, Havana)

incorporating los humildes into the separatist coalition; he also recognized that only by addressing working-class concerns explicitly as a function of nation could workers respond to patria. Indeed, Martí required the allegiance of workers to legitimize the construct of Cuba Libre as a representation of the whole nation and could plausibly find this endorsement only among the cigar workers of Florida. He detected in the Floridian communities the fullness of the ideal of nation: cigar workers organized in peculiarly North American small-town fashion—in Key West, Tampa, Jacksonville, and Ocala: entire townships of Cubans united by a vision of nation and governed by officials elected from among their own ranks. The creation of the Cuban Revolutionary Party in Tampa and Key West in 1892 gave institutional structure and political form to the inclusion of workers in the definition of nation. By 1892 Martí could proclaim that "the working people" were the "backbone of our coalition."[56]

The North was also the place where the process of nation formation was open to women. They shared with men many of the same patriotic concerns, often articulated in similar fashion, most of which had to do with the central issues of independence and sovereignty. Many enrolled in separatist ranks in response to opportunity, much of which arrived in the form of modernity. Women entered into the process of national liberation as a means of personal liberation and vice versa. In this period of transition and rapid change, old gender boundaries were

José Martí with local organizers of the Cuban Revolutionary Party, Key West, 1893.
(Courtesy of Centro de Estudios Martianos, Havana)

difficult to sustain. For instance, in Wenceslao Gálvez's novel *Nicotina* (1898), set in Tampa during the early 1890s, Lucrecia contemplates the imminence of a new separatist war and regrets "not being a man so I too can go and fight." Reprimanded by her father—"Don't speak of those things, child, for women should not get involved in politics, that is unseemly"—Lucrecia retorts: "And why not? Those are backward views!"[57]

Women in exile became "involved in politics" at all levels—as fund-raisers, political organizers, and community leaders. They sponsored bazaars, picnics, and dances; organized theater groups; and collected clothing and medicine for insurgent forces in Cuba. Carolina Rodríguez, Emilia Casanova, Ana Aguardo de Tomás, María Josefa de Moya, Rosalía Hernández, Carmen Miyares, Magdalena Mayorga, and Paulina Pedrosa were only the most prominent women associated with the cause of Cuba Libre. Hundreds more served on the patriotic juntas and in the revolutionary clubs that were established in émigré communities. In sum, forty-nine women's clubs joined the PRC, representing more than 1,500 women, approximately 40 percent of the PRC delegates.[58]

The integration of women in the mobilization of patria introduced different issues about the nature of nationality, about who could participate and under what circumstances, much of which passed directly into the programmatic construct of nation. Although these developments were not entirely new, never before had conditions so favored the discussion of gender issues explicitly as a facet of nation. Patria may still have implied patriarchy, but it was no less true that women in exile contributed in fundamentally new ways to the assumptions from which the formulation and meaning of nation were derived. One émigré *programa político* in 1890 called for universal suffrage and "the progressive emancipation of women with the right to vote and to hold public and official positions." In 1897 Edelmira Guerra de Dauval, founder of Club Esperanza del Valle, issued a manifesto demanding equal rights for women, "the vote for single women and widows over the age of twenty-five, divorce for just cause, and access to public office in accordance with physiological and social laws."[59]

Destierro could be highly disruptive, for even the most commonplace assumptions were challenged daily, especially assumptions about gender roles. In many households the boundaries of production and "public," associated with men, and reproduction and "private," related to women, were blurred as the dislocation incurred by exile reduced the space between "work" and "home." It was but a short step from "public" in pursuit of patria to "public" in the pursuit of livelihood.

The position of bourgeois and middle-class women was particularly complex. They were deprived of status and experienced declining living standards. The same conditions that undermined the traditional male roles of husbands and fathers also transformed the traditional female roles of wives and mothers. Women formerly of comfortable means obtained work outside the home—in the factories, in sales positions, in service sectors. Large numbers of émigré households were headed by women, as men remained in Cuba to fight in a war or were killed or imprisoned. Men preparing to join an insurrection often relocated their families in the United States and then returned to Cuba on an expedition. Women themselves emigrated, often alone or with small children, as widows or after abandonment, in search of opportunities to support their families. Newly widowed Concha Agramonte, like many other women during the Ten Years War, immigrated to New York with her nine children and subsequently obtained work as a seamstress. Juan Pérez Rolo recalled his mother taking the four children to Key West in 1869 on the death of his father to find a job and security.[60]

Throughout the 1880s and 1890s increasing numbers of women joined the wage labor force in the United States. "There were Havana families . . . ," Juan

Manuel Planas recounted of Key West, "who accepted the most humble employment in order to live. Housewives worked as laundresses and the daughters of good families were seamstresses or cooks." Data on employment patterns in the Florida cigar factories are incomplete but suggestive. Between 1887 and 1893 nearly 20 percent of the labor force in Key West (3,000 out of 15,000 workers) and Tampa (1,100 out of 5,900) were women.[61]

Criollas in the United States could not help but note the freedom of movement enjoyed by North American women, the ease and liberty with which they traveled alone, strolled, and shopped unaccompanied. These things were not done in Cuba, certainly not by white women with any real or pretended social status. "When we old-timers were children," Alvaro de la Iglesia remembered, "one never saw a lady on the streets unless she was in her carriage." North American travelers to Cuba were slightly bewildered by the proscription against women in public. Women from the United States on Havana streets alone, observed one U.S. tourist, "were greeted in their progress by the half-suppressed exclamations of the astonished Habaneros, who seemed as much surprised to see a lady walk through their streets, as a Persian would to see one unveiled in his."[62]

These observations, of course, suggested larger issues. The encounter with the North could not but challenge the premises and the propriety of the constraints of women of the colony. The experience contributed to new ways by which women came to reject the assumptions of the colonial condition and develop expectations of a new nationality. Certainly nothing caught the attention of criollas so quickly as the sight of North American women appearing alone in public. "What a pleasure it is to see women here driving their own carriages, often alone, sometimes with a girl friend or young daughter," exclaimed Aurelia Castillo de González, "to see also women alternate with their husbands, sometimes with her in the passenger seat, and sometimes him!" All this occurred without the reputation of the man "suffering in the slightest," commented Castillo de González, without anyone "caring about what they were doing, free and happy," in sharp contrast to those countries of "reclusion and preoccupation."[63]

These were customs that many women adapted to easily and, by implication, customs to which men adapted. Cuban men did not object to their wives and daughters traveling alone on North American city streets. One of the pleasures provided by family travel in the North was the opportunity for women to go out unaccompanied to shop, sightsee, and dine with other women. In New York, men conducted business, visited factories and banks, observed Eusebio Guiteras; their women shopped, attended the theater, and visited Central Park. These ways took hold among many Cuban women who lived in the United States. Carlos Loveira, who had himself spent many years in residence there, would write in *Generales y doctores* (1920) of "girls intoxicated with the feminine freedom that is inhaled in the North" and of the many criollas who "adopted American liberty, roots and all."[64]

These developments suggested other possibilities. Women found in the United States opportunities that were scarcely imaginable in Cuba, including education, professional training, and career possibilities. Few who traveled north failed to notice them. "Women in the United States," Eusebio Guiteras noted in 1883, "who receive a very complete education, have many options available to them to make a living." Aurelia Castillo de González made a similar observation. As in "every civilized country," she wrote, North American women are "formed by physical and intellectual education that create possibilities for an infinite number of lucrative occupations." Castillo de González marveled at conditions designed to assist women in their "campaign of emancipation," central to which was the opportunity for a "complete education."[65]

Women in exile did indeed pursue a variety of professional careers and business opportunities. The three daughters of Dr. Juan Fermín Figueroa and Angela Socarrás Varona graduated from pharmacy school in New York and opened the city's first pharmacy owned by women. Adela Campo de Grillo was the only female pharmacist in Key West. After graduating from the New York College of Pharmacy, María Dolores de Figueroa returned home and became the first woman licensed pharmacist in Cuba. Flora and Leopoldina Quesada ran a school for girls. Ana Otero and Isabel Salazar were self-employed music teachers. Herminia Andrade de Benech in New York advertised her skills as a seamstress of the "latest fashions," Dionisia Estrada in Tampa opened a dressmaking business, and Gertrudis Heredia de Serra operated the "Midwife Clinic of Havana" in New York. The Estenoz sisters ran a *casa de familia*, advertising "Cuban food, Cuban hospitality." After years of education and residence in New York, Camagüey-born Rita Dunau returned to Havana and offered instruction in fencing, cycling, and riding as well as classes in French and English. Julia Martínez completed her secondary education at Notre Dame in Baltimore and subsequently received her doctorate in pedagogy at the University of Havana. María Josefa Granados, who lived in Key West and Tampa between 1886 and 1898, eventually went back to Cuba to establish the weekly *El Sufragista* of the Partido Sufragista Cubano in 1913 and subsequently participated in the founding of the Partido Femenista de Cuba.[66]

Samuel Hazard later told of women in Cuba looking "upon the United States as a country to be dreamed of as a fairy vision, where life and liberty are to be really enjoyed." Hazard recounted one conversation with "one sweet innocent": " 'Everyone is free there now, Señor?' 'Oh yes,' I replied; 'we have no negro slaves there now.' 'No, no! Señor, you don't understand me. I mean the women, too—are they not free?' to which I was compelled to reply they were. . . . '*Es muy bueno, Señor*; it is not so here.' "[67]

TOWARD DEFINITION

The experience in the North influenced decisively how Cubans contemplated a nation of their own. Much in this encounter was incorporated into the narrative of nationality and shaped the way the discourse on nation found expression. In the end, the experience affected the very construct of nation and the character of identity and all but guaranteed the integration of elements of North American moral hierarchies into the formulation of Cuban nationality.

These adaptations implied a change in sensibilities and susceptibilities. The experience in the United States revealed more than alternative value systems. The structure of the North American moral order was fundamentally different from the conventions by which Cubans were formed, and adaptation to U.S. norms was itself a source of moral and cultural displacement. The greater the familiarity with northern culture, the more that culture replaced original values and behaviors and the more complete—and permanent—was the transformation.

Life in the United States provided a vantage point from which to take measure of the colonial condition and contemplate alternatives that revealed themselves in everyday life. Many Cubans were born and spent their formative years in the United States. They learned to play new games and acquired a commonplace acquaintance with attitudes and customs that were wholly unfamiliar in Cuba.

This was a process of adaptation and adjustment, a means to consider new opportunities and abandon old constraints. What made this process distinctive, and in many instances definitive, was the degree to which Cubans found their sense of themselves challenged by the confrontation with a very different world. They observed different behaviors daily, and daily their behaviors changed. The experience naturally influenced their disposition to think in new categories. Their lives changed in ways that could scarcely have been imagined, with implications that could not have been foreseen.

The experience in the United States served to accelerate and deepen Cuban discontent with things Spanish. This was a process that advanced unevenly along many different fronts, often at different speeds. Much was related to the inability of the colonial system to meet Cuban needs. The Cuban presence in the United States was itself an expression of discontent. Cubans traveled north precisely to satisfy needs that could not be met at home. They experienced firsthand another way of life, to which they adapted and which increasingly served as the standard for change in Cuba. But it was also true that their encounters in the United States influenced decisively the way they constructed discontent and conceived of nation, which in turn influenced the way they formulated grievances and articulated aspirations. What made these experiences especially momentous was that they occurred at a time of transformation and transition, during the same period in which Cubans were engaged in the process of change, contemplating the raison d'être of nationhood, creating new social relationships in self-conscious pursuit of how to form and inform nationality, and searching for new means to affirm their separateness.

Over a span of many decades, Cubans from all classes came into close, prolonged contact with North America—its values, its institutions, its ways of doing things. Such contact guaranteed that North American cultural forms would insinuate themselves indelibly into the emerging formulations of nationality at all levels. In habits, in tastes, in attitudes, in other ways too numerous to fully appreciate, with consequences impossible to measure, Cubans participated daily in North American cultural transactions. They became like North Americans, that is, emulation as a means of assimilation, often simply to make their lives easier. They learned English, of course, as a necessary survival skill. But they also used English among themselves, in private correspondence and public pronouncements, often as the vocabulary of code, implying shared experiences and a new consciousness. Governor General Valentín Cañedo noted with alarm the large number of Cubans "who today have mastery of the language with which they communicate among themselves."[68] Language indeed began to enter into constructs of class, status, and nationality, whereby English usage signified an alternative that went beyond Spanish to reach out to an opposing cultural system.

There was no mistaking the signs of transformation, the many ways in which new identity, appearances, behaviors, mannerisms, and idiosyncracies were expressed, often acquired self-consciously and designed specifically to draw attention to differences and distinctions. In *Leonela*, when John Valdespina returns to the island after years of residence in the United States, the revelation that he is Cuban astonishes local residents. "*Criollo!*" Fico Suárez exclaims, incredulous. "No one would believe it!" To which Casimiro responds: "He looks more Yankee." In almost identical language, the protagonist in Miguel de Carrión's *Las honradas* (1919) visits a friend in New York whom he has not seen for two years. The changes are apparent: "You look like a Yankee!" he declares. José Antonio Ramos also understood the nature of these transformations. In his novel *Las impurezas de la realidad* (1929), Ramos portrays Masito del Prado, a student at a U.S. college, returning home with a "new notion of things" and flushed with "intellectual emancipation." Not only are Masito's ideas different from his father's, but also he must invent a new discursive framework within which to communicate to his parents. "Why not speak his mind to his father?" the narrator asks. "If at Bethlehem College, despite being in a foreign country and among people barely tolerant of his old Cuban ways, nobody was scandalized by his opinions. They accepted discussion, even when talk turned to themes disagreeable to North American patriotic sentiment. . . . Why, then, in his own home, did he have to remain silent?" And to his mother's pained plea—"don't look for discussions, my son"—the narrative voice responds: "Discussion? It was precisely discussion that he wished to elevate and ennoble, to move beyond the constant talk about meaningless subjects in which the family whiled away its time together."[69]

Posture and demeanor—ways of holding oneself, gestures, carriage—also revealed telltale traces of the encounter with the North. Carlos Loveira, always sensitive to the nuances of exile, in *Generales y doctores* attributes to Cuca the tendency of "crossing her legs masculine style, the American way"; the act of friends expressing affection for each other physically by embraces and kisses is characterized as *a la Americana*. In Mary Peabody Mann's novel *Juanita* (1887), based largely on her experience as a governess on a sugar estate, eighteen-year-old Carolina Rodríguez—"in all respects Americanized"—home on vacation from a Philadelphia boarding school, is introduced to Ludovico: "Carolina frankly extended her hand to him, in American fashion, he took it mechanically, but hardly knew what to do with it."[70]

Many of these changes, of course, were the inevitable results of living abroad, adapting as a way to cope and making the adjustments necessary to meet the needs of daily life: people attempting to get a grip on an unfamiliar, modern world, to make themselves at home in it, to make it their own. In fact, Cubans displayed a remarkable capacity to adapt and adjust. No doubt this was what Máximo Gómez had in mind when he observed in 1888 that "the Cuban has a great facility to assimilate himself immediately to the country to which he goes."[71]

Adaptation is central to Heredia's narration in *Leonela*: it is a complex process of appropriation, a reassembling of the distinct elements of personality, values, and behaviors around newly perceived truths and newly acquired knowledge. John Valdespina is representative of the colonial condition, transformed by his experience in the North, a *criollo* who returns to Cuba as bearer of modernity and progress. He left Cuba as Juan and returned as John and in the process became someone else. Heredia provided a splendid portrait of his time, a revealing document of transformations of the heart and mind, undoubtedly drawn from his own experiences of expatriation. "John Valdespina was a phenomenon of adaptation," the narrator explains, a sign of changing Cuba, "remade by the influence of another medium, or what amounts to the same thing, of another climate, of another education and of other habits and ideas."[72]

But just as much was willed adaptation, a means through which to draw distinctions and increase the distance from Spain, ways of unbecoming Spanish. It was a conscious attempt to elaborate styles of speech, attire, and etiquette that could be appropriated and claimed to be Cuban. Such a process embodied intense contradictions, many of which would persist well into the next century. But in the short run, adaptation served Cuban needs well. This identity was embedded in the narrative on nationality, simultaneously as affirmation and denial, tradition and modernity, present and future.

The process of adaptation deepened the estrangement between Cuba and Spain, of course—it was supposed to. The determination of Cubans to define themselves as different from Spaniards was, in fact, another way to advance the claim of separate nationality. Contact with the North provided new ways to distinguish between Cuban and Spanish and contributed further to the formation of national identity, in ways intended to meet Cuban needs, understanding, too, that change itself reduced the role of—and eventually the rationale for—Spanish rule.

These developments assumed a variety of expressions as Cubans sought new ways to articulate their dissatisfaction, new means of differentiation and definition, all of which served to promote nationality. Many turned to alternative religions as one more outlet for discontent. Baptists, Congregationalists, and Methodists entered Cuban communities in Key West during the 1860s and subsequently made inroads in Tampa, Jacksonville, Philadelphia, and New York, where they established churches, organized Sunday schools, and operated mission classes. Chapels and church schools filled to capacity as more Cubans joined various Protestant denominations. In Tampa, the Congregational church claimed to have 200 members and twice as many students in its missionary school; the Methodist church operated two schools for girls with a total enrollment of 360 students. The Baptist church in Jacksonville served 500 Cuban members.[73]

One source of the Protestant appeal was the array of social services and educational programs provided by missionaries. They organized free vocational training classes and provided English-language instruction. Moreover, they helped with resettlement and sponsored relief programs, including the distribution of clothing and food to needy émigré families.

But the attraction of the Protestant Church was related less to its capacity to provide material sustenance than to its promise as an alternative moral system. Protestantism was everything that Catholicism was not. It implied modernity and exuded the confidence and optimism so much a part of the North American market ethic that appealed to many Cubans. Protestantism engaged more Cubans in the prevailing capitalist vernacular, and its relevance was both symbolic and practical, the hereafter and the here and now. Missionaries acted as agents of a moral economy in which the assumptions of trade and commerce, commodity, and marketplace found corresponding political forms in individual rights, civil liberties, freedom of choice, and freedom of conscience.

Indeed, Protestantism was very much a part of the larger transformation and served the Cuban purpose by providing one more way to reconfigure identity in order to exclude things Spanish. Certainly it involved changing religious beliefs, a conversion of faith in substantive ways. It represented, too, a means of mobility and a sense of community: rootedness during destierro. In ways that the Catholic Church could not, and in ways that the Spanish church in Cuba would not, Protestant denominations easily admitted the participation of Cubans, both men and women, as lay brothers and sisters, but most especially took criollos into the ministry.

The attraction to Protestantism was itself an expression of the larger discontent. No aspect of colonial life was more closely associated with Spanish rule than the Catholic Church. The identification of Catholicism with colonialism took firm hold, and for many Cubans they were one and the same. The Catholic Church symbolized some of the most odious features of Spanish colonialism: illiberal traditions, authoritarian structures, and the preponderance of *peninsulares* within the church hierarchy. The fact that the Catholic Church in Cuba was dominated by a Spanish clergy, dedicated to the defense of Spanish rule, made repudiation of Catholicism a logical if not an inevitable extension of the rejection of colonialism. Raimundo Cabrera denounced the Catholic clergy as "a power which vies with the military authorities in the exercise of tyranny." José Martí was categorical about the fate of the church in a free Cuba: "when the [old] society has been crushed and another, new society has been created . . . Catholicism must perish."[74]

The embrace of Protestantism resonated with meaning: the religion of the North, the Catholic Other, religious heresy as a form of political dissent. Protestantism subsumed an ambiguous political surrogacy in the evangelical text, a relationship in which the very condition of religious freedom implied a new order where religious preference often suggested political affiliation. Salvador Díaz-Versón recalled his parents' decision to marry outside the Catholic Church during the independence struggle: "They were married in a Methodist church, despite their Catholic upbringings, because of their shared revolutionary spirit. Loyal to the old colonial regime, Spanish clergy had denounced the long and desperate rebellion. Young revolutionaries (and their seniors too) developed a feeling of kinship with Protestant churches."[75]

The public support given by North American churches to the cause of Cuba Libre strengthened the ties between Protestant denominations and émigré communities. The Episcopal Church of Rochester, New York, organized the Cuban Hospital Relief Association. The Brooklyn YMCA sponsored Cuba Libre rallies. The Christian Endeavor Association of the Philadelphia Baptist Temple organized fund-raising drives. In Tampa, Protestant ministers routinely delivered invocations at Sunday patriotic picnics. "The pulpits offered evangelical sermons mixed with patriotism," wrote Gerardo Castellanos García of the San Juan Episcopal Church and the Cuban Methodist Mission in Key West. "One attended the service to pray, to sing, to ask God for independence. . . . Protestantism in Key West and in all the Cuban colonies in the United States was a generous supporter and defender of the Cuban cause."[76] That Cubans of impeccable separatist credentials, patriots such as Fernando Figueredo Socarrás and Manuel Deulofeu, joined Protestant denominations and, further, often served as ordained ministers, reinforced the affinity between Protestantism and separatism.

The ranks of Cuban ministers developed early and increased steadily. Some, like Baptists Francisco Pérez Bueno and Miguel M. Calejo, Methodists Enrique B. Someillán, Eladio Díaz, Manuel Deulofeu, and Joaquín Rodríguez, Congregationalist José M. López-Guillén, and Episcopalians Joaquín de Palma and Juan Mancebo were ordained and remained active in the émigré communities of New York, Jacksonville, Ocala, Tampa, and Key West. Others returned to Cuba. During the 1880s and early 1890s, Protestant churches spread across the island due principally to the efforts of Cuban missionaries. Juan Bautista Báez and José R. Peña started an Episcopal church in Guanabacoa. Arriving in Cuba in 1883, Alberto J. Díaz organized the first Baptist church in Havana. José Victoriano de la Cova established a second Baptist church in Matanzas. Baptist preaching stations subsequently opened in Vedado, Regla, Guanabacoa, Los Puentes, Cerro, San Miguel, Marianao, Batabanó, and Cienfuegos. By the late 1880s Baptists had organized eight churches and claimed 1,800 Sunday school students and a church attendance of 12,000. Enrique B. Someillán and Aurelio Silvera established several Methodist churches. Pedro Duarte and Manuel Moreno founded Episcopal churches in Matanzas and Havana. José R. Peña, an Episcopal layman, conducted services in Havana. Former cigar worker Evaristo Collazo set up Presbyterian missions in Havana, Santa Clara, Sagua la Grande, Camajuaní, and Caibarién.[77]

Missionary work also involved educational projects. By 1890 Methodists had opened several day schools and one Sunday school in Havana. Baptists organized two girls' day schools, one in Matanzas with 80 students and another in Havana with an enrollment of 92. The curriculum included reading, writing, typing, sewing, and English. In Cienfuegos, Baptists established an orphan school for 75 boys. By 1891 Baptists claimed a total enrollment of more than 600 students.

The change in religious identity was a highly complex process of meaning and action that in itself reflected a larger historical transformation. Distinctions between spiritual identity and cultural change were neither clear nor precise. Nor were these distinctions necessary, for in both cases conversion was ideologically driven. Conversion implied a process by which to affirm difference and distinction, often at great personal cost and hardship.

Spanish authorities were not slow to understand the implications of the growing Protestant presence in Cuba. Missionary activity represented a new Cuban challenge, and that it assumed largely religious rather than overtly political forms did not reduce Spanish hostility in the slightest. Harassment was immediate and unrelenting. Revival meetings and Sunday worship were disrupted and often banned altogether. A women's Baptist prayer meeting in Havana in July 1888 was suspended when a mob surrounded the church and screamed epithets and hurled stones into the building. In 1889 a Sunday service in Marianao was halted when the mayor appeared with local police and ordered the assembly to disperse. On another occasion, a Sunday evening service in Havana was suspended when a mob gathered outside the church and made noises with drums and pans and yelled curses and denunciations. Cuban pastors were frequently detained and arrested. Pedro Duarte, José R. Peña, and Alberto Díaz were only some of the most prominent ministers imprisoned.[78]

The growing appeal of Protestant denominations gave one more expression to the deepening crisis of Spanish colonialism. Once again Spanish rule was under assault, but this time Cubans had found a different outlet through which to register their growing disaffection with the colonial regime. Indeed, an act as simple as attending a religious service aroused suspicion and under some circumstances could be interpreted as subversive and in more than symbolic ways did challenge key premises of colonial rule. Access to the pulpit provided Cubans with a platform inside Cuba to dispute the authority of Spain over religious matters and, by implication, refute the authority of Spain over everything else. The defense of freedom of worship raised other questions, of course, and preachers did not hesitate to call attention to the linkages.

For the most part, Protestant denominations attracted to the ranks of the ministry disaffected Cubans who had been recruited in the United States and whose expatriation was itself a function of discontent. Their affiliation with North American Protestantism gave one more expression to the Cuban transformation and one more form to the Cuban pursuit of nationality. Protestant denominations generally appealed to Cubans of modest social origins, principally those with working-class and lower-middle-class backgrounds. The ministry tended to consist of representatives of the expanding middle class, many of whom had been unable to find a niche in Cuba. Some had traveled north in pursuit of education and employment and found both. Others were political dissidents, committed to free Cuba, who detected in Protestantism an alternative but no less effective means to challenge the assumptions of Spanish colonialism. The Reverend José Victoriano de la Cova joined the Episcopal Church while attending college in Portland, Maine. Enrique B. Someillán enrolled in a Presbyterian college in Tennessee during the 1870s. The Reverend Alberto J. Díaz was a physician who served as an officer in the Liberation Army during the Ten Years War. He emigrated to New York to receive medical treatment for war wounds, subsequently became a naturalized U.S. citizen, and joined the Willoughby Baptist Church in Brooklyn.

Protestant denominations provided another way for women to take part in the formation of nation. Many criollas expressed their patriotic purpose through work at missions established in the émigré communities and on the island. Josefina Sánchez, María Chongo, Rosa and Emelina Valdés, Amalia Moreno de Soria, María Morales, and Mercedes Díaz were prominently associated with missionary activities in Key West. They served as Sunday school teachers and colporteurs—"carrying the voice of the gospel with their prayers and exhortations into the homes of many unconverted persons," the Reverend Manuel Deulofeu recalled of Isabel Prieto and his wife Bonifacia.[79] They performed relief work, sponsored an array of social services, and played a vital role in integrating newly arrived émigré families into communities that were both Protestant and patriotic, thereby contributing in yet another fashion to the formation of nationality.

It is not always clear how Cubans interpreted the text of North American Protestantism or what use they made of an evangelical subtext. Few sermons of Cuban ministers during these years are known to have survived. Certain tendencies are evident, however, from the private correspondence and published writings of members of the Cuban ministry. Under certain circumstances evangelical tenets could meet Cuban needs directly. Cuban missionaries may have arrived on the island as representatives of North American denominations, but their message could work only if it served Cuban interests. This was a phenomenon perceptively—though only partially—discerned by the Reverend George Lester in 1892. What made Cubans so effective as "missionaries to their countrymen," Lester observed, was "a strong sentiment of fellowship in the Cuban mind" and "patriotic ambitions in which no foreigner can fully share." Salvation was indissolubly linked to liberation. The Reverend Deulofeu explicitly invoked "the light of the gospel" to make "political emancipation truly effective and enduring."[80]

Protestantism contributed to new modalities of political self-awareness, giving form to the proposition that all who shared a common belief system shared common material interests. Whatever may have been the purpose of North American Protestantism, the selection of Cubans as evangelical agents resulted in the remaking of the church in a creole image around which developed another source of Cuban empowerment, one with Cuban leadership, national symbols, and purpose.

Cubans discerned in Protestantism possibilities for material well-being, prosperity, and progress. A large part of the quest for nationality engaged Cubans in reflections about the nature of national potential and sources of collective contentment. For many, Protestantism held the key. Deulofeu could mull over his experience in the United States and attribute to "the grandeur of the gospel" the joy that had "poured into the hearts of the people of this country" and made for the "myriad of American homes which are true havens of peace and happiness." He enjoined all Cubans "to employ the freedom which they have conquered in elevating their character by means of the gospel, which is the powerful lever that within a few decades, has made of England, the United States, Holland, Switzerland and other Protestant countries greater centers of riches."[81]

Spanish authorities early understood that these were not entirely religious issues. Certainly the Protestant presence challenged the privileged place of Roman Catholicism. It raised doctrinal issues and revived historic enmities, to be sure. But more was involved. The mere existence of Protestant churches in Cuba implied transition toward a liberal secular state, a process that could not occur within existing colonial structures—not, at least, without threatening relationships central to Spanish rule in Cuba. Chief among these ties was the support of both the Catholic Church and the countless tens of thousands of peninsulares, soldiers and civilians, the bedrock of the colonial order, for whom the primacy of Catholicism was synonymous with the propriety of colonialism. This was precisely the point made by Matanzas Bishop Juan Bautista de las Casas in 1890, when he implored the provincial governor to denounce the arrival of two Methodist ministers. "I urge you to issue the opportune orders in the defense of the Apostolic Roman Catholic Church," Bishop Bautista exhorted, "which is the religion of the State, and which the aforementioned heretics and apostates seek to offend publicly, as they have been doing by way of pronouncements that are contrary to the laws of the Nation."[82]

In very fundamental ways Protestantism contributed to the dissolution of the Spanish claim of sovereignty by introducing new forms of pluralism. To challenge the exclusivism of the Catholic Church over spiritual matters was to challenge the authority of the colonial government over secular affairs. Indeed, central to the church-state relationship was the reciprocal support for claims of legitimacy of monopoly authority. The Protestant presence inside Cuba created oppositional space from which to introduce alternative religious forms and challenge prevailing political norms of legitimacy. When the War of Independence began in 1895, Protestants across the island were immediately arrested and exiled. In Matanzas the civil governor ordered the Episcopal minister to leave the city within twenty-four hours. In Santa Clara the Presbyterian church was closed and the minister deported.

The expanding Protestant presence thus introduced a new challenge to a colonial order already on the defensive and in varying degrees of disarray and dissolution. One more breach was opened in the collapsing colonial consensus. Persecution of Protestants provided Cubans still further proof of the Spanish incapacity to evolve beyond structures first devised during the Counter-Reformation. To their already long list of grievances against colonialism Cubans now added the demand for freedom of religion. For many thousands of Cubans who attended Protestant religious services and joined the new churches, Spanish harassment confirmed the logic for and, indeed, the necessity of separation from Spain.

AFFIRMATION OF AFFINITY

Much in the Cuban transformation of the nineteenth century was related to forces originating in the United States. The Cuban presence in the North was driven largely by new needs, many of which the ensuing linkages served to meet. But in the process, Cuban needs were also modified and expanded; they adapted to new possibilities, and once those adaptations had been completed, Cubans had acquired new needs that could be met only in the United States. Throughout the nineteenth century Cubans and North Americans came into close contact and developed binding and permanent ties.

The United States served as a context within which to set goals, formulate expectations, and measure achievements. The experience suggested possibilities for individual improvement and collective advancement derived explicitly from notions of material progress to which Cubans could reasonably aspire. It was predicated on mastery of a body of knowledge and access to technology and new methods, all of which were within reach and with which Cubans came into frequent contact as an ordinary part of their lives. This was a world with which they developed familiarity and to which they adapted. It contributed to the formulation of identity and provided the basis on which increasing numbers would define themselves as Cubans. It provided, too, a context within which to contemplate the future and form reasonable expectations of that future.

Cubans could not help but make comparisons and assign value to the differences. This was one way discontent deepened, for the experience in the North created a framework that set the deficiencies of colonialism in sharp relief. How could the colonial order possibly compare favorably with the breathtaking pronouncements appearing in Francisco Calcagno's novel *En busca del eslabón* (1888)? On arriving in the United States, Sinónimo exults: "Hail! Cradle of liberty of the Americas and beacon of freedom of the world, Hail! Land of the future, defender of progress, and the greatest social creation of humanity. Just as man is the ultimate creation on the evolutionary order . . . so too is [the United States] the final result of all the struggles, all the reversals, the misfortunes, the hopes and the triumphs of all the nations and peoples who have preceded us."[83]

The consensus among those who had traveled in the North was striking. Eusebio Guiteras could hardly contain his awe at U.S. accomplishments, and his commentary established the Cuban condition as the implicit counterpoint in the subtext. "The United States," he wrote in 1883, "is the best example of what history has to offer by way of a democratic regime. . . . The display of greatness and prosperity of the republic is not even what is most impressive. What is truly remarkable is the mobility of each individual and the order that prevails within this mobility. Each person recognizes the course to take, and pursues it with marvelous independence." Guiteras made particular note of the absence of any authority that "orders, directs, and manages." North Americans possessed ways "to exercise their legitimate powers," he observed. "In the first place, they elect. Moreover, they assemble freely, and speak freely, and they have a free press." He concluded: "In the United States, power resides with the governed." Carlos Trelles was also in a state of wonder when he recorded his impressions of the North. From every possible perspective, he pronounced—"material, industrial, intellectual, moral, political and economically"—the United States had "reached a place of promise by virtue of its advanced civilization." It was the "most liberal and richest nation on the planet," where "nobody oppressed anyone else" and which enjoyed a "high level of morality and incomparable material development." *El Progreso*, published in New York, extolled the freedom of the press: "In the United States where the newspaper is an article of fundamental necessity . . . one writes what one wants. . . . How different things are with us." Raimundo Cabrera marveled how North Americans were "taught to live and work for the common good, and not the support of a royal family" and how they were linked by "common affection to a country that assured all its people equal rights and privileges." North Americans had little appreciation of "the value of the rights that no one has ever disputed," observed Cabrera. "Only the man born abroad, like me, under institutions that have oppressed him since birth, can appreciate the importance of republicanism." Manuel Pichardo experienced instant transformation on entering the United States. "Effectively, a man feels more master of himself, more dignified in one's life, more vigorous upon breathing this wholesome air that is without limit," exulted Pichardo. "And I have felt myself becoming a different superior person, my spirit soars with powers I had never known." But his euphoria was short-lived, for he quickly realized: "Ay! Then I come back down upon thinking that this is not me, that I am a foreigner. My memory returns to my beautiful country of the palm trees, so favored by Nature and so mistreated by men. To every new impression that strikes me, in the presence of the greatness that this nation has achieved in such a short time, I am reminded of Cuba and I weep for its backwardness. . . . I admire what the Yankee has known to develop with his efforts, his morality, his patriotism and his customs."[84]

These types of encounters could only contribute to Cuban discontent with their homeland as they knew it. Cubans who arrived in the United States were not slow to notice differences and disparities. Such linkages exposed new incongruities and fostered new dissatisfactions. Experiences in the United States revealed new possibilities, raised new expectations, and inevitably created new demands, most of which could not be reasonably accommodated within the structures of Spanish colonialism—and hence further discredited those structures. The encounter contributed to the manner in which Cubans defined the deficiencies of the colonial system as well as suggested possibilities for transformation into nation. They were understandably impressed with the signs of progress, the streets and avenues, the stores and goods, part of which could be attained, they thought, if Cuba could reinvent itself as a smaller version of the United States. How difficult it must have been to resist the temptation to compare Havana to New York. "I think of Cuba with tears and in pain," Enrique Hernández Miyares, editor of *La Habana Elegante*, wrote from New York in 1894, "despite how much I love her, because of how poorly it measures up in comparison. We too have some good things, of course, but we have many bad things, some of which are horrendous. . . . I am not an annexationist. . . . The issue is in imitating the United States and to reach its greatness, in proper proportion to our size and density of population."[85]

The United States served as both a standard and a source of modernity and offered an alternative framework within which to envision the dismantling of colonial structures. It presented a frame of reference for many Cubans and, inevitably, by this standard of progress and modernity, Havana came up woefully short. Unpaved streets, inferior public services, and inadequate educational facilities were only some of the more obvious deficiencies of Havana compared to New York. The monthly *La Fraternidad*, published by the El Progreso Artistic and Literary Society of Sancti-Spíritus, praised the New York public school system, against which it assessed the condition of municipal schools in Cuba and concluded that local authorities were guilty of "perpetuating an act of continued indifference."[86]

But it was not only Havana compared to New York. Key West and Tampa often served as subjects of Cuban rumination. "Key West is one of those . . . links of civilization and progress," proclaimed Carlos de la Torre in 1893. In Raimundo Cabrera's partly autobiographical novel *Ideales* (1918), Tomás returns to Cuba in 1885 after some years of residence in Cayo Hueso (Key West). He is horrified by the state of a provincial city, and in this instance it is *el Cayo* that becomes the standard by which Tomás takes measure of the Cuban condition. "The streets of the town were virtually deserted. . . . The streetcar, the popular vehicle of urban transportation, was conspicuous by its absence; the coming and going on the streets that ordinarily attest to activity and movement in large cities were replaced by a monotonous silence." And there was more: "The pavement of the streets was gravel—uneven, full of potholes, with deep and open ruts in the middle of the road. Off to the side, on streets without sidewalks, weeds had spread everywhere, like debris. The fronts of houses were in disrepair. The tiles on the roofs were hanging in rickety fashion, supported by four wooden posts driven directly into the ground, without foundation or shafts." And Tomás murmurs disapprovingly under his breath: "Such backwardness! Such backwardness!" Wenceslao Gálvez took note of differences immediately on his arrival in Tampa: "Accustomed to seeing in Havana and Puerto Príncipe the urban streetcars drawn by horses, one is surprised to see here the same cars operating under their own power."[87]

Cubans traveled across the United States, keen observers always, musing on the meaning of what they saw, appraising the North American condition but almost always as a meditation on the Cuban condition. On a visit to New Haven one summer, José María Heredia noticed the shade of tree-lined sidewalks and immediately thought of home: "I cannot help but ask myself why in Cuba, under that devouring sun, so terrible, that beats upon our heads all year long, we have not adopted any of the measures that the Yankees use so cleverly to protect themselves against the heat of only a few days." The public parks, botanical gardens, and zoos in Boston, New York, Philadelphia, and Baltimore made a deep impression on novelist Ramón Meza: "What a source of education, what a source of morality and culture—that is what we do not have and what we ask for." Carlos Trelles marveled at the parks in the United States: "What a marked contrast between American cities filled with these urban lungs, where residents can breathe pure air and the children get exercise by playing, and Cuban cities, where one rarely sees a cluster of trees, where there are no open spaces shaded with foliage, where everything is built up and there is no place for recreation or a way to purify the atmosphere." José Silverio Jorrín was struck by the system of public libraries in "the great cities and the small towns" and the "extraordinary generosity [with which] municipalities and state legislatures fund these libraries, dedicated to the dissemination of general knowledge, of specialized sciences, and the teaching of new technologies." Domingo del Monte was impressed by reform schools, where "punishment was tempered with moral and literary instruction and an apprenticeship in a trade allows them to acquire habits of labor and economy." Del Monte did not fail to draw the moral: "If the government of the island wants to reduce at the source the enormity of the calamities that accompany the ignorance and misery of individuals of the working class who manage to escape the moral influence of primary schools, it should establish in every provincial capital a correction school of such beneficial value."[88] Invidious comparisons all, they added so much more to the deepening Cuban discontent.

It would be difficult, if not impossible, to fully assess the impact of these experiences, the myriad ways in which Cubans responded to the United States and how their responses subsequently influenced behaviors and attitudes. They came to know the United States intimately and were shaped by this familiarity. Contacts of this kind, often decades in duration, could not but affect the way Cubans came to view their own society, contribute to shaping their values, and influence the meaning they gave to their lives. The process spanned the entire second half of the nineteenth century, a transformation so gradual as to become itself a pattern of daily life.

Access to the North increased Cuban familiarity with other possibilities. The experience suggested alternatives to many of the things that troubled Cubans most about conditions on their island. This was a world that they could enter and dwell in, a place where they could size up their own situation and explore new means of self-fulfillment and self-representation.

As the pursuit of Cuba Libre stretched across decades and over generations, susceptibility to North American ways deepened. This process had antecedents in the early nineteenth century, and the political objectives that divided the emigration between *anexionistas* and *independentistas* mattered less than the cultural experiences that united them. Central to the experience of destierro was a search for new forms and different ways to pursue patria and express nationality. As the number of Cubans in the United States increased, as the length of their residence extended from weeks and months to years and eventually to decades, the deeper was the impact of North American ways.

The encounter altered the way Cubans thought about change—its form, its scope, its purpose. The notion of change expanded to accommodate new possibilities and thereby became the means by which North American forms fused with Cuban ones. Domingo del Monte understood this well when he acknowledged the "powerfully seductive spell of the marvelous prosperity and free institutions" of the United States.[89]

Cubans were present as both observers and participants at the inception of North American market culture. Between 1865 and 1900 the value of manufactured goods increased sevenfold, the number of factories quadrupled, and industrial capital increased fourfold. The extraordinary industrial productivity of the United States, with its emphasis on consumer goods, convenience, and comfort, began to gather momentum and transform North American life during the years of Cuban emigration and transition. Cubans experienced life in the United States at a time of remarkable economic development, when success and well-being were increasingly measured in terms of material progress and consumption. If Thorstein Veblen, who wrote during the final years of the nineteenth century, was only partially correct, that the "motive that lies at the root of ownership is emulation" and that to "a great extent this emulation shapes the methods and selects the objects of expenditure for personal comfort and decent livelihood,"[90] the implications of the Cuban presence in the United States at this time were far-reaching, indeed. Distinctive characteristics of Cuban social classes were being formed during these decades, many of them in the United States, at a critical moment—when the potential for consumption was expanding and a great many Cubans were self-consciously seeking ways to express "Cuban" as a means of identity and nationality.

Much of this was related to the larger experience that residence in the United States signified when rapid economic development and widening channels of distribution became identified with improved living standards. The population of Cuban emigrants, which was large enough to constitute a market, was, in fact, the target of advertising campaigns by U.S. retailers and merchants. In the mid-1890s the *Tampa Tribune* introduced a new page, *Edición en Español*, filled with Spanish-language advertisements from U.S. merchants and shopkeepers. And across the United States the pages of the émigré press displayed numerous advertisements of sales and services. Many retail stores established "Spanish departments" and hired Cubans as translators. Devlin and Company in New York marketed "an extensive and fine assortment of ready made clothing" and called the "attention of the Spanish American public to . . . our magnificent assortment." Devlin created a *departamento español* and appointed G. Ruiz as supervisor. Hearns department store—the "most popular clothing store in New York," it claimed—offered Cuban customers "interpreters that will provide personal assistants in all the departments." "Se habla español," advertised Nathan's Shoe Store on Sixth Avenue. At Lord and Taylor, "Sr. Iraola has the pleasure to receive his Spanish-speaking friends." Vogel Brothers clothing store announced with great ceremony the appointment of Eduardo Frías Lay to head its new "Cuban department." Clothiers Simpson, Crawford and Simpson urged "Cuban families . . . who visited their establishment to ask for the Spanish interpreter, the Cuban, Miss Rosario Merlo."[91]

This experience was decisive. For tens of thousands of Cubans, vast numbers of whom would later infuse meaning and purpose to the principal institutions of the republic, destierro provided the sum of processes by which they were brought into a modern condition. These were large sectors of the Cuban bourgeoisie and middle class, party to and involved in social institutions, values, and structures of a specific historical moment in the United States. Their world was transformed and made more complex; the possibility of entering the mainstream of new technological systems, both in their material dimensions and their ideological assumptions, had never been as powerful as it was in the closing decades of the nineteenth century. This offered the potential of a high standard of living through industrial modes of production, organization of large-scale social units for efficient manufacture and distribution, and elaboration of democratic institutions through popular participation.

There was a peculiarly subversive quality to North American materialism. In ways large and varied it contributed to undermining some of the most fundamental social assumptions of the colonial order. The proposition that happiness and comfort could be obtained from material possessions was dangerous precisely because it did not confine its appeal to the tastes of the privileged and powerful. Objects more modest, more domestic, more available to more people seized hold of the popular imagination. Convenience and well-being as common, everyday conditions were among the things to which Cubans adapted, appropriated as their own, and in fact demanded: the pursuit of wealth, Veblen suggested, "for an increase of the comforts of life—primarily for an increase of the physical comforts which the consumption of goods affords."[92] Cubans "manage to live here better than they do in Cuba," observed cigar manufacturer Blas Trujillo; "they live [here] more comfortably than in Havana." New comforts and conveniences, in the end, were simply incorporated into daily life in the United States and assumed to be permanent. Visitors and residents alike soon adapted to these ways, all of which, of course, emphasized the deficiencies of home. "It is well known that there is nothing to which one can become more easily accustomed than good things," observed Enrique Hernández Miyares on returning to Cuba. "For that reason, after being in New York for three days, I believed that I was in my element, as if all that greatness, all that comfort,* and all those things that make life pleasant had been made for me."[93]

It was not that these values were entirely novel, but rather that they spread so quickly among so many people at a time when class structures were in transition and national identity was assuming form. Material wealth and consumption were not simply ends, but a condition that conferred distinction and merit on the possessor, and possession served as the mark of social merit. Few facets of North American life impressed Cubans more than the application of science and

*The italicization of English words in translation signifies original English usage in the Spanish text.

industry to everyday comfort and personal convenience. "This capacity to meet constantly even the slightest desire easily, effortlessly," wrote Dolores María de Ximeno y Cruz of a visit to the United States in 1882, "simply by pushing a button . . . was a great surprise." Ximeno y Cruz was astonished by the ways that household tasks were completed with "easy and rapid solution," without "experiencing even minimum difficulties," and concluded: "They possessed the secret of comfort, to which every citizen has access." Ten years later Aurelia Castillo de González wrote almost in rapture of the "thousands of the ingenious devices that make life so comfortable," such as "the kitchen stove that in one instant is turned on and in another is off." But "what I like the most," she declared, "and would like to take to each house in Cuba, are the electric fans, in the shape of a windmill, that rotate with such velocity that the blades disappear . . . and eliminate the heat to the point where one feels cold." She thought about placing ceiling fans in barbershops; she imagined her husband "shaving himself in Havana, in the month of August, and then ask him if he can reject progress." Manuel Pichardo arrived at similar conclusions. "The *yankee* is also all forethought," he observed; "necessity has been attended to in an absolute sense. A hard-working people, they strive for a high level of relaxation: they have created *comfort*. They possess an invention to satisfy every desire." And the objective of thousands of devices? Pichardo asked rhetorically: "To save labor while obtaining great production. How many instruments have I seen that could be used in Cuba with great benefit. And nowhere with greater benefits than in our country due to the scarcity of labor that exists for all types of work."[94]

These were extraordinary times as the enormous productive capability of the United States gathered momentum, as industrial innovation and technological advances merged with mass production and mass distribution to transform the character of North American life. Perhaps nothing captured as fully the sense and essence of the times as the Chicago Columbian Exposition of 1893, a powerful and palpable affirmation of progress triumphant. Almost every country in the world was represented, including Cuba, which had a sugar and tobacco exhibit in the Palace of Agriculture. But it was the technological display by the United States that deeply impressed Cuban visitors to the fair. They were awestruck and could hardly believe their eyes. Raimundo Cabrera was overwhelmed by a sense of wonder at the "spectacle that lifts our vision into the future." Aurelia Castillo de González described in detail the technological wizardry and the gadgets; she could not always explain how these things worked but never doubted that they did work. "What can we say of a kitchen that does not use coal or fire wood?" she remarked of the model electric kitchen. The "wondrous Ferris wheel," the "spectacular printing presses," "electric generators that use oil piped in from Indiana," the "bewildering assortment of farming machinery" were only some of the "many thousands of ingenious devices" that she saw. Electricity in particular, and all the magical uses to which it was put, was especially remarkable. Castillo de González could not conceal her astonishment at Electricity Hall, a spectacular display of electric trolleys, electrical heaters, and Edison's newest invention: the kinematograph, which visually reproduced moving images and lights. Lights were everywhere, replete with messages and metaphors: light was science, progress, civilization; darkness was primitive, backwardness, barbarism. "This is sheer magnificence," Castillo de González proclaimed, "there is the light of the midday sun indoors, there is the brilliant glow of the latest nicest scientific expression of our epoch."[95]

Borrowed forms enhanced self-esteem and raised status. Creole bearers of "modern" culture to their "backward" society were often prone to embarrassment at the Cuban condition. The experience often induced searching self-interrogations, with predictable laments. Manuel Pichardo, who saw the Cuban exhibit in Chicago, in a moment of pained self-realization, reacted with both dismay and despair over the representation of "Cuban": "And after examining our products, what deductions can we make? Can we be satisfied? No, not in the form in which we have been represented. . . . No, it is not sufficient if we wish to figure more honorably in this civilized continent." He continued: "And what do we offer in the long run? Tobacco—a vice. Sugar—almost another vice. And both products from the soil, in which there is little need for the intelligence, ingenuity or knowledge of man. For us to advance . . . we have to demonstrate before the world, the wealth of our industry, of our manufacturing, of our science and art. With so few years of existence like us, the United States has been able to achieve these levels. . . . To achieve this state of progress, we need . . . liberties and exemptions." The editor of the popular Havana monthly *El Base-Ball* gave similar expression to the Cuban angst: "We take little to Chicago, because we possess little. . . . But with such inferior means we go to Chicago, perhaps with bitterness in our heart, to contemplate what others do and what we too could do if in this body social there were a more determined interest [and] more activity in behalf of reform . . . to break the routines contrary to progress in all spheres of human activity."[96]

The inner anguish caused by the confrontation between the "modern" republic of the North and the "backward" colony in the Caribbean inspired a range of revolutionary representations and visions as both a response and a way to reconcile these experiences. These developments had long-term implications, for they occurred as Cubans were assembling the distinct elements that would distinguish themselves from Spaniards and define themselves as a separate community. Cubans learned the ways in which material goods served to delineate social standing and hierarchy of nations. Consumption suggested socially structured ways that goods could draw lines of social relationships and status markers. The experience in the United States provided knowledge of goods, of their social and cultural value, and suggested how they might be employed as a means of self-definition, which included at once self-improvement and self-development, personal transformation, and national consciousness. Goods could serve both as a symbol of individual well-being and an affirmation of national identity, often a conscious way to classify the social and political realms according to well-defined categories of people.

In due course facets of North American material culture became a means to express Cuban national identity. These forms were appropriated to affirm the ways Cubans differed from Spaniards, to demonstrate that who they were and what they wanted to become were not of Spanish origin. Ultimately, this was a Cuban reworking of North American categories to address their own experiences and meet their specific needs.

Some of this took obvious forms, although the implications were far from obvious at the time. Frequent travel between Cuba and the United States and residence, for varying periods, in the North were still other ways that North American customs were diffused and disseminated throughout the island. This contact, prolonged and recurring, fostered Cuban affinity for things and ways North American.

And it was becoming easier to acquire and sustain these affinities. Mass production was integrated with rapid transportation and mass distribution, with the net effect that large quantities and great varieties of U.S. consumer goods became generally available across the island. Much was introduced directly by Cubans who left the United States with tastes for things North American. Many returned to the island dressed in North American attire, with an assortment of furnishings, merchandise, and wares of the North. Vacationing creole families always allotted sufficient time to shop in New York before their departure. "On their return [to Cuba]," observed Eusebio Guiteras, "men and women go out in a frenzy to sack the stores and shops; and trunk after trunk accumulate little by little, forming a mass of luggage that would give envy to the pharaoh who constructed the great pyramid of Egypt."[97]

A huge array of North American products arrived in the normal conduct of trade and commerce, as the inexorable logic of proximity and convenience took its full effect. Rapid cable communication with U.S. suppliers facilitated the entry of North American commodities into the Cuban market. So did the reciprocity treaty of 1892. Woven wire mattresses, clocks, cameras, plated cookware, lamps, pianos and organs, and such varied domestic appliances as stoves, pepper mills, cutlery, coffee pots, sewing machines, and furniture were only some of the consumer goods that found widespread popularity and a ready market on the island. In 1889 the fountain pen—*pluma automática americana*—arrived in Cuba, advertised as the "modern innovation" that allowed "repeated usage with only one ink fill-up a day." The Expreso Isla de Cuba served as agent for Wells Fargo, Carrington Company, and American and European Express Company of New York. The trade catalog of B. May and Company provides a sample of the consumer goods and products available to Cuban customers, including Lillie safes (*cajas fuertes*), New England Glass Company glassware, paint, cement, lamps, and tools. Every refrigerator in Matanzas, reported the U.S. consul in 1890, was manufactured in the United States.[98] The Collins Company of Hartford supplied *machetes*—advertised as "cane knives"—axes, and hatchets. In fact, so totally did the Collins Company expand into the Cuban market that the trademark signature passed into popular usage as the name of the product: Collins (*coyeens*) was synonymous with *machete*, and thus the battle cry: "¡Hay que sacar los *collins* de sus vainas!" (The Collins must be drawn from their sheaths!). The name of a patriotic club that formed in Tampa 1897 appeared innocuous enough but resonated among those in the know: El Club Collins.

Throughout the 1880s and 1890s the use of continuous-process machines allowed for the mass production of an enormous variety of staples that passed immediately beyond the U.S. market to Cuban consumers. Between 1889 and 1893 the total value of U.S. exports to Cuba rose from $11.3 million to $24 million, with notable increases in agricultural implements ($74,000 to $130,000), hardware ($80,000 to $395,000), carriages ($67,000 to $316,000), sewing machines ($42,000 to $96,000), tools ($115,000 to $244,000), and provisions ($3.2 million to $5.6 million). By the 1890s many Cubans were eating the same canned meats (Libby) as North Americans, as well as bathing with the same soap (Proctor and Gamble), drinking the same milk (Borden), serving the same soup (Heinz), and enjoying the same beer (Pabst)—"American lager-beer is slowly coming into favor," noted James McQuade in 1885.[99]

The distribution of mass-produced machines increased. New light machinery and consumer durables spread across the island, including cash registers (National Cash Register), adding machines (Burroughs), cigarette-making machines (Bosak), pumps (Worthington), printing presses (Mergenthaler), boilers (Babcock and Wilcox), guns (Colt), and elevators (Otis). Singer sewing machines appeared in the 1860s and Remington typewriters in 1887. Retail stores specializing in U.S. ready-made clothing also proliferated. In 1875 Antonio Aedo opened the La Bomba shoe store in Havana which only sold shoes made in the United States. In 1893 Víctor Lopez, owner of the La Barata shoe store, acquired exclusive distribution rights to the Cleveland Shoe Company line. In the same year the Los Estados Unidos clothing store opened in Cárdenas offering a full selection of U.S. apparel. Growing numbers of U.S. bicycles appeared on Havana streets. North American furniture increased in popularity. The houses of *habaneros*, observed William Cullen Bryant as early as midcentury, "are filled with rocking-chairs imported from the United States." The narrator in *Dos amores* (1887) by Cirilo Villaverde speaks of one such home in Havana: "It was clear that in this room there was something of the foreign, or at least the person who lived there had traveled to foreign countries, in which he no doubt learned the art of decorating taste and skill."[100] No self-respecting well-to-do Havana household was without the fashionable New York coupé. "The Cubans are gradually getting into the ways and ideas of American life," observed Joseph Dimock as early as 1859. "A few years since an American horse and vehicle was a novelty here, but now an American buggy or hack is nearly as common on the Paseo as the unwieldy volante."[101]

Nor was the distribution of North American products confined to Havana. Almost all Cuban port cities, on both coasts, maintained direct commercial access to the United States. In many instances the North was the only market for local exports and the principal source of foreign imports. By the mid-1880s all the sugar produced around Matanzas, Cárdenas, Sagua la Grande, Caibarién, Nuevitas, Gibara, Guantánamo, Manzanillo, Zaza, and Trinidad was exported to the United States, as was the fruit grown in Baracoa and virtually all the iron mined in Oriente.[102]

The advanced railroad network, moreover, linked provincial ports with interior districts and rapidly distributed foreign imports throughout remote areas in the countryside. This, no doubt, is what Francisco Ponte Domínguez had in mind when he wrote that the construction of the Matanzas-Sabanilla railroad into Corral Falso in 1849 "carried civilization" into the interior. For Sagua la Grande historian Antonio Miguel Alcover, the completion of the Villaclara-Sagua line in 1858 represented a "work of progress and civilization."[103]

These were the ways that Cubans in hundreds of far-flung towns and villages were linked to a vast outside world that they came to know by its commodities, which they identified as a source of their own comfort and well-being and around which they began to order their lives, at home, at work, and at play. Vicente Méndez Roque described growing up in the 1880s along the tracks of the Ferrocarril del Norte between Puerto Príncipe and Nuevitas on the northern coast. "We loved those trains," he remembered. "The train formed part of our existence, its arrival brought a breath of fresh air into our lives." The railroad linked Méndez Roque to the outside world, if only "to meet or say good-bye to a friend or family member, or to wait for an important message or urgently needed medicine, to look at the passengers in the coaches and observe the novelty of diverse types. . . . The train brought in and took away dreams, hopes, illusions, sorrows." And thus the railroad worked its way into the ordinary existence of rural Cuba. Méndez Roque added: "The train was an integral, familiar, and beloved part of our daily lives. . . . It took us away and returned us home; it was the only way out and the only way into the village."[104]

The maritime link between all the ports in all the provinces along both coasts of the island and the United States as well as the rail network from coastal points into the interior opened virtually all of Cuba to North American imports. Traveling through Villa-Clara at midcentury, Ramón de la Sagra reported seeing a "great number of sewing machines imported from the United States." Sagra found sewing machines everywhere, "not only in Havana, but also in the towns in the interior . . . in Sagua, Cárdenas, Colón and even in remote farms in the country." He continued:

> Cuban women have adopted the machines easily, not only because of the little effort required in order to make elaborate clothing but because they have become the only means on the island that permits them to sew. . . . Now, thanks to the machines, almost all the clothing on the farms and among the rural families can be made, even by young girls who previously had nothing to do. It is curious indeed to see little *mulatas* and black girls of 7 and 8 years of age pushing the pedal and doing the sewing in some families.[105]

Almost four decades later, during the War of Independence, as the Liberation Army marched westward across the distant savannas of Camagüey province, Colonel Eduardo Rosell y Malpica was astonished to discover that "in all the houses women have sewing machines." As he recalled his childhood in Havana during the closing years of the nineteenth century, what Jorge Calderón González remembered most was his mother's prize possession: "Always, all her life, she had a Singer sewing machine, which was the one that lasted the longest." The sewing machine also provided access to new techniques and new styles. "In the remote interior of Cuba," wrote Victor Clark, "30 or 40 miles from any better means of communication than a pony trail, the palm-leaf hut of the country-man often contains an American sewing machine as its only piece of purchased furniture, and Spanish editions of American fashion magazines are to be found in these humble dwellings 30 miles from any post office."[106]

North American products soon became commonplace in Cuba. William Drysdale, who visited a sugar mill near Cienfuegos in 1885, described the "amusements on a sugar estate" and the "boys [with] their amateur photographic apparatus, with which they take pictures of everything in the heavens above and the earth beneath." From Sagua la Grande near the northern coast, the U.S. commercial agent made another observation, with portents all too clear: "The stores are well supplied with American canned meats and fruits, hams, biscuits, etc. In all cases American goods are preferred." Dimock made a similar notation in his diary while touring Cárdenas: "American goods are getting more common."[107]

Features of the North arrived in Cuba in many forms and from many sources. Towns and villages across the island assumed the appearance of U.S. communities. This was especially conspicuous in the boomtowns that sprang up in the mining zones and around the headquarters of the massive railroad construction projects. Tesifonte Gallego García was astonished by the "American appearance" of towns near the iron mines of Oriente and the prevalence of the English language throughout the region. Railroad projects in particular gave rise to new settlements, teeming with engineers, surveyors, mechanics, carpenters, and construction workers, erected almost overnight in the provincial interior. At distant locations, North American enclaves were carved out of jungles and forests. The narrator in Heredia's *Leonela* describes the boomtown of "Smithson-City," a "new world in the district of Jarabacoa," where "the English language with its harsh accent was the voice of command for almost all the workers were Yankees." The narrator continues:

That make-shift town in no way resembled Jarabacoa. It was something new, outside the tropical environment, something that had been born adult from evening to morning. . . . It could be said that it was one of those pleasant settlements on the banks of the Hudson River, transferred in its entirety to the shores of the Cuabellas River for the Cuban sun to make it all the more attractive. The small settlement was especially distinguished by its attractive and modest elegance, which suggested a sharp contrast to the indigence and abandon of neighboring towns constructed of palm bark and mud. Smithson-City had superb shops, a perfectly installed foundry, infirmary, railway sidings, stores, and there, on a near-by height, an elegant if small building, the home of the directing engineer.[108]

Cubans, too, arrived with memories of time and place abroad. After the Ten Years War hundreds of cigar-worker families returned from Key West and settled in a new *barrio* of Havana that they promptly named Cayo Hueso. The neighborhood to this day retains its resemblance to nineteenth-century Key West, with its wide streets, wider curbs, and distinctive elements of the architect of *el Cayo*.[109]

Progress arrived in Cuba in the form of things North American: technological advances great and small, innovations permanent and ephemeral, the newest and the latest. Cubans stood in awe of the prodigious accomplishments of the North, many of which were already transforming the way they lived on the island. U.S. companies operated the utilities in the principal cities. In the early 1850s James Robb of New Orleans completed the first gasworks in Havana to the wonderment of habaneros. In 1877 the gasworks was acquired by the Havana Gas Light Company of New York and reorganized ten years later as the Spanish-American Light and Power Company of New York. The Santiago Gas Light Company provided lighting to the Oriente capital. During the 1880s North Americans constructed the first ice factory in Havana; with a production capacity of thirty tons daily, it made the capital self-sufficient in ice. C. and A. Beatty of New York supplied Havana with a fleet of new omnibuses. In 1890 the city of Cárdenas reorganized its fire department around a newly acquired fleet of steam-powered fire engines from the United States. In the same year Runkle, Smith and Company completed construction of Havana's modern waterworks. Telephone service arrived in Havana in 1881 and expanded rapidly across the island: to Cienfuegos a year later and Santiago de Cuba by 1884. Havana possessed a municipal telephone exchange by 1889, only a decade after the establishment of the first commercial exchange in the United States. M. T. McGovern and the Compañía Eléctrica de Cuba, a General Electric subsidiary, introduced elec-

tricity to Havana with the installation of a 100-kilowatt generator at the Tallapie-
dra docks in 1885, three years after Edison's invention. Electricity reached into
the provinces, first in 1889 when Cárdenas installed a steam-power electrical
generator; Cienfuegos, Santa Clara, Camagüey, and Santiago de Cuba followed.
By 1890 the Edison Spanish Colonial Light Company was operating in Matanzas,
Cárdenas, and Sagua la Grande.[110]

Tourism played a part in these developments, as the requirements of comfort
obliged hoteliers in Havana to offer accommodations at least equal to those
meeting the standards of North American travelers. Hotels were transformed
into "sumptuous establishments, where electric lights, reading rooms, elevators
and other comforts of American origin have been introduced." Pleasantly surprised during his travels in 1891, Elliott Durand wrote glowingly: "The hotels of
Cuba have been remodeled and reconstructed to such an extent that they are
scarcely inferior to American houses of the same relative class."[111]

The very notion of progress was potentially subversive, capable of undermining the established order and radically rearranging the hierarchy of values and
authority to the point where the promise of the new undermined the premise of
the old. In its central assumption, the proposition of progress tended to challenge colonial conventions and undermine the beliefs and practices by which
they were sustained. Ideas that joined together progress, science, and technology,
formulated in paradigms of modernity and civilization, had a powerful appeal
to those seeking to overturn the traditional order. They created another source
of differentiation in colonial society, one that also implied values of those who
were "advanced" and those who were "backward." In *Cecilia la matancera* (1861),
novelist Rafael Otero tells of a youth who was "smitten by the word 'progress,'"
whereas the term terrified his elders, for whom "'progress' was synonymous
with 'anarchy.'" Nicolás Heredia, in *Leonela*, was fully alive to the larger implications of progress and its capacity to subvert the normative foundations of colonial authority. When engineer John Valdespina announces plans to introduce
the newest agricultural machinery into the Jarabacoa—"I will bring new inventions that save time and are more efficient, and . . . can make possible diversified
agriculture and will bring great wealth to the region"—Captain Maella, the local
jefe de partido, can hardly contain his ire. "Captain Maella looked upon these
innovations with ill-concealed indignation. He could not explain how the Government had given that man the privilege to disrupt the established order. Ever
since the engineer had started working on the construction of the railroad line,
nobody remembered anymore about the first—and only—authority of the district of Jarabacoa." Valdespina may not have been able to see how a railroad—"a
clear sign of civilization and useful means of public service"—could be a source
of suspicion for anyone, but Maella understood: "I am nothing for that insubor-
dinate foreigner, trouble-maker and clearly pernicious. . . . What is worse is that
by his example the simple inhabitants are being incited against me."[112]

North American ways influenced Cuban patterns of entertainment and recreation. Havana nightlife changed, due in part to electricity, in part to new inventions that were brought to Cuba. In 1893 the Café Tacón in Havana advertised new late evening hours to commence with the purchase of the "fonógrafo de Mr. Edison," with "an immense and varied repertoire." Social life changed as creoles found in North American forms additional ways to define themselves. In 1886 the Havana Yacht Club—the name was always in English—was founded by young creoles who had studied in the United States. The Yacht Club organized races, sponsored regattas, and held swimming meets, all of them modeled on North American programs. Other clubs followed, and they too adopted English names: La Caridad Skating Club, El Field Sport Club, El Jockey Club de Colón. By the mid-1890s, the Havana weekly *La Gimnástica* could write of Cuban youths enjoying "la high life habanera." Cycling—excursions and organized competitions—became popular during the 1890s, particularly among women. By 1894 at least four cycling clubs had been organized: El Sports Club, El Club Velocipédico, El Club de Biciclistas de La Habana, and El Club de Ciclistas de Matanzas.[113]

But it was baseball that took hold most firmly. Cubans were introduced to the sport at a critical moment in the formation of national identity, when Cubans were assembling the elements on which to base a separate nationality. The growing popularity of baseball in the United States coincided with the years of immigration. Cubans could not ignore the sport that had captured the imagination of the North American public. José Martí, who was living in New York at the time, commented on the celebrity of baseball with a mixture of curiosity and wonder. "In every neighborhood there is a baseball game," he observed. "Children . . . in New York like baseball and pistols more than they like books. . . . They go into the streets and hide from the police to play baseball in the courtyards."[114]

Cubans early detected in baseball new ways to act out the drama of nationality. They played baseball on college and university teams, in their neighborhoods, and at the workplace. Cubans in Key West formed four baseball teams (Cuba, Fe, Habana, and Esperanza), around which a Sunday municipal league was organized on a ball field provided by cigar manufacturer Eduardo Hidalgo Gato. The Reverend George Lester, traveling through Key West in 1892, could hardly contain his indignation at the "godlessness of this half-Cubanised city, with its Sunday base-ball, its taverns, its lotteries, and its social abominations." In Tampa, the first Cuban team (Niagara Baseball Club) was organized in 1887, only a year after the incorporation of the city, and was followed by two other clubs (Cubano and Porvenir).[115]

Baseball was brought to the island during the 1860s by students returning from North American colleges and universities. By the early 1870s local teams engaged in intermural competition. The first professional team, the Habana Baseball Club, was founded in 1872, followed a year later by the establishment of the Matanzas Baseball Club. In 1878 the Almendares Baseball Club was assembled. In the same year the Habana, Matanzas, and Almendares clubs formally agreed to organize themselves professionally into the Liga General de Base Ball de la Isla de Cuba.[116]

The Ten Years War ended in 1878 and Cubans returned home, many with a new enthusiasm for baseball. Indeed, in the years that followed the popularity of baseball was nothing less than spectacular. The number of amateur ball clubs in Havana increased rapidly throughout the 1880s and included such teams as Fígaro, Fénix, Cometa, Campos Eliseos, Providencia, San Jacobo, and Salud. Havana neighborhood teams (*clubs de barrio*) multiplied: América Baseball Club (Vedado), Progreso Baseball Club (La Víbora), Cerro Baseball Club (El Cerro), Fe Baseball Club (Jesús del Monte), Marianao Baseball Club (Marianao), and Esperanza Baseball Club (Guanabacoa). Also in the 1880s several Afro-Cuban societies organized baseball teams, among them the Universo Baseball Club, the Comercio Baseball Club, and the Varón Baseball Club in Havana and the Fraternidad Baseball Club in Guanabacoa. Afro-Cuban teams were also formed in Matanzas and Cárdenas.[117]

Baseball quickly spread across the island. Virtually every town and city of any size organized at least one team, including San Antonio de los Baños, Trinidad, Regla, Caibarién, Ranchuelo, Santiago de las Vegas, and Calabazar. Some towns like Sancti-Spíritus, Jaruco, Cienfuegos, Guanajay, Sagua la Grande, Güines, Pinar del Río, and Santiago de Cuba had two local teams, and Remedios and Santa Clara had three. Cárdenas had a total of seven teams. Baseball teams were established in towns as far east as Gibara and Baracoa and in towns as small as Guara (pop. 4,500) and Perico (pop. 3,200). "The enthusiasm for baseball," proclaimed the *Revista Villaclareña* in 1892, "grows daily more pronounced. The proof . . . is in the innumerable clubs that exist today." In all, more than two hundred baseball teams were organized in Cuba between the late 1870s and early 1890s. "One can hardly find any Cuban town," declared the popular monthly *El Base-Ball* in 1893, "that does not already claim as its own a club, perfectly uniformed and prepared to play."[118]

As the number of baseball teams increased, competition became better organized. During the 1880s *clubs de verano* formed into city and provincial leagues. The seven teams of Cárdenas inaugurated a municipal championship series during the 1885–86 season. A year later Pinar del Río's two teams formed a municipal league. In the late 1880s baseball promoters in Las Villas organized a provincial championship series among municipal teams representing the cities of Santa Clara, Sagua la Grande, and Cienfuegos.

Cuban clubs also competed with North American teams. More and more clubs from the United States incorporated Cuba into their barnstorming circuit during the winter and spring months. The first U.S. team to play in Cuba, the Bitter Hops Baseball Club, arrived in 1881 to take on Almendares. The Phila-

HIGH LIFE.
FABRICA DE CIGARROS
DEL
BASE-BALL
DE
N. Allones y J. Garcia,
93, San Rafael 93.

Esta fabrica está dedicada á los sócios de **Base-Ball Club**, y á toda la juventud fumadora.

TODOS LOS ESTABLECIMIENTOS
ESTAN SURTIDOS
Del gran CIGARRO
BASE-BALL.
Tiene la especialidad dicho cigarro de no manchar los dedos

A cigarette advertisement from the magazine *El Sport*, November 1886. (Courtesy of the Biblioteca Nacional José Martí, Havana)

delphia Athletics participated in a series of exhibition games against Cuban professional teams in 1886. In 1890 the New York Giants played winter ball in Havana.

Baseball drew mass audiences. The final championship game between Habana and Almendares in 1886 attracted 6,000 fans. Two years later, 5,000 fans watched a contest between Habana and Fe. The existence of a railroad infrastructure contributed to the expansion of baseball, making interprovincial and intermunicipal play possible. The teams of Cienfuegos and Villaclara routinely exchanged rail visits to appear in each other's home ball park.[119] During the championship series of 1888 between Cárdenas and Santa Clara, four special excursion trains transported more than 4,000 fans to the final game.[120]

The popularity of baseball was also reflected in the proliferation of baseball newspapers and magazines, both in Havana and in the provinces, publications that expanded almost as quickly as the number of teams. Among the most popular Havana weeklies were *El Sport*, *El Base-Ball*, *El Sportsman Habanero*, *El Club*, *La Pelota*, *El Pitcher*, *El Catcher*, *El Score*, and *El Pelotero*. The Habana and Almendares baseball clubs had their own publications (*El Habanista* and *El Almendarista*). The Cerro Baseball Club published *La Joven Cuba*. Provincial weeklies included *El Strike*, *El Sportsman*, *La Tarjeta*, and *El Basebolista* (all in Cárdenas), *El Catcher* (Remedios), and *El Short* and *El Villaclara* (Santa Clara).

The names of the magazines raised another complex facet about baseball in Cuba: it was played in English. That is, the idiom of the game required its practitioners to learn elements of English, to formulate their actions, their moves, and their strategies on the field and at bat in the vernacular of the North. Virtually nothing in baseball was translated. As early as 1881, *El Base-Ball* published a glossary describing baseball terms where even definitions could hardly escape from English usage; the guide included such terms as "foul ball" (pelota que al ser golpeada se dirija al terreno *foul*), "passed ball" (cada pelota lanzada por el pitcher que al no ser golpeada se le escape al *catcher*), and "tip" (tocar ligeramente a la pelota con el *bat* sin casi desviarla de su curso).[121]

Baseball in nineteenth-century Cuba presented one means of taking the measure of colonial society in transition—baseball as an expression of change and as an agent of change. Because the game originated in the North, it offered its Cuban practitioners a way to participate in modernity. This was one reason for its appeal. "Associations of this type," affirmed the organizational charter of the Mascota Baseball Club, "are of great utility and powerful factors in promoting material and moral progress." *El Base-Ball* drew the moral explicitly: "We are members of a generation . . . destined to live for science, arts, letters and the professions."[122]

Cubans celebrated the modernity and progress implied in baseball, associated with the United States, and denounced the inhumanity and backwardness suggested by the bullfight, associated with Spain. Baseball became another way to express disaffection with Spain. Cubans subsumed baseball under notions of civilization and bullfighting under barbarism and drew a Manichaean moral: between the Old World and the New, Spain and the United States, the past and the future. The sport of choice assumed powerful symbolic content and affirmed a modern sensibility. José Martí was unequivocal about bullfighting: "a futile bloody spectacle . . . and against Cuban sentiment for being intimately linked with our colonial past."[123]

Many criollos shared this view. "Public festivals have an enormous importance in the life of each nation," observed Enrique José Varona in 1887, "and offer one of the clearest indicators of the level of civilization at which each is found." Varona continued: "In one nation that today calls itself civilized there are men and entire classes found at various low levels in this evolution. . . . They come together to witness a spectacle in which the spilling of blood is the inducement that arouses their sensibilities, and where the [loss of] life of men and animals is the supreme joy that stirs their emotions." Baseball, on the other hand, "introduces into our customs a valuable element of physical regeneration and moral progress." Journalist Rafael M. Merchán described the bullfight as the "most ferocious and cruel of amusements"; writer and baseball player/promoter Wen-

The bullfight ring in Santiago de Cuba, 1898.
(Courtesy of the National Archives, Washington, D.C.)

ceslao Gálvez also drew the distinction bluntly: "Baseball is an enlightened spectacle and the bullfight is a barbaric spectacle." "We categorically reject the bullfight," proclaimed the editors of *El Pitcher* in 1888, and *El Base-Ball* staff writer Antonio Prieto exhorted Cubans to combat the bullfight without respite. "We will organize a crusade against the ignoble spectacle," Prieto vowed, "a disgraceful reminder of the barbaric times of paganism." Carlos Loveira gave further definition to this dichotomy in *Generales y doctores* (1920), in which Ignacio García recalls a Sunday afternoon in Havana before the War of Independence:

> That afternoon, in addition to a baseball game—enlightened, moral, virile, and wholesome—there was a bullfight, a savage sport that did not appeal to the noble and enlightened Cuban disposition. In the rows of seats and boxes of the baseball stadium, swarmed the Cuban multitude of both sexes (*de ambos sexos*). At the barbaric affair, crammed the foreign multitude in which was found, of course, all the police of the city, and among whom, naturally, was not to be found a single Cuban (*hijo del país*).[124]

Certainly baseball served as a means to sharply distinguish between Cuban and Spanish at a time when such distinctions were increasingly assuming political significance. But more was involved. Baseball offered the possibility of national integration of all Cubans, of all classes, black and white, young and old, men and women. Loveira's allusion to the presence of *ambos sexos* at a baseball game was noteworthy. In fact, criollas did not typically attend bullfights, an absence that signified exclusion from one of the more important public activities of the colony no less than exclusion from a function that served as a source of participation in the colonial polity.[125]

From the outset, baseball in Cuba involved women as spectators and fans at hometown games and as participants in banquets after the games. "The truth is," affirmed *El Base-Ball* in 1882, "that women are at least as attentive or more so than young men to the North American game, and they are always enthusiastic for the victory of the club or the players that they support." Almost all clubs formed an honorary board of directors (*directiva de honor*) consisting entirely of women.[126]

Attendance at a baseball game enabled women to move into the public sphere and participate in an important facet of creole social life, one that was from the beginning replete with messages and metaphors of nation. Baseball offered a new attraction, a new source of membership, an opportunity to be publicly partisan in an activity that was perceived to be distinctly Cuban.[127]

The presence of women, moreover, further ennobled baseball among Cubans who interpreted the *afición* of women for the game as still one more confirmation of its gentility and refinement, in sharp contrast to the brutish and bloody bullfight. Wenceslao Gálvez extolled "the delightful company of ladies (*damas*) who contribute to the sustenance of baseball by their presence at the games."[128]

Baseball offered access to modernity, a status to which all Cubans could aspire, and none more so than those disaffected by Spanish rule. Baseball was both symbol and surrogate of opposition at a time when alternative forms of opposition were not readily available. The ball field was a forum on which select individuals played representative roles that were charged with social and political significance. Baseball embodied a critique of the colonial regime simply by not being Spanish. Cubans were in search of new forms to express discontent, new ways to draw differences between themselves and Spaniards, to identify themselves as a people apart and a nation distinct from Spain. They sought to define nationality through forms that were most immediately available, one of which happened to be baseball.

In the capital and in the provinces, among creole elites and in working-class neighborhoods, Afro-Cubans in Guanabacoa and cigar workers in Key West, Cubans played baseball. In the process, they played out a complex drama of a society in transition, of a people contemplating nationhood and searching for means to give form to nationality. The disintegration of Spanish colonialism spanned the entire second half of the nineteenth century. Indeed, the undoing of colonialism was a gradual development in which normative structures were discredited and cultural forms passed into desuetude. During this period Cubans turned to alternative forms through which to repudiate Spanish ways and give expression to an emerging national identity.

Baseball encouraged both local attachments and national allegiance. Nationality obtained new forms of expression when Cubans played North Americans, as the proposition of team loyalty expanded into a source of national identity. Provincial and municipal rivalries brought Cubans together not only to compete but also to promote social integration—townspeople supporting local teams, meeting in behalf of a common goal; such competition offered membership in a national community, a shared identity and a shared idiom during a time of transition. Baseball served as a means by which women were incorporated into the discourse on nation. Women involved with baseball were engaged in the transformation that baseball signified, the affirmation of something Cuban and the pursuit of forms through which to express a separate nationality.

Baseball provided shared images to which common values were assigned and disseminated. Teams were named for the neighborhoods and towns where they were located, and as voluntary associations they offered a degree of popular democracy unavailable in a social order rigidly defined by class, color, and gender. Cubans discerned that baseball possessed the capacity to create a national community out of fans who were racially mixed and socially diverse, thereby offering the possibility of consensus around which to pursue nation. "The game of baseball," observed Benjamín de Céspedes in 1889, "has the means . . . of bringing into close and harmonious commingling the most humble classes with the highest ones, and out of the solidarity created by the supporters of each team emerges a rehearsal for democracy in its most gratifying and basic form."[129]

Cubans consciously used baseball to give form to the moral order from which the vision of nation was derived: a representation of a means of nation no less than an ideal of nationhood. Aurelio Miranda, one of the founders of the Habana Baseball Club, saw the playing field as a classroom, capable of teaching civic integrity and social responsibility, where Cubans could learn that common efforts, mutual assistance, and collective action were indispensable to the formation of nation. Baseball could teach discipline and patience, virtues necessary for successful nationhood. "Knowing how to wait is one of the great qualities of a man, of a people," Miranda insisted. "The baseball player must learn to wait for his pitch, his play, his moment. An untimely move, a base taken prematurely, a ground ball fielded hastily, leads to a game lost. The same as impatience—the absence of the virtue of knowing how to wait, leads to a loss, and often leads even to the loss of a nation."[130]

Spanish colonial authorities, although aware of the implications of the North American sport, were unable to restrict or reverse its growing popularity. That they tried at all no doubt enhanced the appeal of baseball among many Cubans. Colonial authorities viewed the increasing popularity of baseball uneasily, with some uncertainty and misgiving, but they were never quite able to articulate the source of their suspicion. That a sport with which Spaniards had little or no familiarity had so taken hold among Cubans had an unsettling effect on local officials. They sensed the subversive power of baseball, without knowing fully how or why, but recognized almost from the outset that the game from the North changed Cuban interests in ways alien to Spain, and that this alone was sufficient cause for concern. The challenge to colonial rule, Spanish authorities understood, came from many directions and in many forms. The Cuban attachment to baseball, whose conventions and moral universe were derived entirely from the North, could only weaken the Spanish hold over Cuba.

The Spanish concern about baseball's popularity led periodically to demands for the disbandment of teams and a ban on ball games. As early as 1873, soon after the organization of the Matanzas Baseball Club, government authorities banned baseball simply on the ground that it was an "anti-Spanish activity." The ban was revoked a year later, but Spanish suspicions never abated. According to the conservative newspaper *Diario de Cárdenas*, baseball posed a "threat" to "the integrity of the country." In 1876 colonial officials refused to sanction the name "Yara" for a new baseball team in Havana because of its association with the "Grito de Yara" (1868) and the start of the Ten Years War. The selection by a baseball club in Remedios of the name "Anacaona," after a Taína Indian princess who perished resisting the Spanish conquest, was interpreted by local Spaniards as a gesture of Cuban insolence. In 1881 local authorities ordered the dissolution of the Cárdenas Baseball Club after seeing an intramural game and concluding that Cuban players were developing new battle tactics to use against Spanish troops.[131]

The disapproval of bullfighting need not have assumed a concrete form. Undoubtedly many Cubans deplored the practice but saw no reason to make their disapproval public. In supporting baseball, however, Cubans were constructing an alternative moral order, derived explicitly from new normative structures, and for which they affirmed their preference on the basis of a superior morality and a higher level of civilization. Baseball was not merely an alternative to the bullfight; it challenged bullfighting and the moral universe it represented. Baseball carried a political subtext that both formed and gave form to Cuban discontent. The fact that increasing numbers of Cubans were turning away from the Spanish national pastime to take up baseball offended Spanish sensibilities and aroused their suspicion. More than a few Spaniards surmised—correctly—that the Cuban rejection of bullfighting was a thinly disguised repudiation of Spain. Indeed, some Cubans promoted baseball precisely for this purpose, seeking to lure Cubans away from the bullfight, mindful, too, of the political implications of this transformation. "One of baseball's greatest achievements," exulted Wenceslao Gálvez, "is without doubt to have turned our youth away from the [bullfight], an achievement I applaud, even if some *quijote* brands me antipatriotic."[132]

In the early 1890s, as the discontent with colonial rule deepened, even as Cubans prepared for a new war of national liberation, they were playing baseball: in virtually every large city and provincial town, at home and abroad, there were hundreds of teams of all types, professional and amateur, representing a city or playing for a neighborhood. On returning to Havana in 1890 after an absence of several years, Lorenzo Youngman asserted: "It is clear that during these years baseball has expanded and extended almost everywhere on the beautiful island." When he went to Cuba four years later, Spanish poet Manuel Curros Enríquez found a people wholly absorbed in the sport. "Everyone was at baseball—men and women, old and young, masters and servants," he wrote. "I asked what was this thing 'baseball' and I was told that it was a North American game." Curros Enríquez recalled the moment vividly: "I had a presentiment that Spain had died for Cuba." He continued:

> *Yanqui* ways conquer with such finesse. . . . When a people are influenced by another to the extent that they allow even the games of childhood and adolescence to be replaced, how could it not be dominated? The future, which is a people's principal essence, no longer belongs to them. That is why the loss of Spanish sovereignty in Cuba does not date from 1898. It is much earlier. . . . That is why the popularity of baseball made me realize, virtually upon landing in Cuba, that I found myself in a foreign country.[133]

When the War of Independence began in February 1895, colonial authorities immediately banned baseball. Spanish suspicions were confirmed: the sport was indeed subversive. Scores of Cubans abandoned the field of play for the field of war. The ranks of the Liberation Army filled with ball players such as Major Eduardo Machado (shortstop, Habana Baseball Club), Colonel Pedro Llania (pitcher, Almendares Baseball Club), Captain Juan Manuel Pastoriza (pitcher, Almendares), Major José Dolores Amieva Fuentes (outfielder, Matanzas), and Major Carlos Maciá (pitcher, Almendares). Emilio Sabourín, player-manager of the Habana Baseball Club and one of the chief promoters of professional baseball between the 1870s and early 1890s, was a fervent independentista. He was arrested early in the war and deported to the Spanish penal colony in Ceuta, North Africa, to serve a twenty-year sentence. He died within two years.[134]

NATIONALITY IN FORMATION

Much in the Cuban formulation of nationality can be explained by the experience of revelation and reflection in the encounter with the North, in ways perhaps too varied and too complex to fully comprehend. This experience was related to the means by which discontent developed and deepened and the degree to which Cubans attributed their circumstances to colonialism, for which the obvious remedy was independence. The encounter provided them an opportunity to interpret their own traditions and promote new awareness of social realities. Many Cubans had adopted a standard of "progress" that was essentially North American and that served as the basis for articulating what being Cuban meant.

Nationality assumed its decisive and definitive form out of the experience and the environment to which Cubans established a direct and immediate relationship. In many ways nationality was shaped less by self-consciously held political ideology than by the cultural system that informed the way Cubans assessed their own condition. Even exaltation of a political system that embraced notions of "liberty" and "democracy" as the dominant constructs was itself culturally derived.

The process of nation formation assumed an internal logic of its own. Large numbers of Cubans experienced modernity and, indeed, mastered many of its norms and adopted many of its values, by which, in turn, they were formed and subsequently defined themselves. This promoted consciousness of nationality and gave expression to the meaning of Cuban. It also implied "value" to being Cuban, and once value was assigned to nationality the promise of nation could only raise expectations and encourage new aspirations. These were, in fact, some of the most potent sources of hostility toward Spain: the many and varied ways that Cubans perceived that colonial structures denied them the opportunity to realize their full potential.

Cubans became part of the world of the North. They thought a great deal about how the sources of North American achievement and prosperity could be adapted to realize their own salvation and advancement. They observed firsthand or participated directly in many of these developments. Increasingly the possibility of economic prosperity fused with the proposition of democratic institutions and notions of freedom. Democracy and political liberty thus early acquired a material dimension and implied personal well-being and economic security. All Cuba needed was independence, to be rid of the constraints of Spanish colonialism, in order to fully develop and prosper. "Cuba is a country," wrote Varona, "that needs only liberty and independence in order to be a contributor to prosperity and progress in the concert of civilized nations." In *Generales y doctores*, Ignacio García, on arriving in New York, was astonished by

> The tangle of vehicles and pedestrians of that well-traveled avenue of Broadway over which our cable car advanced slowly; the elevated trains on Third Avenue . . . ; the height of the distant buildings of Singer and Woolworth; the clean gardens and parks. . . . All those things that were so different from ours of those years, caused my grandmother to exclaim: "What a marvelous thing, this Liberty!" And the rest of us, who believed that once having obtained the ideal of independence that nothing more would be necessary for the happiness of Cubans, with our eyes fixed on the roof of the trolley, sighed: "Ah! Liberty!"[135]

In José de la Campa González's partly autobiographical novel *Memorias de un machadista* (1937), Carlos is smitten by the promise of North American society. "Oh—the United States! These are a free people! These are a civilized people!"

The narrator comments: "And he naturally desired that this great civilization be channeled to Cuba, that Cuba would be free to introduce these customs."[136]

These developments shaped the way Cubans thought about themselves. National sensibilities took the form they did largely as a result of alternative possibilities that revealed themselves in the United States and generally became available to countless Cubans at the vital time when they were envisioning a nation of their own. Much in the sense of Cuban was borrowed, imported from the North. Cubans derived enormous satisfaction from the North American display of material progress. They, too, aspired to comfort—the English word passed into the Cuban lexicon directly as "comfort" or its corrupted form "confort"; they also were conscious of convenience, to things possessed of value and worth. All of this confirmed the proposition of "Cuban" as modern and civilized and rightfully identified with all things that constituted progress. These had become *their* accomplishments, a part of the material culture and value system claimed as Cuban.

Cuba assumed the appearance of modernity; it exuded progress: steam-powered mills in the 1810s, railroads in the 1830s, telegraph service by the early 1850s, telephones in the 1880s, and electric lights by the 1890s. Cubans could step back and behold with satisfaction the manifestations of progress they called their own. "Who could have told us . . . ," Wenceslao Gálvez exulted in 1889, "that we would have Havana all lit up with electric lights? We are progressing folks, we are indeed." The narrator in Cirilo Villaverde's *Cecilia Valdés* (1882) extolls the new sugar mills, "those symbols of progress and civilization." In *Leonela*, Fico Suárez, after taking his first trip on the new railroad, exclaims: "These great achievements of modern civilization have a way of moving me profoundly." Writer Francisco Faura was almost rapturous in his homage to civilization: "The locomotive, rapidly crossing from one region to another, joins distant points and overcomes distance; the steamship, rapidly crossing the water, overcomes the great spaces in short order; the telegraph wire, carrying thoughts like atoms of light, with extraordinary velocity, facilitates communication; the press, immortalizing ideas, perpetuates genius. These are the triumphs of modern civilization." In a tribute to the history of Villaclara, municipal historian José A. Asencio affirmed that "from its origins [Villaclara] has drawn inspiration from a profound love for the regenerative cause of Civilization and the sacrosanct ideal of Progress."[137]

The discourse on nationality developed at the apogee of the positivist vogue and the attendant emphasis on progress and civilization. The ideology and features of the material culture with which positivism was associated resonated among Cubans contemplating national forms, and for none more than those living in the United States. This was a vernacular with which Cubans abroad became conversant, not perhaps always explicitly as positivist concepts, but rather as paradigms of progress from which came the idealization of nationality.

Increasingly, Cuban discontent had to do with identity. No difference was as sharply drawn as the notion of Cuba as modern and Spain as backward. This issue was not entirely new, of course, for the antecedents of being "Cuban"—as compared to being "Spanish"—had their origins in the previous century. What was different in the nineteenth century was the invocation of nationality as identity based not simply on differences, but on values assigned to what those differences implied. Simply put, to be Cuban was superior to being Spanish. "The Cuban," Varona insisted, "possesses characteristics that denote progress within his lineage (*raza*), and if he is not absolutely more intelligent than the Spaniard, he is certainly of quicker comprehension and less resistant to change. . . . He is more open, more modern, more cosmopolitan. . . . The Spaniard is ill-prepared for the higher necessities of civilization."[138] Antonio Gonzalo Pérez contended that Cuba was "vastly superior," for "quite early in the century [Cuba] began to receive all the blessings of modern civilization." Spain, on the other hand, "situated in a corner of Europe, isolated by custom and tradition and by difficulty of approach, densely ignorant and fanatically religious, lay quite outside the current of progress." Pérez continued: "She is still saturated with the superstitions of the Middle Ages, which is equivalent to saying she is about five or six centuries behind the times. Therefore, it is not extraordinary that the Colony preceded the mother-country in the construction of railways and telegraphs, those valuable agents in the conveyance of modern ideas."[139]

The degree to which Spain lagged behind advances in science, technology, and industry, Cubans suspected, the extent to which it appeared incapacitated by unchanging ways, implied a larger malaise. The fact that Spain lacked the material resources and the technical means of modern development raised the possibility that Spanish normative structures and value systems were incapable of accommodating progress and modernity. "Not only is the level of general culture in Spain very low," pronounced Manuel Villanova in 1889, "but advanced knowledge of the arts and sciences has not reached the level attained in France, England or Germany. It would be easy to compare the works of Spanish authors with foreigners to prove the scientific backwardness of Spain." A year later Alfredo Virgilio Ledón published a small treatise to document "the inferiority of the Spanish race." The degree to which identity with modernity and progress informed nationality was suggested as early as 1882 by Manuel Linares: "If we are to be Spaniards only to represent the Motherland as one of the most backward people in the world . . . we must insist with devotion and resolution: at that cost we do not wish to be Spaniards."[140]

To remain with Spain was to remain in the past and hopelessly outside the mainstream of civilization. "If we want to advance on the path of civilization and progress . . . ," Gaspar Betancourt Cisneros insisted, "it is necessary that we separate ourselves from Spain." In Justo González's novel *Cubagua* (1941), Arturo contemplates the meaning of the 1895 war for independence and writes to a friend: "This . . . is not a war between Cubans and Spaniards, but between the past and the future, between a spirit that renovates and another that petrifies."[141]

Much in the meditation on nation had to do with the notions of progress and civilization. These ideas took firm hold and, indeed, became central to the meaning of Cuban. The particular Cuban genius was in adaptation, the eagerness with which Cubans took to change, especially change that was perceived to improve their lives. This was the special place occupied by Cuba, determined in part geographically and in part historically. Much of what passed for progress arrived in Cuba directly and quickly and hence was easy to appropriate and claim. Identity with progress was total, a condition from which corollary notions of civilization and modernity were derived and around which national community assumed form.

Cubans were mindful of the ways these developments linked them to the United States and the extent to which they depended on the North for the maintenance of standards they increasingly claimed as their own. "From the metropolis the colony receives nothing but grief," Domingo del Monte affirmed, "from the United States, prosperity and civilization." Raimundo Cabrera agreed: "We had the great good fortune to have the Americans export to us the railway in 1836, long before its introduction in Spain, and later on to teach us to make use of the telegraph; these advances directed us on the paths of civilization and progress." How these forms fused in the popular imagination is suggested in *Generales y doctores* when Teresa chides a friend for resisting a popular fashion and taunts: "Americanize yourself, boy! Get civilized!"[142]

Such encounters with the North also informed constructs of gender and civilization. The experience of Cuban women in the United States suggested new gender configurations from which the notion of freedom for women became an attribute of civilization, which was, in turn, at the core of what a free Cuba implied. Aurelia Castillo de González invoked this proposition in her praise of Harriet Beecher Stowe as "proof of what in the future will become of talented women in those countries that march on the now ample road of civilization." María Antonia Reyes de Herrera shared this view: "I believe that upon being educated a woman should not be limited to becoming 'a good housewife,' but that she should be educated as a complete citizen, strong, learned . . . without admitting any difference in intellect other than what is imposed by her greater or lesser intelligence."[143]

To be civilized and, hence, modern, necessarily implied the capacity to incorporate women into nationality, to expand notions of freedom, and to construct new roles and new ways of participation. It became more and more difficult to prohibit in Cuba behaviors that were sanctioned in the North. In the discourse on progress and civilization, to which Cubans had become highly susceptible as the central elements of self-definition, old proscriptions on women—associated with the colonial regime—were becoming increasingly untenable and indefensible. Certainly women who had been educated in the United States or who had lived or worked there did not easily acquiesce to the imposition of old ways.

The schooling of Cuban girls developed into one of the major controversies of the late colony, in which clashing notions of tradition and modernity accentuated the propositions of gender and civilization. The discourse is rich with allusions to a complex code of sexuality and the implications of the control of reproduction and the reproduction of control. Writer Anselmo Suárez Romero reprimanded parents for sending their daughters abroad to be educated. "You have heard that schools in Cuba are in deplorable condition . . . ," he admonished solemnly, "and you have concluded that it is preferable to educate your daughters in foreign schools." Parents like these would never be able to undo the "profound anguish" that such an experience would cause their daughters, who "will find nothing worthwhile in their country" and will "yearn always to return to the country in which their first impressions were formed." Their customs would be "diametrically opposed to those of the land of their birth." They would "listen coldly on some occasions, or with repugnance at other times, or perhaps with contempt some times" to the norms of society. Educator Carlos Saladrigas raised the issue of schooling explicitly along gender lines. Whereas colonial authorities had generally expressed misgivings about the effects of study abroad on Spanish nationality, Saladrigas warned that it threatened traditional gender roles. Sending sons abroad was entirely reasonable, Saladrigas argued, even desirable, to enable them to learn from "nations more advanced and to be introduced to the great factors of moral and intellectual regeneration necessary to perfect civilization." Under no circumstances, however, should daughters go. "The Cuban woman is, in effect, the most impressionable creature on earth. Her vivid imagination, which is one of her most precious attributes, is also the invincible enemy of her happiness." Saladrigas enjoined: "What a very careful education this temperament requires!" To send "these tender creatures abroad," even with the best of intentions, could not be considered as "anything less than an act against nature," for a woman, whose "primary and principal mission evolves within the bosom of the family," had no need for a foreign education. He concluded: "When the young girl recalls with pain the years she lived in a country that appears better than hers, and feels sad, alone, and dejected while on the sacred soil of her country, which for everyone else is so fascinating and beautiful, you can be sure that great harm has been done to her heart. She has forgotten the sacred principles of concord and stability so essential to the defense and perpetuation of the family."[144]

These issues had larger implications. Much in the formulation of identity as modernity and civilization was derived directly from expanding familiarities abroad. "From the personal communications of the many Cubans who have lived abroad," wrote Enrique José Varona, "and as a result of the marvelous facility with which today ideas are disseminated, there has emerged in Cuba an artistic, scientific, and judicial culture that while not general throughout the island is nonetheless extensive. In the cities and towns, the life that the Cuban is developing reaches very high on the scale of civilization."[145]

The premise of Cuban as civilized resonated among proponents of nationality, bourgeoisie and middle class alike, among workers and shopkeepers. It served as a source of national community and shared identity, for the invocation of civilization as a paradigm of progress always implied that Cubans belonged and Spaniards did not. This proposition had enormous vitality, one that subsumed under the sources of "Cuban" modern sensibilities as the basis of separate nationality. It went to the heart of why Cubans were not Spanish. The narrative of civilization served as the larger discursive framework within which representations of nationality acquired form to distinguish between Cuban and Spanish. "There exists in Cuba," Raimundo Cabrera insisted, "a people endowed with all the qualities and elements necessary to attain a high degree of civilization and prosperity." Journalist Fidel Pierra agreed. Spanish civilization was "pernicious," he declared, and it was necessary for Cubans, "at a very early day, to blot out even the last vestiges of it from the island." Spain had revealed its "incapacity . . . as a nation to evolve a civilization promoting and securing the well-being and happiness of those living within its folds." Cubans, on the other hand, were "endowed with those [qualities] of ready adaptability to new and more favorable media"; they possessed "a great capacity for rapid and solid improvement and advancement."[146]

Colonialism itself was proof of Spanish backwardness, a New World anachronism, an obstacle to democratic institutions that offended standards of progress and ran counter to all that was commonly understood as modern. The persistence of Spanish colonial rule in Cuba, wrote José Mayner y Ros, was "in defiance of civilization and progress."[147]

This was a peculiar anguish—very Cuban: experience and familiarity with a wider world, of greater possibilities, and a powerful impulse to participate. In travel abroad, Cubans learned firsthand what was happening elsewhere and in the process could appreciate what was not happening in Cuba. It is from this perspective that the liberation movement of the 1890s must be understood: a mobilization to create a modern secular state, the primary attributes of which were informed by notions of progress, social justice, and democracy, a movement so self-consciously advanced that it would not be reproduced again until 1910 in Mexico and 1917 in Russia.

Through much of the nineteenth century, Cubans defined themselves through denial. They distanced themselves from Spain, differentiated themselves from Spaniards, and otherwise discarded those forms that identified them as Spanish.

But Spain was not the only specter that menaced the realization of nationality. The invocation of progress provided a useful way to expel Spain, but it also acted to exclude Africa. The premise of Cuba as civilized could not easily accom-

BINDING FAMILIARITIES 89

modate the presence and participation of hundreds of thousands of people of African origin. If Spain was perceived as an obstacle to the realization of nation, Africa was seen as a threat to the endurance of nationality. Spain was backward, Africa was primitive. If Spain could hold Cuba back, Africa could drag Cuba under. Spain and Africa had endowed Cubans with tendencies contrary to the very notion of progress. For Diego Vicente Tejera, nothing perhaps was as detrimental to "the project which we propose of creating a republic sincere and strong" as the Cuban proclivity for indolence. "This indolence," argued Tejera in 1897, "is natural for us. . . . White Cubans descend from Spaniard and Cubans of color from Africa, two races equally lazy."[148]

In expelling Spain it was also necessary to expunge Africa. Denial of African no less than of Spanish was key to the kind of identity sought by criollos. Years earlier Antonio Saco had been blunt: "[The] Cuban nationality of which I have spoken, and the only one that should concern all sensible men, is that formed by the white race." The population of color, people of African origins, could not be admitted into "nationality" simply for not being "sensible."[149]

For much of the nineteenth century, slavery had served as one of the great divides of colonial society, separating not only whites and blacks, but also whites who defended slavery and whites who opposed it, an alignment that often corresponded with those who supported colonialism and those who were against it.

But the issue of the African presence in Cuba transcended the debate over slavery. Long before slavery was abolished in 1886 and especially after, the primary concern was race relations and how the hundreds of thousands of Cubans of African descent fit into the formulations of nation that were being finalized in the late nineteenth century. On the eve of the abolition, people of color, both slave and free, constituted one-third of the total population, approximately 500,000 out of 1.5 million inhabitants. The abolition of slavery raised new questions about the character of national community and the means and implications of incorporating people of color into nationality. The image of savage spirits loomed large in the creole imagination throughout the nineteenth century, always in the form of slave uprising and race war. The dismantling of slave structures occurred concurrently with the assembling of the elements of nationality, and the two developments were not unrelated. The subtext of nation had, in fact, become very much a narrative about race relations, and increasingly it was all but impossible to contemplate discarding colonial structure without first putting to rest the specter of race conflict that had long united defenders of Spanish rule and divided supporters of Cuban independence.

The fear of postcolonial race conflict could be addressed only insofar as the final representation of Cuba Libre was able to devise a way to accommodate people of color into nation. Nationality itself offered a means of mobilization and the promise of integration. Indeed, one of the most important social functions of nation was to formulate a construct that transcended racial identity and that subsumed race as a subcategory. Nation promised salvation to all, but especially to people of color—an entirely plausible formulation because it implied community and offered membership, something real and important, something that racial identity could affirm in only narrow terms. The exaltation of "Cuban" implied equal status for all. The proposition of nation was all-encompassing, accessible, more relevant to more people, something to surrender to and subordinate all competing identities to, and, of course, into which all were welcomed unconditionally.

People of color could join—and indeed their participation as equals was actively solicited—in the struggle for nation, for on no other terms could creole separatists reasonably expect to obtain the cooperation of a population whose support was vital to the triumph of independence. "Martí knew," writes Gerald Poyo, "that Cubans of color would have to be accepted as equal partners in the nationalist movement before they would embrace it unconditionally."[150]

But the proposition of equality in this instance implied a discourse among whites, principally an exhortation to admit the participation of blacks in an undertaking that was always conceived as "national" but, in fact, one in which blacks had little role in defining. Indeed, the incorporation of blacks was essential to complete the representation of the whole nation in the category of Cuba Libre. Martí needed to explicitly include Cubans of color in the separatist amalgam and could safely do so without threatening the balance of social forces that had assembled around Cuba Libre. Blacks could be admitted into the formulation of nation on terms of equality as defined by whites. Perhaps more important, the proposition of equality was a message directed explicitly at people of color, under which was subsumed as subtext a coded warning against the contrivance of racial constructs. To affirm color, to proclaim black with pride, was divisive and justified white hostility. Martí denounced "racial divisions" and the "difference of race" because they obstructed "the achievement of national well-being." But he also asked people of color: "What must whites think of the black who prides himself on his color?" And this was not entirely a rhetorical question, for Martí provided the answer: "The black man who proclaims his race, even if mistakenly as a way to proclaim spiritual identity with all races, justifies and provokes white racism."[151]

The imperative of nation thus foreclosed the invocation of race, presumably by both whites and blacks, under the aegis of racial equality. "Equality" between the races within racist structures, however, promised to institutionalize racism. Cuba could not, under these circumstances, but default to racial categories, organized around assumptions of racial hierarchies in which white assumed a racelessness as it enjoyed a privilege of white, while Cubans of color were obliged to struggle to obtain "equality."

The participation of Cubans of color in the creation of nation was conceived in narrow terms, specifically in the context of the defense of the project of Cuba as a free and sovereign nation. Manuel Sanguily outlined these relationships explicitly. The project of "the Revolution," as he referred to the Ten Years War, "in its origins, in its preparation, in its initiative, in its program and direction, that is, the Revolution in its character, essence, and aspirations was the exclusive work of whites. The man of color was summoned by them and by them situated *for the first time in the history of Cuba* in a position to take part in and to lend service to the cause, and given the opportunity to distinguish himself as much as the whites." Sanguily continued:

> It was necessary for the white Cuban to make the Revolution, that *he alone* challenge the considerable forces of Spain. For that reason he ruined himself, he sacrificed his life, his wealth, the peace of his home, the future of his children. The black was at the time a slave, and he who was not a slave was something of a pariah. One was going to risk everything. The other risked nothing, but stood to gain everything, to win in the end liberty and personal dignity. . . . The Cuban, his former master and now his liberator, his only salvation, summoned him to his own banquet, led him with a fraternal embrace and from then on converting him into his comrade (*compañero*) and imbued him with a new spirit and a magnificent ideal, generous determination, and moral excellence.[152]

Blacks would be welcomed in the discourse of nation as long as they adopted the vernacular of nationality and embraced the assumption of the transcendent nation. They could participate as an actor of nation, but not agency. People of color were to be fitted into nationality, but only insofar as they accepted specific premises of nation, formulated by those who saw themselves as the bestowers of liberty.

This transformation would be accomplished by education and preparation. There was no reason to fear blacks after independence, separatist leader Rafael María Merchán predicted in 1896, for the future republic would "fill the Island with schools and all types of means of civilization, so that all would acquire the aptitudes demanded by society." Cubans of color would "not forget that they owe to whites the abolition of slavery." Merchán concluded: "No, we do not fear blacks: over them as over whites, will be the law." Manuel de la Cruz argued along similar lines, noting that the "fear of the black was a legitimate apprehension" at an earlier time, when the "greed of Spanish slave traders inundated the island with Africans" and Cuba was "subjected to an invasion of savages." But conditions had changed, de la Cruz insisted, for the "glorious revolution of Yara" (1868–78) had "transformed the slave into citizen." In any case, there was no doubt that whites were assured of "continued predominance by virtue of their numbers, force, and culture."[153] The authority of whites over blacks, insisted philosopher Raimundo Menocal, was not based solely on force, but on a "civilization and mentality . . . so superior that it is reasonable that [whites] will retain their ascendancy and will maintain blacks in perpetual dependency until their extinction." The civilization of blacks is "primitive, fetishist, and patriarchal." In Menocal's opinion, the "tendency of the black race can not predominate in this country nor should [blacks] be permitted to influence our society in the slightest."[154]

The declared intention of the arbiters of nation was to educate and convert, to incorporate the masses of people of color into nationality. In fact, their actions produced the opposite effect. It is at least arguable that creoles had a stake in preserving cultural distinctions among people of color to maintain racial barriers and social hierarchy. These were precisely the sentiments Martín Morúa Delgado, himself a man of color, attributed to the creole protagonist in his novel *La familia Unzúazu* (1896):

> Now that the slave has disappeared, the black remains. We want liberty, complete liberty; but our slave of yesterday cannot become our equal of today. . . . Physical slavery has been virtually eliminated, [but] we insist resolutely . . . that the black consider himself "black" for his entire life among us; that the freedman (*liberto*) develop his mental capabilities in the conviction of his indisputable inferiority as he makes his way through our society. In that manner two absolutely necessary acts basic to our future stability will have been achieved: the expectations of the black will not rise and our former privileges will remain consolidated. . . . In this manner there will be no reason to fear race conflict. Cuban liberty will be patriotic reality.[155]

The degree to which the proposition of civilization served as the subtext of independence and the relationship of civilization and independence to formulations of race and nationality appear with remarkable clarity in Tomás Justiz y del Valle's novel *El suicida* (1912), set in the early 1890s. Julio proclaims to his mother: "We are preparing ourselves to enter the twentieth century with dignity. . . . Cuba will never be truly civilized as long as one Spaniard remains. It is necessary to kill them! War without quarter!" To which his mother exclaims, "The blacks will rule then!" and Julio responds: "I prefer them. The black can be domesticated, the Spaniard can never be civilized." How this configuration subsequently informed the narrative on race and itself acted as a means of social control was suggested in Justo González's *Cubagua* (1941), in which the black protagonist Homobono characterizes the Afro-Cuban condition in the 1920s: "We blacks have to recognize that much of the benefits we have achieved we owe to whites. The principles of equality and human liberty, the abolition of slavery, and the benefits of civilization enjoyed by blacks are the result of the achievement of whites."[156]

The formation of national identity was a complex process that involved negation and affirmation as one and the same imperative, often as the same set of acts and attitudes. In this pursuit Cubans appropriated all means available, a process in which they looked out and forward, but hardly ever looked in and back. In a discourse otherwise rich and ranging, dedicated almost entirely to identity and nationality, a coherent approximation of history was conspicuous by its absence. The idea of history as a narrative framework of a common past, to be shared and celebrated, a way to validate the authenticity of nationality, was not invoked in the construction of "Cuban." If, in fact, as Immanuel Wallerstein suggests, identity is most of all a function of the past, and "pastness" is a "central element in the socialization of individuals,"[157] then the apparent absence of categories of the past indicates that much of what became usable as "Cuban" was derived or appropriated from the present.

These were years in which consciousness was in transition, identity was in flux and in formation, and Cuban energies were expended almost entirely in creating usable forms in the pursuit of nation. Cubans did not situate themselves in a past; in fact, they lacked a coherent notion of an instrumental past. They invoked few symbols from which to claim continuity and derive legitimacy. To be sure, an occasional allusion to Hatuey and Taíno resistance to the Spanish conquest drew the obvious moral. So, too, did invocation of the unsuccessful independence conspiracy in 1811 organized by the black carpenter José Antonio Aponte. However, creoles could scarcely imagine that their efforts were even remotely connected to the struggles of Indians and ex-slaves. Nor did the filibustering expeditions of the 1840s and 1850s provide much in the way of sustenance, for these had been in the main annexationist plots, a proposition that after the 1870s had been discredited and all but repudiated.

The process began, as Ramiro Guerra y Sánchez correctly suggested, with the Ten Years War, as Cubans proceeded to invent a usable past. "The Ten Years War had another even higher purpose in the history of Cuba and in the process of the definitive creation and consolidation of Cuban nationality," Guerra affirmed, adding: "A nation (*patria*) is in its essence a historical essence, a moral entity with a past and a future. It needs to possess a spiritual patrimony of glory and heroism, of epic and legend. There does not exist a strong people or robust nationality that does not possess it. Before 1868, Cuba in large measure lacked this patrimony, and the Ten Years War created it in magnificent fashion. After Zanjón, and notwithstanding defeat, Cuba possessed a rich patriotic tradition to revere and cherish."[158]

The denial of Spain and Africa as sources from which to affirm "Cuban" created a condition of enormous complexity. These circumstances propelled Cubans to devise alternative normative structures and new cultural forms to advance distinctions and differences. The formulation of nationality was conditioned in large measure by the encounter with ways North American, both on the island and in the United States, from which Cubans borrowed freely and adopted unabashedly, elements that in the end they made their own.

To be Cuban on these terms was to formulate nationality around North

American structures. That national identity embraced civilization as a condition of material progress made Cuba especially susceptible to North American cultural forms, from which it was in part derived and on which it depended for its continued vitality. Much of what became Cuban began as North American and, indeed, gave impetus to the ways and things they would share thereafter.

These developments should by no means serve as grounds for doubting the authenticity of Cuba Libre or questioning the power of the independentista ideal. The drive for nation was a force of enormous resonance, around which emerged a consensus of enduring vitality. These were powerful sentiments, not to be trifled with or dismissed lightly.

Throughout the nineteenth century Cubans and North Americans drew toward one another to satisfy the needs in the other that could not be easily met among one's own. They exchanged seasonal visits, North Americans traveling south in the winter, Cubans heading north in the summer, finding comfort and rejuvenation in each other's mineral springs and baths. North Americans traveled south in search of the past, Cubans went north in pursuit of the future. They invested in each other's country, operated hotels, and exchanged the material goods and services of modernity and progress. They developed connections that assumed structural form and in various ways provided elements through which each found a sense of completion.

Cubans could borrow and adopt freely and frequently from North American cultural forms, but the process implied selective appropriation and always adaptation. Before this process could occur—and indeed the only terms under which it could occur—there had to exist already a notion of *cubanía* to which were added variations as a means of affirmation. Something had to exist for these new forms to take on the meanings they did in this particular context. Separatists may well have invented new traditions, but they could not have devised just any new tradition: it had to be congruent and fit within some recognizable set of distinctive cultural parameters.

Much of what passed for nationality as a claim of distinction and independence was based less on representative institutions than on representation of nation as popular political legitimacy. Certainly Martí had taken an important step toward the development of new political structures in the Cuban Revolutionary Party, but the language of Cuba Libre remained embedded in a popular voluntarist vernacular. It thus became possible for Cubans to incorporate and accommodate within the larger metaphysics of nationality elements of North American forms and still defend the proposition of a separate nationality. Such were the conjunctures of national identity. Cuban self-definition early incorporated as a major formative element resentment of U.S. policy designs on Cuba and hence set into place the central tension of Cuban nationalism: emulation of North American ways, especially as those ways could materially improve life for Cubans, and resistance to the United States because it posed a threat to a separate nationality.

2

PERSISTENCE OF PATTERNS

These immigrants will take back to their homeland the habits acquired in this great school of democracy.
—Diego Vicente Tejera, Key West, October 1887

Cubans who have lived in [the United States] have taken on many of America's ways and are a seed whose sowing is sure to bring good to the island. Others who frequently visited the United States have also contracted some of America's energy, enthusiasm and zeal and will further the welfare of their country more for having been to the most progressive of the nations of the world.
—*Havana Post*, July 24, 1900

The influence of the American intervention has been both beneficent and far-reaching. . . . A ferment of new ideas as to ways of doing things and ways of existing has been spread among the common people. The visit of the Cuban teachers to the United States exercised a broad educational influence in this direction. The oral teaching of the American, his bitterest criticism and denunciation, and all the driving he may do as an employer, will slide off a Cuban like water off a duck's back. But he will be imitated. If an American settler puts up a windmill or buys an improved plow, a market for those things is at once created in his vicinity. Suspenders have superseded belts since the American occupation. When American ladies adopted the palm leaf hats of the country as a comfortable and becoming head gear, the Cuban ladies followed their example. [The United States] will bring with it a large fund of imported customs of a sort intended to elevate the prevailing standard of living, that will add to the intellectual resources of the people, and that will increase their familiarity with modern inventions, improvements, and processes.
—*Bulletin of the U.S. Department of Labor*, 1902

Cuba is simply over-run with Americans of all ages, of all conditions of life, of all professions, and of no professions. From the gray-haired many, down to the newsboy selling his papers in the street, Americans are in evidence. Years ago the rush was to the west of the United States; now the tide has turned southward to Cuba. . . . From appearances, many seem to think that they will find the streets here paved with gold to be had for the picking up.
—*New York Times*, May 7, 1900

Cuba Libre cost Cubans dearly. Not all suffered equally, of course, but most suffered some, and many suffered much. These were the decades of recurring cycles of Cuban rebellion and Spanish repression, first the Ten Years War (1868–78), then the Little War (1879–80), and finally the War of Independence (1895–98): in all, thirty years of intermittent revolution and repression, random depredation alternating with systematic devastation, successive acts of reprisal and revenge, of pillage and plunder, of homes destroyed and lives disrupted.

THE LONG WAR

Ruin came in many forms, and for many Cubans it came at the hands of the Spanish. The crime was "infidelity" (*infidencia*), broadly defined as "treason, rebellion, insurrection, conspiracy, sedition, sheltering rebels and criminals, communication with the enemy, seditious or subversive expressions, pronouncements, and conversations, public demonstrations, references, and everything else of a political nature tending to disturb tranquility and public order or in any other way attack the integrity of the Nation."[1]

The punishment was confiscation or attachment of property (*embargo de bienes*). Among the first tried for infidencia were the leaders of the insurrection, many of whom came from the ranks of the creole bourgeoisie. Some of the most valuable properties, personal as well as commercial—sugar plantations, coffee estates, tobacco farms, and ranches—were embargoed. The Aldamas in Havana and the Pedrosos of Matanzas were among the many prominent families to lose sugar mills, coffee estates, ranches, and *haciendas*. Urban properties (*fincas urbanas*), mainly retail stores, factories, rental properties, and homes, were also seized. José Morales Lemus lost eighteen fincas urbanas in Havana and Guanabacoa. Colonial officials took four urban properties of attorney Néstor Ponce de León, including his home and law office, together with the library, office furniture, and legal records. Many others anticipated confiscation and hastily liquidated, often at enormous losses. Inocencio Casanova, a planter in Cárdenas, sold a sugar estate valued at $1 million for half that amount and immediately fled with his family to New York.[2]

Spanish authorities also seized liquid assets, savings accounts, and personal property, including jewelry, furniture, and works of art. By the end of 1870 the colonial government had confiscated the stocks, bonds, and securities held by José Morales Lemus, Ignacio Alfaro, Cristobal Madán, and Antonio Ponce de León, among others, valued at more than $2 million.[3]

The confiscations delivered devastating blows against the property-owning classes and foreshadowed the demise of the creole bourgeoisie. Many who had known a more or less comfortable existence immediately suffered the loss of wealth and status; others plunged into indigence and debt. Many never recovered. They were deprived of their principal source of income and the means of a livelihood. Thousands of families lost the savings of a lifetime and property accumulated over several generations: homes, farms, businesses, stores, professional offices—almost anything of worth. As early as 1870, the total value of assets and properties seized was nearly $20 million.[4]

Then, of course, there was the war itself: it released powerfully destructive forces, sometimes as a matter of policy, planned and deliberate, often by chance or mishap. Perhaps the reasons mattered little, for the results were the same. Creoles on both sides of the conflict—loyalists as well as separatists—suffered enormous property damage in the war zones. The losses were staggering. (See Appendix Table 2.1.)

Cuban woes did not end with the cessation of the Ten Years War—they merely assumed different forms. The 1880s were difficult years as declining sugar prices and shrinking markets plunged the economy into chaos. Sugar estates across the island changed hands at accelerating speed as planters struggled desperately to stave off financial failure and personal ruin. "Out of the twelve or thirteen hundred planters on the island," the U.S. consul in Havana reported tersely in 1884, "not a dozen are said to be solvent."[5]

The effects were immediate and far-reaching. Commerce contracted, banks collapsed, factories closed. Unemployment soared. The cost of living increased, even as wages and salaries plummeted. Food prices mounted. Rents in Havana and its suburbs increased. So did evictions. The jobless became the homeless as the unemployed took to the streets in search of shelter and subsistence. Rural workers migrated to overcrowded cities looking for jobs, only to join the swelling ranks of the urban unemployed. In 1888 the governor of Havana denounced the "disagreeable spectacle offered by the great number of individuals of all classes who are continually found asleep or given over to idleness in the promenades and other public places."[6]

The combined effects of war and economic depression were telling. In Cienfuegos the value of rural and urban property declined by half. The previously opulent city of Trinidad experienced a downturn as business houses failed and retail shops closed. Matanzas was especially hard hit. "Firms are going into bankruptcy every day," reported the U.S. vice consul in 1884; "planters are discharging their laborers and threaten—to save themselves further disaster—to abandon their estates. . . . All credits are denied even to the most substantial and men are wondering how and where they will obtain the means to live."[7] Between 1862 and 1883 the island lost two-thirds of its taxable wealth. (See Appendix Table 2.2.)

The depression of the 1880s accelerated the disintegration of the creole bourgeoisie. Planters across the island plunged deeply into debt, desperate to stave off insolvency, and in the end lost everything. Some sought to survive by selling off parts to save the whole, but, of course, it was only a matter of time until the sum of the parts equaled the whole.

Bourgeois families experienced rapid downward mobility. Many lost their entire wealth and eventually their homes. They abandoned the stately mansions in El Cerro for more modest structures in Vedado and Almendares.[8] Many descended into the ranks of the middle class and were obliged to work as salaried personnel in the professions or in commerce.

These were not the best of times to join the middle class, however. Vast numbers of professionals and salaried employees were themselves in crisis, as they faced declining living standards, indebtedness, unemployment, and eventually emigration. Many middle-class Cubans were also victims of expropriation, losing homes and farms, shops and professional offices, as well as savings and sources of income. "It is not the labourer that is to be pitied," commented the British consul in Havana in 1889, "but the middle-class creoles, who, unfit for rough manual labor, and unskilled in handicrafts, can find no employment on a par with their physical or intellectual capacity."[9]

The economic depression that followed war was itself followed by another war: a new separatist insurrection in 1895 and three more years of devastation and destruction. The insurgency expanded rapidly across the island, from east to west, into all six provinces. It was a brutal conflict, a war of excesses, disruptive and destructive at every turn. Spaniards were ruthless in their defense of colonial rule, Cubans were relentless in their demand for national sovereignty. Contending forces laid siege to the largess of the land, preying upon the bounty of its resources, consuming or destroying crops and livestock and practicing pillage of every kind as the normal method of warfare.

In 1896 Spanish general Valeriano Weyler arrived in Cuba and immediately moved against the privileged and propertied, no less than the poor and powerless, to eliminate opposition wherever it was found. Arrests and deportations were so sweeping that they appeared at the time to be indiscriminate and random, for it was impossible to imagine that repression on this scale could actually be by design. In fact, it was deliberate. This was organized terror, the wholesale extermination of tens of thousands of Cubans suspected of complicity, real or imagined, actual or potential. General Weyler realized that his forces could not defeat the Cuban Liberation Army without first destroying the rural communities from which it emerged, on which it depended, and into which it dissolved: it was necessary to wage war against hundreds of thousands of peasants, farmers, and rural workers—against, in short, the entire civilian population of the countryside.

Weyler did not hesitate. In mid-1896 he inaugurated a reconcentration program: the relocation of the rural population into a network of internment camps. His forces scoured the countryside to round up Cuban civilians slated for the reconcentration camps. Young Spanish soldiers, many of them still adolescents, ordered to defend the honor of the *Madre Patria*, acquitted themselves by burning villages and planted fields, destroying food reserves, razing homes,

Ruins of residential neighborhood, Victoria de las Tunas, 1900.
(Courtesy of the McKeldin Library, University of Maryland at College Park)

and seizing livestock. Animals that could not be driven into Spanish zones were slaughtered. Any resource—human or material—of potential use to the separatist armies was destroyed when it could not be removed. The longer the war continued, the more desperate the Spanish became and the deeper they descended into depravity. By the end of the year, a stillness had settled over vast expanses of the Cuban countryside. The farms were untended, the fields unworked, the villages uninhabited. Entire communities disappeared. Vast stretches of rural Cuba were reduced to wasteland.

Peace came in August 1898, and only then was it possible to fully comprehend the dimensions of the devastation. Three decades of war and depression had visited unimaginable suffering and incalculable losses on the Cuban people. The War of Independence had been especially cruel in its conduct and consequences. It had been total war, a campaign in which pillage and depredations of all kinds were adopted as a cost-effective means of waging war and in which the systematic destruction of property became an acceptable, if not a preferable, way to defeat the enemy. Total, too, in that the war had involved almost everyone in nearly all the one thousand towns and villages of the island, by choice or by chance, and where the distinction between civilians and combatants lost any useful meaning, where neutrality was suspect, and where security was often to be obtained only behind battle lines, rarely ever outside them, and never between them.

The effects of the war could be seen everywhere. Houses in the interior were roofless and in ruins. Roads, bridges, and railroads had fallen into disrepair. Where towns and villages once stood, there remained only scattered piles of rubble stone and charred wood. Mines had closed. Commerce was at a standstill and production paralyzed. Agriculture was in ruins, and from everywhere in Cuba came reports of farms in distress and farmers in despair. What had been lush farming zones were now scenes of scorched earth and singed brush. Huge areas of the island's most productive regions had been desolated. Years later the U.S. Tariff Commission concluded that two-thirds of Cuba's wealth had been consumed by the war. Tens of thousands of small farms, coffee *fincas*, tobacco *vegas*, and cattle ranches simply vanished. Hundreds of sugar mills and hundreds of thousands of acres of sugar land were reduced to charred rubble and barren fields. Of the 1,100 sugar mills operating in 1895, only 207 survived the war.[10]

Travelers to the island that first autumn of peace were uniformly appalled by the extent of destruction. "I saw neither a house, nor a cow, calf, sheep or goat, and only two chickens," one journalist reported from Camagüey. "The country is wilderness," a "desert," another correspondent wrote from Las Villas.[11] U.S. general Fitzhugh Lee gave a chilling account of conditions in Pinar del Río:

> Business of all sorts was suspended. Agricultural operations had ceased; large sugar estates with their enormous and expensive machinery were destroyed; houses burned; stock driven off for consumption by the Spanish troops, or killed. There was scarcely an ox left to pull a plow, had there been a plow left. Not a pig had been left in the pen, or a hen to lay an egg for the poor destitute people who still held on to life, most of them sick, weary, and weak. Miles and miles of country uninhabited by either the human race or domestic animals were visible to the eye on every side. The great fertile island of Cuba in some places resembled an ash pile, in others the dreary desert.[12]

Treasury Department agent Robert Porter described a people "left enfeebled by deprivation and too weak to take up their occupations," inhabitants "huddled half starved in miserable huts near the towns and cities," a "hungry and discouraged native population [standing] listlessly on the streets and in the public places," where at "each station the railroad trains were boarded by half-starving women or children begging for bread or coppers." Ramiro Guerra y Sánchez recalled those days of his youth vividly: "We were a people in ruin; a little country, in misery, starving. Our only source of strength was our hope, combined with a firm and energetic determination to endure and live on."[13]

Peace found a people prostrate in almost all the towns and cities and almost everywhere in the countryside. Want and despair permeated the island, with neither relief nor remedy in sight. Life assumed a nightmarish quality as a war-weary people went about the task of reconstituting their households and resuming their lives in the midst of desolation and devastation. The losses were incalculable. Property damage, of course, could be assessed and in many instances verified. But material destruction constituted only a part of the harm. What could never be fully known, or perhaps even imagined, was the human suffering, the despair, the heartache. The war was won through much sacrifice and almost unbearable hardship. Hundreds of thousands of Cubans had perished. Households had been disrupted, homes destroyed, families broken, lives shattered. Because many survived in sound body did not always mean that they were well or whole. Countless numbers bore their pain in their memories, in sadness and sorrow, haunted by the loss of persons and places that had once given their lives purpose and meaning. They carried on with broken hearts and inconsolable grief: widows and orphans, parents who lost children and children who lost parents, the untold numbers who lost entire families, the maimed, the infirmed, the aged, homeless, and jobless—all of whom could not even begin to imagine how to put their lives back together. Few, indeed, were the Cubans who had not suffered in direct and personal ways.

Vast numbers never fully recovered. Many spent the rest of their lives in mourning. Others found renewed purpose in seeking to avenge the dead. Spanish conduct of the war had filled many Cubans with an enduring hatred of Spain and of all things Spanish. Much could be neither forgiven nor forgotten. In the years that followed newspapers across the island periodically reported the mysterious murder of Spaniards, assaults and assassinations of former officers in the Volunteers, arson and vandalism against Spanish property, crimes that were rarely solved or punished—like a desultory blood feud that persists long after the participants recall why it began. That was how the War of Independence ended.

Cubans had triumphed over Spain, but at enormous cost borne by two generations over three decades. They had sacrificed personal assets and family fortunes, great and small, in support of independence. Many had abandoned their shops, businesses, and professions, others had discontinued their educations or disrupted their careers to free Cuba. Some of the most prominent military and political leaders of the insurrection had come from families of means, with property and professions, with plans and prospects. After the war they had nothing. They lost their possessions to tax collectors or creditors, to punitive confiscations or the ravages of war. They were without homes, without money, without jobs.[14] "There are many families in Santiago who 18 months ago were in comfortable circumstances," wrote the U.S. consul from Santiago de Cuba, "and who to-day are paupers, selling the remaining pieces of furniture in their homes in order to buy bread, with no future before them but starvation, or a bare subsistence on charity." Pawnshops flourished as families liquidated what remained of their personal possessions and household property in one last effort to hold on a little longer. Pawnbrokers developed into an unscrupulous lot, prompting the *Diario de la Marina* in 1899 to urge authorities to regulate transactions "to prevent usurious abuses."[15]

After 1898 it was unclear how things would get right again, how Cubans would find the means to reclaim what had been formerly theirs and make a place for themselves in the country they had struggled to create. The war had shattered life as they had previously known it; few knew how, or where, or with what to begin anew. Countless numbers were destitute, without income or employment, without any kind of representation. In *Sombras eternas* (1919), Raimundo Cabrera portrays his protagonist in poignant terms: "Without the old home in which he had established his household and managed to put aside modest savings after twenty years of work, his farm destroyed and in debt, he was now obliged at 45 years of age to start all over again with the difficult task of making a living, and feeling very old."[16]

Opportunities were few and prospects were bleak. The resources to restore farms and revive commerce, to rebuild homes and resume careers, were simply unavailable. As Cubans surveyed what their victory had wrought, more than a few contemplated a cruel denouement, indeed. Perhaps they had created a future in which there was no place for them. "Where do I start?" a soldier asks himself in Salvador Quesada Torres's partly autobiographical short story, "El silencio" (1923). "I have suffered much, a great deal, so much that were I to describe my suffering in detail it would result in a sorrowful book. . . . It is the story of humble men like us who liberated Cuba and today have nothing to eat. In my own land . . . I find myself without protection or assistance."[17] "You know," General Alejandro Rodríguez confided to a friend in 1899, "that abandoning my interests and family, I was among the first to reach for arms and support the revolution." He added: "I who have served my country, for which I have sacrificed everything, cannot even have my family at my side for a lack of means to support it. I cannot embark on any business or reconstruct my farm due to a lack of funds. I see myself perhaps forced to emigrate in search of bread in a strange land."[18] Captain Carlos Muecke wrote sorrowfully of his comrades, whose "property whether in town or in the country has been destroyed and they must begin anew. . . . [they] have sacrificed all—[their] houses, even their clothes are gone . . . without money they cannot rebuild their houses, restock their farms, refit their offices, or go to work."[19]

The war had ended in 1898, but not entirely the way Cubans had envisioned. Spain had been defeated, to be sure, and at least that part of the Cuban purpose had been achieved. But the U.S. intervention of 1898 changed everything. The separatist project had been successful on every count except perhaps the one that mattered most: it failed to produce power. Cuba Libre had been conceived as an endeavor of national mobilization, in pursuit of which Cubans had endured a war of ruinous proportions and in whose behalf they had purposefully laid waste to the land and willingly impoverished themselves. A free Cuba promised empowerment, a country for Cubans to call their own, a place where they could ensure the ascendancy of Cuban: power to affirm nationality; power at the service of national community—without mediation, without intermediary;

power to articulate identity and shape the institutional structures of nation; power to advance the primacy of nation as the basis on which to constitute nationality.

An immense and heterogeneous constituency had organized around Cuba Libre, for which free Cuba had promised advancement, improvement, and betterment. Enormous amounts of material resources and a moral subsidy had been expended in behalf of independence. Cubans of all classes had given all they had to Cuba Libre, keeping nothing in reserve, and for many nothing remained. Their sacrifice and selflessness had been predicated on a vague but commonly shared notion that victory would enable them to recover what they had lost: their homes, farms, and estates; their shops and offices; their jobs—in short, everything that had been formerly theirs. In his novel *Ideales* (1918), Cabrera depicts a creole family exiled during the war, its property confiscated and its home in Havana seized. "Cuba will be free," a friend consoles, "and all who are abroad will return and we will once more be prosperous and happy."[20]

A separate nationality implied integration into national community as the basis of well-being and security. Nationality elevated each member of the community: it promised status and dignity. To a society where status was often the prerogative of property, nationality promised that self-respect and pride would be available to all, openly and equally. Cuba Libre held the possibility of mobility, the founding of a nation in which Cuban interests formed the sacred trust for which the republic was to be created and charged to defend and uphold. Cubans had entered into a covenant, as they understood their commitment, a social contract in which they devoted themselves to bringing into being a republic dedicated to defending their interests. "The Republic," observes the narrator in Arturo Montori's novel *El tormento de vivir* (1923), "affectionate and paternal, was obliged to care for its children, the Cubans, who had suffered so much to create it":

> Especially the poor, the émigré workers who took bread from the mouths of their loved ones to raise money for the Revolution, the peasants who abandoned their families to all sorts of horrors and misery to join the insurgent ranks, and all . . . who endured humiliation and were prepared to take whatever risk required for the cause of liberty. They would now be, surely, the pampered children, the favored ones of the new situation, in which their needs would be met with affectionate solicitude, against the abuses of the strong, merchants, bourgeois, planters, owners of enterprises, all the new owners of the wealth, mostly foreigners.[21]

DESIGN WITHOUT A PLAN

Cuba had been wrested from Spain, but it had also been wrested from Cubans, if only for a time. But that was time enough to set in motion far-reaching and long-lasting changes. After 1898 the North American presence extended in many directions and in many forms, almost unchecked, with little to impede its advance and almost nothing to limit its influence. The North Americans entered an environment of unimaginable desolation and destitution. With vast resources at their disposal, they early learned to exact Cuban acquiescence to their needs. Even the distribution of food to the hungry served as a means of social control.[22]

Such conditions severely limited the Cuban capacity to articulate and advance national forms independent of North American authority. Certainly Cubans carefully monitored the political impulses of U.S. representatives, wary of North American territorial designs and prepared to resist attempts to restrict or otherwise compromise Cuban independence and national sovereignty. The notion of a separate nationality never lost its grip on the popular imagination and persisted as an ideal of enormous vitality from which the strategies of popular mobilization of an entire generation were derived. This proposition resonated throughout the early decades of the republic, one unreservedly supported by the vast majority of Cubans.

But Cubans also had other immediate concerns. These were difficult times, when the Cuban people were especially susceptible to North American ways. The U.S. presence decisively influenced how they constituted themselves as a nation. It suggested the models and modalities from which Cubans devised their national identity and provided the principal constructions by which to contemplate matters of vital importance, from the type of households to be organized to the choice of careers, from religious preferences to social affiliations.

To have pursued alternative possibilities would have necessarily challenged the very premises of the North American presence in Cuba and invited an armed confrontation whose outcome was far from certain. In any case, many Cubans were already familiar with, or had adapted to, North American cultural forms. Much in the value system that mediated the U.S. presence had been previously accepted by the Cuban people and thus was unlikely to offend their sensibilities, which were at least partially derived from North American sources. In fact, some of the most important and binding adaptations had been set in motion well before 1898, over decades of close and frequent encounters with the United States, many of which were subsequently reinforced in Cuba and offered mobility in an environment increasingly dominated by North American cultural forms.

These circumstances also offered opportunities to North Americans and, indeed, were very much at the heart of what made Cuba such highly contested terrain. It was not only that large numbers of Cubans faced impoverishment, but also that their condition made them vulnerable to expulsion or extinction. That Cuba was governed by North America during the immediate postwar years made a difficult situation worse. This was not a Cuban government and not of Cuban choosing; most important, it was not of the same moral universe. Numerous Cuban farmers, large and small, appealed to the U.S. military government for assistance such as credits, low-interest loans, and subsidies to assist recovery, but to no avail. "Many requests have been made by the planters and farmers to be assisted in the way of supply cattle, farming implements, and money," military governor John R. Brooke reported in 1899, "and all were rejected." Brooke explained:

> The matter has been most carefully considered and the conclusion reached that aid could not be given in this direction. The limit has been reached in other means of assistance to the verge of encouraging or inducing pauperism, and to destroy the self-respect of the people by this system of paternalism is thought to be a most dangerous implanting of a spirit alien to a free people.... The real solution ... is through the medium of banks.... This system would not destroy or impair the self-respect of the borrower; he would not be the recipient of charity, but a self-respecting citizen working out his own financial salvation by means of his own labor and brain.[23]

Treasury Department agent Robert Porter agreed, insisting that private savings, not public subsidies, was the answer to Cuban woes: "Savings banks must ... be established, for no people can become permanently prosperous where thrift is unknown and where there are no opportunities for saving the surplus earnings of the population."[24]

Convictions so strongly held by those in power had significant consequences. U.S. appropriation of public revenues and refusal to sanction public assistance sealed the fate of thousands of farmers. Without capital or income to revive ruined estates, replace destroyed machinery, or replenish stock, and without collateral to borrow and negotiate, property owners were doomed. Farmers large and small found themselves without the resources to carry on. Unable to resume production or to pay outstanding debts, property owners were forced to sell out, often at great losses. Between 1898 and 1900, farms were changing hands at the rate of nearly four thousand a year.[25] "There are ... many abandoned estates," U.S. consul Ross Holaday reported from Santiago de Cuba, "which were destroyed during the wars in Cuba, the owners of which are either too impoverished to again establish and operate them, or they do not desire again to undertake planting." Correspondent Albert Robinson agreed: "Any number of the old estates can now be purchased at almost any price." Havana newspapers were filled with classified advertisements offering farms, estates, and plantations, urban properties and private homes, shops and stores, at highly reduced prices. A "magnificent sugar mill" valued at $400,000, with an annual production capacity of 60,000 sacks, was advertised for $100,000. Patricio Ponce de León sold Central Indio for one-tenth of its $250,000 value—"leaving [me] with a large family to support," he despaired, "and absolutely without resources."[26]

Property values plunged. "Real estate," *Diario de la Marina* reported in mid-1899, "is worth less than half its former value." Farms in San José de las Lajas sold for one-fifth of their original worth. Property valued at $1,000 per *caballería* (33.3 acres) before the war was selling for $100–200 afterward. "Land, at this writing," reported two U.S. consular agents in 1898, "can be bought in unlimited quantities at from one-half to one-twentieth of its value before the insurrection." "Good land can be had from $5.00 to $100 per acre," wrote army chaplain Francis M. J. Craft from Pinar del Río in early 1900. "In some parts of the island land can be had, in large tracts, as low as $2.00 per acre." Sumptuous mansions on Prado, Galiano, San Rafael, and Monte sold for as low as $4,000. A classified in *Diario de la Marina* captured the tenor of the times: "For sale at the best prices: rural estates and urban property. The public can acquire fine furniture, valuable jewelry, and large paintings at low cost."[27]

What was a bane for Cubans was a boon for North Americans. Cuba beckoned: opportunities for the taking, quick returns and high yield, were depicted variously as "virgin land," a "new California," "a veritable Klondike of wealth." Leonard Wood was euphoric about the "magnificent country" that was "practically undeveloped," about its "extreme fertility and richness," a land that was "wonderfully fertile" offering "wonderful opportunities for industrious Americans" and "bound in the future to become the seat of great wealth and prosperity." The possibilities were everywhere and everywhere promising. "The island may be called a brand-new country," exulted Wood.[28]

These were powerful images—the promise of fortune, of work and livelihood: appealing under any circumstances, they were especially compelling to North Americans at the close of the century. In the 1890s the U.S. economy sputtered and stalled, producing one of the most serious economic crises in the nation's history. The panic of 1893 announced the onset of years of dislocation and distress. Bank failures and suspensions occurred in rapid succession, bringing ruin and destitution to tens of thousands of families. A total of 160 national banks, 172 state banks, 177 private banks, 47 savings banks, 13 loan and trust companies, and 16 mortgage companies folded. Credit steadily contracted, bankruptcies and business failures increased in number and value, factories closed and farms went under, liquidations and foreclosures escalated, brokerage firms collapsed, and across the United States financial and commercial dislocation paralyzed entire sectors of the economy. Railroad companies went into receivership, industrial production declined, and sales plunged. Wages followed as the number of hours worked and weekly pay declined and joblessness rose. Unemployment soared from 728,000 (3 percent of the wage labor force) in 1892 to 2.8 million (11.7 percent) in 1893 and 4.6 million (18.4 percent) in 1894. Between 1895 and 1898 unemployment leveled off and remained constant at 3.6 million, or approximately 14 percent of the wage labor force.[29]

It was now the turn of North Americans to escape hard times. They migrated to war-ravaged Cuba by the thousands, shipload after shipload in successive waves, each larger than the one before, people of all social types—among them carpetbaggers and camp followers, peddlers, prostitutes, and petty thieves, hustlers and hawkers, swindlers and speculators—in search of opportunity and fortune, in flight from one of the most devastating depressions in U.S. history. Unemployed and unemployable, landless and luckless, they swarmed to Cuba in pursuit of dreams. For the countless numbers who had lost jobs, businesses, farms, and homes, the opportunities for beginning anew were irresistible, indeed. As early as November 1898, correspondent Stephen Crane wrote from Santiago de Cuba of the arriving "vanguard of a caravan of indigent Americans looking for fortune in this new country."[30] To these must be added the officers and soldiers of the U.S. army of occupation, journalists and job seekers, tourists and missionaries, and the thousands of others who would loosely qualify as "business people": vendors, shopkeepers, and traveling salesmen, merchants and agents, wholesalers and distributors, brokers, contractors, and sales representatives, money lenders and land developers. "The hotel registers," the *Havana Post* commented, "show for January and February 1899 the names of men whose wealth mounts up into the hundreds of millions who came on no idle tour of inspection but who meant business."[31]

They went to Cuba in search of deals and bargains, pushy, aggressive, conquering, searching through the rubble of an island, among a people in distress, for "good buys." Havana was filled with foreigners, straining the capacity of existing hotels and boardinghouses, racing about in a frenzy, creating confusion and commotion, people dashing about in search of the best deals, always amid rumors of better deals. Correspondent Franklin Matthews, who was among the many thousands arriving in Havana during the first weeks of the U.S. occupation, recalled "snatches of conversation . . . of Americans planning to get an option on this or that public works, or arranging to enter into some business venture." This was the "second army of American occupation," commented Matthews, "thousands of men who really had legitimate business on the island [and] hundreds who were mere adventurers in business, syndicate-chasers, franchise-grabbers, political contractors and the like." Novelist James Gould Cozzens described Havana during these days with texture and point of view: "Habana was full of such people; adventurers, misinformed idiots, knaves, murderers, thieving contractors, corrupt officials, lease hunters—every form of rogue and rascal. It was then the last and worst American frontier, with the ethics and atmosphere of all frontiers; life, depraved and violent; honor, nonexistent; and fabulous money loose for the stealing." Charles Pepper wrote of "scum floating across the Gulf," of a "whole class of . . . buzzards" and "American braggarts" who "swaggered through the town with their hands in their pockets and their hats tilted back." Trumbell White, who was there at about the same time, described similar conditions, if with greater circumspection. "The influx of Americans to Havana was rapid after the city was accessible to them," White wrote. "Havana was soon thronged with speculators of all classes. Adventurers found their paradise and all sorts of frauds were attempted in competition with legitimate business enterprises. Real estate, rents and franchises rose in price with startling rapidity. Certain phases of the life reminded one of the boom towns and mining centers of our own west in the bonanza days. Hotels were crowded and at every order there were men with options worth fortunes, which they were willing to sell dirt cheap."[32]

Thousands arrived for the cheap land: abundant and available, it was land for the taking, a place to start anew. Development approached boom proportions, and in many quarters the island assumed the appearance of land rush camps. North American real estate offices opened across the island. J. E. Barlow and Company, which established an office on Prado in September 1898, was the principal agent for the sale of urban real estate to the U.S. government, including office buildings, storage facilities, warehouses, and the one thousand acres on which Camp Columbia was constructed. Barlow also developed the suburban subdivision of Buena Vista, proclaimed as the future "Newport of Havana." The H. P. Wilkinson Real Estate Company advertised "lands for sale in all provinces of the Island." William H. Redding Realty, offering "the most desirable real estate in Cuba," provided one more confirmation of the demise of the creole bourgeoisie in its advertisement for "hundreds of the choicest lots situated in the most aristocratic neighborhoods in Vedado, including the old homestead of the Count of Pozos Dulces, with all its buildings . . . considered the most valuable property in all Vedado."[33]

Land development syndicates proliferated. (See Appendix Table 2.3.) Speculators and developers fanned out in the countryside in search of ruined plantations and abandoned estates on which to tender low offers to desperate and debt-ridden landowners. Many were get-rich-quick schemes, unscrupulous and fraudulent, taking equal advantage of insolvent Cuban sellers and unsuspecting North American buyers. Vast parcels of land were purchased at depressed prices, subdivided into tracts, and sold at inflated values.

North Americans arrived as entire households, parents with children, often extended families; as settlers and small farmers, ranchers, fruit growers, and truck gardeners; as individual homesteaders and commercial farmers. By 1905 approximately 13,000 North Americans had bought land in Cuba. This was a new generation of self-styled pioneers—in flight from economic hardship and in search of new opportunities, a new beginning, a new life—consciously reenacting the drama of the U.S. frontier. They engaged in all types of farming and animal husbandry: from growing alfalfa and cotton to producing pineapples and strawberries, from beekeeping to cattle ranching, from raising chickens to breeding ostriches. Slowly but inexorably Cubans lost possession of their farms and estates. M. W. Brown from Cleveland purchased an estate near Cabañas on which he planted cotton and fruit trees. B. C. Kent from Chicago invested his life's savings in a 333-acre vegetable farm near San Cristobal. Mr. and Mrs. A. P.

Milem from Oklahoma bought 70 acres in Cabaiguán on which they planted fruits. F. H. D. Prentiss of New York acquired 2,000 acres in Mariel. J. W. Paine of Boston bought 18,000 acres near Consolación del Sur. Walter F. Hogheins of Buffalo purchased the defunct coffee estate of Rafael García in Sancti-Spíritus. Adam Gray from Cincinnati arrived in 1901 and acquired the 600-acre estate "Doña Juana" in Rancho Boyeros. E. P. Ansley and W. F. Winecoff from Atlanta bought 66,000 acres from the bankrupt Pastor family of Santiago de Cuba. Lohr Berry from Grand Rapids obtained 16,000 acres in Camagüey from the Díaz family.

The Reciprocity Treaty of 1903 provided further incentive to develop real estate on the island. The treaty conceded to agricultural imports from Cuba a 20 percent tariff reduction—a discount designed to favor growers in Cuba over other foreign producers but, in fact, one that also made farmers in Cuba competitive with growers in California. Waterborne freightage of two days to New York was one-quarter the cost of rail transportation from the Pacific coast. Farmers in Cuba were thus in an excellent position to capture a large share of the lucrative northern markets for winter fruits and vegetables. Florida had previously supplied some of these needs, but a series of record freezes in December 1894 and February 1895 had wrought havoc on Florida agriculture. Thousands of citrus farmers and fruit and vegetable growers were ruined. The local economy collapsed, property values plunged, and many residents lost their jobs, homes, groves, and farms. Indeed, much of the citrus industry of Cuba after 1898 was developed by failed farmers from Florida who gathered what remained of their resources and resolved to start anew in warmer latitudes.

North American settlements and agricultural colonies sprang up across the island. These U.S. enclaves were organized around family farms and locally owned fruit-packing companies, in towns populated largely by North Americans, with shops, churches, and homes identical to those left behind in the United States. At least thirty-five North American agricultural colonies were established in all six provinces, some bearing such improbable names as Ocean Beach (Pinar del Río), Riverside (Las Villas), La Gloria City, Garden City, Boston, Palm City, the Ceballos Colony, and Columbia-on-the-Bay (Camagüey), Omaja [i.e., Omaha], and Bartle (Oriente).[34]

The Isle of Pines in particular attracted North American settlers. By the terms of Article VIII of the Platt Amendment, the Isle of Pines was excluded from Cuban territorial boundaries pending future negotiations between Cuba and the United States. In the years that followed, even as the Isle of Pines continued under nominal Cuban administration, hundreds of North American families acquired nearly $22 million in property holdings. An estimated 4,850 registered U.S. property owners claimed to own more than half of the island. North Americans established a ubiquitous presence. A total of 2,000 residents made up more than half of the total population. The new settlers soon overran the older towns of Nueva Gerona and Santa Fe and established new communities, including Columbia, McKinley, Palm Grove, Westport, San Francisco Heights, and Santa Barbara Heights. They organized ten churches and nine schools, with classes taught in English by North American teachers. English became the dominant language and U.S. currency the medium of exchange. U.S.-owned land companies and real estate developers proliferated; they included the Isle of Pines Company, Isle of Pines Land and Development Company, Santa Fe Land Company, and Almacigos Springs Land Company. Colonists established one bank (National Bank and Trust), owned three hotels (Santa Rita Springs Hotel, Santa Barbara Inn, and the Burnside), and operated numerous small businesses, including the Cash and Carry Store, American Hardware Company, Santa Barbara Nurseries, Bradley's Fertilizer Works, and Brunswick Café, Royal Palm Café, American Café, and Café Donovan. Almost all import merchants were North American, many of whom maintained direct contact with U.S. suppliers. Two weekly newspapers, the *Isle of Pines News* and the *Isle of Pines Appeal*, were published in English. A variety of community organizations—the American Club, Pioneer Club, Santa Fe Social Club, Card Club, Hibiscus Club, and others—served as centers of social activity. Irene Wright, who visited the island in 1908, observed that "American residents there have made the Isle of Pines an American community in everything except political status." She explained:

> Americans are in the majority of the population; American money is not only the official, but the actual currency of trade; the prevailing architecture outside the towns is unreasonably American; American ministers preach from the pulpits; American automobiles and spring wagons have replaced the clumsy oxcart . . . to facilitate shipments of fruits from orchards and gardens owned by Americans, producing for American markets. There are maps published, on which lands whose proprietors are American are colored red; these maps show that, literally, Americans own the Isle of Pines.[35]

Other North Americans went to postwar Cuba in pursuit of employment and livelihood, seeking business and investment opportunities. The island was filled with job seekers, contract workers, and entrepreneurs of all types. North American soldiers were among the first beneficiaries of the intervention. They arrived early and were not reluctant to parlay their official position to business advantage. Many were volunteers, swept up by the patriotic euphoria of 1898: officers who had interrupted business and professional careers, enlisted men who had abandoned jobs as mechanics and artisans, and the untold numbers who came from the ranks of the unemployed. Many U.S. military men remained in Cuba. "Soldiers who are discharged here at the expiration of their enlistment," observed one correspondent, "find no trouble in securing work with good pay, especially if they have any trade or education. One, a plumber by trade, found that he could get a good position in the city, so he secured his discharge from the

Fortunes in Cuba

A SHORT ROAD TO A COMPETENCY AND A LIFE AMID TROPICAL DE-LIGHTS FOR THOSE WHO ARE AWAKE TO THE PRESENT OPPOR-TUNITY.

The Cuban Colonization Company

OWNS and holds deeds for two large tracts of the best land in Cuba, situated on the north coast in the Province of Puerto Principe, the most fertile and healthful portion of the island. This region is being rapidly colonized by enter-prising Americans, who own and are develop-ing thousands of plantations in the immediate vicinity of our holdings. We are selling this valuable land in small tracts, from five to forty acres each, at a low price, payable in monthly installments. It has been practically demonstrated that this soil will pro-duce abundantly all kinds of tropical fruits, sugar cane, coffee, tobacco, cocoanuts, etc.

The purchaser of land from us will have no taxes to pay for the first three years, and can have a warranty deed as soon as his land is paid for.

An advertisement for La Gloria City agricultural colony in Camagüey (Puerto Príncipe) province. (From James M. Adams, *Pioneering in Cuba: A Narrative of the Settlement of La*

A discount of 10 per cent. allowed from regular prices when full payment is made at time of purchase.

An Insurance Policy.

In case of the death of any purchaser we will issue a warranty deed to his or her estate without further payment.

REMEMBER — That a 10-acre Orange Grove in Cuba, four years old, is worth ten thousand dollars, and will net you from three to six thousand dollars annually.

REMEMBER—That in Cuba you can have fruits ripening every month in the year.

REMEMBER — That what you would pay for winter clothing and fuel to keep you warm in the United States will keep up a home in Cuba, where the winter months are perpetual June.

REMEMBER—That in our location are combined a delightful and healthful climate, pure and abundant water, and a rich and productive soil.

Send for illustrated booklet and leaflets, giving information concerning prices, etc.

CUBAN COLONIZATION COMPANY.

MAIN OFFICE,

ROOM 367, ARCADE,   CLEVELAND, OHIO

BRANCH OFFICE, -- -- HOOPESTON, ILL.

... OFFICERS ...

DR. W. P. PEIRCE, President and Treasurer.
W. G. SPIKER, Vice-President and General Manager.
G. W. HANCHETT, Assistant Manager.
W. P. PEIRCE, JR., Secretary.
JAMES PEIRCE, Assistant Secretary.

Gloria, the First American Colony in Cuba and the Early Experiences of the Pioneers [Concord, N.H., 1901]).

Residence of Mr. and Mrs. W. E. Schultz, Santa Fe, Isle of Pines, 1901.
(Courtesy of the Library of Congress, Washington, D.C.)

service. He now makes $6 a day working at his trade. Others are making from $60 to $100 a month. A surgeon here last year with one of the volunteer regiments is now located permanently in Havana."[36]

Many officers and men serving in the military government subsequently became landowners and successful businessmen. Major Eugene F. Ladd was the army auditor at the time he purchased an orange grove in Santiago de las Vegas near his brother's cotton and pineapple plantations. Customs appraiser Captain W. F. Smith of the New York 202d Volunteers acquired a ranch outside of Havana. Major S. S. Harvey resigned his commission to open Harvey's American Headquarters Hotel. Captain Ed Smith of the Rough Riders, Captain George Evans of the Forty-ninth Iowa Infantry, and Sergeant Arthur Willis of the Missouri Volunteers were only a few of the many U.S. veterans to be mustered out in Cuba and to buy farms and plantations on the Isle of Pines. Major Orland Drucker purchased a farm in Bejucal. While serving a tour of duty in Puerto Príncipe, Colonel Cushman A. Rice acquired a cattle ranch in Camagüey. Captain A. W. Putnam resigned his commission to organize a land development company to colonize Paso Real in Pinar del Río. General George C. Reed formed Las Uvas Land Syndicate in Pinar del Río, which was managed by Major James E. Runcie of the judge advocate's office in Havana. Captain Tillinghast L. Huston resigned his commission in the engineer corps and founded the T. L. Huston Contracting

Residence of T. M. Symes II, Santa Fe, Isle of Pines, 1901.
(Courtesy of the Library of Congress, Washington, D.C.)

Company, the Huston Concrete Company, and the Huston-Trumbo Dredging Company. He obtained the lucrative contract to dredge Cuban ports and improve Havana harbors and eventually went on to own the New York Yankees. Captain Osgood Smith of the 112th New York Infantry became a successful Havana attorney and executive secretary of the American Chamber of Commerce in Cuba. By 1907 Sergeant Frank Steinhart, who had served as the chief clerk of the occupation, had become president of the Havana Electric Railway, Light, and Power Company.

The larger significance of the North American intervention, and certainly the enduring consequence of this presence, had less to do with political relationships than with social realignments. It was embedded in the ways in which U.S. normative systems and moral hierarchies worked their way into everyday life, primarily in the form of a vast cultural transfer, one that was facilitated by the great material impoverishment of Cubans in 1898. This allowed for the introduction of North America's accumulated technical knowledge, advanced industrial systems, new machinery, capital flows, new business organizations, and modern building innovations, all of which came loaded with meanings and metaphors as well as models of identity and modes of self-representation. New mass-producing and mass-distributing enterprises established themselves all over the island. New technology, advanced production modes, the latest transportation systems, and modern industrial organizations were introduced. All in all, this process of reconstruction began from a condition of almost total ruin; in the course of such regeneration, much of what was old passed into desuetude and what was new promised deliverance.

Members of the Hibiscus Club, Isle of Pines, 1901. (Courtesy of the Library of Congress, Washington, D.C.)

The North American presence assumed its most visible form in postwar reconstruction, a sweeping undertaking that reached virtually every community on the island. This was a time of putting lives back together, of fresh beginnings and new hopes. But it was also rebuilding on North American terms, a rearrangement of Cuban institutions to accommodate U.S. needs. The project of recovery was appropriated by North Americans and conceived almost wholly within the moral order of the North. Most of all, it implied realigning social relationships and reassembling what commonly served as the means of security in such a manner as to guarantee that success would come easiest to those most conversant with North American ways.

The scope of the reconstruction under North American auspices is incalculable. New forms were injected directly into Cuban institutional representations, virtually unchallenged. What was particularly noteworthy about the postcolonial order was the U.S. capacity to mobilize vast resources on a prepossessing scale, made all the more potent in an environment of desperate need. The larger significance of these developments was the degree to which North American ideas and practices so thoroughly overwhelmed those of Cuba and in the aggregate defined a market culture derived from North American models and from which Cuban national structures subsequently evolved. Enormous energy was deployed in reconstruction efforts, generally as state-sponsored public works

Hotel Plaza, owned and operated by the Development Company of Cuba, located in the Ceballos agricultural colony in Camagüey (Puerto Príncipe) province. (From Development Company of Cuba, *Ceballos: The Garden Spot of Cuba* [New York, n.d.])

and private investments, characterized by a massive infusion of capital and technology, all of which implied attitudes and values that contributed to the synthesis of national identity. The rebuilding process reinforced the structural links of Cuban value systems to North American sources, which served as a repository from which to assign form and content to nationality and to which Cubans would thereafter remain indissolubly connected.

North Americans took over completely and immediately set about repairing, rebuilding, and reconstructing—in all, a monumental commitment to public works programs and infrastructure development across Cuba. Scores of public buildings were repaired or rebuilt. New bridges were completed. The construction of new roads and highways began early, as did the clearing, repairing, and paving of old streets and thoroughfares. New methods were introduced to the building of rural roads, which were constructed as all-weather macadam to withstand seasonal rains and periodic flooding. Bridges, culverts, and road-beds routinely employed heavy stone packing. Roads linking Guanajay-Mariel, Matanzas-Cidra, Güines-Cuatro Caminos, Camagüey-Santiago de Cuba, and El Caney-Santiago de Cuba were only some of the most important construction projects completed after 1898. Within a decade, the total length of highway had increased from 256 to nearly 2,481 kilometers. More than 4,000 kilometers of new telephone and telegraph lines were laid, as new service linked Havana, Matanzas, Cienfuegos, Santa Clara, Camagüey, Las Tunas, Bayamo, Palma Soriano, San Luis, and Santiago de Cuba. As early as 1900, Havana was connected by telephone with almost all towns within a 75-mile radius. In 1910 Havana became

Reconstruction in Santiago de Cuba during the U.S. military occupation, 1901, is vividly illustrated in these before-and-after photos.
(Courtesy of the Library of Congress, Washington, D.C.)

the first city in the world to install an automatic telephone system on a multi-exchange basis.

Havana teemed with activity. Gangs of survey teams, construction crews, builders, and wreckers seemed to be everywhere, and at times they were. Wharf and pier construction expanded to accommodate the surge of maritime traffic. Old streets were repaired, new ones were put in. New public buildings were erected, and old structures received modern electrical fixtures and plumbing facilities. "Very nearly every street in the city shows builders are at work," commented one observer in 1900; "houses are either being built a story higher or new ones being built."[37] The water system was improved. A comprehensive sewerage system was introduced, and new water pipes were installed; electric streetlight and natural gas networks were augmented. New private homes were equipped with hot and cold running water and indoor bathrooms. The parks were cleaned, repaired, and landscaped with walkways, playgrounds, and fountains. Additional light and power systems powered city streets and store signs. A New York corporation, the Havana Electrical Railway Company, completed a new electric trolley system in 1901. Fifteen miles of track linked downtown Havana to the suburbs via two main lines: one from the harbor entrance west to the Almendares River through Vedado and the second from the northeastern sector of the city south to El Cerro and the Jesús del Monte suburbs.

The new trolley changed the demography of the capital. Residential patterns were transformed. The suburbs grew in spectacular fashion. Property values soared. New areas were opened to real estate development, particularly for the expanding middle class, which was now able to move out of the congested city center but still return to work. Passenger service increased markedly, from 10,000 daily on the old horse-drawn cars to 60,000 daily on the new electric trolley. At the Guanabacoa terminus, new parks, pavilions, picnic grounds, and a baseball stadium were constructed. Nowhere, perhaps, was the change as dramatic as in the suburb of Vedado, much of which was completed by North Americans. "There is a building boom on in Vedado," reported the *Havana Post* soon after completion of the trolley in 1901, "and at present there are more houses in the course of construction than there have been at any one time for the past ten years. Nearly every vacant lot in that suburb has been purchased by someone for a site for a home."[38]

Reconstruction and renovation proceeded throughout the island, including modern waterworks in Matanzas and Santiago de Cuba, sanitation projects and new streets in Matanzas; a new sewage disposal system in Puerto Príncipe; new water systems in Nuevitas and Ciego de Avila; a modern drainage system in Cienfuegos; repaired streets in Santa Clara, Remedios, and Sagua la Grande; waterworks in Guantánamo; rural roads for Las Tunas, Puerto Padre, and Holguín; improved harbors in Bahía Honda, Caibarién, Gibara, Baracoa, and Manzanillo.[39] A new water system was introduced in San Antonio de las Vegas.

Construction of the Contramaestre Bridge over the Cauto River, 1902.
(Courtesy of the McKeldin Library, University of Maryland at College Park)

"Waterpipes are being laid over all the town," related a visitor in 1900, "and [it] is to be supplied with water in a modern fashion. Up to now the people have had their water hauled there from long distances in large barrels."[40] In almost every provincial city and town new roads were constructed and old ones repaired. Among the health and sanitation projects were the expansion of ditches, drainage systems, and garbage disposal systems and improved street cleaning.

Extensive work was undertaken in the port cities. Harbors and basins were dredged, new docks and warehouses were built. Old wrecks were removed from shipping lanes and channels. Waterfronts were cleaned. Navigational aids to guide maritime traffic along coastal points and into ports and harbors were repaired and expanded. Beacons, buoys, and lighthouses increased along both coasts. In Cárdenas, the harbor was dredged, the channel was deepened, and a new wharf with a railroad terminal was linked to the existing rail system, all at a cost of $1 million. The harbor of Matanzas was dredged to the Yumurí and San Juan Rivers, and the channel in Cienfuegos was deepened to reach the Cuba Central Railroad terminals.

All of these projects involved North American builders and contractors, architects and engineering firms, law offices and advertisers, thousands of North American workers, huge amounts of U.S. capital, and enormous quantities of U.S. material resources. The Thompson-O'Brien Engineering Company was one of the largest contractors engaged in state-sponsored projects and private construction, including the building of two new electrical plants in Havana, sugar mills, bridges, and canneries. Purdy and Henderson erected the National

Habana. Lonja del Comercio.
Produce Exchange.

Lonja de Comercio, Havana, constructed between 1905 and 1909 under the supervision of Purdy and Henderson. (Author's collection)

Bank of Cuba building, the Cuban Telephone Company, the Plaza Hotel, the Centro Gallego, and the Havana Yacht Club. The Huston Contracting Company was associated with such important projects as the Havana Electric Railway, Havana Central, Cuba Central, and the Santiago Street Railway. Almost all of the steel bridges built in the first decade of the republic were constructed by Huston Contracting. Frederick Snare built the Havana Central Railroad Station and new wharves in Matanzas. The American Bridge Company and the Union Bridge Company of New York installed most of the railroad bridges. McGivney and Rokeby secured the sewer contract in Havana and subcontracted out to its subsidiary, the Cuban Engineer and Contracting Company. The Ford and Patterson Company and the Cuban Construction and Contracting Company built artesian wells in Sagua la Grande, Sancti-Spíritus, and Santa Clara. The Cast-Iron Pipe and Foundry Company from New York was the principal source for cast-iron water and gas pipe. The National Concrete Company manufactured blocks, tubing, and tiles of cement. The Cuba Lumber Company of Delaware sold shingles, doors, shutters, and blinds. The General Construction Company obtained the contract for new school buildings in Havana—using "a design similar to those built in the states," noted one observer.[41] The Standard School Furniture Company supplied schools with desks, chairs, and tables.

North American construction firms worked city streets and rural roads. The Pan American Construction Company and the Havana Construction Company shared most of the contracts for paving municipal streets. The Cuban Quarry Company of New Jersey provided the cut stone for building and road construction. The Tropical Engineering and Construction Company, incorporated in Cuba but owned entirely by North Americans, developed the waterworks system in Santiago de Cuba. The brick paving contract for Havana was held by Tennessee Paving Brick Company. Parker, Waugh and Company built the new customhouse of Havana. The M. J. Dady Engineering Company from Brooklyn dredged the Cárdenas harbor.

Utility services increased. The Spanish-American Gas Company distributed gas fuel for motors and cooking. The Delaware-based American Water Works Company modernized the Matanzas water system. A Boston consortium operated the waterworks of San Antonio de los Baños. The largest ice manufacturing plant and cold storage facility in Havana was built by Krajewski-Pesant Company. The B. E. Hambleton Company erected a municipal ice plant in Santiago de Cuba, and the Cuba Construction Company built a modern ice factory at Batabanó.

Electrical services expanded. The Spanish American Light and Power Company, the Mutual Incandescent Company of New York, and the Cuban Electric Company modernized the capital's electrical system. The Cienfuegos, Palmira and Cruces Electric Railway and Power Company, incorporated in Maine in 1903, developed a water power plant on the Hanabanilla and Negro Rivers and offered electric power and railway transportation across Las Villas province, including Cienfuegos, Palmira, Cruces, Lajas, Sagua, Rodas, Sancti-Spíritus, Ranchuelo, Santa Clara, Remedios, Caibarién, and Placetas. In 1905 the Cuban Electric Company opened a modern plant in Vedado and provided expanded service to Havana, including Vedado, El Cerro, and Jesús del Monte. Electricity arrived in Los Palacios in the same year and was immediately followed by an ice plant and a steam laundry. By 1909 electricity had reached Guanabacoa, Regla, Marianao, San Antonio de los Baños, Batabanó, and Aguacate. Several years later a new electric plant and an ice factory were built in Morón. A second modern electric trolley system was completed in Santiago de Cuba in 1907 by a New York–based syndicate organized by U.S.-trained engineer Eduardo Justo Chibás. New electric trolley systems followed quickly in Camagüey, Cienfuegos, and Matanzas. The Interstate Electric Company of New Orleans introduced modern electrical systems to sugar estates, including electric railroads for hauling cane, electric cranes for hoisting cane, electric elevators, and electric mill machinery. The Regla Iron Works Company installed Otis elevators in the Pasaje Hotel. The new warehouse built by the American Tobacco Company on Zulueta also included two freight elevators by Otis. The Lykes Brothers constructed the first modern meatpacking plant. The American Machinery and Export Company of New York provided sawmill machinery, sugar mill and traction steam engines, and cane loaders. New piers and wharves were constructed by the American Dock Company. The Ward Steamship Line purchased vast tracts of waterfront property in Havana and in the major provincial ports, constructed

Camagüey Railroad Station, ca. 1910s.
(Courtesy of the McKeldin Library, University of Maryland at College Park)

new warehouses, and modernized loading operations. The Mooretown Salt Company developed the salt flats of Cayo Romano.

Railroad projects were undertaken across the island. Old systems were modernized and new ones organized. The Santiago Railroad Company, the Cuban Eastern Railway, and the Guantánamo Railroad were only some of the most prominent rail ventures in the postwar years. The most ambitious railroad enterprise was undertaken by the Cuba Company under William Van Horne. The Cuba Company acquired an estimated 50,000 acres of land for rail stations, construction sites, towns, depots, and a right-of-way 350 miles long. Its trunk line extended through the center of the island, from Santa Clara through Camagüey province to Santiago de Cuba—nearly 550 kilometers of new track. By 1902 all six provinces were linked by railroad, enabling travel between Havana and Santiago de Cuba in less than twenty-four hours. The Cuba Railroad opened the eastern provinces to economic development: Alto Cedro to Nipe Bay (1905), giving rise to the new town of Antilla; Cacocúm to Holguín (1906); Martí to Bayamo, Palma Soriano, and San Luis; and Bayamo to Manzanillo (1911). In sum, about $30 million was invested in railway construction.[42]

The ramifications of reconstruction projects were far-reaching. Government building codes raised construction standards. This period also saw the introduction of new building materials, including reinforced concrete, and new building methods, as well as modern fixtures and fittings. New electrical systems and modern plumbing were installed, including running water and bathroom fixtures. Previously, flushing devices were unknown and the wiped joint was nowhere in use. These developments, in turn, had other effects. "Modern installations for running water and sanitary equipment made the bathroom a priority in turn-of-the-century planning," wrote architectural historian Carlos Venegas Fornias. "No longer tucked in a corner at the back of the building, the 'connecting' bathroom, a symbol of republican comfort, became an integral part of the home."[43]

Public works contracts were awarded primarily to U.S. architects, builders, and contractors, who in turn employed workers from the United States, including plumbers and carpenters, riveters, electricians, machinists, mechanics, welders, bricklayers, stonemasons, teamsters, and technicians. Virtually all of the engineers employed in the paving and sewer construction of Havana between 1899 and 1909 were North Americans. U.S. workers posted and repaired telephone lines. The American Bridge Company hired hundreds of construction workers in the United States for railroad projects in Cuba. And hundreds of U.S. bricklayers, welders, and ironworkers were employed in the construction of United Fruit Company facilities in northeastern Cuba. The construction projects of the Cuba Company, including railroads, warehouses, wharves, and hotels, were completed mostly under the supervision of workers from North America. The number of U.S. plumbers in Cuba was sufficiently large to result in the formation of a local union chapter in Havana—Local No. 200—to which no Cuban belonged, reportedly for lack of qualifications.[44]

Professional practices expanded. The American Hospital and Clinic, the Anglo-Saxon Hospital—"only American graduated nurses in attendance"—and the American Osteopathic Institute provided a range of health services. Among the North Americans were dentists Elton Goodfellow, W. H. Keller, W. F. Metzger, C. W. Orland, Byron Rhome, D. M. Sabater, B. M. Sims, James Warner, and Erastus Wilson; physicians T. M. Calnek, Wiley Forsythe, Frank Hart, David Jacobson, H. D. Kneedler, and Clifford Ryder; as well as optometrist Harold Rollins, chiropodist J. M. Palmer, and chiropractor Edith Pierce. Dr. M. Johnson opened a pharmacy on Obispo. The International Drug Store prepared "prescriptions . . . by a competent graduate American clerk." Carlota the Wonderful, who relocated her practice from Atlantic City to Havana, billed herself as the "only true clairvoyant in Cuba."[45]

The number of law offices, insurance companies, and banks also increased. New law firms included Page and Conant of New York, Lucius Lamar, and Hugh Grosvenor and Company. Among the insurance companies to operate in Cuba were the Norwich Union Fire Insurance Company, Maryland Casualty Company, Mutual Life of New York, Pan American Life Insurance, and Standard Life

Insurance Company. These concerns wrote life, fire, marine, and workman's compensation policies throughout the island. By the 1910s large sectors of Cuban industry, sugar mills, manufacturing plants, and retail stores were insured by U.S. companies, which meant, too, that safety and security practices increasingly conformed to U.S. standards. New North American banking and financial institutions included the Guarantee Trust Company of Georgia, Fidelity and Deposit Company of Maryland, Buffalo Colonial Loan and Deposit Company, North American Trust Company, National Bank of Cuba, and Bank of Havana. The Colonial Loan and Deposit Company financed housing construction in Vedado.

The island saw a proliferation of English-language newspapers and magazines, almost as many as Cubans had published in the United States. (See Appendix Table 2.4.) The leading Havana dailies, including *La Lucha*, *La Discusión*, and *Diario de la Marina*, published English-language sections.

THE ORDER OF THE NEW

In these years Cuba teemed with North Americans—many thousands of soldiers and workers, journalists, colonists, and tourists, farmers and settlers, developers, contractors, and builders—generating a greater demand for goods and services, almost none of which could be met locally. So large was this presence that it constituted a market: vast numbers of customers and clients with needs of every kind.

The results were predictable. More North Americans arrived to meet these needs, and the products and services they introduced soon transformed the character of daily life for Cubans across the island. Hotels, guest houses, and boardinghouses increased in every province. J. L. Thrower opened the Hotel Thrower on O'Reilly Street. The Cuba Company operated Casa Grande in Santiago de Cuba, the Hotel Antilla, and the Hotel Camagüey. Other hotels included the American Hotel in Santiago de Cuba, the Park Hotel in Guanabacoa, and the New York Boarding House, Columbia House, Bay State House, and Hotel Belvedere in Havana. The International Hotel in Vedado advertised itself as a "modern hotel, [with] electric lights, hot and cold water, rooms with private baths." The old Pasaje Hotel in Havana added forty new rooms in 1899 and installed an electric elevator; its rooms were "furnished in American style."[46]

Bars in Havana multiplied: in 1899 the Washington Saloon, Yankee Bar, New England Bar, New York Bar, and Texas Bar opened in rapid succession. Charles Christian's Manhattan Bar followed in 1900. Soon there were more restaurants and cafés: the American Tea Room, California Restaurant, and Chicago Restaurant. Charles Shaw advertised that his new Park Restaurant offered "strictly first-class American cooking." The Gay Broadway on Prado sold "fine ice cream, wines, and beer." John E. Rogers operated the Elite Café, Charly Lum owned the American Union Restaurant, and E. W. Nelson opened the Studio Restaurant.

On Teniente Rey the Hail Columbia Restaurant, which opened in 1899, proclaimed: "Our cooking is strictly American and our customers are Americans." El Cosmopólita described itself as "the only restaurant in Havana where American cooks are employed . . . the only place in Havana where American pies are served." Dave Echemendía and Sam Myers inaugurated an oyster house known as the Manhattan Café. Harry Eckstein operated the Delmonico Café. W. H. Speed opened the American Soda Shop providing "ice cream soda and American soda water at American prices: the finest glass of soda water from the coldest fountain in Havana." The Greater New York Café advertised service "conducted in American style." El Boulevard Café opened on Empredado for "business men who seek their lunch there during the noon hour"—and eating habits in Cuba began to change.[47]

New entertainment programs replaced Spanish productions. The Alhambra Theater in Havana, formerly the principal venue of Spanish *zarzuelas*, reopened in 1899 under the name of the American Café with a newly refurbished music hall for nightly stage shows. Hotels, cabarets, and theaters contracted vaudeville acts, minstrel shows, and burlesque companies from the United States. The Myerson Vaudeville Company played successively in Havana, Matanzas, and Cienfuegos. The Payret Theater was leased to a North American burlesque company. The Washington Casino, which opened its doors in 1899, was committed to a "continuous performance with the best American and home talent." New theaters included the Jardín Americano, featuring nightly performances by the "Cuban Extravaganza Company." William Davidow's Casino Americano advertised "first class artists from the States" and booked only acts from the United States. Cuban- and Spanish-owned establishments switched their programs to North American productions. In 1899 D'Estramps and González introduced into the Cuba Theater "a high class vaudeville show" with two performances in English nightly.[48] In 1900 the Sells and Gray Circus made the first of its annual visits to Cuba.

Retail shops of all types opened in and around Havana. The American Creamery advertised "products from home." D. B. Davis established the Vedado Grocery and enjoined prospective customers to "call on me for anything you need in the line of American groceries," and James Lisberger operated an American grocery in Cienfuegos. Carl Zager opened the California Meat Market in Vedado. W. D. Crosbics installed Crosbies Chicago Market, which sold "Swift & Co. meats, choice butter, fish, and fresh vegetables." The New York Meat Market on Aguiar Street offered the "most complete assortment of meats . . . kept on ice in our spacious refrigerator." Louis Frohock arrived in Cuba in 1899 and opened the "Cash and Carry" grocery store on O'Reilly Street. In the same year, the American Grocery also appeared on O'Reilly to provide a wide assortment of food lines from the United States. "I recall when at the entrance to O'Reilly," Alejo Carpentier reminisced, "a shop called the American Grocery opened, which sold North American canned goods in competition with Spanish and French products. That seemed like an extraordinary innovation."[49]

Retail stores proliferated and were themselves among the principal means by which ways and things North American were disseminated inside Cuba. The newest methods in laundering and dry cleaning were U.S. enterprises. The Troy Laundry Machine Company proceeded to install up-to-date steam mangles across the island, fit neighborhood laundries, and equip laundry factories with the newest machinery. The American Eagle Laundry in Havana proclaimed "American clothes washed American style by Americans." The New York Steam Laundry Company operated El Tío Sam Cleaners. Others included American Dry Cleaning and Dyeing, Lindsay's American Clothe Dry Cleaners, and Cuban-American Dry Cleaning Company. Knight and Wall Company of Tampa established a hardware store in Havana that sold nails, barbed wire, iron and galvanized pipes, paint, stoves, cooking utensils, farming implements, and wagons. Charles H. Thrall offered electrical supplies. The Cuban Electrical Supply Company advertised "electrical supplies of every description in stock for immediate delivery," including motors, dynamos, generators, and gasoline engines. Daniel Lebeuf sold "American stoves." The Brunswick-Balke Collender Company installed bar fixtures, billiard tables, ice boxes, and bowling alleys. Champion, Pascual and Weiss opened a furniture and office supply store on Obrapía and received the exclusive distributorship for Underwood typewriters. In Havana, James B. Clow and Sons offered modern bathroom and toilet fixtures and the latest plumbing lines. In Cienfuegos, Guy Wisewell opened a store of *instalaciones sanitarias modernas*, including bathroom fixtures, sinks, and plumbing installations. Harry Zimmerman advertised as "the only American barbershop in Havana." The Southern Express Company, Wells-Fargo, Adams Express Company, and Cuban and Pan-American Company were the major private carriers. The American Second Hand Store on San Rafael bought and sold used furniture, tools, and clothing. W. H. Cox established a bicycle distributorship, and James Rand opened a shoe repair shop.[50]

Advanced technology appeared in the form of accessible consumer goods. In 1900 Charles Repp opened the American Talking Machine Company, which carried a full line of phonographs, gramophones, vitaphones, and records. In 1905 H. J. Hagen established the exclusive dealership for Victor Talking Machines and distributed a new line of phonographs. Two years later Anselmo López opened a store on Obrapía to sell the newest "Grafófonos Columbia" and Columbia records.

With the arrival of new clothing lines, fashions changed. Charles Berkowitz's La Moda Americana on San Rafael sold ready-made women's dresses and men's suits, all advertised as "the latest fashion." Haberdasher Melvin Schwartz opened La New York—"Havana's American clothing store" with "clothes that 'breathe' of Broadway"—to sell lines of U.S. clothing and furnishings. In 1900 J. A. Rowell

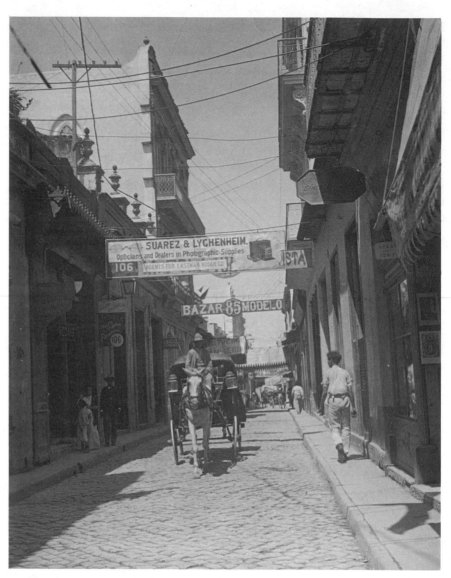

San Rafael Street, Havana, in full commercial revival, 1901. (Courtesy of the Smithsonian Institution, Washington, D.C.)

and Company, wholesale hatters and shoe dealers, established a new store on Obispo. The Steinberg Brothers operated El Escudo Americano—"the best American haberdasher in Havana"—selling Hart Schaffner and Marx clothes and Manhattan and Arrow shirts. Berns and Company and Gent's Clothing Company both specialized in men's fashions. Ben Projan and L. J. Reisler operated the Gotham Store on O'Reilly, advertising "high grade American clothing." The A. W. Conradson and Company established the American Taylor Shop.

Morley's American Dressmakers offered the "latest New York style." Larry Spero was the "only American tailor in Cuba to get an up-to-date tailor made suit . . . cut and made in the latest American style," and the Wheeler Shoe Company on Prado was the "only American shoe store in Havana."[51]

This vast transfer of North American goods and services included bakers (Cosmopolitan Bakery), beauty salons (Carter Sisters Beauty Shop, Bonnie Brown Beauty Parlor), musical instruments (Universal Music Company), opticians (Anglo-American Optical Company, Cuban-American Optical Company, American Opticians), stationery and office supplies (La Casa Wilson, Frank Robbins and Company, Harris Brothers, H. W. Swan), photographers (Graphic Works, American Photo Studio, Todd Photograph Company), newspaper stands (American News Company), and at least one mortician (Cumberbatch and Company).

Hundreds of U.S. manufacturers opened sales offices and agencies throughout Cuba. Billard and Company dispensed soda water equipment and soda fountain machinery. The American Machine Company established an agency to distribute sawmill equipment. Stockell, Pearcy and Company represented the Millburn Wagon Company and the Sechler Carriage Company. Hubbel, Nichols and Company—"the only strictly American agricultural implement house in Cuba"—sold disc plows, mowers, carriages and wagons, shovels, wheelbarrows, and rakes. The Lykes Brothers from Florida engaged in a brisk business replenishing Cuban livestock herds. The Crossmann Brothers Seed Company of Rochester and Griffen Brothers Nursery of Jacksonville opened branches in Havana. U.S. manufactures of all types, including sewing machines, office machines, and light machinery, as well as heavy machinery, such as dynamos, motors, conveyor belts, and complex agricultural equipment such as harvesters and reapers, established direct sales and service outlets.

The market that emerged in postcolonial Cuba thus replicated the demands of the U.S. market and was one that U.S. manufacturers were uniquely qualified to enter. Imports tripled from an annual average of $10 million between 1895 and 1898 to $30 million during 1899–1902 and increased again to nearly $50 million in 1905–7. U.S. ships crowded into Havana harbor, loaded with commodities such as livestock, machines, building materials, foodstuffs, and an enormous array of consumer goods. "The harbor is growing lively with shipping," wrote Stephen Crane from Havana in September 1898. "The time to make 2,000 percent on the sale of provisions in Havana. The wharves are now piled high, and there is still even more in the bay."[52]

The U.S. merchandise pouring into Cuba soon accounted for a large share of wholesale orders and retail sales. The Reciprocity Treaty (1903) added further logic to this connection by conceding a pricing advantage to imports for which there already existed a preference, thereby guaranteeing U.S. products a privileged place in the Cuban market. By 1909 more than 50 percent of Cuban imports originated from the United States. "Articles of American manufacture or production are . . . offered for sale almost everywhere," U.S. minister Herbert Squiers reported as early as 1904. "The demand for American shoes has largely increased. . . . American watches and clocks are frequently seen as are also American soaps, shirts, corsets, hosiery, dry goods in general, typewriters and foodstuffs of every description in which we control the market." Only two years later Thomas Rees wrote of the "high class wealthy ladies of Cuba" dressed in "beautiful garments of the latest style, mostly imported. They dress no different from any lady of New York, Chicago or any other American city."[53]

Increasing numbers of Spanish and Cuban retailers switched to North American lines. The Havana shoe store La Granada acquired exclusive rights to distribute Banister's shoes for men. Manuel Rodríguez opened the American Meat Market, and José Valle sold "American fashions" at his San Rafael clothing store. P. P. Elijalde and Company on O'Reilly Street advertised an inventory of furniture from twenty-eight different U.S. manufacturers. The Peletería Washington on Obispo sold shoes with the same "elegance, distinction and beauty of the city of Washington," and El Aguila Americana advertised the "latest styles of Arrow collars and shirts." Pedro Vázquez sold "American furniture for bedroom, dining room, hall or office." Raúl Acebal Suárez opened La Casa Blanca clothing store—"organized along modern style"—and invoked the White House in Washington, D.C., as emblematic of the fashions of that "great nation of the North." F. A. Baya was the distributor of Spalding sporting goods, including baseball gloves, catcher's masks, bats, boxing gloves, punching bags, tennis rackets, and baseball score and rule books.[54]

Across the island local retailers and merchants increasingly turned to North American suppliers for consumer goods and foodstuffs. The logic of reciprocity could hardly have resulted in any other outcome. Carreras Brothers and Company in Havana purchased its dry goods supplies in New York. In Cárdenas, Celestino Revuelta, proprietor of La Vajilla dry goods store, obtained his hardware supplies from the North, and Guillermo Fernández, owner of La Escocesa, secured his supply of shoes for men, women, and children from U.S. manufacturers. In Caibarién, wholesalers Hernández and Mata bought foodstuffs from New York, while the R. Cantera house acquired its inventory from Chicago and Mobile. La Vasconia dry goods store in Sagua la Grande, owned by Severino Arruza, received its hardware and glass products from the United States. Imaz and Company in Caibarién obtained hardware goods from Louisville and farming equipment from Indiana. In Cienfuegos, Sánchez Cabruja and Company turned to suppliers in New York, Chicago, and St. Louis, and Cardona and Company obtained agricultural equipment from Iowa.[55]

Local retailers adopted new business names to trade on new market conditions: the O.K. women's shoe store, Yankee Casa Cubana, La Boston clothing store, and Los Americanos bed store. La New York advertised itself as "Havana's

Los Estados Unidos General Store, Antilla, ca. 1905. (Courtesy of the McKeldin Library, University of Maryland at College Park)

American clothing store." J. Murillo opened La Americana pharmacy. A. W. Lazcazette's Black Cat Café operated "according to American ideas." Victoriano García opened Los Estados Unidos clothing store. Eduardo Domínguez, owner of the Metropole Café, advertised his expertise at "mixing American cocktails and American drinks of all kinds." Diego Pérez's American Restaurant offered an "American breakfast at any hour." At El Habanero laundry, owned by Gerardo Núñez, "all work is under the direction of a chemist and American management." The Matalobos brothers opened the "Uncle Sam" beauty shop. The "Fonda Cubano-Americana" employed bilingual advertising: "*A comer barato*. 50¢ square meal. English spoken."

Cuban professional practices traded on associations with the North. Dr. Serafín Loredo called himself an "American physician," and Dr. Arístides Agramonte advertised his medical degree from Columbia University. Alfredo Comas noted his residency at Maryland General Hospital, and dentist José Reposo made mention of his degree from the University of Pennsylvania. Attorney Félix Martínez Giralt publicized his Columbia University degree. Undertaker Ricardo Marín advertised his funeral parlor as the "house commissioned by [the United States] to attend to the burial of 191 victims of the *Maine*."

Increasingly, too, Cuban and Spanish merchants organized business and professional enterprises under English-language names. Rafael Díaz opened the Latest Fashion clothing store on Obispo, and Eduardo Pérez Moreno operated El Dandy linen shop. Vicente Vallejo González founded the Vallejo Steel Works. Carlos Torre operated the American Hat Store. The Reciprocity Supply Company, dealing in home interiors, was owned and operated by Gaspar Contreras and Antonio Suárez. The Quiñones Hardware Corporation, S.A., opened in

1916. Carlos Márquez and Narciso Alvarez organized the West Indies Express Company. Vicente Milián owned the Havana Fruit Company. Carlos Zetina opened La Pansy Shoe store. Francisco López was the proprietor of the American Style clothing store. Dentist Manuel Larrañaga—"educated in the United States"—established his practice under the name American Dental Parlor and used "all the modern equipment." Jesús López Guerrero operated the Health Protection Institute. Dental surgeon José Gálvez Guillén called his Havana office the New York Dental Parlor, and Dr. Antonio Lladanosa opened the Gabinete Electro-Dental Americano.[56]

North American advertising methods arrived early and immediately proceeded to inform and hence transform local market culture. In September 1898 George Benson—identifying himself as an "advertisement contractor" in newspapers in Havana, Matanzas, Cienfuegos, Cárdenas, Santa Clara, Puerto Príncipe, and Santiago de Cuba—established an advertising agency in Havana and solicited contracts from manufacturers and merchandisers in the United States.[57] Advertising agencies introduced billboards, developed newspaper copy, and organized publicity campaigns. Franklin Matthews was astonished by the prevalence of U.S. advertising during a visit to Havana in 1899. "Everywhere . . . there were brilliant lithographs advertising various brands of American beer. It was a wonder that some enterprising agent had not plastered the sides of Morro Castle with these signs. One would think, from the number of them in town, that we were simply a nation of beer guzzlers."[58]

Advertising firms expanded rapidly after the turn of the century. In its first year the West Indies Advertising Company, which opened an office in Havana in 1900, was reported "busy painting large displays of Borden's Condensed Milk . . . on the walls all over the city."[59] Three years later the Advertisement Company of Cuba caused something of a local sensation in Havana by constructing a billboard measuring 100 by 10 feet. W. B. Fair located the office of the Havana Advertising Company on Prado. William Scott opened a sign company on Prado and announced the availability of modern electric signs, whereas the W. B. Elliott Company specialized in billboard advertisements. In 1907 the Liga Cubana de Publicidad formed with Walter Stanton as president and Rafael Fernández and J. A. González as vice presidents.

Advertising worked powerfully to foster a new consumer culture, defining status, civilization, and modernity as acts of consumption. A wide array of commodities, including soap and toilet products, patent medicines and prepared foods, clothing and household goods, especially those manufactures that enjoyed decreasing cost and low per-unit prices, early flooded the Cuban market. As advertisements for new ways resonated with themes of progress and civilization, old habits and traditions were slowly displaced. Fleischman and Company, for example, informed "the people of Cuba" that "one of the important duties we owe to ourselves is the proper care of our health":

Bread made through the use of injurious ingredients and by unscientific fermentation is unhealthful. Sour bread is dangerous. Sweet bread is delicious and healthful. Compressed yeast is now used in all of the principal bakeries of Europe and America. . . . Bread made with the use of Fleischman & Co.'s compressed yeast is the best. If this is not so, why has compressed yeast taken the place of fermented dough in most civilized countries of the world? Are the people of Cuba not entitled to as much as the people of other civilized countries? . . . If you are satisfied to eat an inferior bread made by a process which the people of other civilized nations have long since discarded, don't mention the subject to your baker at all and you will continue to move along in the same old way.[60]

Already market forces had begun to appropriate and transform facets of nationality. The relationship between national forms and market culture was complex from the outset, always in flux, changing in response to context and circumstances. It was not simply that economic hardships of the postcolonial environment may have persuaded well-meaning men and women, genuine patriots and dedicated *independentistas*, to abandon the cause of Cuba Libre to attend to urgent personal matters such as family—parents, children, and their future well-being. The very formulation of nationality already incorporated the concepts of civilization and modernity as central, defining tenets, an identity construct that was particularly susceptible to North American market forces. Identity fused with commodity. National sensibilities evolved under specific historical circumstances in which the affirmation of "Cuban" could not but draw upon those forms that were most readily available.

The postcolonial condition implied, by definition, transition and transformation, often as conscious efforts to create cultural distance from the discredited past. Circumstances provided the occasion to affirm and act out rejection of old ways, through new conventions and conduct, new patterns of association, and new forms of recreation. The lasting impact of the North American presence, and, in the end, its capacity to implicate Cubans into the normative assumptions of U.S. hegemony, was related to the extent to which the new forms themselves provided the moral and material basis for daily life after the war.

That so much of the impetus driving postwar reconstruction originated from the North had far-reaching implications. What contributed mightily to the appearance of Cuba as modern and technologically advanced, based on U.S. models, was the degree to which that reconstruction, whether in the form of public works or—especially—private buildings, was completed under the direction of North American planners and designers.[61] Many construction projects of the early republic were directed by Cuban architects, engineers, and builders educated or trained in the United States, including Alberto de Castro, José Toraya, and Leonardo Morales. Cubans in the employ of foreign firms, engineers like U.S.-trained Domingo Galdós (Cuba Company), Joaquín Chalons

(Steel Ore Company), and Félix Carabarrocas and Evelio Govantes (Purdy and Henderson), were obliged to adopt U.S. standards and specifications. In one more fashion, transformation implied distance from the colonial past. Carlos Venegas Fornias wrote:

> [Havana] rejected the old colonial order and its architectural past. In the opinion of most, Havana should have abandoned its look of an old-fashioned Spanish city built according to outdated models of urban planning and become a completely modern metropolis. . . . An ideology of progress led builders to turn their backs on history and look for new directions in the international repertory and to the introduction of new techniques of construction, such as reinforced concrete. Building itself became more organized with the appearance of American contractors and better professionally managed local construction firms. Cement consumption skyrockets to sixty thousand tons a year.[62]

North American entrepreneurs situated themselves in strategic places of the Cuban economy to influence the refashioning of Cuba—its environment and the ordinary life of its citizens—in the image of the United States. They were assertive proponents of doing things in Cuba the way things were done in the United States. And because they controlled the resources and the access to resources, because they occupied positions of influence and power, they succeeded in transforming the world of the Cuban familiar around North American forms. L. Scott Thompson, general manager of the Portland Cement Company in Cuba and chairman of the Good Roads Committee of the American Chamber of Commerce of Cuba, was an indefatigable advocate of road improvement. "I can't travel over the roads in the States," he declared, "without thinking about what a fine thing it would be if Cuba could have roads that would even come near to those fine highways up there. . . . And that would be a fine thing for Cuba, just to have roads like that."[63]

North Americans built new factories, designed new office buildings, and introduced new styles of home architecture across the island. The J. H. Mathews Company of New York constructed the bottling plant for the Tropical and Palatino breweries. N. E. Allen owned a brick plant in Cienfuegos that was designed and constructed by the American Clay Machinery Company of Willoughby, Ohio. Andrés Gómez, a former resident of Philadelphia, owned a city block in Havana on which he planned to construct an office building. He returned to Philadelphia to engage North American architects and builders for the project, which was announced to be "modern in every way." The Siboney Cigarette Company of Havana hired New York architect Milliken, Inc., to design a new factory "along modern lines."[64] The Frank Robins building on Obispo was planned by architect Francis O'Keefe. The Barraqué office building on Amargura was a replica of a New York commercial structure. The new Presidential

Central Railway Station, Old Havana, designed by U.S. architect Kenneth Murchison, 1912.
(Courtesy of the Biblioteca Nacional José Martí, Havana)

Palace was constructed by General Contraction Company and the interior designed by Tiffany Studios of New York. Schultz and Weaver conceived the Sevilla Biltmore Hotel, Concha Beach Club, Cuban-American Jockey Club, and Casino Nacional. New York architect L. A. Abramson designed the YMCA building in Havana. New York engineer Thomas T. Allard built the Almendares Bridge, and Kenneth Murchison devised the Central Railway Station in Old Havana. Barclay, Parsons and Klapp directed the construction of the Havana Customs House. The National City Bank in Havana was designed by the New York architectural firm of Walker and Gillette and built by the Starrett Brothers of New York. "Office buildings . . . seem to have been bodily transported from New York," commented one traveler in 1920.[65]

Residential dwellings bore an unmistakable resemblance to homes in the North. Many of the smaller and more modest houses constructed after 1902 were modeled on the bungalow of southern Florida; indeed, the word *bungalow* passed directly into the vernacular to describe this style of architecture. The housing boom in Vedado was dominated by North American architecture. Homes with wide porches, expansive lawns and gardens, and tree-shaded grounds were especially popular. "Americans have bought much ground and are building many beautiful houses," commented Minister Squiers in 1906, "houses of much better quality and more graceful architecture than is to be found in the average Cuban dwelling."[66] Missionaries introduced chapels, churches, and houses that were distinctively North American. The residential zones of North American employees on U.S.-owned sugar plantations and in railroad and mining centers reproduced communities in the United States. "Felton is a pleasant American community," noted the local U.S. consul of the Bethlehem Steel Corporation zone in Oriente, "it has two excellent hotels and a brick and stone guest house, while attractive dwellings furnished to American employees are modernly equipped."[67] North American agricultural colonies in Cuba reproduced small U.S. towns. Long after most U.S. settlers had departed, Sydney Clark toured the Isle of Pines. He observed that the "small towns, such as Columbia and Santa Fe, once eager and flourishing, are now like the ghost towns of California's Mother Lode." Clark found that Nueva Gerona looked "like a small town of Georgia or Tennessee that broke its tether, strayed to a strange pasture and became a stranger's property."[68]

A new world was in the making. Perhaps, under the circumstances, it could not have been otherwise. Cuban institutions had experienced varying degrees of dislocation and disintegration. Progressive impoverishment over three decades, climaxed by the enormously destructive war of 1895–98, had rendered many property-owning families—perhaps the majority of them—powerless to defend their interests, without the credit or capital to liquidate outstanding debts, without the means to resume production, without the resources to return to their professions. Family units had been shattered and household arrangements disrupted, class structures were in disarray, property relations were in transition. The war had all but demolished the world known by most Cubans. In the years of transition that followed, many structures around which colonial society had been organized and regulated passed into disuse. Many of the reference points in people's lives had disappeared or no longer worked. New behaviors had to be learned. Familiar boundaries had vanished. The disruption of the lives of tens of thousands of families was of sufficient magnitude to constitute a threshold between old and new. Cubans had returned to ruin, to incalculable material losses and irreplaceable human ones, but most of all to circumstances so radically changed as to cause a rupture with memory. Places to which they had been previously anchored by memories no longer existed. In Luis Felipe Rodríguez's short story "El despojo" (1928), Iznaga returns home after the war to find that he is "a stranger in his own land."[69]

Old landowning elites were among the first to be incorporated into North American structures. They managed to escape total ruin by exchanging deeds for stocks and relinquishing positions of ownership for a seat on corporate boards of directors. Others exchanged property for posts as overseers of the land they had previously owned. They became resident managers and administrators—employees, in a word—and lived off salaries and commissions. The process had its antecedents in the years before the war and was accelerated afterward. In 1893

Benjamin Perkins and Osgood Walsh of New York purchased the 60,000-acre Constancia estate from the Apezteguía family and then hired Julio J. Apezteguía as resident manager. The war ruined Hipólito Dumois, owner-president of the Banes Fruit Company. In 1899 he sold his land to the United Fruit Company, which subsequently hired him to serve as administrator.[70] This practice continued during the early years of the republic, as planters increasingly traded titles for stocks and salaries, sometimes selling outright to U.S. buyers; such planters included Miguel Díaz (Perseverancia), José López Rodríguez (Conchita and Asunción), Melchor Bernal (Lugareño), Enrique Zulueta (Habana and Vizcaya), Pedro Arenal (Socorro), Pedro Laborde (San Miguel del Jobo), and Juan Ruiz de Gamiz (Yaguajay). In the novel *Sombras eternas* by Raimundo Cabrera, Torcuato del Pazo exchanges his warehouses and tobacco farms in Vuelta Abajo for "a considerable number of stocks and a position on the board of directors in an American company." In José Antonio Ramos's play "Tembladera" (1918), Joaquín Ortega faces a similar choice but resolves to hold on: "The proposal of the *yanquis* would have left me as administrator . . . with double salary and some stock. . . . But that would have been to admit our impotence and indolence."[71]

Other Cubans found employment with North American enterprises. Indeed, an entire generation of entrepreneurs, businessmen, and managers was formed by their association with U.S. concerns. Many joined U.S. commercial, financial, and industrial firms and earned a living by distributing U.S. manufactures and managing U.S. franchises. A large number made careers of serving North American interests as advisers and agents, notaries and negotiators, translators and interpreters, brokers and buyers, and as sellers. General José Lacret Morlot established a real estate consulting office. "Having a practical knowledge of the entire island," he advertised in 1902, "[Lacret Morlot] offers his services for buying and selling farms and plantations, mining properties, native timber, and all kinds of leases. . . . For corporations and private individuals."[72] Alcides Betancourt joined with H. J. Cooper to form a land, mine, and timber brokerage firm and advertised his "expert examination and reporting on lands and titles."[73]

Many secured a livelihood as attorneys serving North American interests. Rafael A. de Calzadilla dedicated his practice to translating legal documents. Pablo Desvernine (LL.D., Columbia) represented the New York law firm Coudert Brothers, whose clients included the Havana Gas Company and the Cuba Company, all the while he was secretary of government in the military administration. Alfredo Poey was associated with the Havana law office of Page and Conant before establishing his own practice in 1900 to represent North Americans in Cuba: "He is not only familiar with laws of Cuba but the United States. He speaks English as well as Spanish and his knowledge will be of great advantage to his clients," asserted Poey's advertisement.[74]

Rafael R. Govín worked for the tobacco firm of H. B. Hollins of New York. Guillermo Domínguez Roldán served as legal counsel for the Equitable Life

Insurance Company of New York, and Fernando Sánchez de Fuentes represented Fidelity and Deposit Company of Maryland. Cosme de la Torriente was retained by Central Railway. José Antonio González Lanuza, who had been secretary of justice in the military government, joined with Norman Davis to organize the Trust Company of Cuba. Rafael Manduley and Gonzalo de Quesada represented the Cuba Company. Nicasio Estrada Mora was managing attorney for the Havana branch of the Buffalo Colonial Loan and Deposit Company. José Ramírez de Arellano was appointed legal adviser for the Standard Life Insurance Company. Domingo Méndez Capote represented the Ward line, Pan American Insurance Company, Havana Commercial Company, and Sinclair Cuba Oil Company. Orestes Ferrara and Pelayo García established the law office of García and Ferrara to represent U.S. companies, including the Cuban Engineer and Contracting Company, McGivney and Rokeby, and the Cuba Company. Luis Fernández Marcané, Antonio Sánchez de Bustamante, and Arturo Mañas Urquiloa were only some of the most prominent attorneys who served as legal counsel to North American corporations.[75]

Many Cubans found jobs as sales representatives and agents of U.S. companies. The Fuller Brush Company hired local representatives in Havana for direct sales across the island. Mario Solomon represented Heinz soups in Matanzas, and Oscar Cintas was the exclusive representative—and eventually vice president—of the American Car and Foundry Company. Enrique Cárdenas represented the R. A. Hutcheson Fruit Company of New York and Emilio Delgado, the John Lucas Paint Company of New York. Víctor G. de Mendoza represented Babcock, Wilcox and Company. Luis V. Placé was an agent for the Ward and Munson Steamship Line, José Morales de los Ríos was assistant manager of the New York and Cuba Mail Steamship Company office in Havana, and José Lallaude worked as the Havana representative of the Southern Pacific Company. Ricardo Avellano was sales representative of Harris Brothers. Pedro Velásquez served as vice president of the Cuba Lumber Company. Alfonso Hernández, as the sales agent of Parson Brothers of New York, sold newsprint to Havana newspapers, and Magin Badia distributed fertilizer for Swift and Company. Zaldo and Company, founded by brothers Carlos and Teodoro (both Fordham graduates) represented U.S. contractors and figured prominently in the success of the Cuba Company. In 1903 the Zaldo brothers joined with H. P. Booth, president of the Ward Line, to organize the Cuba Construction Company.

Increasing numbers were employed by U.S. banks and insurance companies. Francisco Figueredo was the comptroller of the Havana branch of the Guarantee Trust Company of Georgia. In 1900 the North American Trust Company established a branch in Cienfuegos and appointed "a local board of directors" consisting of Vicente Villar, José Cabrija, Carlos Trujillo, Manuel Hartas, and Adolfo Orifa, reported the *Havana Post*, "whose business ability and knowledge of the situation is of great benefit to the bank." Joaquín Capilla represented the Equitable Life Assurance Society in Havana.

The growing North American presence acquired a momentum of its own, contributing to conditions that further expanded the U.S. community. The establishment of many new corporations, businesses, and stores, for example, created an additional demand for accountants. North American accounting firms followed U.S. investments and early included Judd and Company, William P. Field and Company, and Rockey and Company. Staff, Mather and Hough arrived in 1911. Peat, Marwick, Mitchell and Company, Deloitte, Plender, Griffiths and Company, and Price, Waterhouse and Company opened offices in Havana during the early 1920s.

Virtually all U.S. companies in Cuba, as well as many Cuban enterprises, employed the services of North American accounting firms. These agencies introduced modern accounting systems on the island. They taught accounting in Cuban schools and collaborated with the government in the development of a curriculum for a professional program at the University of Havana. North American firms established the dominant methods of accounting by which the first generation of Cuban accountants were trained. Except for the senior partners in the Cuban branches, virtually all agency personnel were Cuban.[76]

These associations integrated a large number of Cubans into North American systems. In representing the interests of U.S. concerns, most were obliged to meet company standards and adopt corporate practices. U.S. businesses taught them management principles and modes of operation. Thomas O'Brien explains how the American and Foreign Power Company reorganized local office culture, imposing on Cuban white-collar employees work habits, office values, and personal conduct that often "ran contrary to many of their own beliefs and interests."[77] Business practices and trade methods were determined largely by headquarters. Franchise holders were required to attend training sessions in the United States, participate in annual company conferences, and maintain close contact with the home office. Many also attended annual trade and professional meetings in the United States. For almost all of the eleven years that Manuel Carranza represented the National Cash Register Company in Havana, he attended the annual summer international conference of company agents in Dayton, Ohio.

Countless other Cubans remained in the United States after 1898, forming the émigré communities in Key West, Tampa, Jacksonville, Philadelphia, and New York. Many subsequently played an important role as bearers of North American ways: as vendors of U.S. merchandise, representatives of U.S. manufacturers, and agents of U.S. interests. Some returned to Cuba as employees of U.S. companies, opening branches and distributorships on the island. Fidelity and Deposit Company of Maryland selected Charles M. Echemendía, a Cuban executive at the Baltimore headquarters, to open its Havana branch in 1899. Ernesto Mantilla, previously Cuban consul in New York, returned to the island as trade representative of the U.S. Worsted Company. When the Singer Sewing Machine

Company enlarged its sales and service operations "to organize Cuba and conduct business precisely as . . . in [the United States]," it hired all fifteen new managers from the Cuban community in Tampa. Years later Sears, Roebuck and Company selected Tampa-born and U.S.-educated Aurelio Prado to head its Cuba operations.[78]

Expanding reconstruction projects provided a powerful boost to local economies. Many Cubans, through employment with U.S. enterprises in the development of railroads, sugar mills, and public works programs, found themselves deeply implicated in transformations of far-reaching consequences. Germán Alvarez Fuentes recalled the arrival of the railroad to Camagüey and the many ways that it altered daily life. "With the opening of the offices and the workshops of the railroads," Alvarez Fuentes noted, "the city quickly prospered":

> These centers of work served as great schools, where so many, men as well as women, were educated and where they perfected their skills, where they began to receive a good income for their work. Without the offices and shops of the railroads the city of Camagüey would have been only slightly larger than Trinidad or Sancti-Spíritus, and no more. But the new blood, the influx of culture and progress brought to Camagüey by the railroad was something that reached all sectors. . . . The railroad was at one and the same time a school and shop, culture and education, something akin to an awakening, a general arousal that knocked on all the doors of the city and province. Women and men filled the schools, obtained new jobs; others . . . devoted all their hours, day and night, to the study of stenography, typing, English, accounting, telegraphy, plumbing, carpentry, machinery, and office work. . . . The railroads provided the great school of life in which all received the aptitudes necessary to set the example for the rest of the city.[79]

Cubans employed by North American enterprises crossed cultural thresholds in other ways. Thousands of construction workers hired by U.S. companies and supervised by U.S. personnel acquired familiarity with North American standards, experience with U.S. methods, and access to U.S. tools. "A large majority of the Cuban workmen of this section," wrote John R. Stanley from the Manicaragua Valley in Las Villas in 1902, ". . . are employed by American capital, and are, as a result, accepting American implements in the way of agriculture, etc., and preferring the American mule many times to the yoked steers. These symptoms, though small, are visible signs of facilitated labor, and thus are one of the many things that turn the tide in favor of Americanism."[80]

In the cities and in the countryside, construction sites bustled with activity, port cities teemed with maritime traffic, wharves and warehouses filled with an array of foreign imports, and everywhere, it seemed, the island was on the mend. Families were reunited as well as begun, careers were resumed, and the future was recovered. These were remarkable years of revival and renewal, of opportunity regained and possibilities restored. Cubans could once more contemplate the future with a measure of certainty, perhaps even optimism: the future as a foreseeable condition for which to prepare, in which one could think again of constituting a household, making a place for children, and satisfying family needs. "It is unforgettable," comments the narrator of Francisco Díaz Vólero's novel *Amor, patria y deber* (1921), "the moral change that took place among the Cuban people when the United States arrived. Those sorrowful faces, furrowed by traces of pain and uncertainty . . . changed radically and people became full of life, with hope abounding; weeping changed to laughter, melancholia to enthusiasm."[81] There was, perhaps, no more powerful testimony of rising confidence and renewed expectations after the war than the dramatic increase in fertility rates. Between 1899 and 1907 the population under five years of age increased by 162 percent, from 130,876 to 342,652.[82]

What was especially striking about the recovery was the degree to which Cubans drew on U.S. representations of material progress and moral well-being to prepare themselves for the future. The presumption of the North American presence was central to the rendering of what was generally accepted as "normal" and all but guaranteed that North American forms would be incorporated into what became Cuban.

The expansion of U.S. market structures presented new consumption options and fostered new fashions, new habits, and new modalities of self-representation. Some of this was familiar, of course, for Cubans who had had previous contacts with the North had acquired direct knowledge of these possibilities. What was different after 1898 was the sheer scope of the North American presence, the power of its appeal, the ubiquity of its forms, and the way it seemed to represent status and security. Things and ways North American resonated modern and offered a means to affirm success and material well-being. In the end, they were routinely appropriated in the restoration of postcolonial normality.

The infusion of vast quantities of capital goods and technology from the United States also meant that the North American presence provided the structure around which daily life in the new republic organized. North American cultural forms insinuated themselves at every turn. They constituted the material constellation by which Cubans arrived at a sense of themselves and suggested the perspective from which to contemplate possibilities of success and well-being. Many could choose from only what was at hand or within reach to make a place for themselves in their own country. Fashions, for instance, began to change almost immediately. "The youth who previously imitated French styles and combed and cut their hair with a certain distinction," observed Wenceslao Gálvez in 1900, "now use suspenders and part their hair in the middle, leaving them with a hairstyle that was always associated with philosophers." Gálvez continued: "The university is full of students with hair cuts *á la americana* and hair styles of the same origins, with a part down the middle and two pigtails on

The raising of the Cuban flag announcing the establishment of the Cuban Republic, May 20, 1902. (Courtesy of the Smithsonian Institution, Washington, D.C.)

the side. Everyone can comb their hair as they wish, of course, but the youth of today will soon shape our future, and so it is natural that upon seeing them so fond of *yanquismo* one becomes alarmed."[83]

Much of what passed for Cuban, and from which national identity was derived after 1898, was drawn from an environment dominated by North American cultural forms. Cubans were surrounded by the artifacts of market culture and the ethos that gave them meaning. The power of these conventions lay in their capacity to persuade Cubans that they were superior and worthy of emulation. Countless numbers subscribed to these conventions, which became the framework for piecing their world together again. Values associated with North American market culture gained usage and utility because they served as a means to mediate the Cuban encounter with the new order, a way to negotiate space inside Cuba. Consumption emerged simultaneously with the republic as the context in which the concept of modern was articulated and affirmed.

Recovery was characterized not merely by reconstruction and rebuilding, but also, and especially, by a rearrangement of consciousness of what was familiar. It was only a matter of time until most Cubans ceased to pay attention to the origins of the material structures and normative standards of their everyday lives. Market culture became so well understood, so fully integrated into daily existence, that it assumed the appearance of the ordinary, in which most felt more or less at home because it was, in fact, home.

The moral was not ambiguous. These were difficult times in which to hold on to old ways. In an environment of material want and institutional collapse, new forms served as the principal means through which a multitude reassembled their world and resumed their lives. Many Cubans daily confronted the need to make urgent decisions, often under unfamiliar and unpredictable circumstances. Most people came to terms with reality as they found it. They improvised and compromised, adapted and adjusted. What was clear from the outset was that resources and access to resources were controlled largely by North Americans and that frequently economic security could be achieved only by accommodation to the U.S. presence.

The changes wrought by war shaped the character of much of the next half century. The sheer destructive power of the conflict had shattered the material basis of existing class structures. Perhaps the single most salient feature of the postcolonial order was the weakness of the old creole bourgeoisie. Colonial class hierarchies in which status was ascribed and inherited had collapsed. In their place were structures that made social mobility more possible than ever before, perhaps more achievable than anywhere else in Latin America. Cubans could strive for success and aspire to mobility by dint of their own efforts, or at least they believed they could. Access to wealth and power was not available equally to all, to be sure. Considerations of race and gender, for example, narrowed possibilities for many. But the principle if not the promise of mobility had indeed taken hold.

Status was early associated with the adoption of foreign ways and most readily accessible through the consumption of goods and services originating from the United States. This was a gradual and complicated process, spanning the early decades of the republic, for consumption increased with the growing availability of U.S. manufactured products, consumer commodities, and household merchandise—goods mass-produced and priced within the reach of many people. The possibility of possessing these goods was one of the most powerful sources of Cuban productivity and, in fact, played a central role in defining the Cuban middle class. Ordinary people were disposed to work harder and longer, for they saw the prospect of improving their status and raising their standard of living through hard work. The greater the availability of consumer products, the greater the incentive for emulative consumption. The promise of the North American ethic, to which increasing numbers of Cubans subscribed, was contained in the notion that happiness was based on material well-being, which could be realized through hard work. Loló de la Torriente was deeply impressed by "the virtues of the North American people: . . . the capacity and discipline for work." This is also a salient theme in the novels of Carlos Loveira. "From my time in the United States," remarks one of his characters in *Los inmorales* (1918), "I acquired one North American virtue, which is a pity that we have not imported to our unlimited fondness to imitate everything *yanqui*: it is the virtue of work."[84]

Many Cubans subscribed to the market ethic that was so much a part of the postcolonial environment. The models available suggested that emulation was the key to success, specifically the adoption of new work habits and new attitudes toward work. Julio Villoldo perceptively noted these changes among Cuban youth, whom he described in 1917 as having broken with "old traditions and past prejudices." The changes were remarkable. "Youths from very fine and old family lineages," wrote Villoldo of the new generation, "do not disdain to be contractors, brokers, real estate agents, salesmen of famous automobiles, promoters of all products that represent life, movement, action." This break with the past gave rise to a new generation of merchants, managers, and entrepreneurs. "Even in the lower classes, among the humble citizens, a true revolution has been in progress. At present a large number of young men are dedicated to mechanics, others are employed as chauffeurs. All aspire to follow the example of other countries: to become imbued with the spirit that has taken over the universe." Years later, Alejo Carpentier remembered the Havana of his youth:

> All efforts extended toward making money, toward making a living, . . . stimulated by the growing Americanization of a city where already the food stores were being called *grocery*, where there were American bars in all parts, when the invasion of the American cigarette, American products, the North American automobile, North American clothing, everything, was a daily thing, and becoming stronger and in a certain sense more subjugating. That world fostered among the people such a drive to make money that to be a writer, artist, intellectual or painter was seen as useless, and was totally frowned upon by the bourgeoisie.[85]

At about this time *El Fígaro* published a series of articles paying tribute to the "self made man"—always used in English—in business and commerce. Retailer Francisco García was praised as "giving the impression of a winner, of the *self made man*, who without outside help or external assistance has succeeded by virtue of his intelligence, his acuity, and his hard work." Merchant Bernardo Barria Ortega was also included among "the young men worthy of the support and praise of good citizens for being precisely a type of *self made man*."[86] In the short story "Estrenos" (1935), Armando Maribona describes his protagonist Jorge in just these terms: "He knew . . . how to make his way through life and understood the organization and progress of the company he had founded. He yearned to succeed, to become powerful, and he was succeeding. He was a *self made man*, full of enthusiasm and energy. He was logical [and] poised."[87]

Jesús Castellanos was not altogether happy about these developments and, in his essay "Rodó y su 'Proteo' " (1910), contemplated with chagrin the emergence of the *hombre práctico*, a type he identified as the Cuban counterpart of the North American self-made man. "Our country today provides the most sorrowful display of scandalous utilitarianism and disregard to what signifies reflection, art, and poetry," complained Castellanos. The national intellectual level had declined, a development caused by the rise of the hombre práctico, the man "who specializes in a form of productive work and beyond which he finds nothing worthy of contemplation." In short, "The *hombre práctico* is the machine to make money without concern for society."[88]

These were years of dynamic U.S. economic expansion and increased industrial output—goods and services in search of new markets—and it happened that Cuba was among the first new markets in which U.S. producers could expand without political obstacles or trade barriers. North American consumer durables and nondurables alike transformed Cuba in fundamental ways. All that was new was transferred to Cuba, from simple household appliances to complex industrial technology, machinery and mechanical aids, advanced transportation modes and modern communication systems, and the newest conveniences and latest advances in the building trades, including household plumbing systems, electrical fixtures, elevators, telephones, and architectural innovations. "There has been evidently a great field for dealers in plumbers' supplies and fixtures," commented an architect who visited Cuba in 1907.[89]

The amenities that had amazed so many in the North, such material benefits of civilization as electric trolleys, telephones, skyscrapers, and paved streets, reached the island within a few decades. That these beacons of progress were imported mattered less than that they affirmed the Cuban claim to modernity, so essential to the discursive structure of national self-representation.

In the short space of ten years Cuba had catapulted into modernity. Almost everywhere there was evidence of progress: improved urban transportation systems, paved roads, modern buildings, up-to-date comforts and conveniences. Countless Cubans who had already developed an affinity for these innovations now claimed them as their own. "Cárdenas as a modern city . . . will have its appearance totally changed," observed one visitor in 1900. "From all perspectives, Cárdenas is a new city, *a la americana*, and its trade proves it."[90]

In Havana, the changes were remarkable. New public buildings and commercial structures, no less than private homes, contained the latest technological advances, including indoor plumbing, electrical fixtures, modern home furnishings, and built-in appliances. The Reina Mercedes Hospital had a new plumbing system, an electric power plant, and entirely new concrete floors. The Michigan

Stove Company of Detroit installed gas ranges in many new houses constructed after 1902. *Habaneros* could behold the new trolley system, gaze up at new buildings, and marvel at the modernity that had descended upon them. "The development of Havana during these past several years is truly extraordinary," *Diario de la Marina* editorialized in 1907. "The new and beautiful constructions within the city, the improvements and construction of houses in the downtown neighborhoods, the expansion and creation of new neighborhoods—all indicate the vigor with which our urban life evolves." Eduardo Anillo Rodríguez later recalled those times. "Havana was completely transformed," he wrote in 1919. "Priority was given to sanitation improvements. The first buildings constructed of cement and iron were built during those years. The first electric trolley was completed in 1901, the parks and promenades were improved, and the streets in Havana and other cities were repaired." Anillo Rodríguez concluded: "We received a free country worthy of membership in the concert of civilized nations." Miguel de Carrión's novel *La última voluntad* (1903) was set in the new Havana, in which "furniture, attire, buildings, the streets and the women experienced a transformation that was as radical as the political change that had occurred." This is no doubt what Columbia University–trained architect Leonardo Morales had in mind when he reflected on national developments since independence. "The revolution in Cuba was one of the most complete in our history," affirmed Morales in 1926. "It not only changed the regimen of government, but it also changed our costumes and appearances. It is in architecture where we have seen the most radical change establishing a pronounced difference between our colonial architecture and the republican actuality." It was left to Alejo Carpentier, in *El recurso del método* (1974), to give poignance to the ironies associated with the transformation of the capital:

> [T]he first skyscraper was constructed—five stories and an attic. . . . The old city, with its two-story houses, was quickly transformed into an Invisible City. Invisible because, transformed from horizontal to vertical, there were no longer any eyes that could see it and know it. Each architect, determined to make his building higher than the ones previously constructed, thought only about the particular aesthetics of *his* facade, as if it could be seen from one hundred yards off, when in fact the streets, planned to accommodate one car at a time . . . were only six or seven yards wide.[91]

Few visitors to Havana could fail to be astonished by what were commonly identified as Cuban achievements. "Today I have walked along various streets of Havana," commented Dominican writer Francisco del Castillo Márquez in 1905, "and in all its aspects it is a great city which enjoys the marvelous life of civilization: all its streets are asphalt, paved and macadamized, and their cleanliness obliges me to compare them with Belgian and Dutch streets. On many of them are found homes of magnificent modern construction of three, four, and five floors." Rubén Darío similarly wrote of the "astonishing material progress Cuba has made in every order of things."[92]

These were the standards Cubans adopted and called their own, the models employed to affirm modernity and progress, success and status. Under North American auspices Cuba was reborn modern. These elements of modernity were assimilated into the everyday environment and served as the material correlates around which "Cuban" assumed form. Retail trade, with its capacity to supply people directly and immediately with products for everyday use, expanded everywhere. Ways and things North American reached virtually every *municipio* on the island. They arrived as tobacco, mining, and railroad companies. The new Guantánamo Naval Station was a presence of another type, with equally important local effects. The growth of sugar mills transformed life in scores of communities and perhaps nowhere more dramatically than along the northern coast of Oriente in the towns of Puerto Padre, Gibara, Banes, Mayarí, and Antilla. The new sugar mills introduced electric power plants, advanced technology, railroad networks, modern roads, new forms of recreation including sports and the cinema, and employment opportunities that provided still more occasions to incorporate Cubans into North American structures. "The village of huts is now being transformed by the [United Fruit] Company," navy captain George L. Dyer wrote of Banes in 1900.[93]

The North American reach broadened in other ways as well. Sales representatives, vendors, and jobbers fanned out into all the provinces, each an exponent of North American material culture and a new way of life. The thousands of Cubans employed by North American banks and insurance companies, utilities, commercial houses and retail stores, and contractors and builders also participated in this world. Missionary stations, with their emphasis on social programs and educational projects, introduced into remote regions a complexity of new work habits and new recreational forms, an etiquette of gender relations, and a myriad of new customs. The expansion of the agricultural colonies and many thousands of individual farmers and homesteaders brought Cuban communities in the interior into contact with new methods. As early as 1905, the establishment of Los Palacios Colony in Pinar del Río was accompanied by an electric light plant, a steam laundry, an ice plant, and tractors to construct new roads. La Gloria Colony Transportation Company operated a pole tramway to Nuevitas Bay; La Gloria Telephone Company installed the first telephone system in the region. North Americans on the Isle of Pines introduced all-weather roads, electric power plants, a turpentine factory, sawmill factories, packing plants, ice factories, and telephone service.

During these years North American conventions passed directly into Cuban usage. Christmas gained widespread acceptance, popularized mainly by Cuban missionaries in the nineteenth century. "We celebrated the Christmas tree this year," the Reverend Alberto Díaz wrote from Havana in 1887, "and took one of the theaters, where we gathered 2,000 children and over 3,000 adults. The Sunday school has expended over $300 in toys, dolls, preserves, ice-cream and rent of the theater."[94] After 1898 North American missionaries continued to observe the holiday; they decorated Christmas trees and distributed gifts to children, customs that spread as the missionary presence grew on the island. During the U.S. occupation, the military government observed Christmas as an official holiday, for which employees received early pay and extended vacations. North American merchants and retailers introduced marketing strategies to promote Christmas as a Cuban holiday, practices that Cuban and Spanish retailers were quick to adopt.

Christmas also insinuated itself into a larger and more complicated discourse on nation. The affirmation of modern necessarily implied repudiation of all that persisted of the colonial period, especially customs derived from Spain. The celebration of December 25 instead of January 6 (Kings' Day) represented a negation of one more part of the colonial experience. Renée Méndez Capote recalled the joyful anticipation of awakening on December 25 to the gifts left by Santa Claus. "The Magic Kings never brought us anything," she wrote. "The Magic Kings gave gifts only to the children of Spaniards, not to children of the liberators (*mambises*). That is what *mamá* always told us and it never occurred to us to ask the Magic Kings for anything."[95]

These were years of revival and renewal, of high expectation and constant experimentation. José de la Campa González wrote of the moment with perspicacity in *Memorias de un machadista* (1937). The protagonist overhears conversations "in his own language, but that nobody seemed to understand." The narrator observed: "Another new Cuba had arisen, strange, incoherent, in which all that was discussed was of horse races, of football, of baseball, and non-stop discussions of the United States, with a ridiculous ambition of speaking English . . . [and] a stupid adoration of everything that was from the United States."[96]

It might have been easy to dismiss interest in the English language as a "ridiculous ambition" were it not for the fact that this preoccupation was itself product and portent of the changes overtaking postcolonial society. Cuba was reborn modern, and much of the narrative of this modernity was in English. English intruded itself as the language of government and of trade and commerce; spoken by tourists and colonists, it was overheard on the street and in cafés and restaurants, written on storefronts, and read in advertisements and newspapers. The ubiquitous sign "English spoken here" appeared in department stores like El Encanto and La Filosofía, in retail shops, and in professional offices. "Maybe it is time that we proclaim that Spanish is also spoken here," *La Lucha* suggested in 1901.[97]

English transformed Spanish and increasingly passed for Spanish. English entered Spanish as part of the popular vernacular. *Diario de la Marina* often complained about the frequent use of such words as *precinto, colector, super-*

visor, and *reportar*—"the many barbarisms, as unnecessary as they are ridiculous." Moreover, "It is not so trivial as many foolish people believe but, on the contrary, profoundly affects the future of the Cuban people, whose first sign of doom and ruin will surely be first the corruption and later the complete disappearance of their language."[98]

English was the language of transition and transformation. It promised entrée, a way up and out: access to employment, economic security, and social mobility in an environment where most jobs—certainly the better-paying ones—were most readily available to those who knew English. The English language had become the idiom of opportunity, and the relationship between language and livelihood was self-evident. English served as a means of social demarcation, a way to distinguish the old and traditional from the new and modern, a way out of the past and into the future. In this environment the vernacular of dominant discourse appeared in English, without which opportunities for advancement could be delayed if not denied altogether.

Among the first Cubans to reap the benefits of the new postcolonial order were those possessing bilingual skills. Appointment to civil positions and public office during the U.S. military occupation was often awarded on precisely these grounds. "Orders have been issued," a correspondent wrote from Santiago de Cuba in 1898, "that English-speaking Cubans shall have the preference in appointments to office."[99]

The "preference" for "English-speaking Cubans," of course, favored the former residents of the North who had returned after the war by the thousands. Their arrival coincided with the onset of the military occupation, as the United States set in place the bureaucratic structures to administer the island. Familiar with North American customs and fluent in English, émigrés early obtained preferential access to public office. Correspondent Charles Pepper reported in 1901 that émigrés who knew English were "of great value in filling the offices" in the military government. "Their intelligence was quick and they could understand something of American administrative methods. . . . It was inevitable that these Cubans should obtain the most responsible positions and the best-paying ones, for their services were of great value." As early as 1899, the U.S. consul in Cienfuegos announced the return of large numbers of émigrés, adding: "As they speak English they have more readily found employment and appointment at the hands of the United States officers." In the same year chief of Havana customs Fred Bach noted that of the twenty-four Cubans in his employ, "only two served in the late war. Plenty of these men served at Key West or New York, but in the field—never." Major John Logan informed his superior that the customs subcollector in Sagua la Grande "was a Cuban who went to the United States in 1868 and did not return until December 27, 1898, when he arrived with the appointment of sub-collector from the [U.S.] government in his pocket."[100]

Emigrés used their language skills to mediate the encounter between the

United States and Cuba; in fact, they became one of the principal means by which North American norms were transmitted to the postcolonial moral order. They served as interpreters and translators, architects and engineers, teachers, clerks, bookkeepers and accountants, police officials and army officers, city councillors, mayors, provincial governors, and civilian cabinet members. Few, indeed, were the major appointments in which English did not loom large—for instance, General George Davis writing in behalf of Guillermo Dolz Arango for governor of Pinar del Río: "speaks English fluently which will be a great convenience"; General William Ludlow on Juan Ruis Rivera for governor of Havana: "speaks English fluently and well" and on Mario G. Menocal for Havana police chief: "speaking English fluently, and with an American education as an engineer"; General L. H. Carpenter in behalf of Alcides Betancourt as a civil secretary in Camagüey: "his services will be very necessary on account of . . . his thorough acquaintance with both Spanish and English"; Leonard Wood supporting Alejandro Rodríguez for mayor of Havana: "A man of unquestionable honesty and ability, speaks English well and is decidedly friendly with Americans"; General James H. Wilson on José Antonio Frías for mayor of Cienfuegos: "he speaks English with facility," and on Carlos Yznaga for mayor of Trinidad: "he speaks English perfectly"; and General Wilson on Governor Pedro Betancourt: "speaks good English and has all the qualities of an American gentleman."[101]

Numerous civil positions were staffed with alumni of North American schools, many of whom were U.S. citizens. Engineer José Ramón Villalón (Lehigh University) was appointed secretary of public works, and Pablo Desvernine (Columbia) served as secretary of finance. Perfecto Lacosta was secretary of agriculture, commerce, and industry (in 1900 he visited Cincinnati briefly to cast his ballot in the U.S. presidential election).[102] Demetrio Castillo Duany (New York Business College) became governor of Oriente; General Pedro Betancourt (University of Pennsylvania), governor of Matanzas; and Emilio Núñez (also Penn), governor of Havana. Engineers Esteban Duque Estrada (Stevens Institute of Technology) served as chief of public works in Pinar del Río; Manuel Coroalles (Rensselaer), as director of public works in the city of Havana; Juan Miguel Portuondo Tamayo (Columbia), as chief engineer of the Matanzas–Las Villas military department; José Primelles Agramonte (Columbia), as chief engineer for Havana province; and Sotero E. Escarza (Rensselaer), as engineer of Cienfuegos. José Celedonio del Castillo, an engineering student in Boston, was named lighthouse inspector. Carlos M. Rojas (Harvard) served as mayor of Cárdenas, and Fernando Figueredo Socarrás (Rensselaer) was appointed chief of Cienfuegos customs.[103]

The degree to which the economy revived around North American forms was a further inducement to learn English. The moral was unambiguous: English was the route to advantage and advancement. Well-paying white-collar positions—accountants, clerks, bookkeepers and secretaries, managerial staff and sales personnel—as well as low-paying jobs—as servants, maids, housekeepers, cooks, and laundresses—often required facility in English. "The more progressive merchants have hired clerks who can speak English," one correspondent reported from Havana as early as December 1898, "and this class of labor is in great demand. Other Cuban and Spanish clerks are assiduously learning English. Interpreters are commanding good wages, and at the hotels they have all they can do. Even the bootblacks are soliciting trade in English, and the beggars whine, 'Please give me a cent.'"[104] Years later novelist José Soler Puig, in *Un mundo de cosas* (1989), depicted occupied Santiago de Cuba as a place where "Cubans who knew English found employment immediately in the customs office, in the post office, in public works, in city government, because the chiefs of the government offices were all Americans. Those who did not speak English had no alternative but to toil and reach for the pick and shovel, working like a *peón* on the many projects the Americans began upon their arrival, paving streets and constructing roads."[105]

Classified advertisements from these years provide powerful corroboration of the extent to which English had become important to livelihood. The American Grocery wanted a wagon driver who "must be sober and industrious and must speak Spanish and English." H. C. Swan advertised for a clerk "who can wait on customers. Must speak English and Spanish." The Jones Dairy of Vedado was seeking a "boy to deliver milk" who "must speak some English." An office supply company wanted "an educated boy, 14 to 18 years of age, who speaks good English." In 1900 the telephone company announced an expansion of services and new openings for operators "who speak both English and Spanish."[106]

New office work created other opportunities for Cubans with English-language skills. Employment agencies were organized specifically to fill the need for bilingual typists, stenographers, and secretaries. The Public Stenographers and Employment Agency was established in 1906 to supply "the leading firms, hotels, etc., with their stenographers." The Stenographic and Translating Bureau offered "competent stenographers, expert translators . . . for government, leading hotels, banks, and firms."[107]

Bilingual secretaries and stenographers were especially in high demand. In advertising for a typist, the Frank Robbins Company stipulated: "Do not apply unless possessing thorough knowledge of English." The Lonja de Comercio sought "a young gentleman of presentable appearance and absolutely fluent in verbal translation from English to Spanish, and vice versa, as interpreter for business purposes." The J. C. Metz Company of Havana needed an "office boy who speaks Spanish and English." In Santa Clara, the Cuba Company was looking for a bookkeeper "experienced and speaks and writes English and Spanish." A commercial house advertised a promising bookkeeper position for a young man with one primary qualification: "It is indispensable that he possess English." A large U.S. corporation required "the services of a man who can handle the credit end of the business. Knowledge of English and Spanish essential." A merchant in Oriente province wanted a bookkeeper "at once, must be thorough office man and speak English and Spanish," and a Havana merchant house wished to hire a "messenger and office boy—must know English and Spanish." The Cuba Trading Company advertised for an "English-Spanish stenographer. Must know both languages well."[108]

The burgeoning tourist sector—hotels, travel agencies, and shipping lines—was in particular need of bilingual employees to act as tour guides, interpreters, chauffeurs, ticket agents, and sales personnel. The Hotel Nuevitas in Havana advertised for a desk clerk who spoke "Spanish and English with perfection." The Hotel Belvedere required a "waiter for the dining room, one that is courteous and speaks English," and the American Tea Room sought "a waiter or waitress who speaks English." Many domestic and low-paying positions had a similar language requirement. This 1901 classified was fairly common: "Wanted: a servant for general housework. Must speak English."[109]

Cuban and Spanish merchants also demanded a bilingual staff in an economy where linkages to the United States were central. North Americans were suppliers and vendors, clients and customers, making bilingual clerks, secretaries, cashiers, and sales personnel all the more necessary. This was particularly true in retail trade. New department stores, perfume and linen shops, and specialty stores of all types, whose clientele often consisted of North American visitors and residents, were obliged to hire staff fluent in English. When Julia and Félix Zahonet announced plans to open two variety stores in Havana, they advertised new positions "for various young Cuban women who speak English."[110]

The moral was not difficult to divine. In an environment where North American conventions were in the ascendancy, English was indispensable to opportunity and mobility. The value of English was self-evident, as the *Havana Post* reminded its readers:

> The street conductor who is able to speak English is a much more valuable asset to the street car company and worth more money than the one who cannot. The stenographer who is able to work in both languages receives all the way from $20 to $50 a month more than the one who knows Spanish alone. A good interpreter receives all the way from $2.50 to $5.00 a day, though he may be a weakling and men much stronger get only a dollar a day. A prominent Cuban railroad official has confessed . . . that he holds his high salaried position solely because along with his railroad knowledge he is able to speak English.[111]

Carlos Loveira captured the essence of the new reality in *Los inmorales* (1919) through his protaganist, who during his time in New York "went about acquiring something invaluable in our latitudes in the struggle to make a living: the English language." Even more to the point, he asserted: "To know English is to have a guarantee of never being without a job."[112]

Much energy and ingenuity went into learning English. "I am practicing English without rest," wrote Gualterio García to a friend in 1898, "and I write and read a great deal. What is difficult for me is to speak it correctly, for it is very hard to think in Spanish and speak in English." Some offered to exchange Spanish lessons for English ones. "Cuban gentleman," one classified advertisement read, "speaking little English, wishes to exchange Spanish for English with educated person." According to another, "Cuban young lady will exchange Spanish for English lessons with English lady." Still another proposed: "Spanish for English: A Cuban graduate of a university, wishes to find someone with whom he can practice the English language, either by exchanging lessons or by giving his services in the business office of some American house without salary."[113]

Many people found novel ways to learn English. Francisco García, a sugar mill employee in Las Villas, took a course transcribed on phonograph records. Eduardo (Eddy) Chibás was taught by a Jamaican carpenter employed in his father's factory.[114] Years later, as the expanding sugar estates of Camagüey and Oriente hired contract workers from Haiti and Jamaica, some Cuban mill administrators assigned Haitians to field work and Jamaicans to the mill, a division of labor intended to make Jamaicans available to help Cubans practice their English.[115]

Parents were quick to understand the implications of the growing North American presence and adopted a variety of measures to prepare their children for the new order. These were calculated strategies devised by parents concerned about the well-being of their children, reasonable and rational responses to a presence that seemed both ascendant and permanent. Some families sought English-speaking friends for their children. "A boy 13 years old," read a *Havana Post* classified, "wishes to find an American or English boy his age, or a little older, for a playmate, with the object of practicing his English." Families of means employed English-speaking governesses, teachers, and tutors. The Mendoza family advertised for "an American woman to care for two small girls," and Mrs. Arango sought an "American woman to handle a three year old child." Mrs. Andreu advertised for "a governess for teaching the English language to a girl of 13 years. I wish her to live in my home." One Cuban family wanted a "female teacher for daily classes in English for two small boys." In 1914 the Beers Employment Agency advertised "more than ten openings" for "governesses and nursery governesses for the best Cuban families." Renée Méndez Capote recalled starting her home English lessons at age seven under a "formidable Englishman from London who arrived to give classes early every day at 6:45 A.M."[116]

Many Cubans sent their children north for English instruction. "In 1904," future chess master José Raúl Capablanca recalled, "I went to the USA to learn English and prepare myself to enter University." José García Pedrosa, recounting his youth in Cienfuegos, noted that his father had "foreseen the necessity of having the English language." Between 1910 and 1916 the five García Pedrosa children were enrolled in U.S. schools: Rogelio at Rensselaer, María and Emilia at Mount St. Vincent Catholic School in New York, and Luis and José at Manhattan College.[117]

Nothing, perhaps, was greater confirmation of the degree to which North American cultural forms had insinuated themselves into Cuban life than the marketing of the English language as a means to success. English-language instruction developed into a big business. In 1899 Charles Pepper wrote of a "wave of English teaching that has swept over the island." Berlitz opened an office in Havana in 1905 with a simple, pointed advertisement that surely resonated in postcolonial Cuba: "Time is money. Learn English and you will earn money. Learn it at the Berlitz School and you will make time."[118] Two years later Berlitz had branch offices in Cienfuegos and Matanzas.

The number of *academias* and *colegios* dedicated to English-language instruction proliferated, including El Colegio Ingles de La Víbora, Academia de Idioma Roberts, the School of Conversational English, the School of Linguistry, and the Cortina Academy of Languages. Many of them were organized by Cubans who had lived or studied in the United States. Juan Antonio Barinaga—representing himself as "Cuban, married and educated in the United States"—opened a number of Academias de Inglés in Havana, advertising "a special method, the most modern and most rapid style . . . the only way to learn to speak English with Boston pronunciation." Luis B. Corrales's Gran Academia de Comercio maintained that English was "the language that dominates the world of commercial transactions," and Academia Baralt urged "heads of households" to "secure the future of your children with English." In 1901 Francisco Herrera founded the Academia Mercantil y de Idioma, which offered full programs in both day and evening sessions, including English-language classes, business mathematics, and bookkeeping. The Colegio Patria was established as an elementary school with "special classes for English-language instruction."[119]

In time, private instruction was offered either in the home by individual tutors or in small classes, day or evening, for young and old. José Cuervo, identified in an advertisement as "Professor of English," guaranteed "English in two months: practical classes, especially to be understood by the Americans." Another "professor of English" promised "success in a few months" at "modest prices." Carlos Greco offered to teach English in the home "in a very short period of time, using rapid and appropriate methods."[120]

North Americans also made a living by teaching English. Thomas H. Christie used "modern and practical methods," and Henry Brown, Hilda Rafter, Jeanne Orval, Mary Mills, and a Mrs. James were among the most frequent advertisers who provided individual English-language instruction in the home. One reason for the popularity of North American missionary schools was that they presented an opportunity to learn English at little or no cost. "The people are willing to send their children to American teachers," Baptist Reverend W. W.

Barnes reported in 1911. "A knowledge of English helps the man or woman that has to work earn a higher salary. For that reason many of them want their children to learn English. The first thing that fathers ask about is the study of English." Quaker schools along the northern coast of Oriente, Miguel J. Casado recalled, were "praised by everyone," for they offered "a chance to study English in every grade." "Knowledge of the English language is a very great business and social asset to the Cuban," Una Roberts Lawrence wrote of the Baptist experience, "hence every Cuban wishes his children to learn English, and the mission school, with its director from the United States, provides this advantage much more efficiently than the public school with its Cuban teacher who has never lived in an English-speaking land." Episcopal bishop Albion Knight despaired over the inability to meet student demands. Writing in 1907 about the "large influx of Cuban children into our parochial schools," Knight reported: "This increase is so great that we are unable to supply accommodations for the children who desire to enter, nor are we able to open schools at all the places making requests for them."[121]

The prevalence of English created particular opportunities for women in offices. The nature of office work was transformed by the increased use of typewriters, calculators, adding machines, cash registers, and stencil machines. Typewriters especially gained widespread usage after 1898, especially in commerce and manufacturing, in banks and professional offices. "The Remington typewriter," commented the *Havana Post* in 1900, "has had an extensive sale in Havana since the arrival of the army of occupation."[122] Between 1903 and 1905 the total value of typewriters imported from the United States more than doubled—from $31,000 to $70,000. "There are very few countries," reported the *Commercial and Financial World* in 1906, "that can show such a rapid increase in the demand for these machines as in . . . Cuba."[123] The expansion of the government bureaucracy and the revival of the economy, the development of complex functions of cost accounting and increased computation, new systems of paperwork, and wide use of telephone and telegraph services revolutionized the demands of the postcolonial labor market, creating new kinds of jobs and new categories of employment. New banks, insurance companies, shipping lines, hotels, and travel agencies also needed clerks, typists, and secretaries.

The growing North American presence provided a powerful impetus for the employment and advancement of women, especially those fluent in English. In 1899 military governor John Brooke opened civil positions in the military government to women. In 1901 Isabel Ríos was appointed postal superintendent in Gibara, the first woman to hold this post anywhere in Cuba. Adelaida Rodríguez, who had lived in New York, obtained employment as a clerk in the Superintendent of Schools office. Returning from Key West, Emilia de Córdoba assumed a clerical position in the Department of Public Works. "To the Cuban woman in general," observed a traveler in 1905, "the American intervention and influence were a godsend indeed; as, for the first time in four hundred years, the gates of opportunity were opened to her."[124]

In an economic environment dominated by North American practices, women with fluency in English enjoyed uncommon advantage over men who did not and could compete with men who did. Such advertisements as an R. G. Dun and Company classified in Havana—"Wanted immediately: an English speaking boy or girl, capable of writing on the typewriter"—and one by Sussdorf and Zaldo Company—"Wanted: stenographer, either male or female, with knowledge of English"—suggest how fluency in English could facilitate women's assimilation in the labor force. The Cuban Trading Company sought "Lady telephone operators. Must speak Spanish and English." One advertisement in 1903 offered a monthly salary of $150 to "young men and women who know how to take short-hand in English and translate it into Spanish." Monroe and Company needed a "young man or woman who has knowledge of English and Spanish to take care of office."[125]

The number of women who entered the wage labor force increased significantly in the twenty years between the censuses of 1899 and 1919. The supply of typists enlarged from 6 to 901 and telegraph and telephone operators from 5 to 321. The number of women in sales went from 36 to 235. Nurses increased from 284 to 727, and teachers more than tripled—from 1,502 to 5,172. Indeed, during the early years of the republic women registered notable gains in almost all occupational classifications, including sales, stenography, bookkeeping, and banking. Some employment categories that did not exist for women in 1899 but appeared in 1919 were manufacturing (420), office workers (740), government employees (1,274), pharmacists (200), clergy (213), and attorneys (6).[126] Visiting Cuba in 1910, Charles Berchón was struck by the "large numbers of women who were teachers, in charge of bookkeeping and typists in the large businesses."[127]

These developments must be seen as both opportunity and necessity. It was not always clear that women joined the labor force out of choice. Some did, of course, but many did not. These were difficult times, and for many families the employment of women often signified the difference between maintenance and indigence. Even after the war many middle-class women continued to work outside the home, in large measure as a result of the devastation wrought by the conflict. The war had shattered households and reorganized family structures. Women had assumed new roles and larger responsibilities. Many had lost spouses and were obliged to work outside the home—often outside the country—to support themselves and their families. A great many women had sole charge of the family. In 1899 Cuba had the highest proportion of widowed to married women in the Western Hemisphere: fifty-one per hundred, or one widow for every two wives.[128]

Perhaps what mattered most was the availability of opportunities for which women could qualify and compete. Women in increasing numbers pursued educations specifically to work outside the home. The Academia Comercial inaugurated two stenography programs "exclusively for ladies," each three months long and paid for in small monthly installments. The Esther Colegio was founded in 1907 for "girls and young ladies." The Minerva Academia de Comercio offered classes in English and typing, and the Cuban-American College provided "students of both sexes" day and evening classes in English, stenography, and typing. The Business College of Boston opened a branch in Havana in 1901 with a "separate department for the education of young ladies, where they will be attended with such care and with such interest as if they were in a private school for young ladies." Juan Antonio Barinaga advertised that he was free two hours a day to "offer those hours to heads of family who preferred that their daughters be educated in the home."[129]

The presence of women in offices, in business and government, in the professions, soon assumed a logic of its own. The demands of economic reorganization, directed and driven largely by U.S. capital, contributed to an environment in which the employment of women was not only admissible but also necessary. Women assumed expanded roles in the postcolonial economy, a process that integrated them into the public realms of the republic—as members of the labor force, as customers and consumers, as representatives of their own interests— even as it incorporated women into the formulation of nationality.

These were some of the ways in which Cuba assumed the appearance of normality at the start of the twentieth century. The process signified diffusion of the new and the novel, the modern and the current, on a huge scale. All of this was promptly appropriated and incorporated into the familiar: elements around which postwar reorganization proceeded, creating at the same time the circumstances in which everyday life assumed ordinary appearance around North American structures. Cubans set about the task of rebuilding their lives under very difficult circumstances, where the material elements and the moral imperatives of what passed for normality were largely North American ones. They served as the principal means to resume daily life and reassemble an inhabitable world.

These were complex social processes, for they involved the incorporation of a new hierarchy of values into Cuban life. Tens of thousands of Cubans of all classes—children and adults, men and women, black and white—were integrated directly into North American structures at virtually every turn: as customers, clients, coworkers, as employees and business partners, in professional organizations and voluntary associations, at school and in social clubs, in church and on teams. The postcolonial environment was dominated by an array of agencies that transmitted North American cultural forms, with which a vast number of people were obliged to come to terms daily in ordinary ways. This process of negotiation, often irrespective of outcome, was arguably the single most decisive determinant of an emerging national identity.

North American ways expanded into communities across the island, not only as goods and services but also as the moral order from which those goods and services originated. Under many circumstances, these conventions were all-encompassing, which made it almost impossible to contemplate alternatives or, for that matter, to entertain doubts that they were anything but predominant and permanent. Many Cubans integrated North American values and customs into their own lives. Such conventions provided the choices from which Cubans routinely selected the means of self-definition and personal advancement. They insinuated themselves into public and private spheres, into households and workplaces, into the meanings assigned to daily life and the preparations made to meet the future. Much of what passed for everyday and ordinary—what was "Cuban," in a word—was, in fact, a product of normative affinities derived in large measure from North American formulations, henceforth inalterably part of the physiognomy of postcolonial Cuba. These conditions shaped the social environment in which the first republican generation was formed and whose moral authority reached well into the 1950s.

These were enormously complex circumstances under which to arrive at nation and national identity. North American conventions were in the ascendancy, unchallenged and in some instances unchallengeable. Whatever may have been their hopes and objectives in 1895, whatever may have been their expectations of Cuba Libre, vast numbers of Cubans after 1898 were confronted with a new and constantly changing reality to which so many others seemed disposed to adjust. Probably for all the reasons everyone else had—for alternatives were pitifully few—Cubans increasingly acquiesced to the new order as a way to get on with their lives. Accommodation and adaptation were a practical response to reality, a way to assess what needed to be done, always with the assumption that this response would solve the most urgent problems and meet the most desperate needs. There was nothing especially dramatic about these adjustments, certainly nothing that was immediately apparent. They were simply decisions made and actions taken, often routinely, to cope and make do, and it is unreasonable to suppose that more than a handful of Cubans were alive to the larger implications of these transformations. These were a people longing for normality. It happened that normality assumed form around the North American presence and much of what subsequently passed for ordinary and everyday, of what often evolved into what became Cuban, was assembled from what was most commonly available. It may have been difficult to contemplate a future in which North Americans would not occupy a place of prominence, and thus preparation for that future necessarily implied accommodation with the North American presence and mastering the practices on which that presence was based.

Reality could speak for itself. The North American presence promoted itself and enjoined all to submit. The power of its appeal was in the promise of transformation, rendered in terms that registered among countless Cubans. The moral was embedded in the concept of imperialism as an enterprise of civilization, of mission and uplift. "We must lift them up by a generous, a noble Christian series of efforts," exhorted General Oliver Otis Howard in 1898. "It is our God-given mission, and the whole Christian world is watching to see if the great American republic is equal to the strain." Leonard Wood agreed. "We are dealing with a race that has steadily been going down for a hundred years," Wood commented in 1900, "and into which we have to infuse new life, new principles and new methods of doing things."[130] Secretary of War Elihu Root provided a slightly different rationale for the same goals:

> We are trying to give the Cuban people just as fair and favorable a start in governing themselves as possible, and to help them avoid the conditions which have subjected Hayti, Santo Domingo, and the Central American Republics to continuous revolution and disorder.... The great difficulty with which they have to contend is that they have had no experience in anything except Spanish customs and Spanish methods which have grown up for centuries under a system opposed to general education and self-government. To succeed in their experiment, the Cubans must necessarily acquire some new ideas and new methods.[131]

The notion of mission informed virtually every facet of the North American purpose in Cuba. "We are missionaries," proclaimed Alfred Wilby, president of the U.S. Plumbers Local 200 in Havana. "To the plumbers of America will be entrusted the great work of clearing this city of the dread scourge of yellow fever.... Let us be mindful of the importance of the position we occupy, and let us always strive to raise the standard of plumbing and do our utmost to fulfill our part of an undertaking which our government has commenced." Protestants also promised civilization. "There must be a great deal of uplifting, of change, of improvement," affirmed one missionary. "The moral standards must be raised, and new ideals must be introduced. The Cuban people have . . . new habits to form, new customs to adopt, before they can reach the condition of civilization which they ought to have."[132] Luther Wishard, head of the YMCA, justified the establishment of the Cuba branch on the grounds of "the civilizing influences the Association affords."[133]

It seemed to matter little that many Cubans had already adopted their own propositions of civilization, many of which were derived directly from U.S. sources. North Americans failed to distinguish between normative structures, around which many Cubans had given meaning to their lives, and political attitudes, central to which was the concept of a separate and sovereign nation. That these two contradictory value systems could coexist was not readily obvious. Rather, the affirmation of sovereignty—in other words, rejection of annexation to the United States—was construed as evidence of Cuban backwardness.

The task of civilization was thus formulated in terms of "Americanization" in which a modified hierarchy of values and altered modalities of behaviors served to prepare Cubans for eventual absorption: to become so much like North Americans that they would relinquish their claim to Cuban. Americanization was conceived as a fundamental change of consciousness, for the logic of its legitimacy was in the act of relinquishing a separate nationality.

This effort was conceived in terms of a gigantic education project. "It will take time to accomplish what is yet to be desired," Wood acknowledged. "It can be achieved only slowly and may best be attained through a system of education."[134] Attention during the U.S. occupation centered on the new public school system as agent of Americanization. Textbooks were Spanish translations of North American texts. History books contained U.S. history; indeed, the teaching of history served as a means of Americanization, a way to reconfigure memory around another past. The *Manual para maestros* (1900), the text used to train Cuban teachers, exhorted Cubans to understand the importance of U.S. history. Students were to "compare the thirteen colonies that gave rise to the United States with Cuba during its colonial period" and "to learn how the American people gradually resolved the problem of self-government, thereby forming some idea of the enormous task that currently confronts Cuba." It concluded: "In this manner the history of the United States will shed much light on the current needs of this island and the responsibilities that its citizens must assume."[135]

Cuban public schools were organized around a civic training program in which children acquired familiarity with North American institutions by organizing model governments and playing the roles of elected officials. The "City Schools," as the program became known, was based on a system widely used in New York immigrant neighborhoods to facilitate assimilation.[136]

The City Schools program extolled the virtues of the North American political system over Latin American forms. There existed a "natural tendency of human nature," the City Schools charter affirmed, for the "physically and mentally strongest individual to domineer or 'boss' other individuals" and "make himself rich at the expense of the people." This "natural tendency" was illustrated by the "chronic revolutionists in Central and South America, where the people are impulsive and easily led by hot-headed orators who do not like to have other hot-headed orators for their public officers, to collect exorbitant taxes and blackmail from the people so they can live in ease and luxury without doing much work." The charter continued:

> But the orators that are out of power would be glad to have the same opportunity to collect taxes and blackmail, such as the Cubans have been accustomed to pay to the officers of the crown, and live in luxury without much work. So they make fiery speeches and incite a lot of men to get out their machetes and guns and kill or drive away the other orators. In Colombia that sometimes happens as often as four times a year, and is utterly destructive of every interest of the people. Cuba hardly wants to be governed by that kind of orators [*sic*], with machetes and guns.

The charter stressed the importance of leadership by "statesmen," leaders who encouraged "honesty, purity, cleanliness, industry, thrift, and prosperity and lead the people to abide peaceable [sic] by the decisions of the majority." Cubans were urged to "learn from the experience of other citizens" and "to look at the unsuccessful republics to see the cause of their misfortunes and at successful republics to see the cause of their success, for good government helps the people to be prosperous, clean, healthy, and happy, and bad government tends toward failure, filth, disease, and misery." In other words, "The United States is the most successful of all human governments."[137]

The success of Cuban public schools, according to U.S. authorities, depended on the adequate training of teachers. In early 1900 the military government completed an ambitious program designed to train Cuban teachers at U.S. colleges and universities. In July 1900 the first contingent of 1,300 Cuban teachers went to Harvard for two months of instruction. Other U.S. schools also organized special programs for Cuban teachers. The New York State Normal School at New Paltz established an educational program that invited thirty Cuban teachers annually.[138]

Formal instruction was only part of the program. Officials hoped that the experience in the United States generally would have a salutary effect on Cubans. "I believe that this body of teachers," Root wrote to the president of Harvard in 1900, "going back after their experience here, and scattering into every municipality in Cuba, will carry back more of saving grace, for peaceful and prosperous Cuba than the whole power of the Government could accomplish in any other way."[139] This view was shared by the *Havana Post*. "The teachers now in Boston," the *Post* commented editorially in July 1900, "will come back more or less Americanized and will do their share toward getting Cuba out of the old Spanish rut."[140] For Leonard Wood, the value of the Harvard program was "not so much from what they learned from books and lectures, as from what they saw and absorbed from observation."[141]

The long-term effect of the teachers' project is impossible to measure, of course. It was not merely that the first generation of public school children of the republic received instruction from teachers trained in the United States. At least as important, many of the participants subsequently went on to occupy prominent positions in all facets of public life.[142]

TERMS OF ADAPTATION

The process of Americanization must not be presumed to have been thrust upon Cubans as empty vessels. The extent to which North American ways passed increasingly for Cuban was often related less to the purpose for which these forms were designed than to the use Cubans made of them in their daily lives. Cubans were not passive recipients of new values. Appropriation of new conventions was driven by an internal logic of its own, central to which was the expectation that innovation would serve self-interests. Cubans found themselves almost daily obliged to negotiate encounters with North American structures, an interplay that over time shaped the way they arrived at a definition of self and nation. Accommodation depended primarily on the degree to which North American modalities met everyday needs, a process that was often both selective and pragmatic and always designed as a strategy to make do and do good. By drawing from everyday life in the postcolonial environment, much of which was formed and informed by North American value systems, Cubans developed a complex but highly usable means to define nationality.

Much in subsequent accommodations was, in fact, calculated to defend the proposition of nation, in the conviction that for "Cuban" to retain its resonance as a separate nationality there had to be parity with the United States. The cultural meanings of these accommodations were embedded in larger social constructions of nationality, many of which were derived explicitly from North American sources and provided methods and modalities to defend the proposition of Cuban.

Adaptation implied a peculiarly material basis by which to define and defend Cuban. Parity meant comparable standards of living, of participation in the prevailing currents of modernity, and membership among the "civilized" nations of the world. These were propositions central to the definition of nationality and defense of nation. As early as 1897, Benjamín Guerra, the treasurer of the Cuban Revolutionary Party (PRC), acknowledged that Cuba was a "satellite" and "under the influence of the United States." "But," Guerra hastened to add, "she will revolve and have an orbit of her own. She will not lose her identity."[143]

The claim to modernity could be sustained only insofar as the challenges to the notion of Cuba as civilized were eliminated. The Cuban encounter with North Americans, in the United States and on the island, must be viewed as an effort to fashion an understanding of and gain mastery over those forces changing daily life. That many chose to adopt and appropriate, to be sure, facilitated U.S. penetration, and perhaps more than a few gave themselves entirely up to the premises and promises of market culture on North American terms. For many other Cubans, however, the process of appropriation and adoption became the means to defend nationality. These were not conditions without contradictions, of course, and recognition of the resultant tensions became one way to give form to resistance and work out complex questions of national identity.

One of the most carefully crafted renderings of the concept of adaptation as redemption was advanced by Colonel Eugenio Silva, a former officer of the Liberation Army and a graduate of U.S. schools. Silva invoked "Americanization" as a strategy to defend *Cubanidad*. "It is necessary that we Americanize ourselves as a precise means of conserving our nationality," he insisted, for "the more we know . . . the more will we be in a condition to sustain our rights and liberty." This meant "improvement in all means of procedures in public and private life"; Cubans "should learn to live in comfort." "Is it not a shame that in Cuba people still live in ground huts," Silva asked ruefully, "and that there is not an appropriate place for taking a bath in the majority of our rural houses?" These questions affirmed the confidence that Cubans could aspire to more, that the standards by which they would take measure of their condition could be nothing less than those of the highest level of civilization and modernity. This was at the heart of defending nation. Redemption was possible only through the elimination of disparities that tended to create unequal relations. What, then, could be more pernicious to the proposition of a separate nationality than to permit disparities between Cuba and the United States to create in the public imagination doubts about the value of Cuban: that to be Cuban was inferior to being North American, in some way backward, behind and beyond the pale of civilization. Silva detected in North American ways the material and moral means to defend his nation: "The more we know them and the more we use their excellent educative system which has indisputably placed them at the head of civilization, the less cause and less fear will we have of being absorbed by them, so long as we are considered as their equals. . . . I maintain that it is necessary that we must survive as a free and independent nation, that we Americanize ourselves." "Americanization" was invoked explicitly as a concept of "enlighten-ment," which involved "improving [Cuban] customs, physical and moral de-velopments [and] better living." Silva urged the development of national indus-try, commerce, and agriculture, "copying the methods which have given results in the United States."[144]

This theme found many variations in the early decades of the republic. It loomed large in the meaning of nationality and *patria*. In Alberto Lamar Schweyer's novel *Vendaval en los cañaverales* (1937), Gonzalo Maret reflects on hearing a description of Cuba as a backward country: "I couldn't deny it. We are! What is worse is that we believe that in denying it we are patriotic, when in fact it would be better to recognize it and avoid it." Maret continues: "We ourselves opened the way for the foreign exploiter and what's worse is that we rely on him, for were it not for the investment of capital from the North, we would be in the same backward condition in which we found ourselves when the colony ended. And I do not want a *patria* without hygiene, without guarantees, without roads and full of illiterates. . . . The *patria* is not an abstraction, but a comfortable reality and only the people comfortably situated . . . feel the advantage of nationality."[145]

Similar arguments were employed as the rationale for learning English, mas-tery of which promised individual advancement and collective progress. "We must study English not only as a means of culture, but as a most valuable accomplishment in the economic struggle in which he who knows English has a tremendous advantage," argued educator Ramón Gómez de Rosas. "It has been recognized that the more we understand English the better we can advance ourselves as individuals, and consequently, as a nation. To study English is seen to be not only a personal opportunity, but an act of patriotism." Raimundo Cabrera made a similar argument: "Cubans should know English . . . in order to improve their knowledge of how to be free, to consolidate their independence."[146]

These formulations were central to meanings assigned to schooling in the North, to participation in sports, to carriage and comportment. Cubans learned early to assess their own well-being according to North American standards, by which they were surrounded and to which many saw the necessity to subscribe if only as a means to defend the proposition of becoming and being Cuban. These conditions placed immense pressure on prevailing forms of nationality, for it was uncertain that the material requirements around which national identity developed could be easily sustained through sugar exports. The ensuing gap between the ideal and the reality all but guaranteed to periodically plunge into crisis many of the dominant paradigms on which nationality was based.

3

IMAGE OF IDENTITY

All those spectacles that offer "attractions" for the "tourist": the races, boxing, the cabarets. They are a disgrace. The foreigner comes here to find what is not permitted in his country.
—Francisco José Castellanos, *Poca cosa*, 1915

By all means and any means the American visiting Cuba should get acquainted with its women.
—Basil Woon, *When It's Cocktail Time in Cuba*, 1928

North American travelers wish to find . . . friendly and peaceful natives, guitars and songs, beaches and mountains, a great deal of sun and as much moon as possible. In short, all the pleasures of the primitive and colonial, while relying on airplanes, ships, railroads, and cars, and modern and clean hotels and restaurants, and at prices no higher than they are accustomed to paying in the United States.
—*Carteles*, December 14, 1947

We must admit that every trip we make to Cuba reveals to us more clearly one sad reality. . . . Spanish culture is being rapidly supplanted and replaced by everything American that can possibly travel there by ship, air or wireless. When the Cuban goes shopping he invariably specifies, "*Americano, por favor*," even when buying such things as wines and laces, which are European specialties. . . . Of course, this tremendous admiration for everything American works to the advantage of the tourist, who finds himself very much at home the moment he sets foot in Havana, where he is received and welcomed everywhere.
—Tana de Gamez and Arthur R. Pastore, *Mexico and Cuba on Your Own*, 1954

Things North American arrived in Cuba in many forms, in ways that were always changing and hence serving as a source of further change. But change originating from U.S. sources often signified transformation as accommodation to North American needs, around which Cuban forms subsequently assumed recognizable shape. Much of what became Cuban, in fact, was a product of North American summonings and subsequently served as the means by which North Americans developed a familiarity with Cubans.

TRAVEL AS TRANSFORMATION

Nowhere did North American demands reconfigure Cuban life as dramatically as through tourism. Although travel to Cuba had its antecedents in the nineteenth century, not until the 1910s did the opportunity to develop a mass tourist market present itself. Several events occurred at once. The suspension of U.S. travel to Europe during World War I immediately created alternative vacation sites. Tourist promoters in Cuba were quick to react. As early as 1914, U.S. railroad interests, shipping executives, hotel operators, and retail merchants formed the Cuban Commercial Association for the purpose of "attracting foreign travel to Cuba."[1] Five years later, at the behest of the local U.S. business community, the Cuban government created the National Tourist Commission to promote travel to the island.

Increased travel was also related to transportation advances in the United States. Rail connections improved; steamship service increased. Railway travel to southern ports expanded, and by the late 1910s it became possible to transport passengers comfortably and efficiently to Cuba via southern ports from almost anywhere in the United States. Rail lines and steamship companies joined together to coordinate schedules and improve service. The Seaboard Coast Railroad and the Peninsular and Occidental Steamship Company offered daily service to Cuba: the fifty-six-hour trip from New York to Havana provided direct service from Pennsylvania Station to Key West aboard an electric-lighted Pullman train with drawing room, sleeping, and dining cars. The Peninsular and Occidental also joined with the Atlantic Coast Railway Company to coordinate two weekly trips between Tampa and Havana, with scheduled rail service from New Orleans, St. Louis, Chicago, and New York. The Illinois Central Railroad Company introduced two daily routes from Chicago and St. Louis to Havana via New Orleans and Tampa. Illinois Central integrated upper midwestern routes, including those from Minnesota, Wisconsin, and Nebraska, into the Cuba travel network. Southern Pacific joined with the Ward Line to offer rail service from Portland, San Francisco, Los Angeles, San Diego, and Denver to New Orleans with continuing steamship service to Havana.

Steamship service also expanded. The Pacific Steam Navigation Line, Panama Mail Steamship Company, Clyde Steamship Company, and Cunard operated weekly New York–Havana schedules. The Great White Fleet (United Fruit Company) traveled from Boston, New York, and New Orleans to Havana and from New York to Santiago de Cuba. The Vaccaro Line (Standard Fruit and Steamship Company) offered passenger service between New Orleans and Havana. The Munson Steamship Line carried passengers from Baltimore, Jacksonville, Miami, and Mobile to Havana. The Eastern Steamship Line inaugurated Miami-to-Havana service.

Air travel began in 1921, when Aeromarine Airways, Inc., inaugurated daily air service between Key West and Havana. In 1928 Pan American Airways scheduled daily flights from Key West to Camp Columbia Aviation Field. Havana thus became one of the first cities in the world to operate an international airport. Air service increased dramatically in the decades that followed. Pan American Airways, National, Braniff, Chicago and Southern, and Cubana Airlines scheduled hundreds of flights weekly between Cuba and points north, including Miami, Tampa, New Orleans, Houston, New York, and Chicago.

Changes within the United States also enhanced the appeal of travel to Cuba. Postwar prosperity and economic growth had expanded the ranks of the middle class. The workweek shortened and vacation time lengthened. More people had more disposable income and more leisure time for the pursuit of personal pleasure and entertainment. The 1920s were years of cultural transformation, shifting moral boundaries, and changing lifestyles. Change did not always come easily, of course. Popular tastes often outran official morality; in fact, at times it seemed that they were running in different directions. State legislatures had banned horse track betting during the 1910s, and tracks were eventually closed in New York, Louisiana, and California. The Volstead Act of 1919 ended the legal sale and distribution of alcoholic beverages.

It was precisely these activities, outlawed in the United States but available in Cuba, that gave tourism one of its defining characteristics. Travel in the 1920s shaped a larger narrative of choice and free will. Much of the North American fascination with Cuba then and thereafter was as a place to work through the contradictions of competing moral imperatives. This was Cuba as site of negotiations, as means and metaphor for liberty and license, independence and indulgence. What made this contact so decisive in Cuba was that as a result of their overwhelming presence, North Americans were able to establish as dominant discourse the concept of "Cuban" as a function of their needs, around which much of what subsequently developed as "Cuban" assumed form.

From the outset the Cuban tourist industry was driven by North American tastes and preferences. Under the circumstances it probably could not have been otherwise, for the principal impulse behind the development of tourism originated from among North Americans themselves. The travel market was obviously North American, around whose needs the tourist infrastructure developed its definitive characteristics.

Travel to Cuba began slowly and increased steadily, from nearly 33,000 visitors in 1914 to 36,000 in 1915 and 44,000 one year later, reaching spectacular levels in the decades that followed: from 56,000 in 1920 to 90,000 in 1928, to 178,000 in 1937. Between 1920 and 1940 more than two million U.S. tourists visited Cuba. Travel resumed after World War II and escalated in the 1950s: from 120,000 in 1946 to 194,000 in 1950, to a record 356,000 in 1957.[2]

This travel included a visible high society: the rich and the famous, visitors whose presence conferred on Cuba the status of chic, glamour, and fashion. This was Cuba for the socially prominent and the smart set: trendsetters like

Gloria Vanderbilt, Dwight Morrow, and Mayor Jimmy Walker; celebrities such as Charles Lindburgh, Amelia Earhart, Irving Berlin, and Will Rogers; film stars like William Powell, Norma Talmadge, Gloria Swanson, and Gary Cooper.

Tourism was not limited to the well-to-do and well-known personages, however. On the contrary, what made travel to Cuba noteworthy was its appeal to the mass market, the large number of middle- and working-class North Americans who found Cuba accessible and affordable. Havana became a popular site for conventions and trade meetings: the Brotherhood of Locomotive Engineers, Allied Traders of the Baking Industries, Alabama Press Association, Southeastern Laundrymen's Association, National Editorial Association, and Shriners were among the many U.S. organizations to meet there. And, of course, periodic inundations of sailors and marines on liberty filled the streets of Havana and Santiago de Cuba with a boisterous presence. "The day of our departure a great fleet of American destroyers landed," Hart Crane wrote of his last day in Havana in 1926. "The streets immediately became torrents of uniforms."[3]

Cuba offered an ideal vacation spot: a foreign country with Old World charm and a felicitous winter climate located close to the United States. This was the background and setting, always conceived as ambience. In fact, the success of tourism depended less on the allure of things foreign than on the availability of things familiar. Indeed, herein lay the immediate impact and the long-term significance of U.S. tourism: its power to modify setting and meaning of ordinary life around North American familiarities to which vast numbers of Cubans had become accustomed.

Changing moral codes and lifestyles in the United States during the 1920s implicated Cuba almost immediately. Prohibition, for example, had sweeping consequences. Unemployed bartenders and saloon keepers found jobs in Havana as bars and cabarets that closed in the United States were reopened in Cuba. William Caldwell's Neptuno Bar advertised "choice American food and the best liquors money can buy. A favorite gathering place for Americans." Harry McGabe's Gold Dollar Bar presented "60 beautiful dancing girls." Tom Morris from Cleveland owned the American Busy Bee Bar—"open day and night"—promising the "largest glass of beer in Havana for 10 cents." When Prohibition forced Ed Donovan to close his bar in Newark, New Jersey, he packed up the chairs, tables, mirrors, hanging sign, and the bar itself and relocated on the Prado. Pat Cody also reopened his New York saloon, Jigg's Uptown Bar, in Havana. Peter Economides, formerly chief barman at the New Orleans Café in midtown Manhattan, became proprietor of the Café Suzerac. John Moller from Brooklyn opened Ballyhoo Bar, and George Harris operated George's Winter Palace. Harry McGabe opened the Rialto Café, also on the Prado. Other establishments followed: the New Orleans Café, Winter Garden Bar, Muldoon's Café. The Seminole Café offered "nothing but genuine American and Scotch whiskey. Best draught beer in town."[4]

Bars multiplied prodigiously, and there seemed no limit to the number that could remain in business. By the 1920s about seven thousand bars operated in Havana. "If there is any city with more bars than Havana," commented U.S. consul Carlton Hurst, "I have still to see it. Literally hundreds of them crowd the smaller thoroughfares especially at the street corners, often in connection with grocery stores, and are surcharged with bottles of every kind."[5]

Liquor distributorships also proliferated. So did distilleries and breweries. W. A. Kennerly relocated his Roanoke, Virginia, distillery in Havana. The Havana Distilling Company—"which represents considerable American capital," reported the U.S. chargé d'affaires Edward Reed—opened a large plant at El Cano to manufacture rye whiskey, Scotch, and other liquors. In 1920 the Cuba Cervercera Company purchased the entire factory of the U.S. Brewing Company of Chicago, increasing its production capacity to five million liters of beer daily.[6]

The familiar world of North America was reassembled in Cuba: familiar brand names, familiar food, familiar language, and familiar amusements. This was one more way that North American cultural forms were transmitted to Cuba. "The home lover," the *Havana Post* asserted in 1924, "those who think they cannot get along without just what they have been used to all their lives can find it right here in Havana." The paper observed: "Time was when it was difficult to find what they termed 'good American cooking' here. Now there are plenty of places. . . . One may go out in the great open spaces or he can remain in the thickly crowded districts and mingle with his own kind. . . . A man may see the American baseball. . . . One is not deprived of his own form of religious worship, whether he be Catholic, Protestant, Jew, Christian Scientist or Oriental."[7]

Hotels owned and operated by North Americans were designed for the comfort and convenience of North American guests. Old hotels were refurbished and passed under new management. The old Seville was acquired by John M. Bowman, head of the Biltmore chain, and reopened in 1919 as the Seville-Biltmore. The new Havana Biltmore appeared in 1924, becoming the twelfth Biltmore of the Bowman group. Walter Fletcher operated the Hotel Plaza, modeled on the New York Plaza and using the same suppliers for its silverware, china, and glassware.

The number of new hotels increased. W. T. Burbridge opened the Miramar Hotel; Dwight Hughes, the Albany Hotel; and John A. Richardson, the Hotel Lincoln. Following in quick order were the Hotel Vanderbilt, Hotel Packard, Hotel Cecil, St. Louis Hotel, Hotel Biscuit, Hotel Bristol, Savoy Hotel, Hotel Saratoga, Hotel Pacific, Hotel Palace, Boston Hotel, Miami Hotel, Hotel Parkview, Hotel Ambassador, and Hotel Washington—all sounding familiar and always referred to in English. George Koenig from Miami promised that his Hotel Seminole would be a "first-class American café, lunch, and restaurant." The New Ritz Hotel advertised "American management." Roy Wake operated the Clifton House, "making a specialty of American home cooking and baking."

Mrs. H. Weidemann called her Hotel Brooklyn the "American headquarters" for "strictly American cooking." The Riverside House in Vedado was a "strictly up-to-date American house with all modern improvements and home comforts." J. E. Harrigan, proprietor of the Hotel Harrigan on Neptuno, provided "all American beds." The Hotel Royal Palm promised its guests a "homelike home for those away from home": "At the Hotel Royal Palm you will find all those little comforts that tend to make you feel at home. All help . . . speak both English and Spanish, and therefore can intelligently interpret your desires. Beds have American springs and mattresses. All rooms have telephones with direct connections with any phone in the United States or Canada. . . . Restaurant serving American food at reasonable prices. Meals like mother used to make."[8]

U.S.-owned hotels reached across the island, including the Hotel New York in Camagüey, the Hotel Burnside in Nueva Gerona, and the Castle-Pullman Hotel and Hotel Happiness in Varadero. The Cuba Company operated La Casa Grande in Santiago de Cuba, the Hotel Antilla, and the Hotel Camagüey.

New restaurants appeared in Havana almost as quickly as hotels. The New American Restaurant opened in 1920 on San Rafael. The Havana Tea Room—"under the management of American women"—offered "home made pies, pastry, cakes, and waffles . . . in quiet and pleasant surroundings." Fanny's Place on O'Reilly advertised itself as "famous since 1917 for its American home cooking." Anita Carter operated the Green Parrot: an "American dining room offering pancake and waffle breakfast 6–10 A.M. and businessmen's lunch 11–2 P.M." Geyer's American Restaurant assured prospective customers that "only English speaking waiters [were] employed." The McAlpin Café proclaimed itself "a real American cafe: not an imitation, but a spacious, beautifully appointed AMERICAN eating place. The large dining room is socially favored for dancing and cabaret each evening until midnight."[9]

North Americans dominated key sectors of the tourist trade. The Royal Blue Line Company, incorporated in Boston, operated two tourist buses in Havana. Simon Blumberg ran the Royal Palm Line. Mr. Foster's Sightseeing Trips conducted escorted tours in Havana. John Heimbinder from New York managed the American Guide Association, an organization of uniformed guides that accompanied sight-seeing tours. James Arnold operated the Cuban-American Sightseeing Company, and Robert C. Massman managed Havana Tours, Inc.

Cuban and Spanish entrepreneurs competing for the tourist business had no choice but to also cater to North American tastes. English-language names prevailed. Ramón Rodríguez opened the Armenonville Cabaret as an "American night club," meaning "that the program, show and atmosphere will be entirely American with plenty of 'whoopee,' " designed "to cater largely to the American tourist trade." Segundo González's Hotel Harding—advertised as the "house of normalcy"—boasted that its restaurant was "justly celebrated as serving the best American meals in Cuba." Other Cuban- and Spanish-owned hotels included

The newly opened Hotel Manhattan, described as "the pride of Havana," 1919. (Courtesy of the Biblioteca Nacional José Martí, Havana)

the Hotel Chicago (Vicente Castro), Hotel Pennsylvania (José Valiela), Park House Hotel (Francisco García), Hotel Manhattan (Antonio Villanueva), Hotel New York (José Morgado), and Hotel Ohio (Teodoro Miranda). The Hotel Telégrafo offered "American coffee" and the Gran Hotel América "American cuisine." The Hotel Almendares promised "efficient American-style service." Juan Ferrón opened the Alaska Café—"a new café to cater to American trade," reported the *Havana Post* in 1924. At the American Restaurant, Diego Pérez provided a "real American breakfast any hour." Francisco and Gustavo del Barrio identified themselves as "Frank and Gus del Barrio, proprietors" of the New York Bar. Benito "Benny" Rego managed the Winter Garden Bar. Sloppy Joe's Bar was owned and operated by José Abeal.[10]

Cuban entrepreneurs often hired North Americans to run their facilities. When Pablo Mendoza built the Hotel Almendares in 1920, he appointed Henry Albert as manager. In the same year Ignacio Montalvo and Federico Torralbas

Tourist postcard beckoning North American travelers to Cuba, ca. 1920.
(Author's collection)

Sloppy Joe's Bar. "First port of call, out where the wet begins," read the postcard inscription. (Author's collection)

opened the resort Balnearía de San Diego with North American management and staff. Antonio López, owner of the Isla de Cuba Hotel, advertised "English-speaking employees," as did the Hotel Paris in Matanzas and the Hotel Louvre in Havana. The Carabanchel Hotel and Restaurant boasted of "the most competent English-speaking waiters." La Zaragozana and La Diana restaurants had "English-speaking waiters." The Oriental Park Hotel in Marianao offered the services of an American barbershop. The Hotel Inglaterra in Havana and the Hotel Venus in Santiago de Cuba dispatched interpreters to meet tourists at dockside.[11]

It was precisely the juxtaposition of the foreign with the familiar, the old with the new, to be abroad without being away that was at the heart of the Cuban appeal to North American sensibilities. Cuba offered antiquity without sacrificing modernity, access to the exotic with minimum exposure to risk. "So near and yet so foreign," a popular tourist postcard proclaimed.

Again and again tourists marveled at the convenience of pleasure. "I have never been in a place with the same charm of this one," exclaimed Alice Voorhies of Cleveland, "and think, it's so close to home." Edith Cochran of St. Petersburg agreed: "It seems so wonderful to arrive in an entirely foreign city after only a few hours ride from the States." "It is one of the most picturesque and unusual cities of the world—in spite of its nearness to us," commented U.S. diplomat Norval Richardson. "Havana has many modern conveniences—fine hotels and restaurants, quick transportation, and all that," affirmed Blanche Madsen of Portland, Maine, "but at the same time it has the charm of an Old World city,

Hotel Almendares, Marianao, ca. 1920s. (Author's collection)

with its old Spanish architecture, its many places of historic interest . . . and the charm of a foreign tongue." Edward Sceery of Paterson, New Jersey, concurred: "Before I came here I did not myself realize that it has the advantages of modern cities and at the same time is so foreign." Chicago stockbroker Smith Holden predicted that more Americans would travel to Cuba "when they realize the charm of this foreign country that lies so close to their doors, . . . where they can have all the pleasures and interests of foreign travel and at the same time the convenience and attention they have been used to at home."[12]

The importation of the familiar for North Americans also established familiarities for Cubans. Tourism created a demand for a vast array of U.S. goods and services that inevitably led to daily Cuban usage. North Americans arrived bearing change, often unknowingly; in search of novelty, they also introduced novelty simply by their demeanor and their needs, by the clothes they wore and the way they behaved: hundreds of thousands of visitors whose very presence suggested the possibility of alternative models of self-esteem and new modalities of self-representation.

Travel on this scale must be viewed as a complex process, for it was one of the principal ways that Cubans and North Americans arrived at renderings of one another, serving as both a point of reference and a source of emulation. The presence of North Americans was itself product and portent of changing lifestyles, of transitions and transformations, noteworthy for their capacity to rearrange existing moral hierarchies. The familiar world of the Cuban developed in large measure as a consequence of the North American demands that Cubans were obliged to accommodate. Goods and services provided to satisfy North

Oriental Park Race Track, Marianao. The grandstand boasted a seating capacity of ten thousand. (Author's collection)

American tastes at the same time shaped Cuban tastes. Cuban dispositions no less than preferences were inevitably influenced by those elements so prevalent and accessible in everyday life.

Havana offered countless new amusements and new forms of entertainment. The Oriental Park Race Track opened in Marianao in 1915 and was immediately proclaimed "the finest [racetrack] on the American continent." Golf arrived when the Trust Company of Cuba hired contractor Frederick Snare to construct the Havana Country Club in Marianao. On completion, el Country Club boasted a spectacular eighteen-hole golf course and a membership roster of 1,500 North Americans and Cubans; it soon acquired a reputation as "the sportiest course in the Western Hemisphere."[13] In 1929 a New York architectural firm designed the eighteen-hole course for the Country Club de Santiago de Cuba. Golf courses subsequently opened at the Almendares Country Club, the Rovers Club, and the Biltmore Yacht and Country Club.

Boxing also came to Cuba during these years. Previously prizefighting had been limited to U.S. soldiers of the military occupations (1898–1902 and 1906–9). The few gyms that existed in Havana were operated by North Americans, the most prominent of which was the Academia de Boxeo established in 1910 by ex-boxer John Budinich. Prizefighting as a professional sport had not taken hold in Cuba, due in part, suggested sportswriter Jess Losada, to the Cuban sensitivity—"a purely colonial characteristic"—that "if you touch my face I'll kill you."[14] Boxing lacked pomp and panache, but most of all it lacked a paying public.

This changed after 1914. Boxing initially arrived in Cuba as a tourist attraction, mainly championship bouts between North American boxers during the

A view of the golf course at el Country Club, Havana, ca. 1920s. (Author's collection)

high tourist season. Noting the sudden surge in boxing matches in 1915, the weekly *Gráfico* commented: "There is at this moment an attempt to popularize in Havana a sport virtually unknown until recently. We refer to boxing." In the same year the new Havana Stadium was inaugurated with the championship middleweight match between Young Ahearn and Willie Lewis as the main event. But it was the "great white hope" contest between Jack Johnson and Jess Willard at Oriental Park in April 1915 that won boxing a mass audience. The publicity campaign and press coverage in the weeks leading up to the bout aroused enormous public interest as more than five hundred sportswriters from around the world arrived in Havana to cover the event.[15]

Weeks of prefight publicity had the desired effect. On the day of the bout, Oriental Park filled to capacity. Press accounts estimated an audience of 30,000 fans, approximately 25,000 of whom were Cuban.[16]

Two new boxing arenas were added, el Ring Cuba in 1918 and el Black Cat Ring in 1919, both operated by Cuban impresarios José María Villaverde and Angel Rodrigo Vivero. In 1920 a professional boxing association was formed (el Havana Boxing Committee), followed a year later by a government regulatory agency (Comisión Nacional de Boxeo y Lucha).[17]

The popularity of prizefighting spread across the island. National championship rankings were established in all weight divisions. By the mid-1920s Cuban boxers appeared on U.S. fight cards and soon earned prominence in professional boxing circles. In 1929 Kid Chocolate (Eligio Sardiñas) became the first Cuban to be ranked internationally. He won the world junior lightweight crown two years later and the featherweight championship in 1932.[18] By the 1930s, boxing had

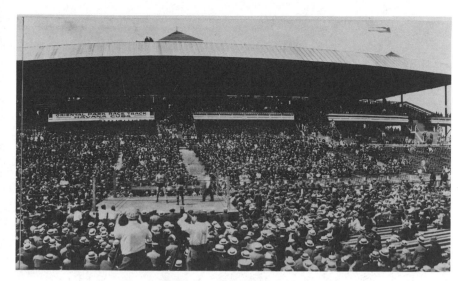

A panoramic view of the Jack Johnson–Jess Willard fight, held at the Oriental Park Race Track, Marianao, 1915. (Courtesy of the Library of Congress, Washington, D.C.)

become a national passion. A new boxing magazine, *Nocaut* (knockout), enjoyed wide circulation. The success of Kid Chocolate inspired a new generation of professional boxers. Subsequent champions included welterweights Kid Gavilán (Gerardo González) and Benny Kid Paret.

Other forms of recreation accompanied the expansion of tourism. A miniature golf course opened in Vedado. By the early 1930s *golfito* was the rage among Cuban youth. "Upon its introduction," reported a correspondent in 1931, "the miniature golf course was visited only by North American tourists and residents. Within a few days, Cubans began to invade the course and today we have Cuban champions in men and women's miniature golf."[19] Palisades Park—named after the New Jersey park—opened in 1920. A sprawling amusement park complete with roller coaster, Ferris wheel, and carousel, it gained widespread popularity, mostly among Cubans, attracting crowds of 6,000–10,000 daily and often as many as 15,000 on weekends.

Nightclubs, cabarets, and hotels routinely booked orchestras and performers from the United States. The Cascades Orchestra of New York played at the Seville-Biltmore. The Hotel Bristol engaged Chuck Howard and His Orchestra. The Paul Whiteman Orchestra and Jerry Freeman and His Orchestra played at the newly opened Presidente Hotel. The Plaza Hotel booked Hugh May and His Jazz Boys and the Don Lanning Orchestra. The Joy Palace in Miramar engaged the dance team of George and June Ball. The Max Doling Orchestra opened at the Blossom Inn. In 1922 John Philip Sousa played at the Teatro Nacional. In 1927 the Ziegfeld Follies had a ten-day engagement at the National Theater. Cuban proprietor Pablo Mendoza of the Hotel Almendares booked Coleman and His

Kid Chocolate (Eligio Sardiñas), world junior lightweight champion (1931) and feather-weight champion (1932). (Courtesy of the photographic archives, *Bohemia*, Havana)

Celebrated Orchestra of New York and the Michael Borochowsky Orchestra of Chicago.

Entertainment reached new heights of grandeur with the opening in 1928 of the Gran Casino Nacional in Marianao. Nothing quite like it had ever been seen before. Designed by New York architects Schultz and Weaver and interior decorator Renee Lewis, the Gran Casino represented the North American rendering of tropical opulence. Capable of seating one thousand people, the palatial restaurant-nightclub included an immense gambling room as well as an elaborate dance floor and stage area from which extravagant floor shows alternated with dance orchestras. The casino immediately acquired an international reputation as the "playhouse of the Caribbean" and set the standard for elegant dining and fashionable nightlife. The dining area, wrote Consul Carlton Hurst, "is always crowded with beautifully gowned and bejeweled women. The center of the floor is cleared for fancy dancing by professionals and the space is then retaken by the public. . . . In the rooms beyond are the roulette tables where thousands of dollars change hands in the course of the evening. People walk out at intervals on the broad terrace to see the fountain with colored lights playing on the marble figures of the dancing nymphs."[20]

The Gran Casino Nacional underscored the salient feature of tourism in Cuba: the capacity of North America to arrange the physical environment of Cuban life around its own needs. What passed for Cuban was, in fact, often of North American origin. From the Havana Biltmore in the 1920s to the Havana Hilton and the Riviera in the 1950s, U.S. motifs dominated hotel construction. The Seville-Biltmore Hotel and the Concha Beach Club were designed by Schultz and Weaver. The Hotel Nacional, completed in 1930 and hailed as the "quintessential Cuban hotel," was designed by New York architectural firm McKim, Mead and White; construction was supervised by Purdy and Henderson Company. The Nacional's Grand Ball Room was decorated by New York designer Robert E. Locker; the floor plan was completed by Hasbrock Flooring Company of Long Island.

Never before had the exaltation of things Cuban so thoroughly passed into the popular imagination. Cuba was chic, Cuba was in vogue: morning golf at the Country Club, afternoon races at Oriental Park, evenings of formal dining at the Casino Nacional and dancing at the Plaza Hotel roof garden. Travel writer Joseph Hergesheimer proclaimed Havana "a city both fashionable and rich." Sydney Clark described the times vividly: "Cuban articles, Cuban music and that vague substance known as Cuban atmosphere became the rage of smart circles in both hemispheres."[21]

Comparisons were perhaps inevitable, and they too accentuated the vogue of things Cuban: the "Cuban Riviera," the "Riviera of the Caribbean," and the "Nice of the Atlantic"; the Gran Casino Nacional was the "Monte Carlo of Latin America," and the Prado was the "Champs Elysee of the winter time." Havana

Above and opposite: Kid Gavilán (Gerardo González), world welterweight champion (1951). (Courtesy of the photographic archives, *Bohemia*, Havana)

was described variously as "a little Paris," the "Paris of the West Indies," and the "Paris of America." It was "the substantial rival of resorts like Monte Carlo and the Venetian Lido," asserted one travel writer.[22]

Havana seemed to have cast a spell over North Americans. It was "a paradise on earth" (Olive Gibson) and a "veritable fairyland" (Pauline Bychower), a sensation echoed by Anaïs Nin—"I have been transported to Fairyland"—and Hart Crane: "It's a funny little metropolis, more like a toy city than a real one." "Days there fly by as if on wings and one feels as if living in a land of enchantment," wrote tourist Nina Hawkins. "I thought I'd died and gone to heaven," was National Airlines flight attendant Alcyone Hart Barltrop's first impression of Havana.[23]

Images of Cuba were transmitted in newspapers, magazines, and periodicals, in travel articles and tourist books, and in advertisements of travel agencies, railroad companies, steamship lines, and airline carriers. Havana was the subject of motion pictures, poems, odes, and songs. The sights and sounds of Cuba— real and imagined—served as a Hollywood staple for decades. Between the 1930s and 1950s Cuba was the setting of scores of films, including *The Girl from Havana* (1929), *Under Cuban Skies* (1930), *Cuban Love Song* (1931), *Havana Widows* (1933), *Weekend in Havana* (1941), *Moonlight in Havana* (1942), *Cuban Pete* and *Club Havana* (1946), *Holiday in Havana* (1949), *Havana Rose* and *Cuban Fireball* (1951), *Santiago* (1956), *Affair in Havana* (1957), and *Pier 5 Havana* (1959). Cuba appeared in the fiction of Burnham Carter, James Gould

Nocaut sports magazine enjoyed a brief existence during the early 1930s. (Courtesy of the Biblioteca Nacional José Martí, Havana)

Cozzens, Graham Greene, Ernest Hemingway, Josephine Herbst, and James Street and in the poetry of Hart Crane, Theodore Dreiser, Robert Frost, Langston Hughes, and Wallace Stevens.

But it was in the lyric of popular music that the North American narrative on Cuba acquired its greatest resonance. The lyric could celebrate the most fanciful notions of the island through wistful yearnings and wishful thinking. Indeed,

Gran Casino Nacional, Marianao, the "Monte Carlo of the Western Hemisphere," ca. early 1930s. (Author's collection)

few countries in the world have been the subject of more popular songs than Cuba. (See Appendix Table 3.1.)

Cuba entered the North American imagination in many forms, but principally as a place of pleasures unavailable at home—where one could do those "things" that usually were not done anywhere else. Access to alcoholic beverages during Prohibition was an early tourist attraction. "Never has so much beer, rum and Daiquiri been consumed in so short a time," a tourist wrote home. Visitors availed themselves of the opportunity to drink immediately on arrival. "I have seen people leaving incoming ships," commented Consul Hurst, "who have stopped at bars on their way to the hotel taking alcoholic drinks. By the time they reached the hotel they could scarcely ask the reception clerk for a room."[24]

It was not merely the availability of alcoholic beverages, however. The opportunity to drink carried a subtext of individual freedom and indulgence. It implied license for excess. "Here the tourist finds that touch of the tropics of which he has read," the *Havana Post* proclaimed:

> The somber mantle of Volsteadism is not draped over this happy island, where personal liberty is something to be enjoyed openly and not spoken of with bated breath within the murky precincts of an evil smelling speakeasy. Here the tourist . . . may, if he chooses, "take a whirl" at the lottery or other games of chance prohibited by an element which in his homeland seems desirous of removing the spice of life from the reach of the worker and relegating it to those able to pay for the luxury of violating popular laws.[25]

Pages 184–86: Covers of sheet music, ca. 1910s–1920s. (Author's collection)

Correspondent J. J. Van Raalte extolled Havana as the "paradise of the cocktails," the "ideal country of personal liberty," adding: "When we come here again next year we should bring with us the Statue of Liberty, to place in the port of Havana, where it properly belongs." Cuba was the "land of the free," affirmed one visitor, where "all forms of pleasure will flourish until the sun advances along the meridian and the mighty throng of visitors turn their faces northward again." Among the major appeals of Cuba, Basil Woon declared, was "personal liberty carried to

the Nth degree," by which he meant: "You may drink as much as you want to, . . . you may lose as much money as you desire in the Casino, you need not carry your marriage certificate with you, and you may stare at the pretty señoritas." Isabel Stone agreed: "Three hundred years ago our forefathers came to America in search of 'life, liberty and the pursuit of happiness.'" She continued:

> Today in ever increasing numbers, Americans are flocking to Cuba . . . to pursue life, liberty and happiness according to the twentieth century version.

Nor are they waiting for such slow transportation as a sailboat. Nothing less speedy than an airplane satisfies many of these emigrants, in whose minds White Rock is fast being confused with Plymouth Rock as a synonym for freedom. The native Cuban proudly names his country "Cuba Libre," Free Cuba. . . . The visiting American places his own interpretation on the word "free," a composite picture in his mind's eye of legalized racing, lottery tickets, brass rails, sophisticated night life and the most enlightened divorce law in the world.[26]

Cuba was constructed intrinsically as a place to flaunt conventions, to indulge unabashedly in fun and frolic in bars and brothels, at the racetrack and the roulette table, to experiment with forbidden alcohol, drugs, and sex. "An all-round pleasure laboratory," exulted one visitor; a "booming playground," proclaimed another. "America's finest playground," affirmed a third tourist, "where gayety rules supreme," offering "every aid to extravagance." "It is hot, it is 'wet,' it is, in its easy tropical way, Wide Open," wrote Bruce Bliven. One could "sin" without consequences. Cuba was a place, Sidney Clark rhapsodized, where "conscience takes a holiday." "Of course, I feel rather sinful about running over here to Havana," admitted Wallace Stevens. Cuba should be called the "Isle of Self-Indulgence," a journalist suggested, "for self-indulgence brings us here, just as the hope of gold lured the early Spaniards to come over. . . . The early Spaniards came here to find gold; we come here with gold to indulge ourselves in our so-called bad habits."[27]

The notion that Cuba existed specifically for the pleasure of North Americans took hold early, lasted long, and was central to the meaning associated with being a U.S. tourist in Cuba. One advertisement asserted: "Cuba. So near and so friendly is a storehouse of inexhaustible sun and gaiety for the Americans. . . . It might be said that nature has purposely placed this Holiday Isle of the Tropics at the door of the great American nation for the pleasure, repose and health of its inhabitants."[28]

Tourism in Cuba traded on the proposition that North Americans were privileged visitors who, by virtue of nationality, were exempt from the rules they were expected to live by at home. In Cuba, they could do whatever they pleased. They were free to act out the individual behaviors that replicated the complex hegemonic hierarchies defining Cuba's relationship with the United States. Arriving in Cuba from the Canary Islands about this time, Francisco González Díaz recorded his impressions of U.S. tourists: "Every *yanqui* defines and imposes the primacy of his country in the smallest acts, in the slightest gestures. Each citizen of the United States travels with his citizenship in his suitcase, with an authoritarian and overbearing *yanquismo*. Each one moves about the world bolstered by a sense of a supreme power that authorizes him to speak overbearingly and give orders."[29]

North Americans appreciated their privileges. "There is one thing more than another that strikes arrivals from the United States . . . ," observed *New York Times* correspondent Henry Ilsley, "and it is the unrestricted opportunity to do as one pleases; each to enjoy himself in his own particular way . . . with no thought of breaking the laws of the land or being criticized." Lyricist Marion Sunshine described Cuba as a place "Where the palm trees smile up at the sky / Where you do as you please, there go I." One tourist described Cuba as "a place where you can get anything you want"; another wrote home that Havana was a "town [where] you could do anything you want, and know nothing is wrong."

"The idea of freedom to do just as one pleases . . .," commented vacationing Hollywood director Bryan Fox, "is most appealing." Basil Woon commended Cuba to his readers as a place "satisfyingly foreign" and "so completely exotic that [Americans] may be as superior as they please." The tourist "may become drunk and noisy," Adolphe Roberts noted, "he may commit any small offense, and the regular police will not touch him. They will steer him into the hands of the tourist police, whose members . . . will take him, if necessary, to their station house, sober him up and guide him to his hotel without having made a charge against him. . . . He will be helped in an argument or fight by a tourist police-man, who generally will give the short end to the Cuban involved." "It's great to be an American in Havana," exulted a visitor, "to be free to consume an inordi-nate amount of booze."[30]

Forms of personal gratification banned in the United States were pursued assiduously in Cuba. Drug trafficking flourished; indeed, heroine, cocaine, and morphine were only slightly less available than Scotch, gin, and rum. As tourism increased, so did drug consumption. "The wrong use of opium, heroine, mor-phine, and other harmful drugs, a few years ago almost unknown here," the *Havana Post* complained as early as 1916, "is now growing rapidly and heroic measures will have to be adopted if the state is to curb the destructive habit." One visitor "noticed Americans as patrons" of opium dens, adding: "There are at least a dozen opium joints running full blast within the well known Havana district."[31]

The most enduring North American images of Cuba were formed during these years and served as the principal narrative depicting the island: Cuba evoked romance and exuded sensuousness. Romance was everywhere, for the taking. Havana "was made for romance," proclaims the narrator of Burnham Carter's short story "Journey by Moonlight" (1940). It was "hyper-sensual and mad," concluded Hart Crane, "i.e., has no apparent direction, destiny or pur-pose; Cumming's paradise." "Havana is a veritable city of romance," exclaimed one visitor; "the last refuge of romance and romantic living," insisted another. In 1924 a tourist rhapsodized: "It seems that in this part of the world the moon shines its brightest and the spirit of romance that breathes in the air on a moonlight night in Cuba is irresistible. The tall graceful palms swaying in the breeze; the stillness of the night, undisturbed except by the sound of the ocean, washing the shores, the luxuriance and fragrance of the vegetation, all combine to lend a complete sense of enchantment and contentment."[32]

Romance was the staple of the lyric of popular music: "Havana, gay ren-devous for romancers," affirmed "Cuban Cabaret"; "Cuban Moon" proclaimed Cuba "the Island of romance," and on the "Sidewalks of Cuba," one would be "intoxicated by romance."[33]

The notion of romance was, in fact, a euphemism for sex and seduction, the rendering of Cuba as a setting for amorous adventures. The "air was instinct with seduction" as Joseph Hergesheimer described Havana. "Cuba—the very name conjures visions of romance, beautiful women, soft music–filled nights and cigars," Hyatt Verrill wrote. *House and Garden* was slightly more circumspect: "A certain amount of sin, naturally, is to be expected in a city as whole-heartedly devoted to love and romance as Havana. . . . All this Latin temperament and the beauty of Cuban girls, who are well aware of their enticements, having a tendency to unsettle susceptible Americans and induce erratic behavior." Helen Lawrenson attributed Havana's appeal to "atmosphere," a condition "so toxic, so insidious, so hypnotic" that it "casts a spell over the hearts of men." She was convinced that "something in the air" had "a curious chemical effect on Anglo-Saxons, dissolving their inhibitions and intensifying their libidos": "Travelers . . . find in Havana a seduction more potent than anywhere else, even though much of the time they are unaware of its exact nature. The intrinsic basic quality of Havana is a deadly magic which permeates the very air which flows through the city, inescapable and inseparable, and which can only be defined, in the last analysis, as Sex. It is, without any doubt, the sexiest city in the world."[34]

Havana was gendered precisely around these formulations. "Havana is like a woman in love," insisted travel writers Consuelo Hermer and Marjorie May. "Eager to give pleasure, she will be anything you want her to be—exciting or peaceful, gay or quiet, brilliant or tranquil. What is your fancy? She is only too anxious to anticipate your desires, to charm you with her beauty." Milton Guss invoked a similar analogy: "La Habana strikes me as a gal with a split personality. By day she can be a reserved lady of Spain. And by night she can remove her mantilla and really let her hair down." Helen Lawrenson likened Havana to the "geographical counterpart of Zola's *Nana*"; like Nana, "the city exudes an essence, fragrant and fateful, of delight in love. In the streets the dark, warm, carnal life throbs with an endless ease and grace." Decades later Georgia Anne Geyer characterized Cuba during these years as "America's most beautiful mistress," and Andrei Codrescu referred to "the heyday of American good living in Cuba, when the whole country was a cheap and bountiful mistress."[35]

Cuba was the site of sex with women of the Other, exotic and mysterious, primitive and carnal, passionate and governed by libidinal impulses, and often articulated in explicitly racial terms. "It was the exotic strangeness of the adventure," explains the narrator in William McFee's short story "The Roving Heart" (1935) as protagonist Edward Brownlow contemplates a visit to Cuba: "He was an American, and underneath that he was English; and he had a double hereditary lease in the belief that foreign women possessed the secrets of love undreamed of by the girls of his own race." "Something in the tropics and the people, the Spanish!" Joseph Hergesheimer speaks through his protagonist in the novel *Cytherea* (1922). "Those dancing girls in gorgeous shawls, and they haven't any clothes underneath; and that nakedness, the violence of their passions, the danger and the knives and the windows with iron bars, stir me. It's all so different from New York." Waldo Frank contemplated Cuban women in his dreams: "A woman passes. The hips and the high heels are jazz; the arms and breasts swathe her in Andalusian softness; under the blare of her rouge, Africa mumbles." Edmund Whitman wrote that "a sailor with a quarter . . . may expect to find some strapping African willing to accommodate him behind six sacks of sugar on the wharf." Sydney Clark directed his readers to Paula Street, "a red light district of black hue, where burly negresses call raucous invitations to passing males and clutch at their sleeves." E. L. Stafford dedicated one stanza of his ode to Havana to the "glorious women": "Eyes smoldering lakes of fire Radiant, fathomless with the woman glow, old as eternity, Charming, with languid glances over fans."[36]

Nowhere, perhaps, did the themes of sex and seduction recur as often or resonate as distinctly as in the lyrics of popular music. The discursive structure of the lyric allowed for clever phrasing, play on words, and double entendre. Through innuendo, insinuation, and inference, popular music contributed to some of the most enduring representations of Cuba. Irving Berlin's Cuba was "Where dark-eyed Stellas / Light their fellers panatellas." The Harry Waxman lyrics in "My Cuban Pearl" told of "her wicked glance / And vamping Spanish dance," adding: "You ought to see how she shakes her naughty wiggy wee / She's all there I'll say, she's some girl." In "A Cabana in Havana," Tom Seymour wrote: "And how she'd look at me / And softly say 'Si si' to all I planned." In the Moe Maffe lyric, Havana was depicted as "the only spot where you get what may be the lot of any maid." The promise of "Down In Old Havana Town" was "Ev'ry señorita seems a little sweeter," where the "girls are hot tamales," a place "to see those dark eyes glisten / Those red lips kissin." Edward Heyman's "Cuban Cabaret" celebrated Havana as the "gay rendezvous for romancers," a "city of fiery dancers" with "eyes burning with desire":

> I'm excited by your glance,
> Invitation to romance
> In a Cuban cabaret.
> Like the cigarette that you hold in your hand,
> Love's a spark that soon flickers out when not fanned
> And so give me all your love
> Tomorrow night, you will dance again for someone new
> When I'm far away from you.

The Marion Sunshine lyric of "Cuban Belle" alluded to the "languid eyes":

> When she starts to sway,
> All I can say, is well, well, well. . . .
> Oh, it's hard to tell, where she gets her spell,
> But believe it or not, a spell she's got. This Cuban belle.
> She's got rumba on her hips, Bacardi on her lips,

But her foot it never slips, Cuban to her finger tips:
Take Garbo to dine with you, and Joan Crawford bring her too.
Long before the evening' through,
You'll be telephoning who?[37]

These possibilities passed directly into the representation of Cuba as tourist site. The sense of expectation was central to the appeal of travel to Cuba: a chance encounter, a flirtatious fling, a sexual adventure. The opportunities were said to be everywhere, and the promise of sex with Cuban women was itself a subtext of the tourist narrative. "The young girls of Havana are radiant, good-looking, chic and expertly flirtatious," reported a travelogue. "They are aware of their charms and see no harm in displaying them with becoming modesty." Basil Woon described in detail the "dark, seductive beauty" in Havana: "At least two out of every three girls on the street . . . are pretty, and half of them, if you like the lissome, languorous, warm-eyed, dark-skinned, vividly-colored type, are beautiful. And even this percentage is beaten by Santiago and Cardenas, not to mention Matanzas and Trinidad." Sydney Clark's travel guide called attention to the "thousands of young girls of shopgirl class and lower. . . . Their complexions are like petals, of some unknown flower between pink and brown, their figures as dainty as a midsummer-night's dream. Their breasts are generously rounded, in the abundant manner of the tropics, and the girls are not unaware of their charms." These were the images that also gained familiarity in the United States in the fiction of Warren Miller ("Cuban women with their magnificent breasts and hips") and Graham Greene ("brown eyes, dark hair, Spanish and high yellow, beautiful buttocks lean against the bars, waiting for any life to come along").[38]

Cuba as a place of sex, sensuality, and seduction took firm hold. The images filled the popular culture. "I always thought of Cuba as a place to fall in love," Jake comments in the play *Rum and Coke* (1986), "well, maybe to seduce is a better word." In the film version of Damon Runyon's *Guys and Dolls* (1955), Sky Masterson (Marlon Brando) plans the seduction of Salvation Army worker Sarah Brown (Jean Simmons) by taking her to Cuba. All the scenes purporting to represent Havana are of bars and cabarets, and predictably the Brando-Simmons *mambo* sequence climaxes in a bar brawl. Cuba as site of seduction is confirmed as Brando speaks of "magical bells for lovers, full of rum and music on a make-believe island." The moral was not lost on the movie audience. "Once [in Cuba]," wrote film critics Jay Nash and Stanley Ross, "she succumbs to the ambience, the rum, the music; he can have her if he wants her." Ernest Hemingway was characteristically more blunt than Damon Runyon. In *Islands in the Stream*, Henry and Willie are in Havana "hunting girls." Affirms Willie: "We want whores. Nice, clean, attractive, interesting, inexpensive whores. That can fuck."[39]

The appeal of Cuba as a place in which to abandon inhibitions and flout conventions crossed gender lines. North American women also seemed to have often traveled to Cuba with similar expectations, although the evidence is less clear. Cruise ships were filled with female passengers. The Cunard Line estimated that 65 percent of their passengers were women, traveling alone or in groups. Travel writer Barbara Dubivsky confirmed Cunard data. "Along about this time every year," Dubivsky wrote in December 1951, "hundreds of briefly liberated young working girls stagger up the gang-plank of cruise ships, bringing their savings in the form of new clothes and a round-trip passage to southern places. Most of them are fully prepared to meet loads of interesting people."[40]

Images of the "Latin lover" had long assumed a place of prominence in North American perceptions of the male Other. Schoolteacher Irma Sutton was not reluctant to "praise Cuban men," whom she found "polite, efficient and in many cases possible aspirants for Ramón Novarro's part in the films. It is rather curious to see so many sideburns and dark complexions and canes in real life instead of only in the movies." The lyrics of "The Week-End of a Private Secretary" narrate one experience:

> I went to Havana to look at the natives,
> To study their customs, their picturesque ways.
> In searching for some local color,
> I ran across a Cuban gent, and he was such a big sensation,
> I forgot the population.
> He showed me the city, he taught me the customs;
> My trip to Havana was quite a success.

The narrator in Juan Arcocha's novel *Los muertos andan solos* (1962) recounts the ease with which Rogelio picked up American women at Varadero: "The women who vacationed there had a very clear idea of what they were looking for, and hence it was a matter of allowing themselves to be picked-up." Musician Charlie Barnet recalled his days in Havana as a "gigolo": "Cruise ships would arrive regularly . . . and there were lonely women looking for thrills in a foreign country. My headquarters was Sloppy Joe's, a popular bar all the tourists visited. For a fee I would take the women to all the night-spots, as well as to sex shows if they wished. I was able to make pretty good time with some of them." Helen Lawrenson described the "boatloads of hopeful females who go down there every year on cruises, trusting to find a nation of Cesar Romeros." Lawrenson herself had taken a five-month vacation in Cuba, an experience on which she based a 1936 *Esquire* article, "Latins Are Lousy Lovers." In that essay she addressed such matters as "Latins in bed," the way "they meet you at the bar for cocktails at five-thirty [and] make violent love to you," and the way they "boast of their prowess, their anatomical proportions and their methods." Almost twenty years later Lawrenson returned to Havana and revisited this theme: "A walk on the streets of Havana is something every woman owes to herself once in her life time. . . . Nowhere in the world does a woman get such concentrated, consistent, and flattering attention as on the streets of Havana. There the ogle is raised to the level of a fine art." In the Twentieth-Century Fox film *Week-End in Havana* (1941), Nan Spencer (Alice Faye), a sales clerk at Macy's department store, travels to Cuba to visit the "countless bars and numberless nightclubs" in search of romance. She is hopeful that the "tropical magic" and "moon of temptation" will provide the ambience in which she can say "*adios* to my heart." In a 1957 flashback episode of *I Love Lucy* ("Lucy Takes a Cruise to Havana"), secretaries Lucille McGillicuddy (Lucille Ball) and Susie MacNamara (Ann Southern) seek "romance, excitement and adventure in Havana," specifically "to meet the men of our dreams." It is on this occasion that Lucy meets Ricky Ricardo (Desi Arnaz).[41]

Perhaps no image was so firmly fixed and widely held as Havana as a place of vice—an "extraordinary city," recalled Graham Greene, "where every vice was permissible and every trade possible." "One of the last of the world's sinful cities," proclaimed the *Saturday Evening Post*. *Time* magazine described Havana as "one of the world's fabled fleshpots," and *Variety* reported: "Havana is prepared to put on any kind of show a Yankee from home might desire."[42] This was the Havana of sumptuous bordellos and squalid brothels; of sex on the streets, on stage, and on the screen; of pornographic theaters and bookstores. G. L. Morrill described his encounters at "every other house . . . a seductive señorita at the door or window, with extended hand or winsome voice urging you in Spanish or broken English to forsake the counsel of your mother's Bible."[43]

Prostitution flourished. Sex shows and live pornographic theaters proliferated. The Shanghai Theater and the Tokio Cabaret offered nightly pornographic performances; the Tokio advertised: "Come when you like, do what you please, and let your conscience be your guide." The estimated number of prostitutes in Havana increased from 4,000 in 1912 to 7,400 in 1931. By the late 1950s about 270 brothels operated in Havana, with more than 11,500 women working as prostitutes.[44]

Descriptions of brothels routinely appeared in tourist guidebooks. Adolphe Roberts recommended the "refined prostitution" available on Virtudes Street, "institutions" that were air-conditioned and well furnished and offered drinks at moderate prices. Here the visitor would find the "tapestried and mirrored rooms where the salaciously-inclined may witness startling scenes in the flesh or by means of moving pictures." Roberts specified that the "girls constitute the main attraction. . . . Any one of them may be taken from the premises." *Terry's Guide to Cuba* gave tourists precise directions to Havana's waterfront red-light district—"the prurient spot resorted to by courtezans, varying in complexion from peach white to coal black; 15-year-old flappers and ebony antiques; chiefly outlanders who unblushingly loll about heavy-eyed and languorous, in abbreviated and diaphanous costumes; nictitating with incendiary eyes at passing masculinity; studiously displaying their physical charms or luring the stranger by flaming words or maliciously imperious gestures." Sydney Clark recommended Oficios Street: "many prostitutes, most white or near-white ply their trade here with conscientious zeal, greeting any in-coming male as though he were a dear friend from childhood days."[45]

Not for the first time, Cuba insinuated itself into the North American imagination, became implicated in North American transformations, and was in turn shaped by those transformations. This was an environment summoned into existence for North Americans. They did not "discover" paradise, they created it. Cuba met North American needs so fully that it had to have been invented by them. They found in Cuba the perfect Other: foreign but familiar, exotic but civilized, primitive but modern, a tropical escape only hours from home in which to flout conventions, a place to live dangerously but without taking risks.

Cuba became associated with indulgence and abandon, and visitors were rarely disappointed. Ernest Hemingway liked Cuba because it had "both fishing and fucking." Tennessee Williams would reminisce about his "riotous weekends in Havana," and Ava Gardner fondly recalled the Havana of her honeymoon in 1951 as an "American playground, complete with gambling houses, whorehouses, and brightly lit cafes, every other one boasting a live orchestra. Traffic, lights, bustle, cigar smoke, pretty girls, balmy air, stars in the sky, they all combined to form a Latin town that aimed to please." Hoagy Carmichael remembered everything as "tropical"—"tropical nights, tropical beer, tropical music, tropical girls, tropical moon, tropical mood"—and was unabashedly nostalgic about the "strangely blonde Havana B-girl" who "danced divinely." Carmichael wrote: "The beer was strong. The rumba music, the first I had heard, gave me a tingle . . . it was a wonderful cruise." Graham Greene delighted in Havana "for the sake of the Floridita restaurant (famous for daiquiris and Morro crabs), for the brothel life, the roulette in every hotel, the fruit machine spilling out jackpots of silver dollars, the Shanghai Theatre, where for one dollar and twenty-five cents one could see a nude cabaret of extreme obscenity with the bluest of blue films in the intervals." When bored with the bars and brothels, Greene went in search of "a little cocaine," and nothing "was easier." Historian Neill Macaulay also recounted his time in Havana: "The whorehouse I visited . . . was furnished with spotless, linoleum-topped tables and chairs arranged around a small dance floor. There was a brightly bubbling jukebox with rock-and-roll records, and a bar. The girls, all teenagers, were dressed in shorts and halters. All were white and several blonde, though their eyes were unmistakably Latin. It was a place where American high-school and college boys of the 1950s came to relieve their sexual tensions in surroundings that were not forbiddingly foreign." This must have been what John Sayles had in mind in his novel *Los Gusanos* (1991) when he wrote of "the Casa de Rock, where boys from the University of Miami would come to fuck little blonde Cuban girls who spoke good English and wore ponytails and blue jeans just like the little blonde girls they were afraid to fuck back

Havana nightlife by day. (Courtesy of the photographic archives, *Bohemia*, Havana)

home." In Havana U.S. ambassador Arthur Gardner could only observe with mounting incredulity and lamely lament: "The masses of people who come here are bent only on pleasure and think of Cuba except in terms of fun, rum and nightclubs."[46]

North American tourism was at once the cause and effect of other changes. As nightclubs and cabarets expanded, nightlife assumed extravagant proportions. Big-name performers arrived from the United States to play for North American audiences. In 1939 Martin Fox purchased the Villa Mina estate in

Marianao and constructed the Tropicana nightclub. Small clubs, bars, and dance joints proliferated, bearing such names as Dirty Dick's, Hollywood Cabaret, Pennsylvania, Johnny's Dream Club, Tally-Ho, High Seas, Skippy's Hideaway, and Turf Club.

In the 1950s more than twenty new hotels were completed, and gambling establishments increased. In 1951 Florida developer Jerry Collins opened a greyhound racetrack in Miramar. In the same year a new, modern amusement park called "Coney Island" operated in Havana. The Riviera and the Hotel Capri introduced casinos in 1957; these were followed by the Montmartre, Sans Souci, and Tropicana nightclubs. The Capri hired actor George Raft as the casino host. Other casinos were installed in Havana at the Hotel Nacional, Plaza, Seville-Biltmore, Deauville, and Comodoro; in Cienfuegos at the Jagua motel; in Varadero at the Internacional; and on the Isle of Pines at the Colony Hotel.

The U.S. underworld was also attracted to Cuba. Indeed, the reach and range of organized crime on the island increased dramatically in the 1950s with the hearings of U.S. senator Estes Kefauver, which had the net effect of forcing criminal elements to relocate their gambling operations elsewhere. "It was the chill of the Kefauver hearings which to a large measure induced the Americans to seek warmer and more hospitable grounds to the south," reported *Variety* in 1953.[47] Once again, like Prohibition, North Americans seemed content to exorcise their demons by exporting them to Cuba. The Fulgencio Batista government obligingly modified existing gambling regulations to permit any nightclub or hotel in Havana worth $1 million or more, and more than $500,000 outside the capital, to operate gambling casinos. The stage was set. "These are wonderful things that we've achieved in Havana," proclaims Hyman Roth (Lee Strasberg) in the film *Godfather II*, "and there's no limit to where we can go from here. . . . We have now what we have always needed: real partnership with a government. Here we are, protected, free to make our profits, without Kefauver, the Goddamned Justice Department and the FBI—90 miles away, partnership with a government."

By the late 1950s, organized crime had assumed control of the major hotels and casinos in Cuba. Tens of millions of dollars were invested in luxury hotels, nightclubs, and gambling casinos. The "famous Cleveland gambling syndicate," *Life* reported, including Sam Tucker, Moe Dalitz, and Wilbur Clark, operated the Parisién Casino of the Hotel Nacional. Norman Entratter from Las Vegas controlled the Venecia in Santa Clara. Harry "Lefty" Clark, described by the *Miami Herald* as "the dean of the U.S. gambling underworld," went to Havana in 1956 and immediately took over the Tropicana casino. Norman Rothman operated the Sans Souci and later passed it on to Santo Trafficante, who also managed the Capri. Meyer Lansky provided most of the $14 million used to construct the luxurious Riviera Hotel. Lansky operated the Montmartre, Seville-Biltmore, Internacional, Comodoro, and Havana Hilton.[48]

Tropicana Casino: "Where you can try your luck at the most fascinating games in a distinguished atmosphere," advertised the Tropicana. (Author's collection)

In the 1950s gambling receipts exceeded $500,000 monthly. "This is going to be another Las Vegas," an anonymous gambling promoter boasted to *Life* correspondent Ernest Havemann, "only like Las Vegas never imagined." The *Havana Post* concurred, observing that Cuba was bidding for the title of "the Las Vegas of Latin America." During these years Lucky Luciano was planning to transform the Isle of Pines into the "Monte Carlo of the Western Hemisphere," with luxury hotels, lavish gambling casinos, and elegant brothels. "Without any question," recalled mob attorney Frank Ragano on the CBS news documentary "The Last Revolutionary" (July 18, 1996), "there wasn't a better place in the world for a mobster to operate a business than in Havana, Cuba. That was a great time there, anything you wanted was there, was available."[49]

North American crime figures became a familiar sight in Havana, ranging from the high-profile mobster to the small-time hood and hustler. In fact, the underworld presence assumed the proportions of a migration. Mobsters "have moved into Havana in such force," reported one observer, "that the town looked like a haven for the underworld in exile." The *Miami Herald* described an "invasion of Cuba by the U.S. underworld." "You walk into one of these new gambling joints," reported *Newsweek*, "and it's like walking onto the set of a Grade-B gangster movie. Every thug you ever saw east of Las Vegas who can get up the plane fare is walking around one of these casinos in a white silk evening jacket acting like a head waiter." Longtime Havana resident Milton Guss also noticed the change. "The tide of gambling has washed a lot of American undesirables ashore," he observed ruefully. "There is no shortage of American hoodlums in Cuba." In 1958 former prime minister Manuel Antonio de Varona appealed directly to Estes Kefauver for assistance. The introduction of "big gambling," Varona explained, had resulted in the arrival of "several well-known American racketeers," adding: "These strange elements are extremely dangerous to the Cuban people, since they are not only fostering many vices among my fellow citizens, but acting as potential instruments in the hands of an unscrupulous tyrant. Nobody can fix a limit to these characters, once they have enough power to act. They could become a powerful force to undermine or destroy any person or institution firmly determined to fight corruption on the island."[50]

REPRESENTATION OF RHYTHM

The expanding tourist presence introduced changes that were both profound and permanent, transformations to which the Cuban people adjusted as a normal part of daily life. But some of the most noteworthy changes involved what tourists returned home with, impressions made and tastes formed as a result of their experiences in Cuba. Travel on this scale served as a source of dynamic exchange by which cultural forms were transmitted in both directions.

Such travel played a substantial role in shaping the way "Cuban" was rendered in the United States. This involved a complex transaction by which the North American notion of "Cuban" acted to change or otherwise modify Cuban self-representation as a means of success and advancement. Music was an important medium of this encounter and often gave "Cuban" decisive form in the popular imagination.

The cultural transformations of the 1920s carried North Americans deep into the realms of previously forbidden musical idioms, where melody mattered less than rhythm and dancing was expressed less in prescribed steps than experienced through permissive body movements. The fixed choreography and dance etiquette of Victorian social dancing were abandoned for dances that allowed improvisation, syncopated rhythms, and the physical intimacy of the dance floor embrace. Men and women assembled together in public places to move their bodies to the rhythms of such new dances as the turkey trot, camel walk, bunny hop, fox-trot, and tango. Dance became a way to explore the exotic and the primitive, an opportunity to experiment with personal freedom, a way to assert being. "Not to dance was not to exist," declared music publisher Edward Marks in 1934.[51]

Between the 1920s and the 1950s Cuban music was a pervasive force in the development of popular dancing in the United States. North American appropriation of Cuban musical idioms was accompanied by adaptation and alteration, largely commercial transformations to meet local market conditions. The music arrived loaded with images, and therein lay its appeal: license to deploy energies associated with the tropics. In the course of successive adaptations and arrangements, substance mattered less than form, from which emerged the representation of "Cuban" on North American terms.

Music in Cuba was in transition. The *son* arrived in Havana during the late 1910s and within a decade had gained widespread popularity. With its origins in Oriente province, the *son* fused Spanish melody and African rhythm. And for this reason, the *son* was rejected by fashionable society. It was *oriental*, a polite way to imply that it was African; it was unsophisticated, another way of saying that it was of the underclasses. In 1919 soldiers dancing the *son* in Guanabacoa were arrested and charged with immorality. As late as 1929, composer Luis Casas Romero denounced the *son* as a "true disgrace" to national music, a reflection of the "ignorance and degeneration" that had contaminated Cuban music.[52]

Nevertheless, enthusiasm for the *son* spread. From simple origins, the *son* continued to strengthen its style through the 1920s and early 1930s and soon became the standard fare in local nightclubs and cabarets, in theaters and music halls. The number of *son* bands increased. Between the 1920s and 1940s, nearly fifty bands (*conjuntos*) were performing in a variety of venues in Havana.

This was part of the musical ambience that delighted North Americans. The *son* offered precisely those qualities U.S. tourists sought in Cuba: it possessed melody and rhythm, it was polished and primitive, it was lush and sensuous, eminently danceable—the perfect musical accompaniment to romance, "a dance of Dionysian movement," wrote musicologist Cristóbal Díaz Ayala.[53]

North Americans were captivated by the *son*, which they often mistook for the *rumba* and misspelled as *rhumba*. The rumba was actually an exhibition dance performed by a man and a woman, typically as a sexual pantomime. People danced the rumba in working-class bars, waterfront cafés, and dance halls, the dockyard clubs (*fritas*)—in "the darker dives of the city," commented Sydney Clark. The rumba was explicitly sexual, as the performers danced to a script of courtship and consummation. "Lewd and licentious," wrote music critic Earl Leaf; "remarkably lurid . . . candidly sensual and of generative inspiration" and "danced to orgiastic music in some hot little *bohío* . . . undeniably frank," echoed Clark.[54]

The rumba was distinctly African and dismissed contemptuously by the Cuban middle class. Edith Pitts remembered that it was popular only among "the lower social elements," a "dance seldom mentioned in polite circles." Sydney Clark described the rumba as a "writhing African jungle dance . . . never countenanced on the island except in the lowest negro halls." It scandalized delicate sensibilities and evoked racial phantasms. In a letter to the State Department in 1920, U.S. minister Boaz Long objected to the "syncopated music of Africa" that seemed to be gaining popularity. "The 'rumbas,'" he warned, "are danced with sensuous music and the dances themselves often become indecent. . . . It is undeniable that sensuous songs and dances have the effect of developing a mob spirit. In the case of the negro they may arouse a sense of racial solidarity."[55]

The popularity of the *son* and the rumba might well have remained confined to working-class neighborhoods, among the poor, and in the bars and fritas

Typical Cuban Rumba - Havana

Professional rumba stage dancers, Havana, ca. early 1930s. (Author's collection)

along the waterfront. However, such Cuban musical genres attracted a wider audience, which is to say that they found a market and acquired commercial value. They conjured up exactly what many North Americans traveled to Cuba for: sex and sensuousness, the lewd and libidinous, the quintessential representation of the primitive, the exotic, and the erotic. "There is something about [rumbas] so reminiscent of voodoo," mused Edmund Whitman after a visit to Cuba, "of drums beating up the misty valley, of dark-skinned men and women prancing around the bonfire, that once known . . . can never be forgotten." One tourist came upon a band playing "native Cuban music with the native instruments, and it made you feel you were off in the jungles." Ted Shawn recalled his first encounter with the rumba: "I felt as if I could not possibly remain a spectator, but must spring out onto the floor and to the strains which seem to move in my blood like some rich, old heady wine." Shawn vowed to return to Cuba, convinced that "here I know I will find something near to Nature's breast, a measure of the cosmic rhythm that I seem to hear calling me from afar during those enchanted Havana nights."[56]

North Americans filled the cabarets and local dance halls to observe and to participate. In one such cabaret in Havana, Joseph Hergesheimer came upon "men and women doing [the rumba], galvanized by drink and the distance from their responsibilities, animated by the Cuban air, . . . prodigiously abandoned." The men were mostly "commercial gentlemen and stiff brokers," the "genial obese presidents and managers of steamship companies . . . invariably accompanied by their wives, who, for the most part, endeavored to re-create the illusions and fervors of earlier days." Herbert Lanks visited a club where a "gal in close-fitting bronze skin" whirled "out on the patch of floor and melts into an ultra-seductive version of the sensuous rumba." Lanks continued:

> Her slim, tense, dancer's body weaves and melts its way into the music and into the senses. A tom-tom beat in the savage, sensual music beats every trim line of her body into every tired brain. . . . The tourist . . . forgets that he is a bald-headed businessman from Manitowoc; he is swept away by the tropic night and the tom-tom beat and the weaving bronze body; he is part of something young and strong and fierce and ageless as the jungle and unquenchable as the fiery heart of Africa.[57]

Music served as both source and setting of the North American meditation on sex and sensuality. Emphasizing the movement of hips and lower body, Cuban dance offered a powerful representation of tropical sensuality. The music was necessary to the pursuit of romance and seduction. In the motion picture *Weekend in Havana*, Nan Spencer (Alice Faye) was downright rapturous about "romance and rumba," the "enchanting rhythm" and "the primitive beat of the bongo drum and the sensuous sigh of the violin."

Sensuous music, stimulating primitive impulses, aroused romantic urges.

The lyrics of North American popular music were filled with allusions to the "effect" of music. The lyrics of "Blame It on the Rhumba," for example, clearly established the relationship:

> If I find romance in your arms while we dance,
> Blame it on the rhumba, blame it on the rhumba.
> I feel a thrill and my heart won't be still,
> Blame it on the rhumba, blame it on the rhumba.
> And while the music is playing,
> While the lights are low,
> I'm not to blame if I say "I can't let you go."
> So why be discreet if our lips chance to meet,
> Blame it on the rhumba, blame it on the rhumba.

"The Last of the Rumbas" carried a similar moral: "Rumba taught me romance / Made me fall in love / And lose my heart in your dance." So did "In the Madness of the Rumba": "In the rumba you implore me / In the rumba you adore me."[58]

North American tastes helped bring the *son* and the rumba out of the fritas and fringes of the Havana underclass and into the fashionable supper clubs and high society night spots in Cuba and the United States. North American market forms quickly appropriated Cuban idioms, and in the process they were transformed and subsequently emerged as the dominant commercial expression of Cuban music. At the center of this complex process was the diffusion of the musical genres by which Cuba would be represented. For respectable Cuban society, bourgeois and middle class alike, the notion that the *son* or the rumba symbolized Cuba was as inconceivable as it was inadmissible. Secretary of Education Juan J. Remos denounced nightclubs that featured the rumba and urged the government to "take charge of tourists and steer them away from Havana cabarets." Visitors could not understand Cuba by visiting such places, Remos insisted, "for neither they, the dance nor rumba music were typical of Cuba."[59]

At issue here was the extent to which North American tastes and market forces combined to shape the image of Cuba, independent of how the dominant classes may have wished their nation to be represented. "The better people in Cuba," observed music critic Maurice Zolotow, "cannot figure out why Americans prefer the rumba to the more austere danzon, which is the favored dance of the Cuban upper class."[60]

To the dismay of the Cuban middle class, the *son* and the rumba enjoyed rapid commercial success in the United States. Cuban music gained access to the U.S. mass market as a result of several circumstances. Certainly timing was important. North Americans were in the throes of social dancing, and "tropical" rhythms fit perfectly as the sound score of the times. Tourism also facilitated the crossover of Cuban idioms. Back home, tens of thousands of U.S. visitors to the island were instrumental in creating the demand for Cuban music. North American orchestras and jazz bands booked for the tourist season in Havana returned to the United States playing versions of the *son* and rumba. New York band-leader Emil Coleman, for instance, was one of the many to add rumba numbers to his repertoire. According to a 1932 account in the *Havana Post*, Jerry Freeman and His Orchestra succeeded "in infusing into their music the languorous appeal of native melodies" at the Gran Casino Nacional.[61]

This was a time when U.S. manufacturers were mass-producing phonographs and seeking new overseas markets. Record sales were specifically intended to increase the demand for phonographs. As early as 1920, RCA Victor was advertising in *La Lucha* "new Victor records" identified as *danzón, guajira, punto guajiro*, and *rumba*.[62] The growth of commercial radio broadcasts also broadened the audience for Cuban music.

Throughout the 1920s U.S. phonograph companies recorded Cuban music; by 1925 hundreds of Cuban records filled their catalogs.[63] In 1928 promoter Juan Castro accompanied RCA Victor representatives across Cuba in search of vocalists and orchestras to record. During this trip RCA Victor signed the Miguel Matamoros Trio to a long-term contract. North American music publishers also rushed to the island to buy Cuban compositions, often at shamelessly low prices. In 1929 Herbert Marks, while honeymooning in Havana, purchased Moisés Simons's composition "El Manisero." Supplied with English lyrics by Marion Sunshine and Wolfe Gilbert, "El Manisero" was published in the United States in 1930 under the title "The Peanut Vendor." In the same year Don (Justo Angel) Azpiazu and His Orchestra introduced "El Manisero" in New York. Presented in an overture version, "The Peanut Vendor" was staged as a vaudeville production, with lead singer Antonio Machín appearing on stage pushing a peanut cart.[64]

The spectacular commercial success of "The Peanut Vendor" inaugurated one of the most remarkable periods in the history of popular music in the United States. "The Peanut Vendor" quickly topped the list of best-selling sheet music, reaching the 1 million mark by 1940. By the end of the decade, no less than thirty different recordings of the song had been released, including versions by Louis Armstrong, Guy Lombardo, Duke Ellington, Woody Herman, and Xavier Cugat.

The success of "The Peanut Vendor" revealed the enormous commercial potential of Cuban music. What became known as the "rumba craze" had begun. Music publishers and recording companies reacted immediately. The Southern Music Company even organized a rumba sheet music club. Record sales soared. Suddenly, it seemed, an insatiable demand for the rumba had developed nationwide. In 1931 *Variety* reported:

Cuban dance music . . . has attained sudden popularity in America and [is] growing in favor. . . . Cuban music is more sprightly and peppy than the slow melodic music which has been crooned and danced to for the past several seasons and serves as a pleasant variation to public taste, yet it is slow enough to take the place of the music of the crooners without any radical change. The dancing public, particularly the youngsters, have been dancing slowly for some time and therefore find this slow Cuban rhythm adapted to their purposes.[65]

Popular dancing was transformed. "More plain Americans," reported Earl Leaf, "are taking *rumba* lessons than any other social dance except the fox trot." Rumba lessons accounted for more than 60 percent of the total business of the Arthur Murray dance studios, providing in one year earnings in excess of $14 million. "Dance floor addicts have gone in so intensely for these idioms," commented *Variety*, "that the fox-trot's status as the dominant form may soon be relegated to second place."[66] In 1935 Paramount paired George Raft and Carole Lombard in the film *Rumba*, further boosting the dance's appeal.

Perhaps no person played a more prominent role in popularizing the rumba in the United States than Xavier Cugat. Born in Spain and raised in Cuba, Cugat pursued a brief but unsuccessful career as a classical violinist in New York. Moving to Los Angeles, he earned a modest living as the head of the dance orchestra "Xavier Cugat and His Gigolos." Cugat's genius was his ability to integrate Cuban musical idioms with familiar North American orchestral sounds. His most successful recordings transformed the *son* and the rumba into elegant orchestral arrangements. "Americans could not become acquainted with the intricate and intoxicating rhythms . . . ," Cugat explained, "which are especially rich in a variety of dance forms. It was too rapid, and it was necessary for me to play many of these compositions at first at a much slower tempo until they could be comprehended and appreciated." Cugat possessed an engaging stage presence— "I knew the American people . . . were crazy for a personality, so I decided to become a personality"—and was a consummate charmer, in constant dialogue with his audience, often in self-effacing heavily accented banter. "Cugie," as he was popularly known, understood his dual role of popularizer and performer; he also recognized the importance of forming a public taste for Cuban music. He pointed out the need "to render the *son* into really a slow American fox trot," adding: "I played melodic foxes and gradually insinuated the claves and maracas to soften them"—and instantly he had carried North Americans across a new dance threshold.[67]

These were not always authentic performances, but Cugat recognized the significance of authentic *performers*. He played across the country, in small towns and large cities, on college campuses and in concert halls. Cugat employed a troupe of ruffled-sleeved professional dancers and always fronted his orchestra with an attractive woman, beginning with the adolescent Rita Hayworth (née Rita Casino). Dancers would demonstrate new steps and proceed to mingle among club audiences and lead patrons back to the dance floor—all very much the Cugat trademark. By the early 1930s Cugat had established his band as the house orchestra at the Waldorf-Astoria, and for the next thirty years he interpreted Cuban dance music for U.S. audiences.

In the late 1930s a second Cuban dance captured the attention of the North American dancing public. The *conga* was associated with Desi Arnaz, who in 1933, at age seventeen, moved to the United States with his family to escape the political turmoil of post-Machado Cuba. Arnaz first played with Cugat, then formed the "Siboney" combo to perform in Miami Beach. He compensated for his limited musical talent and training with showmanship and stage presence. Drawing on memories of the carnival street processions (*comparsas*) of Santiago de Cuba, Arnaz introduced the conga and immediately launched a new dance sensation. The conga, a processional line with the kick on every fourth beat—festive, simple, and very danceable—soon reached a national audience.[68]

In the Cugat tradition, Arnaz was very much a "personality," playing the role of Cuban at least as much as he played music. He enjoyed a brief motion picture career in the role of a Cuban bandleader, first in the Universal film *Cuban Pete* (1946) and later in the Columbia release *Holiday in Havana* (1949). In the title song "Cuban Pete"—identified in the published score as "a swing novelty"—Arnaz proclaims that he is the "hottest guy in Havana" and the "king of the rhumba beat / the dance of Latin romance."[69]

Cuban music passed into the mainstream in many forms. Some of the most popular recordings of 1930s and 1940s—and among the most commercially successful releases—were Cuban compositions to which English lyrics had been added, including "The Breeze and I" (Andalucía), "Always in My Heart" (Siempre en mi corazón), "Let Me Love You Tonight" (No te importas saber), "Maria My Own" (María la O), "Yours" (Quiereme mucho), "Come Closer to Me" (Acércate más), "From One Love to Another" (Danza Lucumí), "Say Si Si" (Para Vigo me voy), "Two Hearts That Pass in the Night" (Dame de tus rosas), and "Green Eyes" (Aquellos ojos verdes). The 1941 Jimmy Dorsey recording of "Green Eyes" sold nearly one million copies.

Music served as a popular way to create and disseminate images of Cuba, to define and interpret it. The island loomed large in the North American imagination. The endeavor to explain it, and to communicate that explanation to a larger public in the United States, assumed a variety of artistic expressions and constantly influenced all facets of the North American performing arts. Among the tens of thousands of tourists to visit Cuba was George Gershwin, who enjoyed a vacation noteworthy for its excesses at a time notable for excesses. "I spent two hysterical weeks in Havana," he recalled fondly, "where no sleep was had, but the quantity and quality of fun made up for that." Between visits to the bars and brothels, however, Gershwin became intrigued by Cuban rhythms and percussion instruments. In 1932 he completed the orchestral piece "Cuban Overture," adopting the melody from the *son* "Echale salsita" by Ignacio Piñeiro and featuring in the coda an array of Cuban percussion instruments.[70]

Other North American composers found inspiration in Cuba. Harl MacDonald in 1935 wrote *Rhumba Symphony: Reflections on an Era of Turmoil*. The work, John Tasker Howard asserted, "succeeded admirably in presenting graphically the modern restlessness, the hectic, brooking emotionalism, and the avid lust for wild and fiery pleasure that outwardly characterize much in the present era."[71] The Cuban influence on Morton Gould's *Latin-American Symphonette* (1941) was apparent in the movements called "Rhumba" and "Conga." Quinto Maganini composed *Cuban Rhapsody* and Aaron Copeland *Danzon Cubano*. North American choreographers sought to define Cuba in dance forms. Katherine Dunham created such numbers as "Cuban Slave Lament" and "Havana Promenade." The theatrical piece "Rumba to the Moon" was the work of Charles Weidman.

In the late 1940s and early 1950s the *mambo* seized hold of the North American imagination. The origins of the new Cuban dance were variously attributed to Orestes López, Antonio Arcaño, Arsenio Rodríguez, and Israel "Cachao" López, but it was pianist Dámaso Pérez Prado's arrangements of the mambo, presented in a big, brassy band sound with trumpets, saxophones, and trombones, backed by a powerful rhythm section—all influenced by Stan Kenton—that captured the *afición* of the North American public. Pérez Prado's treatment of the mambo in the 1950s was similar to the approach adopted by Cugat and Arnaz for the rumba and the conga in the 1930s and 1940s: to popularize by means of showmanship and theatrics. His audiences were taken by his onstage antics, his high kicks that soon developed into high jumps, loud grunts of "Uh!" as he spun in the air. "Prado is a natural showman," wrote Johnny Sipel in 1951, "combining his batoning with dancing and kicking. His enthusiasm projects to the payees as well as sidemen, who work standing up and weaving and bobbing in rhythm."[72]

The mambo overnight became a national phenomenon, riding a wave of popularity that swept across the United States. Pérez Prado drew overflow dance audiences nightly. "The largest crowd the Zena Ballroom [Los Angeles] has ever seen went wild in its enthusiasm over Pérez Prado and his band," wrote *Down Beat* in September 1951. Two weeks later Ralph Gleason reported from San Francisco: "Pérez Prado has swung into Sweet's Ballroom and 3,500 people followed. Prado's audience dances, my friends—young and old they kick out."[73]

The mambo was in demand everywhere. "Dance bands drifting in from the hinterlands report loud and persistent requests to 'play a mambo,'" reported Bill Simon. "Mambomania!" proclaimed *Newsweek* in 1954, adding: "The mambo is the biggest exotic dance craze to sweep the country in a quarter century." Walter Waldman agreed: "In terms of dedicated hypnosis, nothing like the effect of the mambo on its exponents has ever been witnessed in contemporary America." From Chicago *Variety* reported: "Mambo fever has gripped the windy city"; from New York it announced: "New York is beginning to shake from the hips down as the mambo fever continues to spread around town."[74]

Mambo became the dominant motif at nightclubs and in dance rooms nationwide. The Encore Room in Chicago changed its name to Mambo City. Another Mambo City opened in Los Angeles. Other new clubs included the Mambo Club in New York, El Mambo in Miami, and the Mambo Room in Cleveland. When Roseland sponsored "Mamborama," the Palladium countered with "MamboScope." The Hartford Statler featured a weekly dance program called "Mambo at the Statler." Carnegie Hall presented the lavish stage show "Mambo Concerto," and the Los Angeles Shrine Auditorium promoted the "Mambo Jambo Revue." The Savoy Ballroom and the Apollo Theater declared Mondays as "Mambo Nights." Dance studios rushed to add mambo lessons to their offerings. "Dance studios find a course in mambo these days is as essential as a time payment plan," reported *Down Beat* in 1954. The Palladium hired dance instructor Joe (Killer Joe) Piro to offer free mambo lessons on Wednesday evenings. Mambo also received more airtime on radio. "With the rapid spread of the mambo beat in the last year," observed *Variety* in 1954, "pop disc jockeys are now programming an increasing number of such platters on their shows." Increasingly bands adopted "mambo" as part of their name. Cal Tjader reorganized his group as the Modern Mambo Quintet. Others included Carlos Molina and the Mambo Men, the Charlie Velero Mambo Band, and the Peacock Mambo Combo. Record revenues soared. By the mid-1950s mambo record sales topped $5 million. In 1955 Paramount released the movie *Mambo* starring Silvana Mangano and Shelly Winter.[75]

The mambo influenced virtually all genres of popular music. The dance was such a commercial success that in mid-1954 RCA Victor limited its weekly single record releases exclusively to mambos. "Music publishers and record companies have caught mambo fever," reported *Variety* in 1954. "They've opened up all the valves in the current mambo push and are flooding the market with variations on the theme, hoping to cash in on some of the gravy before the law of diminishing returns sets in." There seemed to be no end to mambo recordings. Jazz musicians were among the first to record mambo titles. Errol Garner made an album under the title *Mambo Moves Garner*. Cal Tjader released *Mambo with Tjader*. Others included Sonny Rollins (*Mambo Jazz*), George Shearing (*Cool Mambo*), Billy Taylor (*Early Morning Mambo* and *Mambo Inn*), Shorty Rogers (*Mambo del Crow*), Stan Kenton (*Mambo Rhapsody*), Duke Ellington (*Bunny Hop Mambo*), and Count Basie (*Mambo Mist*).[76]

Dance orchestras released scores of mambo recordings, including the Duke Jenkins Orchestra ("Mambo Blues"), Woody Herman ("Woodchopper's Mambo"), Sonny Burke ("More Mambo"), Ted Heath ("Manhattan Mambo"), Les Brown ("St. Louis Blues Mambo"), Pete Terrace ("Invitation to the Mambo"), and Lester Young ("Another Mambo").

Popular recordings with mambo titles reached the top of the charts in spectacular fashion, although it was never clear that they had much to do with the Cuban rhythms from which they presumably derived inspiration. Vaughn Monroe's "They Were Doing the Mambo" rose to number one on the charts and was followed almost immediately by Perry Como's "Papa Loves Mambo." Rosemary Clooney sang about the "Mambo Italiano," and the Honeydreamers recorded "Irish Mambo." Other recording artists with successful mambo titles were Eartha Kitt ("Mambo de Paree"), the Five DeMarco Sisters ("Mambo Is the Word"), Mel Tormé ("The Anything Can Happen Mambo"), Gary Crosby ("Mambo in the Moonlight"), and Sophie Tucker ("Middle Age Mambo"). Ruth Brown climbed to the top of the rhythm-and-blues charts with "Mambo Baby," which encouraged other entries in that category such as Big Maybelle's "New Kind of Mambo" and the Sheppards' "Cool Mambo." Bill Haley and the Comets recorded "Mambo Rock." Country and Western versions included Darrell Glenn's "Banjo Mambo" and Sheb Wooley's "Hillbilly Mambo." In the category of children's music, the Lennon Sisters recorded "Mickey Mouse Mambo." Classical music was represented by Jan August's recordings "Bach Mambo," based on a Bach fugue, and "Minuet in Mambo," inspired by a Paderewski opus. Sonny Burke recorded "Longhair Mambo," based on a Mozart composition. The Melino Orchestra made "Mambo à la Strauss." Among the stock of Christmas releases in 1954 were Pete Rugolo's "Jingle Bell Mambo," the Smith Brothers' "We Wanna See Santa Do the Mambo," Jimmy Boyd's "I Saw Mommy Do the Mambo with Santa Clause," and the Billy May Orchestra's "Rudolph the Red Nosed Mambo." Novelty items included the Frankie Yankovich Orchestra's "I Don't Want to Mambo Polka" and the Irving Fields Trio's "Davey Crockett Mambo."

The mambo entered all show business venues. "Almost all dance halls and night clubs now require its band to have at least some mambos in their books," reported *Down Beat* in 1954.[77] In the Las Vegas Thunderbird, Les Barker fronted a flashy *Mambo Cuba Revue*, complete with chorus and dancers. In New York, the Chateau Madrid, Latin Quarter, Stork Club, and El Morocco booked mambo bands. Leonard Bernstein incorporated a mambo sequence in *West Side Story*. Las Vegas stripper Lili St. Cyr used a mambo number for a "Latin" act in her stage show. Radio City Music Hall included a mambo for the precision tap line in its *Noche Caribe Revue*. The *Sonja Henie Ice Revue* staged a "Songs of the Islands" production featuring mambo numbers on ice. The *International Revue* at the Las Vegas Desert Inn included a pair of chimpanzees, Tippy and Cobina, who played the maracas and miniature timbales, and Ringling Brothers and Barnum and Bailey Circus in New York introduced mambo-dancing elephants.

Demand for the mambo had not yet fully waned when another Cuban dance captured the North American imagination: the *cha-cha-chá*. Developed by violinist Enrique Jorrín, Orquesta Aragón, and José Fajardo in the early 1950s, the cha-cha-chá was in many ways the opposite of the mambo: rather than brass, it relied on strings and flute; it was light, crisp, and melodic. The rhythm was catchy and, compared to the pulsating mambo, simple. Most of all, the dance was eminently learnable.[78]

Sheet music cover of Perry Como's hit "mambo" recording, 1954. ("Papa Loves Mambo," words and music by Al Hoffman, Dick Manning, and Bix Reichner. Copyright © 1954 Shapiro, Bernstein & Co., Inc., New York, and Al Hoffman Songs. All rights reserved. Used by permission.)

The cha-cha-chá gained instant popularity among all age groups. Indeed, the commercial success of the cha-cha-chá was astounding. "It is king," proclaimed music critic John Wilson. "At the present moment, cha cha has . . . flooded onto almost every dance floor in the country. . . . A nation-wide chain of dance studios reports that it is now the most popular dance among its pupils."[79] Sam Cooke was absolutely correct when he recorded "Everybody Loves to Cha-cha-chá."

Few commercially successful recordings, however, would be characterized as authentic. Most of the commercial success of the cha-cha-chá accrued to main-stream North American dance bands, which exaggerated the simplicity of the rhythmic patterns often to the point of novelty. Its most profitable application was in the reworking of U.S. standards in new rhythmic patterns. By the late 1950s the cha-cha-chá had insinuated itself into all genres of popular music. After the commercial success of the "Tea for Two Cha-cha-chá," recorded by Tommy Dorsey Orchestra with Warren Covington, in 1958, the market was glutted with endless cha-cha-chá renditions of familiar songs, including Guy Lombardo's "Exactly Like You Cha Cha," Lester Lanin's "Over the Rainbow Cha Cha," Lawrence Welk's "Cha Cha Polka," and Enoch Light's "I Want to be Happy Cha Cha." Edmundo Ros recorded the *Hollywood Cha-Cha-Chá* album, which rendered popular film scores like "Three Coins in the Fountain," "Tammy," and "Love Is a Many Splendored Thing" into cha-cha-chá rhythms. Christmas re-cordings were predictable: "The Christmas Song Cha Cha" by Hugh Winterhal-ter and "Rudolph the Red-Nosed Reindeer Cha Cha" by Hernando Hopkins.

The popularity of Cuban dance music between the 1920s and 1950s was remarkable. Cuban idioms transformed popular music in the United States. Nightclubs and cabarets nationwide reinvented themselves as they imagined "Cuban" to be, and for a time "Latin" served as the dominant ambience of North American nightlife. In name and decor, clubs projected "Cuban": among them, the Latin Villa in Kansas City, the Latin Quarter in Boston, Chicago, Miami, and New York; the Latin Casino in Cincinnati and Philadelphia. Clubs with the name "La Conga" opened in New York, Miami, Los Angeles, and Cleveland. The Club El Chico appeared in Greenwich Village. Other New York clubs included the Cubanacán, El Toreador, Havana-Madrid, Yumurí Club (later, Birdland), and El Bongó. The Uproad House became the Cubanola Club, and the Cuban Casino opened on Forty-fifth Street. The Spanish Villa was launched in Baltimore. Oth-ers followed: the Fiesta Room in Cleveland and Cuban Village and the Rhumba Casino in Chicago. The Habanita in Los Angeles was a replica of Sloppy Joe's in Havana. El Chico in Pittsburgh adopted a "rhumba-conga atmosphere," a 1940 *Variety* review noted, complete with a "tropical bar" covered in burlap and bamboo, a lounge with Monterey furniture, and a main dining room "walled with Spanish palm, California stucco and dotted with wrought-iron arches and railings, Castilian paintings, over-hanging miniature balconies and swinging palms." The Statler Terrace Room in Cleveland was renamed the "Cuban Terrace" and renovated in a "conga-rhumba motif" that boasted a "complete Latin-American atmosphere in decor, combining palm trees, statuettes of Mexican peons, sketches of Havana life and a dash of South America in its murals." The jazz-based Music Box changed its name to "La Bamba" and switched to "Latin music." Bob Fosse secured one of his earliest dancing jobs at the Cuban Village in Chicago, wrote his biographer, where waitresses wore "Cuban costumes."[80]

Cuba also provided the motif and the music for scores of revues and stage shows. The Yacht Club in San Francisco presented *Carnival in Havana*. The Lucerne in Miami Beach featured *Havana Mardi Gras*. *Night in Havana* opened at the New York Holiday Theater, *Cuban Nites* at the Chicago Palace, and *Holiday in Havana* in Miami.

The vogue of Cuba was especially prominent in new album recordings, among them Stan Kenton's *Cuban Fire!*, Ray Bryant's *Cubano Chant*, Tito Puente's *Cuban Carnival*, Shorty Rogers's *Afro-Cuban Influence*, Luis Tiramni's *A Touch of Cuba*, the Stanley Black Orchestra's *Sophisticate in Cuba*, Mark Monte and the Continentals' *Dancing at the Habana Hilton*, the Richard Heyman Orchestra's *Havana in Hi-Fi*, and Kenney Dorham's *Afro-Cuban*. Percy Faith released the album *Malagueña: Music of Cuba*, whose liner notes beckoned the reader: "There is more to Cuba than rum and sugar, more than gambling and good times, more than historic shrines and beautiful scenery. There is music, fascinating and unusual music, and it is constantly in the air."

From fashionable supper clubs in midtown Manhattan to the Los Angeles Coliseum, from Harlem to *el barrio*, from nightclubs in Seattle to summer resorts in upstate New York, Cuban rhythms were in vogue: the obligatory fare of virtually all orchestras, dance troupes, and singers in cabarets, nightclubs, and ballrooms, highbrow and lowbrow alike, in big cities and small towns. The Hipp nightclub in Baltimore booked Chiquita, "a Cuban, in a torrid rhumba on toes, with some of the grinding and bumps a bit too strong for family patronage." The Versailles of New York installed Panchito—a "crack rhumba band," proclaimed *Variety*—and added the Rodolfo D'Avalos ensemble of eight dancers to demonstrate "the advanced rhumba tempo, called the conga." It was the "prime motif as the new show is Latin," according to *Variety*. The Colony Club in Chicago booked the DeMarco's rumba team and the Fernando Rhumba Orchestra. And from Detroit, *Variety* reported: "As far north as this spot . . . [the public] is red-hot for the conga and rhumba. Some niteries have gone overboard for the Spanish stuff and most of the others cash in on the current craze with the *rhumba* and conga evenings."[81] Dolita DeSoto, billed as "a Spanish gal from Cuba [who] knows her *rhumba*," performed at the Club Villa in Seattle. Earl's Club in Washington, D.C., featured Ted Rodríguez and La Conga Dancers, and the Charles Fredericks Orchestra in Minneapolis came "through commendably with sampling of . . . Cuban dancing." In 1956 a young singer by the name of Maya Angelou debuted at the Keyboard Club in Beverly Hills; *Variety* described her as an "Afro-Cuban song stylist, . . . still an unpolished performer but there's a potential here for topdrawer stuff."[82]

The mambo and cha-cha-chá were also fashionable among the three hundred hotels and bungalow colonies in the borscht belt stretching across the Catskills, including Grossinger's, the Concord, Tamarack Lodge, the Pines, Ridge Mountain, the Granite, Loch Sheldrake, the President, Raleigh, Esther Manor, and the Willow Lane. On summer evenings in the 1940s and 1950s, the Catskills pulsated with Cuban rhythms. Bands large and small, well known and never to be known, played to appreciative audiences. "Latin music was created by the Cubans and Puerto Ricans," recalled Catskills comedian Jack Eagle, "but somehow the Jewish people became addicted to it." Hotels hired dance instructors for the season and organized dance classes for guests. Adolphus "Doc" Cheatham, a member of Machito's Band, spoke fondly of his playing days at the Concord: "The people up there were mostly Jewish, not Latin, but they loved the band. . . . All those places in the Catskills have instructors, and every day they're teaching the people how to do the Latin dances, and when the people have learned they naturally want the music to go with the steps."[83] Jackie Horner, a dance instructor at Grossinger's in the 1950s and a self-confessed "mambonick," recalled the decade as "mambo time," when "Latin was all the craze." The "rumba had come in during the '40s and was still going strong," Horner noted, "but everyone wanted mambo and cha-cha." This was the world from which emerged Francine Lassman of Brooklyn—"an alumna of the Jewish Alps," quipped Joey Adams—who married Xavier Cugat, changed her name to Abbe Lane and subsequently became known as "the Latin Bombshell."[84]

The success of Cuban idioms contributed to the creation of what passed under the all-inclusive, generic name of "Latin" music. In the 1950s "Latin" became one of the dominant genres of the U.S. recording industry. New releases of old standards employed Latin arrangements. "Capitol is Latinizing Billy May's Crew and other labels are doing the same," reported *Variety* in 1954. Booking agencies expanded their Latin acts. In 1953 the Show Artists Corporation established a Latin department. Mercury Artists Corporation created a Mambo-Jazz department and added more than one hundred Latin acts to its roster. Publishers similarly expanded their Latin American catalog. The major recording companies acquired more Latin groups—"the Latino Vogue has moved over to the major disc labels," observed *Variety* in 1953. Coral records signed Pupi Campos; Columbia, José Fajardo, Joe Loco, Rita Montaner, and Edmundo Ros; Decca, Alfredo Brito, Bebo Valdés, and the Cuarteto Caney; and RCA Victor, Pablo Beltrán, Pérez Prado, Cuarteto D'Aída, Orquesta Aragón, Conjunto Casino, Beny Moré, Noro Morales, René Touzet, Tito Rodríguez, and Tito Puente.[85]

The number of Latin recordings by North American artists grew at an astonishing rate. Peggy Lee released *Latin à la Lee* and Nat King Cole did *Cole en Español*. Charlie Parker recorded *Charlie Parker Plays South of the Border*. Law-

rence Welk produced an album entitled *A Musical Trip to Latin America*. Cal
Tjader albums included *Tjader Goes Latin*, *Latin for Lovers*, and *Latin Kick*. Fred
Sateriale's Big Band album *Broadway Latin American Party* set popular show
tunes to Cuban rhythms. George Shearing released *Latin Lace* and Jack Con-
stanza recorded *Latin Fever*. Other albums included *Dance to the Latin Beat* (Al
Stefano Orchestra), *Hugo Winterhalter Goes Latin* (Hugo Winterhalter Orchestra), *For Latin Lovers* (Carmen Cavallaro), *Lush and Latin* (Freddy Martin Orchestra), and *Skitch Henderson Plays Latin Favorites* (Skitch Henderson).

"Latin" was fashionable and marketable. It seemed obligatory for commercial
success; indeed, for a time everything appeared, as they said in the trade, "to go
Latin": vocal groups like the Latins from Manhattan and such dance teams as the
Latin Lovelies and the Lucky Latinos. The Latin-Aires played at the Hollywood
Mocambo, the Latineers vocal group performed in New York, the Los Latinos
wire-walking act opened in Los Angeles, and the Latin-Ettes played at the Latin
Villa in Kansas City.

To capitalize on the popularity of Cuban dance music, many North American
dance bands adopted new names: the Savoy Havana Band, the Havana Novelty
Orchestra, the Havana Royalty Orchestra. The Milton Shaw's Rhumba Orchestra played at the Plaza Persian Room, the Herbie Collins Rhumba Unit in
Atlantic City, and the Don Astrow Rhumba Band in Pittsburgh. The Terry
Sisters' Rumba Band opened at the New York Rainbow Room to decidedly
mixed reviews—"being non-Cubanos, their bumps, postures and breaks are all
studiously applied, lacking the insouciance of the Hispanic originals," commented the *Variety* reviewer.[86]

Many performers reinvented themselves to pass for Cuban. New York–born
Puerto Rican José Calderón became known as "Joe Cuba" and dancer Pedro
Aguilar from Puerto Rico as "Cuban Pete." Trumpeter Bill Coleman recalled
playing with the band of another "Cuban Pete": "Pete was an Algerian but most
people who knew him thought he was from Cuba. . . . The music that Cuban
Pete's orchestra played was Cuban style."[87] The New York dance band Arturo
and His Cuban Rhythm consisted of Angelo Ilardi (Arturo), Sanzone Vicent,
Dave Goldfarb, and Antonio Cibelli. The Phil Green Orchestra reorganized as
"Don Felipe and His Cuban Caballeros," and the Rimac Carioca Orchestra was
renamed the "Rimac Cuban Orchestra." In 1949 Japanese musician Tadoaki
Misago organized the Tokyo Cuban Boys Orchestra. It was no longer clear what
"Cuban" meant: it could be almost anything that was remotely "Latin," or
vice versa.

The commercial appeal of "Latin" persuaded numerous North American
musicians to adopt Spanish stage names. Alfred Mendelsohn became known
as "Alfredo Méndez," Harvey Averne was "Arvito," and Alfred Levy organized
a successful Latin band under the name "Alfredito." Arranger Ben Pickering
worked under the name "Roberto Rey." The Gerald Bright Band was reorga-

nized as "Geraldo and His Orchestra," and the Arthur Ross Orchestra changed to "Arturo and His Gay Caballeros." Louis Katzman directed the Brunswick house orchestra, the Banda Nacional, under the name of "Luis Medrano." And the La Playa Dancers—billed as an "authentic Rhumba team"—were actually Grace and Bob Conrad.

The popularity of Cuban music also increased the demand for Cuban bands and dancers. "The rhumba conga fans," according to *Variety* in 1941, "prefer to have this class of music interspersed by Latin-American combinations because of the native color lent to the rhythms by the foreign language vocals." And, indeed, some of Cuba's most talented musicians appeared in the United States: Alberto Socarrás, Eliseo Grenet, Ernesto Lecuona, Alberto Iznaga, Don Azpiazu, Antonio Machín, Miguelito Valdés, and Frank Grillo (Machito), among many others. "There are now more and better rumba bands in Manhattan than there are in Havana," reported Maurice Zolotow in 1940. "The nimblest Cuban rumbaists and congaists have departed their native land for the chiller but more lucrative bourn of the United States, where everyone seems to be dancing the rumba." By the early 1940s promoters in Cuba were lamenting the flight of Cuban musicians and the U.S. "grab of Cuban talent." "The sad truth of the matter," commented one observer, "is that there is more worthwhile Afro-Cuban talent around New York, Miami and other key cities than in the entire republic."[88]

It is not clear that Cuban music was always defined as Cuban, for as often as not it was subsumed under the undifferentiated genre of Latin music, a category that could also include the *tango*, *merengue*, *bomba*, and *samba*. But "Latin" was indeed generally Cuban, certainly in its most successful commercial form, such as the *rumba*, *conga*, *mambo*, and *cha-cha-chá*. Commercial success on this scale, of course, could not have been achieved without substantial adaptation of authentic rhythms and original phrasings; original practitioners would probably have found the new arrangements unrecognizable. The vast numbers who took to the dance floor, however, would not have known this. Even in its most adulterated form, it was still exotic stuff, for any dance that demanded even the slightest free movement of hips and shoulders suggested sensuality and abandon.

Yet the success of Cuban music did not always signify success for Cuban musicians. In most cases, it did not. Cuban musical idioms created a market that was beyond the reach of all but a few Cuban musicians. The principal beneficiaries were North American entertainers who succeeded in adapting Cuban idioms to North American tastes. The possibility of fame did attract thousands of Cuban musicians to the United States, but generally to no avail; in fact, at the height of the popularity of the mambo and cha-cha-chá during the mid-1950s, about five hundred Cuban musicians in New York were unemployed.[89] Cuban musicians and dancers often appeared as types, exactly as *Variety* suggested—for "native color"—appropriately tropical and exotic, outfitted in colorful attire, typically satin shirts with full, ruffled sleeves and brightly colored scarves.

The vogue of Cuban drew on familiar representations, mainly those images created by the interplay of popular culture and market forces. The result had less to do with Cuban realities than with North American constructions. Once these representations of "Cuban" took hold, however, they became the primary way that Cubans gained access to the North American market.

Decades of close, recurring encounters with North Americans had enabled Cubans to envision themselves as they might be seen by others within the hierarchy of values that gave "modern" meaning and resonance. They often looked north for validation. Benito Rivadulla Pascual expressed chagrin in 1928 over the growing number of peanut vendors who crowded the parks and prom-enades of Havana, peddling their products to tourists and residents alike. Riva-dulla Pascual could imagine how North Americans might interpret the peanut vendor. He could, in other words, see himself as the Other in North American eyes. Peanut vendors, he worried, "negate the refinement of Havana and the customs of a modern population. . . . Vendors who daily and from the early hours . . . disturb the public not only by their presence but with the constant ringing of their bells." And what, Rivadulla asked rhetorically, "what would the thousands of foreigners who are today our guests think upon seeing these misfits who are a negation of a cultured population?"[90]

The irony, of course, was that only a year later the spectacular commercial success of the song "Peanut Vendor" in the United States transformed the pea-nut vendor into one of the enduring representations of Cuba. In 1932 the peanut vendor was again employed as the rendering of Cuban in the MGM film *Cuban Love Song*, where Terry (Lawrence Tibbet), a marine stationed in Cuba, falls in love with Nenita (Lupe Velez), a local peanut vendor. Not for the last time, images Cubans sought to negate were precisely the ones that succeeded in repre-senting Cuba as a commodity. The contest for control of representation and self-identity was rarely easy and almost never won. The "Peanut Vendor," originally a *pregón* that in the Cuban context was seen as novelty and folkloric, became in the North American context the representation of Cuba.

These were critical issues, for they drew Cubans into a complex negotiation of self-representation. If the United States served as the place of personal fulfill-ment and professional accomplishment, it was necessary to conform to what popular tastes and market forces proclaimed "Cuban" to mean. Success in the north could often be obtained only by acquiescence to prevailing U.S. represen-tations of "Cuban." The adaptation had widespread implications, for it required Cuban complicity in North American constructions, to become what North Americans believed "Cuban" to be, for how else could one reasonably expect to gain access to this market? Decca records promoted orchestra leader Bebo Val-dés as the "Glenn Miller of Cuba." Singer Miguelito Valdés's attempt to cross over to mainstream nightclubs included a 1945 engagement at the San Francisco Mocambo Club, where he was billed as the "Cuban Bing Crosby." Xavier Cugat recalled hiring Miguelito Valdés as a vocalist at the Waldorf-Astoria: "I insisted that he sing no numbers that would shower ringsiders with his excessive gyrations and explosions." Recognizing that he was "stifling the artistry of Valdes," Cugat relented some but eventually fired the singer because he "irritated the customers."[91]

North American tastes demanded commercialization of the rumba, conga, mambo, and cha-cha-chá to the point where the music was transformed beyond the reach of Cuban composers and musicians. Many of them dedicated their talents to commercial forms in an attempt to gain access to this market. Nevertheless, it was a market in which they could not compete. Simply put, they could not produce credible adulterations such as "Papa Loves Mambo" and the "Davey Crockett Mambo." In the process, much creative energy went into the development of execrable material, little of which succeeded but had the net effect of subverting the authenticity of the genre. Cuban music was transformed as fully as it was transforming. The U.S. market turned the rumba into a genteel ballroom dance almost beyond recognition. No Cuban musician could have discerned that the mambo compositions of Antonio Arcaño and Arsenio Rodríguez bore any relationship to "Hillbilly Mambo" or "Mambo Italiano."

The vogue of "Cuban" transcended music. During these years, Cuban no doubt acquired its most enduring representation in the character of Ricky Ricardo. I Love Lucy debuted in 1951 and continued until the end of the decade. It may have been inevitable that the Desi Arnaz role was shaped by the rendering of Cuban most prominently fixed in the North American imagination: a rumba orchestra leader at the Tropicana nightclub who periodically performed renditions of "Babalú Ayé." In the episode "Lucy Meets Bob Hope" (1956), Ricky buys "a piece of the Tropicana" and changes the name to "Club Babalú."

Although it is impossible to fully comprehend how this image of Cuban was understood or otherwise contemplated by the public, the series clearly attracted a huge audience. Indeed, I Love Lucy was one of the most-watched programs in television history—by the mid-1950s it typically drew 50 million viewers weekly. By one reckoning, everyone in the United States had seen at least one episode of the show.[92] "It's unlikely that anyone between the ages of 6 and 60 . . . hasn't been able to identify Desi," affirmed Down Beat in 1953. "Lucy and Ricky were not merely characters in a domestic comedy," TV critics Donald Glut and Jon Harmon insisted. "They were real, they were loved. . . . They would become an American institution."[93]

Ricky Ricardo as "real" and the Cuban as an "American institution" suggest the reach of I Love Lucy. An entire generation derived, in varying degrees, its image and impression of "Cuban" from the television program. Ricky Ricardo conveyed all the information that many viewers would ever know about Cuba. He easily reinforced the dominant images: rumba band leader, heavily accented English, excitable, always seeming to be slightly out of place and hence slightly vulnerable, perhaps even childlike and nonthreatening. Ricky was "a combustible combination of cockiness and stubborn authority," wrote Michael McClay in an official history of the series, "mixed with a fiery Latin temperament tinged with vanity—and a hilarious accent." He served as an easy foil for Lucy's schemes; Ricky as an object of mockery and mimicry was one of the series' recurring thematic elements. Embarrassed by Ricky's English in one episode, Lucy hires a tutor for their baby and pleads with Ricky: "Please promise me you won't speak to our child until he's nineteen or twenty."[94]

Whatever else *I Love Lucy* may have been about, it possessed a subtext about Cuba. Cuba always seemed to be implicated in Ricky's behavior. In "Be a Pal" (1951), Lucy seeks to surround Ricky with "things that remind him of his childhood" and proceeds to decorate their apartment in what she imagines Cuba to be: palm trees, Mexican *sombreros*, a flock of chickens, and a mule. In another scene, Lucy breaks out into song, lip-synching to a Carmen Miranda recording. In the episode "Lucy Meets Bob Hope," after Ricky performs an energetic dance number, Bob Hope asserts: "That'll set Cuba back a hundred years." In "The Ricardos Visit Cuba" (1956), Lucy manages to cause havoc in the Ricardo household and the next day laments: "After what I did last night, Cuba might cut off America's sugar supply!" In "Lucy Is Enceinte" (1952), Ricky has had a bad day at the club and frets: "Oh, what a business. Sometimes I think I go back to Cuba and work on a sugar plantation." In "Ricky Needs an Agent" (1955), Lucy encourages him to consider a movie career by remaking old films: "Gone with the Cuban Wind," "Seven Brides for Seven Cubans," and "Andy Hardy Meets a Conga Player."[95]

The most successful Cuban performers in the United States were types, musicians who shared several traits in common. Xavier Cugat, Pérez Prado, and Desi Arnaz, in his brief motion picture career and as Ricky Ricardo, played off their antics and accents, lending themselves to caricature and self-parody, and implicated their music in novelty in ways that would have been inconceivable for Tommy Dorsey, Benny Goodman, or Stan Kenton. Along the way, they created an image of Cuban that others would be obliged to conform to as the price of success in the North. They possessed finely tuned commercial instincts and showed remarkable talent in adapting Cuban idioms to North American tastes. "I am accused of not playing Cuban music the 'way it is,'" Cugat once defended himself in an interview in Cuba. "Fine. That is exactly the reason for the great success of Cuban music there. Without immodesty, I can say that the rise of our music is due to my efforts. Don Azpiazu, for example, played our music 'as it is.' I can assure you that he reached a very small public, and nobody remembers his orchestra. Has the same thing happened to me? Oh no! In any city of the United States they know the Cugat orchestra. . . . In that way, Americanizing the Cuban somewhat, which continues being Cuban, I can answer you, one reaches the mass audience."[96]

Things and ways Cuban, once under the sway of U.S. market forces, were transfigured as a function of commercial imperatives. A people for whom the proposition of civilized and modern was central to national identity were cast in the role of the North American Other, as exotic and primitive. "The tourist is a type . . . who has become tired of civilization and seeks the primitive," observed Eladio Secades. "To create the primitive where it does not exist is one of the ways to promote tourism." Chilean Tibor Mende, on visiting Havana in the early 1950s, readily understood the drama unfolding before him: "In exchange for [North Americans'] dollars, *habaneros* obligingly provide them all the illusions of the tropics. Cuban orchestras . . . play on a lavishly decorated stage, the black rhythm palpitates amidst the rays of light and bodies continue the playing of the sinister sound of the drums of the Congo; heard in the darkness are the sounds of exotic *rumbas*, of *congas* and *mambos*."[97]

4

POINTS OF CONTACT, SOURCES OF CONFLICT

When one speaks of the *centrales* of the dominant power of North American capital, one usually assumes that the radius of their operation is limited to the production of sugar and close relations with *colonos*. . . . This is far from reality. Each *central* situated in the bowels of our countryside consolidates the entire economic system of its region and dominates it politically and economically. The administrator has at his disposal all the public functionaries and security forces. And against them neither the law nor any protest is practical.
—Leví Marrero, February 25, 1937

Here [Banes] . . . were luxurious lawns and impressive tropical homes. Here American and Cuban employees of United Fruit played polo, swam in their pleasant swimming pools, and shopped in boutiques for American goods, which arrived regularly and smartly by ship. Here one found . . . a burgeoning and upward-striving middle class of Cubans who lived like Americans, prayed like Americans . . . and expected more out of life like Americans. Banes had more ties to New York than to Havana. . . . Everybody used the beaches and the golf courses, and on the Fourth of July, the Americans and the Cubans held a huge picnic at the American Club. . . . Life was fun in Banes, life was positivistic, life was American and therefore the future!
—Georgie Anne Geyer, *Guerrilla Prince*, 1991

We are being invaded—and you know it—by Methodists, Baptists, Jehovah's witnesses and Christian Scientists. North American Bibles are part of the furniture of our rich houses, like Mary Pickford's photograph in a silver frame, rubber stamped with her familiar "Sincerely yours." We are losing all our character.
—Alejo Carpentier, *El recurso del método*, 1974

We have been very much pained by samples of Protestant civilization given to the Cubans by fellow Americans. . . . A U.S. naval ship has been stationed in the harbor for several days, and the sailors give terrible illustrations of what vile liquor will make of man. Drinking, carousing, gambling, singing, shouting, entering houses and insulting women, breaking windows, shutters, etc. It makes our faces tingle with shame. And the Cuban does not know any better than to take them for typical Americans. What can they think of us?
—May Mather Jones, Quaker Missionary, Gibara, February 1901

Among us he who wishes to be heard needs to be brief, very brief—unless he talks about baseball.
—José Antonio Ramos, *Entreactos*, 1913

Baseball was a serious matter. One time, the Cienfuegos ball club brought a black ball player from the American Negro Leagues to strengthen the team, and the poor guy made an error and Cienfuegos lost the game. They had to take the guy out under cover and accompanied by 20 or 30 policemen for the people had concluded that he had been bought and wanted to kill him.
—José B. Fernández, *Los abuelos: Historia oral cubana*, 1987

 The North American presence derived much of its moral authority from its capacity to implicate vast numbers of Cubans in its purpose. In some cases it could create an environment in which alternatives were all but inadmissible. The authority of U.S. corporations, in particular, extended across the island and nowhere with greater effect than in the communities of the interior. A single corporation often represented the principal economic activity of a region, which meant that it was the major employer as well as the primary source of revenue in the form of payroll, taxes, and local buying power. For this reason, the corporation was in a position to arrange the pace and purpose of daily life around its own needs.

THE MEANING OF THE MILL

Communities were transformed into company towns, managed and maintained as a function of North American interests. The Cuban Portland Cement Company in Mariel owned the houses of its one thousand employees. Portland provided utility services, including running water and electricity, and local transportation. North American personnel lived comfortably on Cayo Masón on Mariel Bay, in cottage-style residential neighborhoods with access to the company school staffed by U.S. teachers, a local post office, a hospital, and a commissary. Other corporate enclaves appeared in the mining centers operated by the Bethlehem Steel Corporation, U.S. Steel Corporation, Freeport Sulphur Company, and Eastern Steel Company, dominating the towns of El Caney, Firmeza, Daiquirí, Ponupo, Felton, Nicaro, and Bayamo.

Perhaps the most powerful and certainly the most pervasive corporate presence could be felt at the sugar mill. U.S. control over sugar production increased rapidly after Spanish rule ended. As early as 1899, R. B. Hawley purchased the Tinguaro mill near Colón and the Mercedita property in Cabañas. Hawley organized the Cuban-American Sugar Company and established the Chaparra sugar mill in Puerto Padre; he subsequently bought San Manuel and Delicias. U.S. investors acquired 80,000 acres near Santa Cruz del Sur and formed the Francisco Sugar Company in 1901. William Van Horne, on incorporating the

Cuba Company in New Jersey in 1900, proceeded to acquire 300,000 acres on which to construct 350 miles of railroad and organize the Jatibonico and Jobabo sugar mills. The United Fruit Company built the Preston and Boston mills on hundreds of thousands of acres of land it obtained in northeastern Oriente. Within a decade of Cuban independence, virtually the entire northern coast of Oriente had passed into the hands of North American sugar corporations.

North American interests proliferated across the island. The Niquero mill was constructed by the New Niquero Sugar Company. The Warner Sugar Refining Company, established in 1906, acquired the Miranda, Amistad, and Gómez Mena mills. Edwin F. Atkins consolidated family holdings near Cienfuegos around the Soledad, Florida, and Trinidad mills. The Atlantic Fruit Company took over the Tánamo mill, the Matanzas Sugar Company purchased the Jesús María mill, and Thomas A. Howell (West Indies Sugar Corporation) assumed control of Alto Cedro, Cupey, Santa Ana, and Palma mills in Oriente. In 1916 the newly organized Cuba Cane Sugar Corporation took possession of seventeen fully equipped mills, including Mercedes, San Ignacio, Jagüeyal, and Lugareño. Four years later Milton Hershey completed construction of the new Hershey mill in Matanzas and subsequently acquired Rosario and Carmen. In Matanzas province George Loft of Loft Candies bought the Dulce Nombre mill, and Hires and Company acquired Dos Rosas. Other mills passed to the North Americans: Jaronú and Cunagua (American Sugar Refining Company), Macareño (Caribbean Sugar Company), Punta Alegre, Baraguá, Tacajó, and Báguanos (Punta Alegre Sugar Company), Vertientes, Pilar, and Estrella (General Sugar Company), Isabel and Los Caños (Guantánamo Sugar Company).

Within twenty-five years of the founding of the republic, U.S. control of sugar production was the most salient feature of the Cuban economy. North American ownership increased from 29 mills in 1905, accounting for 21 percent of the production, to 64 mills in 1916, representing 53 percent of the harvest, to 75 mills in 1926, accounting for 63 percent of total production.[1]

North American mills created within their jurisdiction self-contained communities managed as facets of corporate operations, directed largely by North American personnel. The mill town (*batey*) assumed the appearance and character of a small city—"distant little cities implanted in each sugar mill and its environs," commented one observer. The sugar factory was surrounded by office buildings, machine shops, and foundries; some distance beyond were homes, schools, churches, and hospitals; hotels, banks, and retail shops; baseball fields, tennis courts, and golf courses; social clubs and theaters. Such enclaves replicated the customs and class divisions of home and were largely indifferent to the world of Cubans beyond them. An estimated 27,000 people lived on United Fruit property. "The company employees lived in a self contained environment particularly in the Preston where I resided," recalled Richard Smith, who grew up at United Fruit. "The company provided housing, transportation, shopping facilities (mostly food), water, milk, social clubs, golf and tennis facilities, horse-back riding and plenty of beaches. There was rarely a need for the company employees to venture much beyond the confines of the plantation." George Braga could boast of the Rionda corporate holdings, two-thirds the size of Rhode Island, which included eight sugar plantations. "On them . . . lived some 40,000 people," according to Braga. "The maintenance of the mill towns, the schools, the hospitals, the churches, all came under our supervision and were our responsibility." Chaparra consisted of nearly six hundred homes, churches, six schools, one hotel, three movie theaters, a Masonic lodge, a dry cleaners, a telegraph and post office, a pharmacy, a dental clinic, and a company hospital; it was "without exaggeration one of the finest in the republic, after those of Ha-vana." Journalist Carlos Martí described Chaparra as a "flourishing and pros-perous population" that had acquired "a manner of living according to the needs of modern civilized life," including "comfortable and modern [houses] equipped with electricity provided by the company." All the homes possessed "a supply of drinkable water in sufficient quantity for all their needs, provided by an aqueduct constructed by the company, with each house having installed a plumbing system and shower outlets to meet all the needs of the residents." Eva Canel agreed. "Chaparra is almost totally urbanized," she affirmed: "It has very wide streets on which families gather; there are modest homes and elegant *chalets*. There is a very comfortable hotel where employees eat well at prices imposed by the company. There is bustle, there is movement: men of all kinds, races, and types, women well dressed, flirtatious, and as daring as in Havana."[2]

North American personnel lived in segregated quarters, districts known vari-ously as *la zona americana* or *el barrio americano*. They existed as ideal repro-ductions of home—"a little segment of North America set down on the edge of vast rolling fields of cane," commented William McFee in his short story "At the Villa Agostino" (1935). In 1960 Warren Miller visited Nicaro and observed how much it looked "like the Pennsylvania of my childhood." Neighborhoods where the North Americans had formerly lived had "trees and gardens, lawns, big houses." The batey replicated the "American way of life," with all the conventions and conveniences of home. "Employees' residences stand along both sides of the clean, graded street where shade trees are planted," observed Irene Wright of the Boston mill. "Facing on this street is a ball ground, where the children romp. There are also tennis courts. Opposite the main office building is a park." Cor-porate executives occupied spacious homes—*chalets*, the Cubans called them— with gardens and lawns, often attached to golf courses and tennis courts, with access to exclusive country clubs. The North American zone of the Palma mill was "magnificent," with "elegant *chalets* built on splendid avenues. . . . It is entirely possible to imagine that one is in the aristocratic neighborhood of some great capital." The size and location of homes mattered, of course, for they served to fix the social demography of the batey. "Here the manager has his

Home of the administrator of the Jatibonico sugar mill, Camagüey province, ca. 1920. (Courtesy of the McKeldin Library University of Maryland at College Park)

sumptuous dwelling," noted Harry Franck, "his heads of departments their commodious residences, the host of lesser American employees their comfortable screened houses shading away in size and location in the exact gradations of the local social scale."[3]

North Americans created model communities, giving attention to symmetry and structure, balance and order, always with a larger purpose: to affirm power and progress. The community at Hershey was, in fact, called the "Model Town." "Its 200 or more attractive bungalows," observed T. Philip Terry, "stand in symmetrical squares flanking gardens that face shaded avenues aflame with tropical flowers." The Model Town was fully equipped with telephones, electric lights, theaters, dancing pavilions, an amusement park, a baseball field, and the company Hershey Hotel—"all the requisites of a modern American town," proclaimed Terry. "Typical of the larger American-owned mills of Cuba," was the way Charles E. Chapman recalled Hershey. "Everything about the place is spic and span,—good mill, ball-field, neat cottages, and attractive grounds."[4]

Mill towns symbolized the promise of the "American way of life," having to do with a high standard of living, good health, and well-being. From Hershey, Herbert Lanks wrote:

At the model plan in Hershey the company has done much to help its employees toward a higher standard of living. Comfortable modern homes have been built for them, making the town a model for the whole countryside. Various clinics as well as education and social services have been established to go with the physical improvements. A clear attempt has been made to raise the children to a higher standard of living, and the result was particularly noticeable in the appearance of the children on the streets. Whereas in other towns and villages there are always a number of ill-kempt street urchins begging for money, here all are well dressed, playing together in an orderly manner, and with respectful answers to questions when spoken to.[5]

Preston was a model New England community, with paved, curbed, and tree-lined streets, hotels, bungalow-style homes with lawns and gardens, possessing "all the accompaniments of a comfortable American town," wrote Terry. "I was proud of Preston for various reasons," exulted Sydney Clark, "all summed up in one, namely that the community was *kept up*. The streets were in repair, the dwellings neat and well painted. Each dwelling had a lawn and the grass was cut, the hedge trimmed. . . . Neatness, promptness, cleanliness, snap were obviously the planks of the Preston platform."[6]

To Cubans, the North American communities suggested an idyllic existence: comfort and convenience combined with leisure and luxury, a way of life that appealed to Cuban sensibilities. One visitor to the Francisco mill described 130 houses "with gardens, well-aligned and freshly painted," of "American construction of wood," and "everything very pretty, very poetic, very chic." The North American mill town of Rafael Estenger's youth appeared in his novel *El pulpo de oro* (1954): "The streets were straight and clean, without deep ruts or pot holes, without flies buzzing around in the shop or café." Walfredo Rodríguez Blanca described one community with "luxurious *bungalows*, surrounded by trees, with spacious patios, often a tennis court and manicured lawns on wide streets. . . . In some houses there are even pools and houses that are mosquito-proof."[7]

The North Americans' privileged existence stood in sharp contrast to the surrounding everyday Cuban reality. Disparities assumed many forms and often appeared in the most unremarkable manner. Rodríguez Blanca's allusion to screens was significant. Few fixtures associated with U.S. households seemed to rankle Cubans more than screens (*tela metálica*). Screens were as ubiquitous as they were conspicuous. They were, of course, quintessentially colonial, something that most Cubans could not have articulated explicitly but instinctively suspected. That screens were identified with privilege was certain. But the issue was more complicated. Screens suggested aloofness, a way that North Americans distanced themselves from the daily experience of living in Cuba. On arriving in Hormiguero in 1946, Katherine Ponvert found the "housekeeping facilities" in the *casa de vivienda* to be "backward, unsanitary, extravagant and generally unworkable." Ponvert did not hesitate: "I settled down to making plans for modernization. . . . My first act was to screen the whole kitchen wing, including the long open gallery leading from the dining-room to the kitchen. [Chef] Eulogio claimed this made it airless! But I insisted, preferring less air and thousands less flies." The North American houses in Preston, observed Luis Felipe

The Preston *batey* of the United Fruit Company, with the sugar mill in the background. (From Frederick U. Adams, *Conquest of the Tropics* [New York, 1914])

Rodríguez, had "a very disciplined look and very *snob*. The principal residences were enveloped by screens, probably to keep mosquitos from entering and prevent Liborio from looking in."[8]

The use of screens was one of many markers that delineated the great social distances between the "American way of life" and Cuban life. "Windows defended by screens," observed Armando Leyva, "where they lived very well indeed." Communities coexisted, often contiguously, but they were unmistakably different. Banes was divided into two well-defined sectors separated by the Banes River: the *barrio Americano* for United Fruit personnel of the Boston mill and the Cuban zone. Erna Fergusson, who visited Banes in 1946, described it as possessing "its own set-up for human living on a civilized scale." She continued: "It is always fun to visit one of these transplanted patches of the United States in a foreign land; they are so much alike, so altogether like home. Wide porches with screens, doors that really catch and shut tight, rows of high-backed rocking chairs; indoors all the home magazines, ping-pong tables, an out-of-tune piano, and a faint scent of antiseptic." Fergusson was quick to note the differences between what she called "company town" and "Cuban town." Company town reminded her of "any garden village at home with flower and vegetable beds, a lawn, clotheslines and a driveway." She observed "young people . . . coming home from tennis or swimming, older people from golf, pianos sounded from the houses and chatting from the screened porches." Fergusson concluded: "This was the way salaried folk live." Cuban town appeared "pleasantly colonial," where people gathered in the evening by "long windows with iron grills," inside "lighted rooms with tiled floors, tidies on pianos and tables . . . and painted or plaster saints on the walls." The homes in a company town were adorned with "hibiscus and butterfly bushes and rampant bougainvillea, royal purple or candent red"; the homes in Cuban town had "artificial flowers in tall vases."[9]

On visiting the North American zone, Alberto Quadreny wrote, he could hardly contain his astonishment: "It appears that we have entered another country. All the houses were beautifully constructed and well painted, . . . doors and windows covered with screens to keep out flies and mosquitos, with gardens, some of them as fine as those of Vedado and some parts of Havana and Marianao." Many of the schools and shops were "as good as in the capital," with railroad lines—"the finest railroads in Cuba"—that were "vastly superior to our public railroads." A month after Quadreny published his article, Rafael Rojas Domínguez wrote to *Carteles* about the other Banes. "I am familiar with all the zones that Quadreny writes about," Rojas Domínguez explained. "I do not know of any sewerage or of the paved streets that he mentions. Those cute houses with screens . . . no doubt exist, but the people who live there with all the comforts of modern life are the high officials. And how do 80 percent of the workers of those mills live? In miserable thatched huts, with sad and starving children, full of parasites and tormented by hunger: senior United Fruit employees live in those expensive houses at the cost of this misery."[10]

Carlos Forment also distinguished the "American Banes" from the "Cuban Banes." The American Banes was a community of "*chalets* and *bungalows*, each one surrounded by a garden, on wide cement-paved streets always meticulously maintained clean. Inside each home was found: a refrigerator, a radio, curtains, windows doubly protected by glass and screens, bathrooms and abundant water that runs through indoor faucets." Evenings were filled with "gatherings, visiting, music, cocktails, and week-end promenades." The Cuban Banes, on the other hand, created "the opposite impression," with "the cleanliness of the streets ignored, unpaved, homes with faded paint, a small park inadequate for the needs of the community, and a city government that can no longer continue with so many expenses."[11]

The power of the mill extended far beyond the confines of the batey, inevitably drawing on the surrounding communities to meet North American objectives. The extent to which this proximity and ensuing familiarity shaped Cuban life is incalculable. Indeed, at times the capacity of the mill to transform the human and material environment seemed unlimited. Corporate entities played an important role in disseminating North American cultural forms, all as a function of "doing business," to be sure, but with the net effect of introducing into remote areas of the island "modern" ways, to which countless Cubans became accustomed. Cuban-American Sugar transformed Puerto Padre. Before 1900, Carlos Martí wrote, the region was largely "unworked savannas and overgrown woods . . . upon which had been raised a prosperous and flourishing community, in whose confines are found all the necessities of modern civiliza-

Panoramic view of the Delicias residential zone, ca. 1920s. (Courtesy of the photographic archives, *Bohemia*, Havana)

tion." Martí marveled at the sights he beheld. "The lines of its streets and the constructions all corresponded to the present epoch of advance and industrial and urban progress," he affirmed. "All the sidewalks are made of cement. Public lighting is provided by the electrical plant at the Delicias mill." In Camagüey, Santa Cruz del Sur was practically a Francisco company town. Many of the 60,000 residents depended on the mill for employment. The company introduced electricity, operated an ice factory, and provided mail and telegraph service.[12]

The mill was arguably the single most dominant factor in the life of neighboring towns and cities. It created an environment that possessed the means and commanded the resources to refashion the moral and material world of the tens of thousands of men and women who resided within its reach. Mills supplied the jobs and the payroll on which many local residents depended. "The Atlantic Fruit Company is the staff of life for Sagua de Tánamo," commented a traveler in 1915. More than 5,000 local residents worked at Atlantic's Tánamo mill. Almost all employment in Santa Cruz del Norte (pop. 3,500) was linked to Hershey. Morón (pop. 86,000) was dominated by Cuba Cane. The town of Vertientes did not exist until the construction of the mill of the same name and on which it became totally reliant. United Fruit controlled three-quarters of the land of the *municipio* of Banes and half of Mayarí, a territory encompassing almost 300 square miles. Few, indeed, were the families of Banes (pop. 20,000) and Mayarí (pop. 61,000) whose livelihood was unconnected to United Fruit. The "entire country surrounding Nipe Bay," asserted an observer as early as 1912, "including the towns of Saetia, Felton, Preston and Banes, is owned outright by American corporations. . . . In other words, every human being in this district is either an employee of, or a contractor for the United Fruit Company or the Spanish American Iron Company."[13]

The mills had other effects, many of which reached deeply into local sensibilities. Perhaps it could not have been otherwise. The sugar company summoned into existence a moral order that required varying degrees of accommodation and emulation to achieve a livelihood and well-being. Cubans were obliged to deal with the mill on its terms. This meant, of course, acceptance of the dominant corporate modalities, including business methods and management style. But it implied more, for this comportment was necessarily related to a value system that insinuated itself into virtually all aspects of Cuban life.

In ways too many to calculate, often with consequences too complex to contemplate, the mill acted as a powerful transmitter of North American cultural forms. Holidays regulated much of the social life of the mill, including Christmas, Washington's Birthday, the Fourth of July, and Thanksgiving. Residents of the mill communities were drawn into North American commemorations, as well as parties, picnics, and parades and dances, banquets, and receptions. James Gould Cozzens incorporated his memories of Tuinicú at Christmas time in *Cock Pit* (1928), where "a full Christmas day" was observed with a party for children, "with an authentic Christmas tree, shipped at some expense from lands where Christmas trees grow," and "brilliantly decked and set about with small hills of toys." Local town dignitaries were frequently guests at these functions. The American Club of Preston invited local elites of Banes, Antilla, and Mayarí to participate in Fourth of July celebrations. Movie theaters operated in almost all mill communities, and almost all featured U.S. films. Chaparra had two theaters, which, Carlos Martí observed, were at "the high level of those in the capital with regard to films shown."[14]

Sugar corporations occupied an important position in local commerce. Many mills acquired foreign trade privileges through subports that received merchandise directly from U.S. suppliers from which it was distributed throughout the mill retail network. "As we now have our own port," reported the manager of the Manatí Sugar Company, "no doubt we shall import many goods, and after we complete the [railroad] line to Lagunas, we shall import considerable merchandise for Tunas and other points." Remote rural communities obtained access to foreign imports through company stores. Household products, consumer goods, clothing, tools, machines, and foodstuffs were distributed through retail outlets managed by sugar mills. George Braga recalled that the company store at Tuinicú was stocked with "saddles, French perfumes, liqueurs, whiskey, boots, bolts of cotton and silk, yokes for oxen, machetes, watches, live birds, beans, canned goods and rum." The volume of retail sales at Preston, mainly in the form of groceries, clothing, hardware, and household merchandise, was valued at more than $700,000 annually. United Fruit operated a total of seven retail stores dealing almost exclusively in U.S. products. The Cuban-American Sugar retail department at Chaparra received all its merchandise from the United States. "Nothing that these enterprises consume," commented a Cuban journalist regarding Cuban-American Sugar mills, "comes from the country, but is all imported from abroad." The combined retail sales of the three Cuban-American Sugar mills (Chaparra, Delicias, and San Miguel) exceeded $2 million annually.[15]

Local consumption patterns were transformed by the distribution of U.S. food products, beverages, clothing, and household goods. The company store was a place where "a ruddy-complexioned *yanqui* offered canned wonders with foreign names," wrote Dora Alonso. Katherine Ponvert remembered the retail business of Hormiguero: "When the farmers have some spare ready cash, they ride into the batey and buy their favorite fare—American canned goods. One delightful character of the batey, named Fundoro, told . . . with pride that his child didn't drink orange juice, he provided canned apple juice for him." Gonzalo Mazas Garbayo's short story "Mi señorita" (1930) alludes to one of the many ways these transformations occurred: "In the grocery store of the mill, the commercial instincts of the owners—to ingratiate the Americans—led to the substitution of guava bars for cans of marmalade bearing the name of a millionaire from Chicago."[16]

These changes were particularly evident in the towns surrounding the sugar corporations, including Banes, Puerto Padre, Palma Soriano, and Santa Cruz del Norte, among many others. "In no Cuban town is the American influence as noticeable as Banes," observed Carlos Forment. It was "a bilingual city," with retail stores selling U.S. products and catering to North American tastes. But Banes was also different in the attitudes and values of its citizens. "The Cuban people here offer an admirable example," wrote Forment, "influenced by the Saxon spirit, adopting its virtues of saving, of comfort, and confidence in their own effort." Contact with North Americans had "propelled Cubans toward success and self-improvement, in victorious competition of efforts that defines definitively our superiority when we resolve to improve ourselves."[17]

Local dependencies developed in other ways. In a budgetary environment where national expenditures to meet provincial needs were notoriously inadequate, municipal governments were always alive to the opportunity to obtain additional revenue. Mills often functioned as dispensers of resources and sources of patronage, as philanthropic agencies and agents of good deeds. U.S. companies made contributions for civic improvements, social services, and community charities, including orphanages, schools, clinics, and recreation. Many of them operated scholarship programs for college educations in the United States. Mills often subsidized public works. United Fruit donated $50,000 to the city of Banes for the construction of a sewerage system. Sancti-Spíritus honored the Tuinicú mill for the "philanthropic work" that "gave life and powerful support to the municipal treasury."[18]

The mill created an environment where North American structures prevailed, where the formal and informal networks of power and persuasion combined to define the terms of social interaction. The company could reasonably assume that philanthropy would be accepted with appreciation and repaid with gratitude, always implying a measure of indebtedness that could best be liquidated through acquiescence to the mill's interests. This was a way to preempt protest and prevent opposition. Years later Katherine Ponvert recounted her uncle's reaction to the attempts to form a labor union at Hormiguero:

> Don Elie felt justifiably that he had always paid the highest wages and given his employees the most benefits. Our batey families had always received free electricity, free ice and free milk. Countless men, their wives and children had been helped and financed through illnesses; their houses were maintained; their parks and surroundings, already beautifully landscaped, were kept up. We provided a primary school and a church service on Sunday at the chapel. Don Elie was truly and personally hurt, and I do not think he ever throughout the rest of his life quite recovered from the shock and disappointment of this movement.[19]

In *Vendaval en los cañaverales* (1937), Alberto Lamar Schweyer describes a strike against the "Goldenthal Sugar Company" when Mr. Goldenthal is urged by his niece to summon the authorities: "What do you care what the Cubans say? Forget them! Didn't you do what you could for them? Haven't you created ten scholarships for the children of your employees to study in the United States? Didn't you concern yourself every year when you went to Palmares to distribute toys to the children? If they are not happy with this, what more can you do for them?"[20]

Cubans gained access to the realm of the mill through different points of entry. An inexorable reciprocity linked the mill to neighboring communities, reinforced by local institutions, mutual needs, and common interests. Missionaries played an important part in this order. Many U.S. mills promoted evangelical projects and early enlisted the Protestant presence to serve the mill's interests. The United Fruit Company dispensed land, construction materials, and financial support to establish Quaker churches and schools in Holguín, Gibara, Banes, and Puerto Padre.[21] United Fruit also provided Methodists with three hundred acres, water, and electricity at no charge to establish the Agricultural and Industrial School at Guaro. Hershey sponsored a Presbyterian agricultural school in Aguacate. The Episcopalian Brooks Home and School in Guantánamo was subsidized by the Guantánamo Sugar Company. Episcopalians also operated a secondary school on the property of Constancia Sugar Company.

Under the circumstances, missionary schools were obliged to help integrate Cubans into North American structures and the larger normative system on which they were based. The Methodist school at Guaro received operating subsidies from United Fruit, Atlantic Gulf Sugar, and Bethlehem Steel, whose representatives served on the school board and determined policy regarding admission, curriculum, personnel, and so forth. Students were socialized to view as normal—and to survive and succeed in—an environment shaped by the primacy of North American interests, to which they could obtain access only after having mastered the appropriate skills and attitudes. The Methodist Agricultural and Industrial School taught English and introduced students to North American methods, thereby preparing them for employment with United Fruit. "The training afforded the boys," observed Irene Wright, "is intended to form them into competent employees." Students came to know United Fruit officials, recalled Edgar Nesman, the former director of the Methodist school, and "were looked upon kindly because they had graduated from the United Fruit–sponsored school." José Reyes completed his education at the Quaker school in Puerto Padre and was immediately hired by Chaparra. Among those in the graduating class of 1912–13 of the Quaker school in Banes was Fulgencio Batista, who promptly obtained a job in the railroad department of United Fruit.[22]

Missionaries occupied an anomalous place in this world. Whether by choice or by chance, they often found themselves serving the mill's interests. Protestant ministers and mill personnel mingled, they collaborated and reinforced each other's presence; in the process, large numbers of Cubans were drawn into the value system around which everyday life was experienced. "We are a little world to ourselves," reflected Quaker missionary Zenas Martin from Banes in 1902.[23] But it was also a complex world, an extensive network of mutual interests maintained in delicate equilibrium, governed by unstated assumptions and shared notions of what was normal. The realm of the mill was sustained by interlocking needs and overlapping interests. None of this was necessarily insidious, of course. Rather, people came to terms with reality and seized opportunities wherever they found them. It simply happened that the terms of that reality were largely defined by North Americans.

This is not to suggest that missionaries were never troubled by the anomaly of their circumstances. The defense of Cuban well-being often forced missionaries to confront the privileged place of foreign capital. North American hegemony was rarely monolithic, and even the consensual context of domination was subject to conflicting interests and competing needs. Many missionaries were decent men and women of conscience who played an important if unwitting role in discrediting structures inimical to Cuban interests.

This was a complex process. Missionaries in pursuit of their goals could not long remain indifferent to the excesses of North American hegemony and in the process contributed to subverting the power of its assumptions, although it is far from clear that this was their intent. Methodists seemed especially troubled by their association with United Fruit, unable to reconcile their commitment to the social gospel with the abuse and exploitation they confronted daily. The Reverend Paul Acker could not contain his disgust in Preston, "where we American business people draw the resources from the land, but do not identify ourselves with the people," adding: "The Cuban nationals live like animals and we are doing practically nothing to help them raise their standard of living." Richard Milk, director at Guaro, often complained of "the abuse of foreign business firms" and of "feeling daily and hourly the shadow of one of the world's greatest imperialistic concerns virtually dictating every movement and almost one's very thoughts." Edgar Nesman recalled "the righteous indignation" of the Guaro staff, "indignation at injustice, exploitation, immorality, and living conditions." Methodists wanted to "teach the students critical analysis," Nesman explained, "to think through social and economic problems, to be independent thinkers and reflect on social and economic forces governing their lives, and yet we realized that we were inhabiting a zone of United Fruit."[24]

On the other hand, many Protestant ministers were completely under the influence of the sugar company. Quaker minister Zenas Martin eventually became a prosperous *colono* for United Fruit. The Reverend Pedro Fernández of Puerto Padre worked as a banker for Chaparra. Methodist minister Rafael Verdecia Hernández, who taught English at the Centro Escolar in Preston, was transferred to the United States, where his three children—Samuel, Marta, and Carlos—completed their high school education. When Verdecia Hernández resumed his ministry in Cuba, Samuel obtained employment in the Agriculture Department of United Fruit and Marta and Carlos were hired by the Nickel Processing Corporation in Nicaro. The nature of this order is poignantly illustrated in the short story "Un pueblo del interior" (1924) by Sergio la Villa. The local Protestant pastor, a simple man, "was himself simply one more possession of the mill," writes Villa. "Cuban by birth, but educated in a college in South Carolina, he liked avocados because they were 'exotic' and was totally unfamiliar with the multiple ingredients of the Cuban stew (*ajiaco criollo*), to which he preferred *corn flakes*. And thus, adapted by education and custom to foreign habits, he lived happily among the American colony that had invaded his native region and that by exploiting it had changed its structure and spirit."[25]

Cubans were selectively admitted into mill management. The North American presence was a privileged one, possessing and preemptive, controlling and corrupting. The mill hired Cubans as technicians, functionaries, consultants, and attorneys, without whom the mill could not have functioned. The personnel records available indicate that thousands of Cubans were on the payroll in virtually every capacity. According to the office personnel registry for Tuinicú, they were employed as surveyors, physicians, machinists, accountants, inspectors, clerks, electricians, teachers, technicians, engineers, and artisans.[26]

Cubans who reached the upper levels of administration were typically educated in the United States, mostly men who had made the adaptations necessary to move among North American conventions with confidence and conviction. Mario G. Menocal, administrator of Chaparra, was a graduate of Cornell University. Ernesto Fonts y Sterling, administrator of Delicias, had studied at the New York Military Academy. Ignacio Valdés, the head of the Hormiguero office, attended a North American boarding school. Economist Fernando Berenguer wrote of one Cuban mill employee, "Americanized, full-faced and clean shaven, wearing blue-jean overalls and smoking a large pipe; Cuban by birth and a resident of the United States, where he had taken out American citizenship, of which he boasted. He looked upon other Cubans with disdain and was seen only associating with foreigners." In *Vendaval en los cañaverales*, Lamar Schweyer describes Márquez, the highest paid Cuban in the "Goldenthal Sugar Company," as a "native of Cienfuegos but educated in New York, a drinker of whiskey and a smoker of a pipe and an American citizen." In Luis Felipe Rodríguez's short story "Los subalternos" (1928), Rogelio Cárdenas of the "Yucayo Sugar Company" was the only Cuban permitted to attend the American Club: "He speaks English with its proper guttural and nasal accent. He orders his clothing from Chicago, smokes American cigarettes and is always seen with a copy of the *New York Times* in his pocket. This Cuban played tennis with the missies and properly consorts with his boss Mr. Norton. Rogelio Cárdenas . . . is profoundly convinced that to be Cuban is a misfortune, for he believes, like Mr. Grey, that Cubans are scoundrels and slouchers."[27]

Opportunities for advancement in the North American mill were often limited, mostly by virtue of nationality. Cubans in administration generally were lower or middle managers. The Cubans in the office of the "Goldenthal Sugar Company" were mostly cashiers, bookkeepers, and secretaries supervised by North Americans. "One could advance from bookkeeper to pay master and from cashier to chief of administration. But no further if one were Cuban."[28]

Cubans often reached positions high enough to see firsthand the world to which they were denied access. Pedro Menéndez Victorero studied in North American schools and completed a civil engineering correspondence program in the United States. Advancing rapidly in the Central Sugar Corporation, he reached the second highest position in the railroad department. "And it was here," Menéndez Victorero recalled, "that I began to feel the difference between being Cuban and being *yanqui*, for the latter were well paid, they were housed in comfortable homes, with all expenses paid, and further enjoyed all the privileges that were denied to Cubans, to such a degree that we were never invited to any of the social functions at the administrators' home (*casa de vivienda*) . . . despite the fact that we were very close to the American supervisors and despite the fact that we always presented ourselves correctly dressed and conducted ourselves in the manner that was expected." Félix Peña, the protagonist in "Los subalternos," second in charge in the mill office, "feels the humiliation of his subordination. And for that reason he had resolved to quit the office of the Yucayo mill. . . . But, because it is practical and necessary, he does not want to leave without acquiring experience in the Yucayo mill."[29]

Salary differentials were also a source of ill will. Cubans who inhabited this world occupied a complex position of ambiguity and ambivalence: privileged by local standards, subordinated by company norms. It would have been difficult to ignore the anomaly of their situation. What they often shared, albeit in different ways, was a sense of alienation, of being Cuban in Cuba, for which they were the object of discrimination.

Many Cubans developed intense hostility toward the North American sugar company, even as they depended on it for their livelihood and well-being, where they confronted daily conditions that set in relief the vast, often unbridgeable distances of being outsiders in their own country. In Pablo Armando Fernández's novel *Los niños se despiden* (1968), Lila revealed an abiding hatred of the Deleite mill: "Because it is not ours. Nothing of this is ours, not the land, not the mill, not the *batey*, not the cane, not even the people who aspire to be like them and who in a certain way are."[30]

This sense of lack of place, of not belonging, created a peculiar angst for Cubans, one of alienation and estrangement in their own land. The Nipe Bay region, observed Librado Reina in the short story "Resurrección" (1927), had "a concentration of foreigners," where "the one who was in the minority was the Cuban," where "the Cuban does not feel as if he were in his own country and where he participates in the ceremony of a liturgy that erodes national bonds and impoverishes."[31]

The discourse on nationality was often complicated by the understanding that to challenge the terms of the North American presence also implied the necessity to confront the role of Cuban complicity. So deep were the layers of Cuban participation, so structural was the Cuban integration into the North American normative systems, that to challenge the U.S. presence effectively risked evisceration of the social system.

Vast numbers of Cubans found themselves in complicated circumstances. They had joined with North Americans in collaborative relationships, often out of conviction, but also out of convenience, or need, or opportunism. Their participation in this order was vital, and, indeed, there was no other plausible explanation for the resilience of North American hegemony. That so many went along, however, did not necessarily mean that they approved of or were untroubled by their circumstances. Many were in positions similar to that of Pedro Menéndez Victorero, who had successfully completed a North American correspondence course in engineering and mechanical drawing but was obliged to work for a U.S. sugar company: "Despite the hatred of the situation of humiliation to which I was condemned and subject, due to the necessities of life, I went to work for an American company, the Caribbean Sugar Company."[32]

The mill closed in on itself and reproduced an idealized version of North American moral order: a world as self-contained as it was self-serving, exercising an authority that reached as far as its interests warranted. Its influence extended into the community through existing power relationships. Company administrators were often longtime residents of the island who over the years had developed extensive networks among local elites. Armando Leyva described North Americans in Banes, many who had been there for fifteen years, who lived well and who "notwithstanding their foreign nationality enjoyed the solid and felicitous friendship with the local families."[33] Such relationships were shaped by binding reciprocities and in the aggregate constituted a complex network made and maintained through patronage and the skillful allocation of resources.

Early on, the sugar company became an influential player in local politics. The mill could tip the balance of local power struggles, facilitate the ascendancy of one contender over another, and provide resources to those political groups favorably disposed to the company's interests. The mill often furnished campaign funds and delivered votes. In Estenger's *El pulpo de oro*, Henry Rawson, manager of the Nebraska mill, selects employee Raimundo Peñafuerte as candidate for a seat in the House of Representatives, "to defend the interests of the Company." The mill proceeds to hire local politicians to obtain the votes, offering to pay $10 for each vote cast for Peñafuerte. In the partly autobiographical novel *Cubagua: Historia de un pueblo* (1941), Justo González writes of the association between the administrator Mr. King and Patricio, the mayor of Cubagua: "Nothing contributed as much to make [Patricio's] political influence as decisive as the cooperation of the sugar mill. The many people he had helped place in jobs, the farmers who needed loans against their crops, for whom he had acted as intermediary, and all who feared that they might some day have need of his services, represented votes cast for him." No doubt James Gould Cozzens witnessed similar transactions during his residence at Tuinicú. His novel *The Sons of Perdition* (1929) depicts the "United Sugar Company" near the town of "Dos Fuegos," where Mayor Pepe Rijo was stamped by the "great label *United*":

> As Alcalde of Dos Fuegos, he felt, unprotesting, like the Company's property. He would never have been alcalde had [General Administrator] Mr. Joel Stellow wanted somebody else for mayor, Chief Man. Without any explanation, the *Administrador General* put a hand under Pepe, [and] lifted him above everyone else. . . . Pepe was made alcalde because he was too simple to offer any obstacle to Mr. Stellow. . . . Pepe knew. The mere mention of Mr. Stellow's name restored to him that sensation of his smallness, his helplessness, of the smallness and helplessness of all of them in the hollow of the Administrator's hand.[34]

The extent to which local officials were actually working in behalf of mill interests is, of course, largely a matter of conjecture. But that they were involved is indisputable: mayors and governors, town council members and senators, justices of the peace, magistrates, and judges, soldiers and policemen—all, at one time or another, were caught up in the plans and policies of the sugar mill.

Mills engaged in graft and corruption as the normal cost of doing business. The American Sugar Refining Company, for instance, made huge payments to obtain tax relief for the Cunagua and Jaronú mills.[35]

A powerful network of interlocking interests bound the mill to local officials. Politicians and power brokers frequently appeared on company payrolls. The Macareño mill hired the former director of customs at Antilla, Rafael Ramos, as sugar contractor and agent. Tomás Hernández Avila, former contractor and *mayoral* for Spanish-American Sugar, served on the *ayuntamiento* (town council) of Puerto Padre. Ladislao Guerra y Sánchez was elected mayor of Guantánamo after twenty-five years of employment with the Guantánamo Sugar Company. Chaparra administrator Mario G. Menocal became president of the republic; his successor, Eugenio Molinet, later served as secretary of agriculture under Gerardo Machado. Cuba Cane superintendent of mills Miguel Arango was the Liberal Party nominee for vice president. Fulgencio Batista had worked for the railroad department of United Fruit. President of the House of Representatives Orestes Ferrara and Senator Antonio Sánchez de Bustamante sat on the board of directors of Cuba Cane. Senator Luis Fernández Marcané was senior United Fruit counsel in Cuba. United Fruit's legal affairs was divided into two departments: one at Preston under Angel Navarro, a nephew of Marcané, and the other in Banes under Rafael Díaz Balart, the town mayor.[36]

Few, indeed, were the municipal and provincial politicians from northeastern Oriente unconnected to United Fruit. Another mayor of Banes, Delfín Campañá, had previously served as an office superintendent. Juan Arnais González had been mayor of Mayarí and inspector of labor accidents for the Department of Agriculture in Guaro before joining United Fruit in Preston. One brother, Mario Arnais Herrera, was a member of the Mayarí city council; another brother, Gabriel Arnais Herrera, was mayor of the Cuban sector of Preston. Oscar Quintín Silva Muñoz worked in the commercial department of United Fruit before assuming the post of secretary of the municipal administration of Banes.

Employment also served to expand and consolidate influence over local authorities through kinship networks. Ramón Sierra García, a Banes power broker, was the second chief of United Fruit's cattle division, a position from which he arranged jobs for no less than sixteen relatives—brothers, sons, nephews, and in-laws—as office clerks, guards, overseers, and cattle hands. Friends and family of local politicians were frequently hired as goodwill gestures and shrewd networking. Representative Santiago García Cañizares of Santa Clara obtained an office position at the Tuinicú mill for a member of his staff. The governor of Santa Clara interceded with Tuinicú for a job for a friend. In González's *Cubagua*, the mayor's son is hired as a company attorney fresh out of law school.[37]

In return, the mill could reasonably expect a wide variety of concessions and considerations, including favorable court rulings, exemptions from local ordinances, police and military assistance, special tax waivers, port regulation exemptions, and special import licenses. As early as 1915, the Department of Government in Havana received a formal complaint against the ayuntamiento of Banes that the municipality was not collecting taxes from United Fruit. "The complaint intimates," reported the *Havana Post*, "that the members of the city council have private reasons for being so considerate of the company's interests." In one Oriente municipality, all government officials, from the mayor to the justice of the peace, owned *colonias* that sold cane to the local North American mill. Charges by workers and small landowners of mill wrongdoing were routinely dismissed. "The administrator of the mill is always right in the eyes of the authorities," commented an observer.[38]

The sugar company was emblematic of almost everything that was wrong in Cuba's relationship with the United States: the powerlessness, the degree to which the mill constituted a world unto itself in which Cubans had no rights except those conceded by the company and to which existed neither remedy nor redress. "Cuba for the American mill owner," says the peasant protagonist in Raimundo Cabrera's novel *Sombras eternas* (1919), "is what it was for the old *peninsular*: a colony, a land for exploitation, and the Cuban a serf."[39]

Of course, the mill could not function unassisted. A vast, complex network of overlapping and mutually reinforcing interests involved local politicians and judges, army officers and police officials, religious leaders and community authorities in the company's interests. The mill reigned over a domain of immense proportions, an entity responsive only to the logic of the market and accountable only to the authority of shareholders. "The sugar mills are independent states within the Cuban State," concluded Carlos Forment. "It appears inconceivable to me," affirmed José Comallonga of the National Association of the Sugar Industry, "that one of those corporations possesses 165,800 acres cultivated like oceans of cane, without there being in so vast a territory a single *bohío*, not one Cuban, without a single native *colono*, and hardly any Cuban employees; with its own sub-port, buying everything directly; its own customs collector, with its own police force. In sum: everything, everything, everything American. Is this not a State? Is this not a foreign State on Cuba soil, connected to Cuba only physically?"[40]

The image of the North American sugar company was thus fixed in the Cuban imagination. Years later Marcial Ponce reminisced about Preston: "The laws of the country did not apply there. It had its own laws and one had better be very careful about obeying them." "The law?" asks the protagonist in Lamar Schweyer's *Vendaval en los cañaverales*. "There is no law here except the Company," proclaims Nida in Cozzens's *Son of Perdition*. "In the sugar mills only the will of the representative of the company rules." The mill, explains the narrator, "has managed to convert itself into a foreign fiefdom in the heart of the island." In effect, "They can do whatever they want to the Cuban on his own land." Indeed, seignorial analogies were commonly drawn to describe the world of the sugar mill. Henry Rawson of the Nebraska mill in Estenger's *El pulpo de oro* is said to "live like a king in the sugar zone." Virginia Schofield, a former resident of a United Fruit enclave, made a similar comparison: "United Fruit Company officials lived like nobility and kings." Methodist minister Edgar Nesman agreed: "They ruled as if they dominated a kingdom. Authoritarian, totalitarian, everyone and everything under their control. A colonial aristocracy. And all administered out of Boston."[41]

The image of the mill outside and above the law assumed a powerful resonance in the narrative on nationality. Because the North American presence was so visible, and so visibly privileged, it aroused resentment and revulsion. The reach of the sugar company extended over tens of thousands of Cubans, who were subject to its authority without recourse. Such a presence challenged the very concept of nation: huge areas of the island beyond the reach of national authority. This reality evoked the idea of a *Cuba irredenta*, of expanses of national territory needing to be returned to Cuban sovereignty. Sergio la Villa characterized the North American mill as "a type of American ship anchored on land, with Cuban servants and crew, but with an American officialdom." Walfredo Rodríguez Blanca concurred: "Effectively, we have on this island a Republic and various private 'territories' belonging to North Americans."[42]

THE PRESENCE OF THE NAVAL STATION

The establishment of the U.S. naval station on Guantánamo Bay in 1903 created a North American enclave of another type, one that also transformed daily life for the surrounding communities. The impact was direct and dramatic and most keenly experienced in the cities along the southeastern coast, including Santa Cruz del Sur, Manzanillo, and Santiago de Cuba. But it was in Caimanera, on the western side of Guantánamo Bay, and in the city of Guantánamo, north of the base, that the naval station dominated Cuban life. Caimanera and Guantánamo acquired their definitive form through their principal economic activity: servicing the naval station. The regional economy developed specifically around the needs of U.S. service personnel, which meant, too, that the ties between local communities and the naval station were structural and reciprocal. The base provided the major source of revenue on which the livelihood and well-being of thousands of households depended. The arrival of the fleet announced boom times. During the 1920s the city of Guantánamo (pop. 15,000) was visited annually by an estimated 25,000 servicemen, whose business, one observer affirmed, "contributed mightily to the trade of this city." A small café operator reported that earnings increased from $200 daily with ordinary base personnel to $1,000 a day when the fleet dropped anchor.[43]

Merchants prepared orders and acquired stock timed with the arrival of the sailors and marines. In 1927 Guantánamo suffered a severe blow when the fleet commander confined servicemen to the naval station. "Business in Guantánamo City is stagnant . . . ," noted the U.S. consul in Santiago de Cuba, "many firms being particularly bad off because they stocked up in anticipation of the Fleet's visit . . . and were left with goods unsold." When the following year the fleet wintered in Puerto Rico, the effect on Guantánamo and Caimanera was devastating. "Bills in Caimanera involving considerable sums," related an observer in 1928, "are usually paid 'when the fleet comes in,' and merchants now find themselves heavily stocked. Financial ruin faces smaller merchants. Rooming houses will suffer, farmers in the country will be unable to dispose of produce and cigar dealers are hurt. Hurt too are car owners and bootleggers."[44]

Much of the commerce of Guantánamo depended on the naval station. Local merchants and retailers regularly supplied fresh fruits and vegetables to the base commissary. "Base personnel," reported one local observer, "constitute one of the most permanent and plentiful sources of livelihood of the city of Guantánamo." When the town learned that the *Missouri* was arriving, Pedro Suárez recalled, "all the businessmen were overjoyed. At one time the *Missouri* represented the presence of five thousand Marines in town who generated all the earnings for the length of three or four months." Most retail shops stocked North American products. Local establishments bore distinctly U.S. names, including the Washington Hotel, the Kentucky House, and the Roosevelt Hotel. So did bars, nightclubs, and cafés: the Gold and Silver Bar, Pan-American Club, Roof Garden Bar, Arizona Club. The city of Guantánamo "is becoming a Monte Carlo," *La Lucha* declared as early as 1905.[45]

The naval station became an integral part of daily life in Guantánamo. Hundreds of dependents of base personnel established residence in the city, and North American ways took a firm hold. Guantánamo was "the most Americanized city in the whole of Cuba," proclaimed the *Times of Havana* in 1958:

> The money that goes daily into the vaults of the several local banks is more than half Uncle Sam's currency, left here by personnel on their frequent visits for entertainment or shopping from the sprawling U.S. Naval Base. . . . Most shopkeepers and tradesmen—and even street urchins and professional beggars—can hold their own in conversation with visiting gobs and marines who flock into town by the hundreds and thousands each week-end. Unlike any other Cuban city with a mere seventy thousand population, Guantánamo provides all sorts of entertainment, from side street honky tonks to modern night clubs and a gambling casino. In all of them one is more likely to hear English spoken than the native Spanish.[46]

The impact of the base on Caimanera was especially pronounced. Among the 7,000 Cuban residents in Caimanera there lived an assortment of North American social types: unsavory individuals such as hustlers, gamblers, pimps, and bootleggers as well as a community of retired naval personnel who remained to operate bars and cafés. Naval contractor George Gillings and retired chief petty officer Jim Beauzay ran a local hotel. During Prohibition ex-naval personnel in Caimanera conducted a flourishing bootlegging trade with the naval station, especially the service personnel of the fleets. An average 2,000 to 3,000 servicemen visited Caimanera weekly. Caimanera could not but yield to the logic of its location, as a small, desultory fishing village of several hundred households was transformed to serve the needs of the naval personnel—"an extension of American territory," pronounced *Bohemia* in 1938. Gambling houses and casinos multiplied; bars and brothels proliferated. "Caimanera is the Barbary Coast of Cuba," wrote George Wally, "where American sailors on pass from only across the bay . . . stay overnight to make whoopee in sailor fashion."[47]

But mostly Caimanera was squalor, a mixture of the seamy with the sordid, a place of rural wretchedness and misery. It lacked hospitals and schools. It was often without adequate water supplies and was almost always a place of questionable sanitary conditions. On more than one occasion naval authorities declared the village off-limits due to health concerns. Caimanera received the dubious distinction of being identified in Ripley's *Believe It or Not* as one of the filthiest settlements in the world. Few who visited the place disagreed. "The entire town of Caimanera beggars description as to its moral and sanitary defects," asserted U.S. consul H. M. Wolcott in 1917. "The streets are mud holes during the rainy season and are entirely without public light service. Close by the docks and scattered among the few places of legitimate businesses are saloons and houses of prostitution of the most degraded type. There is no place of amusement or recreation here that is not an immoral influence." Thirty-five years later Methodist minister Ira Sherman arrived at substantially the same conclusion: "Caimanera is literally the most God-forsaken town I've ever seen."[48]

The economy of Caimanera relied largely on its cafés, cabarets, and casinos, its bars and brothels. More than eight hundred women worked as prostitutes in nearly fifty brothels. Most brothels were named after different states in the union—among them, "Maryland," "New York," and "Florida." More than thirty bars catered exclusively to U.S. servicemen. One district of the town, known locally as "Brooklyn," was reserved for officers and petty officers. "No mere gob or marine may set foot in . . . [the] aristocratic dance hall," commented an observer. "One has to be 'brass bound,' as they say in the navy . . . for the enlisted man gets 'his' on the other side." Ira Sherman walked the streets of Caimanera one night in March 1952 and counted no less than three hundred sailors in the houses of prostitution. "It really is sickening," he wrote at the time, "and certainly such as to make one rather ashamed to be an American in this community." Years later Sherman remembered it vividly: "Caimanera as a whole depended to a preponderant degree on the patronage of the U.S. navy people in the bars and houses of prostitution which gave the casual visitor to the town the impression that there was virtually nothing else there at all. It seemed that there was very little employment of any kind in the town itself not directly related to

U.S. servicemen from the Guantánamo Naval Station arriving at Caimanera on shore leave, ca. 1940s. (Courtesy of the photographic archives, *Bohemia*, Havana)

those bars and houses, although I suppose there may have been a small grocery or two."[49]

North American servicemen became something of a permanent fixture. Often thousands of sailors and marines, on liberty after months at sea, were determined to let loose and plunge into dissipation, often with predictable results: barroom brawls, street fights, and conflicts with local police. Former marine James Manning recorded his experiences at the naval station during the late 1940s in fictional form:

> Damn kids. Why don't they keep them on their cursed ships? These Latin ports, these unobtrusive people are not prepared for the hordes of sailors and marines pulling liberty in their front yards. Young men at their sexual pinnacles, pulled out of the States for the intrigues of foreign ports with their infatuated imaginations. Having their first excursions from behind the barriers of moral restrictions drawn by parents and home towns, then these Caribbean ports, with their basic potentials to please the appetites of these soaring Phaethons with gnawing insides, equal to moral chaos and civil lethargy.[50]

The economic impact of the base affected virtually all Cuban households. The receipts generated by servicemen on leave made a huge contribution to the local economy. By the early 1950s, moreover, the U.S. Navy had developed into one of the largest local employers. About two thousand residents of the city of Guantánamo worked on the base as carpenters, mechanics, electricians, plumbers, painters, welders, truck drivers, gardeners, seamstresses, cooks, and maids. The base generated a payroll of almost $4 million annually.

The proximity of the naval station to Caimanera and Guantánamo set in sharp relief the disparities between Cuban communities and the North American zone. This was a world to which thousands of Cuban workers gained access daily as they traveled back and forth between two starkly different environments. The naval station was equipped with a hospital, swimming pools, a 27-hole golf course, tennis courts, bowling alleys, basketball courts, and an outdoor motion picture theater—the whole of which resembled a resort. The base was an "extension of American territory," observed one Cuban journalist, "where the American life-style prevails, with all the comfort, conveniences, the sanitary precautions, ventilation, discipline, and order required in such a location. . . . Hundreds of homes are in perfect geometric alignment, each one with ample gardens decorated profusely with roses and flowers, with very clean streets, illuminated at night with a profusion of lights. The Cuban can visit that zone only after having been declared healthy and having his baggage checked, almost as if he were arriving to another country of scrupulous sanitary regulations." On the other hand: "Near the naval station the city of Guantánamo vegetates, feted and dirty, the other side of the coin: dressed in rags. The town gives the impression of disaster, depression, and squalor. . . . It is because of the decadence of spirit and the environment of miasma that so much filth can coexist with so much garbage."[51]

The abject moral and material plight of Caimanera belied the Cuban claim to membership among the modern nations of the world. It was not that similar conditions did not exist elsewhere in the republic. They did, of course, and in some locations were worse. What made Caimanera different was that it was both visible and visited by North Americans, thus serving as the basis on which the North would judge Cuba. "Does it not occur to our leaders," Herminio Portell Vilá asked plaintively in 1954, "that the naval station serves as a window through which hundreds of thousands of North Americans have seen a Cuban community mired in backwardness, without hygiene, and in misery? Caimanera has more than 10,000 residents who live in shocking conditions of poverty and backwardness, virtually at the doorsteps of a North American community on Cuban soil in which hygiene, comfort, and civilization are the characteristics of the towns of the United States."[52]

THE EVANGELICAL MISSION

North Americans established their presence throughout Cuba, from east to west, in all provinces, in the cities and in the countryside. They arrived as individuals, as families, often as entire communities; as investors, industrialists, and entrepreneurs; as landowners and miners; as merchants and manufacturers; sometimes as small companies and often as large corporations. They arrived as distributors of wares and dispensers of ways in their person, self-possessed and single-minded in their purpose. Most of all, they arrived with an unshakable confidence that the future belonged to them. Few Cubans could see any reason to doubt their certainty.

The North American presence assumed many forms, not everywhere the same, of course, and not always with the same effect. But the pattern of the process was the same. The presence of North Americans always seemed to change things. They seemed capable of rearranging the material elements and moral imperatives of everyday life around their own needs, to which everyone else was subsequently obliged to negotiate accommodations as a means of well-being and livelihood.

What gave North American cultural forms their particular resonance and, indeed, their enduring resilience was that they took hold locally, precisely because they seemed relevant to daily life as experienced in even the most remote communities. Protestant missionaries were particularly successful in establishing a local presence. Churches and schools appeared almost everywhere; most towns and villages had at least one active preaching station. "Every considerable village in Cuba," an observer commented as early as 1901, "had at least one Protestant minister . . . with, generally, two or three women auxiliaries." Missionaries were dedicated, determined, and driven. They suffered adversity and privation, often toiled under wretched circumstances, yet persisted. Methodist missionary David Carter wrote poignantly of his experiences:

> I have worked to the limit of my strength. I have endured hardships not a few, I have traveled thousands of miles in second-class Cuban cars. I have slept in dirty, vermin-infested beds. I have eaten unwholesome and unclean food in wretched little Cuban fondas. I have spent weary hours toiling through the deep mud of Cuban roads on old poor beasts scarcely able to carry me—the best that could be hired—reaching my destination so stiff and sore I could scarcely dismount and my hands and face blistered by the sun. I have threaded my way through dense forests scratched by briars and thorns and covered with mud. I have forded swollen streams so deep and dangerous that the muddy waters came up midway the saddle skirts.[53]

Missionaries arrived at the onset of the military occupation in 1898, initially in scattered numbers and subsequently in successive waves; they represented the principal Protestant denominations in the United States. They staked out spheres of influence in all provinces and in almost all *municipios*. Methodists began their work in Havana, then extended their activities into Matanzas, Cárdenas, Cienfuegos, Manzanillo, and Santiago de Cuba. Presbyterians located in Havana, Artemisa, Cárdenas, Bejucal, Caibarién, Camajuaní, Remedios, San José de los Ramos, and Placetas. Episcopalians proclaimed the island a missionary diocese, with a resident bishop in Havana and mission stations in Matanzas,

A Baptist church in Cabaiguán, n.d.
(Courtesy of the Biblioteca Nacional José Martí, Havana)

Bolondrón, Unión de Reyes, Isle of Pines, and La Gloria. Baptists fanned out into all six provinces. Congregationalists moved into Havana, Guanajay, San Antonio de los Baños, Guanabacoa, and Matanzas. Disciples of Christ established themselves in Havana and Matanzas. Quakers spread along the northern coast of Oriente into Puerto Padre, Holguín, Gibara, and Banes. Pentecostalists set up missions in Havana and Cárdenas.

In fact, so many denominations arrived in Cuba at one time that evangelical competition quickly got out of hand. In 1902 an interdenominational conference convened in Cienfuegos to impose order on these missionary projects.

HAVANA, Cuba. La Primera Iglesia Presbiteriana.
The First Presbyterian Church.

A Presbyterian church in Havana, n.d. (Courtesy of the Friends Historical Collection,
Guilford College, Guilford, N.C.)

A Quaker schoolhouse in Banes, 1925. (Courtesy of the Friends Historical Collection, Guilford College, Guilford, N.C.)

The resulting comity plan established zones of influence for the larger denominations: Northern Baptists were allotted Oriente and Camagüey, while Southern Baptists received Las Villas, Matanzas, Havana, and Pinar del Río. Quakers and Methodists divided eastern Cuba between them. Presbyterians and Congregationalists settled in the western provinces. Episcopalians operated in Havana, Matanzas, and Santiago de Cuba.

Early evangelical efforts centered on humanitarian projects, specifically philanthropic work and social programs. Missionaries entered an environment of dire need, dispensing goods and services where little of either were readily available. They sponsored relief work and organized extensive programs to aid victims of the war. They distributed tools and supplies, seeds, and agricultural equipment to farmers. Methodists delivered food supplies to reconcentration camp victims in Cienfuegos and opened the Industrial Asylum for orphans in Cárdenas. Presbyterians founded an orphanage in Cárdenas. Episcopalians organized shelters in Havana, Guantánamo, Matanzas, and Bolondrón to care for orphans and dispense food supplies to reconcentrados. Virtually all of the principal denominations dispatched physicians and nurses and established clinics and dispensaries where medical services were provided at little or no cost.

Protestants also organized schools. Indeed, perhaps no single undertaking so fully engaged the material resources and moral resolve of the Evangelicals as education. They offered private education at modest cost and often at no cost at all. At the time, the public school system operated in varying degrees of disarray and disrepute; public schools were understaffed and underfunded, if they existed at all. Missionary schools thus met real and immediate needs. Moving into all municipios of the island, they provided instruction from kindergarten through high school, vocational and technical training—in agriculture, industry, and mechanical trades—and business schools and four-year colleges. Their projects included schooling for boys and girls of all ages, adult education, programs for the handicapped (the blind and deaf), boarding schools for children of the well-to-do, and asylums for orphans.[54] Methodists established a network of *colegios* for girls in Matanzas (Irene Tolland College), Marianao (Buena Vista), and Cienfuegos (Eliza Bowman), as well as schools in Camagüey (Pinson), Havana (Candler), Santiago de Cuba (Wesley), and Guaro (Agricultural and Industrial School), and elementary schools in Havana, Santa Clara, Vedado, Camagüey, and Santiago de Cuba. Presbyterian Robert L. Wharton founded La Progresiva in Cárdenas, modeled on the U.S. academic curriculum. Other Presbyterian schools opened in Havana, Caibaguán, Caibarién, Güines, Nuevo Paz, and Sancti-Spíritus. Episcopalians launched the Cathedral School (Havana), the Brooks Home and School and the Sarah Ashurst Episcopal High School (Guantánamo), La Trinidad (Morón), and the Industrial School (Matanzas). In 1905 the Church of Christ opened McClean College (Havana) and El Discípulo College (Matanzas). Southern Baptists founded the Cuban-American College (Havana), the Woman's Training School (Santa Clara), high schools in Colón and Batabanó, and elementary schools in Mariel, Colón, Cruces, Trinidad, Cárdenas, Sancti-Spíritus, and Consolación del Sur. Northern Baptists organized the Colegio Internacional (El Cristo) for boys and girls and elementary schools at Manzanillo, Baracoa, and Guantánamo. The Adventists founded the Antilles High School in Santa Clara. Quakers established Los Amigos school in Holguín and a network of elementary schools and *colegios* in Banes, Antilla, Gibara, and Puerto Padre.

Missionary educators often replicated the race-driven curricula strategies common in the United States. The large number of blacks in Limonar shaped the curriculum of the local Episcopalian school. "Because of the prevalence of blacks in this locality," Bishop Albion Knight explained in 1907, "I have selected this point as the place to locate an industrial school for the negroes modelled on the plan of Hampton, Tuskegee, and Lawrenceville."[55]

Missionaries consciously assumed the role of agents of civilization and progress, dedicated to moral regeneration and the introduction of new habits of sobriety, thrift, industry, and discipline. "For nearly 400 years Cuba was isolated and had no actual contact with progressive ideas or ideals," Bishop Knight affirmed in 1916. The encounter was rendered as a contest between "two differ-

A Quaker Sunday school class, Gibara, 1910. (Courtesy of the Friends Historical Collection, Guilford College, Guilford, N.C.)

ing ideas of civilization": the conception of civilization "that belonged to the period of the explorers in the time of Columbus" and the idea of "civilization which prevails today in the most enlightened countries in the world." One missionary wrote of the "by-products of the Gospel in Cuba," chief among which was "the creation of a purer civic atmosphere." This new environment called for "self-control, civic integrity, truthfulness and honesty in business, . . . desire for purer politics, [and] opposition to Cuban vices of sensuality and gambling." The relationship between education and moral uplift was palpable. "The ignorance of the people on all lines is appalling," declared Quaker May Mather Jones from Gibara in 1901, "and the standard of morals for this and other reasons is very low." The Reverend E. P. Herrick wrote eloquently about preparing the "children of the Antilles" for "the duties and responsibilities of citizenship." Missionary Howard Grose described Cubans as "ambitionless and ignorant and improvident," with "indifference to pursuits that demand patient investigation, hard intellectual effort, or scientific accuracy," whose condition had "kept [their] mind free from any anxiety as to making provision for the future." Grose recounted a conversation with a local farmer who, when asked why he did not cultivate more of his land, replied: "What is the use? When I need money I pick off some bananas and sell them. I get for them twenty or twenty-five dollars, which lasts me a long time. When I need more money I pick more bananas." Concluded Grose: "What a distance they must be lifted, if they are to reach a real Christian civilization!"[56]

The immediate impact, and indeed the larger significance, of the evangelical mission was more than a change of religious faith. "Conversion" also implied a change of behavior and new attitudes toward life and living. Both were mutually reinforcing. The power of Protestantism lay in the fact that it was spiritual as well as practical, theological as well as temporal, otherworldly as well as worldly. The transition from colony to republic, accompanied as it was by the expansion of U.S. market forms, placed missionaries in an important transitional role. They provided still one more way that the normative foundations of the postcolonial reality were rearranged around North American hierarchies. The goods and methods they introduced anticipated the messages and meanings they proclaimed, and vice versa. Missionaries arrived bearing representations of the North; as cultural artifacts and consumption preferences, they served as advocates of a moral economy that celebrated commodity and commerce and in the process advanced the idea that individual mobility and material well-being were within everyone's reach. Missionaries self-consciously imagined themselves as harbingers of progress and modernity, a state of mind that had less to do with religious affiliation than with national identity. May Mather Jones was eloquent about the conditions in Gibara, "the place where . . . Columbus, on his first voyage, landed." She continued:

> But, alas! How little advancement has been made! The people are almost a hundred years behind the times. The Cuban farmer brings his produce to market in a large double basket thrown over the back of his horse something after the manner of old fashioned saddlebags. . . . The coming of the Americans and the introduction of American ideas has caused a ridiculous blending of the ancient and modern, for instance, side by side with the above we have an electric light plant and a telegraph office. . . . But in spite of his slow, plodding life, the average Cuban is anxious to learn and this makes the outlook hopeful, though his mind is yet as uncultivated as the hills and plains where he makes his home.

Northern Baptists set out explicitly "to mold the [Cuban] character." This endeavor presumably involved the elimination of differences whereby Cubans were to be assimilated into a new moral order in which all would be judged by a single standard. "The missionary work represented by Protestant missions is the best hope for the future of Cuba," affirmed Howard Grose. "There must be a deal of uplifting, of change, of improvement. The moral standards must be raised, and new ideals must be introduced. The Cuban people have generations of bad training and no training to outgrow, new habits to form, new customs to adopt, before they can reach the condition of civilization which they ought to have."[57]

Much of evangelical education drew on the belief that discipline and self-possession would produce uplift and upward mobility. Missionaries served as conduits of market culture, offering the promise of participation as the reward for self-restraint, central to which was education: a tangible opportunity for self-improvement. This was the central premise of educational strategies and the proof of the promise. The prospects for evangelical success turned on the capacity of this experience not only to make the new postcolonial reality comprehensible but also to make it negotiable and accessible.

Educational programs represented one of the more important ways that North American ways spread across Cuba. Schools provided moral authority for individual action and beliefs and promised empowerment at a time when change and transition were the most salient facets of the postcolonial environment. Education offered a means of inclusion in the new order, a way to obtain preparation and the necessary skills to compete.

The sources of the missionary appeal were many and mixed; indeed, the appeal itself was different to different people at different times. The fact that many children attended Protestant schools was itself both product and portent of the new order and suggests the degree to which Evangelicalism was perceived to offer economic security and social mobility. Indeed, for vast numbers, Protestant schools offered the most readily available means to obtain preparation to negotiate ordinary encounters with the new order. This became one more way to make sense of change and get through the period of transition. Moreover, Protestant education figured prominently in Cuban survival strategies: it provided a way to cope with change and get through the period of transition. Missionaries could endeavor to remake the everyday world of Cuban communities and in the process integrate individuals into the larger value system around which postcolonial Cuba reorganized. James Gould Cozzens inhabited that world briefly as a tutor on the Tuinicú sugar estate, an experience that later found narrative form in *Cock Pit*: "Those Protestant ministers whose duties were never done, whose manifold activities and good works kept their churches in a turmoil of classes, benefits and uplifting programs all the week through, and whose obligations extended to the last details of the individual lives of their flock."[58]

But this framework also provided a standard by which to measure the efficacy of capitalist structures on their own terms. The promise of the paradigm could be judged within the moral and material standards suggested by the evangelical project. That the evangelical church became so involved in everyday life would have important implications over the long run. Perhaps without realizing it, and certainly without meaning to, the very missionary project that integrated Cubans into the new market culture also enabled them to envision alternative possibilities and shape expectations derived from the ethic of hard work and good deeds. In its most successful form, it could create the incentive to participate—to motivate the farmer to grow more bananas, for example. But expectations unmet could serve as a powerful source of mobilization. The failure of market mechanisms to accommodate Cuban needs fully and fairly could generate discontent and dissent and eventually discredit the very structures they were designed to celebrate.

Interests sometimes converged, but almost as often they clashed, frequently at the same time, always as an element central to the Cuban–North American encounter. Much of the U.S. purpose was designed to incorporate Cubans into the new order, to help Cubans define themselves and their needs to facilitate their integration into the structures of North American material culture. Certainly the evangelical church shaped aspirations, but it also fostered needs that, in the end, there was no way of meeting. Without fully recognizing the inherent limitations of dependent capitalist structures of an export economy to accommodate Cuban interests, however, they set in motion the forces that would contribute to discrediting market relationships. Cubans acquiesced to this agenda largely in the belief that it promised personal fulfillment and material well-being. But it is unclear whether North Americans gave much thought to the implications of their success.

The Protestant mission was a complex undertaking. It was, to be sure, preeminently concerned with the spiritual, with salvation and the hereafter. But it also understood the need to address temporal matters of livelihood and the material conditions of the here and now. At a deeper level, and only partially distinct from spiritual salvation, missionaries aspired to nothing less than reordering the value system of everyday life: to engage Cubans in dialogue whose terms they sought to control and whose structure transmitted the assumptions of North American moral hierarchies. "To us, who study the Cuban situation from a moral standpoint," explained the Reverend J. Milton Greene, "it seems that the radical need of this people is the introduction of a new religious system under which a remedy can be found for intellectual stagnation and which will substitute for merely external rites and ceremonies . . . of the heart, the discipline of character and the regulation of daily life." The Protestant promise arrived embedded in the concept of moral uplift, insinuated in the idiom of the market as a means of material well-being. The formulation was central to the credibility of the evangelical purpose and the long-term success of the church. "It is difficult to see," observed J. Merle Davis in 1942, "how a virile church can ever arise in an economic order that gives employment for less than half of the year."[59]

North American missionaries were fundamentally engaged in a project of transformation, the central premise of which was to confront Cubans with their defects of character and the deficiencies of their condition and offer a remedy to both through redemption as an act of rearranging the normative hierarchies of everyday life. Howard Grose wrote of the evangelical success in "changing lives," introducing new "moral standards" by which Cuba would acquire "a new conscience, a new consciousness, a new creed." Reverend Greene frowned on prevailing child-rearing practices, because "the children grow up lawless, willful and selfish, without the first element of self-control in their character." Cubans revealed a "lack of intellectual initiative, . . . the absence of industrial conscience, of personal integrity, of domestic purity, of mutual confidence, and of social morality." Quaker Benjamin Trueblood wrote of Cubans "kept in ignorance" who "pass their time lounging, sleeping, . . . smoking, gambling at cards, and in various pleasures, often of the lowest animal kind." Yet he believed that the island had a promising future if "the right influences" were brought to bear. Baptist Henry Morehouse agreed. Cubans had to be taught "how to behave themselves," he insisted, and, using the analogy of the "blasting of rock from the quarry," he added: "They must be hammered and shaped for their respective places and assembled and arranged for service according to the architect's design." Richard Milk of the Agricultural and Industrial School wrote explicitly of "the changed life [as] the basis for all religious and moral progress." The Reverend David White argued that the evangelical church "must not think solely of converting a man to a new outlook on life, but must create new possibilities of living for him." The church was enjoined to "put before these people new creative tasks" and "reach out beyond Sunday giving each day both content and meaning." Methodist Edgar Nesman introduced a 4-H Club to provide "suitable character building experiences." Students were expected to undertake projects for which they were "personally responsible." Activities expanded in other directions: "The club is now in the process of learning how to hold a democratic meeting," Nesman wrote in 1954. "It is exciting to watch the progress of youngsters brought up in an authoritarian culture as they learn to work together, each holding some responsibility for the success of the group."[60]

In the end, missionaries were less successful in converting Cubans into pious Protestants than in disseminating cultural forms of the North American market system. It was not only that missionaries sought to bring Cubans to a new faith. They were also determined to change the way Cubans lived. They sought to transform the nature of the Cuban condition by reordering the material circumstances and redefining the moral framework of daily life. Quakers and Methodists organized industrial programs to promote crafts and cottage industries to make Cubans "independent of the one-crop system." Emphasis was given to production and marketing: "to teach students in school and people in their homes to make things that can be sold." The Methodist Agricultural and Industrial School sought to promote "changes in understanding, attitudes, and skills." Its major objective was to prepare youth "for adequate social and spiritual adjustments to meet the complex problems of modern life" and "for democracy by trying to practice democracy at all levels within the school structure." The Colegio Presbiteriano in Güines adopted a curriculum designed to neutralize the "marked individualism of the Cuban temperament" by promoting a "co-operative spirit" among the children. Students were organized in cooperative societies to manage departments, from which they derived income and experience. "What purpose is there in religion if it doesn't change the lives of people?" asked the Reverend Carroll English in 1955. "If it changes people, it changes culture."[61]

The evangelical mission envisaged spiritual rebirth as the source of material well-being and specifically to improve the living standards of all Cubans, especially among the urban working classes and rural poor. Families of modest social origins were among the most receptive to the evangelical message. In *Cubagua*, Justo González—himself a Methodist minister—set his memories in a fictional town where "all the converts were of humble condition." This depiction was corroborated by the Reverend Arthur Gray, who described Cuban congregations as belonging "to what is called the 'working class.'" Students at the Agricultural and Industrial School were "very largely young people of impoverished family circumstances." Merle Davis estimated that workers, farmers, and the unemployed constituted 30 percent of church membership, followed by housewives (29 percent) and students (23 percent): "a constituency . . . drawn almost entirely from the lower middle class, the very poor, and the humblest ranks of society."[62]

Protestant ministers were directly concerned with the material condition of their congregations, without which the spiritual message could not reasonably be expected to possess relevance or resonance. This certainly was conceived as a subtext of the evangelical message—a strategy, in a word. But sufficient evidence exists to suggest that it was received as the dominant text, in which case it was not dissimilar to subversive narrative. Under certain conditions, evangelists could direct Cubans to specific forms of self-awareness of their condition and almost always around North American notions of well-being and good living. The power and, indeed, the promise of the evangelical project were related directly to the degree to which Protestants summoned a vision of moral uplift and material upswing. North American Protestants invited Cubans to join a righteous community based on spiritual tranquility and material well-being, on justice and equality. The emphasis was on free will, on ideals of civil liberties and civic virtues, on natural rights and individual responsibility.

This was very seductive stuff and could not but have been received with anything less than expectation, although it was not always clear how these formulations would improve the Cuban condition. Baptist minister M. N. McCall alluded to abject conditions in the countryside, to the "forgotten man of Cuba," whose "government has talked about improving his living conditions but has done almost nothing." McCall pledged to "take a message of hope and salvation which changes and lifts all life out of such conditions." Bishop Albion Knight drew the moral explicitly along class lines. "The native people who are being reached," he acknowledged, "belong usually to what is ordinarily known as the lower class of people." More to the point: "The lower class realizes that there has been something wrong in the order of things that such conditions should exist, and thus with this class there is more or less of discontent and inquiry, and their minds are more open and ready to receive new truths which may be presented." Baptist Una Roberts Lawrence was categorical about the role of evangelical education in motivating "the Cuban . . . to advance his own interests" and predicted: "Education creates a desire for better living conditions, makes boys and girls discontented with old ways of doing things, rouses their minds to wanting some opportunities better than the past offered their parents. Contact with the world will help bring it about, and certainly the awakening power of a vital form of Christianity will play no small part in it."[63]

The evangelical mission thus summoned Cubans to aspire to goals that often were simply unattainable. Hopes were raised and expectations created, then dashed. Episcopal bishop Hiram Hulse gave clear meaning to the evangelical purpose in a 1930 sermon in Havana. "Charity is no longer the contemptuous tossing of a coin to a beggar," insisted Hulse, "but becomes an attempt to put him on his feet and make it possible for him to earn his own living. Christian civilization begins to grow with its different ideals from heathen civilization. The state is seen in its true light as intended for the protection of the individual and so every man has a chance to make the most of himself and not be exploited by the more powerful." Years later, in almost exactly the same terms, Methodist Edgar Nesman recalled the emphasis of sermons "not on giving alms to beggars, but upon assisting the beggar to get on his own two feet to provide for himself, to take charge to do something about his lot." In fact, under the conditions prevailing in Cuba, the missionary exhortation to achieve self-sufficiency as a means of self-fulfillment was ill-adapted if not ill-conceived, something that did not begin to become apparent until the 1950s. Nesman realized that perhaps "the way the young person was taught is not really practical for the conditions that actually exist. . . . Closely related to this is the fact that there is just no economic opportunity. . . . No land is available and there are no other professions open, especially without capital."[64]

Vast numbers of Cubans had been intellectually and ideologically shaped by the power of rational argument and positive knowledge, by principles of equality and equity, but were increasingly obliged to experience life as a contradiction between the professed evangelical worldview and the real world of material and social inequality. In many ways, Cubans were prepared to inhabit a world that did not exist—not, at least, in Cuba—but whose oft-proclaimed superiority was routinely transmitted as an article of faith. The extent to which the evangelical imperative may have contributed to discrediting the prevailing order may never be known. But the countless thousands who embraced the Protestant vision were obliged to contemplate their disappointment and consider alternative ways to act on their newfound sense of the possibility of a better life. That Cuban Protestants were so fully represented in the revolutionary struggles of the late 1950s is, of course, suggestive.

Information on church membership is incomplete or otherwise unavailable and hence must remain largely speculative. About 350 organized churches, and at least as many chapels and preaching stations, spanned the island. By the 1950s several hundred thousand Cubans had joined a total of 500 congregations, by which time Protestant ministers outnumbered Catholic priests and Protestant churches and chapels outnumbered Catholic churches.[65]

By midcentury, too, even as the Catholic church continued to be dominated by Spanish priests, Cubans filled positions of prominence in the clergy of almost all other denominations, including the Baptists (Moisés González, Antonio Martínez, Mario Casanella, Anastasio Díaz), Methodists (Carlos Pérez Ramos, Manuel Viera, Angel Fuster), Presbyterians (Raúl Fernández Ceballos, Sergio Arce, Alfonso Rodríguez Hidalgo), and Quakers (Juan Serra, Maulio Ajo, Manuel Garrido de Catalá). Of the total 23 Episcopal clergymen, 21 were Cuban. Cubans were especially well represented among Presbyterians, Baptists, and Methodists. Of the total 1,592 Protestant religious workers, more than 85 percent (1,367) were Cuban. In 1940 Merle Davis reported: "The Cuban Evangelical movement is notable for the small number of its foreign missionary workers and for the withdrawal of a large proportion of missionary evangelistic workers from the field with the turning over of this side of the work to Cuban leadership."[66]

The emergence of a Cuban clergy had far-reaching implications. Most immediately, it transformed the composition of the ministry. But more important, it produced a new pluralism. Cubans appropriated the evangelical narrative as a moral and ethical imperative by which to address the national condition. This is not to suggest that Cubans created a new church. They did not. Rather, they transformed the discursive framework of the evangelical mission and in so doing created a new source of power, one dedicated to a national purpose and directed by Cuban leaders. They moved into positions from which to identify injustices and articulate grievances and thereby to create new forms of dissent and provide new ways of popular mobilization. Merle Davis was not the only person who believed that Cuban dedication to *patria* could be a valuable means to defend the church without considering that devotion to the church would also serve to defend patria.[67] Cubans may have indeed adopted the evangelical vernacular and conducted themselves according to its practical dictates. But it was a framework that allowed Cubans to engage North Americans on their own terms and to define Cuban needs as different and distinct.

Evangelicalism had gained adherents from precisely those Cubans who detected in the message of the mission the means of uplift and improvement—just as North Americans had hoped. Cubans adopted and altered the evangelical text to the point where it had acquired special resonance, relevant specifically to daily needs. Under no other circumstances could the Protestant narrative have so seized the popular imagination.

BASEBALL AND BECOMING

The expanding North American presence also was accompanied by new sports and other recreational forms. The Jockey Club was founded in 1899 and included on its board of directors U.S. generals John Brooke, Fitzhugh Lee, William Ludlow, and Adna Chaffee and Cubans Perfecto Lacosta, Saturnino Lastre, Mario G. Menocal, and Rafael de Cárdenas. Two years later John Diamond opened a bowling alley on Zulueta and advertised: "Ladies and gentlemen are cordially invited. Absolutely American style."[68] Havana acquired three skating rinks: the Novelty Skating Rink, the Broadway Skating Rink, and the American Roller Rink operated by the Richardson Ball-Bearing Skate Company of Chicago. Auto racing began in 1903 with the founding of the Cuban Automobile Association under the leadership of Enrique J. Conill, Julio Blanco Herrera, Ramón Mendoza, and Honoré Lainé, all former residents of the United States. Two years later the Cuban club affiliated with the International Association of Automobile Racing. Havana was selected to host international winter races, attracting drivers, automobile manufacturers, and visitors from around the world.

In the years that followed, clubs centering around North American sports proliferated across the island. The Almendares Yacht Club was chartered in 1901, followed a year later by the Havana Sports Club. Also in 1902 the Vedado Tennis Club—all the names were in English—was founded by Cubans who had taken up tennis during previous residence in the United States. The Vedado Tennis Club expanded into baseball, basketball, and football.[69] The Riverside Yacht Club sponsored such activities as swimming, handball, and ice skating. Other sports clubs were organized in Cienfuegos, Matanzas, Varadero, Sancti-Spíritus, and Santiago de Cuba. In 1916 President Mario G. Menocal appointed Richard Grant athletic director of the University of Havana, which organized a football team under the direction of U.S. coach James Kendrigan. The university and the Vedado Tennis Club inaugurated annual football games, and by the 1910s the University of Havana football team regularly played U.S. college teams.

Sports took hold among all classes, men and women, in the capital and in the provinces. Team sports engaged all sectors of Cuban society, social clubs as well as professional associations, schools, and corporations. The team became one of the most prevalent forms of Cuban social organization, endowed with the capacity to create membership and promote community.

Baseball recaptured public attention immediately after the War of Independence, when professional teams—Habana, Fe, Almendares, Marianao, Santa Clara, and Cienfuegos—resumed play. Public attendance increased. Sunday ball games in Havana routinely attracted five thousand fans weekly. Quaker missionary Zenas Martin expressed dismay at the sight of "thousands of the people" attending the Sunday baseball game in disregard of the Sabbath. The crowds attending ball games in Vedado in the summer of 1900 strained the capacity of the new trolley system, on one occasion causing a near riot. "The management knows that there are always a lot of baseball games going on in that district on Sundays," complained the *Havana Post*; "they should have put on an extra car or more to accommodate the crowd."[70]

In neighborhoods throughout the capital, children took to the streets to play ball. In 1901 the *Diario de la Marina* denounced the "plague" of youngsters playing baseball on the city streets: "Repeated complaints arrive to this office concerning the real scandals occurring on public streets by boys playing baseball. The laws of the city prohibiting those games are ignored and the police appear to be incapable of enforcing them." Ball games were held anywhere open space permitted, and by 1910 the mayor of Havana ordered that baseball be confined to ball parks. "This action," reported *La Lucha*, "tends to avoid the frequent small games seen on the streets and in vacant lots in the city, which often result in bodily harm to passers-by and damage to property, and also to reduce the number of vagrants who devote their energies to the sport during the day instead of being more gainfully employed."[71]

Baseball expanded rapidly on the island. In Santiago de Cuba, Baptist missionary H. R. Moseley attributed the decline of Sunday school attendance to the sport. "Since the introduction of Sunday baseball . . . ," he complained in 1901, "we find it difficult to hold the boys." Driving across Cuba in 1909, Ralph Estep reached the small town of Macagua (pop. 907): "Being Sunday, it was a day of celebration. There had been a baseball game in which the Pinks beat the Blues. Cuba is baseball crazy. Each country team has dainty cotton flannel suits, which they put on after the game for the purpose of parading around the town." Missionary Una Roberts Lawrence made a similar observation: "Baseball has started on a wave of popularity that promises to place it in the forefront of the amusements of the island. In the afternoons you can drive in any direction from Havana and in the open spaces near the villages and towns there will be a ball game in progress."[72]

Amateur clubs increased. Some teams adopted patriotic names such as Libertad, Patria, Demajagua, Patriota, Independencia, and '98. Provincial and municipal teams proliferated. So did the school teams, from the University of Havana to secondary and elementary schools, private and public. Teams formed among the various branches of the armed services. Fashionable social clubs of Havana and in the provinces organized baseball teams and established leagues. Corporate teams included Cubaneleco (Cuban Electric Company), Club Teléfono (Cuban Telephone Company), and Club Ferroviario (railroad employees), as well as Partagás and La Corona (individual cigar factories). Many North American corporations sponsored company teams and promoted trade league play. Teams were formed by the Juraguá Iron Company, the Nicaro Mines, and the Cuban Mining Company. Almost all of the larger sugar mills sponsored company teams. Children's teams also multiplied. The Asociación de Béisbol Infantil (Cubanitos) consisted of 1,600 boys between the ages of nine and thirteen organized into sixty teams. It did indeed seem likely, as one observer commented in 1954, that Cuba had more baseball teams per capita than any other Latin American country.[73]

Baseball leagues increased almost as rapidly as teams, among them the Professional League, Semi-Professional League, Social League, Inter-Provincial League, Youth League, Commercial League, Confederation of Cuban Workers (CTC) League, Popular League, National Amateur League, and Mining League, as well as provincial and municipal leagues, including the Liga Popular in Las Villas and the Liga Municipal of Santiago de Cuba. The Sugar League, which consisted of mill teams, produced some of the fiercest rivalries in Cuban baseball, such as Delicias versus Chaparra and Senado versus Lugareño. Katherine Ponvert recalled the intense team rivalry between Hormiguero and Soledad.[7]

Corporate ball clubs were designed to serve the interests of sponsoring companies. North Americans adopted the conventional wisdom that baseball could promote hard work, cooperation, and discipline—the traits most esteemed by employers. Certainly company teams improved morale and goodwill, and, of course, a successful team contributed to a favorable public image. Teams also promoted corporate identity and loyalty to the company. Manuel Rionda considered a $100 donation to the Elia mill baseball club as a business expense. The Sugar League provided a welcome distraction during the summer months of inactivity, idleness, and unemployment associated with *tiempo muerto*. Rionda expressed concern about dead time between harvests, when "the men having nothing to do and no other topic to discuss they naturally talk about their imaginary grievances and create discontent." Baseball was an effective way to pass idle time. "As the laborers will have a great deal of time this Dead Season," reported the administrator of the Manatí mill in 1928, "we have decided to prepare a large field in front of the railroad station so that they can have their base-ball and foot-ball games." Some U.S. officials believed that baseball could serve as a means of social control. James Sullivan, the U.S. minister in Santo Domingo, wrote:

> The American national game of baseball is being played and supported here with great enthusiasm. The remarkable effect of this outlet for the animal spirits of the young men, is that they are leaving the plazas where they were in the habit of congregating and talking revolution and are resorting to the ball fields where they become widely partisan each for his favorite team. The importance of this new interest to the young men in a little country . . . should not be minimized. It satisfies a craving in the nature of the people for exciting conflict and is a real substitute for the contest on the hill-sides with the rifles, if it could be fostered and made important by a league of teams in the various towns in the country . . . [this] well might be one factor in the salvation of the nation.[75]

Baseball also represented economic opportunity. Players recruited from the mill labor force were paid over the course of the dead season. The players of the Tuinicú Stars baseball team, for example, received five dollars per game.[76]

Many players developed their skills sufficiently to play in the professional leagues in Cuba. Some reached the major leagues in the United States. Pedro Gómez played for the United Fruit Company before moving up to the Cuban professional leagues and eventually to the Washington Senators, by which time he had adopted the nickname of the mill from which he came: Preston. Orestes "Minnie" Miñoso had played for the España mill team, Tony Taylor for the Alaba team, and Miguel (Mike) Cuéllar for a mill team in Santa Clara. Antanasio (Tony) Pérez was among the last ballplayers from the Sugar League to reach the big leagues after 1959.

Company teams could also foster player solidarity and worker unity. The evidence is scattered and largely anecdotal, and far too much information is lacking to determine with any precision the meaning of company teams for employee players. Teams did give workers the opportunity to come together, travel, and discuss topics of mutual interest. Manuel Fernández Chaveco, a United Fruit Company ballplayer, recounted the ways that baseball facilitated union meetings: "You know we couldn't meet in public, so we had to meet during our baseball games. We'd hold a big game and during it hold our planning meetings."[77]

Baseball held the promise of mobility and the possibility of success and stardom, a way up and out of poverty. Many Cuban big-league players shared backgrounds of poverty and hardship. Edmundo "Sandy" Amorós came from a "family [that] was poor and illiterate and worked in the cane fields." Miñoso recalled hard economic times when his family was forced to take "refuge in what could only be described as a shanty in the sugar cane areas of La Lonja." "Our baseball has acquired the status of a basic industry," commented Jess Losada in 1946, "like sugar cane, coffee, and politics. . . . For the new generation there are two goals, two ambitions: a seat in the legislature, where the *guanábana* is always ripe, or a flannel suit of the ballplayer that is valued across the continent at dizzying prices." In Juan Arcocha's novel *Los muertos andan solos* (1962), Rogelio had pitched in the Amateur League for La Progresiva. "He would have liked to play professional baseball," the narrator explains, "and indeed was even scouted by the Washington Senators." But his arm gave out, and he could no longer pitch: "Rogelio had always thought that was the greatest opportunity of his life and he had lost it. He would have liked to have lived in the United States and earned a great deal of money."[78]

And, indeed, much of baseball in Cuba was connected to and sustained by baseball in the North. The Cubanitos developed institutional ties with similar organizations in the United States, including the Little League, the Pony League, and the Babe Ruth League. Cuban teams were often incorporated directly into U.S. professional baseball leagues. The Havana Cubans club was organized by Clark Griffith and Roberto Maduro in 1946 to play in the Class B Florida International League. Cuban baseball made an important advance in 1954, when

Maduro established the Cuban Sugar Kings franchise in the AAA International League.

Connections with organized baseball in the United States assumed many forms and worked powerfully to promote affinity and identity with U.S. baseball. Exhibition play expanded. The arrival of major league clubs always provided excitement and expectation to Cuban baseball. Local fans delighted in watching home teams play—and especially defeat—major league clubs. And Cuban teams often acquitted themselves in impressive fashion. In 1908 the Cincinnati Reds lost seven out of eleven exhibition games to Habana and Almendares, and the next year Connie Mack's world champion Philadelphia Athletics lost four out of eight games to the same teams. Also in 1909 the American League champion Detroit Tigers dropped eight out of twelve games to Habana and Almendares. In the years that followed, almost all of the major league clubs played in Cuba—often during spring training games, sometimes in postseason tours—including the Cleveland Indians, Brooklyn Dodgers, St. Louis Cardinals, Boston Red Sox, Pittsburgh Pirates, and New York Giants.

Cubans came to know North American major leaguers firsthand, for many competed in Cuba during the off-season. Celebrity ballplayers often made well-publicized and highly remunerative appearances, especially during the tourist season. In 1920 Babe Ruth received $2,000 a day for ten days to play several exhibition games with local ball clubs. Increasingly, too, major leaguers played for Cuban professional leagues during the off-season. "Winter ball," as it was known in the United States, allowed North Americans to gain experience and perfect their skills on high-caliber teams. Some of the most successful major leaguers played winter ball on Cuban teams, including, for Cienfuegos: Brooks Robinson, Carl Erskine, Gene Mauch, Sal Maglie, Billy Herman, Don Zimmer, and Joe Black; for Marianao: Roy Campanella, Jim Bunning, Charlie Lau, and Don Newcombe; for Almendares: Tommy Lasorda, Dick Williams, Bob Allison, Roger Craig, Gus Triandos, Jim Grant, Bobby Bragan, Bob Skinner, Billy Hunter, and Willie Mays; for Habana: Ken Boyer, Bill Virdon, Hoyt Wilhelm, Dick Sisler, Wally Moon, and Eddie Kasko. Tommy Lasorda recalled his playing days in Havana fondly—"they took their baseball very serious. Very, very seriously."[79]

Contact with North American clubs and ballplayers changed the character of Cuban baseball. Most directly, it confirmed that Cuban ballplayers could compete at the major league level. They learned that they could hit Christy Matthewson and strike out Ty Cobb. Knuckleballer José Acosta struck out Babe Ruth three times. The major leagues became the standard by which Cuban performance was measured, the standard to which Cuban ballplayers aspired, and the standard that Cuban fans came to expect and demand.

Cuban ballplayers early appeared on many major league rosters. Perhaps more than any other single factor, it was the growing presence of Cuban players in the major leagues that made U.S. baseball so much a part of Cuban life. The list was long and impressive: in the 1920s and 1930s it included Adolfo Luque, Manuel Otero, Pedro Dibut, and Rafael Almeida (Cincinnati); José Acosta and Jacinto Calvo (Washington Senators); Armando Marsans and Angel Aragón (New York Yankees); Emilio Palmero and Joseíto Rodríguez (New York Giants); and Miguel Angel González, Oscar Tuero, and Pájaro Cabrera (St. Louis Cardinals). Others followed in the 1940s and 1950s: Sandy Amorós (Brooklyn Dodgers); Roberto Estalella, Conrado Marrero, Pedro Ramos, and Camilo Pascual (Washington Senators); Minnie Miñoso (Chicago White Sox); Tony Taylor (Philadelphia Phillies); and Willie Miranda (New York Yankees). "The rush of Cubans to the big leagues may cause an appeal for an amendment to the immigration laws," quipped New York sports columnist W. O. McGeehan in 1919 after the Cardinals, led by pitcher Oscar Tuero, had defeated the Giants. "St. Louis and Cincinnati would be out of the league altogether if it were not for their Cuban allies. And to think that Spain had Cuba for all those years without even developing a ballplayer good enough for the Philadelphia Athletics." In fact, so large was the influx of Cubans that White Sox general manager Frank Lane predicted the displacement of American youth from the major leagues. "There is one thing about the Latin-Americans from the Caribbean sector," Lane affirmed in 1952, "they not only love to play, but they're hungry for money. They prove it on the field. They really hustle. I'm afraid the boys in this country have seen too much soft living. They drive cars before they're out of high school. Everything is handed to them on a platter. They no longer have that driving power, motivated by the fierce determination for gold and glory."[80]

Baseball culture had indeed taken hold on the island, the most noteworthy feature of which was the creation of a vast and knowledgeable baseball public. Fans in Cuba followed major league pennant races and the World Series with at least as much enthusiasm as fans in the United States. Major league teams and players were well known and big-league baseball was daily sports news in Cuba. From the conservative *Diario de la Marina* to the communist daily *Hoy*, papers filled with news about the major leagues, including AP and UPI wire stories of the previous day's games, complete with game summaries, box scores, and league standings. In the 1930s radio programming inaugurated live broadcasts directly from the United States. Havana station CMW (Voz de las Antillas) provided a play-by-play broadcast of the 1934 World Series. In the 1950s Cuban television began live broadcasts of major league games.

The fact that Cuban players were often members of pennant-contending teams and appeared in World Series games provided additional excitement. The remarkable sixth-inning catch by Dodger left fielder Sandy Amorós in the seventh game of the 1955 World Series off Yogi Berra, with no one out and the tying runs on base, and then doubling Gil McDougal at first base and clinching the winning game (2–0) of the first Dodger World Series victory, made Amorós a hero in both Brooklyn and Cuba. "The most spectacular catch of the series," Roy

Camilo Pascual (Major Leagues, 1954–71) played for the Washington Senators, Minnesota Twins, Cincinnati Reds, Los Angeles Dodgers, and Cleveland Indians. (Courtesy of the National Baseball Hall of Fame Library and Archive, Cooperstown, N.Y.)

Campanella later declared. For one brief moment, the World Series victory belonged to Cuba. "Amorós, hero of the year," proclaimed *Carteles*. *Bohemia* published a full-page photograph of Amorós over the caption: "His performance in the World Series has produced intense joy in our nation." His deeds signified a "triumph and corroboration for the quality of our sports" and "assure him a place of honor in the history of the pastime of Cuba."[81]

Life in Cuba often focused entirely on the U.S. World Series. The autumn of

Orestes "Minnie" Miñoso (Major Leagues, 1949–64) played for the Chicago White Sox, St. Louis Cardinals, and Washington Senators. (Courtesy of the National Baseball Hall of Fame Library and Archive, Cooperstown, N.Y.)

1932 was a time of deepening political crisis in Cuba. The anti-Machado forces had assassinated Clemente Vázquez Bello, president of the Senate; the government responded with the murder of Representative Gonzalo Freyre de Andrade and his two brothers, Leopoldo and Guillermo. Representative José M. Aguiar was gunned down at his front door. October also saw the World Series between the New York Yankees and the Chicago Cubs, and Cuban attention seemed transfixed not on the national crisis but on the national pastime. Mariblanca Sabas

Pedro "Pete" Ramos (Major Leagues, 1955–70) played for the Washington Senators, Minnesota Twins, Cleveland Indians, New York Yankees, Philadelphia Phillies, Pittsburgh Pirates, and Cincinnati Reds. (Courtesy of the National Baseball Hall of Fame Library and Archive, Cooperstown, N.Y.)

Alomá could hardly contain her indignation. "We are irresponsible!" she thundered. "The bodies of five prominent Cuban figures are still not even buried, and I hear many men of my country heatedly debate the possibilities of the New York American League team against the Chicago National League team. Five assassinations right here in the capital that have not in the slightest diminished the

Edmundo "Sandy" Amorós (Major Leagues, 1952–60) played for the Brooklyn Dodgers and Detroit Tigers. (Courtesy of the National Baseball Hall of Fame Library and Archive, Cooperstown, N.Y.)

extraordinary enthusiasm of the Cuban fans. Days that should be given to mourning have been spent by the radio that is transmitting the World Series."[82] Nothing changed in the ensuing years except that pennant races and World Series play claimed even greater attention. "Business comes to a halt for a few hours each day of the series games," deplored the *Times of Havana* in 1958; with a sense of relief, it added: "Now that the World Series has ended life can be expected to return to normal both in the United States and Cuba." Fidel Castro would recount to Dan Rather on the CBS documentary "The Last Revolutionary" (July 7, 1996) how, during the height of the insurrection against Fulgencio Batista, the guerrilla commanders halted operations to listen to the final game of the 1957 World Series between the New York Yankees and the Milwaukee Braves.[83]

The Cuban connection to U.S. baseball certainly transformed the character and quality of the sport in Cuba. But over the longer run, it also contributed to changing the nature of baseball in the United States. Not all of the best Cuban players reached the major leagues, of course. Nationality could obscure racial categories but only up to a point, beyond which considerations of color prevailed. And it was precisely color that barred many of the greatest Cuban ballplayers from reaching the major leagues, including José Méndez, Martín Dihigo, Cristóbal Torriente, and Luis Tiant Sr. "It is clear," feature sports writer Manuel F. de la Reguera observed in 1936 after the Cuban defeat of the Cincinnati Reds and St. Louis Cardinals in successive exhibition games in Havana, "that racial prejudice prevents many Cubans from playing on the best teams of the majors. Their quality is clearly demonstrated in the exhibition games when the color line is removed and their talents are fully manifested."[84]

Baseball directly involved Cubans in the complexities of North American race relations, a process fostering multifaceted collaborations that eventually contributed to changing the very character of baseball in the United States. Barred from the big leagues, black ballplayers in Cuba and the United States joined together to sustain a level of quality equal to the standards and traditions of the major leagues.[85]

African American players could not help noticing the growing Cuban presence in the major leagues and immediately understood the implications. The Cuban success in reaching the big leagues suggested possible strategies to overcome racial barriers in the United States. The presence of Armando Marsans and Rafael Almeida in the major leagues, commented the *New York Age* in 1911, "is of great significance and will have great bearing on the future destiny of colored men in baseball"; it predicted: "With the admission of Cubans of a darker hue in the two big leagues it would be easy for colored players who are citizens of this country to get into fast company." The *Age* noted that "the Negro in this country has more varied hues than even the Cubans" and suggested that "until the public got accustomed to seeing native Negroes on big leagues, the colored players could keep their mouths shut and pass for Cubans."[86]

In fact, African American ballplayers did contemplate the possibility of reaching the big leagues as Cubans. Catcher Irwin Sandy played with the Providence Grays of the National League and with Baltimore of the American Association as "Vicente Nava." On several occasions management encouraged talented black prospects to assume Cuban identities. One club in the New York State League offered outfielder John Donaldson $10,000 to visit Cuba, adopt a Spanish name, and report to the club as a Cuban. Quincy Trouppe later told of being encouraged by a scout to go to "a Latin country and learn Spanish," suggesting that speaking Spanish would ease his way into the major leagues. John Bud Fowler, released from white teams in the early 1890s, experienced difficult times on the barnstorming circuit. "It was hard picking for a colored player this year," he wrote in 1895, "I didn't pick up a living; I just existed. If I had not been quite so black, I might have caught on as a Spaniard or something of that kind." In the 1976 film version of *Bingo Long Traveling All-Stars*, Charlie Snow (Richard Pryor) studies a "Spanish phrase book" and practices speaking a heavily Spanish-accented English. "From now on," he announces midway through the film, "I am going to be known as Carlos Nevada"; "I am going to break into the majors as a Cuban!"[87]

"Cuban" was also incorporated into the identity of several clubs of the old Negro Leagues. One of the first professional African American ball clubs called itself the "Cuban Giants." Organized in 1885 by the waiters of the Argyle Hotel in Babylon, New York, players sought to pass for Cuban at a time of deepening racial tension in the United States. "The team was sensitive to mounting racism," wrote Janet Bruce, historian of the Kansas City Monarchs, "and as 'Cubans,' clowning in a gibberish Spanish on the field, they were safer from white fans when they defeated white teams." Sol White, who played for the Cuban Giants, recalled that when the "first team began playing away from home, they passed as foreigners—Cubans, as they finally decided—hoping to conceal the fact that they were just American Negro hotel waiters, and talked a gibberish to each other on the field which, they hoped, sounded like Spanish."[88]

Other teams followed this practice. The Cuban X-Giants was organized in 1896 by former Cuban Giants. There were also the Long Branch Cubans, An-sonia Cuban Giants, Genuine Cuban Giants, Havana Red Sox, and Jersey City Cubans. Sid Pollock, the owner of the Indianapolis Clowns, organized the Cuban House of David club managed by Ramiro Ramírez. In the original novel *The Bingo Long Traveling All-Stars and Motor Kings* (1973) by William Brashler, the team played "the big teams like the Detroit Cubans" and often contemplated barnstorming across Cuba.[89]

Cuban teams, for their part, Anglicized their names and enjoyed considerable success competing against teams in the Negro Leagues. In 1899 the Cuban Stars inaugurated annual summer trips north, which continued through the 1930s. Other teams included the All-Cubans, Stars of Cuba, Santiago Stars, and Havana All-Stars. The Cuban team in the Florida International League was known by its English name, the Havana Cubans, as was the AAA International League team, the Cuban Sugar Kings. At various times Cuban teams joined the National Negro Baseball Association (1920), Negro National League (1922), and Eastern Colored League (1923). The National Negro Baseball Association consisted of the American Giants (Chicago), Chicago Giants, St. Louis Giants, Monarchs (Kansas City), ABCs (Indianapolis), Marcos (Dayton), and Cuban Stars, desig-

1—Gonzalo Sanchez, catcher.   2—Sam Lloyd, short stop.   3—Ricardo Hernandez, outfielder.   4—Preston Hill, outfielder.   5—Grant Johnson, short stop y second base.   6—Luis Padron, right fielder.   7—J. H. Magrinat, outfielder.   8—Carlos Moran, third base.   9—Camilo Valdes, mascota.

JUGADORES DEL "HABANA."

A team portrait of the Habana Baseball Club with African American players, 1911. (Courtesy of the Library of Congress, Washington, D.C.)

nated as a traveling team and consigned to play its entire season on the road. The Eastern Colored League also incorporated a Cuban club, the New York Cubans, managed by Alejandro Pompez, made up primarily of Afro-Cubans, including Martín Dihigo, Luis Tiant, Ramón Bragaña, Silvio García, Lázaro Salazar, and Francisco Correa.[90]

Cubans also appeared on the roster of Negro League teams. José Méndez, Cristóbal Torriente, Martín Dihigo, José Colas, José Burgos, Luis Márquez, and Luis Tiant, among others, played variously with the Memphis Red Sox, Chicago American Giants, Pittsburgh Crawfords, Birmingham Black Barons, Homestead Grays, and Kansas City Monarchs. And African American ballplayers played winter ball in Cuba. Among the members of Cuban teams were John Henry Lloyd (Philadelphia Giants), Grant Johnson (Brooklyn Royal Giants), Bruce Petway (Chicago Leland Giants), Joe Williams (Royal Poinciana), Dick Redding (Lincoln Giants), and Frank Duncan (Philadelphia Giants). This experience allowed many African Americans to become full-time professional ballplayers and earn a living during the off-season. Cuba also offered greater social space within and across ambiguous racial boundaries. This was not a racially egalitarian society, to be sure, but it stood in sharp contrast to the rigid and explicit color barriers that prevailed in the United States. Pitcher Max Manning recalled one trip to Havana: "We got on the train in Philadelphia, and we had to stay in a colored only compartment. We couldn't ever leave to get some food. When we finally arrived in Cuba, we were treated as heroes. We could stay at any hotel, eat at any restaurant."[91]

In an integrated environment African Americans received confirmation that they could play at least as well as whites. They faced some of the best major leaguers: as batters against big-league pitching, as pitchers against big-league hitting. African American players on Cuban teams excelled against visiting major league clubs. In the 1910 Detroit Tigers–Habana series, Ty Cobb batted for a .370 average, whereas John Henry Lloyd hit .500, Grant Johnson .412, and Bruce Petway .390—all against major league pitching. In competing with major leaguers, both from Cuba and the United States, African Americans took measure of their abilities against big-league standards and thus competed as equals. Frank Duncan and Newt Joseph, who often played in Cuba, concluded that Cuban major leaguers were not as good as black ballplayers from the United States. Quite a few Cubans, they observed, "who on account of their white skin gain entry into the big leagues . . . come home and play in the [winter] league, but as a rule, as strange as it might seem, they do not measure up to the high standard of the American Negro ballplayer." Adolfo Luque of the Cincinnati Reds was "a splendid pitcher in the big leagues but can't win against the colored boys in the Cuban league." Pitcher Emilio Palmero of the Washington Senators had "failed to come up to the standard against the colored hitter," and catcher Miguel Angel González of the St. Louis Cardinals "did not show extraordinary ability."[92]

In the Cuban leagues black players from the United States developed the confidence that they could compete with the best white players in the majors. "I knew we were ready in 1942," recalled pitcher Dave Barnhill. "I played against quite a few big leaguers in Cuba. I pitched against Bob Lemon. I played against Johnny Mize." For pitcher Max Manning, the experience in Cuba was decisive. He later reminisced about defeating the Almendares team made up of Solly Hemus, Danny Gardella, Chuck Connors, and Max Lanier: "That game gave me a big boost. I always had an inner confidence in myself in terms of major league competition. I never had any inner doubts in my mind about that."[93]

The Cuban connection had lasting consequences for the development of baseball in the United States. Baseball in Cuba provided an environment that was unavailable in the major leagues. Teams were fully integrated: black and white Cubans played with and against black and white North Americans. Within the ambiguity of Cuban race relations, a condition noteworthy for blurred color lines and shifting racial dichotomies, black and white ballplayers from the United States were free to mingle, to play together on the same teams and on opposing teams, which would have been all but inconceivable in the United States.

Baseball in Cuba contributed to transforming major league play in the United States. U.S. racial barriers were first broken in Cuba. White major leaguers received their first experience of integrated baseball while playing winter ball in Cuba, where they developed professional respect and personal ties with African American players. Integrated baseball in Cuba served as a transition to integrated baseball in the United States. Dodger pitcher Carl Erskine later reflected that Cuba was "a good training ground" for playing on an integrated team. Black and white ballplayers from the United States, knowing no Spanish, were often drawn together as visitors in a foreign country. In a comprehensive history of the Negro Leagues, Donn Rogosin wrote of the friendship that developed in Cuba between Willie Wells and Johnny Dunlap of the Boston Braves, who became roommates while playing for Almendares. "One day, while at the race track," Rogosin wrote, "Dunlap spied Early Wynn, who was pitching for Havana that year. 'Earl, come on over and have a beer,' invited Dunlap. Wynn took one look at Dunlap's dark-complexioned companion and said, 'I don't drink with niggers.' 'What'd you say?' quizzed Dunlap. 'You heard what I said, I don't drink with niggers,' responded Early Wynn. Dunlap swiftly got up and broke Early Wynn's jaw. Wynn pitched no more in the winter league that year."[94]

Thus it was that Cuba served as the site of preparation for the integration of major league baseball. Branch Rickey opened the 1947 Dodgers spring training camp in Havana, in part to avoid the hostile segregationist environment of Florida, in part to field an integrated team in an environment where mixed teams were the norm. Four black ballplayers joined the spring training that year: Don Newcombe, Roy Campanella, Roy Partlow, and Jackie Robinson. Baseball was changed permanently.[95]

It was not at all clear that Cubans were mindful of their role in the transformation of baseball in the United States. Most were absorbed in meanings that were special inside Cuba. Baseball had become a national passion. Its popularity cut across lines of class and age and transcended boundaries of race and gender; it appealed to urban residents and rural inhabitants and united Cubans of all political and ideological persuasions. A 1953 survey revealed that more than 70 percent of all Cubans considered themselves baseball fans, including 82 percent of the men and almost 60 percent of the women. More than 75 percent of the upper class (*las clases pudientes*), 67 percent of the middle class, and more than 75 percent of the working class were identified as baseball *aficionados*. The Cuban people, *Bohemia* commented, regarded baseball "as something very intimate, something very much theirs, as a nearly sacred institution." Fan support of the "national sport" was unlimited "in sacrifice, in emotion, in money. [There] is no other activity . . . that commands as much popular sympathy as baseball." By all standards, *Bohemia* concluded, baseball had long ceased to be a "private business" and assumed the form of "a great public spectacle of positive national preponderance." Writer Mario Vidal made similar observations. "Is there anyone in Cuba today, young or old, man or woman, rich or poor, who does not talk about baseball in all parts at all times?" Vidal asked rhetorically. Enthusiasm for baseball had "displaced political discussions . . . and the high cost of living. The citizen can do without everything: without bread, without meat, without lard: he has baseball. Sports fanaticism has done away with all other fanaticisms. Neither communism nor fascism: baseball. Sports stars have eclipsed the great political leaders. Not a single one of them, not even the most popular has mobilized the masses in Cuba the way baseball is currently doing." Historian Herminio Portell Vilá, who often wrote about sports, always took note of the special place of baseball. "On the afternoons, any day while there is sun light," he observed, "on Saturdays and Sundays, there is no space in this capital that is not filled by groups of boys playing baseball and imitating the gestures, mannerisms, and ways of professional ballplayers, whose names they often adopt as nicknames." Portell Vilá concluded: "The picture that I have just described can be seen in Guanabacoa and Marianao, in Matanzas and Artemisa and everywhere in the country: it is a madness of baseball." Gustavo Robreño recalled his youth in his partly autobiographical novel *La acera del Louvre* (1925). "In theaters, in cafés, in clubs and at dances, in the *paseos*, everywhere in fact, baseball was discussed," muses the protagonist. "Young and old, rich and poor, all were afflicted by the contagion. I would not dare attempt to distinguish with any certainty who in Cuba enjoyed the greatest popularity: whether it would be Montoro, Sanguily, Fernández de Castro and Figueroa—our acclaimed political leaders—or Carlos Maciá—the best player of his time—[and] Adolfo Luján the durable pitcher."[96]

Political leaders of all party affiliations and ideologies sought to identify themselves with baseball. "Many politicians," observed a traveler in 1957, "use the ball park to advance their personal campaigns and make it a point to be seen in attendance there as an election nears." Colonel Fulgencio Batista threw out the first pitch to inaugurate the new season in 1935. The following year President Miguel Mariano Gómez tossed the first ball to begin the 1936 championship series—one of his last public acts before being ousted by Colonel Batista. Of the start of the 1936 season, *Bohemia* commented: "Our most important and distinguished personalities, as much from politics as from government and sports, were present to witness the games."[97] At least one ballplayer, Baldomero Acosta, parlayed his popularity to win elected office as Liberal Party mayor of Marianao.

Local politicians were not the only ones who sought to generate goodwill through baseball. In 1955 U.S. ambassador Arthur Gardner established the "Arthur Gardner Trophy," awarded annually to the outstanding player of the Cuban winter league. The first two awards were given to Camilo Pascual and Minnie Miñoso. Indeed, throughout the 1950s the U.S. embassy promoted baseball in Cuba as part of a larger Cold War strategy. In 1950 cultural affairs officer Jacob Canter urged the U.S. State Department to create a program to allow Cubans to train in the United States during which "players would be introduced to other aspects of American civilization besides that of baseball." Three years later a new cultural affairs officer reminded the State Department that "baseball provides an unusually good opportunity for reaching primary USIS [U.S. Information Service] target audiences." Similarly, pro-U.S. groups in Cuba detected in baseball a way to improve U.S.-Cuba relations. The Comité Nacional Acera del Louvre supported the game as a part of its efforts "to promote friendship" and "work for the spread of American type democracy." The Comité Nacional repeatedly affirmed its support of baseball "for the moral and physical improvement of our youth and the betterment of relations with the American people."[98]

Through good times and bad, in periods of economic depression and political crisis, baseball persisted as a source of national identity and collective unity. During the 1920 stock market crash sports writer Guillermo Pi described the "multitudes crowded in front of the entrance to Almendares ball park, the streets leading to the stadium covered by an ocean of Fords (*fotingos*)." Pi concluded: "The people love their favorite sport, despite the times and all calamities. It is the temporary panacea of all their woes." During the economic collapse and political crises of the 1930s, fan enthusiasm escalated. Baseball seemed to offer stability and continuity at a time of uncertainty and insecurity. Adolfo Font reflected on the meaning of increasing ball park attendance: "Baseball, during our most difficult national struggle, has united Cubans in a close and sincere embrace. . . . In these hours of uncertainty, in these times when Cuban society is so divided, [baseball] serves anew to recreate affection, true patriotism, and the serenity of all."[99]

Many observers noted the capacity of baseball to bring Cubans together, to unite otherwise politically divided and ideologically diverse factions around the all-encompassing category of nationality. This was one more way that a sense of nation assumed form. Cuban appropriation of baseball must be viewed as a highly complex process of socialization and national dialogue. Participation provided access to equality, an opportunity to compete and prevail within a North American framework and thereby affirm the value and validity of being Cuban by meeting—and surpassing—standards set and recognized in the United States.

Cuban achievements, attained within structures and rules to which all participants subscribed and were subjected equally, provided a basis on which to measure self-worth and demonstrate the capacity to compete and prevail. In Felipe Rodríguez's "Los subalternos," sports offered Cuban employees of the "Yucayo Sugar Company" parity with North American administrators. "At this mill," protagonist Felipe Peña explains to administrator Ted Darling, "those of us from here have only had the option of watching you all play tennis. I am going to organize the boys around sports, . . . to play against you in anything, and win, to prove that they too have the stuff of top quality, what you call 'concentration' and what I call the 'aptitude for collective effort.'" The narrator concluded: "From that day Felipe Peña . . . began the task and in a short time the Cubans had organized a sports club . . . and they won and lost in baseball and tennis. . . . For the first time in his life Felipe Peña looked upon his friends and brothers with pride, without feeling like a subordinate. . . . This small achievement made him aware of a realizable hope: that our Spanish America has a defined path toward civilization . . . by way of collective work to give competition value and importance."[100]

Sports offered the basis on which to stake a claim to membership in the community of civilized nations of the world. "It requires little study," José Sixto de Sola affirmed in 1914, "to see that in all countries, and especially those who in this century are in the forefront of civilization, sports of all types are accorded increasing importance." Success in sports competition contributed to "forming and fortifying the pride that each citizen has in belonging to the nation from which such deeds and persons originate." Sola drew his moral explicitly: "In sports, Cubans are notable and outstanding; their success has been complete, extraordinary, and at times simply marvelous." It was necessary to recognize the importance of sports "to the cause of Cuban nationality." Cuban success, especially in competing with the foreigner, provided "pleasure and pride in being Cuban." This was a way for Cuba to attain stature in a world otherwise dominated by such great powers as England, France, Germany, and the United States. "The remarkable triumphs of Cubans in the sports of those countries . . . ," Sola insisted, "well out of proportion to the size of the national territory and the number of inhabitants, necessarily obliges that our name as a civilized nation . . . reaches the highest levels of glory." He asked rhetorically: "How can it not be important—very important—that among those countries, and especially in the North American Union, where sports are accorded the highest honor among activities considered noble and exalted, that the name of Cuba be accorded esteem, consideration, and respect?"[101]

Sports provided a way to project an international presence, and hence promote national esprit de corps, a means of affirmation and a source of differentiation, of parity and prestige. The subtext was embedded most notably in baseball as Cuba worked through a complex relationship with the United States. "What Cuban who has attended a baseball game between Almendares [baseball team] and one of the great North American major league teams that has visited us in recent years," Sola asked, "has not felt linked to our players and the rest of the fans by a powerful bond?" He continued:

> What a magnificent event, and rich in sentiments useful for Cuba. . . . A multitude of ten, twelve or fourteen thousand souls, overcome, waiting breathlessly, for a Cuban triumph. And after having obtained the sensational victory, this same multitude, on its feet and acclaiming the players with a frenzied clamor, subsequently pouring like torrents throughout the city, carrying joy to all parts of the city, a joy that passes from the city to the rest of the island, becoming unanimous from Maisí to San Antonio [i.e., from one end of the island to the other].

Sola concluded: "What is it that produces such intense enthusiasm, so deliriously, so unanimously? Ah! It is the national sentiment. They are all Cubans and they feel Cuban." José Soler Puig's novel *En el año de enero* (1963) captured some of this sentiment as Juan muses: "I love Cuba. It's my country. . . . I want it to progress, that it be the first in the world. I am delighted even when Camilo Pascual wins a game, up there [in the United States], in baseball. And I don't know Camilo nor do I care what kind of person he is. Only that he is Cuban." In similar fashion Jess Losada observed in the 1936 St. Louis–Habana series that Julio Blanco Herrera, the Tropical Beer magnate who constructed the Tropical Stadium, had "achieved what no provisional government had been able to accomplish: bringing together all sectors and beliefs. In the Tropical Stadium gather fraternally the conservative, the liberal, the republican, the communist, the Auténtico, the *abecedario*, the *panista*, the influence peddler, the soldier, the hustler, and the loudmouth." Almost twenty years later José Agustín Martínez, after attending a Cuban Sugar Kings ball game at Gran Stadium, similarly observed: "It was remarkable, the wholesome joy, the patriotic spirit of that mass of humanity that shook the air with its yells, with its songs, with the explosions of delirious support for the players who defended at that moment in the public imagination, the national flag as if we were in full war and that was actual combat between two armies, and not a passing sports event." Mario Guiral Moreno, who saw the Havana Sugar Kings defeat Syracuse in 1955, commented on the "special significance" of baseball, its capacity "to awaken patriotic sentiment among our people."[102]

Baseball figured in the continuing national narrative of progress and modernity, a means to verify and validate the claim to civilization. Baseball suggested a moral code as well as an ethical order to inspire private life and inform public conduct. Renderings that resonated in the nineteenth century continued to shape the Cuban association with baseball in the twentieth. Physician José Antonio López del Valle thought much about the sport, about its greater meaning and value. Baseball was "a school for practical philosophy," with lessons for all facets of life: "It teaches us 'to want' to win and 'to know' how to lose. To realize maximum efforts for victory and have gracious resignation in defeat. To sit down on the 'bench' when it is not our time. To concentrate energies and apply them at the precise moment. . . . To love the flag. The power of unity." These virtues were useful not only in a person's daily life, but also for the life of a nation. According to López de Valle:

> [Baseball] is a school of discipline and respect of the decision, of obedience to orders, of submission to authority. There are, to be sure, infractions. But they cost dearly immediately. They are the causes of defeats, and public condemnation of those who make them. . . . It is a school to learn and a magnificent stage on which later to display agility, fortitude, and dexterity in the realm of ideas and actions. . . . And everything is in a congenial ambience, of democracy, of cordial camaraderie, in fresh air and an open field. . . . It creates a spirit of tolerance, of goodwill, of forbearance, and true brotherhood: of love!

Columnist Hernández Travieso addressed the larger implications of baseball: "To know how to lose with elegance and grace is as important for a citizen of a democracy as knowing how to win without bluster and contempt for the defeated. It is the essence of democracy. It is that phrase coined by the Anglo-Saxons, 'to be a good sport,' that perhaps contains the secret of the success of their political institutions, and in our not knowing it—not when we win or when we lose: the failure of ours."[103]

The notion of baseball as a "school" had other applications. The creation of the Cubanitos was in large measure inspired by the regenerative powers attributed to baseball. "To take a boy off the streets by way of baseball," wrote Armando Villegas of the promise of the Cubanitos, "to see him through school and discipline him for the future, to shape his character and [promote] good habits, in that manner to fight illiteracy and juvenile delinquency—that is the fundamental objective of the Cubanitos."[104]

Nationality was subsumed within the narrative of baseball. The team represented nation in Pan American games, the Caribbean World Series, and Central American competition. Nowhere perhaps was this issue of identity so sharply etched, however, as when Cuban teams played North Americans. These meetings were replete with meaning and metaphor. It seemed always to have been thus—when Cuban teams played against U.S. teams in spring training exhibition games and postseason play, when they joined the Florida International

League and later the AAA International League. Cubans always seemed to imply a subtext in the competition with North Americans. During a series of exhibition games between St. Louis and Habana and Almendares, Jess Losada characterized the Cardinals as "representing royalism [and] Habana and Almendares were democratic forces. It was, hence, a class struggle." And when a Cuban umpire called a close play in favor of St. Louis, "the fans disagreed, and they came to their feet as an imposing mass and cried out that the empire had sold out to *yanqui* imperialism."[105]

The English language obtained another point of entry through sports. Indeed, it would have been all but impossible to understand basketball, boxing, and baseball without English. Basketball relied on such usage as "los oficiales del floor," "el varsity femenino," "el time keeper," "el foul," "el coach," and "el referee." Boxing called upon phrases like "un star bout de 5 rounds," "van al clinch," "el ring del Havana Boxing," "el campeón mundial light weight," "regresa en pos de un come back," and "su jab izquierdo y el uppercut derecho." *El Mundo*'s account of Rocky Marciano's defeat of Joe Wolcott in 1953 included such phrasing as "un formidable uppercut," "el knockout," "el primer round," and "estaba groggy." But it was most of all baseball about which it would have been impossible to report or read without knowing the game in English. A *La Correspondencia* account of a baseball game in Cienfuegos used such terms as "el fuerte team," "un fly a primera out," "López da un foul," and "el sexto inning."[106] The language used in the sports section of *El Mundo* during the early 1950s suggests the degree to which baseball was a game understood in English:

El score final	Un flai al center
En el primer inning	Salió de su slump
El double play	Notable infielder
Unico hit	Con Fonseca at bat
El primer rally	Buenos hitters
Después de haber sido out	Un squeeze play
Un infield hit	Un wild pitch
Un lineazo entre center y right	Sobre el average de 300
Un juego de extra-innings	

English words were also rendered phonetically in Spanish. To knock out became "noquear," to jab was "jabear."[107] In baseball, this practice produced a new vernacular:

jonrón (home run)	roleteó (rolled out)
tubey (two-base hit)	pitchear (to pitch)
tribey (three-base hit)	fildeador (outfielder)
batear (to bat)	aut (out)
flai (fly)	straik (strike)

Baseball reached deeply into the popular consciousness and, in ways not dissimilar to those in the United States, provided the means to assemble representations of reality. It insinuated itself into popular idioms and provided allegories for daily living. Cuban idiomatic expression drew heavily on baseball metaphors to describe conditions and circumstances unconnected with the sport. To be "entre 3 y 2" (between 3 and 2) was to be under intense pressure calling for decisive action. "No pasó la primera" (did not reach first base) signified failure. "Tirar una curva" (to throw a curve ball) suggested deception. "Batear un jonrón" (to hit a home run), "botar la pelota" (to hit the ball out of sight as in a home run), and "dar un batazo" signified great success, whereas "no llegar a jonrón" meant achieving only partial success. To "ponchar" (to be punched out as in a called strike three) referred to a mishap or defeat ranging from having a flat tire to failing a test. "Es un flai" (It's a pop-up) signified an automatic out and thus implied failure and disappointment. "Bola" (ball) found many usages: "no tener nada en la bola" (to have nothing on the ball) was to be without influence, whereas "tener mucho en la bola" (to have much on the ball) was to be very intelligent; "una bola de humo" (a full ball, i.e., "smoke") was to be exceptionally talented, whereas "llegar como bola de humo" was to arrive rapidly; to have "la bola escondida" (hidden ball) was to succeed through subterfuge; "cambiar de bola" (to change balls) was to change one's opinion, and "tirarle a alguien con la bola mala" was to deceive someone; "aclarar la bola" was to explain an idea. "No haber por donde batear" (no place to bat) described a problem without a solution. "Tirar una nokel bol" (To throw a knuckleball) was to prepare an ambush, and "coger fuera de base" (picked off) was to take by surprise. To be "un pitcher de grandes ligas" (a big-league pitcher) was to excel in something. "Batear las dos manos" (to bat as a switch hitter) was to be bisexual; "jugar en las dos novenas" (to play on both teams) could also imply bisexuality or taking both sides of an issue. "Quieto en base" (remain on base) referred to staying put or remaining silent.[108]

Baseball metaphors also entered the vernacular in wholly improvised fashion as a way to communicate a condition in the most fundamental and hence most comprehensible form. Visiting Holguín in 1937, Jess Losada recalled the Machado years, when Captain Arsenio Ortiz, known for brutal repression of the opposition, was dispatched to Oriente to end antigovernment activities. Losada likened Ortiz to "the dictator's closing relief pitcher" (pitcher tapón) in the Oriente region." When in 1960 Fidel Castro denounced U.S. support of dictators in Latin America, he alluded to the practice whereby an incumbent dictator was "benched, retired to the bull pen for a while in order to use him again" (se lo pusieron en un banco, lo retiraron al 'bull-pen' un tiempo para volverlo a usar). In Robreño's *La acera del Louvre*, Pepe objects to the use of a baseball analogy to characterize his misfortune. "I am not talking about baseball at this moment, nor do I think it appropriate to mix the sport in this serious matter"—to which the protagonist responds: "Well, I do: facets of baseball have relevance to all situations of life."[109]

Cubans also played a major role in disseminating baseball elsewhere in Latin America. During the nineteenth century Cubans emigrated throughout the Caribbean and almost immediately on arrival established ball clubs. As early as the 1870s, émigrés went to the Dominican Republic to organize sugar production in the southeastern plains of San Pedro de Macorís and La Romana. Baseball soon followed. Shortly thereafter, the brothers Ignacio and Ubaldo Alomá arrived in Santo Domingo from Cienfuegos and within months had organized two baseball teams. During the 1890s Havana cigar manufacturer Emilio Cramer went to Caracas to establish La Cubana cigarette factory. Together with other émigrés and Venezuelans, Cramer organized a Caracas city league of five teams. At about the same time, the Cuban émigré community in the Yucatán introduced baseball in Mérida and Progreso. The local municipal teams suggested the origins of the organizers: Cuba Baseball Club, Habana Baseball Club, and Matanzas Baseball Club. In the 1920s and 1930s Cuban teams traveled throughout the region to play local teams. In the late 1950s the Cuban Triple A club, the Cuba Sugar Kings, played a series of exhibition games in Mérida and Managua annually. Cubans also comprised the largest group of foreigners playing in the four-team (León, Boer, San Fernando, and Granada) Nicaraguan league. León, Boer, and San Fernando were managed by Cubans Tony Castaño, Fermín Guerra, and Roberto Ortiz. Cuban umpires called the games.[110]

5

SOURCES OF POSSESSION

Havana's infatuation with the movies continues to grow. Women alternate shopping with mid-day forays to the movie theater and many children, upon leaving school, have their parents' permission to pass away the time enjoying motion pictures until the dinner hour.
—*La Lucha*, June 15, 1929

The Cuban woman has abandoned her placid and tranquil life of colonial times. In referring to women we mean the women born in the Republic, because those of the colony with rare exception retain the colonial mentality. . . . The young Cuban women of the republic, the working women of the middle class, of the petty bourgeoisie and the proletariat, manifestly reveal a triumphant and progressive enthusiasm for advance.
—*Carteles*, April 20, 1941

We lack initiative, originality. We do not like to create, but imitate. And that is the way we have been from time immemorial.
—*Carteles*, June 1919

Our identity is not only theoretical—it is eminently intuitive.
—Noel Navarro, *El nivel de las aguas*, 1980

Why are these Cubans like us in so many ways?
—Erna Fergusson, *Cuba*, 1946

Cubans as a whole are plausible.
—Ruby Hart Phillips, *Cuba: Island of Paradox*, 1959

Cuba was in transition—again: not the type of transformation associated with political upheaval or economic dislocation but, rather, change in the form of adaptation to different cultural modes and new social conventions, yet with consequences no less far-reaching and all-encompassing. Some changes were immediately apparent, with obvious implications. Others were simply portents, and only the prescient few could imagine what they signified. Change was the salient condition of daily reality, relentless, often irresistible, and that it was not always readily discerned was itself indicative of the degree to which it had become a part of the familiar environment in which the first republican generation came of age.

BETWEEN IMAGE AND IMAGINING

Cuba had become a very different place in the decades following the end of Spanish colonial rule. The population had almost doubled, from 1.5 million in 1899 to 2.8 million in 1919. Part of this increase—approximately 272,000—was through immigration, but most of the new residents were Cuban born. Indeed, the full dimensions of postwar fertility rates revealed themselves in dramatic relief in the census of 1919. Nearly 60 percent (1.5 million) of the total Cuban-born population of 2.5 million was under the age of twenty-one, almost half of whom were between ten and twenty years old.[1] A distinctly young population—the majority of Cuba's inhabitants—was being formed during the 1910s and 1920s, years of remarkable cultural developments and rapid social transformations.

War again was the source of change, but this time it was war in Europe, and it was prosperity, not depression, that produced the change. World War I crippled European beet sugar production and led to a sharp decline in the world supply of beet sugar, from 8.3 million tons in 1914 to 4.4 million tons in 1918. The increase in the world price of sugar was not long in coming: from 2.05 cents a pound in 1914 to 4.30 cents in 1918. But the best times did not arrive until after the war, when the price of sugar jumped to 9.2 cents a pound in 1919 and continued to rise steadily thereafter. In 1920, the year of dazzling prosperity—the "Dance of the Millions"—the increase was stunning: 10 cents in March, 18 cents in April, 22 cents in May. The value of the sugar crop more than doubled from the previous year, from $455 million in 1919 to more than $1 billion in 1920.

World War I occasioned one of the most spectacular economic booms in Cuban history. Scores of new sugar mills, mostly North American, were rushed into construction and then production. Vast new acreage passed under cane cultivation. Producers could not find ways fast enough to clear new land. Miles of virgin forest land were cleared ruthlessly, with thought given only to efficiency and economy. Some used fire as a cost-effective means to clear the land. The United Fruit Company resorted to dynamite. Teresa Casuso recalled these years of her youth:

> I remember, in Oriente, the great impenetrable forests that were set aflame, whole jungles that were fired and razed to the ground to make way for the sugar cane. My parents were in despair for that lost wealth of beautiful, fragrant tropical wood—cedar and mahogany and mastic, and magnificent-grained pomegranate—blazing in sacrifice to the frenzy to cover the country-side with sugar cane. In the nights the sight of that flaming horizon affected me with a strange, fearful anxiety, and the aroma of burning wood floating down from so far away was like the incense one smells inside churches.[2]

These were years of astounding prosperity. "Sugar for two years has been a gold mine," Franklin D. Roosevelt confided to his diary during a visit to Cuba in

1917. "Rampant prosperity," proclaimed the trade journal *Facts about Sugar*; "astonishing prosperity," the *Havana Post* agreed. Cuba had "more money at hand than it can spend," marveled one North American businessman visiting Santiago de Cuba in 1918; he remarked about "the amount of wealth to be seen in that city of one-story dwellings," adding: "The poorest shack has a lot of valuable furniture." Another observer calculated that the wealth generated by sugar was "almost as great as the per capita wealth produced by all the farms, all the factories, and all the mines of the United States"; he concluded: "Perhaps no other city in the whole world has proportionately as large a wealthy population as Havana."[3]

Few who visited Cuba during these heady years could contain their astonishment at the spectacle of opulence. "Cubans spend money with both hands," commented a visitor, "and they could teach us Americans about the art of extravagance in the construction of beautiful houses and the purchase of jewelry, clothing from Paris, and large automobiles." U.S. consul Carlton Hurst recalled: "Everybody in Cuba had money. . . . People started to erect sumptuous villas in Country Club Park, Almendares and elsewhere, magnificent automobiles were imported from the north."[4]

The war had one more decisive effect: it served to divert Cuban trade away from Europe to the United States. North American imports increased from 59 percent of the total to nearly 80 percent. The value of U.S. imports soared from $68 million in 1914 to $404 million in 1920, a movement of capital goods and consumer durables of huge proportions, a seemingly endless flow of commodities of every imaginable type. The harbors were crammed with sea vessels of all kinds—merchant ships and mail steamers, freighters and lighters, ferries and floating dry docks—all servicing a volume of trade so vast as to overwhelm port facilities. Merchandise could not be unloaded fast enough. "The harbor is full of ships and also full of lighters," reported a Havana merchant in September 1920, "in some places lying six and eight deep against the wharves, loaded with merchandise of every description." As sea vessels crowded into the ports, merchandise piled up on piers and wharves. By 1920 the problem of congestion had reached desperate proportions. Incalculable quantities of foodstuffs perished in transit. The danger of spoilage due to port bottlenecks was sufficiently great to threaten the supply of food imports. Merchant houses, department stores, and retail shops had tens of millions of dollars in merchandise hopelessly tied up in the ports. El Encanto department store stated that $2 million worth of seasonal goods were backed up on lighters and on the docks. "It is the universal agreement that the ultimate cause of congestion, not merely in Havana but also in the other Cuban ports," according to one trade official, "has been the very rapid growth in Cuban commerce which has far-out-stripped the facilities for handling this trade. Cuban prosperity has been so rapid and so great that even if no other difficulties had presented themselves, it would not have been possible with existing physical equipment to have handled satisfactorily the growing commerce."[5]

Trade and transportation expanded together. In 1915 an all-rail route between Cuba and the United States was completed with the inauguration of rail car ferry service between the Key West terminal of the Florida East Coast Railroad and the Havana terminal of the United Railways. Henceforth, fully loaded freight cars originating from any point in the United States could be transported directly to any station in Cuba without having to reload. Each steam ferry was equipped with four standard gauge tracks with a capacity of thirty freight cars and an ability to complete the trip in seven hours. "Among the curious sights of Cuba," commented a traveler in 1920, "are box-cars from as far off as the State of Washington basking in the tropical sunshine or the shade of royal palms hundreds of miles east of Havana."[6]

But it was not only that goods arrived from the United States more efficiently. They were also distributed across Cuba more effectively. Transportation systems expanded as railroads, electric trolleys, and highway construction increased. Additional rail service linked almost all regions of the island: a total of twenty railroad lines that by the 1930s extended 9,000 miles. The Central Highway was completed in 1931 and opened the full length of the island to motor vehicle traffic. More than 5,000 miles of highway and roads linked virtually every *municipio* in Cuba. Increased foreign trade was carried by thirty shipping lines operating out of nearly twenty port cities along both coasts and in every province.

Communication systems also improved. The expansion of telephone service, especially the Havana–Key West telephone cable, further integrated Cuba into the U.S. market. Indeed, this was one of the primary justifications for the cable. "Telephonic connections between this country and Cuba," U.S. secretary of commerce E. F. Sweet predicted in 1919, "would undoubtedly facilitate the very large commercial transactions which are passing each year between the two republics. . . . The heavy American investments in Cuba and the large Cuban business of American exporting and importing houses would receive valuable assistance from direct telephonic connections between the chief Cuban trade centers and the United States."[7]

It is impossible to comprehend the total impact of these developments inside Cuba or how they insinuated themselves into everyday life. Prosperity created new opportunities for the growth of U.S. imports, principally consumer goods and household merchandise. Cuba was an extraordinary market, undergoing dazzling economic expansion, fully integrated into the communication and transportation network of the United States and, perhaps most important, entirely susceptible to the appeal of U.S. imports. Prosperity did not remain at spectacular levels, of course, but the influence of these years reached well into later decades.

The North American presence was ubiquitous, expanding in all directions at once. At every point that this presence made contact with the prevailing order of Cuban life—almost everywhere—it challenged, it contested, it changed. It became a permanent condition, at once a way to take measure of the world and be measured by it.

The reorientation of Cuban trade from Europe to the United States affected all sectors of commerce. It altered the way Cubans experienced daily life, and it changed the habits and preferences of an entire generation and beyond. Although there were many sources of these transformations, none perhaps had a more immediate impact than motion pictures. The movies conveyed new forms and alternative modalities, while at the same time fostering emulation of North American ways and increasing demand for North American products. Precisely because film represented select and stylized versions of life in the United States, it became one of the most influential transmitters of North American ways.

World War I had interrupted European film production and all but halted film exports. By the late 1910s European films had lost the Cuban market to U.S. producers. "Danish and Italian movies were displaced by Hollywood films," recalled Marcelo Pogolotti. Loló de la Torriente remembered the 1910s and 1920s in a similar fashion. "The movie theater screened fewer films of [Francesca] Bertini and [Pina] Menichelli," she wrote in her memoirs, "to show Mary Pickford, Douglas Fairbanks, and the vamp role of Theda Bara, so mysterious and so sensual. In addition, adventure movies were supplemented with western movies, with William Hart as hero, or a war film, with Rudolph Valentino in the lead role of 'The Four Horsemen of the Apocalypse.' "[8]

The large North American community in Cuba also generated a demand for U.S. films; in fact, much of the capital for the early expansion of motion pictures inside Cuba originated from within this community. In 1916 attorney Alexander Kent organized the Red Feather Cinematograph Company and purchased the Campoamor Theater. Red Feather subsequently acquired a total of ten theaters in Havana and the provinces, emerging as the first theater chain in Cuba. Many of the larger movie theaters were operated by their North American owners, further facilitating the distribution of U.S. films. Theater owners were also affiliated with film distributors. The Campoamor showed Universal films exclusively. The Fausto theater was operated by A. L. Pritchett and presented Paramount films. Three North American film distributors dominated the Cuban market: the Caribbean Film Company (Paramount), Liberty Film Company (Fox), and Universal Film Manufacturing Company (Universal). They were soon joined by United Artists of Cuba (1921), Metro-Goldwyn-Mayer (1923), and First National Pictures (1925).[9]

U.S. motion pictures not only displaced European films but also contributed to the decline of other forms of entertainment. The Cuban theater fell on hard times as acting companies disbanded and the number of theaters available for stage productions dwindled. The popularity of motion pictures, especially with the advent of sound, sealed the fate of the Cuban stage. Throughout the 1920s attendance declined and playhouses were converted to picture houses. "With the passage of time," lamented *La Lucha* in 1929, "only memories link us to the prestige of what was once theater art, which has declined in such a demoralizing way . . . as a result of the extraordinary interest created by film, which has been transformed into the lord and master of the public." The newspaper continued: "And thus we do not have actors and singers; everyday their numbers become fewer, as they depart to find work under other skies where motion pictures are not found in such an advanced state of development. . . . We notice with deep dismay that our principal playhouses are permanently inactive. . . . The theater, with its many traditions, is dying." Stage actress María Guerrero was incredulous. "It is truly strange," she remarked. "I do not believe that I am in Havana, the city of culture par excellence; it seems that all that artistic taste has departed and that a new race has taken over." Marcelo Pogolotti recalled a neighborhood theater that was "transformed inexorably into a movie house, swept along by the currents of the times . . . showing only cowboy movies and feature [films] of the kind that starred Pearl White or the fantastic adventure type." Visits by theater companies from Spain, France, and Mexico declined and runs were shorter. Pogolotti reasoned: "The theater languished under the reign of Hollywood."[10]

The popularity of U.S. films was unrivaled. The speed with which they increased was surpassed only by the thoroughness with which they dominated the Cuban market. Alejo Carpentier writes that these were the years of "the massive invasion of North American film that filled the movie theaters," a time when "movie theaters multiplied prodigiously all over Havana [and] when, in the end, there were movie theaters in every neighborhood, movie theaters everywhere . . . when movies entered into daily life." The dominance of U.S. motion pictures was all but complete by the early 1920s. "The moving picture industry has been brought entirely from America," Joseph Hergesheimer observed during a visit to Havana in 1920, "the theaters plastered with Douglas Fairbanks' set grin, William Farnum's pasty heroic, and Mary Pickford's invaluable aspect of innocence. Never, in the time I was in Cuba, did I see a Spanish actor or film announced." A year later Charles Sawyer, manager of the Caribbean Film Company, proclaimed Havana to be "one of the most important markets for motion pictures outside the United States" and added: "No country in the world has a keener appreciation of U.S.-made pictures than Havana, and when I say that I mean Cuba. They are just as familiar in Cuba with the stars of the screen, they are just as partial to them and just as ready to voice their appreciation of good picture acting." In 1923 the British consul all but conceded the Cuban market to U.S. filmmakers:

> The proximity of the United States is almost fatal to the films of other countries. Not only are all the American film stars well known to the Cuban public, but both the Spanish and American papers in Havana constantly grant publicity and a number of American cinema magazines are in circulation in Cuba. Advertising is intense. Theater owners and others have only to run over to Florida (some 96 miles) or even up to New York (60 hours) to see

the latest films and purchase them on the spot, and most of them have agents and correspondents in the United States who send particulars of all new films and report on their suitability for the Cuban market.[11]

Theaters expanded rapidly. By 1920 Havana had more than forty movie theaters, with an average seating capacity of 650, or a total of 26,000 seats for a population of 500,000. Many could accommodate 1,000 patrons and some up to 2,500. The Trianón theater, completed in 1920, provided seating for 1,200.[12]

Motion pictures spread into the provinces, in both large cities and distant towns and villages. Between 1912 and 1920 the number of movie theaters in Cuba tripled—from one hundred to three hundred—representing a total seating capacity of nearly 150,000 for a population of three million. Movie theaters operated in more than fifty cities and towns. The first cinema in Nuevitas (pop. 4,400) opened in 1909. Jobabo (pop. 2,200) had a movie theater in 1919. Cabezas (pop. 900) had two. So did the town of Pedro Betancourt (pop. 4,800). Jovellanos (pop. 7,300) and Bolondrón (pop. 3,700) each had one movie theater.[13] The town of Júcaro (pop. 1,250) inaugurated its new theater in 1920 with films starring Helen Holmes and Douglas Fairbanks. Esteban Palacios Hoyas recalled the heightened expectation with which the residents of the Matanzas town of Los Arabos (pop. 2,300) anticipated the screening of new Shirley Temple and Laurel and Hardy pictures. Small towns and cities, places like Consolación del Sur, Placetas, and Güines, showed matinees for children. In Caimanera, near the U.S. Naval Station, the local cinema offered weekly matinees to accommodate prostitutes who worked in the evenings. "At present there are few places of amusement in smaller towns," observed Idaless Westly, who traveled into the interior in 1921. "Nearly every town I have been in has a picture show. . . . The Cubans are great movie fans, but in many places the 40¢ price forbids many of them to go more than once a week. They cheer the hero and hiss the villain and get so excited over a Helen Holmes film of twelve or fourteen years ago that the theaters are as noisy as an American football field."[14]

Between the 1930s and 1950s the number of theaters increased markedly, as did movie attendance. By 1955 nearly 550 motion picture theaters, with a total seating capacity of 370,500, were distributed across the island. (See Appendix Table 5.1.) More than 500,000 persons attended movies weekly, accounting for more than $92 million annually. Perhaps as many as 200 additional theaters, mostly equipped with 16-millimeter equipment, with a total seating of about 40,000, operated at sugar mills, rice plantations, tobacco *vegas*, and coffee farms during the harvest season. Tuinicú, Hershey, Tinguaro, Preston, Chaparra, España, and Francisco were only some of the larger mills to have cinemas. Katherine Ponvert recalled life at the Hormiguero mill, where "twice a week there were movies shown in the small moving picture theatre on the batey."[15] Private social clubs and *liceos* also established movie theaters. The Sociedad El Liceo in Matanzas operated a theater for the exclusive use of its members.

All through the 1940s and 1950s Cuban audiences saw first-run U.S. motion pictures. North American movies emerged as the most widely available form of commercial entertainment. The number of first-run films increased from 380 in 1950 to 465 in 1951 to more than 500 in 1955, accounting for 85 percent of all new releases.

Havana boasted some of the world's most lavish movie theaters, which were themselves a source of national pride, including the Maxim, Nacional, Payret, Galatea, Colón, Fausto, Neptuno, Campoamor, Miramar, Rialto, Regina, Prado, and Riviera. By the late 1920s they were among the first theaters in the world equipped for sound. They were also among the first to install air-cooling equipment. The Encanto theater advertised "el *comfort*" of the "Carrier Cooling System" with almost as much prominence as it announced the main feature. Air-conditioning arrived in the late 1940s. In the mid-1950s the Nuevo Radiocentro contracted with North American technicians to install the screen and projection technology for the first Cinerama theater in Cuba. "The arrival of Cinerama," exulted columnist René Jordán, "is an event of major importance: only the principal cities of the world possess it. In today's world Cinerama . . . is a modern institution that finally has made its way to our country."[16]

And, indeed, motion pictures served to corroborate Cuba's place in the forefront of civilization. Cuba always seemed among the first to adopt and display modernity, and from the outset movies offered proof of progress. As early as 1920, *La Lucha* declared: "In Cuba, as in all countries of the world who live *a la modern* and take to their bosom all developments that tend to disseminate progress, we feel today the effect of the celluloid magic transformed into the silent movie."[17]

Movie theaters provided a way that even the most remote rural communities could celebrate modernity in their midst. Motion picture theaters served as confirmation of the modern condition. José Manuel Carballido Rey's short story "Octubre de 1926" (1983) was set in a small unnamed village—"hardly four blocks"—where the narrator proclaimed the opening of a movie theater a "great accomplishment, an event of enormous importance for the progress of our community." In Lisandro Otero's novel *Arbol de la vida* (1990), the narrator comments on a visit to the small town of El Jobo: "The movie theater, with ambitions of the Second Empire, reminded one of the opera house of Paris." The town historian of Nuevitas described the opening of its first motion picture theater as an "important step on the path of progress." Ernesto Brivio wrote of the "innumerable quantity of cinema houses, among which the 'Rodi' and 'América' can compete with the best ones in the largest cities in the world." In 1949 Senator Alfredo Hornedo opened the Blanquita theater in Miramar, "the world's largest and most modern theater."[18] The Blanquita theater could seat nearly 7,000 patrons in air-conditioned comfort and was equipped with the latest film projection technology. In 1955 North American Herb Copelan opened the Vento Drive-In, which could hold 800 cars.

Perhaps nowhere in Latin America did U.S. motion pictures so thoroughly saturate a national market as in Cuba. Proximity to the United States accounted for some of this, of course. The large number of provincial ports with direct links to the North opened the island to film imports even as the modern railway system facilitated the distribution of films in the interior. A large moviegoing public existed in the provinces. Sugar production had summoned into existence a huge rural proletariat that, for at least half of the year, had disposal income and for whom movie attendance constituted an important leisure activity.

Attendance cut across class lines, among young and old, men and women, black and white. "People having little else to do," commented an observer in 1920, "spend their leisure hours at the cinema. The negroes flock to these places. Every negro washerwoman thinks she must go every night." A 1956 survey indicated that adolescents attended movies at least once a week. Former domestic servant Inocencia Acosta Felipe recounted her memories of the movies to Oscar Lewis: "I loved the movies. . . . We took in a movie every night and saw some of them as many as three or four times, because the *barrio* movie houses were cheap and we could afford to go often. My favorite star is Ingrid Bergman. . . . I think we went to every movie theater in Havana just to get out of the house. The truth is, we didn't have a comfortable home. It was a single room, with no TV or anything."[19]

Movie attendance developed into one of the salient facets of Cuban life. Néstor Almendros remembered Havana as a "paradise for a film buff," where the "large audience kept many commercial theaters in business." In small towns motion pictures provided relief from the tedium of everyday life, a way to escape, a place to go to, something to do. Guillermo Martínez Márquez's short story "El poema eterno del amor que nace" (1926) is set in Yaguaramas (pop. 1,200), a village with barely "two parallel streets more than one block long," but where the townspeople gathered weekly on Sunday evening to watch movies, "the only diversion of the people." Hortensia de Varela used the short story "La casona del pueblo" (1932) as personal narrative: when the "quiet repose of the evening enveloped the town," youth contemplated the remorseless choiceless-ness of their free time—a stroll in the park, parlor conversation, or the movies. The protagonist in Luis Adrián Betancourt's novel *Expediente almirante* (1977) proclaims that films served "to fortify our ideas and our hopes, something that helps us have a reason to live and to die, but most of all something that entertains, something that takes us away from this world. I don't like a film in which I get all choked up or one that reminds me that there are unsolvable problems in the world."[20]

For communities of the interior provinces, films provided a window to the outside world, a means of transport to distant places and remote times, always possessed of the capacity to inform the imagination and alter consciousness. Samuel Feijóo long retained vivid recollections of an evening in his childhood village of Caonao (pop. 260) when a traveling circus came to town and screened a silent movie. "I lay down on the mat over the grass," he recounted. "Amidst the great applause and shouts of the peasants, I feel my childhood, the films that made my childhood joyous. Cowboys, landscapes of desert cliffs, the clothes of women of old times, covered wagons. . . . I carry this epoch with me." Of his youth in Holguín, Reinaldo Arenas wrote:

> On payday I would go to the movies, which was the only magical place in Holguín, the only place where one could escape from the city, at least for a few hours. . . . I would sit in the *gallinero*, or top balcony, the cheapest seats, where I could sometimes see up to three movies for five cents. It was a great joy to see those people galloping over the prairies, hurling themselves down mighty rivers, or shooting each other to death, while I was dying of boredom in a town that had no ocean, no rivers, no prairies, no forest, nothing that could be of interest to me.

The experience may have been decisive for Arenas: "Perhaps influenced by those movies . . . I started to write novels."[21]

Films touched the lives of many tens of thousands, in direct and often very personal ways. Marcelo Pogolotti recalled the summer vacations of his adolescence, when "I would gorge myself of afternoon movies . . . with Mary Pickford, the Gish sisters, Theda Bara, Olga Petrova and Pauline Frederick [and] cowboy movies with William S. Hart." From exile many decades later, José Pardo Llada described his youthful infatuation with motion pictures: "I saw so many films that at the age of fifteen I won all the prizes by answering the movie questions on the contest programs." In a moving *testimonio* of a resident of El Cerro, Joaquín Santana revealed poignant truths associated with a local movie house over the span of years:

> Here we saw "The Time Machine."
> Here we loved Kim Novak and shot it out with Jesse James the afternoon he attacked our stagecoach.
> From here we headed out to Okinawa, to Iwo Jima and landed and fought on the beaches against the Japanese. . . .
> We came here to dream with our eyes open. We would be pilots, *cowboys*, spies, romantic singers. . . .
> From here we raced down the highways, bundled in our leather jacket like James Dean, looking for a death we did not understand, and despising the home and family, in revolt and brutal, and looked at the world with indifference. . . .
> Here we loved and hated.
> Here we were formed and deformed.
> Here we forgot, in the matinee shows, we forgot that we were poor.
> Here we were the owners of Lassie and Rin Tin Tin.[22]

It is difficult to imagine any other country where North American films formed a more prominent part of popular culture. Hollywood captured the public imagination, and all the evidence suggests that moviegoers in Cuba were as hopelessly if happily immersed in movie star culture as audiences in the United States. Hollywood became part of daily life around which the familiar formed, an object of Cuban fantasy and fascination. Hollywood news became a staple of the Cuban mass media, developed into a full-blown Cuban genre, and eventually contributed to the creation of a popular culture of film. Articles about the private and public lives of movie stars—their marriages and divorces, their triumphs and tragedies—were standard fare. A conspicuous headline in *La Lucha* on March 21, 1920, announced: "Celebrated Actress Mary Pickford Obtains Divorce," followed a month later by a feature on "Mary Pickford: The Most Popular Woman in the World."[23]

Periodicals addressing the film industry appeared early. *La Gaceta Teatral y Cinematográfica* and *Cuba Cinematográfica* were both founded in 1912. The monthly magazine *Cinelandia*, devoted to photographic features about Hollywood, was started in 1920. Indeed, all the leading magazines and newspapers regularly published articles and features on Hollywood happenings. "Las Pascuas en Hollywood" described how movie stars celebrated Christmas. Particularly popular were articles on Hollywood styles and fashions, under such titles as "La elegancia en Hollywood," "Secretos de bellezas de Hollywood," "Sombreros que se usan en Hollywood," and "La modas de Hollywood."[24]

Film stars assumed larger-than-life proportions, and the way they lived on and off the screen was a source of interest and influence. Their views on a wide range of subjects seemed to matter and often served as a means to take bearings by way of the constellation of the North. *Vanidades* published a survey in which Marlon Brando, Mitzi Gaynor, Robert Wagner, Russ Tamblyn, and Kim Novak responded to the question, "How should a single girl conduct herself?" Another survey asked Stewart Granger, John Derek, Burt Lancaster, and Frank Sinatra "What makes a woman irresistible?" Gregory Peck expounded on "the ideal woman," and Yvonne de Carlo described "the ideal man." Studio publicity photographs demonstrated the kissing styles of Eleanor Parker, Joan Crawford, Lauren Bacall, and Humphrey Bogart.[25]

Gossip columns flourished. Some arrived as translated copy of syndicated features by Drew Pearson, Louella Parsons, Dorothy Kilgallin, Earl Leaf, and Hedda Hopper. Others were compiled locally. (See Appendix Table 5.2.) *Social* published "Notas del celuloide." *Bohemia* featured Arístides Pérez Andreu's column "Cinematográficas," María Garet's "Vida diaria en Hollywood," and Leonara de Andrés's "Modas de Hollywood." *El Fígaro* published Luis Pérez Sureda's "Cinema-Crónica." *El Mundo* carried columnist J. M. Valdés's "Tablas y Pantallas" and Marta Marina Cisternas's "La vida en Hollywood." *Vanidades* published Gonzalo de Palacio, "Del cine y sus estrellas"; Jess Losada, "Revista de

Cine"; Isabel Margarita Ordext, "Chismes de Hollywood"; Francisco Marrero, "Conozca la vida de los artistas"; and Don Basilio, "Un observador en Hollywood." *Grafos* featured Alberto Rondón's "Un minuto con . . . ," a monthly interview with film stars (e.g., "Una minuto con Greta Garbo" and "Un minuto con Joan Crawford"). *Carteles* published columnist Agustín Aragón's "Chismes y murmaciones cinelándicos." *Carteles* also assigned Mary M. Spaulding (née María Melero) to Hollywood, where she prepared a weekly feature, "Crónicas de Cinelandia." Spaulding obtained lengthy interviews with movie stars from whom she usually elicited flattering comments about Cuba, thereby creating a direct bond between her readers and Hollywood. She also secured personalized photographs that subsequently appeared in *Carteles*. Full-page photographs thus were signed "Para *Carteles*, Sincerely, Gloria Swanson," "To *Carteles*, Sincerely, Pearl White," and "Success to *Carteles*, Shirley Mason." *Vanidades* published scores of interviews with movie stars, including Debbie Reynolds, Rock Hudson, Jane Russell, Audrey Hepburn, Lana Turner, Grace Kelly, John Wayne, Joan Crawford, and William Holden. *Bohemia*, *Carteles*, and *Vanidades* frequently used studio publicity photographs of movie stars on its cover.[26]

The sale of photographs of film stars developed into a brisk business. Mass-produced signed photographs of stars sold well and were often displayed in homes beside family portraits. The Photo Cinema Star Company was one of many retailers in Havana to distribute 8-by-10 publicity photographs of popular actors and actresses. In 1924 the Polar brewery used studio photographs to promote beer sales, offering customers a collection of ten photographs of such celebrities as Gloria Swanson, Lon Chaney, Jackie Coogan, and Noah Berry in exchange for fifty bottle caps of Polar beer. Photographs of Hollywood stars adorned the walls of many homes. Armando Couto visited a home in Havana that was decorated "with all the things available in the *Ten Cent*"—among them, a picture of "the Sacred heart of Jesus displaying his bleeding heart . . . along side a photograph of Robert Taylor." In Wenceslao Gálvez's short story "Cinemanía" (1932), the protagonist had amassed a vast collection of photographs: "I die for the movies and practically live for the movies. . . . There is no movie star, especially among the men, that does not occupy a place in my alcove and in my thoughts. The way my sister Elvira works to know about the lives of the saints and my brother Tadeo learns about the lives of the presidents of the United States, I yearn to know about the lives and wonders of movie stars."[27] As late as 1991, the author visited the home of a colleague's family in Havana whose living room wall held photographs of José Martí, Camilo Cienfuegos, Ernesto Che Guevara, and Marilyn Monroe. Writer Pico Iyer must have had a similar experience in Havana, for in *Cuba and the Night* (1995) he places his protagonist inside a home "where you could see Che and Michael Jackson and Jesus on the Cross all at once."[28]

Hollywood fully entered the realm of the Cuban familiar. Every year Cuban media engaged in much speculation about who would win the Academy Awards. Periodically, *Vanidades* published a quiz (¿Que sabe Ud. de cine?) asking readers to match a column of names with the photographs of movie stars. Crossword puzzles commonly used first names or surnames as clues for a Hollywood star: "The name of an actress" read the clue of a 1934 *Bohemia* crossword, asking for "Carole." Horoscope charts were routinely published with photographs of movie stars to represent astrological signs: Betty Grable for Sagittarius, Lauren Bacall for Virgo, Ava Gardner for Capricorn, and so on.[29]

Hollywood also traveled to Cuba and thereby fostered familiarities of other kinds. The island was a popular vacation site. Actors and actresses, producers and directors, press agents and distributors were among the most celebrated North American visitors to Cuba and always received considerable media attention. Samuel Goldwyn, Alice Terry, Ramón Navarro, Norma Talmadge, Gloria Swanson, Dorothy Gish, William Powell, and Tom Mix in the 1920s and 1930s and Ava Gardner, Errol Flynn, Eleanor Powell, Gary Cooper, Johnny Weismuller, and Marlon Brando in the 1940s and 1950s were only some of the most prominent film stars to vacation in Cuba. They made themselves generally available for local interviews, they spoke fondly of the charms of Cuba, and they usually endeared themselves to the Cuban public. Tom Mix reminisced about his military service in 1898 as a Rough Rider, recounting war stories detailing his contribution to Cuban independence. Norma Talmadge proclaimed Cubans to be "so affable, splendid, and hospitable." Marlon Brandon announced his "extraordinary fondness for Havana at night. The moon is truly beautiful in Cuba. The atmosphere is exquisite." During a visit John Wayne affirmed: "Lovely people, beautiful landscape, wonderful music."[30]

It may be impossible to assess the full impact of U.S. films on the formation of popular culture and public norms, or how behavior and conventions portrayed on film influenced the standard of self-definition. Motion pictures were accessible, and certainly silent films reached a huge audience without mediation. In their North American context, feature films were cultural artifacts, as much a chronicle of changing times as a source of change, subject always to the logic of everyday life. They reflected values and reinforced behaviors in transition; they permitted a people to see themselves, or versions of themselves, from which to contemplate new possibilities, and promoted a shared identity in the way they experienced themselves as members of a single nation.

But these same films assumed different meanings in Cuba. More than reflect change they often suggested change, pointing to possibilities beyond the otherwise daily realm of the commonplace. They could create a yearning for a different life. The medium possessed the capacity to transport viewers immediately and simultaneously across different spatial and social thresholds. This could be subversive stuff, capable of undermining even the most time-honored truths. Unlike North Americans, Cubans did not see themselves on the screen. They saw representations of alternative ways of being, the possibility of new habits and manners, ways to move beyond prevailing social boundaries. Films acted as a means by which transformations occurring in the United States could be instantly transmitted to Cuba, and in this sense there was probably no more effective agency of mass impression. In what must be considered a remarkable and complex engagement, motion pictures contributed to an anomalous condition in which North American modalities could encourage lifestyles, foster consumption patterns, and shape popular tastes independent of the capacity of national structures to sustain the material base for these practices and preferences.

Motion pictures set into sharp relief the complexity of mutually interlocking and overlapping normative systems and the ways these convergences reproduced and reinforced themselves. The power of film lay in its capacity to project a version of reality—of objects, persons, and places—that provoked a reassessment of everyday life. That North American films enjoyed such a dominance was itself the result of complex circumstances, which, in turn, released new forces that worked to incorporate Cuba more directly, more fully, into the world and ways of the North. It would be facile, of course, to suggest that film alone acted as the agency of social and cultural transformation. It did not. But film did provide powerful representations of new moralities, of other possibilities of behavior, as well as new ways of conduct and comportment, all of which served as a catalyst for change inside Cuba. The effect of film on standards, fashions, manners, and aspirations cannot be underestimated. Under certain circumstances, film could sustain the logic of North American hegemony, for it possessed the capacity to both represent and reinforce as commonplace dominant paradigms of the North.

Timing was important, too, for North American motion pictures arrived in Cuba during the formative years of the first republican-born generation. These were years of passage into adolescence and young adulthood as a normal facet of the life cycle, only it happened to involve the single largest generational cohort in Cuban history. The postcolonial generation, now coming of age, was especially susceptible to new ways of self-expression and self-representation. These youths were formed in a world radically different from that of their parents. They made movies their own and in the process adopted attitudes and behaviors unknown to the previous generation. "The youth of today are self-assured, bold," proclaims Inés in Ofelia Rodríguez Acosta's novel *En la noche del mundo* (1940). "It has nothing to do with the past."[31]

Behaviors were derived from the range of possibilities offered by new circumstances. Much of what originated from the North came in the form of scripted behaviors. Hundreds of thousands of young men and women, the demographically defining generation of twentieth-century Cuba, came of age during years of remarkable cultural change, when the forces of ideological formation and social deployment were shifting into the public realms of the media and the market. Motion pictures served to mediate these worlds, both as source of representation and means of reproduction, and in the process suggested narrative structures around which to arrange everyday life in a changing moral universe.

Men and women of all ages, black and white, filled movie theaters weekly, there to contemplate circumstances very different from those familiar to them. Year after year Cubans found in motion pictures new vantage points from which to contemplate their own lives. Film possessed the means to rearrange the value hierarchies by which to experience ordinary life, for the power of North American motion pictures was in their capacity to universalize the moral and material assumptions of the medium and its model. Film celebrated a different reality and in the process offered a standard by which to take measure of daily existence.

It was not always easy to distinguish between conditions portrayed on the screen and the reality of life in North America. Cuban audiences were typically not in the best position to make these comparisons. Films presented an alternative moral universe and a different view of success and happiness; they redefined standards of beauty and added deeper social meanings to consumption. They depicted values and possibilities that, simply by virtue of having been filmed, often implied validation. North American film narratives gave visual form and moral credibility to notions of right and wrong, paradigms of good and evil.

Movie theaters assumed the function of school—a place to learn about the outside world, about other ways of doing things, about history and current events. "Cinema," affirmed the *Revista Habanera* in 1914, "can be a magnificent element with which to educate the people, with its treatment of scientific affairs, travel, industry, and other similar themes." Solita Solano wrote of "the good influence" of North American movies as a means of "education for the Cubans who do not travel outside their country." Guillermo Cabrera Infante recalled seeing motion pictures at age three: "I was looking at films before I learned to read at the age of four—in other words I could read in the movies before I could in books. To me, the cinema has actually been more than a school, it has been an education." Movies frequently offered many Cubans a way to learn English. "I and my family go very often," said one moviegoer in 1936, "we enjoy the pictures very much, and my children as well as myself have greatly improved our knowledge of the English language by going to see pictures often." In the novel *El caserón del Cerro* (1961), Marcelo Pogolotti wrote of Paulina Bengochea, for whom "Hollywood movies, the only ones shown at the time, constituted the principal source of education." A Havana journalist recounted a conversation overheard between a young girl and her father in a local movie house: "Papá, there are many things that seem appropriate [as seen in film] given that they are commonly done and yet in school they tell us it is bad. You have to take me out of there, for it is at the movies where one really learns." And at least one critic thought that children were learning too much at the movies. "In those shows that are announced especially for children," wrote J. M. Morales in 1917, "or those that they attend, the lesson that is generally offered is such that, right here in Cuba, children have committed crimes that were inspired by some movie; and not a few girls have learned things that many women do not know even at an advanced age."[32]

The formulations of film entered the popular imagination early, and their influence was apparent everywhere. New store names appeared during the 1930s: the *bodega* "Tarzán" and one called "King-Kong." Cubans acquired sufficient familiarity with U.S. motion pictures to permit the use of Hollywood metaphors and models as a dominant modality of national narratives. In José Antonio Mases's short story "Los ladrones" (1973), the protagonist obtains his weight from a pay scale on a printed ticket "on the other side of which was the date and a picture of Rock Hudson, smiling, youthful."[33] It is impossible to fully ascertain the extent of Cuban familiarity with Hollywood. The evidence suggests, however, that Hollywood reached deeply into the commonplace and became a part of what routinely passed, unnoticed, as normal and natural. The fact that Mases assumed that his readers would recognize the name Rock Hudson itself indicates the degree to which Cubans had developed a familiarity with Hollywood.

Familiarity on this scale could not help but rearrange the cognitive categories by which Cubans came to recognize themselves and represent each other. The dominant frame of reference, that is, the means to represent reality and make sense of the world, was increasingly derived from North American formulations. Under the circumstances it was perhaps inevitable that representation of Cuban could often be best accomplished through the use of forms and types most readily accessible and widely recognized: Hollywood images. In Enrique Serpa's short story "Una mujer depravada" (1937), Laura is said to possess "a spirit like Mae West, something like a wicked cocktail of gin, whisky, rum and tequila concealed in an innocent fruit-like taste, like a 'Mary Pickford,' for example." The narrator in Miguel de Marcos's novel *Papaíto Mayarí* (1947) pledges his love to his sweetheart by vowing forever to carry her "from branch to branch, the way Tarzan carried Jane." One character in Luis Ricardo Alonso's *Los dioses ajenos* (1971) is described as "tall, reddish hair, pointed ears, with the smile of Lon Chaney." In Nicolás Dorr's play *Confesión en el barrio chino* (1984), Violeta possesses "intensely red lips, painted over the lip-line in the style of Joan Crawford." At another point Violeta recalls purchasing a new pair of shoes and leaving the store "walking like Dorothy Lamour." And still later Violeta reflects: "My life has been a movie. A great picture in Technicolor made by MGM. With song and laughter. With scenes in which the Marx brothers appear and starring Judy Garland." In Luis Santeiro's play *The Lady from Havana* (1991), Rosa proclaims her desire to be "a Mary Pickford with black hair." Pablo Armando Fernández alludes to Hollywood throughout *Los niños se despiden* (1968): Lila is compared to Ava Gardner, Hortensia looks like Olivia de Havilland, Carlotica resembles Joan Crawford, Mimina is likened to Shirley Temple, and Aleida looks like Jean Harlow. In Edmundo Desnoes's novel *Memorias de subdesarrollo* (1965), Sergio recalls "living with Emma, the brunette [who] remotely resembled Greta Garbo." Guillermo Cabrera Infante has been especially given to the use of movie stars to represent his characters. In *Tres tristes tigres* (1965), a friend of the narrator resembled Lew Ayres, "the honest dramatic cliches written on his face." Irena is "a cute little blonde, a doll who would have looked like Marilyn Monroe if the Jívaro Indians had captured her and reduced her down to size, not only shrinking her head but her body and all the rest—and I mean *all* the rest"; Cuba Venegas has "a hair style a little like a *mulata* version of Veronica Lake." A friend's mother "was very young and very beautiful, a bit like a Cuban Myrna Loy." The protagonist on a date, not wanting "to be at the moment a typical Cuban . . . but rather to be like Andy Hardy meeting Esther Williams," thus appears on a balcony "with the elegance and almost the same walk of a David Niven of the tropics"; and he is "playing the part of a man very much of the world, *a la* Cary Grant." In *Infante's Inferno* (1979), almost all of Cabrera Infante's characters have some resemblance to Hollywood stars: Rosita is "a life-sized version of Shirley Temple"; Carmen is "a beauty with black hair, parted down the middle and . . . looked like an imitation of Hedy Lamarr"; Juliet is a "genuine brunette who nevertheless reminded me of that false blonde of my childhood, Jane Powell, all total tits and green eyes"; a woman in a theater is "a beauty in the dark, . . . a virgin version of Gene Tierney"; and a woman aboard a bus "bent her head, a little like Lauren Bacall in 'To Have and Have Not.'" In the play *Su cara mitad* (1992) by Matías Montes Huidobro, Raúl reminisces to Sara: "You glowed so brilliantly that you did not seem real. You were like an image from the movies. When I was a boy I went to see a Grace Kelly movie, I don't recall which one, and when I first saw you, it was she who came to mind."[34]

At almost every turn, Hollywood served as a reference for recognition. Actor Maiano López was "el Lon Chaney cubano" and Antonio Perdices, "el Valentino cubano." Entertainer Carlos Macías, who used blackface, was billed as "el Al Jolson cubano." Writer Juan Marinello likened novelist Luis Felipe Rodríguez to Charlie Chaplin, "a man who came from yesterday." In 1936 Raúl Roa denounced as reckless a group of overzealous revolutionaries who called for immediate armed rebellion by comparing them to "*cowboys* in western movies who ride into the towns with guns blazing." A news story of a failed holdup attempt against a *bodega* in Quivicán in November 1954 represented the incident as "appearing as if it was taken . . . from the script of a North American western" and "an episode in a gangster movie customarily seen in the local movie houses." In describing his hometown of Bada in Oriente to Oscar Lewis, Carlos Pérez used similar imagery: "Have you ever seen those towns in western movies with the railroad tracks running down the center and the houses lined up on each side? Well, Bada is a town like that." Camagüey and Oriente provinces—Cuba's East—the undeveloped hinterland of the island, found most common representation as the U.S. West. Alberto Quadreny described the areas around Holguín as "el *Far West* cubano," and Antonio Iraizoz wrote of Morón as "un poco el *far west* cubano." Max Lesnik likened government repression in Oriente in 1956 to "the North American west of the last century [where] terror ruled." As late as 1996—and offering testimony to the resilience of Hollywood as a source of metaphor—former University of Havana rector Juan Mier Febles expressed concern about the growing disregard of Marxist tenets: "There are those who do with Marxism what Goldwyn-Mayer does with the MGM lion. It roars at the beginning of the picture, and never again appears."[35]

Films provided formulas around which to assemble reality into recognizable categories. Pilot Alvaro Prendes recalled meeting his flight instructor in the United States, "a typical North American, and like John Wayne or Humphrey Bogart, never smiled, a real tough guy." The U.S. instructor subjected Cuban cadets to difficult drills, "but only to get our reaction—at least that's how I had always seen it done in North American movies." And when successfully completing the program, Prendes affirmed: "That's the way it happened in the best film productions; everyone knew it: it is *fair play*. The good guy in the end prevails and is transformed into a hero by virtue of justice and dignity." In 1958, as the political crisis in Cuba deepened, *Bohemia* pleaded for honest elections, predicting that in that manner "victory would be obtained and the national crisis would be resolved in a *happy end* worthy of Hollywood." And when a family crisis is settled successfully in Luis Adrián Betancourt's novel *Expediente almirante* (1977), the protagonist proclaims: "A true *happy end*."[36]

The reach of the dominant narratives rendered in North American films extended to mass audiences across the island. By 1929 writer R. Suárez Solis could proclaim confidently that "the American, through his motion pictures, is more faithful to life than the European." The Western movie exuded North American values: the individual as hero, confronting insuperable odds in the defense of virtue and justice, righting wrongs and avenging grievances, and always prevailing. Through the Western Hollywood fashioned the imagery of the North American past, a history arranged as a morality play defined in Manichaean dichotomies of good versus evil. Ofelia Rodríguez Acosta grew up with North American films and could incorporate the experience into her prose with sensitivity and subtlety. "Films interested her a great deal," the narrator comments on the protagonist in *Sonata interrumpida* (1943). "Those figures: moving about silently on the screen aroused her fantasies. . . . The shows about the *cow boys* excited her a great deal. There was always a staged fight, in a violent way, between good and evil, and she, in a cold sweat remained in a state of anxiety at the edge of her seat until the fight was settled. Fortunately, the good guys invariably triumphed over the villains." Wenceslao Gálvez developed an abiding admiration for North Americans through motion pictures. "I most admire the American hero," Gálvez wrote. "Such a haughty way of risking great dangers. They always come out triumphant in all their undertakings: if they get knocked down, they do not suffer from the blow. It might be said they are made of rubber. Sometimes I wonder if this is related to their penchant for chewing gum."[37]

The influence of North American films reached into some of the more igno-minious facets of national life. The gangster movies of the 1930s were especially popular and seemed to have even influenced the Cuban form of political vio-lence. The drive-by machine-gun shooting, so much a part of the film genre, became a prominent motif of political warfare in Havana. The method was familiar to moviegoers: the speeding car, the burst of machine-gun fire, the getaway. In 1935 an attempted assassination of journalist Ramón Vasconselos involved a speeding Ford from which machine-gun fire originated. Four years later Marianao mayor Pedro Acosta was machine-gunned in a shooting modeled on the Hollywood gangster film. The protagonist in Enrique Serpa's novel *Con-trabando* (1938) enjoyed the "gangster shoot-out" on film. "I once saw a film in which a gangster killed four men with a portable machine gun," he exclaimed. Cabrera Infante recalled that street clashes between the Batista police and revo-lutionaries "reminded one of certain movie gangsters, immolated simulating, emulating Dillinger or Bonnie and Clyde on the screen."[38] The very word *gang-sterismo* passed directly into popular vernacular to describe shoot-outs and gun battles among armed groups of opposing political persuasions.

Films also affected prevailing standards of self-representation. Notions of beauty and body were in transition, and the influence of North American pref-erences was dramatic. Through much of the late nineteenth and early twentieth century, the idealized *criolla* form was round-faced and full. Visitors to Cuba often commented on the appearance of Cuban women, and they arrived at a striking consensus. Joseph Dimock described women in Havana as possessing "magnificent proportions," observing that in a local theater "of the hundreds of ladies present, I saw but two or three of delicate figures. I should judge the average weight of the ladies to be about 160 lbs." Maturin Ballou wrote of "a roundness of figure that leaves nothing to be desired in symmetry of form." "As a rule, she has a round figure, not large, but inclined to dumpling-shape," noted James Steele in 1881. "Whatever else she may be, she is never what the Americans call 'scrawny.'" Carolina Wallace made a similar observation nearly twenty years later: "I will remark *en passant* that flesh is an important factor in beauty here. To be slender and thin is considered ugly and worthy of commiseration." Cuban writer Benjamín de Céspedes disdained "bare-boned body" (*cuerpo huesoso*) among women, proclaiming instead preference for women in the "full flowering of their beauty" with the "gracious expansion of their lines and curves that acquire matronly artistic proportions."[39]

But times had changed. What previously had symbolized a leisurely mode now signified a state of lethargy associated with backwardness and indolence. "Thinness is the symbol of true beauty," the Cuban Institute of Physical Beauty proclaimed in 1924. "The languid life that women of tropical countries lead, aggravated by the lack of exercise and the hereditary tendency of *dolce far niente*, make creole beauties age early and prematurely lose the lines of youth." The institute promised to fulfill the "dream of the modern daughters of Eve: the acquisition of an elegant and svelte figure in a short time." In 1928 *Bohemia* declared that "thin women are in vogue." The beauty consultant at *Social* agreed: "It can be said that women in the United States have reached the highest level of beauty." Writer Marisabel Sáenz asserted outright that Cuban women were "not attractive in the exact meaning of the word" and that "there were not many attractive women." She attributed the "Cuban type"—"disproportionately heavy, with amply endowed hips, abundant breasts and skinny lower body," a condition she characterized as a "deformation"—to the "mixing of the races . . . but mostly to physical inactivity and indolence to which women of our country are addicted." Sáenz concluded: "Today the women who provide the model that should be followed are the movie actresses. The extraordinary beauty of Joan Crawford, in our opinion, possessing one of the most perfect bodies that could today be admired, is envied by untold numbers of girls all over the world."[40]

The deepening dichotomy found its way into popular literature and perhaps nowhere with greater nuanced understanding than in Lesbia Soravilla's novel *El dolor de vivir* (n.d.). "Women of all types walked about the streets," the narrator remarks. "Some of the *criollas* were of opulent hips, as if models of Ruben, with olive complexions, large and languid eyes, busts of generous proportions, indolent and sensual like seductresses." The new generation was different:

> To contrast with the survivors of a type of classic woman increasingly rare . . .
> there were the slender figures, like insects, with the tight skirts around their
> straight hips, with their knit hats tilted over their ear. . . . Atop four or five
> inches of heels, they take public places by storm with their shrill snobbery,
> their eagerness to become foreign (*extranjerizarse*) and their delirium with
> Hollywood. The blondes dress like Greta Garbo, the brunettes like Clara Bow.
> Some speak English or mix in any banal conversation their Americanisms,
> which strike a chic note.[41]

Motion picture renderings of beauty and body, no less than glamour and grace, quickly gained ascendancy as dominant standards of physical appearance. Films offered the ideal to which all were enjoined to aspire, models that over time gained currency among both men and women. Columnist Don Galaor heralded "the ideal type" and "the standard measurement" as 34–28–34. Hollywood had created a universal "sex-appeal," Jaime Deristel affirmed. "Now . . . a woman without *sex-appeal* is an insignificant being. . . . Today the charm of a woman is in her sexual attraction, in her *sex-appeal*, in her mysterious aura. Of all the modern inventions, film has been designated to bring to the world this form of sensuality, thanks to its stars."[42]

Film narratives on beauty and sex appeal were not confined to appearance. On the contrary, they were at least as much about being and becoming, about survival strategies, status, and success. Hollywood did not merely transmit North American notions of beauty. The ideals presented in movies could seize the popular imagination precisely because they arrived scripted with subtext. Cuban audiences appreciated film as a morality play, and women in particular were conscious of the larger meanings of film narratives in their own lives. These issues were discussed in private and debated in public. Ofelia Rodríguez Acosta wrote at length about Norma Shearer as "the woman of the free spirit" and Pauline Frederick as "the woman who seeks in her lover a provider rather than search for honest work as the material sustenance upon which to liberate her capacity to love."[43] The point here is the extent to which North American modes defined the parameters of public discourse, to which Cubans responded and around which—as model or antimodel—they assembled the hierarchies that gave meaning to their lives.

Motion pictures suggested a world of collapsible social barriers, where resourceful women, through charm and glamour, could rise above dreary circumstances. Upward mobility, success, and happiness were all linked to personal appearance and charm in Cinderella formulas. Roles played by North American actresses easily fit within the Cuban frame of reference and underscored the appeal of motion pictures. The moral was in mobility, a message that registered in the Cuban imagination.

The possibilities were available to almost everyone. Young women became more conscious of their own bodies and began to scrutinize those of North American actresses and imitate their physical characteristics and mannerisms. *Vanidades* published monthly "Beauty Secrets of American Stars" in which Rita Hayworth, Olivia de Havilland, Ginger Rogers, and Eleanor Powell, among many others, discussed the use of cosmetics, perfumes, clothing, diets, and exercises. Jean Harlow disclosed her "beauty secrets" in *Bohemia*. The monthly *Grafos* published a regular feature, "La técnica del make-up," that included, for example, advice on the use of mascara by Fay Wray, rouge by Loretta Young, and lipstick by Carole Lombard. *Carteles* presented "Hairstyles of Hollywood" and selected Greta Garbo as an ideal type. Doris Day, Janet Leigh, Maureen O'Hara, Anne Baxter, and Esther Williams revealed their "Hollywood beauty secrets"; Grace Kelly, Lauren Bacall, Audrey Hepburn, and Marilyn Monroe discussed their "hairstyle secrets"; Cyd Charisse provided helpful hints on how to "maintain the ideal figure." Paulette Goddard related how she used "glamour" to advance her career. Barbara Paine revealed "what all women should know about men," Joan Crawford explained "how to seduce a man," and Leigh Snowden discussed "the importance of how to walk": the "way a woman walks reveals her personality. Walk with chest raised, maintain your head high, and go about humming very softly a tune that you especially like." Readers were told that it was "the way that Marilyn Monroe walked that made her famous." Women were also taught how "to manicure their nails the way the movie stars do." A syndicated column by Sara Hamilton described "what Hollywood stars ate," and Edith Head, supervisor of the Paramount wardrobe department, suggested colors to match personality. In *Vanidades* screen stars served as a means to learn about the inner self. In one article readers were asked to select their favorite actress from a group of photographs as a way to "discover their true personality." Mary Spaulding wrote eloquently of Hollywood "experts on feminine beauty" and the "absolute rules to determine the beauty of a woman." Spaulding's ideals included Claudette Colbert ("who knows as much of torrid passion as she does of tenderness"), Mae West ("her appeal is physical"), and Clara Bow ("lips like ripe fruit, magnificent and expressive eyes, ample and arousing curves"). Spaulding commended Hollywood actresses for their "perfect noses" and "ideal legs." María Julia de Lara, in her weekly column "Salud y Belleza," extolled the perfect back— "smooth, clean and most of all without those masses of fat that disrupt the purity of the lines"—and used MGM actress Thelma Todd as a model. Lara wrote eloquently about "beautiful cheeks" and gave as examples Claudette Colbert and Ruby Keeler, the "aesthetics of thighs" such as Ida Lupino's, the "ideal hands" as possessed by Katharine Hepburn, "desirable hips" like Claudette Colbert's, and the "beautiful nose" of Katharine Hepburn and Jeanette MacDonald.[44]

Magazines and newspapers were filled with columns and feature articles offering advice on how to obtain the ideal shape based on Hollywood standards. RCA Victor marketed a new line of phonographs claiming that to do the Charleston (*charlestonear*) was the best exercise to acquire a Hollywood form. "Do you desire a figure like Esther Williams?" asked one article in *El Mundo*; it urged women to take up swimming as the "perfect way to refine and round off curves, like Esther Williams." Ida Jean Kain dedicated her syndicated column (*Mantenga la línea*) to exercise and physical fitness as the means to shapely figures like Hollywood actresses. The ideal waistline, Kain asserted, was twenty-four inches. "The majority of women yearn to have a figure as svelte as those of the screen stars." Kain offered advice on exercise and revealed movie star "secrets": Eleanor Powell practiced tap dancing as a way to thinner thighs; Janet Leigh recommended roller skating for shapelier legs. Versions of the North American ideal reached all ages.[45]

Shirley Temple, in particular, enjoyed widespread popularity in Cuba, where Shirley Temple dolls and coloring books found a lucrative market. *Vanidades* published a page of cutout dresses for a paper doll version of the young actress. In the short story "Las navidades de Shirley Temple" (1935) by Berta A. de Martínez Márquez, Sarita is the happiest child in Havana for having received a Shirley Temple doll. The Shirley Temple image quickly became a popular way for parents to present their daughters. Throughout the 1930s, national contests were organized to select the best Cuban Shirley Temple look-alike. In 1935 Myrna

Echeverría was selected as "la Shirley Temple cubana." Bella la Rosa reminisced about her life in a local circus, where her younger sister Felicia—"with friz-zled blonde hair" and billed as "the Cuban Shirley Temple"—sang and danced nightly dressed like Shirley Temple.[46]

North American ideals of beauty and body captured the popular imagina-tion. Probably nothing was more influential in disseminating the ideal of North American forms than motion pictures. They took hold early and held on fast. "The North American woman today is one of the leading examples of the world," declared columnist Isabel Margarita Ordext as early as 1916; "her ele-gance no less than her beauty are indisputable." The effects were remarkable. "My mother's feminine ideal was Joan Crawford," Cabrera Infante recalled. "Today," announced health and beauty consultant María Julia de Lara, "the angular figure of the incomparable Greta Garbo reigns"—and forthwith pro-vided a diet for a "rational weight loss" program. *El Mundo* columnist Sandra proclaimed Deborah Kerr—"serene, tender, dignified, and modest"—as the "ideal woman." Marge Champion possessed the ideal legs. *Vanidades* selected Lauren Bacall, Ava Gardner, Dorothy McGuire, Jennifer Jones, and Janet Leigh as "the types of women that most men desire." In Soravilla's *El dolor de vivir*, Mario comments to Belita: "You look like Greta Garbo, exactly like Greta, in your eyes, in your mouth, in your smile"; and the narrator added: "That was the most that a modern girl could aspire to." Actor Otto Sirgo described the "ideal woman" as having "the eyes of Joan Crawford, the face of Ava Gardner, the bust of Jane Russell, the legs of Cyd Charisse, the warmth of Leslie Caron, the culture of Deborah Kerr, and the *sex-appeal* of Sophia Loren."[47]

Dominant idealizations served as the standard by which vast numbers judged themselves and others and, indeed, offered the means of personal fulfillment. "Accustomed as we are to seeing so many beautiful women on the screen in a continuous display of perfection," wrote Mary Spaulding, "it is natural that we would compare ourselves and not be grateful to Nature for what it has done to us. It is not ingratitude: it is simply the logical condition of being human." Spaulding offered as a remedy "the art of plastic surgery"—"It is a flourishing field, as prosperous as the film industry itself." She concluded: "Who can deny the influence of motion pictures in every aspect of present day civilized life. . . . They are a school more instructive and more important than all the text books written to date. We discover ourselves, thus, face to face with this art form which to enhance its enormous prestige has made it even possible to improve body parts poorly made by Nature." The moral was clear: one controlled one's fate by controlling personal appearance. "A nose can change a future," contended Maida Soto, demonstrating with "before and after" photographs how Gina Lollabridgida and Jan Sterling improved their appearances—and their lives—through plastic surgery.[48]

That these concepts were embedded in distinct racial categories did not necessarily preclude access to all. On the contrary, the power of U.S. market forms was in their capacity to intimate inclusion. Blacks could aspire to these standards, if admittedly with additional assistance. "Men and women, do you want to whiten your skin?" asked an advertisement in *Carteles* for a cream produced by J. Rouseau and Company of Chicago. The M. Trilety Company of Binghamton, New York, demonstrated "how one could have kissable lips." A diagram showed a brace strapped around the face and fitted over the lips that was guaranteed "to reduce thick, fleshy, and protuberant lips to the point of leaving them in a normal size. If you use it for two months during the night you will obtain lips that can rival those of the most famous beauties of screen and stage." M. Trilety also distributed a home device to reshape the nose. Employing a picture of a black woman, the 1921 advertisement in the magazine *Social* had a straightforward message:

> Nowadays it is absolutely necessary to be concerned with one's face if one expects to become something and advance in life. . . . It is worth being as attractive as possible. Do not let others form negative opinions of the appearance of your face, for this prejudices your well-being. The success or failure of your life depends on the good or bad impression formed by you. . . . With my apparatus you can now correct defective noses without necessity of surgery, quickly, with security, and permanently.

Allyn's Hair Straightener Cream, manufactured by the Continental Beauty Supply Corporation, was advertised in *Bohemia* as "specially created for people of color." Endorsements obtained by Continental Beauty Supply included those of Beny Moré, Celia Cruz, and Pérez Prado.[49]

Films offered far greater access to the world of the North. For the countless Cubans who had never experienced North American life firsthand, motion pictures provided a connection unobtainable by any other means. Movies suggested new ways for men and women to act and interact, new codes of moral conduct and different ways to experience life. They stimulated the social imagination, introduced new manners and new models of psychological fulfillment, and as part of mass culture possessed the power to serve as a means of unity. If the conventional historiographical wisdom concerning the role of motion pictures in the United States as agency of "Americanization" is only partially correct —specifically, film as an instrument for the integration of immigrants into a broader national consensus through shared cultural forms and common social values—the implication of U.S. films in Cuba must be considered far-reaching indeed. North American modes often became Cuban models. Silent films, in particular, employed a highly comprehensible—and transmittable—stylized method of communication in which image, gesture, and look informed the narrative and suggested a text of explanation. Movies offered new ways of walking, of sitting, of moving the head and shoulders, a new gait, a new gesture, new poses and postures. Movie stars represented stylized dispositions and defined the demeanor of a generation.

Careful observers saw these influences take hold over Cuban youth. "The movies," commented Jess Losada, "have produced a male *standard* that inspires youth everywhere. They look upon the star as the ideal of their dreams. They aspire to be like Clark Gable, Robert Taylor, Gary Cooper or Errol Flynn. . . . These actors wear the best clothing that could be made for men. . . . It is logical that youth have the desire to try to imitate them. They even follow the example of these leading men in the way they make love." Losada concluded: "Movies are unquestioningly the principal classroom for love, urbanity, and aesthetics of today's youth." Rodolfo Arango described the "numerous young men who have taken it upon themselves to imitate Rudolph Valentino." They "dedicate themselves entirely to imitating Valentino in their attire, in their walk, in their hair styling, in their sneezing—in everything. They saw only movies of Valentino and later, upon returning home, stood before the mirror to practice the gestures of the actor, and above all, the lowering of the eyes." In Pepita Riera's novel *Tú vida y la mía* (1949), José Luis cannot contain his astonishment at the changes among young women: "Another group of girls, far more aware of life than their years, leave you amazed with their mannerisms and gestures of coquetry; some believe themselves to incarnate some movie star. I can assure that on this very day I have danced with Lana Turner and Rita Hayworth." In a Luis Sáez short story, the protagonist is "looking despairingly, with the cigarette on the tip of his lips, in the style of James Dean."[50]

It is impossible to determine with precision the degree to which films popularized and promoted North American ways. The evidence is scattered but suggestive. Certainly the medium provided a complex form for discerning previously unrevealed possibilities for self-transformation. "Film . . . is hypnotizing humanity," observed José Juan Tablada. "It is the most powerful instrument for the Americanization of the rest of the planet. How can the masses . . . resist the fascinating influence of the movies? How can one not adopt the fascinating norms that are therein advanced, from the superficial . . . to the profound."[51]

The relationship was manifest, if not always measurable, as the influence of Hollywood reached across the island. Women of all social and economic classes "desire to look like a movie actress," noted Lesbia Soravilla; "even domestic servant girls put on an attractive appearance of refinement and polish on their day off." Almost all popular magazines published weekly photo features of Hollywood styles and fashions as worn by movie stars. Men's fashion writer Algernón linked motion pictures to posture, hair styles, and speech and mannerisms. "The current rage of thin mustaches and long hair," he wrote in 1944, "is a reflection of the movie star."[52]

Women did not misinterpret the premise and promise of screen glamour. The meaning of Marilyn Monroe resonated among Cuban audiences. Blondes filled the Cuban imagination, each associated with a specific demeanor representing the full spectrum of screen types from Mae West and Jayne Mansfield to Kim Novak and Doris Day. It did indeed appear that blondes had more fun. Writer Sara Hernández proclaimed that "gentlemen preferred blondes"; moreover, "They are not only preferred by the public, of both sexes, but many men consider them the fulfillment of their dreams." Many of Cuba's most prominent female performers appeared as blondes, including Elena Machado, Violeta Jiménez, Alba Marián, Marta Pérez, Velie Martínez, Josefina Rovira, and María Brenes. The Elvis Presley and James Dean looks were also imported to Cuba. By 1957 a columnist wrote of the "Elvis craze" in Havana, and almost immediately the "Elvis look" was adopted by several prominent actors and singers, including Pedrito Rico, Pepe Amador, Carlos Alberto Badías, Carlos Barba, and Pedro Vargas.[53]

The power of film to shape preferences seemed to have no limits. North American versions of beauty served as the most readily accessible model on which Cuban ideals were derived. Film stars populated the world of Cuban sexual fantasies. In *Memorias de subdesarrollo* (1965), Sergio contemplates the women known to have visited Ernest Hemingway in Cuba: Ava Gardner, Ingrid Bergman, and Marlene Dietrich—the women "I would use [as] *pin-up girls* for masturbation." Pablo Medina recalled dreaming of "American women—blonde, tall, with fair freckled skin and long shapely legs, just like movie stars . . . [with] ruby-red lips and the curves of their calves accentuated by high-heeled shoes." Visiting a nightclub featuring Mirta, described as "Cuba's Marilyn Monroe," Warren Miller had occasion to learn of the preference of patron Julio Manduley: "Men adore [Mirta] for some reason. I myself find her fat. She is too Cuban. I like better the tall, broad-shouldered women such as Ann Sheridan and Joan Crawford. . . . I like the thin ones, all bones and passion, such as Ida Lupino. I myself feel that there is more soul in a thin person than in a fat one."[54]

These were compelling images inscribed with complex messages and possessed of the capacity to induce discontent with the Cuban condition and foster identities with norms of the North. The power of Hollywood resided in its capacity to implicate Cuban sensibilities in mythical narratives of the North American experience. In Pablo de la Torriente's short story "Una aventura de Salgari" (1956), the sixteen-year-old protagonist yearns for the land of Buffalo Bill, Red Cloud, Jules Verne, cowboys, and Comanches; he remarks: "Man always wants to follow a course similar to the life of his heroes. And I, naturally, was truly bored in Havana. This city is hopeless. . . . Nothing here looks like the *Far West*." In *Arbol de la vida*, Lisandro Otero's protagonist wistfully recalls "Saturday afternoons at the Manzanares theater, when I admired Flash Gordon and hated the odious emperor Ming, and I was exhilarated by the valor of the North American marines in [the film] 'Guadalcanal' or in 'The Sands of Iwo Jima.'" Pablo Medina provides insight into the ways U.S. motion pictures and television fostered ambiguity and ambivalence no less than a sense of inadequacy, if not inferiority: "What did we Cubans have that could possibly rival the glitter of Marilyn Monroe's lips, the innocence of Debbie Reynolds, the purposeful swagger of John Wayne? Or all those battleships and planes crowding the screens? Or the guts of World War II soldiers with their steely teeth and unshaven faces? Or New York where life was vertical and framed in neon? Or snow or Disneyland or nudist camps or cowboys and Indians or Niagara Falls or Porky Pig?" Medina continued:

> More than anything I wanted to be American and live in a suburb . . . and have a pretty blonde wife who waited on me as Doris Day waited on Rock Hudson. And I wanted to have children like those spoiled brats of American television and I wanted to own a Buick and have martinis at lunch in a wood-paneled bar surrounded by women dressed in black, and I wanted to be Eliot Ness, self-righteously ridding the world of gangsters and booze; most of all, I yearned for the reality of celluloid, truth of fiction.[55]

Gustavo Pérez Firmat lived his dream when he met and married Mary Anne— "the *americanita* of my dreams"—from the New Jersey suburb of Northvale. Through Mary Anne, Pérez Firmat recounted, "I was able to imagine myself as an American teenager growing up in the suburbs," adding: "I also know that the fact that she was American and I Cuban acted as a powerful catalyst in our romance. . . . I loved Mary Anne for all the ways—and they were countless—in which she did not remind me of Cuba or Miami."[56]

Film facilitated Cuban entrée into the normative realms of the North. The experience assumed many forms, of course, and the effects were not always the same or immediately discernible. Motion pictures fostered an understanding of ways and things North American and became one of the principal means to presume familiarity with the United States. "We avidly followed American life through the many imported books and films available to us," wrote Marcia del Mar, "and looked to America for guidance and inspiration." Under the circumstances, it was easy to identify with North American paradigms. Notions of self-presentation, of good over evil, and of life with a happy ending resonated on the island. Heroes easily crossed cultural boundaries: Roy Rogers, Red Ryder, and Superman obtained wide audiences in Cuba. In Raúl González de Cascorro's play *El mejor fruto* (1958), Gustavo liked Hollywood Westerns, "always enjoying how the good guys defeated the bad guys." As a child in the 1950s, Oscar Zanetti admired "the tall, thin character with a raccoon hat and a long Kentucky rifle: Davey Crockett. Alongside him, we hunted in the woods of the American frontier, and we defended the Alamo until our last breath. Years later, I would understand—with disillusion—that in some of these childhood battles I had fought on the wrong side."[57]

Motion pictures also played an important part in enhancing the value of consumer goods. The lines connecting beauty and glamour to success and happiness often passed through emulation of North American ways, especially in the consumption of U.S. products. The larger if not always intended effect of U.S. films abroad was to put the North American way of life on display. Motion pictures depicted a standard of living defined mainly by possession of goods, thereby suggesting the social value of products. New levels of fashion consciousness arrived by way of film, which also defined style. Goods seen on the screen, often props as mundane as appliances, home furnishings, and sundries, were a source of information about usage and utility. U.S. motion pictures intensified Cuban susceptibilities to things North American and in complex ways contributed mightily to the formation of tastes and preferences—demand, in a word—perfectly adapted to U.S. products. Chewing gum, dangling a cigarette from the corner of the mouth, or drinking whiskey, for example, had particular resonance. One study of the influence of U.S. films suggests that Westerns were instrumental in promoting whiskey consumption in the Dominican Republic, as when the cowboy enters a saloon and asks for a whiskey.[58]

These were years of changing conventions, of new and different ways of self-representation, of market-driven definitions of beauty and glamour. The suggestive images offered on the motion picture screen influenced Cuban preferences and in still one more fashion drew Cubans to North American consumption modes. This, no doubt, is what Jorge Delano had in mind when he wrote that the "beautifully designed sets in pictures have aroused in people a desire to live in nicer surroundings."[59]

Products designed for the U.S. market projected into the Cuban market new concepts of gender relations, sexual modalities, and standards of beauty not simply as cultural types but as commodity related, accessible as an act of consumption. Sex appeal was depicted as a commodity to be acquired much like furniture. To participate in this cultural order was first and foremost an act of consumption. U.S. products were appropriated to facilitate social integration and self-definition. Cubans were particularly susceptible to commodity forms as a means of behavioral differentiation and social distinction. They were implicated in this world on the same basis and by the same standards, through the same appeals and subject to the same admonitions, as North Americans. Sales of cosmetics, toiletries, mouthwash, deodorant, and toothpaste replicated U.S. trends. Consumption was driven by new advertising forms, loaded with cultural-bound messages of good looks, glamour, grooming, personal hygiene, happiness, and the promise of well-being.

Advertising was a growth sector in the Cuban economy. North American advertising firms established offices in Havana almost as soon as Spanish rule ended. Their presence expanded in direct proportion to the expansion of trade, or maybe it was the other way around. In fact, many of the major U.S. agencies maintained offices in Havana, including Grant, A. B. Ayers, McCann-Erickson, and J. Walter Thompson. Most personnel in Cuban-owned and -operated advertising agencies were trained in the United States. In almost every important way Cuba was integrated directly into North American marketing strategies. "Sales techniques in Cuba are to a great extent identical to those used in the United States," observed the U.S. commercial attaché in 1955. "Advertising media is identical except that it is in Spanish instead of English." Advertising executive J. Bruce Swigert of McCann-Erickson recalled handling the Havana account for Revlon: "Creative for Revlon, being high-fashion and sophisticated, relied on N.Y. models, who were all international types. We would adapt the copy to Spanish in Havana, but relied on N.Y. graphics. The appeal to the Cuban 'high' that was our market was the same as to the New York or London 'high.'" Advertisements accounted for fully 50 percent of the content of daily newspapers. And what they touted most were U.S. goods and products.[60]

Advertisements became a significant means by which to diffuse North American ways. This was not simply promoting a product. Certainly ads urged people to buy U.S. merchandise, but they also espoused a way of life and implied a manner of being in the world. The power of advertising was in its capacity to encourage the development of materialist sensibilities on a scale sufficient to sustain consumption as a condition of everyday life. Advertising functioned at least as much to change habits as to create needs and stimulate demands. In this sense, it served as an agency of socialization, for it fostered a specific version of individual interaction and social adaptation as a way to relate to the world at large. Advertising depicted the desirable household and correct attire, summoned a version of what proper bourgeois life ought to be, and subtly educated prospective customers on new norms for consumerism—for instance, more and different clothes and other goods and household items for every occasion. These changes affected almost every facet of daily life, from manners, fashion, and taste to structures of authority, moral values, and the meaning of achievement.

Advertisers understood their market and early learned to exploit Cuban insecurities to promote products. Unemployment anxieties loomed large in the labor force, as much among professional and white-collar employees as blue-collar workers. A labor market that experienced unemployment and under-employment at a more or less permanent rate of 40 percent was particularly susceptible to product appeal based on job security. An advertisement for Strand ties pictured an applicant being turned down for a job: "He failed to obtain employment because of one detail [an unsightly tie]. In moments like these it is indispensable to wear a Strand tie." In an ad for Mum deodorant, "Sr. Díaz" of "Díaz, García & Co." is speaking on the telephone with an employment agency representative. "Send me another employee," he says. "I have to fire the one I have. She is a good worker but I cannot stand her by my side." Then he comes to the point: "And listen, please, when you send me the new stenographer buy her Mum deodorant and charge it to my account." In a comic strip ad for Toni permanents entitled "Rosa Finds Employment," Rosa attributes her successful job interview to her Toni-permed hair.[61]

The larger significance of North American advertising was related less to market transactions than to moral transformations, although they were closely connected. Advertising could disseminate common values to a mass audience, suggesting inclusion as a function of consumption. This potential had far-reaching implications in Cuba. U.S. advertisers understood their task as the creation of a marketplace culture based on shared values and norms. Advertising as an instrument of education thus served as an agency of "Americanization," forging a national market out of an ethnically diverse and racially mixed population. These concerns were very much on the mind of Frank Presbrey, whose 1929 book on the *History and Development of Advertising* served as the standard textbook for a generation. Presbrey hailed advertising as "a civilizing influence comparable in its cultural effects to those of other great epoch-making developments in history." Repeatedly he stressed that if advertising "did not first educate [it] would not sell the article which the manufacturer is seeking to distribute," central to which was the forging of a shared national identity. The role of advertising in producing a homogeneous national character was vital to its success. Presbrey insisted:

> To national advertising . . . has recently been attributed most of the growth of a national homogeneity in our people, a uniformity of ideas which, despite the mixture of races, is found to be greater here than in European countries whose population is made up almost wholly of people of one race and would seem to be easier to nationalize in all respects. . . . This factor . . . appears as the most important of all influences in blending and welding into a whole the variegated patterns of American customs, costumes, manners and habits.[62]

The capacity of North American advertising to forge national character as a function of market had significant consequences in Cuba. Its success depended on its ability to appropriate symbols and influence other forms of communication even as it taught new consumption behavior. "We used the same kind of demographic information one might use to expand from N.Y. to the west coast," recalled J. Bruce Swigert of McCann-Erickson's approach in Cuba, "plus, of course, the things that were peculiar to the market. Kings' Day, for example, was important back then. And we would use Cuban idiom when it seemed to be appropriate. . . . Or on holidays we were more Cuban than the Cubans, paying homage to Martí and all the others."[63]

The narrative reinforced the central assumptions of consumption. Advertising informed the exchanges transacted daily and shaped national sensibilities, the vision of aspirations, and the formation of personal identity. It created the possibility of self-transformation and in the process implied self-command—in a word, empowerment. Self-worth and success were linked explicitly to standard of living, which in turn was associated with consumption. Products promoted a better life, specifically "the American way of life," around which to arrange beliefs and behaviors. The accumulation of goods promised to increase comfort and luxury and lead to higher social standing, all of which were expected to produce well-being and happiness. The act of consumption was often accompanied by the promise of contentment and success: to enhance self-esteem, allay self-doubt, and increase self-confidence. Consumption offered the appearance of reality and the possibility of personal transformation within a broader narrative of material possession. At still one more point Cubans were implicated in North American formulations.

The extent to which advertising influenced behavior is difficult to ascertain. Advertisements provided explicit narratives of image and usage, specifically the notion of possibility as an outcome of consumption. The combined impact of motion pictures and advertising was far-reaching indeed. These two mediums provided a subtext replete with meanings and messages, principally in the form of prescriptive narratives and sources of new knowledge on how to live, appropriate modes of behaviors, correct dress, and proper tastes. Linkages between success and self-representation, on one hand, and consumption and happiness, on the other, were set in sharp relief. Products promised entrée to desirable lifestyles and ideal personal relationships. Identity was by prescription attainable by assembling a self from the materials most readily available. Success and status were achievements of appearance, in the display and in the demonstration. "Eating isn't enough anymore," proclaims Oscar in Eduardo Machado's play *The Modern Ladies of Guanabacoa* (1991). "We need different things. They've invented the automobile, a washing machine, a light bulb, and it's not what you eat anymore, it's how you cook it. Not just food, what kind of plates you eat it on." Success was to be presented exactly the way Gustavo Pérez Firmat remembered his father, "who loved the outward signs of wealth more than wealth itself."[64]

U.S. products were scripted in the form of injunction: new possibilities for self-fulfillment, new ways of self-presentation, and new strategies for success based on more efficient personal hygiene, better grooming, new eating habits for better health. These products arrived encoded with messages of modernity, of being of the times and up-to-date. Advertisers of U.S. products early recognized Cuban susceptibilities. Perhaps no theme in the marketing of products was as prominent as "modern." "We thought that Cubans were interested in being 'civilized' and 'up-to-date,' " recalled J. Bruce Swigert.[65] Merchandise was proclaimed modern to foster Cuban identity with "modern" countries. "Now in Cuba," read an advertisement for Proctor and Gamble, "similar to the United States, France, and England, millions of housewives in Cuba use Tide." A vast array of women's products promised modernity: Maidenform urged women to "pause, look and see the very modern figure you will reveal in your Maidenform Brassiere"; "the modern woman uses Kotex." Helene Curtis offered "the invisible hair net for the modern woman," and Colgate toothpaste enjoined Cuban women "to laugh without fear of ridicule, for the modern woman smiles displaying her clean and healthy teeth, symbols of refinement and feminine beauty." The "very twentieth century woman," Stacomb hair cream insisted, "would never use conditioners that would dry or discolor the hair." Kellogg's Corn Flakes maintained that "the active child needs instant energy. That's why the modern mother serves this breakfast source of energy." Salem cigarettes boasted of a "modern filter," Pepsi Cola was the "modern soft drink," the Kodak Brownie was "a modern design." Cutex advertised "the modern preparation to remove cuticles"; Squibb's was "the modern toothpaste for the modern woman." Hotpoint exhorted: "Live well *a la moderna* with Hotpoint appliances." General Electric advertised "elegant and distinguished appliances for the modern home," "the modern kitchen for the modern woman," and "modern tools among which those powered by electricity are the most numerous and practical." U.S. Keds were "manufactured by modern methods," Schaeffer produced the "modern fountain pen," Gillette encouraged "shaving *a la moderna*," and Mum roll-on deodorant came in "a modern applicator."[66]

On occasion, the product was explicitly "the American way of life," a condition attainable by the consumption of U.S. products. McGregor clothes promoted its new line of women's slacks as the "American Look"—the name in English; they possessed "stylized lines with the new tendency of American fashion." Kellogg's cold cereal was the "American breakfast"; the ad provided an illustration of the "typical American family" gathered around the breakfast table with the message: "A good breakfast, American style, will give you more energy and vitality all day long." Columnist María Subira urged her readers to "accustom yourselves to breakfast with fruits, cereals, oats, cream of wheat, cornflakes, puffed rice and cocoa." Admiral advertised "a group of high quality household goods that will provide your family with the highest level of American convenience, luxury and economy." Pond's offered to share the "beauty secret known by millions of women in the United States": there was nothing "more important for a woman who wishes to be admired and considered elegant and 'chic' as a delicate and smooth complexion." And a soap manufacturer declared: "Among the beautiful women of the South in the United States, from New Orleans to Key West, Woodbury soap is nine times more popular than any other brand."[67]

This was a vast, complicated system, interlocking and overlapping, reinforcing and reciprocal. That it did not respond to a larger design did not mean that it lacked a logic. U.S. products appeared to be endowed with properties capable of fulfilling dreams inspired by motion pictures, and certainly this was the message conveyed by advertisers. Beauty and, by implication, success and happiness were available to everyone through consumption of the appropriate products.

Cuban familiarity with Hollywood served advertisers well, for they were able to parlay recognition of film stars into endorsements of U.S. products in the Cuban mass media. Virginia Mayo, Don Ameche, and Tyrone Power were only a few of the headliners to endorse Colynos toothpaste in advertisements published in *Bohemia*, *Carteles*, and *Vanidades*. Joan Blondell and Dick Powell recommended Pepsodent. John Wayne favored Camel cigarettes in *Bohemia*. Colleen Moore—"famous for her beautiful hands"—endorsed Cutex; so did Doris Kenyon: "Cutex is indispensable for my dressing room," she was quoted as saying. June Allyson, Cyd Charisse, Deborah Kerr, Esther Williams, and Elizabeth Taylor vouched for Lustre-Creme Shampoo. Woodbury soap announced in one ad that "108 favorite actresses of the New York stage" and in another that "352 Hollywood stars" selected Woodbury Facial Soap as "the best soap for their skin." An advertisement in *Carteles* showed a woman applying Tangee lipstick accompanied by an endorsement from Gary Cooper: "Lips that men like to kiss."[68]

The popularity of motion pictures coincided with the expansion of advertising for North American beauty products and items of personal hygiene. Marketing strategies were both product and promoter of larger social changes overtaking Cuba. The business of beauty flourished after the 1920s, when consumption of lipstick, nail polish, rouges and powders, hair dyes, mascaras, lotions, and creams increased dramatically. Manufacturers offered the promise of glamour, and Hollywood films carried the moral to its inevitable conclusion: beauty was indispensable for happiness and well-being. "Beautiful actress Dorothy Dalton attributes her stupendous success to her beautiful skin," attested the manufacturers of Kulux skin cream. "It is known that the beauty that produces that irresistible attraction," insisted the makers of Palmolive soap, "that seduces, that captures the heart of a man, that the whole world admires, is simply the beauty of the natural immaculate skin, fresh and soft, full of life and youth." The use of Palmolive "in the morning, afternoon, and before retiring" would "result in radiant skin and greater happiness." Cutex advertised a manicure set with the admonition that "enchanting finger nails are today a social necessity." Hopkin's Oriental Cream promised the attainment of "happiness and joy that comes with a pure and impeccably beautiful skin." According to the makers of Ipana toothpaste, "a lovely mouth was the first requisite of beauty. More poems have been inspired by the female smile than any other feature of a woman's face." Hind's facial cream alluded to new fashions when it asked: "Does your face appear older than your shoulders? Protect your face, neck, arms and hands by using Hinds Cream daily." A campaign of Pond's Cold Cream variously showed photographs of "Ana," "Adela," and "Paquita" displaying a diamond ring and the accompanying bold-lettered text: "You too will triumph in love."[69]

Methods of mass production, systems of mass media and mass distribution, rapid communication, and efficient transportation all worked to integrate countless Cubans into a new social order codified by a consumption ethic. This development signaled the ascendancy of a new cultural vision in which consumption of U.S. products and subscription to the normative system from which they were derived combined to forge a moral commitment around the promise of the market. Renderings of the North American consumer ethic within the Cuban context contained a powerful, liberating resonance, and, indeed, this was a major source of its appeal. It offered a new generation the means to challenge old ways. Commodity promised an enlarged social space for self-expression. Under certain circumstances the North American market ethic could redefine the space in which to develop alternative behaviors and values. The power of the market was in its capacity to consolidate national character around the promise implied in consumption.

Many Cubans arrived at definition through encounters with commodity. The market served as the point where culture and social structure intersected and interacted. Cultural change suggested more than new lifestyles and new sensibilities. It implicated social structures themselves, as possibilities of self-expression expanded as a function of consumption and at the same time developed the capacity to challenge existing value hierarchies. In this sense, consumption culture had a powerful, galvanizing effect by seeming to place the possibility of freedom and equality within everyone's reach.

Nowhere did these dramatic developments register with greater resonance than in the lives of women. Many of these changes had their antecedents in the previous century and were themselves the product of transition from colony to republic. These developments enabled numerous women to escape abject dependence on fathers and unhappy relationships with husbands. Divorce, which was legalized in 1918, created new possibilities for independence. So did education. The increase in high school and university enrollment was noteworthy. In 1899 a total of 1,400 women over the age of fifteen had received a formal education; by 1919 the number had increased to nearly 14,000. Almost one-quarter of the University of Havana enrollments in 1929–30—1,300 out of 5,600—were women.[70]

These advances portended improvements of other kinds. Extended education widened horizons and created new employment opportunities. Women entered the labor force in increasing numbers—as professionals, secretaries and stenographers, sales clerks and office clerks, telephone operators, factory workers, teachers, and nurses. With a disposable income and increased freedom of action, women became consumers.

In part these circumstances were related to necessity, in part to opportunity. Economic need often obliged women to seek work outside the home as a result of a changing calculus in the household economy. Family budgetary pressures sometimes acted as a strong incentive for women to join the labor force. But it was no less true that the rapidly expanding North American enterprise replicated U.S. modalities and provided many new job possibilities. U.S. retail chains mushroomed across the island. So did U.S. manufacturers. F. W. Woolworth entered Havana in 1924 and subsequently moved into Matanzas and Cienfuegos. Sears arrived in 1942. The Arrow Shirt company opened a factory in San Antonio de los Baños. The Aetna Knitted Fabrics Company of New York established a plant in Guanabacoa. Arrow and Aetna together hired nearly 700 workers, mostly women. Woolworth's employed more than 1,000 sales clerks, most of whom were also female. Almost all the 300 sales personnel at Sears were women.

The presence of North American enterprises had other consequences. Command of English offered women opportunities for equal employment and advancement unavailable by any other means. A 1957 advertisement by Hemphill Commercial School in *Vanidades*, a women's magazine, made the point explicitly: "There is no difference in the social and economic advance between men and women who know the English language." Columnist Isabel Margarita Ordext, who was herself bilingual, urged women to learn English—a "language very useful today"—to guarantee their job security. In Pogolotti's *El caserón del Cerro*, knowledge of English enables Paulina to obtain employment with the "International Highway Company" in the worst days of the Great Depression, when "it was easier for a camel to pass through the eye of a needle than to find work."[71]

In the 1920s a new generation was reaching maturity in the midst of dramatic cultural change. Many young women had experienced this change firsthand as residents or students in the North and went home with high hopes. "Cuban girls who return from American colleges and schools," observed Solita Solano in 1920, "expect that when they obtain the vote they will find the remedy to many of the ills that exist in Cuba. They want the same liberty that American women have. They want to work in a profession or in an office. . . . They want to have their own careers." While visiting Havana in 1922, Anaïs Nin noticed that "the younger girls, educated abroad are returning with knowledge and ideals, so that for Havana, as for every city, one can count on the gradual influence of progress." In Federico de Ibarzabal's short story "Un escándalo social" (1926), Rosa has recently returned from the United States with different gestures and manners and is "given to certain topics of conversation at any given moment." Rosa was "too modern, maybe ultramodern."[72]

Social change was partly market driven. El Encanto department store was not slow to recognize the implications of these developments. The "evolution of women's customs and intelligence," a store advertisement affirmed, in a "society that readily accepts those measures that improve and refine customs," placed Cuba "among the top of progressive countries." Specifically: "The modern woman, freed of thousands of old-fashion prejudices, now no longer 'goes shopping,' in the sense of passing the time away. She now goes to shop, which is not the same thing." Accordingly, El Encanto announced the availability of credit cards made out in the "modern woman's name" on her own account.[73]

Motion pictures also contributed to these conditions in portraying confrontations between the new and the old. Screen roles depicting all social types, encoded with meanings and messages, reached receptive audiences across the island. Films disseminated the new chic and bravado. Many women identified with North American types, emulating their behaviors and styles. Mary Pickford, for instance, enjoyed enormous popularity in Cuba: "The ingenue, delightful, the eternal youth" was the way *La Lucha* described her in 1926. Her quest to be economically independent and morally liberated, to work as a means of personal fulfillment, manifestly modern and perpetually youthful and pure, registered in Cuba. Women contemplating alternative modalities of being and behavior found in Pickford a model of style and point of view. Rodolfo Arango wrote of the young women who became obsessed to be "more brilliant than Mary Pickford."[74] The flapper, personified by Clara Bow, Joan Crawford, Gloria Swanson, and Norma Talmadge, endowed with freedom and energy, able to flirt with abandon, to dance and party, youthful, spirited, daring, and responsible only to herself, found a larger audience among women of all classes.

Films could not help but invite invidious comparison and expose contradictions and in the end suggested an alternative set of conditions to which to aspire. In the novel *El placer de sufrir* (1921), Alfonso Hernández Catá describes Elvira, who "often went to the movies . . . and upon seeing images of other countries where women could, without suffering a loss of reputation, earn a living became angry at the fate that had her born in a backward country of such wretched conditions."[75]

The invocation of the North assumed many forms, of course, and these changed over time. The enfranchisement of North American women in 1919 provided a powerful incentive to Cuban women and, indeed, served as a constant point of reference. Political developments in the United States resonated in Cuba and often led to the mobilization of Cuban women, who in any case maintained that they were as qualified to vote as their North American counterparts. Columnist Florisa de Neveres praised the United States for having elevated "women to the same social level as men" and for "restoring political rights to the capriciously named weaker sex." Ofelia Domínguez spoke for many when she alluded to the success of suffrage in the United States: "The great American nation has converted its daughters into citizens. Apparently, only the countries of Latin origins maintain the Roman principle of our inferiority."[76]

Dress and demeanor became still another way to affirm modernity and influenced all aspects of women's lives as personal style found expression in new fashions. Here, too, the immediate impact and lasting effects of World War I came into play. Much of Cuban chic had previously originated in Europe; although it never ended completely, the predominance of European fashion in Cuba diminished considerably after 1914. "In normal times," commented Isabel Margarita Ordext in 1915, "Paris is and will be the arbiter of women's fashions; but in times of war the United States has demonstrated that it can satisfactorily resolve these important matters."[77]

North American fashion spread rapidly and soon established a commanding presence on the island. New styles inundated the Cuban market, aided in part by the popularity of U.S. motion pictures. In addition, new mass production techniques and new distribution methods made apparel and accessories available to greater numbers of women. Through mass imports of North American ready-made clothes, lower middle– and working-class women acquired a new sense of belonging and participated in new forms of self-representation. Retailers had an extensive selection of ready-made clothing: the latest styles at the lowest prices. These fashions were most evident in Havana, but they also appeared in almost all large provincial cities. Stores in Santiago de Cuba, reported U.S. consul John Griffiths as early as 1920, "compare favorably with the shops of Havana and many American cities. . . . American custom-made clothes sell well, particularly summer weights. Popular brands of American clothing are handled exclusively by certain stores."[78]

Almost every aspect of women's dress changed, often dramatically. Women wore less clothing: fewer undergarments, shorter hem lines, lower necklines, sleeveless tops, and form-revealing silhouettes. Mass fashion made U.S. apparel accessible to women of even the most modest social origins. New low-priced clothing imports provided a means to project status and demonstrate upward mobility. Under some circumstances, clothes could facilitate the invention of a usable self by which mobility might even be realized. Secretaries, sales clerks, telephone operators, and teachers, among others, led the transition to new styles and inevitably to new ways. "There is not a single poor woman," Ana María Borrero wrote in 1936, "who can not sustain the illusion of being well-dressed. There is not one working girl who can not display an ensemble of three colors to attend church on Sunday. . . . These well-dressed people have a radio in the living room and curtains on the window. My washerwoman, wearing an inexpensive copy of Jean Patou and a copy of a Reboux hat, assumes the behavior of a lady."[79]

The changes were apparent to all observers. "The styles imported from the United States and seized with such enthusiasm by the girls," noted "El Curioso Parlanchín," the pseudonym used by one thoughtful commentator, "has accelerated the change of private customs and provided wider freedom." He continued:

> This change in the life of women, this start of women toward work outside their home, this economic independence, were translated into radical changes of women's customs, in the loss of authority of the father of the family over his female progeny. From a young age women became accustomed to spending the day far from home to go out alone, to deal with men unknown to their fathers and to be governed, not by the father or the husband, as before, but by their boss or bosses who exercised more authority over them than their father.[80]

The new woman became readily recognized and passed directly into popular fiction. "Look at that woman who is so satisfied with herself," remarks the narrator in Luis Felipe Rodríguez's *La ilusión de la vida* (1910). "She is a typist who every day . . . thinks about Obispo Street [stores] with sweet nostalgia, out of which she will later leave, carefree and cheery, under the sumptuous color of a new dress." Loló de la Torriente, writing about the 1920s, recalled Charito Guillaume, "a salesgirl [who] had a good salary that permitted her to dress with certain good taste and wear fine shoes that completed her discreet elegance." This was also the way Mercedes Millán described the 1950s to Oscar Lewis: "You saw women factory workers and office clerks, mere employees, well dressed with high-heeled shoes and fashionable, matching purses and beauty-parlor hairdos."[81]

The introduction of North American mass fashion into the Cuban market had important implications. Stuart and Elizabeth Ewen argue persuasively that mass-produced clothes in the United States acted as a powerful agency of "Americanization." "Fashion and presentability," they suggest, "were, increasingly, categories imposed upon modern industrial citizens. To turn away from the pull of fashion was to remain alien and different; to stand 'outside the gates.' To embrace fashion was to move ahead with society."[82]

These factors resonated in Cuba, only on a larger scale. North American mass fashion served as a way that vast numbers of women presented themselves, the means through which consciously to lay claim to participation in currents that were both main and modern. Cubans and North Americans not only shared similar fashions, but, more significant, they invested similar psychic faith in what clothing could do for them.

It was not only that women looked different. They also acted differently. Fashion symbolized larger shifts in gender boundaries and always as a prelude to further change. New styles of self-representation often announced different behaviors. Women found new forms of self-expression and self-definition. It mattered less that these forms were foreign than that they were not imposed by Cuban men, for whatever else these changes signified, they helped women gain greater control over their lives. These were years of swift adjustment to opportunities that were becoming available every day, most of which had something to do with personal freedom: of movement, of social circles, of political associations, of sexuality. Middle-class women took up smoking in public as a statement of fashion and freedom. Many earned their own money. Women of "respectable" families went out unaccompanied to shops, to movie theaters, to nightclubs. The modern middle-class woman increasingly traveled by automobile, a potent symbol and source of independence and mobility. Indeed, advertisers and automobile dealers frequently pictured women as drivers, often accompanied by male passengers, thereby creating visual images of female independence. The automobile offered new opportunities for mobility—in short, new freedom from old confinements. "Automobile ownership was no longer limited to a few," recalled Loló de la Torriente. "Henry Ford had captured the market by improving the buggies and inundated Havana with the small cars. Horse-drawn coaches had all but disappeared. New styles dictated new uses. Some women began to drive automobiles and, dressed with short and tight skirts, with boy-like hairstyles, put the city on joyful notice that they demanded new ways in the life of women." Pogolotti's *El caserón del Cerro* describes Paulina's "acquisition of an automobile [which] immediately opened a much more attractive vista. Not only was it going to reduce the hardship of confinement but it was also going to eliminate much troublesome facets of her life." Rodríguez Acosta, in *Sonata interrumpida*, wrote of women "who took the liberty of sitting behind the steering wheel and moved about this way, driving their car—brazenly, some people would say—through the principal streets of the capital." For Isabel Margarita Ordext, the automobile was confirmation of the "spirit produced among our women by modern education, . . . a product of our time indispensable for the woman in all spheres of her activities: as a sports woman, as a lady of high society, and last but not least . . . as a patriot, becoming for her one of the necessities of daily life."[83]

In these times of rapid social transformation, North American lifestyles intruded at almost every turn and increasingly became more accessible. In Graziella Garbalosa's *El relicario* (1923), the protagonist contemplates her future as mother and wife but adds: "I have to tell you that when I envisioned those scenes, automobiles were already replacing the coaches, trucks were replacing ox-carts and wagons, the tight, short skirt had long been the rage . . . and women were learning to type and take short-hand rather than working at sewing and baking. My ideal then was an innocent anachronism."[84]

This was a world very much in flux. Generational differentiation accelerated in an environment of rapid cultural change, driven in large part by U.S. products and paradigms. Social change played off cultural change as market forces, mass production, and mass communication combined to shape consumption as a means of self-representation. The environment encouraged women self-consciously to expand the boundaries of traditional constraints and enlarge the social space of their presence on their terms, in pursuit of their needs.

Cuban women inhabited a complex, conflicting environment. Motion pictures summoned imaginings of new lifestyles and, reinforced by U.S. market forces, suggested the ideal and the means of self-fulfillment. Films offered new sources of information, telephones provided a new form of communication, trolleys, taxis, and automobiles presented new means of personal transportation. Old restrictions were no longer possible to enforce. Cubans traveled more freely, with greater ease and efficiency, which meant, too, that they had far wider opportunities to move about in public and meet new people, of all classes and colors, from all walks of life, to have chance encounters. In Miguel de Marcos's *Fotuto* (1948), Yolanda and Fotuto became "sweethearts as a result of the trolley."[85]

Nothing may have symbolized the challenge to old ways more than changing

A Ford advertisement in the Havana magazine *La Mujer Moderna* (*Modern Women*), March 1926. (Courtesy of the Biblioteca Nacional José Martí, Havana)

hair styles. Bobbed hair arrived in Cuba in the early 1920s, introduced on the film screen, in movie magazines and advertisements, and by the thousands of tourists who entered Cuba annually. The meanings that Paula Fass ascribed to short hair in the United States were also relevant in Cuba: explicit sexuality, independence, allowing women "to feel equal with men and unencumbered by a traditional symbol of her different role."[86] Suggestive and sensuous, short hair captured the imagination of many Cuban women. It connoted liberation and a more informal, carefree existence. Sexuality was, of course, implicit. Bobbed hair ended the symbol-laden dichotomy of hair worn in public and in private. By 1924 one beauty consultant proclaimed bobbed hair not only "a popular style but a symbol of the progress of women in our century."[87]

In a culture where long hair among women was traditionally revered for its powerful symbolism, the significance of short hair was immediately understood. Resistance came from many quarters. Eva Fabregas's memories were vivid: "I recall how bitterly I cried the day my mother arrived home with her hair cut short, deprived forever of that immense mat of hair that reached her hips." Anaïs Nin wrote in her diary: "Mother had her hair cut short, what is now called bobbed hair. . . . It makes Mother look years and years younger, independent somehow, even if at first it shocked and troubled because of its extremely modernized appearance." Men often responded to bobbed hair with ire and indignation; the new style even led to divorce. Far more tragic consequences were not uncommon. In July 1926 María Hernández fled to the Marianao police station seeking refuge from her husband, who had vowed to beat her to death for having cut her hair. Periodically, the Havana press reported that an irate husband had murdered his wife for the same reason.[88]

Short hair prevailed, however, gaining acceptance from almost all quarters across the island. By 1924 bobbed hair contests were being held in the larger provincial cities. A year later fashion writer Carolina Adela Alió could exult that "bobbed hair has triumphed in Cuba."[89]

The times were different, and almost everyone sensed the differences. "Today things have changed completely," commented Emilio Roig de Leuchsenring in 1923. "Girls enjoy a great deal of freedom; they do not live permanently locked up in their homes. . . . In our time girls can go out often, as much alone as accompanied with sisters, cousins and friends: to the cinema, to the park and the Malecón, to stores, to the drugstore to make telephone calls, to the grocery to weigh themselves, and to many other places that offer magnificent opportunities to meet their boyfriends." In *Sonata interrumpida*, Rodríguez Acosta gave narrative voice to the changes overtaking women through her protagonist Fernanda: "Daily she met more people; she visited parts of the city previously unknown. She herself had acquired an air of emancipation. . . . She had also cut her hair, and smoked. Both acts were no longer a source of scandal. On the contrary, they constituted the style of higher society." The narrative continued:

Men were becoming accustomed to women out on the streets alone. The movies had powerfully influenced this gain. . . . Work also contributed to this tolerance. The necessity to go to the office, private or government, to stores—which filled with female employees—or the University, institutes, schools and academies—in which the proportion of women increased significantly—also contributed to the end of old ways. . . . But it was the movies: the conjunction of social style and the development of an industry that was taking hold which, perhaps, more than the feminist discourses, contributed most significantly to the liberation of women in that epoch.[90]

Relations between women and men were also in transition. These changes signaled a complex process of renegotiating prescribed gender roles that was both resented and resisted by men. What men found particularly objectionable about the new styles was the degree to which changing behaviors blurred gender boundaries and women appropriated the independence traditionally associated with men. Roger de Lauria lamented the passing of the old days, "not because that era was more moral than ours, but because women then possessed delicacy and refinement unknown by [women] of today." Lauria denounced the "girls of today" who freely gave "themselves half-dressed to the arms of their boyfriends." Whereas "before love was to be eternal and now it is ephemeral. Before the woman was divinely complex. Today she is simple, easily bored. . . . There is no need, unfortunately, to conquer her. She surrenders herself, without need of romantic pursuit."[91]

The new freedom for women challenged traditional sexual hierarchies and found recurring expression in two prominent literary themes: adultery and divorce. "In times past it was relatively easy for a husband to know if his wife was cheating on him or not," asserted Emilio Roig de Leuchsenring. "The husband today presumes his wife's fidelity on faith. Today the wife goes out unaccompanied, or inadequately accompanied. . . . Today she . . . visits many homes and uses the telephone. Automobiles move quickly across great distances. And there are hundreds of movie theaters open in the afternoon. . . . Not even the expert surveillance system of the great European sovereigns would permit a husband to be entirely certain that his wife is faithful." In the Bartolomé Galíndez short story "Infidelidad" (1929), the taxi as a means of mobility is placed at the center of a wife's infidelity. In José Giralt's "Lo irremediable" (1929), Raquel justifies leaving her husband "because he was too *démodé*, as the French say, because he was an avowed enemy of many modern activities that I enjoy and which I consider indispensable for a woman who considers herself truly elegant." Raquel's musings continue: "Imagine, my ex-husband did not permit me to smoke, did not permit me to swim at the beach in plain view of everyone, did not permit me to go to the Club alone to play bridge or mah-jong. In short, he prohibited me from doing the many things that today are done by *chic* women, and that, you understand, made me look ridiculous among my circle of friends." But the moral of Giralt's story is in the conclusion, when Raquel sees the error of her ways and asks for a reconciliation that is denied, leaving her to regret her lifestyle. In *Sonata interrumpida*, Rodríguez Acosta speaks through her newly married protagonist, Mónica. "You see," Mónica explains to her husband, "I, the rebel, the indomitable one, have by my own actions and free will ended up in slavery. I had envisioned myself playing all roles except that of housewife. I believed that I carried in myself an adventurer's spirit and now it seems that I have nothing but a domestic spirit. Fortunately, there is the possibility of divorce in any circumstance of emergency."[92]

New lifestyles acted in other ways to guarantee North American forms prominence and permanence. As more women entered the labor force, more of them came to believe that their livelihood depended on their good looks and appearance. Cosmetics and wardrobe were defended as necessities—not luxuries—as the belief took hold that one's fate depended on the face and body presented to the outside world. Fashion-conscious women thus acquired needs of other kinds, which created new opportunities for North American products. "For women who use short hair," read one advertisement, "a Gillette is ideal to keep the neck clean." The growing presence of women in the workplace also produced a demand for U.S. products. "Are you too tired to work?" asked an advertisement for Lydia E. Pinkham's Vegetable Compound: "A girl who earns her living—whether in a store, office, factory or home—realizes the necessity of regular attendance at her place of employment. For this reason she works on day after day. Even when she becomes tired out and run-down. . . . Thousands of girls have found that Lydia E. Pinkham's Vegetable Compound has helped them back to a normal physical condition."[93]

Women moved into all public spaces, for the modern woman was active not only in the marketplace but also in athletics. "Cuban women," affirmed sportswriter José Losada, "do not want only to be beautiful; they also want to be strong and agile." Women's participation in sports—especially North American team sports—increased markedly during the 1920s. Women employees of the Cuban Telephone Company organized a company basketball team in 1929; other companies followed. Social clubs and sports clubs also established women's basketball teams, including the Loma Tennis Club, Club San Carlos, Vedado Tennis Club, Fortuna Sports Club, and Víbora Tennis Club. By 1930 more than fifty clubs had organized athletic activities for women. Schools formed basketball teams as well. By the early 1930s, women's basketball championships among the clubs and in intramural competition enjoyed widespread popularity. "In the last six months," observed Adolfo Font in 1932, "women's sports activities have increased considerably, to such an extent that in this regard we have progressed remarkably."[94]

Fashions permitted women to challenge old ways and in so doing served as a conduit by which vast numbers were incorporated into the ethos of North

American consumer culture. This was a complex process, not without contradictions, for the means by which women renegotiated gender boundaries also established new social limits. Consumption may have delivered women from old oppressions, but at the same time it introduced new burdens for them to bear. The pursuit of prescribed forms of beauty and body derived from North American models drew countless women into a relentless and time-consuming—to say nothing of costly—pursuit of the ideal. In the process many found the source of their bearings had shifted to the North. In a larger sense all Cubans were involved in this process and with long-lasting consequences, for they had been persuaded to see themselves through the eyes of North Americans and to regard their external appearance as a measure of their character and the basis of their claim to modernity.

These assumptions fell into distinct racial categories. The dominant modality of popular culture in postcolonial Cuba came as white. The North American presence had actually increased the complexity of race relations in Cuba. Color lines were subsequently more deeply etched, racial discrimination was more openly practiced. It would be unduly facile, of course, to suggest that the United States introduced racism into Cuba. Race relations in Cuba were the product of complex historical circumstances. But the arrival of the North Americans had substantial consequences. The United States had intruded itself in 1898 at a critical juncture: the institutional basis of a more equitable society had been created within the separatist polity, one that appeared capable of ameliorating some of the more egregious practices of the colonial regime. Race relations in Cuba at the close of the nineteenth century were in flux. Cubans of color had distinguished themselves in all sectors of the separatist project. They had occupied positions in the provisional government and in the Cuban Revolutionary Party (PRC); they were fully represented within the command structure of the Liberation Army. Through their sacrifice and their struggle in behalf of nationhood, Cubans of African descent had established their claim to a place of respect and responsibility in the republic.

The policies of the U.S. military government arrested and reversed the gains achieved during the war; indeed, they revived and reinforced many of the most deleterious aspects of race relations in the colonial regime. Appointments to public office were limited mainly to whites. Blacks were underrepresented in the Rural Guard and municipal police departments and officially denied commissions in the newly created Artillery Corps. Moreover, they were systematically excluded from political participation through narrow suffrage restrictions. The net effect of those restrictions was to exclude most blacks from voting during the U.S. military occupation. Secretary of War Elihu Root was exultant on learning that "whites so greatly outnumber the blacks" in the final registration rolls and congratulated Governor General Leonard Wood for the "establishment of popular self-government, based on a limited suffrage, excluding so great a proportion of the elements which have brought ruin to Haiti and San Domingo."[95]

Cubans of color lifted their voices in protest against the U.S. policies. "The news that positions in the Artillery Corps are reserved for whites only," declared one Cuban, "is such terrible news for Cubans and for the *patria*. That I could not help but to shed tears." He continued:

That the Americans have their own customs and conventions in the United States is a matter that does not concern us. . . . What does concern us is that these Americans, who say they have come to bring peace to Cuba, upon departing . . . leave behind a well-established peace among all inhabitants of Cuba, and not the discord that they have planted in a sector of our people since the intervention by refusing to appoint them to positions in public administration.[96]

U.S. policies had long-term consequences, setting in place practices that persisted well into the republic. Cubans of color were hardly in a better situation at the start of the republic than they had been at the end of the colony. Like many whites, blacks had lost homes and farms and were without resources to resume their lives. But they also came up second best in the distribution of public offices and faced additional difficulties in the emerging labor market. The place of blacks in the labor force continued almost unchanged from the colonial regime. Some observers argued that conditions for blacks had actually deteriorated. Based on a visit to Cuba in 1905, Arthur Schomburg drew these conclusions:

During the colonial days of Spain the Negroes were better treated, enjoyed a greater measure of freedom and happiness than they do to-day. Many Cuban Negroes were welcomed in the time of oppression, in the time of hardship, during the days of the revolution, but in the days of peace . . . they are deprived of positions, ostracized and made political outcasts. The Negro has done much for Cuba. Cuba has done nothing for the Negro.[97]

Perhaps the most pernicious effect of the North American presence was the extent to which explicit racial delineations acquired respectability in everyday life. North American customs had a direct impact on local behavior. That the large resident U.S. community practiced discrimination openly and unabashedly could not help but influence Cubans. "The negro thinks himself as good as the white man," the North American daily *Havana Sun* editorialized in 1902, "and perhaps he is, but that is no reason why the white man should be forced to associate with him. . . . There is no country upon the face of the earth where an objectionable person would be allowed in either a hotel or a cafe. A proprietor has the right to reserve his tables."[98]

The large degree to which U.S. structures served as the basis for reconstruction and recovery in postcolonial Cuba validated the use of color as a condition of livelihood. In the 1920s and 1930s race insinuated itself at every turn—explicitly and directly. A North American dentist could advertise a "practice confined to the white race." The Washington Saloon displayed a large sign: "We cater to White People Only." The American Grocery needed a "clerk to wait on customers. Must be white." A sugar mill sought a "first-class white male English-Spanish stenographer"; a family advertised for a "neat girl (white) as cook and for general house work."[99]

Not surprisingly, Cuban institutions could also seek white-only employees with impunity. The Banco Nacional advertised for a "white office boy [who] must speak English and Spanish." Even in the early 1950s, classified advertisements in *El Mundo* specified a "young white woman to cook and clean house," a "white servant girl," a "white maid," and a "white nanny." Not until 1951 did the leading department stores of Havana, including El Encanto and Fin de Siglo, hire blacks to work behind the sales counters.[100]

The increase in U.S. tourism, almost all of which was white, also helped to deepen racial divides. North American visitors conveyed the biases and bigotries of their time, to which hotels, restaurants, cabarets, and shops—both U.S.-owned and Cuban-operated—were disposed to cater. It was good business. The Plaza Hotel advertised for "two white waiters speaking English." The Hotel Presidente sought "two white waiters and room boys." Langston Hughes was twice denied entrance to tourist spots, once to a cabaret and on another occasion to a beach leased to U.S. tourist operators. In his short story "Little Old Spy," Hughes wrote of "American steamship lines [that] at the time would not sell colored persons tickets to Cuba." Frank Duncan and Newt Joseph, African American ballplayers for the Kansas City Monarchs, often traveled to Cuba to play winter ball and noticed changes. "Years ago no segregation was thought of," they wrote in 1929, "but now it is everywhere. . . . It is said that the American white tourist brought race prejudice to the island. Soon after the island became a Mecca for winter tourists the signs of prejudice and segregation showed on the surface."[101]

North American prejudices were easily transposed into a Cuban ambience and could serve as the rationale for discrimination in Cuba. In Juan Arcocha's *Los muertos andan solos* (1962), Silvia opposes the admission of blacks to the Tropicana nightclub: "In the first place, if they are allowed in, they will be the first to feel badly because they would not know anyone and everyone would make fun of them. . . . There are thousands of places where they could go and be among their own kind without the need to be at the Tropicana. Do you think that American tourists could continue going to the cabaret if they were to be full of blacks?"[102]

Racial categories in Cuba were rarely as fixed and formal as in the United States, and perceptive observers of race relations almost never failed to notice the huge interstices within Cuban racial hierarchies. Nevertheless, the dominant narrative on nationality continued to form explicitly around the racial categories and sought to exclude those who had not embraced the prevailing social and political ideas of nation. The concepts of civilization and modernity evoked a familiar subtext: the rejection of Africa in the formulation of Cuban. Juan Giró Rodés considered these issues in religious terms: "It is enough already of such ignorance, of such cretinisms, of such fetishisms," he wrote in 1955. "We worship God in church or in the privacy of our homes . . . and hurl into the air such pieces of wood representing false deities, false idols, such as Changó, Yemayá, and Ochún, that date back to dark Africa, with its totems, its polytheists religions and the cult of blood. The idea . . . transplanted from the heart of Africa and imported with the first slaves must disappear from our homes and mind. A better Cuba, a greater nation, more united, more cultured, more civilized . . . can not be achieved paying homage to Changó, Yemayá, and Ochún." *Rumba* was also rejected as representation precisely because it evoked blackness as Cuban. The rumba implied not simply primitive but specifically African. North Americans seemed to believe, Mario Sorondo y Tolón protested, "that we Cubans are all black." José Montó Sotolongo denounced the use of *africanismos* as a representation of Cuba and urged his compatriots to act in a manner that refuted the popular images of Cuba. "In fact," he insisted, "one cannot take very seriously a country of vulgar, lascivious African dances." Montó Sotolongo discredited the "civilization of folklore—African dance—as representing 'Cuban culture.' We do not know who to call savages: the wretched individuals who because of their primitivism can do nothing else . . . or those who try to have the world believe that these are expressions of Cuban culture today."[103]

THE PROMISE OF POSSIBILITIES

These were remarkable years, a time when Cubans passed more fully under the influence of ordinary assumptions of North American market culture. The dazzling display of consumer goods—through image and usage—the appearance of abundance within reach, notions fostered largely by the North, suggested that everything was available to everyone. The expectation of consumption increased rapidly, by example and emulation, and played an important role in shaping Cuban sensibilities.

Much had to do with tastes and affinities, the ability to behave in new ways and have access to alternative lifestyles. These possibilities were at once a measure of well-being and a means of self-definition and always an affirmation of preferences shaped in an environment increasingly dominated by North American material forms. At the core of this process was not just the increased availability of goods, but the degree to which products influenced lifestyles, determined individual expression, and shaped identity and values. There was so much more to want, so much more to buy, so many more ways to differentiate. The profusion of consumer goods continued, most of which had been unknown to previous generations: refrigerators, electric kitchens, furniture, phonographs, radios, tools, and a dazzling assortment of wearing apparel and accessories. An immigrant peddler praised his Cuban customers, for "they loved to buy and buy."[104] The demand for consumer items extended widely and in one way or another involved huge numbers of people in the broader North American market. By 1923 Cuba ranked sixth in the world as an importer of U.S. merchandise.

Goods possessed the capacity to disseminate and legitimize prevailing value hierarchies. The narrative on goods had a subtext, for it not only promoted a product but also advanced a way of life, providing a framework for defining self-worth and measuring achievement in ways seldom doubted and rarely disputed.

Identity with progress and civilization only accentuated Cuban susceptibility to the notion of consumption as an act of self-definition: the possession of merchandise as a marker of modernity and ratification of participation in new and contemporary ways. It was in the act of consumption that the concept of progress and the narrative on nationality intersected. The representation of "Cuban" as civilization, predicated explicitly on the idea of modern as material progress, placed extraordinary demands on nationality. To be Cuban was to be implicated in market forces as a condition of everyday life. In ways profound and permanent, daily negotiations summoned visions of access to a better life presumed available to all—a promise that might have been reasonable within the broader logic of the assumptions of North American market culture but was increasingly disconnected from Cuban economic realities.

So much of what passed in the rendering of national identity, that is to say, of what conferred value on nationality, was derived from association with modernity in its material forms. This implied a belief in progress, in the possibility of personal betterment, as a means through which national identity acquired many of its defining characteristics. Nationality resonated precisely because it implied the promise of progress. Material goods offered a variety of socially meaningful traits as visible symbols of status, a way, too, by which to construct usable social space both public and private. The use of North American products to delineate social hierarchies had far-reaching implications indeed. Cubans experienced progress principally through its North American representations, in such varied forms as fashion and cosmetics, radio, television, and telephone, machines and motion pictures, appliances and automobiles. Living standards were rising and the very way Cubans experienced daily life was changing.

Perhaps the most profound cultural transformations occurred during the 1920s, as the first republican-born generation entered adulthood. The timing was decisive, for it coincided with the rise of mass consumption, primarily the diffusion of goods, previously considered luxuries, to the middle and working class. It was impossible for everyone to participate equally in mass consumption, of course, but what had changed were expectations, as the belief that these goods were in reach of the ordinary family took permanent hold.

Probably nothing characterized this period more than the tide of U.S. consumer imports. Endlessly it seemed, in ways that were as conspicuous as they were ubiquitous, North American products appeared: in store windows, in department stores, in newspaper and magazine advertisements, in mail-order catalogs. And what met the eye did not even begin to take in the full dimension of U.S. imports. Their value catapulted from $25 million in 1902 to $272 million in 1919. During the Dance of the Millions in 1920, the value of U.S. imports reached a stunning $404 million, thereafter declining in the depression, but increasing again after World War II: from $436 million in 1947 to $577 million in 1957.[105]

The 1930s and 1940s were decades of slow economic recovery, almost all of which had to do with expanded trade with the United States. The renegotiated reciprocity treaty of 1934 further stimulated U.S. imports to Cuba. Between 1934 and 1941 the amount of Cuban trade with the United States as a portion of the total increased from 67 percent to 86 percent. World War II further favored U.S. imports, as Cuban commerce with Europe declined and in some instances— most notably with Germany, Italy, and France—ceased altogether.

Trade patterns persisted after the war. For the next fifteen years North American imports accounted for nearly 80 percent of Cuban trade annually, averaging more than $430 million. Not since 1920 had the value of U.S. imports surpassed the $400 million mark; after 1945, it was achieved almost yearly.

These figures could only hint at larger, more complex developments. The postwar years were noteworthy for the renewed expansion of North American structures. Telecommunications systems improved. So did transportation. The Cold War loomed large in these developments, and the "American way of life," with its emphasis on material well-being and individual self-fulfillment, was a formulation invoked explicitly as the idealized alternative through which to counter the challenge of communism.

Consumption served a practical function, to be sure, but it also possessed symbolic value. In the short space of the early decades of the republic, the lives of untold Cubans had been transformed. A varied array of consumer goods had become available and affordable. Ready-made apparel, principally as North American fashions, emerged as the dominant line of clothing for men and women. Electricity, indoor plumbing, and hot and cold running water passed from novelty to necessity, from being limited to the upper class to becoming available to the middle class and eventually the working class. The number of commercial laundries and dry cleaners, mostly North American, grew in the larger cities.

The transformation of daily life was remarkable. It was a short and perhaps inevitable step for Cubans surrounded by such material accomplishment and technological innovation to celebrate progress. These achievements added to the enjoyment of life. The connection between material progress and personal well-being was not new, of course, but never had it involved so many people. "We are going to live the joys of a true life," Oscar explains to Cecilia in Garbalosa's novel *La gozadora del dolor* (1922). "We will live as beneficiaries of the advances of civilization: electric light, a gas kitchen, a bath in warm water, an automobile, and a telephone."[106]

Circumstances did seem to confirm the proposition of Cuba as modern and civilized. In a novel by José Antonio Ramos, *Las impurezas de la realidad* (1929), Havana is rendered in exquisite detail: "White drill suits, impeccable, brilliant diamonds, silk shirts, automobile drives along the Prado, high class visitors, women loaded down with precious stones, palatial residences, uniformed servants, *manicures*, polar bear furs, *roof gardens* with dancers, gambling salons, champagne. And Caruso in maillot singing 'Maria Panchivira.' " And the narrator says of the protagonist: "Impossible for him not to involve himself in the maximum expression of culture, of refinement, of civilization. He had to feel proud as a Cuban of that Havana."[107]

Much in the Cuban capacity to participate in this order was related to the extent to which North American technologies insinuated themselves into Cuban life to improve or otherwise enhance the daily environment in direct and personal ways. Nothing was as central to the Cuban claim to modernity as possession and application of technology in ordinary life. The possibilities offered by these changes revealed themselves slowly, often in unremarkable usage but with long-term consequences.

Telephone service on the island expanded rapidly. The Cuba Telephone Company, incorporated in Delaware in 1909, was subsequently acquired by the International Telephone and Telegraph Corporation. The Automatic Electric Company of Chicago installed two modern exchanges in Havana. In 1915 an estimated 1,600 miles of long-distance lines and 67,000 miles of wire, operated by 34 exchanges, 8 of which were automatic, linked nearly 33,300 telephones in 220 cities and towns. By 1921 Cuba had the largest number of telephones per capita in Latin America: 1.06 telephones for every 100 inhabitants, followed by Chile (0.44:100) and Brazil and Mexico (0.22:100). The city of Havana had 5.9 telephones per 100 people, followed by Caracas (3.8:100) and Mexico City (3.7:100). By one account, in 1916 Havana had more telephones per capita than any other city in Latin America, more than London, Paris, and Vienna, and three times the number of Madrid. "Our modern city of Havana," Gerardo del Valle exulted in 1927, "has proportionally the greatest number of telephones in the world and with regard to the number of calls, we dare affirm that it is greater than cities ten times larger in proportion." Del Valle noted that *telefonomanía* had reached such a point that "when the necessary moment arrived that a private home had to reduce household expenditures, the invention by Bell is hardly ever included on the list of reductions." In the same year, the professional trade publication *El Arquitecto* reminded its readership that "the telephone is no longer something that can be ignored or remembered at the last moment when a house is constructed. It is essential."[108]

In 1926 the number of telephones had doubled to 64,000 and served 327 towns and cities. By 1945 there were 74,000. Ten years later, nearly 150,000 telephones were in service across the island, by which time the telephone had become a vital feature of everyday life. The average Cuban subscriber made between 14 and 15 calls per day, as compared with 8 or 9 calls per subscriber in South America and 5 in the United States. "The Cuban people are among the most telephone-conscious in the world," affirmed the U.S. Department of Commerce in 1956.[109]

Modernity arrived in Cuba in many forms but rarely in isolation. On the contrary, new methods always seemed to be accompanied by the promise of other innovations. Electricity transformed the island, not simply as another commodity but as a source of twentieth-century sensibility. Electricity was linked directly to structures of social reality that were capable of advancing economic progress and reinforcing material well-being.

Electric power also expanded quickly after 1898, almost entirely under the auspices of U.S. power companies. Havana obtained its power from the Havana Electric Railway and Light and Power Company. The Electric Bond and Share Company provided electricity in Santiago de Cuba. The city of Camagüey contracted with H. A. Warhle and the Camagüey Electric Company to supply public lighting for the municipality. Most small companies were subsequently consolidated under the control of the Cuban Electric Company. By 1930 electric power reached virtually every large provincial city, including Pinar del Río, Matanzas, Morón, Cárdenas, Cienfuegos, Ciego de Avila, Santa Clara, Camagüey, Guantánamo, Manzanillo, and Santiago de Cuba. By 1956 the Cuban Electric Company brought power to nearly 650,000 users in almost 300 communities across the island. Sugar mills and mining companies operated independent power plants and furnished electricity to the homes and businesses of nearby communities. The Chaparra Light and Power Company, a subsidiary of the Cuban-American Sugar Company, served Puerto Padre, Auras, Holguín, and Gibara. Hershey provided electricity to Santa Cruz del Norte. The 1953 census reported that nearly 60 percent of the 1.2 million households on the island and more than 90 percent of homes in Havana used electricity.[110]

The expansion of electricity created other opportunities and contributed to new needs. This was North American electricity, standardized as Alternating Current (AC), 110 volts (60 cycles), rather than European Direct Current, thereby establishing an exclusive market for U.S. electrical products. Once Cuban households were wired, the possibilities for product acquisition were virtually unlimited. The application of electricity to household tasks immediately generated a demand for additional consumer goods. A wide array of household electrical appliances became generally available in Cuba at the same time they appeared in the U.S. market, which suggests the extent to which both markets were integrated into the same mass distribution system. The electric light was followed by small appliances, particularly irons, toasters, coffeemakers, and fans, and later by larger consumer durables, including washing machines, refrigerators, freezers, electric ranges, and air conditioners. Appliances previously considered luxuries reserved for the wealthy soon became generally perceived as necessities for everyone. National City Bank president Charles Mitchell could scarcely contain his amazement at the transformations. "High power lines are being constructed right and left," he observed in 1924. "In the homes, all modern conveniences which have been introduced in [the United States] following the development of electricity, are now taking hold throughout Cuba. In short, the Cubans are improving their scale of living in this and in other things."[111]

Almost from the outset U.S. power companies endeavored to create a market based largely on individual and household use of electricity. Cuba's comparatively slow industrial development all but precluded extensive commercial use of electric power. Certainly sugar mills and railroad companies were quick to adopt electric power. The Amistad mill in Güines was fully electrified by 1913. Delicias converted to electricity the next year. Others quickly followed. By the 1950s nearly 140 mills had been electrified.

The rapid expansion of electric power by private users contributed to the expansion of electricity across the island. Electric power often went first to small towns and cities by way of independent corporate users, which then provided service to local communities. The Cuba Railroad Company installed a power plant in its terminal in Antilla for the operation of its yard, warehouses, wharves, and hotel and sold surplus current to households and small commercial users in the growing town.[112]

Because most mills furnished their own power, a large single market for the commercial use of electricity did not develop. No less important, Cuba's principal industry—sugar production—was seasonal and could not generate adequate profits for electric companies. The success of electricity as a commercial venture in Cuba was thus conceived from the outset as dependent primarily on the creation of a market for electrical appliances.[113]

Marketing strategies were designed to heighten public appreciation of electricity as a necessity of modern living. The linkage of modernity with comfort and convenience was itself the central proposition used to encourage electricity consumption and increase the sale of electrical appliances. The General Electric Company (GE) was the major promoter of electricity through product acquisition. "Three times a day and between meals," GE claimed for its Hotpoint line, "there are jobs that Hotpoint products can do and nuisances that can be avoided. For breakfast Hotpoint makes coffee and toast, and prepares any other dish—at the same table! In a Hotpoint kitchen lunch and dinner can be prepared more quickly and easily than by any other means. The Hotpoint iron does a splendid job and with a Hotpoint vacuum cleaner it is no bother to have the house *always* clean and resplendent."[114]

The sale and distribution of U.S. appliances increased rapidly after the 1920s.

Mass production lowered the price of most products, and efficient transportation facilitated distribution. U.S. appliances thus assumed a ubiquitous presence.

As electricity expanded, so did the retail stores selling electrical appliances. The Frank Robbins Company, Mahan and Jewett, La Independent Electric, and the Cuba Electrical Supply Company were only some of the most prominent retail distributors of U.S. manufactures. The homes of families throughout the island were filled with an assortment of consumer goods, appliances, and home furnishings. The sale of irons, toasters, fans, mixers, electric clocks, and vacuum cleaners increased, as well as of freezers, washing machines and driers, dishwashers, and room air conditioners. Between 1947 and 1948 more than 30,000 refrigerators were imported. "The Cuban market was promising," observed Jorge Quintana, "and visionary eyes enthusiastically sought ways to win control of the market. They counted upon the high level of Cuban civilization and that hedonistic instinct of this public to surround itself with comfort and hygiene."[115]

These were powerfully confirming images. For Graziella Garbalosa, the "advent of electricity" was "a characteristic of democracy" that, together with motion pictures and the radio, provided "delights at low cost and little bother." The advent of electricity, *Social* proclaimed, "created a great demand for electrical appliances and accessories, in the factories as well as the home, to such an extent that at present the majority of the better houses of Cuba use electric kitchens, fans and lamps." Electric refrigerators and ovens were "found in the remotest parts of the island" and "rapidly being adopted by all," and finally: "This development places us on par with the comfort of any of the most modern countries in the world."[116]

Radio was formally inaugurated in 1922 with the transmission of the national anthem and a live speech by President Alfredo Zayas. Expanded programming stimulated sales, which in turn increased programming. Broadcast stations increased across Cuba. The Havana-based PWX (later CMC), owned by the Cuban Telephone Company, functioned as a national network. Stations were established in the provinces, including CMHM (La Voz de Las Villas), CMJK (La Voz de Camagüey) in Caibarién, and CMKA (La Creación) in Santiago de Cuba. By 1933 a total of 62 stations were in operation, placing Cuba fourth in the world after the United States (625), Canada (77), and the Soviet Union (68).[117]

The sounds of radio transmissions filled Havana streets; indeed, a bewildering cacophony of broadcasts characterized daily life in the capital. "This thing of radios descended upon the island like a calamity," bemoaned the protagonist in Rodríguez Acosta's *Sonata interrumpida*. "In private homes, in each department of office buildings, in every shop and café, there was one of these apparatuses that people insisted upon raising to its maximum volume. To the horrendous noises that already had made Havana a scandalous city was added the blare of radio transmissions."[118]

Radio broadcasting provided a new form of national entertainment that attracted a wide public in Cuba. Chain broadcasting integrated stations across the island into a single network, thereby creating a national audience tuned daily to the same programs. José Baró Pujol hailed the advent of radio for its capacity to reach the most isolated communities on the sugar plantations and in remote farming villages and mining towns: "It is precisely there that radio can provide the greatest services and benefits to those who in their distance from the large population centers stagnate in their unproductive boredom."[119]

Mass production and mass distribution made radio affordable and accessible to customers of all social classes in all towns and cities. Sales of radio sets soared, increasing in value from $85,000 in 1925 to $650,000 in 1929 and $1.5 million in 1952. By 1958 an estimated 160 radio transmitting stations were broadcasting through more than one million radios.[120]

The appeal of radio was in its capacity to serve both as a possession and as a medium: radios could confirm modernity and hence corroborate participation in the advance of civilization. The radio was "a formidable instrument, . . . a transcendental factor of progress," affirmed the columnist who wrote under the name of Juan de la Habana in 1935. Cubans could feel proud that their achievements had placed them in the company of civilized nations, Gerardo del Valle had asserted in 1932. "Radio has arrived to join with film and the press," he wrote, "to provide us with universal revelation of deeds and ideas."[121]

Radio was one more means to disseminate North American ways in Cuba. No medium reached as many households as radio. Its potential for advertising U.S. products was recognized almost immediately. Indeed, radio broadcasts often gave more airtime to commercial announcements than to entertainment. One Havana station broadcast 1,400 commercial announcements daily.[122] Much of radio programming was underwritten by U.S. corporate sponsors. CMQ radio programs included *La Novela Fab*, *La Novela Palmolive*, *Rapsodia Philco*, *Noticias Mundiales de la General Motors*, *Jueves de Moda Camay*, and *Cocina Frigadaire*. *El Reporter Esso* was an international news program with reports supplied by United Press International. Bayer aspirin sponsored the *Bayer Radio Hour*, with music by the Orquesta Bayer. Majestic appliances sponsored the *Majestic Hour*, featuring such prominent musicians as Ernesto Lecuona, José Echaniz, and Pablo Miguel. *Un Concierto General Electric* provided weekly broadcasts of opera and classical music, and the Havana branch of General Motors Interamerica Corporation sponsored Sunday broadcasts of the Havana Philharmonic.

Radio melodrama (*radionovela*) could also transmit North American ways. Such popular series as *El derecho de nacer*, *Lo que pasa en el mundo*, *La mentira*, *Yo no creo en los hombres*, and *El dolor de ser pobres* depicted lifestyles associated with the promise of the market. "The North American myth of prosperity within reach of everyone," observed Reynaldo González in his study of radio programing during the 1940s and 1950s, "or at least *comfort*—'you too can own a Buick'—was disseminated in a society supposedly open to all possibilities."[123]

Considerable programming in the 1950s was carried in English, mostly recorded material prepared by the U.S. embassy and the U.S. Information Service (USIS). CMQ transmitted such shows as *Books on Parade, America Speaks, Town Meeting, Cross Country USA*, and *Invitation to Learning*, all broadcasts provided by the U.S. government.[124]

As part of national programming, Cuban radio stations also broadcast directly from the United States. In 1924 WEAF in New York and PWX in Havana experimented with chain transmission possibilities. In 1927 Cuba and the United States agreed to a frequency realignment to permit listeners on the island to receive U.S. stations, including by 1929 WGY (the General Electric station) from Schenectady and WHAS from Louisville. North American broadcasts soon became a permanent feature of Cuban radio. By the 1940s Cubans could hear such programs as *Superman* and *Swing and Melody*. A 1946 survey indicated that nearly 20 percent of the population listened to *Tarzan*. Each week WGY broadcast the *Lucky Strike Music Hour* directly from the Hotel Regis in Rochester. Broadcasts of WHAS included weekly music programs played by the Great Northern Railroad Band. "Let the reader sit at any moment by the radio and listen to the broadcasts of our stations," Juan de la Habana complained. "He will despair at the foreign music over the air waves, more foreign music by Cuban singers. . . . Is our poverty of music such that a tenor to a troubadour have to depend . . . on foreign sources." Fifteen years later folklorist Samuel Feijóo blamed radio for the decline of popular musical forms as a result of the commercialization of national musical forms.[125]

The impact of television was far greater. In 1950 Cuba became the first country in Latin America to broadcast TV programs. Eight years later it was among the first countries in the world to transmit color broadcasts.

Television enjoyed a remarkable expansion in the 1950s. Four broadcast companies dominated national programming. The largest Havana station, CMQ-TV (Channel 6)—"based on American methods and ideas," observed the trade weekly *Variety*—was owned and operated by Yale graduate Goar Mestre.[126] CMQ operated stations in Havana, Matanzas, Santa Clara, Camagüey, Holguín, and Santiago de Cuba. Telemundo (Channel 2) had stations in Havana, Cárdenas, Camagüey, Santa Clara, Jatibonico, Las Tunas, and Santiago de Cuba. Unión Radio Televisión Nacional (Channel 4) maintained facilities in Havana, Holguín, and Santiago de Cuba. RHC-Cadena Azul (Channel 11) broadcast from Havana, Matanzas, Santa Clara, Ciego de Avila, Camagüey, and Santiago de Cuba. Cádenas Oriental operated in Santiago de Cuba.

The sale of TV sets soared. In 1951 alone nearly 25,000 sets were imported; the figure increased to 30,000 the following year. By 1955 about 150,000 sets were in operation; four years later the number rose to almost 400,000. Moreover, these are conservative estimates, for they were based on official import data. In fact, an estimated 30 percent of all television sets in use were purchased on the black market. Many more were bought by Cubans shopping in the United States. In 1952 the U.S. commercial attaché expressed skepticism of official import statistics, "which do not reflect sets brought back by returning travelers to the United States or brought in through unauthorized channels." Even at the official 400,000 figure, however, Cuba ranked second only to the United States in per capita television ownership. By the late 1950s, Cuba ranked ninth in the world in total TV sets and fourth (after the United States, England, and Canada) in the number of TV channels.[127]

Television programming served as a point of reference for vast numbers of households. A comparatively inexpensive means of entertainment, TV viewing quickly developed into a principal source of leisure activity, especially in lower-middle-class and working-class homes. The estimated number of television sets in use does not accurately represent the size of the viewing public, for it was common practice for friends and neighbors to gather together to watch TV shows. One marketing survey in 1951 reported that there were 7.9 viewers per television set.[128]

Television provided another point of entrée of North American cultural forms. Its rapid expansion far exceeded local programming capabilities. The demands of continuous broadcasting, in large measure driven by the competition for advertising revenues and the high cost of production, encouraged Cuban operators to rely chiefly on North American programming. This was cost-effective broadcasting, for imported U.S. movies and serials were far less expensive than producing comparable programs locally. Cuban television was filled with old grade B Hollywood films of the 1930s and 1940s. "Television is paradoxical progress that has served to revive the old cowboy movies, the tearful melodramas now shown in episodes, and the musical varieties from the time of the invention of the vitaphone," observed Eladio Secades in 1957.[129]

North American TV programs were imported directly into the expanding Cuban market. *El Show de Liberace* and *The Cisco Kid* made their debuts in 1954. *El Show de Frankie Laine* followed the next year and quickly became, *El Mundo* asserted in 1955, "one of the favorites of the Cuban public." In the same year *El Show de Eddie Fisher* premiered. In 1957 *Lassie* was aired every Sunday evening, by which time Broderick Crawford could be seen weekly on *Highway Patrol*. Other popular shows included *El Sargento Preston, Hopalong Cassidy, Annie Oakley, Robin Hood, Las Aventuras de Rin Tin Tin, Bat Masterson, La Vida Legendaria de Wyatt Earp, Mike Hammer, Detective, Alfred Hitchcock Presents,* and *Superman*. Years later Gustavo Pérez Firmat remembered the television "where my brothers and I watched our favorite American programs, 'Wyatt Earp' and 'Highway Patrol.'"[130]

North American influences were not limited to program imports. Many local productions were modeled on successful U.S. shows. Quiz shows became standard fare. In 1957 Telemundo introduced *El Programa de los $64,000* as the newest quiz show on Cuban TV. Indeed, quiz shows were so popular that Cuba ranked second in the world in the amount of money awarded on television programs.[131]

Other U.S. genres were imitated, including soap operas. In 1957 Cuba's version of *Queen for a Day* (*Reina por un Día*) had become so popular that Telemundo expanded the original thirty-minute format to a full hour. In the same year CMQ introduced *This Is Your Life* (*Esta es su Vida*). *El Hit Parade Cubano* was inspired by its U.S. equivalent, and *El Club Rock 'n' Roll* was modeled on American Bandstand.

The Cuban television industry developed close linkages with its North American counterpart, from which it derived its principal modalities and formats. CMQ was affiliated with NBC. Virtually all technology and equipment came from the North, which meant that technicians were trained in the North. So were many producers, announcers, directors, and managers.

TV programming provided yet another outlet for the marketing of U.S. products. Kellogg's sponsored *Lassie* and Tide, *El Programa de los $64,000*. Other shows included *La Cocina Mágica Hotpoint* and *A Bailar con Colgate*. Advertisements were ubiquitous, "a jungle of commercials," complained one observer."[132]

Nor was it simply a matter of popular entertainment forms disseminating North American consumption values through commercial advertisements. In fact, advertisers often participated in program development as an extension of marketing strategies. J. Walter Thompson in Havana devised a new radio domestic comedy described as the "scene usually in the kitchen, featured by the old family retainer cook (maybe a Jemima), middle-aged Mama who is receptive to modern ideas, and little Miss Bright-Eyes, just coming home from school."[133]

These were porous forms and easily lent themselves to penetration and manipulation. The USIS was especially active in influencing the content and format of programming in collaboration with U.S. companies and their advertisers. In the early 1950s the embassy approached local firms that distributed U.S. merchandise "with a view of having them eliminate advertising in the communist daily *Hoy*." "It is believed," second secretary Henry Holt predicted, "that the reduction of this advertising will have an effect on the financial status of the newspaper." At the same time the embassy urged U.S. company representatives, mainly of Fab, RCA Victor, and Studebaker, all advertisers in *Hoy*, to close their accounts with the paper. On another occasion, the embassy urged A. E. Denari, director of U.S. Rubber International, to cancel U.S. Rubber's sponsorship of a popular TV program on CMQ because the "well known Communist orchestra leader Enrique González Mantici figured prominently." González Martici was subsequently fired and replaced by another band leader, who, the embassy reported, "although slightly tainted, was not believed to be a Communist," adding: "It is hoped to secure similar action from other American firms in the near future."[134]

It was perhaps the automobile that most fully transported Cuban sensibilities across the threshold of modernity. The automobile early seized hold of the popular imagination and quickly became a national obsession. It symbolized progress and modernity, available for purchase and possession. The automobile occupied a strategic and complex place in the rendering of national identity and individual self-representation. Indeed, probably no other product so fully possessed the capacity to corroborate civilization as the Cuban condition. The first cars arrived in 1899, coinciding with the end of Spanish rule, and served as the ideal representation of the promise of the postcolonial future. As early as 1900, the *Havana Post* wrote of the "automobile craze sweeping the island." Sales skyrocketed thereafter. "Without wishing to appear as prophet," *El Fígaro* predicted in 1901, "it can be said with some certainty that the automobile will soon replace the carriage of today."[135]

The number of car dealerships increased rapidly in Havana and the provinces. Sylvester Scovel, a former *New York World* war correspondent in Cuba, established the Havana agency for the White automobile. J. W. Schafer opened a dealership for the Winston and Pope Waverly automobiles in 1903. Oscar Arnoldson operated the exclusive agency for the Columbia Electric Vehicle Company. J. L. Stowers opened the Pope Automobile dealership. In 1905 Walter Fletcher Smith established the Olds Motor Works agency, and F. E. Barnhardt opened the Havana Garage Company to service the new line of Oldsmobile touring cars. Lange and Company sold Willys, Overland, and Hudson. La Cuban Auto Importing Company handled Cole and Stutz. The Garage Moderno owned by José (Pote) López Rodríguez operated the Buick dealership. By the late 1910s and early 1920s, more than 150 different makes of cars and trucks circulated on the streets of Havana.[136]

But it was the Ford—*el fotingo*, as it was popularly known—that enjoyed the greatest initial success and made it possible for many Cubans to own automobiles. The first dealership to sell Fords was Shumeway and Ross, established in 1913. The next year the Ford Motor Company set up an exclusive dealership in Havana with the Lawrence B. Ross agency. Ford dealerships subsequently opened in Matanzas, Cienfuegos, and Santiago de Cuba. By the 1950s Ford maintained thirty-five dealerships across the island. Quaker missionary Zenas Martin in Holguín had reported as early as 1915 that the purchase of the Ford by a local druggist had started something of a trend, and within six months thirty automobiles were circulating about town. "Sometimes our streets take on quite a city air and one finds himself looking up and down when crossing them," he commented.[137]

The success of Ford was due primarily to the capacity of assembly production to keep prices affordable. By the 1920s the Ford runabout could be purchased for less than $300, making the fotingo among the most affordable cars in Cuba. Assembly production also guaranteed the availability of standardized parts at

A one-cylinder Oldsmobile, owned by the mayor of Remedios, Rodolfo Lussó, 1901.
(Courtesy of the Biblioteca Nacional José Martí, Havana)

modest prices. Ford dealers carried an inventory of parts and accessories as well as offered a reliable service warranty—"Ford cars, Ford parts, Ford service," advertised Lawrence B. Ross. For those without the money to pay immediately, Ford offered generous credit terms, available to almost all buyers, and thereby provided middle- and working-class families the opportunity to own an automobile. Through the "Plan Ford," "any family—even if it lives off the most modest income," could buy a car through a weekly payment schedule. "You too can own an automobile without its cost causing difficulty," Ford advertised. "Thousands of families that were earning little, believing that the joy associated with possessing their own car was beyond their reach, have discovered that through this Plan they can easily and opportunely realize their dreams."[138]

Affordable and available in large numbers, the fotingo assumed a populist image—the "democratic Ford" is the way the protagonist in Félix Soloni's novel *Merse* (1926) describes it. The Ford was one of the most celebrated developments of the decade. The narrator in Rodríguez Acosta's *Sonata interrumpida* recalled the arrival of the fotingos: "Some small vehicles, odd looking and dangerous, began to circulate. They were called 'Ford' automobiles. They were an extraordinary occurrence in every sense, and produced a true revolution: not only in the trade and industry but in the spirit and relations of people." The "streets are full of Fords," observed Wallace Stevens during his visit to Havana in 1923. Pedro

Martínez Inclán, who estimated in 1925 that seven thousand Fords traversed Havana streets daily, complained: "One has to seek protection in the doorways from the thousands of . . . automobiles and trucks, and especially of the immense number of 'Fords' that race about at a dizzying speed giving rise to such a great number of accidents that were they to be published it would not be believed by people in other countries." *Gráfico* agreed and demanded some measures of control: "We are all agreed that the Ford automobile has arrived to fill a need in transportation with the indisputable advantages of low cost and speed. . . . [But] to talk about the Ford automobiles we are obliged to call attention to something that could develop into a serious threat to the majority of people who walk along our very narrow streets, above all along Obispo, O'Reilly, San Rafael, and Prado."[139]

That most car dealerships in Cuba were North American owned and operated ensured the privileged place of U.S. automobile imports. World War I also dealt a decisive blow to European car imports. Of the 5,117 automobiles imported to Cuba between July 1921 and July 1922, 4,722 were North American. But it was the sheer productive capacity of North American industry and the service facilities in Cuba that guaranteed the success of U.S. cars. "The chief source of supply [of motor vehicles] is the United States," reported the British consul in Havana in 1923. "This is due to the low initial cost of manufacture by mass production, standardized parts . . . and especially to the excellent service stations for the U.S. cars."[140]

North American automobiles exercised a powerful hold over Cuban preferences: a make for every budget, a model for every taste. A one-day auto show in Tropical Stadium organized by Ambar Motors to display the new 1956 General Motors line attracted over 40,000 visitors. For Pablo in Desnoes's *Memorias de subdesarrollo*, it was precisely the prospect of losing access to U.S. automobiles that led him to doubt that the 1959 revolution could succeed: "American cars will never return here. How Cubans love American cars. The Cuban will not put up with a revolution without American cars."[141]

North American automobiles moved rapidly into the Cuban market. The total number of privately registered passenger cars increased nearly fivefold between 1941 and 1952—from 16,000 to 77,000—and rose to 125,000 by 1955.[142] Chevrolet and Ford enjoyed the largest share of the Cuban market, representing 35 percent of new car sales in the 1950s. Also popular were Buicks, Oldsmobiles, Plymouths, and Cadillacs. The Cadillac was especially appealing. "There are more Cadillacs in Cuba than I have seen anywhere else," commented tourist writer Ludwig Bemelmans in 1957. Tana de Gámez and Arthur Pastore made a similar observation: "Havana . . . buys more Cadillacs per capita than any other city in the world." And by the 1950s Havana could indeed claim the largest number of Cadillacs per capita of any city in the world.[143]

Official data on car sales do not tell the whole story, however. In fact, local sales accounted for only a portion of the automobiles actually circulating in Cuba. Differentials between the manufacturers' suggested retail price and the actual showroom price in Cuba stimulated a brisk black market trade of new cars. A 1950 survey indicated that a Buick "Special" priced at $1,925 in the United States cost $3,275 in Cuba; an Oldsmobile "76" selling for $1,900 was priced at $2,970, and a $2,000 DeSoto "Custom" sold for $3,475. It was common for Cubans to travel north to buy new cars directly from dealers in the United States. "Many Cuban nationals brought new cars back on their return from vacation visits to the United States," noted the U.S. commercial attaché in 1952.[144]

These circumstances also gave rise to a flourishing auto theft trade. A far-flung network operating during the late 1940s and the 1950s transported stolen cars from Boston, New York, and Philadelphia, mostly luxury cars and especially Cadillacs, to Key West and thence to Havana by way of the ferry. "Due to the proximity of Cuba," the State Department reported in 1953, "the traffic in stolen cars is on the increase." In 1951 the National Automobile Theft Bureau and the Federal Bureau of Investigation traced twenty Cadillacs stolen in New York to Havana. Two years later thirty Cadillacs stolen in New York were located in Havana.[145] The absence of treaty arrangements between Cuba and the United States made the recovery of stolen automobiles all but impossible, even if located by insurance investigators, for innocent third-party purchasers of stolen property were fully protected under Cuban law.

Automobiles of all types filled the island: cars to enjoy such pleasures as picnics and weekend excursions, cars to flee from the city, and cars to see and be seen in the city. The desire to own a car became a reasonable aspiration for Cubans of even the most modest means. "There are more automobiles there in ratio of the population than in any country in the world," concluded George Musgrave as early as 1919. Construction plans for new houses routinely included garage space for automobiles. "Nowadays one cannot imagine the construction of a *chalet* or of any house without building its own garage," commented *La Lucha* in 1920. With a population ranking ninth in Latin America in 1929, Cuba ranked fourth in the number of automobiles (28,303), preceded only by Argentina (205,000), Brazil (60,800), and Mexico (38,110). On a per capita basis Cuba ranked third after Mexico and Argentina in automobile ownership: one car for each 78.7 inhabitants. According to *La Lucha*, Havana with one car per twenty-three inhabitants compared favorably to New York with one car per twenty-five inhabitants.[146]

Automobile sales also increased as highway systems expanded and roads improved. The completion of the Central Highway linked the island from Pinar del Río to Santiago de Cuba in a single road network, from which numerous transverse roads were subsequently constructed to coastal points north and south. By the late 1950s, almost all towns over 5,000 population had been connected to the all-weather highway system. The completion of the Vía Blanca in

1951 created a superhighway network on the northern coast linking Havana, Matanzas, and Varadero, while a southern system linked Artemisa, Cienfuegos, and Sancti-Spíritus. Municipal roads increased and city streets improved. Havana completed three tunnels during the 1950s, two under the Almendares River and a third under the entrance to Havana harbor. By the mid-1950s Cuba had more than 5,000 miles of all-weather roads, an achievement that prompted the International Bank to comment on the "great and valuable asset in [Cuba's] highways and roads," adding: "Few—if any—countries of the same general economic status have anything comparable to the Central Highway, either in quality or in the extent to which it traverses the national territory."[147]

Improved roads stimulated automobile ownership. By 1958 nearly 170,000 passenger cars were in service across the island. "Before, when the Central Highway was the only road available for long auto trips," Octavio Jordan suggested, "it was much more difficult to win over new customers for the automobile. . . . But the construction of new highways and roads has created a new type of customer who desires to own a car to ride around with his family and entertain himself with short trips near his home."[148]

Automobiles crowded into Havana, in particular. Congestion snarled traffic, and parking problems became commonplace and daily more difficult. "The parking of automobiles on the cross streets of downtown Havana has reached such an extent that it is all but impossible to drive a car through some of them," complained the Havana Post as early as 1924. In Adrián del Valle's novel La mulata Soledad (n.d.), the protagonist reflects on the constant flow of automobiles along the Malecón: "They were mostly privately owned, filled with the beautiful women of Havana high society; others were rentals with red-faced blond-hair tourists; and great numbers of modest Fords and Chevrolets occupied by students, retail clerks, and middle class couples with their children enjoying the drive along the sea drive. . . . He compared the procession with those he had seen in the great capitals: New York, Paris, London, Berlin, Vienna—a great display of the same vanities in different settings. The procession of Havana was truly splendid."[149]

Few travelers to Havana failed to comment on the pervasiveness of the automobile. "Havana itself swarms with motor cars and every Cuban family in good circumstances maintains a car," observed a traveler in 1920. "Nowhere," commented an English visitor a year later, "not even in London, have I seen as great a number of automobiles, from the luxuriant Buicks and Cadillacs to the infinite variety of Fords, each with its own peculiar booter, siren, or horn."[150]

The automobile changed the order and organization of daily life. It would do so, of course, worldwide throughout the twentieth century. But what was noteworthy in the Cuban experience was that these transformations occurred so early, at exactly the same time that the car was redefining the sociocultural landscape of the United States. "Until not too long ago in Cuba," wrote Gustavo

Robreño in 1915, "people left for work very early, but they moved slowly, for reasons of climate, saving their energies for daily work." Robreño continued:

> But behold that urban life intensifies; the wealth, prosperity, and sanitary guarantees of Cuba attract thousands of tourists and immigrants, and under such circumstances, the automobile appears opportunely and expensively, more than in all other parts of the world, in overwhelming disproportion to the number of inhabitants. An avalanche of automobiles of all makes descends over our city, causing congestion on the streets and complicating traffic . . . All of which has led to changes in the physiognomy of the city, and Havana that before looked like the capital of lethargy is today all activity and briskness, thanks to the automobile that has come to revive us, to present us before the world what we are in reality: a hard working people.[151]

Traffic accidents, injuries, and fatalities increased, mishaps that some people took for evidence of progress. "No country that aspires to be among the civilized nations in the world can offer low statistics of accidents caused by automobile traffic," observed Rafael Pérez Lobo. "Nowadays only backward nations and savage countries are those who do not have this demographic record. Civilization has a price and it is ridiculous to refuse to pay it."[152]

Encoded with intimations of nationality and identity, the automobile early occupied a prominent place in Cuban life. By 1927 *Bohemia* proclaimed the car to be an "indispensable means of transportation and not a luxury item." To "acquire an automobile is not to spend a sum of money on an object, or furniture more or less comfortable, or a means of recreation. . . . Money used for an automobile is a useful investment. Nothing has as much value as time and the automobile is a marvelous instrument that saves us time." The magazine continued:

> The automobile is the vehicle of prosperity and progress. Proof of this is provided by statistics: those countries that have the most automobiles are the ones that most fully and quickly develop. One should never look upon the automobile only as a luxury item. . . . Today the automobile is known throughout the civilized world and even in the heart of Africa, before the white man had tread across the land, the automobile, to the dread of the savages, had marked the soil with the tracks of its tires.[153]

Tens of thousands of Cubans possessed automobiles and, in turn, were possessed by them. The car became a Cuban obsession: the automobile as artifact, loaded with meaning and endowed with properties both metaphorical and categorical. In Pablo Medina's partly autobiographical novel *The Marks of Birth* (1994), the narrator fully comprehends the meaning of the automobile: "Felicia was of that generation for whom automobiles were still harbingers of the future, metaphors of hope, products of ingenuity and work, and so in no subtle way manifestations of the achievements of her class. Let there be mobility and the middle class invented the car."[154]

The automobile was integrated into the landscape of Cuban life, around which formed needs that involved self-representation and self-esteem. It served to corroborate the proposition of modernity and progress. "Havana has nothing to envy of the great cities of the world with regard to industrial and commercial advances," *El Fígaro* announced in 1921. "Nowhere else like the beautiful city of Havana has the automobile acquired such a quick and natural quality. The enormous and constant orders asking for cars and more cars have surprised the most famous manufacturers of Europe and the United States, thus demonstrating that the Cuban people adapt quickly to everything that signifies progress." *El Mundo* agreed: "The rapid expansion of automobile ownership has its logical explanation in the fact that the car constitutes without doubt the fundamental element of the modern era. The merchant as well as the industrialist, the professional, the rentier, employees and workers have need for a vehicle to meet their multiple obligations with comfort and efficiency." One historian of the automobile in Cuba was unabashedly exultant for exactly the same reason: "The large number of vehicles that daily fill our streets and roads, producing surprise among many foreigners who visit us, constitutes irrefutable proof of the progress reached by this country and the high standard of living enjoyed in Cuba." Rubén Ortiz Lamadrid arrived at a similar conclusion, if with a different emphasis. "It is as inconceivable," he insisted, "to classify someone as 'rich' for owning a car as it would be for owning a refrigerator." Mario Parajón declared that cars were an absolute necessity of life. "Twenty years ago," he wrote in 1954, "the automobile was a luxury item, a type of indulgence and elegant addition by which the wealthy added to their aura of opulence." But times had changed and so had the place and purpose of the automobile:

> Now the city grows, it widens, it expands into the rural zones at a remarkable pace. The work place is distant from the home. . . . The automobile has lost its character as an embellishment of wealth. It is now an exigency, an imperative, a necessity. The sign of the times seems to be "learn to move about with rapidity," and to move with dispatch one needs four wheels. The twentieth century has created a new type of man: the admirer of the automobile, who is familiar with brands, types, classes, lines, models, the function of parts, ways to enhance the car, and ways to keep it clean and beautiful. Now wealthy families do not own one car, they have four. Now employees, men of modest means, who live off their daily earnings, keep hidden in their drawer the prospect of owning a car.[155]

Attention to care and maintenance developed into a national idiosyncrasy. For many people the car was their most important possession, at once a means of transportation and a measure of status. Considerable self-esteem was invested in the automobile. "In no other country in the world," affirmed Octavio Jordán in 1951, "do cars, even after four or five years of wear, possess such a resplendent appearance as in Cuba. The Cuban is fastidious in matters of cleaning and washing his car. . . . Every foreigner who comes to Cuba is astonished by the good appearance of the automobiles and asks what we do to keep them in such good condition: Cleaning, my friend, water, wax, and rags everyday!" A report on the Cuban automobile market by the U.S. commercial attaché estimated that the average age of cars in Cuba was three and a half years but added: "Automobiles in Cuba have the appearance of being newer than the average age of three and one-half years . . . due to the frequent washing and polishing."[156] In the closing years of the twentieth century, long after the last North American automobile had entered, U.S. cars were still driven across the island, many appearing in as fine a condition as the day they rolled off the Detroit assembly line fifty or sixty years earlier.

CONFIGURATIONS OF NATIONALITY

U.S. consumer imports loomed large over Cuban life. It was not only that merchandise could act as a means of self-identity, although this property should be neither overlooked nor underestimated. At least as important, consumer goods possessed the capacity to replicate the cosmology of the society from which they originated. Products arrived replete with social meaning and messages, of course. But they also came with practical applications that could rearrange the order of everyday life around hierarchies derived from North American normative systems. The consumption of North American products implied acceptance of the idea of personal transformation and social change, a means of self-invention and self-actualization. Consumer goods served specific functions and were themselves instrumental in defining a new moral order. New kitchen appliances introduced notions of utility and efficiency into the household. "Time, which is money in the North American concept," explained *La Lucha*'s weekly home section, "should be the principal consideration in matters of culinary art. . . . The contemporary kitchen has arranged everything in such a manner to make for rapid work, without wasted movements. The system and the organization should save effort, time, and the need to think." The electric fan did not simply add convenience and comfort, General Electric insisted; it also improved productivity. "Comfort and efficiency go hand in hand," GE advertised its new line of fans. "Your office force will turn out more work in a given time and make fewer mistakes if they are comfortable. Fans pay for themselves in increased accuracy and volume of work." General Motors invoked health. "Frigidaire is being installed in all parts of Cuba. It is a necessity in the home for the protection of health, especially the health of children. It prevents acidosis and other intestinal disorders for milk cannot turn sour." White Frost advertised refrigerators as a means of caring for health: "Eliminate visits to the doctor by acquiring today a new White Frost refrigerator."[157]

The extent to which the national market reproduced tastes and preferences of the North was itself the product of a long, complex relationship. Access and availability certainly were factors. But Cuban preferences were themselves a reflection of affirmation, a disposition or a determination to participate in the currents of modernity. Postcolonial Cuba had organized around a market culture of enormous vitality, noteworthy for its capacity to persuade vast numbers to accept its assumptions of nationality based on the proposition of progress. The formulation early assumed the structure of a dominant paradigm in which notions of civilization and progress derived their definitive social content from values associated with material culture.

Material goods were encoded with complex meanings. Because acquisition was associated with status, the act of consumption itself could be a way to obtain gratification and fulfillment. Consumption offered access to modernity, a way to demonstrate progress and a standard of living associated with civilization as a material condition. Consumer goods linked Cubans directly to the market culture of a wider world and in the process became the material basis for affirming parity with the North.

As U.S. capital increasingly extended its control over property, as the old creole elite succumbed to indebtedness and insolvency, land became an increasingly untenable way to fix social standing. The expansion of the middle class, in part the result of the disintegration of the creole bourgeoisie, further redefined the means and meanings of status. Consumer goods acquired greater importance in establishing social standing largely because they were available and accessible. They became the principal markers of status, with an attending emphasis on newness: the newest model, that most up-to-date version, the latest technology. The social sources of Cuban identity had their origins in the nineteenth century, when notions of nationality were assuming their most usable forms. These ideas had loomed large in the formulation of a separate nationality and acted as one of the principal means by which elements of self-definition were employed in the logic of the separatist project.

The proposition of civilization persisted as a prominent facet of national identity. The meaning of consumption was suggested in a complex narrative in which Cuban sensibilities were engaged at perhaps their most vulnerable point: the proposition of Cuba as modern and civilized, a condition very much at the heart of the people Cubans believed themselves to be.

Modernity arrived in Cuba in many forms, much of it transacted by market culture through the consumption of goods to increase comfort and convenience and buyable technologies to improve efficiency and enhance pleasure. The place of these goods and services in the Cuban order of things was established early and, indeed, became one of the primary means to define meaning and assign value to "Cuban."

The appeal of acquisition extended far beyond the middle class. The promise of status through acquisition and accumulation was virtually irresistible precisely because it seemed available to everyone. Cubans inhabited a world of borrowed forms, structures both imported and imposed, and that in the aggregate defined possibility and shaped purpose. This world was sustained by a series of assumptions, central to which was the proposition of access. Market culture presented itself as highly democratic: goods and services associated with well-being and contentment, it contended, were accessible to all. The power was in the promise and in the capacity of this order to inspire hopes and sustain expectations.

A great many Cubans committed themselves to the pursuit of a standard of living derived principally from North American representations. These were not, of course, always conscious decisions but rather were shaped by daily experience. The assumptions of U.S. market culture contributed mightily to the formation of national sensibilities and in varying degrees shaped the basis on which households throughout the island contemplated the meaning of fulfillment and the measure of success.

These assumptions influenced Cubans of all classes, middle class and working class alike, in all provinces, men and women, young and old. In varying degrees and on various occasions they could all aspire to status through acquisition. Material well-being and moral contentment were intimately associated with the consumption of North American goods. Consumer products were artifacts of the promise, salutary and satisfying, the compensation for the work and worry of everyday life. Cuban workers, men and women for themselves and each other, for their children and their parents, toiled for more than just to make ends meet. The market offered fabulous material amenities, creating a longing for goods in the glittering shop windows of consumer culture. And, indeed, how could workers not be susceptible to these purveyors of comfort and convenience, to the means for achieving an equilibrium between work and leisure?

The desire for access to this world of material well-being was one of the salient characteristics of the Cuban working class. The U.S. labor attaché correctly identified the Marxist traditions of Cuban labor—"strongly critical of capitalism and highly nationalistic," he commented—but perceptively noted something else: "Cubans and Cuban labor . . . display an entirely inconsistent desire for high living standards and leisure." In fact, there was nothing at all "inconsistent" about these positions. On the contrary, Cuban workers aspired to higher living standards precisely as a function of nationalism and could plausibly demand participation in these material realms by which "Cuban" had acquired special resonance. North American market forces had, in fact, created an environment in which workers were obliged to employ U.S. standards as a measure of their own well-being. The goal of the "worker in Cuba . . . is to reach a standard of living comparable with that of the American worker," reported the U.S. Department of Commerce in 1956. The first secretary of the U.S. embassy provided a cogent analysis of the ways Cuban workers derived their bearings:

The Cuban worker is ambitious for himself and accordingly responds to incentive. No doubt he is influenced in this direction by manifold propinquity to the United States. In many cases he is acquainted first hand, or through the press, radio or television, with the conditions of the United States and with what an American worker expects in the way of a standard of living. The Cuban worker has wider horizons than the average Latin American worker and expects more out of life in material amenities than many European workers. This is true of both the individual workers and of his unions, many of whose leaders publicly state their goal of winning the same remuneration and conditions for their workers in the United States.[158]

These possibilities became generally available in the 1920s and expanded through the prosperity occasioned by two world wars and the Korean conflict. In *Los niños se despiden*, Pablo Armando Fernández depicts the 1940s in a *batey* port: "The war brought . . . a certain amount of prosperity: new cars, motorcycles, refrigerators, radios, phonographs, living room sets, and an insatiable enthusiasm for other things that had always been associated with the most wealthy and the Americans of the *batey*. And it brought to the port modern houses and new shops and new bars and a cafeteria." Mary Cruz del Pino observed in her 1955 history of Camagüey province that "the people enjoy the most up-to-date advances. With the exception of the poorest classes . . . Cuban homes are furnished with a radio, refrigerator, television and telephone. The number of privately-owned automobiles is extraordinary, even among the middle class. With each passing day life begins to look more North American in its material aspects." Mercedes Millán told Oscar Lewis of a friend's family whose father worked as a cigar maker at the Partagás factory. "They weren't rich . . . ," she recalled, "but they lived well. Their apartment was tiny but they had a television, radio, record player, electric mixer, and toaster—all the appliances that could add to their entertainment or comfort."[159]

Havana exuded modernity. Sixto de Sola wrote in awe of the "magnificent buildings . . . , industries of all type and communication systems . . . , the electric trolleys, and power plants." Carlos Loveira referred affectionately to "our ultra-civilized city of Havana." Alfonso Hernández Catá noted how "contemporary life sweeps away the traditional" and through radio, telephone, telegraph, and the press incorporated the "young nation into modernity." Returning to Cuba in 1918 after an absence of some years, poet José Manuel Poveda could not contain his astonishment: "Never before has my country seemed so foreign to me, so much another, so far beyond my reach, so far beyond my foresight." *Social* observed: "With each passing day, Havana acquires the appearance of the great European and North American capitals. Among the most noteworthy innovations are the magnificent and artistic exhibitions that are offered by agents of the great makers of automobiles in Havana. The salons are splendid and luxurious, a true exposition, where the automobiles of the best and most reputable manufacturers are available for public viewing." Pedro Martínez Inclán was also awe-struck: "On Obispo Street are located buildings as tall as the fifteen-story ones in the North and numerous houses of one or two floors in the immediate vicinity. Beautiful office buildings, show windows filled with merchandise are often as luxurious as to what is found in the stores on Broadway." Spanish tourist José Pla wrote of the adaptation of "North American structures" in the urbanization of Havana, where the "modern neighborhoods of Marianao and Miramar . . . make one think that he is in Los Angeles." Architects and gardeners, Pla noted, "apply to Cuba the photographs taken from *House and Garden*," adding: "Havana is an impressive city and offers an ideal scale through which to enter the United States. In a certain way, it constitutes an initiation to American life—a school for the newcomers to American life."[160]

Modernity specifically implied a condition of material progress based on consumption, convenience, and comfort. In *Tres tristes tigres*, Cabrera Infante speaks through Mrs. Campbell: "If there is anything the Cubans have learned well from us Americans, it is the feeling for comfort." The construction of modern served as model and measure of civilization in which the discursive framework of nationality assumed definitive form. Consumer goods had been incorporated into daily usage, from automobiles to air conditioners, from tele-phones to toasters, fans, furniture, and furnishings of all kinds, to wearing apparel. And if these goods were not owned by everyone, they were displayed in store windows for everyone to see. They served as symbols, possessed of the ca-pacity to mediate the engagements of everyday life. "In Cuba," observed Eladio Secades, "the seasons of the year are not revealed in the climate, but in the display windows of the stores. Suddenly we open the newspaper and the adver-tisement of some merchant informs us that autumn has arrived."[161]

These were the goods and merchandise that comprised the familiar environ-ment of everyday life. It could hardly be surprising that Cubans aspired to possessions that enhanced comfort and convenience. "Comfort is not a luxury," proclaimed Antonio Ricardi in 1955, "but proof of progress." It was now possible to "enjoy a good life, to use electricity in all its applications from the electric kitchen, sewing machines, typewriters and irons, the telephone . . . the auto-mobile, the calculator, radio and television, air conditioners, the movies, news-papers, fine clothing, electric shaver, and food easily and rapidly prepared." These achievements were the products of civilization designed "to meet the needs, convenience, and tastes of future generations." *El Mundo* maintained that "air conditioning, synonymous with health and comfort, is more a necessity than a luxury"; it was "more than a whim, more than a novelty, more than a ten-dency to imitate others; it has become something of a necessity"; "an air condi-tioner in an automobile is not a luxury but an absolute necessity." Ramón de la Sierra, vice president of the Emerson franchise in Havana, insisted that "any man with a job could have an air conditioner in his home." According to columnist Antonio Hernández Travieso, "today the air conditioner is a necessity felt by every Cuban, and no one who has any self-respect can not but aspire to the idea of installing one, at least in his bedroom. It will not be too many more years before each family budget is adjusted to accommodate this need, just as there is no one today who lacks a refrigerator." Adrián affirmed that "a kitchen can not be considered modern if it has only a gas or electric range, or a simple dishwasher, or an automatic refrigerator. Housewives today clamor for a freezer . . . and an automatic washing machine and an accompanying dryer. Garbage disposals and automatic dishwashers are considered virtually indispensable."[162]

The notion of civilization gave powerful resonance to the narrative on nationality and served as the imagery of self-representation: a mixture of pride and self-esteem, of conceit and confidence. "Cuba is the civilizing country (*país civilizador*) par excellence," asserts Pablo in Tomás Justiz y del Valle's play *Ultima esperanza* (1910). "What foreigner comes here to enlighten us about anything?" The narrator of Constantino Suárez's novel *Emigrantes* (1915) makes a similar observation: "In Cuba, it is clear today, Cubans of all social tendencies after first rendering homage to the *patria* profess their second love to the civilizing nation (*nación civilizadora*)." Years later James Weldon Johnson recalled conversations with the Cuban consul in Venezuela who "never exhausted the subject of the comparison of the standards of civilization and social life in Cuba with those in Venezuela; with the judgment always in favor of Cuba." Juan Bosch commented on the "active desire" among Cubans "to improve, everyday to become more cultured, more civilized, wealthier."[163]

Cubans early acquired the vanity of modernity, and nothing changed during the first half of the twentieth century except that this sensibility became much more deeply invested in the claim to progress and civilization. The idea of modern was itself associated with material conditions and inevitably involved vast numbers of Cubans in modern consumer culture.

Much in Cuban self-representation was deeply invested in the formulation of the North American modern. That the material basis of these claims originated principally in the United States seemed to matter little, if at all. Cubans had become conversant with advanced technologies, new manufacturing techniques, and new communication systems. Modernity could thus be claimed as Cuban, and each advance served to reaffirm Cuba's place in this order. "We Cubans scored a success in 1950," Charlie Seigle boasted, "in being the first Latin American country to operate a television station. To date, no Spanish-speaking country has been able to come even close to matching our achievements in television broadcasting." In the matter of soap consumption—"a symbol of contemporary civilization"—wrote Jorge Quintana, Cuba was among the leaders of the world. In all that qualified as a "classical definition of civilization," he insisted, "there is no doubt that the United States would rank first. That is where man has achieved the maximum level of comfort and . . . personal health." However, there were "aspects of the civilizing process (*proceso civilizador*) in which our country is almost equal to the United States." And in the matter of per capita consumption of soap, Cuba was "one of the greatest consumers of soap in the world."[164]

These goods did not come easily to everyone, of course. Many families struggled and sacrificed to purchase even the most basic household appliances. For many, installment buying became a way of life. Much of the capacity to consume on this scale was made possible by creative finance plans adopted by many retail outlets. Consumer credit became generally available during the early 1920s, placing an endless array of consumer goods within reach of countless families.

Credit purchases increased dramatically, from $12.7 million in 1946 to $30 million in 1951. Indeed, by the late 1940s about 85 percent of all retail sales of durable household goods were made on an installment basis. Within a decade, almost all products, consumer durables as well as nondurable goods—mostly imports—were purchased on credit. "Marketing of major electrical appliances was spotty," reported the U.S. economic affairs officer in 1955, "with those merchants who offer liberal credit terms enjoying a relatively large volume. Consumer credit is becoming a regular feature in many lines of merchandising." A 1955 survey by the Banco Nacional disclosed that 90 percent of all electrical appliances were sold on the longest installment plans available, with the minimum 10 percent down. Installment buying, the Banco Nacional noted, "had contributed to placing within reach of the more modest classes goods which, with technical progress, have ceased to be in many cases articles of luxury and have become an essential part of modern life."[165]

Households across the island increasingly adopted indebtedness as a strategy for upward mobility and a higher standard of living. Reyita Castillo recalled furnishing her apartment—with living room furniture, a pair of framed pictures, a vase, and paper crepe flowers—all on installment buying. "The poor have become accustomed to living like the rich," observed Eladio Secades in 1953. "The system of installment buying has altered the family economy. . . . Today everything is paid on installment: from the television set to the funeral processions. And we continue to buy on credit: radios, refrigerators, the great living room lamp, the automobile, the television set." Secades described the "madness of installment buying," where "housewives learn in newspaper advertisements that they can have a television set for 30 cents a day and, of course, they take the plunge."[166]

Considerable ingenuity was employed in the pursuit of consumer goods. Emma Pérez explained the phenomenon of "floating televisions," specifically "the large numbers of televisions that are acquired on credit and soon returned for failure to make the weekly or monthly payment as specified in the purchase agreement. There are many who have a television only for the first month. Cuba is that way." Gracia Rivera Herrera recounted consumer strategies employed by her own family. "Our expenses were larger than our combined income," she disclosed, so one month her mother would pay the installment on the TV but not on the bedroom set, the following month she would pay on the bedroom set but not on the TV, and so on. Rivera Herrera also remembered her father's determination to own a television. "It became very easy to buy one after a while," she said, "10 *pesos* down and 10 *pesos* a month, and we got our own, though we were never able to meet the payments. But *papá* had a plan: he'd pay 10 *pesos* down and the first month's installment, then he'd keep the set for a few more months without paying until finally they'd take it away. As soon as *papá* managed to get another 10 *pesos* together, he'd make another down payment and the whole thing would start over again." Reyita Castillo had another strategy. "They sold radios on installment," she reminisced, "and they provided one week of trial at home at no cost, after which it could be returned for any reason, no questions asked. It occurred to me to ask for a radio of any brand for the trial period. A week later, I'd return it and ask for another brand. . . . Things went on like this for a while, until I was finally able to get the money to make the payments to buy my own."[167]

The narrative on civilization was not without contradiction, of course; indeed, under certain circumstances it could be turned upside down. The proposition of civilization as the source of Cuban self-representation also spoke to the collective conscience. Well-being was not evenly distributed or equally enjoyed. On the contrary, Cuba evolved increasingly into a country of contrasts, where disparities assaulted the sensibilities at every turn: opulence and destitution, wealth and indigence, waste and scarcity. Huge pockets of Third World squalor persisted, especially in the countryside, made all the more egregious by the comparative high standard of living maintained in the cities. Malnutrition, poverty, and illiteracy were acknowledged attributes of the Cuban condition. Many who subscribed earnestly to the proposition of Cuba as civilized were also among those most troubled by the persistent poverty. Civilization implied enlightened sensibilities and righteous community. Cubans had set very high standards for themselves, perhaps unrealistically high. For many, civilization could not advance if vast numbers were left behind, for a civilized people could not be indifferent to privation in their midst. "Indigents, paupers, and the hungry," was what Mariblanca Sabas Alomá saw in 1931, "hungry for so many things, gentlemen, for so many things. . . . And all this is a society that calls itself civilized." Jorge Mañach struck a similar note, if with a different emphasis. "We would like a nation (*patria*) of which we could all be proud," he explained. The difference between "the primitive and the civilized is based essentially on a type of collective generosity": "Society is most civilized and achieves that condition of *patria* only in the sense that assistance is most generous and effective."[168]

It was thus an obligation inherent in the condition of civilization to seek remedies for social inequality and economic inequity. "The number of beggars that scour the streets of Havana, displaying their miseries everywhere, constantly bothering the citizenry with their demands for help, constitutes a shameful and depressing spectacle," editorialized *El Mundo* in 1949. "The problem of mendicancy is one of the great stains that negates our condition of a civilized people. It is necessary to act with firm and responsible energy and to resolve these cases that are an affront and an ignominy to a country that values its social advances." Pointing to deplorable conditions in the countryside, América Ana Cuervo insisted that "surely peasants have the right to live in better conditions as members of a civilized society." Mario Llerena decried a wide range of problems, including air pollution, prostitution, gambling, inadequate public services, and substandard garbage collection: "In Cuba we have at hand everything that modern civilization can offer together with everything that denies and invalidates it." On the problem of infant mortality, physician Fidel Nuñez Carrión was blunt: "It is painful to confess it, but it is the truth. We pride ourselves on being a civilized country, but our infant mortality rates do not permit us to include ourselves among the civilized countries." Pepín Rivero editorialized in *Diario de la Marina* that political violence was incompatible with the "absolutely necessary guarantees that should be enjoyed by the citizens of a civilized society." T. García de Triana complained about the malfeasance in public life: "If we intend to obtain a position alongside of the most civilized countries in the world, we cannot continue prostrate before the cult of the lie." Octavio Jordán waged a campaign for mandatory automobile inspection as a way to reduce accidents. He wrote: "No country that considers itself civilized fails to undertake periodical inspection of motor vehicles, for it realizes that inspection provides security for its citizens and improves the flow of traffic. That is why it is inconceivable that possessing such a high level of civilization we have failed to take this measure here."[169]

There was perhaps no more powerful corroboration of the degree to which Cuban sensibilities had been penetrated by North American attitudes than the capacity of Cubans to see themselves through foreign eyes. Disapproval and disparagement by North Americans were perceived as both a reflection of a harrowing reality and an unbearable source of shame. Cubans were vulnerable to North American manipulation of definition of self in which approval or disapproval served as an overriding determination of individual representation.

This was a complicated response to decades of contact. Increasingly, Cubans came to measure themselves by northern standards and evaluate their achievements and aspirations based on imported models. The Cuban meditation on modernity was formulated largely in a narrative of self-representation vis-à-vis the North as frame of reference and source of validation. It was to the North Americans that Cubans compared themselves, which meant that increasing numbers also acquired the North American sense of the Other, even as it involved themselves. It was especially important that foreigners—usually the code word for North Americans—corroborate Cuban renderings of self, for much in the Cuban version of civilization was assembled from North American sources,

A street scene in Caimanera, ca. 1950s. (Courtesy of the photographic archives, *Bohemia*, Havana)

from which Cubans derived their frame of reference. "All of us like to see the foreign press praise our country," affirmed Herminio Portell Vilá, "and admire our progress and our wealth, which are the results of the efforts of the Cuban people to advance along the path of civilization." This concern was just as often expressed by the fear of being perceived as less than civilized and modern. Portell Vilá was distraught over execrable conditions in the town of Caimanera and how they might reflect on Cuba's claim to civilization. Only months after the triumph of the revolution in 1959, he appealed to the new government to take action: "We Cubans should do everything that is required of us so that the North Americans of Guantánamo respect us as a progressive, civilized, and well-governed people." Until Caimanera "becomes a model city as clean, as prosperous, as well paved, and with all advances of any city in the United States of comparable size, . . . until it becomes an example of the progressive spirit of Cubans, we will be in a position of inferiority." Portell Vilá concluded: "We need a government that . . . concerns itself with the Guantánamo region, where thousands and thousands of North Americans from the naval base have seen the backwardness, poverty, misuse of the resources of the country, and poor conditions of life, to transform into the most convincing evidence of the good that we Cubans can and know how to do."[170]

The tourist road between Havana and Batabanó was a disgrace, wrote one citizen in 1956. "Can we expect the tourist will speak well of Cuba when he returns to the United States? Of course not!" In Arcocha's *Los muertos andan solos*, Rogelio explains to North American tourists in Varadero that Cubans did not go to the beach in the winter. "They laughed and he was ashamed, thinking that they were going to take all Cubans for savages." Carlos Garate happened to be vacationing in New York when the battle cruiser *Cuba* was making a courtesy call to the United States in 1921. While visiting the vessel, Garate met some Americans who asked him how many more cruisers Cuba had. "I answered quickly, with certainty, tranquility, and serenity, almost convinced that what I said was the truth: 'Twenty exactly like this one.' And they responded: 'Twenty cruisers!' and repeated with a mixture of awe and respect." Garate continued:

I had lied, yes, but I had lied in behalf of a great and noble cause. I had lied out of cowardice so I would not have to admit that my country was not a military power. I had lied for fear of the ridicule that I would have incurred upon confessing to our meager naval force, at a time when the Great War accustomed us to count cruisers by the hundreds. . . . I had lied for patriotic reasons and was satisfied with my lie, for it allowed in the minds of people who did not know better the name of Cuba to be associated with the idea of a country endowed with sufficient force to resist conquest.[171]

6

ASSEMBLING ALTERNATIVES

The de-Europeanization of Cuba began with the Republic and after World War I. . . . Paradoxically, Cubans allowed themselves to be swayed more by the customs, ideas, and tastes of the Americans, by means of which they were subjugated and impoverished. Cubans were bedazzled by the power of what they beheld, perhaps thinking that if the Americans' strength was so great, everything of theirs must have been superior and worthy of imitation.
—Marcelo Pogolotti, *Del barro y las voces*, 1982

Notwithstanding the noise made throughout this Republic by the campaign of nationalism . . . our Cuban friends favor American ideas in many lines; every single man . . . whose economic position will permit, sends his children to northern schools. . . . Just remember for a minute how far our friend and business associate, the Cuban, has traveled along the rode of Anglo-Saxons in the last twenty-five years. He believed that ice water was unhealthy, he now has an ice box; he could not live without his noon siesta, today he does not remember the word "siesta"; he is a damn fool on boxing and a worse baseball fan than a Washington government employee, and he has adopted every one of the fifty-seven varieties of New York slang in his athletic proclivities; he has swallowed daylight saving and he has become an addict to divorce and jazz; he has one son an American dentist and another an American engineer, and both of these boys wear balloon trousers.
—*Havana Post*, October 18, 1925

Miami! This is a name that has different meanings for those who live in Cuba. For the merchant, it represents a successful competitor in the tourism sector. . . . For politicians of all persuasions, it is a charming and pleasant refuge which does not require any authenticity other than decent behavior from the moment one reaches its streets. For the wealthy, the spirited youth, and young lovers, it is an enchanting interlude, an inducement to the daring of money, happiness, and love.
—*Bohemia*, February 4, 1934

The conventions of Cuban life were in transition. North American forms increasingly emerged as the primary means of self-representation and the principal sources of self-esteem, specifically as they informed the codes of social interaction and modes of public being. Certainly World War I had contributed to narrowing the range of possibilities available for popular usage. That the circumstances of ordinary life were changing was apparent even to those who experienced change daily; they were especially noticeable to those who returned to Cuba after a period of absence. Loló de la Torriente, who went back after the war, was astonished by what she found. "The war had changed much in the way of life," she remembered. "In regard to Havana, the transformation was notable. Spanish and French influences had yielded to the onslaught from New York that had come to prevail in a manner contrary to our traditions and customs. The place of the *danzón* was challenged by the *two-step* and *fox trot*." In José Antonio Ramos's partly autobiographical novel *Coaybay* (1926), Minón Mendoza, on returning to Cuba after years abroad, reflects on the influences of the fictional country "Norlandia": "Groups at the Jockey Club and the Yacht Club . . . their *one steps*, their *turkey trot*, their *high balls*, their ostentatious servility to money." The narrator continues: "And among his friends, the privileged ones, successful journalists and young professionals, with only a few exceptions, dedicated themselves to the northern habit of spending money, building mansions, buying automobiles, playing in the clubs and going to the races, and traveling at least once a year to New York, to hear Caruso and buy things on Fifth Avenue."[1]

IN PURSUIT OF PURPOSE

The changes were many and manifest. On occasion they were slightly overwhelming. Waves of change washed over the island in rapid succession. This was modernity on a scale never before experienced, much unconnected to the Cuban past, adjustments that contributed to the formation of a generation that derived its definitive bearings in the course of adapting to change.

It was perhaps among those who opposed these changes that the most vivid renderings of new ways found voice: traditionalists who lamented the loss of old ways, men who resented the new freedom of women, women who resisted the shifting moral order. "Today it is so rare to dance the *danzón*," commented *Social* in 1922, "because the *fox trot* has displaced it, tea is more chic than coffee, the American cigarette is better than the Cuban—all of which makes it rare that our magazines cover the national ambience." Five years later Roger de Lauria arrived at a similar conclusion: "The Cuban is unfortunately fading into the distant past. Soon . . . there will be nothing remaining except a stylized caricature of the *yanki* . . . where chewing gum and tortoise shell eye glasses will complete our conversion into puppets 'Made in U.S.' Even the dances have lost the Cuban essence they previously had, and especially the *danzón*. Even in the very Tacón Theater the *fox trot* has dethroned our typical dance."[2]

The transformations were often dramatic. Something fundamental had changed in ways that were deep and defining. "In little more than fifteen years," observed Francisco González Díaz in 1916, "Havana has been completely transformed. We are obliged to repeat the celebrated phrase: *C'est du nord que nous vient la lumiére*. The influence of the great culture of the North . . . is behind this rapid advance of progress, fully visible in all aspects of national activity." The signs were everywhere. "Travelling the streets I often come to think that Havana looks more like an American colony than the capital of a free nation with its own government," wrote Rafael Santa Coloma. "I have visited some cities in the United States and in none of them . . . do their stores identify themselves in Chinese, German or Italian. Not at all: everything there is in English. . . . But here in Havana, where the official language is Spanish, I fear that if matters continue as they are, the day is not too distant when those of us who do not speak English will have to orient ourselves with an 'Official Guide' that our city council will be obliged to publish."[3]

Adaptations occurred in unremarkable fashion, in private and personal ways, mostly as adjustments to changes or circumstances as they presented themselves—often improvised, sometimes planned. The power of U.S. market culture lay in its capacity to render normative assumptions as moral imperatives. These propositions reached deeply into Cuban sensibilities and formed and informed the meanings given to "Cuban."

Much of the narrative of Cuban was expressed in the concepts of modernity and civilization and derived explicitly from North American formulations. But there was more. The notion of progress insinuated itself into hierarchies of values and systems of beliefs; it had to do with those things that conferred status and self-esteem, markers that served to designate and define well-being. These formulations found application and validation in a moral order dominated by North American conventions, as precepts and principles with which to negotiate a place in the greater scheme of things, which is to say that they were the means by which vast numbers developed a sense of themselves and others. They created powerful affinities, often discerned more clearly by observers attentive to detail and nuance. Venezuelan writer T. R. Ybarra could hardly contain his astonishment: "In no other place in Spanish America are these polar opposites of character, of mentality and concept of life that define North and South America so much alike as on this island." Novelist-playwright José Antonio Ramos experienced a poignant moment of self-realization during a visit to Mexico. "I feel very strange," Ramos recorded in his diary. "Mexico makes me think that I am dead, that I am like a Rip Van Winkle or a ghost that is present in the lives of others but without participating. Mexico is colonial Cuba, it is Spain, it is my childhood and my youth. It is at this moment that I realize with the greatest clarity the profound influence that North America has exercised over me. My Dewey pragmatism feels thwarted in the presence of this civilization in which chance governs almost everything." Benito Vilá did not realize how deeply he was immersed in a North American frame of reference when he arrived in Chile as an exile. He recalled how "poor" Chileans were, a fact he attributed to "their inability to think big, and plan appropriately," adding: "Only 6% of households, when we arrived in 1960, had refrigerators in their homes. There was no television. Cars were outrageously expensive, and certainly rare compared to Cuba."[4]

Much of what served as the basis of Cuban life—what governed conduct and conventions, what influenced habits and hobbies, behaviors and mannerisms—was derived from North American sources. U.S. holidays and commemorative dates were observed in Cuba. Mother's Day was adopted almost immediately after President Woodrow Wilson proclaimed its commemoration in the United States in 1913. February 14 was observed as "Día de los Enamorados" or just as often as "San Valentín." The many thousands of students who attended U.S.-operated schools routinely celebrated Thanksgiving Day. Rafael Hernández would fondly recall his anticipation of Thanksgiving while attending La Progresiva. In 1952 Cuba officially adopted the fourth Thursday of November as "Thanksgiving Day" (Día de Acción de Gracia).[5]

Christmas assumed the appearance of the holiday in the North at almost every turn: the Salvation Army hosted a Christmas party, Ruston Academy presented a program of Christmas carols, the Book and Thimble Society hosted a Christmas luncheon, the Trinity Episcopal Church organized a choral performance, Lafayette School sponsored a Christmas dance, and the University Methodist Church held a Christmas bake sale. The Band of Mercy sponsored a Christmas Charity Feast and el Country Club organized a Christmas Day golf tournament. The Novelty Skating Rink sponsored a special Christmas program that included a decorated tree and multicolored lights, with Santa Claus arriving to distribute gifts. Across the island, on U.S.-owned sugar mills, in mining towns and missionary stations, Christmas was celebrated in the North American way. "It's strange about Christmas cards in Cuba," commented one observer as early as 1928. "A stock in one of the largest stores on Obispo carried only those of the American variety—snow scenes, skating, tobogganing, mistletoe and holly and all the rest of northern yuletide offerings. Where can Cuban cards depicting the Christmas of the island be procured?" Newspaper and magazines advertisements pictured snowscapes, northern winter scenes, and snowmen, sleighs, and reindeers. Trimmed Christmas trees could be found in hotel lobbies and corporate offices, in nightclubs and Protestant churches, in department stores and retail shops, especially in Sears and Woolworth's but also in El Encanto and Fin de Siglo. Santa Claus was everywhere: receiving children at El Encanto, distributing gifts at orphanages, and endorsing all types of products in advertisements. At an annual reception for poor children hosted by the Lyceum y Lawn Tennis Club, Santa Claus appeared to distribute gifts and toys. Christmas carols filled the radio air waves and department store public address systems. "One even hears people on the streets whistling Christmas carols, such as 'Jingle Bells' or 'White Christmas,' " commented Sixto Figueras. It was unmistakingly Christmas time in the city. "It certainly seems like Christmas to me," John Snook wrote in December 1957. "All over Havana, everything is set for Christmas. Why right now the TV is on and I hear 'Rudolph the Red Nosed Reindeer.' Just about . . . everywhere you turn the Christmas spirit is there. Santa Claus is answering the telephone in a window on San Rafael. El Encanto, Fin de Siglo, Flogar, and the *Ten Cent* are all decked out." Agustín Tamargo could imagine a North American tourist seeking to buy something "typically Cuban":

> He stares at the store window and what does he see? Santa Claus, Canadian pines, plastic flakes imitating snow and sleds! But—is he going crazy? Has perhaps the airplane mistakenly taken him to another city? When he enters through the glass door, the American is no longer in doubt. Yes—he is entirely mistaken. He cannot be in Havana. Inside everyone is chewing gum, wishing each other "*Merry Christmas*" and "*Happy New Year*," and calling each other by such names as Miriam, Charles, Richard, Bob, Tony, Julie and Willie. . . . The airplane, the damn plane that was to have brought him to Havana, has left him in some Miami neighborhood.[6]

Window displays and store decorations were modeled on North American designs. Some of this, of course, was influenced by the presence of the U.S. retailers and department stores. North American franchises adopted promotional campaigns developed by corporate headquarters in the United States. Many used the promotional materials provided by U.S. product lines. Cuban stores often modeled themselves on U.S. counterparts. Some stores employed North American decorators. Publicity manager Irving Donnin coordinated the window display of El Encanto. A number of Cuban window decorators, like Antonio Suárez of Fin de Siglo, were trained in the United States. El Encanto assumed the appearance of a modern North American department store, installing elevators and later escalators; it was among the first to introduce air conditioning. With branches in Cienfuegos, Varadero, Santa Clara, Camagüey, Holguín, and Santiago de Cuba, El Encanto provided an outlet for an extensive variety of European and U.S. products—"all sorts of merchandise," affirmed senior partner Luis Entralgo in 1930, "specially suited to the American taste." In advertisements, El Encanto identified itself with North American stores: "Yes, American style. You come into El Encanto and it seems to you that you are in one of the fine stores of New York, Boston or Chicago. The departments are arranged in American style. The interior organization is based on that of the great stores in the big cities of the United States."[7] "It [El Encanto] was pure quality," Antonio Barba recalled. "A department store of this type, which is typically North American, of this high quality and variety, was not found anywhere in Latin America, or for that matter, not found in Europe in 1951. It could be compared only with Sak's, Lord & Taylor, and B. Altman's in New York."[8]

Cuban retailers were fully alive to trends and practices in the United States and quick to adopt methods that seemed to work. Lily Ferreiro, who operated a supermarket in Santiago de Cuba, was especially proud of the "all-window front [that] made it look like its counter-part in the United States." Retired druggist Orlando Requeijo recalled his annual trips to Florida to visit pharmacies and drugstores to study the latest merchandising trends and marketing techniques. Year after year, Requeijo adjusted his retail strategies accordingly, adding such merchandise as toys, phonograph records, small articles of clothing, and eventually a soda fountain complete with hot dogs and hamburgers. Indeed, drugstores across the island were a major distributor of U.S. products for everyday use, from common medicines to cosmetics, toiletries, and sundries. "The best equipped stores were the drug stores," Katherine Ponvert recalled of her years in Cienfuegos. "They have always carried a very complete line of American products and all of the best, such as Elizabeth Arden, Revlon and many other cosmetics."[9]

Cuba became an extension of the North American market. Trends in the United States quickly took hold on the island. In a complex process, North American market culture insinuated itself into virtually every aspect of public and private life, in tastes and preferences, as a means of self-representation and merchandise for self-esteem, prescribed behaviors for which appropriate attire was available, or perhaps it was the other way around.

Cubans were surrounded by images and imagery of the United States. The use of the North American experience as model expanded into the many realms of everyday life, from the most intimate aspects of personal relationships to matters of public policy. By ordinary means, often in ways hardly discerned, the North American narrative was a subject of national dialogue. North American mass media was an important conveyor of representations of daily life, and Cuban media forms were based on U.S. formats. *El Mundo* was modeled on the *New York Herald Tribune*. *Selecciones del Readers Digest* reached a circulation of 60,000; *Life en Español*, *Visión*, and *Lo mejor del Catholic Digest* were not far behind. During the 1910s and 1920s most of the fiction published in popular weeklies was written by Cubans; by the 1940s and 1950s, however, most popular fiction was a translation of North American westerns, mystery and detective stories, and science fiction. The translated works of Ernest Hemingway, Bret Harte, Jack London, Pearl Buck, Ellery Queen, O. Henry, and many others became standard media fare.

In addition, considerable official U.S. effort went into the penetration of Cuban media to obtain a favorable representation of "the American way of life." The U.S. Information Service (USIS) disseminated an enormous quantity of news, information, and photographs to Cuban newspapers and magazines. Newspapers published an estimated 5,000 column inches weekly of news provided by USIS. Editorials in the leading dailies, including *El Mundo*, *Diario de la*

Marina, *Excelsior*, and *Prensa Libre*, were often based on USIS information. For example, the cover of the July 5, 1957, edition of *Bohemia*—a portrait of George Washington against a background of the Declaration of Independence—was supplied by USIS.[10]

News agencies and syndication services transformed the character of Cuban newspapers. United Press International and the Associated Press (AP) provided most of the international news published in the national dailies. King Features, the Tribune Service, and Editors Press Service supplied large quantities of material to daily newspapers and weekly magazines. Cartoons and comic strips included Superman, Dennis the Menace (Daniel el travieso), Buck Rogers, Dick Tracy, Roy Rogers (El Rey de los Vaqueros), Little Abner (El Chiquito Abner), Blondie (Pepita), Katzenjammers (Maldades de los pilluelos), Snuffy Smith (Tapón), Felix the Cat (El Gato Félix), Mickey Mouse (El Ratón Miquito), and Donald Duck (El Pato Donald).

Newspapers and magazines were filled with syndicated columns, features, and articles as political commentary and entertainment, advice, gossip and gardening tips, remedies and recipes. Walter Lippmann, Drew Pearson (*Desde Washington*), Walter Winchell (*Desde New York*), Oscar Frawley (*De los Campos de Training*), and George Ripley (*Crealo o no*) were widely read in Havana. The views of North American consultants, counselors, and specialists of all types appeared in translation daily; they dealt with such diverse matters as social propriety and etiquette, dieting and dating, health and nutrition, beauty, fashion and style, child rearing, and homemaking. The columns of Emily Post and Elsa Maxwell were published regularly in *Vanidades*. Other North American columnists offered counsel and suggested guidelines for virtually all aspects of everyday life: how to bathe correctly and how to wrap gifts, ideal careers for young people, how to interpret dreams. (See Appendix Table 6.1.) Syndicated astrology charts and horoscopes also appeared daily.[11]

Cubans were thus implicated in North American narratives about life and living. This was not simply about customs and conventions, but rather a rendering of daily life arranged around the idealization of North American ways. The power of these formulations lay in their presumption of universality and their capacity to foster familiarity with U.S. market culture as a function of the ordinary experience of quotidian existence. North American styles became Cuban standards. Syndicated articles on interior decoration and home furnishings in the United States were presented as a model for Cuban households. Countless feature stories about furniture arrangement, color patterns, and room decorating were based on North American homes. An article on "new tendencies in interior decorating" was accompanied by photographs of the 1952 American Furnishings Convention in New York and featured William Pahlmann's design for living rooms, Edward Wormley's decor for foyers, Stephen Hendrick's arrangements for bedrooms, and Bertha Schaefer's rendering of the "modern living room." An article on suburban living specified "what should be in every home." Another column used New York apartments as models to suggest creative ways to arrive at a "contemporary appearance." A feature by Betty Pepis acclaimed the latest dining room furniture created by New York designer Paul McCobb.[12]

The meanings assigned to these narratives, many of which assumed the reader's access to the world of material bounty, are difficult to assess. One is left only to imagine how Cynthia Lowry's feature in *El Mundo* in October 1952 might have been received by her Cuban readers: "The housewife in the United States, with her beautiful apartment or comfortable house in the suburbs . . . has an electric dishwasher, as well as a washing machine, a freezer, a vacuum cleaner, and a television. The oven is automatic. Bread and cake come already prepared from the bakery. Many foods come prepared and are purchased in the grocery store."[13]

The dominance of North American customs was further ratified by local arbiters of style. *Vanidades*'s monthly photo feature "The Happy and Clean Home of Which We Dream" used as examples the residences of Rita Hayworth, Bette Davis, Ida Lupino, and John Garfield. Another feature in *Vanidades*, "Your House and Mine: Decorated with Style" by Nereyda de Muxo, was illustrated by photographs of North American homes. Leonor Barraqué prepared the text for a photo essay on "la nursery," based on children's rooms in the United States, emphasizing the importance of "comfortable and simple rooms for the sound body and mind of children." M. Millares Vázquez revealed the "secret of success" and "ways to accumulate wealth" as suggested in interviews with U.S. millionaires.[14]

North American furniture styles and arrangements gained early ascendancy in middle- and working-class homes. Heavily cushioned and textile-covered sofas, framed by two small tables, accompanied by one or two sofa chairs, became the dominant layout of *el living-room*. The sofa bed arrived during the 1930s, followed by wall mirrors, coffee tables, and the radio-phonograph console of the 1950s.[15]

Because so much of what passed for chic originated from the United States, moreover, it was logical and perhaps inevitable that Cubans aspiring to careers in fashion design or interior decorating traveled north for their education, thereby reinforcing the privileged place of North American forms. Margarita Sánchez and Ana María Barraqué studied fashion design in New York. Gisela Madrid Castellanos attended the School of Style and Design at the New York Traphagan Institute of Fashion. Elena González del Valle studied interior decorating at Columbia University. Havana department store model Irma Sánchez Maldonado graduated from the Doris Crane Modeling School in Miami. Fashion designers Miguel Ferreras, Luis Estévez, and Adolfo opened establishments in New York.

The North American penchant for personal development extended to Cuba. In 1955 a Dale Carnegie Institute opened in Havana, and syndicated Dale Carnegie columns began to appear regularly in *Vanidades*. Articles by Norman

"Earn more money and secure your future!" exhorted this advertisement for the U.S. correspondence school appearing in *Bohemia* magazine in 1958. (Courtesy of the photographic archives, *Bohemia*, Havana)

Vincent Peale were a customary feature of *Bohemia*. In Teodoro Espinosa's short story "Hay dulces para todas," the protagonist congratulates himself for his erudition: "I am a well-learned man. I read magazines and newspapers, and I know almost by heart—and it is my main book—*How to Win Friends and Influence People*."[16] Newspapers and magazines were filled with advertisements for self-study and self-improvement. North American correspondence programs prolif-erated. Newspaper and magazine ads offered job training and promised secure jobs, higher salaries, and a bright future. Programs covered everything from English-language skills to public speaking, shorthand to short wave, radio and television repair, aviation mechanics and automobile repair, from accounting to air conditioning, from Rosicrucianism to body building. The "new man" of the 1950s was modeled on the physically conditioned Charles Atlas.

North American experts expounded on courtship etiquette and ideal marital relations in *Vanidades*. In his regular column, marriage counselor C. R. Adams declared that twenty years of age was the ideal time to marry, adding that "despite her social and professional development, a woman still sought security in marriage." Priscilla Wayne suggested ways that married women could con-tinue to be lovers to their husbands. Evelyn Whitman discussed the emotional stability women required for a successful marriage, and Paul Popenoe pre-scribed ways for wives to emotionally support their husbands. Marjorie Ander-son explored the issue of career versus marriage for women and concluded that a career could make a woman "a better wife and mother."[17]

North American theories and practices of child rearing were also widely disseminated. Articles and books on the subject published in the United States were often reprinted or summarized in Cuban media. The popular parenting manuals by Grace Langdon and Irving Stout, *The Discipline of Well-Adjusted Children* (1952), and Norma Cutts and Nicholas Mosley, *Better Home Discipline* (1952), were serialized in *El Mundo*. A feature article providing counsel on raising children with above-average intelligence, written by Edith Sterne and originally published in *Woman's Home Companion*, was reprinted in *El Mundo* as well. Psychologist Robert Clark furnished tips on "how to be a good father." Hortensia Lamar prepared a weekly column in *Carteles* summarizing advice offered by North American specialists: one, by psychologist Josephine Ken-yon, recommended ways to raise adolescent girls; another, by physician D. A. Thomas, emphasized the importance of child obedience. Articles prescribed approaches to toilet training and table manners, play and study, grooming, and discipline and punishment. AP syndicated columnist "Sylvia" encouraged par-ents to allow children to play, for it was "the form in which initiative and abilities developed and the only means by which to establish physical and mental coordi-nation." Attention was given to toys and games as a means of developing charac-ter and responsibility. Child psychologist David Taylor Marke urged parents to choose toys that would develop important skills and responsibility.[18]

The connection between counsel and consumerism and, further, the degree to which consumption was linked to well-being and well-adjustment, were often explicit and, indeed, at the very source of the appeal of North American conven-tions. Child-rearing advice emphasized the importance of play, games, and toys in raising well-adjusted children. Parents should encourage their children to use their imaginations and to decorate their rooms with pictures of Mickey Mouse, the Three Little Pigs, and Shirley Temple dolls. To foster self-reliance and self-confidence, Sylvia told parents that it was essential "to buy toys that allow children to engage in activities appropriate to their age." David Taylor Marke suggested how "to select the appropriate toy." In a column published days before Christmas 1952, Marke enjoined mothers "not to raise children clinging to their skirts" and recommended buying them bicycles. "Many parents fear for the safety of their children while they ride around on bicycles," Marke recognized. However, he hastened to add, the U.S. National Safety Council reported that "American bicycles were the safest in the world." To the point: "Consultants agree that the sooner a child rides a bicycle the sooner he acquires a sense of responsibility."[19]

Cuba early developed into a lucrative market for North American toys, as children often received gifts on two holidays: Christmas and Kings Day (January 6). Sales data are incomplete, but during the early 1940s consumers in Havana alone generated an estimated $60 million in toy receipts.[20] The toy market was dominated by U.S. products. As early as 1919, Harris Brothers Company in Havana featured a Christmas advertisement showing Santa Claus shaking hands with Uncle Sam, proclaiming: "American toys rule supreme due to their indisputable superiority, for their ingenuity and their durability. Good mothers should bring their good children here."[21]

In increasing numbers, Cuban children played with toys manufactured in the United States, even as play in the course of the twentieth century gradually replaced work as the principal way to influence the values and skills that children acquired. U.S. games and toys assumed a commensurately larger role in the shaping of childhood preferences and propensities, with far-reaching implications. It may well be impossible to determine with any precision the relationship between toys and personality formation or, for that matter, how games and toys transmit values. What is certain, however, is that tens of thousands of Cuban children, over three generations, played with virtually identical toys, participated in similar games, and read the same comic books as their North American counterparts. Coloring books published in the United States depicted cowboys and Indians, northern fauna and flora, and U.S. cartoon characters. New games and toys in the United States went to Cuba almost immediately. Pogo sticks appeared in the 1940s. The yo-yo had arrived in the 1930s and became something of a rage. "A real craze exists," Gerardo del Valle reported. "At every turn one finds children and adults practicing with the yo-yo. . . . Recipients of the newest expressions of progress and of all the latest trends, Havana could not but give the yo-yo a great welcome." In 1950 the Duncan Yo-Yo Company dispatched a delegation of yo-yo champions on a promotional tour of the island. Los Reyes Magos toy store advertised "clinics" for children wishing to master the yo-yo. In the 1950s the hula hoop appeared.[22]

Retail shops and department stores offered a large assortment of North American toys. Fin de Siglo sold toy army jeeps and navy ships, revolvers, rifles, bows and arrows, electric trains, Chevrolet and Lincoln toy cars, and Bonny Braids dolls. Shirley Temple dolls became popular in the 1930s and 1940s. Sánchez Mola advertised "American toys," including a Fort Apache set with Indians, cavalrymen, covered wagons, and twelve panels of the fort. Garmendia and Company sold children's toiletries with a military theme: a U.S. Army tank contained shampoo; a U.S. Air Force jet, hair lotion; and a U.S. Navy ship, boy's cologne. Baseball was a source of many toys: boy dolls dressed in major league uniforms, big-league team pennants, bats, balls, gloves, and coloring books. Perhaps the most popular items were cowboy and cowgirl suits, complete with guns and holsters, fringed vests, hats, and boots. Sears sold a wide array of cowboy clothing, toy guns, and toy soldiers. El Pasaje shoe store advertised "beautiful cowboy boots, 'Pecos Bill' style." Casa Cofiño sold Indian chief outfits, and Almacenes Ultra offered a selection of outfits of New York City policemen and interplanetary space ship captains. La Filosofía had Indian chief clothing and cowboy suits "with all the trappings."[23]

The popularity of these products was itself an indication of the extent to which the iconography of North American popular culture had seized hold of the Cuban imagination. The merchandise traded on the celebrity of U.S. film and television personalities and could assume name recognition. Cuban boys and girls could pretend to be Hopalong Cassidy, Roy Rogers, and Dale Evans. Almacenes Ultra advertised "a perfect reproduction of the outfit of the famous *cowboy* Hopalong Cassidy," and Sears offered Roy Rogers pants, shirts, and boots and Dale Evans blouses and skirts. In 1955 Fin de Siglo proclaimed itself "the first to offer its children collections inspired by the image of the North American hero, Davy Crockett, 'king of the wild frontier,' " including outfits for boys and girls, handkerchiefs printed with "scenes of the frontier," Davy Crockett bed sheets and pajamas, books and comics on "the history of the great American hero," and a "plastic and metal rifle, manufactured to scale, copying the original used by the hero to hunt buffalos on the wild frontier." Casa Vasallo advertised a "Dick Tracey Wrist Radio," and Casa Cofiño marketed a "Highway Patrol" model car and a Robin Hood outfit, "an exact replica used by North American film and television star Richard Greene." Fin de Siglo also promoted a Superman suit, with pants, shirt, cape, belt, and "a certificate ratifying membership in the Superman Club."[24]

Supermarket chains opened stores on the island after World War II and immediately transformed household economies and family shopping habits. Cubans were drawn to the supermarkets' attractive display of merchandise, varieties of meats, fresh fruit and vegetables, and frozen foods, all located under one roof and sold at reasonable prices. It was all very modern. The U.S.-owned chain Minimax Supermercados—"Minimum prices—Maximum Quality"—expanded in Havana and its immediate suburbs. Proclaiming itself "the most modern supermarket in Latin America," Minimax reproduced the North American shopping environment. Minimax owners, commented correspondent J. Lamar, "knew that the Cuban consumer was ready to adopt rapidly the modern and convenient system of the Supermarket, where in an agreeable environment of cleanliness and comfort—air conditioning and background music—are found all the necessary articles of daily need in the variety and price most desired by the public."[25] A second chain owned by the German Ekloh family arrived during the mid-1950s. Modeled on the Kroger system in the United States, the Ekloh Supermarkets expanded quickly in Havana. The new stores not only introduced a new way to shop but also provided a mass outlet for U.S. products. More than 60 percent of Ekloh merchandise consisted of U.S. imports.

Supermarkets enjoyed wide success and soon threatened the traditional *bodega* with extinction. A series of surveys in 1954 indicated almost unanimous popular enthusiasm for these chain stores. "As a modern housewife," explained Hilda González, "I am certain that the *groceries* have displaced the *bodegas*, and I applaud all undertakings that signify advancement and health for the country, for these *groceries* are an example of cleanliness and give us before the whole world a boost as a civilized country." Gina Casamayor praised the attractiveness and convenience of the "modern type of food services that offer better advantages to the domestic economy." Luis Rolando Cabrera declared the bodega to be a thing of the past: "Progress, with its inexorable march, has decreed the disappearance of *bodegas*. . . . Their place is being filled little by little with *groceries* North American style that today dominate the food stores. . . . They were invented by the *yanquis* and have obtained acceptance."[26]

North American cooking and dining gained popularity as well. U.S. brand names and food lines, no less than cookware, were readily available in Cuba. Cafeteria-style and fast-food establishments opened throughout the 1950s. Eating habits were in transition, and whether due to changes in the pace of daily life or advances in food processing, including frozen foods, what Cubans were eating and the way they were eating, as well as where and how they ate, progressively approximated North American habits. Increased travel to the United States brought many into contact with North American customs and permanently modified Cuban ways. After several weeks in Miami, Roberto Pérez de Acevedo announced his adoption of the "American style" of eating, which included juice, eggs, toast, and coffee in the morning and salad, vegetables, and meat in the evening. "I have actually slept much better," he asserted, "than when I ate two heavy meals and a strong lunch."[27]

North American eating habits also received publicity in the mass media. Jane Nickerson, whose syndicated columns were published in *El Mundo*, offered information on the newest kitchen devices and cooking utensils, with recipes for easy meals, including one on how to "prepare hot dogs for lunch." Adriana

Loredo made a career in journalism by reproducing weekly in *Bohemia* recipes (El menú de la semana) from U.S. sources, usually *Good Housekeeping*, *Woman's Home Companion*, and *McCall's*. "These are good recipes," she assured her readers, "and they 'work.'" But Loredo transmitted more than instructions on the preparation and presentation of food. She was also an exponent of a way of life, offering recipes that were themselves a narrative of the changes overtaking North American households. Demographic shifts, including the movement to the suburbs, smaller families, and the growing presence of women in the labor force, were reflected in recipes appearing in *Woman's Home Companion* and *Good Housekeeping*. In one column Loredo passed on the conventional wisdom of making larger portions "to save as left overs on later occasions." In another she discussed *Woman's Home Companion* recipes for the preparation of complete meals requiring less than thirty minutes. "The secret is to prepare the main meal in advance," she explained, "and simply put the finishing touches on at the time of serving." What was especially important in the recipe, Loredo concluded, was not the meal "but the principle upon which its preparation is based."[28]

Food prepared quickly received increased prominence if not preference in everyday life. Certainly advertisers extolled U.S. food lines whose principal—and most marketable—virtue was speed and simplicity of preparation. But the very availability of these products was a reflection of larger changes overtaking North American households, which insinuated themselves directly into Cuban homes. In a column on the "modern kitchen," *La Lucha* was direct and to the point: "Time, which is money in the North American concept, should rule supreme in matters pertaining to culinary arts. . . . The contemporary kitchen should be ordered in such a manner as to make for fast work, without needless movement. . . . The system and the organization should save on effort, time, and thinking." María Subira, whose weekly feature "Consultas y opiniones" in *Bohemia* was often viewed as the final word on fashion, style, and nutrition, was almost celebratory about JELL-O: "Nothing is more economical, easier to prepare and prettier to look at. . . . It is prepared in one minute. There is no need to cook or dirty one's hands." The "new" Quaker Oats could be "prepared quickly—in one-fifth the time than before. . . . This new Quaker Oats saves time, work, and gas." Cream of Wheat was called simply "Rapid!" An advertisement for Kellogg's Corn Flakes proclaimed: "Although it seems incredible, breakfast in two minutes!"[29]

Other changes were introduced directly by the growing North American presence. In 1954 the new F. W. Woolworth in Vedado offered a complete breakfast, lunch counter service, and a "take-out" department. "Don't worry if you do not have a cook," Woolworth's advertised, "we serve delicious food to take out in a new delicatessen department (*nuevo departamento de delicatessen*). Deliveries to the home—free! We will deliver directly to your home orders valued more than $5.00." A Woolworth's that opened in Camagüey two years later had a "modern department, a lounge for the ladies, a well-stocked bakery, a soda and lunch counter, and a new *delicatessen* department, all air conditioned."[30]

Cubans easily adapted to these developments. "I have recently come to enjoy having breakfast at the *Ten Cent*," comments the protagonist in Virgilio Piñera's short story "El caramelo" (1962), who in the process developed a taste for strawberry pie (*el pie de fresa*). In Lisandro Otero's novel *En ciudad semejante* (1970), Ernestina Guiral is described "pouring syrup over *hot-cakes*" at breakfast. Short story writer Calvert Casey conveyed Cuban sensibilities poignantly:

> The other afternoon I entered that immense storehouse of useful and useless things that we in Cuba call "el Ten-Cén" and that the North Americans built with the name of Woolworth's on the front, that nobody could ever pronounce. It's found all over the world and the one in Havana is the most luxurious of them all thanks to the fabulous success it attained, for when it moved to the corner of Galiano [Street] it was converted to a type of social club for people of all classes.[31]

Woolworth's was part of a larger trend. "The modern Cuban eats hot dogs, hamburgers, hot cakes, waffles, fried chicken, and ice cream," observed resident *New York Times* correspondent Ruby Hart Phillips in 1957. "It has become almost impossible today in Havana to find native foods such as *malanga*, *yuca*, *picadillo*, or *ajiaco*." At about the same time Sydney Clark observed similar developments:

> The American quick lunch has invaded Havana in an impressive way. . . . The Cafeteria America is at the corner of Galiano and Neptuno. It is large, lively, cheerful in its strident way, and will fling at the customer anything in the sandwich line or the salad or croquette or hot cake line. It will serve *Corn Flakes con leche* and *perros calientes* (hot dogs). It will also jerk any kind of soda or furnish any ice cream dish from plain *frozen de chocolate* to a "honey moon". . . . One can eat in the America in twenty minutes. . . . The Hollywood Soda Fountain Restaurant, at Neptuno and Manrique, is more restful to the eye and ear than the America, but will also serve a lot of things very quickly. . . . The Salon Pullman on Consulado is a gaudy red-leather place serving anything from a sandwich to a full meal.

In *Los muertos andan solos* (1962), Juan Arcocha depicts Jorge as "having eaten a hot dog and drunk a Coca-Cola as he always had for lunch."[32]

Many of these circumstances had to do with North American tourism, the demands of which contributed to changes in the Cuban landscape. "Havana has now gone completely US," lamented advertising executive Shirley F. Woodall in 1951. He continued:

> There is not only a Nedick's stand in the park, but a large, clean and imposing Howard Johnson establishment now adorns 23rd and G Sts., complete with

22 flavors of ice cream—imported, sir, by air from the US! This country that has perhaps the largest assortment of wonderful indigenous fruits that [is] to be found in any single country in the hemisphere (and most of them are elegant in ice cream) has to foster a tourist trade whose pampered tastes lead them to insist on stateside ice cream in addition to their traditional bagels. Hell of a note.[33]

The adaptation was striking and it seemed to gather momentum. North American customs passed unremarkably, often unnoticed, into everyday life. They exuded motion and mobility; they created things to do, places to go, such as movie theaters, skating rinks, amusement parks. New habits and new preferences developed. Products acquired status and their users claimed stature merely because of their association with the United States. Felicia Rosshandler recalled her first experience with cornflakes on arriving in Havana from Europe: " '*Es americano*,' the waiter explained . . . , as if that said it all. Imported, expensive, El Kellogg symbolized high-class fare in Havana where, we would learn, anything American was considered chic." The smoking of U.S. brands of cigarettes, especially Lucky Strike, Camel, and Chesterfield, became sign and symbol of chic and smart—all the more remarkable in a country known for its outstanding tobacco products. Indeed, the demand for U.S. cigarettes was so great that an extensive illicit trade developed. One-quarter of the 22 million packages of U.S. cigarettes sold in 1950 arrived as contraband. This was also true for an endless number of products.[34]

New recreational forms and new pastimes, as well as games and novelties of all types, filled Cuban leisure time. Crossword puzzles appeared in the 1920s. Bridge parties early became popular with high society. Mah-jongg arrived in the 1930s. By the 1940s gin rummy was very much in vogue and, according to the official history of the Vedado Tennis Club, "even managed to cause the demise of domino."[35] Canasta parties acquired the status of chic in the 1950s. Bingo arrived at about the same time and immediately captured the popular imagination. Thousands played nightly in private clubs and meeting halls. Some of Havana's most fashionable nightclubs sponsored weekly bingo events and competed with each other in prize offerings. The Sans Souci provided a wide variety of grand prizes, including diamond rings, mink stoles, Cadillacs, and Chrysler Imperials. The Tropicana offered $10,000 as the grand prize. In 1957 a new program aired on local television: "Bingo en Televisión." "Bingo fever has seized the residents of Havana," commented *El Mundo* in 1957. Bowling gained new popularity during the 1940s and 1950s, as bowling alleys opened in Havana, Varadero, Cienfuegos, Camagüey, and Santiago de Cuba. In Camagüey the bowling alleys "Faico" and "La Bolerita" combined bowling lanes with nightclubs. A newly formed Cuban-American Bowling League sponsored annual competition among the social clubs, including the Havana Yacht Club and the Biltmore Country Club. Handball, softball, and squash found a large following. In 1957 an ice skating rink was installed in the Palacio de Deportes. In the same year, square dancing was introduced by the Ministry of Education. Twelve North American square dancing experts were hired to teach nearly one hundred Cuban physical education instructors the finer points of country dancing. Greyhound racing arrived in the early 1950s, operated in Marianao by the Havana Greyhound Kennel Club—the name in English. The grand prize was $20,000; lesser prizes included sixteen Plymouths, round-trip airline tickets to Miami, and tickets to the World Series. Dog shows became popular under the auspices of the American Kennel Club. Dog owners organized breeding clubs like "el Terrier Club de Cuba." In 1958 a new dog obedience school for German shepherds opened in Havana where commands were taught in English. " 'Sit!' 'Stay!' 'Heel!' 'Jump!' 'Come!' " recorded the correspondent for *Bohemia*, adding: "English is used because of the greater severity of the command words, and because of fewer letters and vowels in many words, although it is also true that the training literature used here for this purpose comes from the North."[36]

The economy was changing more rapidly than the language, with new technologies, new machinery, new devices, and new consumer goods never before needed. All were introduced in successive and seemingly endless waves. So, too, were brand names, merchandise, and pastimes. North American popular usage took hold and seemed all but impossible to arrest and reverse. Almost everything, it appeared, relentlessly assumed a North American form.

U.S. products rearranged the cognitive categories of everyday life. They worked their way into popular culture by manipulating specific linguistic and iconic codes and fostered a commercial language that displaced colloquial usage. Brand names gained currency and entered the vernacular in the form of generic representation. Usage implied familiarity, and recognition on this scale suggests the extent to which these forms had passed into popular consciousness. "Frigidaire" became synonymous with refrigerator, "Ace" and "Fab" with detergent, "Delco" with automobile battery, and "Arrow" with dress shirt. "Yale" came to mean lock. ("Minnie puso el *yale* a la puerta," observed the narrator in Federico de Ibarzabal's 1938 novel *La charca*.) *El péter*, from Peter Paul brand, came to signify a chocolate bar, and hence "un péter Nestlé" or "un péter Hershey." In *La última lección* (1924), Carlos Loveira uses "la Gillette" as a synonym for razor blade and "un Ford" for taxi. Often "un Chevi" (i.e., Chevrolet) was also used for taxi. In *En ciudad semejante*, Lisandro Otero uses "un Kleenex" for tissue ("abrió la cartera, tomó un *Kleenex*"). In the short story "Tres timbrazos," Rogelio Llopis describes his protagonist as impeccably dressed, wearing "Florsheim shoes." "Colt 38" meant pistol ("dos morteros no son dos *Colt 38*," comments the narrator in Luis Ricardo Alonso's novel *El palacio y la furia* [1976]). Indeed, guns of all types were represented by manufacturers' names. Juan Esteban Estevanell in *Santiago: 39 grados sobre o* (1980) used "Thompson" for machine gun ("el policía tomó la *Thompson*"), as did Lisandro Otero in *Arbol de la vida* (1990) ("hallé a Sancristóbal con dos *Thompson*"). Otero in particular is fond of using manufacturers' names: "si obtenía un *Remington*," "estuvo a punto de sacar su *Smith & Wesson*," "leventaron el *Winchester* y la *Browning*." Luis Agüero used "Kodak" for camera. In Llopis's short story "Un hombre infame," "un lucky" (i.e., Lucky Strike) is a synonym for cigarette; Luis Adrián Betancourt wrote "encendió un *Winston* de una caja nueva." Eladio Secades referred to "un ches-ter" (i.e., Chesterfield) to mean cigarette ("Deme un *chester*"). So does novelist Edmundo Desnoes, who in *El cataclismo* (1965) characterizes U.S. tourists as "fumando *Chester*." In the novel *Los Robledal*, Hilda Perera describes Juana as "bearing a benevolent smile like Aunt Jemima," and Loló de la Torriente's pro-tagonist in *Los caballeros de la marea roja* (1984) was expected to have "una sonrisa *Colgate*" (a Colgate smile). To describe how closely the protagonist in the short story "De Estupiñán y la ameba" was paying attention, Abel Prieto invokes a familiar image: "with his ears cocked with more intensity than the dog of RCA Victor." During a visit to Havana, British historian Jean Stubbs marveled on learning that the generic name for chewing gum was "Chiclets," that "Marlboro or Chesterfield . . . meant cigarettes," that "detergent was invariably called FAB, and rice was Tío Ben. I was educated in Quaker, for oats; Del Monte, for fruit and juice; and all the major U.S. brands that were no more."[37]

U.S. name brands entered directly into the vernacular. These *cubanismos* appropriated properties associated with the product according to what it was used for. "Echale fli" or "darle fli a alguien," derived from Flit pesticide, was to rid oneself of an undesirable person. "Ser una persona como *Longines*" was to be punctual or precise. "Convertir alguien en *Leonard*," inspired by the Leonard refrigerator, meant to give someone the cold shoulder. "Ser como el *alka selser*," taken from the instant effervescence of Alka Seltzer, described a person who angered quickly. "Hasta donde dice Collín" signified to the very end, suggested by the Collins trademark at the base of the machete blade and hence to thrust the blade fully into an adversary. "Ser alguien un chicle," from Chiclet chewing gum, referred to someone from whom it was impossible to free oneself. "Ser como la magnesia filixs," referring to a very active man, was taken from Phillips Milk of Magnesia, which had to be shaken well before using. For one to "hacerse Vaselina" was to be evasive and duplicitous—that is, to be slippery.[38]

Colloquial usage commonly drew on North American popular culture as a source of representation and, indeed, offered powerful testimony to the degree to which U.S. forms had insinuated themselves into ordinary speech. "Ser al-guien *Rhett Butler*" was someone who had gone out of style. "Quiere ser alguien el *Tarzán* de la jungla" referred to a person who undertook impossible tasks. Olive Oil in the *Popeye* comic strip was translated as "Rosario," and "ser una mujer *Rosario*" described a thin woman. To be "un mister *Scott*" referred to a man married to an unattractive woman, inspired by the Scott's Liver Oil label depicting a fisherman in tow with a codfish. "Echarse un *Cinderella* de película" was to dream or fantasize. "Ser alguien un *Kin Kon*"—as in King Kong—charac-terized one as vulgar and uncouth. "Ser *Ferdinando* el Toro," alluding to Ferdi-nand's preference for flowers over fighting, referred to a gay man. Ripley's *Believe It or Not* acquired full idiomatic status. One sportswriter described "a fantastic triple play on the level of Ripley." "The things that go on in Cuba," affirmed political commentator Antonio Llano Montes in 1955, "appear taken from the pages of Mr. Ripley's 'Believe It or Not.' " In Otero's *En ciudad seme-jante*, Octavio accuses Arsenio of "having accumulated more useless knowledge than Ripley." In Leonel López-Nussa's novel *Tabaco* (1963), Efren responds to good news by declaring: "Incredible! A case for Ripley!"[39]

It is not surprising that Cuban speech was filled with English-language refer-ences to ordinary goods. North Americans controlled the terms of transactions and hence imposed the dominant rendering of everyday narratives. In 1952 "el Coney Island Park" in Havana announced the opening of "el Kiddyland" with such new rides as "el Bubble Bounce" and "el Cuddle Up." U.S. products domi-nated the advertising copy of newspapers and magazines. The names of cosmet-ics, clothing, and home furnishings appeared entirely in English: "Super Stay" lipstick by Dorothy Gray, "Light and Bright" hair coloring by Richard Hudnut, the new Helena Rubenstein lipstick colors "Sunny Coral" and "Pink and Fair," the latest Shulton perfumes "Friendship's Garden" and "Desert Flower," Rev-lon's "Touch and Glow" lipstick, Coty nail polish "Copper Bright" and "Sunset Orange." Clothing lines included Catalina swimwear "Eye Catcher," "Heart Throb," and "Side Glance." Often advertisers assisted the reader with pronuncia-tion: for example, an ad for "Outdoor Girl" skin cream was accompanied by the phrase "Pronunciese 'audor guel' "; "Holeproof" stockings, by "Pronunciese 'jolpruf' "; and Max Factor "Hi-Fi" makeup, by "Pronunciese 'Jai Fai.' " The pro-motion of U.S. clothing lines contributed significantly to the Cuban vernacular:

Pullover, *overall* y pantalones
Pedal-pusher de gabardina
Overall de gabardina
Lindos *Beauty-Kits* muy refajados
Sweaters de lana
Jackets y cazadoras de piel
Fajas y *panties*
Shorts de baño

Society pages relied heavily on English words to describe social events. By the 1950s English had become the principal mode for representing the social world of the Cuban middle class. Column headings for social news in *El Mundo* and *Diario de la Marina* between 1950 and 1958 reveal the prevalence of North American usage:[40]

El gran *beauty fashion show*
Birthday party ayer
Animado *cocktail party*
Canasta party en El Liceo
Baby shower en El Liceo de Matanzas
Gran *fashion show* en el Jockey Club
Fiesta de *teen agers* en el Country Club
La *maid of honor* llevaba un precioso vestido
El *buffet-supper*
Un *candle light party*
Muy animado el *Camp-Fire* del Vedado Tennis Club

In all areas related to entertainment and social events English words figured prominently, either in their original form or as rendered phonetically in Spanish: el night club, un cake, un bar, lonchar (to lunch), el show, el coctel (cocktail), el hit parade, el sandwich, and el jaibol (highball). "The singing of '*Happy Birthday to you*' is obligatory at childrens' and even adults' parties," observed folklorist Samuel Feijóo. In the Sergio Chaple short story "De cómo fueron los quince de Eugenia de Pardo y Pardo" (1978), the assembled guests bellow "el happy-birthday," and in the novel *Segar a los muertos* (1978), Matías Montes depicts "children singing something other than 'happy birthday' "—rendered as *japibertdey*. A popular brand of Cuban cigarettes in the 1920s sold under the name "Olrait" (i.e., "All Right"); another, called "Hit," was described as "cigarros tipo americano." A popular local soft drink was titled "Cuban Boy."[41]

English words became so familiar that they eventually ceased to be italicized in print. "El sandwich" was ubiquitous—for example, "En cualquiera de los cafés podía comprar un sandwich y una botella de cerveza" (Marcelo Salinas) and "Voy a bajar al café para comerme un sandwich" (Arturo Alfonso Roselló). Biui or Biu was Buick, as in Reynaldo Castillo's short story "Clave 26": "Era mecánico de la Biui." Armando Couto recounts a conversation, "¿Puedes prestarme un nickel para la guagua?"—and in Raúl González de Cascorro's play *La muchacha vestida de limpio* (1957), Alejandro asks "Oye ¿tienes por ahí algunos níkeles sueltos?" In Abelardo Piñeiro's novel *El descanso* (1962), the protagonist afirms the honesty of a friend: "es incapaz de robarse un níckel." Alonso characterized a government as "una dictadura *part-time*." *Bohemia* referred to popular songs as "los *hit parades* que reflejan las preferencias del público," and in *Papaíto Mayarí* (1947) by Miguel de Marcos the protagonist declares "hice un *test* muy satisfactorio."[42]

In the world of banking, manufacturing, and retail trade, North American idioms were everywhere: "el staff meeting," "estar en el inside" (often "el insai"), "el slogan," "el business," and words like "store," "grocery," and "standard." In a 1996 interview General Lino Carreras Rodríguez spoke of clearing land as "terrenos . . . fueron buldozeados [bulldozed] hace algún tiempo." Llopis's protagonist in "Tres timbrazos" is fond of whiskey, given as "uisqui" ("mientras yo ingería el tercer uisqui de la tarde"); Enrique Serpa corrupts the English in the short story "Burócratas" ("bebia whisky con agua de seltz"). "El know-how" became distinctly identified as an admirable North American characteristic. "They really do possess all the resources," Pablo explains to Sergio in the film *Memorias de subdesarrollo*, "*el know-how* to develop the economy of the country. . . . The Americans know well how to do things, *el know-how* to make things work." The protagonist in Alonso's *El palacio y la furia* extols the know-how of the Americans: "I guarantee you that the problem is in the development of the economy. Apart from some *mulato* sons of Catalans in Santiago de Cuba, this is a country of Galicians and darkies (*negritos*), two races resistant to progress. . . . What has to be done is to attract more Americans with their *know-how*." In *El Cataclismo* by Desnoes, after the triumph of the revolution Ana Luisa proclaims: "We, the professionals, the educated people, are the ones in charge, the people with the know-how (*el nou jau*), like the Americans say."[43]

The English forms of household furnishings passed directly into the vernacular through advertisements and daily usage. Home furnishing lines included "Beautyrest" mattresses and "Deepsleep" box springs; Community Silverware promoted its "Twilight," "South Seas," and "Morning Star" patterns. Sears advertised "descanse comodamente en este *rocking chair*," "un *studio couch*, el mueble que usted necesita," "un económico juego de *living room*," "un *dinette set*," and "un precioso juego para su comedor o *pantry*."[44]

The sights and sounds of the North reached into virtually every sphere of daily life, with the capacity for self-validation as well as for obtaining Cuban acquiescence. The power of the English language was self-evident in its association with banking, manufacturing, and trade, which is to say with property, prosperity, and power. Some of the most influential enterprises affirmed their presence in English: the National City Bank, Insurance Company of North America, Trust Company of Cuba, Havana Docks Corporation, Cuban Trading Company, Chase Manhattan Bank. Hotels were named after U.S. presidents (Lincoln, Roosevelt, Harding, Washington), after U.S. cities (New York, Chicago, St. Louis, Albany, Boston, Miami), after U.S. hotel chains (Biltmore, Hilton) and other establishments (Ambassador, Parkview, Royal Palm, Riverside, Park House, St. Johns, Hotel Happiness, Surf). Nightlife was in English (Paradise Bar, Sloppy Joe's, Cozy Corner Bar, Savoy Bar Club, Bar OK, Johnny's Bar Club, Dirty Dick's, Johnny's Dream Club, Four Winds, Blue Moon, Hollywood Cabaret, Skippy's Hideaway, Night and Day); so were movie theaters (Atlantic, Ambassador, City Hall, Duplex, Majestic, Miami, Strand, Rex, Roxy, Roosevelt, Palace).

Cubans frequently used English-language names for their businesses, perhaps to be chic—like Armando Hair Stylist, Fair Department Store, Bergens Modas Department Store—or perhaps to inspire confidence and credibility—

Capitolio, a replication of the U.S. Capitol. (Author's collection)

such as the Cuban American Insurance Company (owned by Juan Beltrán y Moreno), Havana Military Academy (Raúl Chibás), Auto Driver Academy (Joaquín Delgado García), Atlantic Gas Company (Nicasio Fuentes Roca), Garrido Travel Agency (Julio Garrido), Havana Shipping Company (Pablo Pérez), Independent Electric Company (Gustavo Madrazo Rodríguez), and Milanés Electrical Supply and Television Company (José Antonio Milanés Alvarez). The Park Avenue linen shop was owned by Manuel Hernández Menocal and Antonio Tijera Domínguez. Directories were filled with Cuban-owned but English-named businesses: Electrical Comfort, S.A., Havana Business Academy, Havana Speedwriting Academy. The Super Cake, S.A., advertised "spectacular wedding cakes"; Tip Top Baking Company sold cakes "para el 'Happy Birthday.' "[45] There were parks such as Reparto Víbora Park, Cienfuegos Park, Oriental Park, Miramar Gardens, and Campo Alegre Park in Luyanó. The main street of fashionable Miramar was Quinta Avenida (Fifth Avenue). The Capitolio was an exact replica of the U.S. Capitol, only smaller. The symbol of the Partido Popular Cubano was the Statue of Liberty. Usage implied prestige and privilege, which were associated with such residential zones as Reparto Biltmore, Country Club Park, and Reparto Lawton, as well as social standing, like belonging to—always written in English—"el Big Five de La Habana" (the Casino Español, Havana Biltmore Yacht and Country Club, Havana Yacht Club, Country Club de La Habana, and Miramar Yacht Club) and scores of other clubs: the Vedado Tennis Club, Lucky Tennis Club, Villa Real Golf Club, Comodoro Yacht Club, Club Smart, Cubaneleco Yacht Club, Jockey Club. Participation in this world was to be part of "la jai," as in "high life." Social clubs in the provinces replicated the style of the

Gibara Yacht Club, Oriente, ca. 1930s, suggesting the extent to which North American forms reached across the island. (Courtesy of the Friends Historical Collection, Guilford College, Guilford, N.C.)

capital and always went by their English names: Country Club de Santiago de Cuba, Camagüey Tennis Club, Gibara Yacht Club, Sports Club de Marianao, and Villaclara Tennis Club, among others.[46]

Provincial clubs served as transmission points for North American lifestyles, sports, and recreational activities. El Country Club de Camagüey hired as athletic director Carl Latimer, from Los Angeles, who introduced canasta parties, swimming, softball, and gym classes. In his novel *Bertillón 166* (1960), José Soler Puig writes of the Vista Alegre Club in Santiago de Cuba—filled with "the smoke of Chesterfield and Camel cigarettes"; "everything there was an ambience of Miami or New York."[47]

Few who traveled to Cuba could fail to perceive the pervasiveness of English. Returning to Havana in the mid-1920s after an absence of several years, Marcelo Pogolotti noticed the changes immediately. "It was sad to see," he recalled, "how the number of billboards on the streets in English had increased, not only as a result of the penetration of North American enterprises, but also as a result of the slavish imitation of Spanish and Cuban businesses." Venezuelan T. R. Ybarra was amazed by the number of advertisements aboard a Havana trolley car. "I counted today," he wrote in 1939, "twenty-four signboards, twelve written in English. All of them praised North American products. Of the other twelve written in Spanish three also proclaimed the excellence of articles manufactured in the United States." This trend became more pronounced with the passage of time. "Hundreds of English words have crept into the Spanish language," observed Ruby Hart Phillips almost two decades later. "Occasionally a publication in Havana rails against the increasing number of English signs, stores with English names, and the encroachment of the English language into Cuban life. But it is a hopeless battle. Words once given common usage cannot be eliminated." Vacationing in Havana about the same time, actor Peter Ustinov was also struck by the North American presence: "The place felt as though it was irretrievably impregnated with American influence, which is not at all the same as saying that it was like the United States. Every advertisement was for an American product."[48]

This tendency was discerned by Cubans with growing dismay. "The cafés, the drug stores, public establishments of all sorts," commented one journalist, "slavishly emulate North American styles, and even copy the names in Cuba with English terms and signs. The typical *bodega* is now called *grocery*, even if operated by a Menéndez. Already the cafés and restaurants have falsified their names: they are now called *cafeterias*, although they lack the one attribute that in their country of origin justifies that name: efficiency of service. The *boticas* are *drug stores* and even a modest stall is called *market*, that is to say, *mercado*." Samuel Feijóo made a similar observation in 1954: "So many names, brands, advertisements, and billboards . . . announce that Havana is losing its national (*criollo*) color and character." Feijóo noted that "the *tiendas* are called *stores*, the *mercados* are *markets* and *groceries*. . . . The residents of Havana now say *porch*, *living*, *hall*, *grocery* for their equivalent in Spanish."[49]

Language can reflect social reality in compelling ways. The extent to which North American usage expanded into Cuban vernacular usage provides powerful corroboration of the degree to which U.S. forms had seized hold of the conventions of daily life. English-language words entered Spanish as a function of social relationships, particularly unequal power relationships. Use of English words and phrases was to be taken as evidence of acceptance and adaptation, but it also served as proof of sophistication.

Although North American ways were most visible in Havana, they reached across the entire island, into both the large provincial cities and the small rural towns of the interior. U.S. consumer goods, household merchandise, clothing, and toys could be found in almost every community. North American retail stores and department store chains expanded throughout Cuba. Sears opened first in Havana in 1942, then in Marianao, and subsequently in Cienfuegos, Santa Clara, Holguín, and Santiago de Cuba; by the early 1950s it was the largest retail establishment in Cuba. Woolworth's operated five stores in Havana and opened branches in Matanzas, Cienfuegos, Santa Clara, Camagüey, and Santiago de Cuba.

North American retailers transformed local consumption habits and shopping practices. Their presence provided an outlet for huge quantities and vari-

A Tip Top Baking Co. cake advertisement: "Happy birthday to you. . . ."
(Author's collection)

eties of U.S. products, often at prices far below those of local retailers. Indeed, the immediate effect of the expansion of U.S. retailers was to drive local merchants out of business. Katherine Ponvert remembered the arrival of Sears to Cienfuegos: "A week before the grand opening I happened to go into town, and the excitement everywhere was intense. Nearly every store was having a big sale. Rusty pots and pans were hauled down from the shelves and offered for next to nothing. The shopkeepers were in despair, and well they might be. Sears has revolutionized shopping in Cienfuegos with its line of bright, shiny aluminum kitchen ware, gay inexpensive open stock chinaware, and electric iceboxes and deep-freezers." Traveling salesmen dispersed across Cuba, especially during the *zafra*, a time when disposable income was plentiful, selling goods and services, promoting new habits and greater efficiency. In the novel *Los días de nuestra angustia* (1962), Noel Navarro depicts traveling salesman Carlos Sánchez on the road in the interior province, selling wares, distributing goods, and placing orders.[50] By the mid-1950s U.S. products could be seen all over Cuba. "No observer with experience in Latin America," the U.S. Department of Commerce reported in 1956, "can fail to be impressed by the variety, quantity, and quality of the merchandise displayed in the provincial towns and cities of the island. While such items as mechanical refrigerators, gas ranges, and television sets are prominently displayed, the strongest impressions are those formed by an inspection of stores carrying housewares, apparel, and foodstuff."[51]

Traces of the North were to be found almost everywhere. "The social leaders of this small city," Ralph Estep had written of Colón as early as 1909, "were very ordinary types in their commonplace imitation of American dressing." While conducting research in Bejucal (pop. 11,000) in the 1950s for his dissertation, George Stabler was surprised to discover the extent to which North American customs influenced the pattern of Cuban life. "In Bejucal there are people who follow the personalities and events of United States politics," Stabler wrote. "More people follow the fortunes of American baseball (particularly Cuban players) and the changes in American women's fashions. Others follow the boxing news very closely. Professionals (doctors, lawyers, teachers, agriculturalists, etc.) receive journals and professional news magazines directly from the United States and also learn of American developments in the fields through their own professional journals." He continued:

American-made machinery and finished goods play an important part in the economy of the city. . . . The many carpentry shops in the city employ American-made power and hand tools. . . . The clothing factories employ American-made sewing machines and use American-made yarn and dyes. The few telephones and telegraph are American-made. The machine shops use American-made machines and repair American-made automobiles, trucks, and other machinery. The people buy and consume large amounts of American-grown rice, beans, lard, hams, and canned goods. The farmers use

American-made plows, machetes, and other hand tools, tractors, pumps, and so on. They may feed their cows American-produced soybean protein supplement or feed their chickens American-produced growing mash. . . . The people of Bejucal watch television on American-made sets, listen to American-made radios, watch American movies, dance and listen to American music.[52]

Few indeed were the communities beyond the reach of North America. Abascal y Moré recorded the changes overtaking the peasant archetype in verse:

> Es tanto lo que el cine lo ha cambiado
> Que ya no quiere usar la guayabera,
> Ni lleva el jipijapa, tan siquiera,
> Que el criollo orgulloso siempre ha usado.
>
> Los usos y costumbres ha imitado
> de otros países ya, de tal manera,
> Que no le agrada mas que lo de afuera,
> a lo típico habiendo renunciado.

Returning to the places of childhood memories in Las Villas, Marcelo Salinas was astonished to discover how "quickly the distinctive characteristics of *criolloísmo* had disappeared: in language, in mannerism, in what gives a people its own physiognomy." Nowhere had this process advanced as far as in the "popular lexicon" of the most remote locations: "Peasants isolated in villages are happy to use the movie argot and enthusiastic to Americanize themselves with [such words as] *olrait* [all right], *sénkeu* [thank you] and *money*." Salinas concluded: "It is inevitable change: the logical consequence of the railroad, the movies, the victrola. Of course, it was painful to see how this Cuba is formed: it is hardly Cuban." Samuel Feijóo had a similar experience in 1954. "It is truly absurd," he observed, "to hear *OK*, *all right*, and *so long* from the lips of a Cuban from the interior. We have seen a Cuban orchestra called RIVERSIDE playing in La Esperanza, Las Villas. Outside of Ranchuelo we have already seen a *night club* built among the Royal Palms. . . . And in the cities these *night clubs* are advertised with neon lights." Visiting Pinar del Río in 1948, travel writer Herbert Lanks commented on local youth: "We were amazed to see how these young people dressed up in this provincial town. As much as in Havana, the girls here went for careful coiffures and styles that would not have been out of place on New York's Fifth Avenue." At the other end of the island, in Jobabo, Oriente, Macías Bustamante was critical of Cuban youth who "think only of smoking 'Camel' cigarettes, dance the *fox-trot*, train for boxing, and imitate the smiles, the walk, the gazes, and the dress of Hollywood stars." In the Armando Leyva short story "El pregón novelesco" (n.d.), the protagonist sees a young man from Santiago de Cuba board the train and "shortly after getting in, he takes off his suit jacket, a defect of *yanqui* customs."[53]

Cubans inhabited a world dominated by North American representations, in ways not always apparent but never ambiguous, and to which aspirants were obliged to conform before obtaining entry. To pursue professional sports, principally baseball and boxing, to aspire to success in the North, often required a combination of adaptation and assimilation into the dominant representative forms. If sports were rendered primarily in English, its participants could hardly do otherwise. Teams often had English names. The Cuban Sugar Kings played in the International League and the Havana Cubans in the Florida League. Sportswriters adopted U.S. nicknames. Jaime Albear of *La Lucha* became Jimmy Albear; José Losada of *Carteles*, Jess Losada; and José Massaguer, Joe Massaguer. Benny Jimmy wrote for *Bohemia*.

Athletes also gave their names in English. Aspiring major leaguers on the Havana Cubans were known as Johnny Gómez, Tony Zardón, Charlie Cuéllar, Eddy Marcos, and Benny Fernández. Major leaguers included Adolfo Luque (who became Dolph), Edmundo Amorós (Sandy), Pedro Ramos (Pete), Orestes Miñoso (Minnie), Dagoberto Campaneris (Bert), Octavio Rojas (Cookie), Miguel Cuéllar (Mike), and Atanasio Pérez (Tony). Others were Willie Miranda, Jackie Hernández, Mike Fornielles, and Pee Wee Viamontes.

Boxing also favored the adoption of professional names in English. The use of "Kid"—instead of *niño*—was a common practice; the most famous were Kid Chocolate (Eligio Sardiñas), Kid Gavilán (Gerardo González), Kid Juancito (Juan León), Kid Tunero (Evelio Mustelier), Kid Nacional (Adolfo Gis), Kid Charol (Esteban Gallard), and Benny Kid Paret. There were many others: Kid Carpentier, Kid Sosa, Kid Sila, el Patent Leather Kid, el Havana Kid, Mario Kid Sánchez. Other Anglicized nicknames included Baby Cuña, Baby Malpica, Baby Palanca, and Baby Face Quintana; Bull Dog González and Rocky Marrero; Young Manuel and Young Blanco; Black Bill and Black Pico.

These adaptive practices were an attempt to create a public persona that would resonate in the world of professional sports in the North. But the custom also extended to entertainers, performers, and musicians who sought to enter the North American market. Among the most successful were Bobby Collazo, Frank Domínguez, Rudy Calzado, the Castro Sisters—the name of the act was always in English—and Richard Egües. Orchestras included Ernesto Lecuona's Los Cuban Boys (changed in 1946 to Havana Cuban Boys), Los Antobal Cubans, Quintana Melody Boys, Don Azpiazú's Havana Casino Orchestra, Los Cuban Jazz, La Orquesta Jazz Queen, Havana Riverside Orchestra, Los Dandys, Los Champions del Ritmo, Orquesta Swing Casino, ABC Boys—named after the ABC revolutionary society—and Los Happy Boys. The dance team of Gladys Mora and Raquel Mota performed under the stage name of Las Cuban Stars.

English names implied access to the world of the North. Their use suggested distinction and difference, an identity drawn from the vernacular of the North implying status and success. North American given names gained widespread popularity among Cubans of all classes. Indeed, such usage connoted a complex social transaction, a practice that was itself the product of an environment that in almost every other way implicated Cubans in North American assumptions. Given names enjoyed periods of vogue. Popular women's names in the 1910s and 1920s reflected the persistence of Spanish usage—for instance, María, Ana, Mercedes, Rosa, Rosario, Isabel, Ofelia, Carolina, Hortensia, Amalia, Paulina, Luisa, Josefina.[54] Names changed markedly after the 1930s. This is not to imply that older forms disappeared, but rather that they were joined by at least as many names of North American origin. In the 1940s and 1950s society page announcements and news stories of events for children and adults, as well as private school yearbooks, reveal that some names were obviously Hollywood-inspired, such as Marilyn Rodríguez, Ivonne Meneses de Tamayo, Constance García, Betty González, Hedy Lluría Vázquez, Dorothy Sotolongo, Mae de la Campa, Mary Caballero, and Elizabeth Pardo.[55] Names like Lincoln Roldán, Lincoln Díaz Balart, Ike Quintana Rivero, and Daniel Lincoln Ibañez were influenced by U.S. public figures. Moreover, Cuban political leaders like Eddy Chibás, Tony Varona, and Eddy Zayas Bazán adopted a "folksy" style by Anglicizing their given names.

The popularity of North American names extended across the island. In Miguel Barnet's novel *La vida real* (1984), Julián travels into the interior: "One of the things I really noticed when I arrived was . . . Cuban peasants of Mayarí and Jobabo calling themselves Frank, Mike or Tony." The practice was especially pronounced in areas where Cubans frequently encountered North Americans—those engaged in missionary work and families living on or near U.S. sugar mills or other U.S. enterprises. Reverend Enrique Someillán became Henry Someillán. Frank País was the son of a Baptist minister. The names of socially prominent Cubans in Banes included Tony Blanca, Betty Ruiz, Nelly Ortuño del Valle, Mike Mas Durán, and Walter Rey Delgado. In the zones around the Guantánamo Naval Station it was not uncommon to find children named Usnavy (or Usnavito/Usnavita) after the markings of "US Navy." A short story writer was named Marines Medero. North American brand names also were a source of names. "Norge" was a common given name during the 1950s. One of the protagonists in the José Manuel Fernández novel *Todo angel es terrible* (1964) is named Norge Peña.[56]

The popularity of American given names suggested the degree to which the vogue of things North American had passed directly into forms of self-representation. Nor perhaps should these developments necessarily be viewed as either exceptional or extraordinary. Cubans could assemble the elements of identity only with the cultural material most readily available, and the fact that this happened to include many U.S. forms spoke less to choice than to chance. North American given names conferred status in an environment in which standing was often expressed in English. The Havana social register and a book listing the elite of Havana society (*Libro de oro*)—both published in the 1950s—include such names as Percy López Morales, Georgette García Montes, Sally Pérez, Mary Kay Inclán, Edith Matamoros, William Aguila Sarduy, Alex Ortiz, Jack Gutiérrez, and Tessie Bengochea.[57]

The selection of names often suggested cosmopolitan and contemporary. The *Libro de oro*, which included the names of children, parents, and occasionally grandparents, suggested a process of Anglicization of names with the passing of generations. Mary Lou Illas was named after her mother María Luisa and Willy Martínez Muñoz after his father Guillermo. There were many other examples: Richard Repilardo (Ricardo), Raymond Suárez (Ramón), Larry Ruiz (Lorenzo), Freddie Santamarina (Fernando), Sammy Verdes Escarra (Samuel), Tommy Pujáns (Tomás). In one case, grandfather Francisco Figueroa Miranda named his son Frank who named his son Frankie.[58]

North American names often had larger implications. Leonor Barraqué described an upwardly mobile middle-class family whose children "spoke English without knowing proper grammar and who were adept at all sports." Barraqué wrote: "This was believed to be necessary to advance socially. Even the names in the family reflected the snobbery (*esnobismo*) of the time. Teddy and Jack, they and their parents being Cuban, the grandparents Spaniards, they felt the need to copy the Saxons, even if it was only in names, because it looked good." In the Gonzalo de Quesada y Miranda short story "Por amor y arte" (1929), "Mary whose real name was María" was renamed by her schoolmates because "she was the best in the English class, read American magazines, and knew how to sing the latest musical hits from Broadway." In *Los dioses ajenos* (1971), Alonso's protagonist Paulina was "called Polly by her mother's family, considering it far more elegant than Paulina. And Polly it remained." Miguel de Marcos wrote about Nicasio, who in the hope of improving his employment possibilities, changed his name to Nickie. In the Andrés de Linares short story "Dos señoritas de vanguardia" (1929), Yale graduate José Martínez changes his name to Joe Martins, "plays golf, parts his hair in the middle and shaves twice a day." As portrayed by José de la Campa González, Carlos Puertas became so infatuated with English that he changed his name to Charles Doors.[59]

Cubans often gave their pets English names. José García Pedrosa once bought a fox terrier whom he called "Happy." In Antonio Benítez Rojo novel *El escudo de hojas secas* (1972), the pet dog was named "Lucky." In *Dreaming in Cuba* (1992) by Cristina García, Tía Alicia named her two canaries Clara and Lillian after Clara Bow and Lillian Gish. The narrator continues: "When Clara laid eggs, however, Tía Alicia changed Lillian's name to Douglas, after Douglas Fairbanks. Their babies were Charlie, May, and Gloria."[60]

These complex social transactions, which reached deeply into the sources of nationality, do not lend themselves to facile explanations. Under the circumstances, Pablo Medina writes, "it was natural for English to become the second, and even more important, language of Havana." As he tells it:

Through consumer goods, movies, and sports it had made its way into the everyday speech of the city. Thus we had our cars: Cadilá, Biu, Ohmobil, Pontiá, Packa, Estudebeique, Plimo; our movie stars: Johngüein, Rohodson, Betideivi; and in baseball, the national sport, we had *estrai guan* . . . and the always exciting *doble plei*. But nowhere was American cultural and linguistic influence more evident than in nicknames. Instead of the traditional Spanish Paco, Fico, and Nico, more and more often one heard Frank for Francisco, Freddie for Federico, and Tony for Antonio. In addition knowledge of English . . . was a true mark of culture and status. And in a mercantile city . . . the ability to transact business in English assured one a solid and well-respected place in the business community.

Oscar Hijuelos conferred distinction on César Castillo's command of English in *Mambo Kings Play Songs of Love* (1989): "He was proud of himself, as in those days it was a mark of sophistication among the Cubans of New York to speak English. At the parties they attended, given by Cubans all over the city, the better one's English, the higher his status." English served as a marker and under certain circumstances could affirm social standing. Gustavo Pérez Firmat recalled his mother, who "fancied that she spoke English like a native, which she didn't really, but she spared no opportunity to flaunt her considerable fluency. She spoke English in the car, at the beach, over the dinner table. When she wanted to speak to my father without being understood by the servants, she resorted to English."[61]

No small part of this process involved self-invention shaped by the powerfully seductive promise of North American ways. There was hardly anything peculiar about young people—and often old—seeking to emulate modalities associated with success and well-being. These were not circumstances of their making but rather conditions of their environment, in which they were formed and which they accepted often unquestioningly as every bit as "Cuban" as the landscape they beheld. North American customs became so much a part of Cuban life that they passed for Cuban. Many were surprised to learn that *el Gato Félix* and *Daniel el Travieso* were not Cuban but U.S. comic strips. "Most Cuban children think 'sandwich' is a Spanish word," observed Ruby Hart Phillips. "No waiter in a restaurant would know what to serve if asked for an *emparedado*." How was one to know that *suéter* (sweater) was not Spanish? Even as Eladio Secades warned of the growing U.S. influence in Cuba, he himself was employing colloquial conventions that perpetuated the use of North American forms in the popular vernacular. Secades criticized the wearing of U.S. college sweaters embossed with school insignias: "El suéter acribibillados de insignios de 'coliches' [colleges]."[62]

Cuban sensibilities were shaped in this environment. Preferences and predispositions, no less than tastes and temperaments, were influenced by these experiences. After all, to master these forms, to become fully conversant with their meanings and incorporate them into a personal cosmology was at the heart of growing up, of making the countless adaptations and accommodations to reality that signified "being well adjusted" in an environment dominated largely by ways and things North American.

These forces influenced educational plans, shaped career strategies, and determined self-representation. Adaptation is the central theme of Eduardo Machado's play *Once Removed* (1986), in which Olga confronts her husband: "You trained yourself to adapt, to be ready to adapt. That's why you studied mathematics at Villanova and learned English." In *Segundo remanso* (1948) Marcelo Pogolotti speaks through his narrator, who pronounces that "the Cuban has an extraordinary capacity for adaptation. He absorbs and assimilates like no one else. He understands the changing reality of things, and wherever he finds himself he integrates without difficulty." This was Sergio's lament in the film *Memorias de subdesarrollo*: "Cubans waste their talents adapting themselves to every moment. People are not consistent." In the novel *Como se va el amor* (1926), Carmela Nieto describes Mariana as a "converted *yankee*," who "spoke English, adopted American summer wear, with American fashions," adding: "The adaptation was in her point of view."[63]

The use of English forms as the medium of self-representation gained in popularity. Contest titles for individual achievement were rendered in English: beauty pageants for "Miss Cuba" were selected from the finalists "Miss Pinar del Río," "Miss Havana," "Miss Matanzas," "Miss Las Villas," "Miss Camagüey," and "Miss Oriente." Other contests included body-building competitions for "Mr. Cuba," couples competing for the title of "Miss y Mister Televisión" and women for "Miss Empleada," "Miss Dependiente," and "Miss Deporte." Singer Miguelito Valdés was commonly referred to as "Mr. Babalú."

The signs were all around, often literally, and the moral was self-evident. Not since the end of Spanish rule was the urgency to learn English as widely experienced or keenly felt as after World War II. English appeared everywhere, everyday, and on occasion it could frustrate even the most ordinary act. In the short story "El azúcar que vuelve a la tierra" (1973) by José Antonio Mases, the protagonist is brought to a puzzled stop at a jukebox coin slot over which is "little *yanqui* lettering: 'Insert coin here.'" Some knowledge of English was necessary to complete crossword puzzles with such clues as "cerveza en ingles" or "hielo en ingles," "uno en ingles," "perro en ingles," "gato en ingles," "señor en ingles," "sentarse en ingles."[64]

North American forms assumed prepossessing proportions and were themselves the salient markers by which many Cubans derived their bearings. Gustavo Pérez Firmat recalled that English was "Havana's unofficial second language," adding: "English permeated my childhood. We watched American movies, drove American cars, consumed American products, and listened to rock-and-roll music." Gilberto Seguí also described the Havana of his youth:

"Mixed in my memory appear the dazzling mirror-walled lobbies of the Rex and Duplex movie theaters, the escalators that went up and down in the stores, the air conditioning, the arrival of television, modern *cafeterias*, the beat of *rock and roll* and the cha-cha-cha, and the *American way of life*."[65]

This was indeed the Cuban condition, presumed normal and permanent; it was hardly possible to imagine any alternative other than negotiation of access and accommodation. The importance of English in this scheme of things was obvious and unquestioned: it was universally understood as one of the principal means of access to livelihood and prosperity. This was the dominant narrative at midcentury, and it is not difficult to appreciate the power of its appeal. "Better employment. More money. Better future," promised one advertisement for the International Correspondence School. "Those who speak English have many more opportunities." St. George's School struck a similar note: "English is a career. . . . Who can deny today that mastery of the English language gives access to better paying positions and allows for more lucrative professions?" Some years earlier *Carteles* had promoted its own English-language program in terms that could not but have resonated:

> Has it not occurred to you the unlimited opportunities that would present themselves, to fill important positions in banks, in commercial and industrial enterprises, hotels, steamship companies, or to raise substantially your salary in your present job or position? If you have the will to succeed and do not desire to remain all your life among laggards for whom the lack of preparation offers only prospects of misery and poverty, learn English, the universal language, and expand your range into infinite horizons.[66]

The moral was unambiguous, and there was no confusing its meaning. In López-Nussa's *Tabaco*, Onelio Capote could dismiss the English language as "barbaric and stupid" but nonetheless recognize its importance: "What matters to me is the commercial value of English. Or the advantages that it can provide me to earn a living." In Héctor Quintero's play *Contigo pan y cebolla* (1965), Lala explains to her daughter: "Nowadays it is more important to know English than to know Spanish. As soon as a young woman learns English, she can join any American company." When the daughter responds that she would be perfectly happy to work as a sales clerk in a shop, "without the necessity of knowing English," Lala responds: "Sure, in a shop, why not? . . . To be on your feet all day, holding packages for your customers, working Saturdays all afternoon, and hope for a meager raise every twenty years. Is that what you want?" A 1953 survey by *El Mundo* on the importance of English to Cuban youth revealed a striking unanimity, represented by the response of Emma Durán: "It is of the greatest necessity for a student to learn English after learning his own language. This will open a much wider door to the future. His personality will develop and distinguish itself and he will have greater opportunity to find employment." In

Havana writer Gonzalo Mazas Garbayo exhorted Pablo de la Torriente to learn English while Torriente remained exiled in New York: "You should not abandon its study, for it will serve you well and provide you with the opportunity of translating short stories from American magazines for our magazines. You know, of course, that translators here receive more money than writers, one of the charming and contradictory things about our beautiful island."[67]

The transformation of Cuban lifestyles was itself a culmination: an entirely logical and inevitable product of decades of close encounter with and constant engagement in North American life. It involved all classes in all provinces, although it was most pronounced among the middle class in Havana. Almost anyone who could live in this way did so, and most who did not wanted to.

The material manifestations of wealth, no less than the social markers of status, the ideological formation of privilege, and the presumption of prerogative were increasingly derived from North American sources. The extent of integration into U.S. normative structures and market culture was, of course, a function of social stratification. To be sure, some sectors were more completely integrated than others. Nevertheless, much of what passed for relatively modest expectations of everyday life—for all classes—was shaped to a greater or lesser extent by the promise of the North American market structure.

Families across the island in varying degrees were formed in this environment. Erna Fergusson wrote of her visit with the Ichasa family in Pinar del Río: "The Ichasas are one of those Cuban families that make you wonder whether you are in Cuba or the United States. Both mother and daughter were educated in the States. . . . With me their talk and manner was [sic] altogether Yankee." In Camagüey, Fergusson met José Morel, the owner of a 265-acre ranch, "educated in the States," who asserted: "We in this family . . . are very American." The García Carratalá family lived in Alturas de Miramar. Sixteen-year-old Sandra— known as "Sandy"—was bilingual; she had studied for three years in Miami and attended Cathedral and Ruston Academy. Her favorite recording artists were Pat Boone and Bill Haley; her favorite movie star was Gregory Peck. Her pets included two dogs, Smokey Joe and Tag-Along Joe. As she contemplated her future educational plans in 1957, she affirmed her intention to attend Wheaton College or the University of Florida.[68]

Patterns expanded and replicated themselves. Families of all social origins adopted whatever ways were within their reach and within their means. The results were evident across the social landscape of the island. The characteristics assumed definable shape, so it became possible to speak of "types" and "typical Cuban families." A news story of a birthday party in Santa Fe for the sisters María Cristina and Silvia María Pérez described a "supper of hot dogs, banana chips, jello and cokes," and "rock 'n' roll [was] danced until it could be danced no more." Congressman Indalencio Pertierra celebrated the birthday of his two daughters Beatriz and Olga María with a "Hill Billy Fair," reported *El Mundo* in

English, with "girls dressed in *gingham* dress and boys in *overalls* and checkered shirts." An account of the Agramonte family hosting a St. Valentine's Day party related that "Cupids hung from the chandeliers" and noted "the selection of Enrique Saladrigas as the King of Hearts and Miss Isabel Agramonte as his queen."[69]

Untold numbers of families sent their children to summer camp in the United States. In the early spring, newspapers and magazines were filled with advertisements of U.S. summer camps of every type. Ethan Allen Camp in Vermont provided hiking, swimming, and handicrafts. Eagle's Nest Camp in North Carolina for boys and girls eight years and up, in its ad in *El Mundo*, offered one additional activity: "Classes given in the English language." Thirteen-year-old Olga Suquet, a student at Lafayette, attended Moss Lake Camp in the Adirondacks every summer.[70]

North American styles became standard in the definition of middle class. This was a world of banquets and brunches, of morning receptions and afternoon teas, of baby showers and business luncheons, of fashion shows and formal dinners, of bridge parties, garden parties, cocktail parties, and canasta parties, of country clubs, social clubs, and yacht clubs, and always of social climbing and status seeking. On any given day of the week, the Havana press provided details of the previous day's noteworthy social events and announced the next day's activities. This was especially frustrating to the USIS staff in Havana, which, seeking to disseminate pro-U.S. information in Cuban newspapers, had to compete with society news. "Far too much space is devoted to social news," complained one official, "sometimes to the extent of 30 or 40 percent of a given issue."[71]

North American fashions were dominant. At a formal dance at the Havana Yacht Club in 1948, Herbert Lanks could scarcely contain his amazement. "We were surprised to see the degree of formal dress worn by both men and women in this warm climate," he noted. "As it was summer, the men were all dressed in immaculate white, although a few appeared in light suits. The women wore shining knee-length formal gowns and immense picture hats, each an individual creation for the wearer. The atmosphere of the affair was much more formal than a similar function in the United States."[72]

North American fashions defined the norms of glamour, from the latest in formal evening wear to the newest beachwear, from suits, sweaters, and sports clothing to overcoats and undergarments, from the latest hairstyles, handbags, and hats to cosmetic lines, shampoos, and soaps. Cubans of all classes chose dress as a way to project posture and position, real or imagined. Daily—in motion pictures and on television, in newspapers and magazines, in advertisements and department store windows—Cubans were presented with representations of status and success based on North American standards. Indeed, nothing else was more accessible to more people.

New cosmetics and clothing lines frequently were accompanied by company "consultants" and "experts" to advise prospective customers on correct usage and appropriate dress. This was not merely promoting a product but also fostering fashion as a means of self-representation. Gladys Price represented Helena Rubenstein products at Fin de Siglo, demonstrating how to apply lipstick, rouge, and mascara. Elizabeth Wyndham was the consultant for Charles of the Ritz cosmetics at Sánchez Mola. The Max Factor Make-Up Studio on San Rafael enjoyed a large clientele in Havana. El Encanto department store regularly hosted representatives of U.S. lines: Virginia Fry to discuss the newest Catalina swimwear, "to clarify whatever doubts you have with regard to the tones and models that correspond best to your figure"; Barbara Lawrence from Revlon "to respond personally to your questions."[73]

Fashion news developed into a genre of Cuban journalism, most of which was devoted to North American trends. Angela Velarde, Leonor Barraqué, Ramona Ballote, and Ana María Borrero wrote about women's fashions. Henry Wotton's *Páginas masculinas* was a U.S. syndicated feature on men's styles published in *Grafos*. Algernón presented a weekly column in *Carteles* on men's fashions, from the newest evening wear in Los Angeles to autumn lines in New York. The feature included commentary on collegiate styles at Yale, Princeton, and Harvard; on vacation wear in West Palm Beach; on shirts and shoes, sweaters, suits, and ties worn by retirees in Miami; and on the preferences of Hollywood actors: William Powell chose "heavy fabrics" whereas Gary Cooper preferred tweeds, Robert Taylor favored the collegiate look and Melvyn Douglas liked sports clothes. Clothing could indeed serve as the measure of a person, but it also affirmed a larger condition of modern. In Raúl Aparicio's novel *Frutos del azote* (1961), Tomás stares in the mirror and repeats the phrase he remembers from a men's fashion magazine: "Smartly accessorized." He thinks: "Not what one could imagine as the average type, the consummate expression in the midtwentieth century of the native from a civilized tropical island."[74]

Fashion shows were noteworthy social events, giving prospective clients a preview of the newest styles in evening wear, casual attire, and sports clothes. Nor did Cubans make the slightest concession to the tropics: furs were among the more popular lines presented on these occasions. Erna Fergusson, who attended one such event in Havana, commented with a hint of incredulity: "On Monday evenings the auditorium offers a brilliant clothes show with imported models, diamonds and emeralds, silver fox and chinchilla. A lady said: 'Americans think we are silly to wear furs, but we like outdoor entertaining—the smartest New Year's party is outdoors at the Country Club—and of course we *need* furs.'" A travel guide reported: "Paradoxically enough, there's a big furor over furs in Havana. The great silver-fox plague raging up North has now spread down to the tropics. Cuban women of means adore mink, ermine, sable, fox, all the precious furs, and wear them lavishly. As a matter of fact, Havana seems to be a Mecca for phony-furs among the poorer women. To own a fur-piece is everyone's ambition, even if it's only a skimpy one-skin scarf of dubious ancestry."[75]

Every year, usually in late November or early December, the most exclusive stores in Havana announced the arrival of the new winter lines of stoles, coats, and capes. La Filosofía advertised "an exclusive collection of fine furs," including mink and fox. Finas Modas offered a "magnificent collection" of mink, ermine, marmot, fox, and squirrel. El Encanto boasted of mink, Norwegian Blue Fox, and silver fox that "drape over the body in a splendid caress of elegance."[76]

North American forms of entertainment and recreation also spread across Cuba. Stage shows, musical revues, and big-name entertainers from the United States appeared frequently. The Ringling Brothers and Barnum and Bailey Circus, the Water Follies, Gene Autry's Rodeo, and the Ice Capades toured the island annually.

North American music gained a wide audience in the 1920s and 1930s. Much of this was related to the expanding presence of North American orchestras engaged to play in hotels, nightclubs, and cabarets during the tourist season. The engagement of big-name vocalists in Havana nightclubs also increased familiarity with U.S. popular music. The most fashionable clubs, including the Sans Souci, Montmartre, Tropicana, and Capri, booked artists like Billy Daniels, Steve Lawrence, Lena Horne, Johnny Mathis, Nancy Wilson, Tony Bennett, Eartha Kitt, Cab Calloway, Johnny Ray, Sarah Vaughn, and Nat King Cole. Cole was especially popular in Havana, particularly after the release of his album *Cole en Español*, which featured several Cuban compositions.

The music of North America reached Cuba in other ways as well. Hollywood musicals, which were popular throughout the 1940s and 1950s, served as an important source of U.S. music. Radio also played a key role in promoting familiarity with music from the North, either through local programming or via direct broadcasts from the United States. As early as 1930, Cubans imported more than half a million phonograph records annually. Jukebox sales soared during this period, and they arrived stocked with U.S. recorded music. The jukebox became a ubiquitous presence across the island—in large cities and small towns, in bars and brothels, in dance halls, cocktail lounges, and nightclubs. One traveler described a scene in a small village near El Caney: "There is a corner cantina at the intersection of two dusty roads. People ride up on horseback. Inside, a monstrous jukebox is roaring. The pieces are all from Hollywood's 1943 crop of musical films, with a few Agustín Lara and María Grever ballads sandwiched in." Guillermo Cabrera Infante recalled that this was the way he learned North American popular music, mesmerized by "the radiant, rainbow chrome Wurlitzer . . . that jukebox which I'd stick to, virtually glue myself to, as with the movies." He continued:

> This robot phonograph bewitched me with its selection system and rotating records, these mechanical, musical movements which preluded more than

preceded the slaving, sensual sound. Though I first had to wait for someone with money (I never had any) to come and drop a nickel in the machine, and choose, if I was lucky, as in a lagniappe lottery, my favorite of all favorites, "At Last." I became a fan of Glenn Miller band . . . [and] the new sound, swing.[77]

The impact of U.S. popular music was immediate and long-lasting. North American orchestras introduced fashionable dance music to a wider Cuban public. Certainly the orchestras and singers were booked largely for North American tourist audiences, at some of the most stylish hotel venues and night-clubs in Cuba. But these locations were also frequented by many middle-class Cubans, who increasingly adopted North American dance as one more expression of fashion. The Charleston and the fox-trot soon displaced the *danzón* as fashionable ballroom music. As early as 1915, music at the Hotel Miramar's weekly tea parties was provided by "a good orchestra playing the latest musical importations from New York." Periodically *Bohemia* published diagrams of the steps to the latest U.S. dances. In his Miami exile, Lorenzo Zequeira recalled fondly attending club dances, where he learned the fox-trot. In 1920 *La Prensa* (New York) reported on a lavish presidential ball in Havana, where the "fox trot predominated among the dancing numbers, although the one-step, the *valse* and *danzón* were also played, with an American music orchestra alternating with a [Cuba] sextet in charge of the *danzón*." "The youth of today," complained a Havana columnist in 1929, "complete devotees of all that is foreign, have completely forgotten our antecedents. . . . Trend-setters have determined that because the *danzón* is old it should be banished from our *fiestas*. . . . But it is not only new trends that are contributing to the demise of a tradition which should never be lost but—and sad indeed it is to admit—also the lack of patriotism of many Cubans of today, for how else can the reign of the Charleston and other foreign dances be explained?"[78]

Cuban musicians also adopted these forms to increase their versatility and improve their opportunities for work. The 1920s were a difficult time for musicians in Cuba. For one thing, the advent of sound in the motion picture industry delivered a rude blow to hundreds of musicians previously employed to provide orchestral accompaniment to silent films. No less important, the expansion of tourism had established North American tastes as the dominant determinant of the local market, thereby effectively excluding Cuban orchestras from the most lucrative venues on the island. In 1929 Cuban musicians protested preferential booking of U.S. bands in local hotels, cabarets, and nightclubs. The Great Depression further sealed the fate of local musicians. By 1931 an estimated 2,000 Cuban musicians were out of work.[79]

Cuban musicians sought to adapt to popular taste and market trends. Song-writers devoted considerable energy to composing fox-trots—in English—for the expanding local market, including such compositions as Esteban Peña's "Don't Make Me Cry," Ramón Moreno's "Beautiful Girls in Miramar," Pedro

Martínez's "Cute Baby," and Ismael Torres's "Oh Broadway!" U.S. popular music increasingly influenced arrangements and orchestration, dance and vocal styles. "Cuban popular music is becoming daily less Cuban," protested one critic. Vocalists progressively adopted the phrasing and mannerisms of U.S. singers. Andrew Salkey noticed the "North American style" of singer Elsa Rivero, who acknowledged: "I used to listen to the records from the States and try to sing like some of the singers." North American vocal harmonies were copied by a number of performers, most notably the Cuarteto D'Aída, formed in 1951. Local orchestras and society bands likewise used North American arrangements and added an ever-growing number of U.S. standards to their repertoire. By 1950 almost half of the music in Havana nightclubs was provided by U.S.-styled bands. At nightclubs and social clubs, at cabarets and cafés, at parties in the home, increasing numbers of Cubans danced to North American music. In the short story "De cómo fueron los quince de Eugenia de Pardo y Pardo" (1978), Sergio Chaple narrates preparations for a birthday party: "Julito put on his portable Silvertone phonograph. We had 'Blue Moon' by Vaughn Monroe; 'Begin the Beguine' by Artie Shaw; 'Perfidia' and 'Moonlight Serenade' by Glenn Miller; 'My Reverie' by Larry Clinton. All this was especially to squeeze together, slowly, nothing difficult to dance." In *Los muertos andan solos*, Arcocha describes a scene at the Havana Yacht Club in 1958:

> There were many people in the grand ballroom of the first floor. The orchestra played "September Song" and many couples were dancing. The orchestra played a slow "blues," "Star Dust." . . . The dance floor filled little by little, and upon finishing "Star Dust" the orchestra continued with a long "potpourri" of old North American melodies. One of the musicians began to sing in English "At Last," in a voice pleasant enough although a bit too soft, trying to imitate the style of Frank Sinatra.[80]

By the late 1940s and the 1950s, a new genre had attained wide popularity. Known as "el feeling"—the name was in English, although occasionally it appeared as *el filin*—the new music was generally a ballad, romantic and sentimental, long-phrasing, that emphasized melody over rhythm and arrangement over improvisation. "El feeling" was influenced by the stylings of Ella Fitzgerald, Billie Holiday, and Sarah Vaughn. Among the vocalists most closely associated with this style were Elena Burke, Fernando Alvarez, Olga Guillot, José Antonio Méndez, Frank Domínguez, Miguel de Gonzalo, and Pacho Alonso.[81]

By the 1950s, too, rock 'n' roll moved into Cuba and immediately found a receptive audience among the youth. Record sales soared as rock stars in the United States became idols in Cuba. In 1957, in a market where previously the sale of 3,000 records was considered to be commercially successful, Elvis Presley sold more than 50,000 copies of "Don't be Cruel" and Bill Haley sold 12,000 copies of "See You Later Alligator." Rock 'n' roll record sales approached

$200,000 annually.[82] The film *Al compás del reloj* (*Rock around the Clock*) was likewise a box office success. In 1956 a rock 'n' roll program called *Melody Time*—the name in English—debuted on Channel 10. A year later the dance show *Club Rock 'n' Roll*, modeled on *American Bandstand* and designed for *rockeadores*, appeared on Telemundo.

Rock 'n' roll was more than just music, of course. It was accompanied by a lifestyle script, with a point of view, a dress code, and a vernacular of its own—the models for which were North American, most notably James Dean and Elvis Presley. In *Macuta La Habana* (1981), novelist Enrique Alvarez Jané describes "the movie poster that attracted people like a magnet. It advertised an Elvis Presley movie and the entrance ways were filled with young people dressed and with hair styles in the American style." One journalist depicted Cuban youth in 1957 as having a penchant for "chewing Chiclets, stylized smoking, and dancing rock 'n' roll." A year later Braulio Robet wrote of the "current rock 'n' roll epidemic among the youth of today, who ostentatiously display their sideburns, *moccasins*, and *blue jeans*." Rine Leal recognized some of the larger implications of the popularity of rock 'n' roll among Cuban adolescents. "They have read and they know," he observed in 1957. "They read that in the United States all the young people dance in the hallways and form the legions of Elvis Presley fans; they know that this is one way to appear modern, bold, and that people talk about them. . . . They want everyone to know that they too do the same things that kids in the North do."[83]

Such associations often implied membership as increasing identity with things and ways of the North. Many Cubans developed a variety of direct ties with the United States on which their ability to succeed in Cuba frequently depended. Professionals were educated and trained in North America, including physicians, dentists, engineers, chemists, architects, attorneys, and accountants, joined U.S. professional associations, and frequently traveled to conferences and professional meetings in North America. Dentist Sergio Giquet attended the annual orthodontist meeting and Ernesto Regueiferos the annual meetings of the American Institute of Architects. Surgeon Antonio Rodríguez Díaz was a member of the American College of Chest Physicians and the Association of Military Surgeons of the United States. Physician Braulio Sáenz held membership in the American Dermatological Association and sat on the American Board of Dermatology. Vicente Pardo served as president of the American Dermatological Society in 1956. Francisco M. Fernández, a Columbia graduate, belonged to the American Academy of Ophthalmology. Angel Vieta, dean of the Faculty of Medicine of the University of Havana, was a member of the American College of Physicians, American Bacteriological Society, and New York Medical Academy. Filiberto Rivero was elected to the Board of Councillors of the Radiological Society of the United States. Attorneys Carlos Angulo and José García Baylleres were members of the New York Bar and the American Law Society of

Washington, respectively. Geographer José M. de la Torre joined the Ethnographic Society of New York. Biologist Carlos Guillermo Aguayo, a Harvard graduate, maintained membership in the Boston Society of Natural History, American Association of the Advancement of Science, American Museum of Natural History, and Brooklyn Entomological Society. Fernando Sagebién, a Rutgers advertising graduate, was a member of the Society for the Advancement of Management, Direct Mail Advertising Association of New York, and American Public Relations Association.

Many Cubans were integrated into North American structures by virtue of their employment with U.S. companies, from large sugar corporations and mining operations to banks, department stores, and small shops and farms. International Harvester had 500 employees. Other firms included Owens-Illinois (200 employees), U.S. Rubber (650), Portland Cement (650), First National Bank (450), Sherwin Williams (300), Cía. Goodrich Cubana (350), Coca-Cola (500), Armour (500), Sears (600), F. W. Woolworth (1,000), and the Spanish-American Iron Company (600). Many upper- and middle-level management positions in local branches of U.S. companies were occupied by Cubans, men like Angel Gómez Puente, vice president and general manager of Bauer and Black; sales manager Carlos de la Vega of Continental Can Corporation; Dupont assistant manager Humberto Villa; manager T. O. Rodríguez of National Cash Register; Gustavo de la Luz, vice president of Remington Rand de Cuba; Eduardo Moreno of Dun and Bradstreet; manager Vicente García of Otis Elevator; and José Medina, vice president of Wells Fargo of Cuba. An estimated 150,000 Cubans were employed by North American enterprises in the early 1950s.[84]

These associations often developed as a requirement of company policy, sometimes as adaptation to corporate culture, occasionally as unabashed emulation of dominant modalities. "Cubans who came into contact with Americans in a technical way," William Dorsey recalled of his years in Havana, "such as [through] chemistry, mechanical training, engineering, techniques of manufacture, etc., were quick to learn the advantages to be had in those new methods, and soon adopted them as the way to go." Local executives and managers, distributors and retailers of U.S. product lines, were often obliged to maintain close contact with corporate offices in the United States. They frequently traveled north for trade shows and training programs. Max de Marchena, vice president of Cuban Radio Philco, annually attended the national Philco convention in the United States. Cuban management personnel of General Electric traveled to the annual GE trade conventions to remain abreast of new product lines and learn of the latest marketing techniques. All but two employees of the U.S. advertising firm McCann-Erickson in Havana were Cubans, executive J. Bruce Swigert remembered, all of whom were trained "the McCann way." Swigert continued: "Also, New York training was available to them. When CMQ was preparing to launch TV in Cuba, we sent our then-radio director to New York for a quick course in the new medium. Later, toward the end of the 50s, it became common practice to get the professional talent—together at corporate head-quarters . . . for seminars designed to improve their skills."[85]

In cases where so many people worked for others, it was inevitable that personality traits and behavioral patterns would conform in varying degrees to standards associated with success. The employment of so many Cubans by North American enterprises affected behaviors and bearings, values and per-spectives, appearances and attitudes. Eladio Secades described Carlos, "a highly placed employee of an American company," who "even though there is no sun wears sun glasses and matches the colors of his ties with his socks." In García's *Dreaming in Cuban*, salesman Jorge "traveled five weeks out of six, selling elec-tric brooms and portable fans for an American firm. He'd wanted to be a model Cuban, to prove to his gringo boss that they were cut from the same cloth. Jorge wore his suit on the hottest days of the year, even in remote villages where the people thought he was crazy." In a column on Andrés Hernández, an employee of the First National Bank and the U.S.-owned Cuban Warehouse Corporation, Arturo Suárez wrote: "His temper, not of the impetuous kind of his father—much too Latin—is more likely mild, a bit stern as occasion demands, modeled after American passiveness, whose learning created in him a sound judgment."[86]

The growing U.S. presence provided other means to foster local affinities with North American ways. The resident North American community increased steadily in the early decades of the republic, approaching 12,000 by the end of the 1950s, with more than half of it residing in the Havana metropolitan area. But numbers alone did not tell the full story, for this was a community whose influence far exceeded its size. It consisted of merchants, manufacturers, and missionaries, corporate executives and mill administrators, bankers, brokers, and retailers, diplomats, civil servants, and salesmen, a formidable presence that represented the dominant order. In the short space of several decades, North Americans controlled key sectors of the Cuban economy: sugar, tobacco, mines and ranches, trade and commerce, communication and transportation, the banks and the utilities. They owned a vast portion of the national territory. They operated the better schools and presided over some of the most prestigious social clubs. They lived in privileged circumstances, both in Havana and on the great sugar estates. They were the money lenders, the landowners, and the power brokers. They bought and sold politicians and policemen the way they bought and sold farms and factories.

The North American presence assumed a variety of institutional forms. Resi-dent foreigners sought to foster a sense of community, a home away from home, by re-creating shared familiarities and developing ways to defend and advance their collective interests. Protestant congregations were established early by the United Methodist Church, the First Baptist Church, the Presbyterian Church, and the Trinity Episcopal Church. The United Hebrew Congregation (Temple

Beth Israel) was founded in 1904. At almost every turn, North Americans gave their activities organizational form. The American Club was formed in 1901. An Anglo-American Club operated in Santiago de Cuba. Contractor Tillinghast L. Huston organized the Havana Camp No. 1 of the United Spanish War Veterans in 1910. The year 1919 saw the organization of American Legion Havana Post No. 1 by World War I veterans and the introduction of the American Chamber of Commerce.

Women's social and philanthropic organizations proliferated. The Woman's Club of Havana was founded in 1910 by Sarah Thurston. Presbyterians established the Book and Thimble Club to promote literary and philanthropic activities. The Mother's Club, formed in 1923, was described locally as "just one big happy family which tries to give the . . . [American] colony a touch of getting together and doing something in a group, just like they did back home."[87] The Santiago Women's Club was organized by Mary Cumings, the wife of a civil engineer with the Frederick Snare Corporation at Moa Bay. A Sigma Alpha Pi chapter, established in Havana in 1926, dedicated itself to "loyalty, purity and service." The Little Theater of Havana was formed as a repertory company in 1943; by the 1950s it claimed more than 150 members—Cubans and North Americans—who were involved in all facets of theater production. Other organizations included the Cuban Association of University Women, St. Agnes Guild, Choral Society, Women's Society of Christian Service, Menorah Sisterhood, Children's Home Society, and Red Cross.

North American charities and reform groups entered Cuba as soon as Spanish rule ended. The Havana chapter of the Woman's Christian Temperance Union was established in 1899. In the same year the American Society for the Prevention of Cruelty to Animals opened an office in Havana and lobbied the U.S. military government to ban bullfights and cockfights. In 1906 Jeanette Ryder organized a Band of Mercy chapter to defend the rights of children and animals. The Salvation Army arrived in 1918 and the Community Chest in 1943.

The larger significance of such organizations was the extent to which they drew Cubans into the moral universe of North America. Across the island, Cubans young and old, men and women, developed a familiarity and a fondness for U.S. customs through service clubs, fraternal associations, and social organizations. A branch of the Young Men's Christian Association (YMCA) was established in 1904 and within the first year enrolled almost 500 Cuban members, mostly clerks, salesmen, and young professionals in the expanding ranks of the lower middle class. YMCA programs played an important role in spreading traditional U.S. athletic and recreational activities, especially sports. The YMCA inaugurated annual bowling tournaments and subsequently sponsored volleyball matches, swimming meets, and track events. In 1905 the association introduced basketball with remarkable success. Two years later *La Lucha* reported: "Every afternoon . . . a number of the young Cuban members may be seen contesting for the slippery leather which they try to toss into the mesh goals. It is gaining in popularity every day." By 1924 the YMCA cited a total attendance of nearly 10,000 participants, by which time its activities also included billiards, chess, checkers, and Ping-Pong. The Boy Scouts arrived in 1913, then the Girl Scouts and Cub Scouts. Scouting (*escoutismo*) developed rapidly, with troops established in Havana, Matanzas, Cárdenas, Cienfuegos, Camagüey, Nuevitas, Antilla, Banes, and Santiago de Cuba. In 1944 *Carteles* extolled the Boy Scouts as a source of "strength and development of citizenship," whereby the boy "acquires habits of character, energy, and faith in the individual and collective effort" and learned that "respect of hierarchies and obedience to legal norms are virtues."[88] By the early 1950s about 2,500 boys and girls belonged to the "Scouts de Cuba."

Civic and fraternal organizations expanded throughout the early decades of the republic. The Loyal Order of Moose Lodge No. 782 of Havana was founded in 1915, with charter members representing the administration of President Mario G. Menocal—among them the president himself, Rafael Montoro (secretary to the president), Charles Hernández (secretary of communication), Oscar Díaz Albertini (director of the Department of Justice), Emilio Núñez (secretary of agriculture), and Colonel Matías Duque Estrada, as well as U.S. and Cuban businessmen George M. Bradt, Alexander Kent, Harry Clews, Hipólito Amador, and José M. López. Membership qualifications were explicit: "The Havana Lodge is open to all Cubans, Spanish and other nationalities who can read, write and speak the English language. We want only good men of the white race, who are in good standing in the community and engaged in lawful occupation."[89] The Rotary Club, dedicated to upholding business values and promoting individual responsibility for the resolution of social problems, arrived in 1916. Profits and public service combined to form both the ethos and the ethic of philanthropic capitalism.[90] The Havana Rotary Club was founded by two Rotarians from Tampa, cigar manufacturers Ernest Berger (Tampa-Club Cigar Company) and A. L. Cuesta (Cuesta Rey and Company), with charter members representing important sectors of the U.S. and Cuban business community.[91] By the late 1920s the Havana club consisted almost entirely of Cuban members. "I expected to speak in English," U.S. ambassador Noble Brandon Judah wrote in his diary of his speech to the Havana Rotary in 1928, "but as all the members of the Club were Cubans, I spoke in Spanish."[92] A total of fifty-nine Rotary Clubs were eventually established on the island, from Havana to provincial capitals and small interior cities. The Shriners Club of Cuba was organized in 1922 and the Elks Club of Marianao two years later. The Lions Club was founded in 1927 and quickly expanded across the island. The Havana Lions, whose membership exceeded one thousand, became one of the largest Lions clubs in the world. In 1945 Ramiro Collazo was elected president of the International Association of Lions Clubs.[93]

Cubans and North Americans mixed socially and professionally. Across the island they held positions together on local chambers of commerce, like the one in Antilla in 1924 that included Julio Martínez, Manuel Guarch, Florentino Garrido, A. B. Oliver, William MacDonald, and E. T. Morton. Among the members of the Cuban-American Jockey Club were Enrique Fontanills, H. D. Brown, Mario Diáz Irizar, Carlos Fonts, Frank Steinhart, and Lorenzo Salmón. The growing alumni associations brought together graduates of U.S. colleges and universities. The board of directors of the University Club of Havana, for instance, consisted of Alberto José García (Fordham), José Caminero (Villanova), Mariano Lora (Wisconsin), Adolfo Arellano (Harvard), and Francisco Fernández (Columbia). Cubans were well represented in individual alumni associations. The charter members of the Cornell Association of Cuba consisted of Chester Torrance, Francisco Landa, A. Hyde, M. F. Galdo, Luis Díaz, S. M. Yzaguirre, Frank Getman, and Mario G. Menocal. Other associations included the Alumni Association of Columbia, the Princeton Club of Cuba, and the Harvard Club. The Havana Petroleum Club was organized in 1957 as a social club for executives of the Cuban petroleum industry.[94]

It is difficult to determine the full impact of these connections. Vast numbers of Cubans were immersed in North American modalities by way of social settings, professional associations, and civic organizations. These affiliations ritualized "the American way of life" and, as expatriates were wont to do, often in an exaggerated manner. Associations served both as sites and sources of North American ways that could not but implicate a great many Cubans. They commemorated U.S. holidays: St. Valentine's Day, Washington's Birthday, the Fourth of July, Thanksgiving, and Christmas. Picnics, cookouts, and barbecues soon became as much Cuban recreational forms as North American ones. The Mother's Club sponsored an annual Halloween party attended by hundreds of Cuban and North American children. The Havana American Legion post observed Memorial Day. The Women's Guild of the Holy Trinity Episcopal Church put on a yearly "Rummage Sale" and a St. Valentine's Day Bridge Tea.

In view of the origins and affiliations of these organizations, it is not surprising that they promoted familiarity with and an affinity for traditions of the North. Some, like the Daughters of the American Revolution, Lions, and Rotary, provided scholarships for study in the United States. The Lions Club of Cárdenas was a spirited booster of U.S. tourism. So, too, was the Rotary Club of Santiago de Cuba. Every Christmas the Havana Lions Club distributed toys and clothing to blind children at the Varona Suárez School in Marianao.

Associations served as sites of Cuban–North American transactions. The combined effects of employment and socialization created powerful affinities and preferences. When Ann Hutchinson was growing up in Havana, "the Americans tried to maintain their national traditions like celebrating July 4th, helping at the USO during the war and knitting for the Red Cross, celebrating Thanksgiving together." Hutchinson noted: "My father in the Lions Club mixed with

Cubans and played golf with them at the Country Club." Rufo López-Fresquet, a Chase Manhattan executive, later wrote of the "great number of Cubans [employed] as administrators and skilled workers" by U.S. firms. "Frequently these workers were sent to the U.S. for training. They associated freely and became friends with the American personnel. Together, they attended meetings of the Manufacturers' Association and of the Lions and Rotary Clubs, and they were invited to the same social events."[95]

The decision to join with North Americans in business clubs, civic associations, charitable organizations, and professional societies no doubt figured prominently in Cuban career strategies. These became places where Cubans acquired familiarity with North American conventions; they presented occasions for exchange and negotiation, adoption and appropriation. North American customs could be studied in the expectation that they would yield secrets of success, something that could be adopted and applied to move ahead. Víctor Muñoz took note of picnics, of the circus and movies, the celebration of holidays like Memorial Day, the Fourth of July, and Thanksgiving. "These people, like no other, have the capacity to transform themselves into children when they need to rest their spirit," Muñoz observed. "Collectively, as members of another country and a different people, we believe that if we could feel like children, as they do, perhaps our national achievements would be greater, perhaps we would reach the high summit where this great country is found."[96]

The ways Cubans entertained conformed increasingly to North American etiquette. Contact with North Americans also changed local recreational habits. Cubans took up golf, tennis, bowling, and handball. Moreover, sexual restrictions were relaxed. Consuelo Hermer and Marjorie May wrote in 1941 of the influence of the Havana Country Club: "Cubans, watching the impersonal, between-sexes camaraderie of the Americans, were encouraged to allow their daughters a similar measure of freedom. In this way, the Country Club can really be credited for the relaxation of the hitherto rigid *dueña* system. Today, daughters of Cuba's finest families lounge or play on the clubhouse grounds with the same freedom our own girls enjoy, and to a certain extent, this attitude has penetrated to other social levels."[97]

BETWEEN ARRANGEMENT AND ARRIVAL

The capacity of North American structures to rearrange the moral order and material basis of Cuban life increased over time. And over time, too, the assumptions of these relationships seemed to acquire an incontrovertible logic, so that for most people the important question—indeed, often the only question—was how best to gain access to the prevailing order. Much of this involved education, of course. But public schools remained in disarray and disrepute through the early decades of the republic and by midcentury were generally discredited among Cubans of all classes.[98] The remarkable expansion of private education was powerful corroboration that public schools had lost public confidence. Public schools were perceived as unable to prepare Cubans to meet the challenges of their time.

So private education flourished and was itself product and portent of the forces transforming Cuba. Between 1926 and 1954 the number of accredited private schools increased from 464 to 776 and were attended by nearly 110,000 children from kindergarten to the eighth grade. An additional 90,000 attended nonaccredited private schools. Fully 35 percent of the total elementary school population attended private schools. Many thousands of other students were enrolled in an estimated 150 private secondary programs of all types—*colegios*, *academias*, and *institutos*—operating across the island.[99]

By definition, private education implied middle class. Indeed, that was precisely the point, for in the popular imagination—and often in fact—private schools promised advantages rarely associated with public schools. Families of modest social origins, lower middle class and working class alike, strained and sacrificed to provide private schooling for their children. Workers earning as little as $40 a month were known to pay as much as $8 a month to enroll their children in these institutions. In Jesús Masdeu's novel *La raza triste* (1924), Miguel undertook "hard work in the factory . . . working well into the night, determined to save the $200 necessary to pay . . . for early months of tuition and appropriate school clothing." A study in 1955 concluded that a typical private school cost almost $350 annually, including tuition, books, and supplies, at a time when the national per capita income was only about $370.[100]

By the 1950s the tendency had become particularly pronounced. "Even persons of quite modest means," the International Bank for Reconstruction and Development reported in 1950, "who cannot really afford it, will stint on other things to put their children in a private school." The bank added: "The extra economic burden thus imposed by the deterioration of the public schools is not inconsiderable, especially for middle-class families." *Bohemia* arrived at a similar view, if with a different emphasis: "Even the lower classes, as soon as they accumulate two *pesetas*, are impatient to send their children to a private school in the petty bourgeois belief that in this manner they are prepared for a better life." The magazine continued:

> While in other countries even presidents of the republic send their children to public schools. . . . here in Cuba this is seen as an indication of a lack of means. Not the children of a president, or of a minister, or of a senator—not even a bank clerk—attend a public school in our country. That's for the "darkies" (*los negritos*) and the rabble (*la chusma*), who have no alternative. It is evident that every day fewer are the Cuban parents of the middle class and even the underclass who send their children to public school.[101]

The proliferation of private schools confirmed that success and security were associated with mastery of North American methods. The emergent educational system favored the middle class over the working class, whites over blacks, the city over the countryside. But in the end it involved almost everyone in some form. The appeal of private education was its promise of entrée to the prevailing order. It was not merely that the U.S. presence had become ubiquitous. North American ways had so thoroughly insinuated themselves into daily life as a condition of well-being that they were seldom considered as anything other than Cuban. Private schools arranged everyday imperatives into commodity form and thereby set in relief the prevailing truths of the Cuban condition.

The promise of private schools was largely related to employment opportunities and economic security. Schools multiplied prodigiously: business colleges (Havana Business Academy, Havana Business University), commercial programs (Hough Academy of Commerce, Baldor Academy, Academia Profesional de Comercio, Hemphill School, Colegio La Luz), and secretarial schools (Academia Pitman, Academia Robiña, Colegio Couret, Tarbox School of English, Havana Speedwriting Academy, Academia Gregg).

Most were modeled on North American programs. Indeed, that was their principal appeal: to equip students with the knowledge and skills necessary to compete in an environment dominated by U.S. conventions. The Tarbox School of English advertised an "American style" secretarial program: "North American companies in Havana call us frequently asking for secretaries with North American training. Prepare yourself for one of these excellent positions! We offer Cubans a modern North American secretarial program in English and of the same high quality of the course offered by the best secretarial schools of New York and with North American teachers." The Havana Business Academy, with an enrollment of 3,000 students, was a member of the American Association of Business Colleges. The business curriculum included accounting, marketing, sales, typing, and stenography, with emphasis on English-language instruction. Havana Business University opened in 1942 as a junior college and subsequently expanded into a four-year program. It held accreditation from the American Association of Junior Colleges and the American Association of Business Colleges. Hough Academy of Commerce promised to "facilitate good jobs," and Hemphill School exhorted Cubans "to increase your salary" and "become master of your destiny." Academia Pitman "guaranteed employment at the end of the course." Academia Gregg advertised that more than 700 of its graduates had found lucrative employment "in the principal national and foreign companies."[102]

English-language training was at the core of the private school curriculum, a reminder that the narrative of Cuban well-being was formulated on North American terms. The moral was often implied in the name of the schools: Roosevelt College, George Washington Institute, Lincoln Academy, el Instituto Edison, Emerson College, Liberty School, la Havana Military Academy.

Almost all private schools provided English-language training. "Pre-primary to eighth grade with English in all grades," advertised the Colegio Oscar Espín.

The Colegio Cubano Arturo Montori offered "primary education totally in English," and the Colegio Academia Bravo stressed its "use of English in all grades under certified teachers." The Instituto Edison, with an enrollment of 3,000 students, proclaimed itself "a modern school" where "English is taught to the boys and girls since kindergarten all through senior high school." Liberty School advertised a curriculum in which "children speak English from kindergarten to sixth grade."[103]

The emphasis on English was especially prominent in business and commercial programs. The connection between English and employment and earnings was presumed to be as self-evident as it was self-explanatory. "Do you know English?" a National School advertisement asked. "Whoever responds affirmatively can earn more money and have better positions." An ad of the Colegio Cubano Arturo Montori addressed parents: "Commerce in English, and in this way you will facilitate the future development of your son. Our commercial relations with the United States oblige us to employ personnel prepared in this field. The Colegio Cubano offers its commercial program totally in English in response to these needs." "Learn English," Hemphill School enjoined, "the language of Progress. Increase your prestige and popularity—and earn more money. Never before have there been as many opportunities for men and women with knowledge of the English language."[104]

The most prestigious private secondary schools were modeled on North American curricula, including Ruston Academy, St. George's School, Lafayette, LaSalle, Calvert School, Columbus, Central School, and Phillips. St. George's School, ostensibly patterned according to the British system, was, in fact, North American. "Our textbooks were American," wrote Felicia Rosshandler, recalling her experience at St. George's, "and our teachers were mostly young, leftover tourists from the United States"; the school "attracted mostly upper-class Cuban girls whose parents wanted them to have Yankee manners." Religious schools included Candler College, Cathedral, the Cuban-American High School, La Progresiva, and Los Amigos. At Merici Academy, a Catholic high school for girls, English language instruction was central; *Merici*, the name given to the annual yearbook, was printed in English. Villanueva University in Marianao was operated by North American Augustinians and affiliated with Villanova of Pennsylvania. Among the most appealing advantages of secondary programs was the preparation of students for admission to North American institutions of higher education. Candler explicitly described its high school program as "adequate preparation for enrollment in colleges and universities in the United States."[105]

Private schools enrolled students from the resident U.S. community as well as the Cuban middle class. In the 1950s Ruston Academy had an enrollment of nearly 600 students in the elementary school program, approximately one-third of whom were Cuban; half of the 150 students in the high school program were Cuban. The faculty consisted mostly of North Americans and Cubans educated

One of the more prestigious private schools in Havana, Methodist Candler College prepared students for the North American curriculum.
(Courtesy of the Friends Historical Collection, Guilford College, Guilford, N.C.)

in the United States. Mario Iglesias had attended Ohio University. Lilia Vivo de Crespo taught sixth grade at Cathedral, where she had herself completed her elementary education; she then attended St. George's School and the Havana Business Academy and eventually received a B.S. degree in elementary education from SUNY–New Paltz. Antonio Santa Cruz, a member of the Havana Business Academy faculty, was born and acquired his early education in Tampa; he subsequently graduated from Catholic University in Washington, D.C.

In curriculum as well as extracurricular activities, in sports and social events, these programs replicated the North American school environment. Ruston student organizations included a student council, debate club, dance committee, ring committee, senior chorus, and cheerleaders. Team sports comprised men's and women's basketball teams, volleyball, and baseball. The Ruston Academy yearbook, *Columns*, depicted scenes that could have easily been from a high school in Muncie, Indiana: photographs of prom night and the annual rock 'n' roll dance contests, highlights of sporting events, theater productions, and scenes from Cafetería Biltmore, a snack bar and popular after-school gathering place. Student yearbook photographs identified "the most popular," "the most athletic," "the most handsome," and "the prettiest."[106]

North American private schools served as sites of complex engagements, a point at which over the years many thousands of young Cubans acquired daily familiarity with U.S. ways and into which they were in varying degrees assimilated. The larger implications of these programs did not escape U.S. government officials, who early recognized the value of private schools in forming attitudes and values. They provided generous if discreet funding to such institutions as the American Central School on the Isle of Pines, Ruston Academy, and Villanueva University. "The indoctrination of Cuban children in the principles of democracy," affirmed public affairs officer Jacob Canter, "and the knowledge and understanding these children obtain of the United States while attending a school like Ruston are perhaps the most effective means of shaping Cuban opinion in the future." By "sharing everyday experiences with American classmates, the Cuban students of these schools are developing at an early age an attitude of friendship for the United States which no amount of adverse propaganda will be able to eradicate." Canter's observations about Ruston were applicable to other private schools:

> Ruston is American more in its methods and objectives than in its curriculum. . . . It attempts to build character; it concentrates on training the minds in the exercise of judgment and understanding rather than to serve as a mere depository of memorized facts; above all, it strives to prepare its students for responsible citizenship in a democratic society. Moreover, by bringing together in the same classroom and in its social and extra-curricular activities Cuban and American students . . . , by teaching the English language and American history, geography, and literature, Ruston is forming in malleable, non-American minds thought patterns that make for attitudes favorable to the United States. The Cuban members of the board of directors are, furthermore, men and women who sincerely admire American ideals and values.

Canter also defended the funding of the American Central School on the Isle of Pines as a way to provide "knowledge and understanding of the United States to children in an area of Cuba remote from American influence." He added: "Except for commercial motion pictures, perhaps the only direct American influence working on these pupils is that of their program of studies and their contact with their teachers."[107]

The extent to which U.S. curricula may have counteracted or otherwise impeded the development of national affinities is, of course, a matter of conjecture. What is certain, however, is that increasing numbers of Cubans worried about the effects of foreign schooling on children's capacity to develop ties to *patria*. As early as 1917, educator Arturo Montori warned against the "anti-nationalist project" of private schools, where "hostility toward the republican institutions of our country was deliberately expressed." Thirty years later *El Mundo* raised similar concerns, particularly about primary education: "It should be the mold of citizenship and the instrument of the State to create community, without distinction or discrimination. That is precisely the instrument that has served to forge unity and patriotic consciousness among many nations that are today leaders of enlightenment."[108]

Over many decades tens of thousands of Cuban children, from the primary grades through high school, from diverse social origins, were formed in this environment. Not all of them were affected the same way, of course, and indeed the impact of the experience was often mediated by circumstances far removed from the classroom. On the other hand, many of these students became part of and party to an alternative moral order, an outcome that was at once cumulative and all-encompassing. In the short story "La vida" (1934) by Arturo Ramírez, the protagonist recalls his daily conversations with classmates, "discussions about baseball, *cowboy* movies and the adventures of Nick Carter, all our favorite subjects." It is not clear how representative young Andrés Balmes may have been when asked in a 1930 student survey to name his favorite author—he responded: "Mark Twain." But certainly he was not alone.[109]

These conditions were themselves products of complex and often elusive social adaptations: conscientious parents seeking to decipher the signs of the times, doing the best they could to prepare their children to meet the future and fit into an environment in which North American forms were the dominant modalities of public transactions. The decision by the Medina family to enroll their children in the Cathedral School was in large measure based precisely on these considerations. "Ever conscious of preparing us for the rough-and-tumble ambience of Cuban society," Pablo Medina recalled, "my parents enrolled my sister and me in an American school." The ways that school prepared young Medina for the "rough-and-tumble ambience of Cuban society" were striking: "By the time I was in third grade, I was all but fluent in English and was reading Mark Twain, Dos Passos, and Harriet Beecher Stowe in the original." Medina was exposed to "expressions and vocabulary and, more important, attitudes and points of view." He concluded: "I learned my second language better than anyone expected and was exposed, if indirectly, to a great deal of American culture, from the game of football to the obsession with holiday decorations to Americans' inborn optimism and generosity." Miguel Barnet recounted the effect of his Cathedral School education more bluntly: "When I completed my studies at a North American school in 1958," he wrote, "I knew very little about Cuban culture, and much less about popular culture and traditions."[110]

In the first half of the twentieth century, many other young men and women of all social backgrounds traveled north for their education: in primary and secondary schools, boarding schools, parochial schools and seminaries, business colleges, military academies, technical and vocational institutes, colleges and universities, and graduate and professional schools. Study in the North, of course, had its antecedents in the nineteenth century. It resumed immediately after the War of Independence. As early as 1899, the U.S.-based Cuban Educational Association provided scholarships and financial aid programs for select Cuban students to study in the United States. The only condition was that students return to the island on graduation.[111] Within two years, about 2,500 Cubans had enrolled in U.S. colleges and universities.

The association was clear in its objectives. The educational experience in the United States, Gilbert K. Harroun, director of the Cuban Educational Association, predicted confidently in a published article, will turn Cubans away "from militarism to the much-coveted pacific methods of our people and Government." Harroun explained:

> The day is not far distant when young men of the type our association is aiding will become factors in the management of their own home affairs, and it is exceedingly doubtful if there can be laid out any line of philanthropic work which will bring so large a return to the people of the United States as that of dealing in these educational futures. . . . The bringing to the United States at this time 2,500 of these worthy, malleable young men . . . and then returning them to their homes cannot but produce a stage of human development that will glimmer as a beacon light in aiding to create a stable, pacific government in the Antilles.[112]

In private correspondence Harroun was more direct. "Doing everything I can for the young men who come to the United States with an honest desire to study the American methods," he wrote in 1899, "and then return to their own land believing such students will be of great aids to their country."[113] A year later Harroun asserted: "If [we] could dispose of a thousand children yearly we could gain in one half of the hundred years which otherwise will take us to Americanize this place."[114] General Joseph Wheeler, a Cuban Educational Association board member, envisioned similar results. The idea was that Cubans educated in the United States "would return home to spread a good work that would knit the island closer to the country to which it owes its benefaction."[115]

The placement of Cuban students in North American schools itself became a lucrative business. In 1921 *Bohemia* established an office in New York to answer inquiries about U.S. colleges and universities. A year later José Comallonga published *Algunas instituciones americanas*, a comprehensive guide to schools in the United States, including elementary and boarding schools, military academies, high schools, colleges, and universities. By the 1940s and 1950s, a number of placement agencies had opened to arrange the enrollment of Cuban students in these institutions. Michael Richardson—identified as an "education consultant"—operated the American Schools Bureau in Vedado, offering information about all types of schools, from military academies to girls boarding schools, from high schools to vocational training programs, in all price ranges, in every part of the United States. The Beers Employment Agency organized a college placement department. Continental Schools, Inc., and Colegios Americanos, U.S.A., provided information about college and universities, military academies, and Catholic schools, as well as summer camps. The Garrido Travel Agency established a "college clearing house" service and marketed U.S. college education with an unambiguous moral to parents: "In North American colleges your

"Do you plan to educate your children in the United States?" asked an advertisement for the school placement service of Continental Schools, Inc., Havana. (Author's collection)

children not only obtain an excellent education and learn the English language, so necessary these days, but they also develop an appropriate personality that enables them to grow and act independently each time they confront the problems that life presents them. In other words: it teaches them to be responsible."[116]

In the first half of the twentieth century the children of some of the most notable Cuban families studied in the North, including the sons of José Martí, Antonio Maceo, Calixto García, José de Jesús de Monteagudo, Juan Gualberto Gómez, Mario Menocal, and Fulgencio Batista. *Diario de la Marina* editor Nicolás Rivero enrolled all seven of his children in North American schools and availed himself of his editorial page to observe: "Perhaps there is some patriot who would prefer death rather than agreeing to become an American. But it is also likely that if this same patriot has children and the means he would send them to study in the United States in order that when they became adults . . . they would struggle in circumstances less disadvantageous than those who came to liberate us. . . . The paternal instinct is very pragmatic, nothing wishful or fanciful." Many Cuban children were sent north early. "At eleven years of age," Demetrio Presilla López reminisced, "my father sent me to the United States. I completed my primary and secondary education in a very strict and very good Methodist college in the South. I subsequently completed my higher education at St. Louis University, where I graduated in chemical engineering." Others followed a track similar to that of Elena Díaz-Versón, who attended the Methodist Buena Vista high school and the University of Miami, where she eventually earned a law degree.[117]

Enrollments increased throughout the early years of the republic. In 1916 a total of 6,000 Cuban students attended primary and secondary schools in the United States. College and university enrollments rose from 139 in 1923 to 261 in 1936, 585 in 1946, and 769 in 1950. Between 1955 and 1958 about 1,100 Cubans enrolled annually in U.S. institutions of higher education.[118]

Study in the North was filled with promise and expectation, the occasion to learn English and become conversant with the methods and skills needed to succeed in an economic environment dominated by U.S. conventions. A North American education provided preparation for managerial and executive positions with U.S. companies. That was a large part of its appeal. In 1957 half of the 1,046 Cuban college students in the United States expressed an interest in finding "employment with the overseas branch of an American business firm upon completion of studies."[119]

The educational experience in the United States assumed many forms and involved men and women from all walks of life. All through the 1920s and 1930s, Cuban schoolteachers participated in annual Chautauqua programs. North American universities sponsored summer programs designed specifically for Cuban students. The University of Alabama annually hosted 100 students for a two-month English-language program. The University of Miami and the University of Florida established similar programs. Traditionally black colleges hosted Afro-Cuban students, many of whom attended summer school. In 1953 Bethune Cookman College in Florida inaugurated a scholarship program for Afro-Cuban students. Exchange programs provided other educational opportunities. In 1950, 25 Cuban exchange students went to the University of Kansas to study meteorology and aviation. Others also received specialized training in the United States. An estimated 200 physicians annually served as residents and interns at North American hospitals and clinics. Many pursued advanced training at U.S. medical schools. Religious leaders often completed their studies in the United States.[120]

Some Cubans studied at U.S. service academies. Demetrio Castillo was a graduate of West Point. Carlos Hevia, secretary of agriculture in the government of Carlos Prío Socarrás (1948–52), graduated from Annapolis and served a tour of duty in the U.S. Navy. So did Juan A. Torella. Indeed, Annapolis designated two slots annually as a "Cuban quota." Between the 1930s and 1950s, thousands of officers and enlisted men were educated and trained in the United States. Army officers routinely attended the Command and General Staff School at Ft.

Leavenworth, Kansas. Virtually all officers of technical and specialized branches of the Cuban armed forces, including aircraft maintenance, communications, meteorology, supply, administration, and medicine, were trained in the United States. Almost all commercial pilots studied there under the auspices of Inter-American Fellowships for Aviation. And all the control tower personnel at Rancho Boyeros airport received their training in the United States.[121]

The U.S. government also subsidized civilian travel and study in the United States. The Point Four Program offered grants-in-aid for in-service training. The Bureau of Mines awarded Luis Miguel López Márquez and Zoila Avalos Balner one-year training grants to attend the University of Maryland. Individual grants were provided by the U.S. Department of Agriculture to study the dairy industry, animal husbandry, and poultry; by the U.S. Department of Commerce to study banking and finance; and by the U.S. Department of the Interior for saltwater fishery technology. Labor leaders received grants for training in labor administration, collective bargaining, and workers' education. "There are few leaders of promise," the U.S. labor attaché noted in 1958, "who have not now had some training in the United States." Teachers, journalists, and editors routinely received USIS grants to travel and study in the North as a way to foster pro-U.S. views. "Cuban editors, commentators, and others in key positions to place information material," reported Ambassador Earl E. T. Smith, "have been provided with special service."[122] *Excelsior* editor Manuel Braña Chansuolme received a grant to visit the United States during the 1956 elections. Braña's visit, explained the USIS officer, would enable him "to send back a series of articles underscoring for Cuban readers the orderly, democratic operations of the American elections," as well as "to stock his mind, and his notebooks, with observations for later articles on various aspects of American life." Jorge I. Martí, managing editor of *El Mundo*, was chosen because of his "generally favorable" editorials. "He knows the United States quite well," commented USIS, "has studied there previously and has consistently maintained a favorable stand on all major issues involving the United States." Columnist and radio commentator Fernando J. Fernández received a grant because he had "turned out a number of articles on American themes, . . . all of them favorable to the United States" and devoted "at least 10 minutes each week" of his radio program "to a discussion of American cultural and social developments." The USIS officer continued:

> The Embassy is in close and frequent contact with Mr. Fernández. He is, so to speak, "on our team." When important people come to Cuba, we inform Fernando, who is sure to cover the visit for his newspaper or discuss it on the radio. He is also readily disposed to help us get other local stories covered if they are of interest to the Embassy, including education exchange projects. . . . Through personal conviction and also, in part, out of a sense of gratitude for his grant, he is working regularly and effectively to help increase the bonds of understanding between the people of Cuba and the United States.[123]

Many Cubans were beneficiaries of corporate scholarship programs. The Moa Bay Company awarded three scholarships annually for the study of metallurgy, mining, and geology in the United States. United Fruit, Hershey, and Cuban-American were only some of the most prominent sugar corporations to provide subsidies for study in North America.

Moreover, Cuban employees were often sent north to receive specialized instruction and advanced training. Technicians at CMQ television went to New York to train at NBC. The Cuban Telephone Company (ITT) sent Luis Medina for advanced study in New York. Chase National Bank of Havana enabled Rufo López-Fresquet to attend Columbia University. General Electric Cubana, S.A., sent Fidel Maymir to Schenectady to complete specialized engineering courses. Cubans were also recipients of philanthropic awards, including the Robert H. Palmer Scholarship for study at Stanford and the John Druys Scholarship to study agriculture at the University of Florida. In 1957 Florence Pritchett Smith, wife of the U.S. ambassador, established a three-year scholarship for the study of fashion, textile design, and interior decorating in the United States. Among the recipients of Guggenheim fellowships were Herminio Portell Vilá, Carlos G. Aguayo, Pedro Joaquín Bermúdez, Isabel Pérez Farfante, Julio Fernández de la Arena, Abelardo Mareno Bonilla, and Leví Marrero. The Cuban-American Institute in Havana distributed funds obtained from the U.S. government and private foundations, including Guggenheim, Rockefeller, and the American Association of University Women, to subsidize study in the North. By 1958 the institute had provided over $500,000 in tuition support for nearly 500 students.

Nevertheless, most students who attended colleges and universities in the United States paid for their own tuition. Of the 1,046 Cubans attending U.S. schools in 1958, 85 percent (787) were self-paid, the highest percentage of all foreign college students in the United States.[124]

Few, indeed, were the Cubans of means who had not studied or worked in the United States. José M. "Pepín" Bosch, president of Bacardí, was educated at Riverview Academy in Poughkeepsie, Villanova University, and Lehigh College. Manuel Quevedo, president of Aerovias Q, attended Park Avenue Institute in Bridgeport and graduated from St. John's University. Goar Mestre received a business degree from Yale, then returned to Havana in 1938 to organize the advertising firm Mestre and Godoy; he eventually went on to control CMQ television.[125] Some of the leading newspaper and magazine executives were educated in the North, including *El Mundo* editor Luis Botifoll (Tulane), *El Mundo* manager Antonio Bernabé (New York University), *Diario de la Marina* editor José Ignacio Rivero (Choate and Marquette), *Avance* editor Jorge Zayas (Columbia), *Social* editor Conrado Massaguer (New York Military Academy), and *Carteles* publisher Alfredo Quílez (Packard Business College). A generation of Cuban architects and engineers completed their studies in the United States. Many of the most prominent planters also studied in the North. Years later, in exile, many of these same alumni of U.S. schools would play an important role in the development of the sugar industry in Florida.[126]

Many Cubans who studied abroad were especially well suited to work for U.S. corporations on the island. They moved easily between the two worlds, concurrently transmitting and transacting complex cultural encodings in both directions. Ricardo F. Portuondo studied at the Eastman School of Business (Poughkeepsie) and subsequently obtained employment with Standard Dredging Corporation of New York. José Ricardo Tarajano (Rensselaer) got a job with Owens-Illinois Corporation. Roberto Goizueta graduated from Cheshire Academy in Connecticut and received a chemical engineering degree from Yale in 1952. On his return to Havana, he obtained employment as a chemist in the Havana Coca-Cola Bottling Company. Thirty years later, in exile, Goizueta became chairman of the board and chief executive officer of Coca-Cola, serving until his death in 1997.[127]

Some of Cuba's most celebrated writers and intellectuals attended school or lived in the United States. After completing his secondary education, José Sixto de Sola promptly enrolled at Betts Academy in Stamford, Connecticut. Jorge Mañach, Luis Baralt, and José Rodríguez Feo all graduated from Harvard. Marcelo Pogolotti recalled his parents' decision to enroll him at St. John's Military School in New York: "In 1916 the idea that high school age youth should attend school in the United States was very much in vogue, as much to acquire perfect fluency in English as to [avoid] the moral and educational inferiority of local schools." Concepción Freyre de Andrade had a similar experience. "When I was fifteen," she recounted, "I was sent to study for a year at a Catholic boarding school in New Jersey to perfect my English."[128] Poet María Alvarez Ríos attended the University of Michigan, and essayist Juan Jerez Villarreal graduated from Northwestern. Pablo Armando Fernández emigrated to New York in 1944 and subsequently attended Washington Irving High School and Columbia University. Jorge Guerra, Rogelio Llopis, Calvert Casey, Humberto Arenal, Edmundo Desnoes, and Ambrosio Fornet were among the many writers who also studied in the United States. Fernando G. Campoamor attended high school in Louisiana, Carlos Enriquez studied business at the Pearce School in Trenton, Luis Rodriguez Embil graduated from Hempstead Institute of Long Island, and José Zacarías Tallet completed his studies at the Heffly Institute of Commerce in New York. Roberto Fernández Retamar taught literature at Yale, and Ezquiel Vieta taught literature at Franklin and Marshall. Mary Cruz del Pino taught Spanish at Wayne State, Antón Arrufat worked for Las Américas Publishing Company in New York, and Heberto Padilla taught Spanish at the Berlitz School of Languages in Rockefeller Center.

There were many reasons to travel north, and the experience abroad remained one of the constants of the Cuban condition. Cubans went precisely because they had always done so; the North was familiar and well known to

Cubans as a place to flee adversity or to seek opportunity, like the exiles in Teresa Casuso's partly autobiographical novel *Los ausentes* (1944) who yearned for a chance "to be someone just one time." Some of this took the form of cyclical migration during both good times and bad: in good times when people had the means to travel, in bad times when they had the need to travel. Cycles of repression and revolution, especially during the early 1930s and late 1950s, obliged many to flee north. In 1932 *Carteles* estimated that 40 percent of the population of Cuba had lived in the United States at one time or other. Moreover, travel to North America increased after World War II. Many migrated north to stay: an estimated 50,000 Cubans obtained permanent resident visas between 1946 and 1956. At least as many arrived on 29-day tourist visas and remained. Hundreds of thousands of others arrived simply to visit and vacation, to study and sightsee.[129]

For all who dreamed big dreams, the North was the place to make it, to fulfill ambitions of fame and fortune. The prospect of success in the United States was seductive. Much in Cuban life had been organized around North American models, often in the form of aspirations and ambitions, as a point of reference and a source of orientation, as destiny and destination. The United States was the place to make good, to be formed and educated, to be confirmed and validated. Models of success no less than the measures of success were derived as a way of life and a manner of being, as something to do and someone to become. The North represented success of consequence, and all who imagined making it—really making it—were obliged to contemplate emigration. In baseball it was the major leagues, and there was no mistaking the meaning of *las ligas grandes*, both as measure and metaphor of success. "All young Cuban ballplayers had the same dream," Minnie Miñoso remembered, "first the Cuban League of professional baseball and then the big leagues of the United States, the most coveted of all goals." He added, "My one dream was to become a professional baseball player, a hero. I determined to become one at all costs." Those who aspired to careers in art, including Concepción Ferrant Gómez, Gloria González, and Natalia Bolívar, studied at the Art Students League in New York. In the world of stage and screen, it was Broadway and Hollywood. Musicians, singers, and actors pursued crowning success in New York. "I was at the top of my life's work," recalled singer Miguelito Valdés in 1943. "Certainly so it appeared to many. But I wanted to advance and I thought about New York." The well-known magician Gil sought wider horizons and emigrated to New York, "the city of great opportunities, of great success." Xavier Cugat recounted the times in his childhood when, walking along the Malecón, "I would gaze out over the horizon, completely lost in my thoughts about New York. How big it was, how it looked, how it must feel to be part of such a large city, how much it had to offer those seeking fame and fortune."[130] Prima ballerina Alicia Alonso developed her career in New York. Ballerina Hilda Moreno also went to New York, changed her name to Morenowa to suggest Russian antecedents, and eventually attained prominence in the Ziegfeld Follies. The North was where the greatness of boxing champions Kid Chocolate, Kid Gavilán, and Beny Kid Paret was confirmed. "My fixation," Kid Chocolate reminisced in Gerardo Chijona's documentary film *Kid Chocolate* (1987), "from the time I was a boy, had always been to get to Madison Square Garden." Rosario García Orellana established her opera career in Philadelphia, where pianist Jorge Bolet completed his training. Pianist José Melis studied at Juilliard. The United States was where the genius of world chess master José Raúl Capablanca was celebrated, where the talent of Desi Arnaz developed, and where artists like Carlos Enríquez, Wilfredo Lam, Antonio Gattorno, and Amelia Peláez traveled to live, study, and work. It was during this migration that José Capote arrived in New Orleans in search of work, met and married Lillie Mae Faulk, and adopted her young son Truman.

Hollywood also became the stuff of Cuban dreams, the place where one could make it in the movies and reach stardom. "My greatest wish in life," exclaimed seventeen-year-old Dinorah, "is to be a great movie star! Ah, if only a Hollywood producer would give me a contract." Mercedes Loynaz—"Miss Cuba 1930"—proclaimed her "greatest aspiration" was to be in the movies. Isis Margarita Finlay—"Miss Cuba 1954"—aspired to appear in films with Montgomery Clift. "There is a kind of show business madness that is becoming common in Cuba these days," reported Eladio Secades in 1957. "It is the madness of the movies, the desire to be a film star, a high fever of celebrity status. It makes women want to become thin and impels men to grow their hair long."[131] One after another Cubans traveled to Hollywood in search of stardom, and some actually reached the big screen. Tomás (Tommy) Milián was a member of the Actors Studio and starred in several Hollywood films. Mike Roldán appeared with Gary Cooper in *His Woman* and with Joan Crawford in *Our Dancing Daughter*. Lilo Yarson was cast in *For Whom the Bell Tolls*, and Sergio Orta had a supporting role with Judy Garland in *Ziegfeld Follies*. Rita Montaner appeared with Al Jolson in *Wonder Bar*. General Manuel Benítez, chief of the national police during the early 1940s, worked as a young man as a Hollywood extra. In the late 1930s artist Enrique Riverón went to Hollywood to work for Walt Disney in the production of *Snow White* and *Ferdinand the Bull*.

The North beckoned: it was the place to find the kind of fame and success that really mattered. Aspirations formed through familiarity with the ways and the world of the North helped rearrange hierarchies of values and contributed to discontent with Cuba, for it was hardly possible to imagine realizing big hopes on a small island. "Famous!" proclaims Laribeau in Carlos Felipe's play *Capricho en rojo* (1948). "If it were in Paris or in New York. I don't want to be famous in this little village of Havana!" Opera singer Victoria expresses a similar view in María Domínguez Roldán's novel *Entre amor y música* (1954): "This United States is great, huge, and marvelous in many aspects; it has singular opportunities for artists." The pianist in Jaime Sarusky's novel *La búsqueda* (1961) announces his intention to leave Havana for New York because "here there is no chance for success," and in José Antonio Ramos's play *Tembladera* (1918), Teofilo proclaims: "I want to go to the United States. Havana bores me, it repels me, it oppresses me." In Piñeiro's *El descanso*, Jorge wants to go north because "here there is not much to do." The protagonist in César Leante's *Padres e hijos* (1967) vows to leave this "damned small country," a "shitty country that destroys everyone."[132]

The high life—*la jai*—was in New York, the place of the chic, world-famous stores—"to live the life," as Cubans were wont to say. New York implied the center stage of the world: to be in New York was to experience the metropolis of modernity. "In our country," Arturo Alfonso Roselló observed in 1953, "there are many . . . for whom Manhattan assumes fully the proportions of a mythical territory." José Antonio Ramos speaks through his protagonist Damasito del Prado in *Las impurezas de la realidad* (1929) in proclaiming New York "the great city, symbol of liberty and fullness of life," a place of "universities, museums, laboratories, shops and factories, technical schools, conferences, concerts, expositions: the intense and active creativity of the Great City." In Edmundo Desnoes's *Memorias de subdesarrollo* (1965), Laura scorns Havana. "One cannot live elegantly here," she declares. "For that one has to live in New York." In the Manuel Douglas novel *The Cubans* (1981), Raquel arrives in New York with a mixture of awe and reverence: "She had heard of New York, read of New York, seen New York depicted in moving pictures and in the newsreels . . . and she wanted New York beyond all imagining." Architect Ricardo Porro recalled New York vividly: "It was a city that I visited since my childhood. . . . New York was naturally a shock for me, one who came from a colonial ambiance, accustomed as I was to our very sensual houses. What a contrast, those skyscrapers that reached such staggering heights! . . . New York radically changed my existence." Laura Gómez Tarafa related that "from the time I was two years old, my family used to go to New York every year, so that it was practically my second home town." Natalia Bolívar's experience was similar: "The family traveled to Miami and New York often, and in New York we went to concerts and the opera and saw the shows on Broadway." In Pablo Armando Fernández's partly autobiographical novel *Los niños se despiden* (1968), the protagonist affirms that he is "obsessed by New York. That city is a state of mind." At another point, he exults: "New York is probably the most exuberant place in the world." New York was "the cafés of Greenwich Village, the restaurants and bars of the East Side, museums, libraries, concert halls, art galleries, the shops of Fifth Avenue, luxury hotels, jewelry stores, banks, travel agencies, boutiques, delicatessens, book stores, universities, perfume shops, private clinics and public hospitals, beauty salons, art theaters, gyms and Turkish baths, tobacco shops, bowling alleys, institutes, apartment houses"—and more: "New York was a private party, sophisticated, glamorized . . . by café society, the international set and the 'In crowd,' it was a popular fair, noisy, robust, coarse, and open."[133]

The experience in the North was ritualized, with the obligatory photographs in New York as proof of presence: in Central Park, in front of the Statue of Liberty, perhaps on Broadway. Few were the family scrapbooks that did not contain at least one photograph of a relative in New York. In Desnoes's *Memorias de subdesarrollo*, Sergio rummages through drawers and discovers old photographs of Laura "everywhere . . . in New York, on Fifth Avenue, in front of the mannequins of the Bergdorf-Goodman windows." Reinaldo Arenas recalled receiving a picture from his uncle "in which he was steering a luxurious motorboat, his hair impeccably groomed even though the boat seemed to be moving at great speed." Arenas later learned that it was a studio photograph, but "in Cuba everybody thought my uncle was driving his own boat." The narrator of Barnet's *La vida real* ponders the "typical Cuban custom" of arriving in New York and "within a few days being photographed on a street in the Bronx or Manhattan in front of a very expensive car, wearing a coat and velvet hat. . . . or standing in front of a luxury hotel and saying: 'I work here.' "[134]

Travel north was a way to act out meanings associated with nationality; photographs corroborated being there, having arrived. Many went north with high hopes, with affection for and attachment to ways and things North American. Through travel it was possible to experience firsthand the realms from which so much of what mattered originated, the very source that formed and informed the Cuban imagination.

This was similar to the Cuban experience of the previous century, except that in the twentieth century it involved many more people. The history of the nation taught exile as a means of redemption and recovery. *Destierro* offered a choice that maintained an external resonance and an internal logic. It possessed its own history and traditions, which were deeply personal, the private stuff of family triumphs and tragedies. Few were the families that did not include at least one voice of expatriation: those first-person narratives told and retold at family gatherings, which in their own way fostered familiarity with the proposition of exile as a function of nationality. This was certainly one way that a family history repeated itself: destierro as a family tradition.

The experience often repeated itself from one generation to the next. People who lived and studied in the United States tended to send their children north. The emigration experience in all of its forms reached deeply into what became Cuban, an experience that replicated itself over generations and evolved into a condition by which vast numbers subsequently defined themselves and developed their children. They were shaped by this experience and, in turn, shaped their children through a similar one. The United States became a place to be formed, to mature, and to learn how to negotiate encounters with a world dominated by paradigms of the North. Thousands of young men and women followed their parents' footsteps north to study and work. Senator Alcides Betancourt (New York Business College) placed his three sons, Mario, Ernesto, and

Alcides, in the New York Military Academy at Cornwall-on-the-Hudson. President Mario G. Menocal (Cornell) enrolled his son in his alma mater. José Miguel Tarafa (New York Business College) sent his son Fernando to New York for study. Novelist and former New York resident Raimundo Cabrera enrolled his son Ramiro in City College. Leonardo del Monte (Louisiana State University) sent his daughter Lydia to his alma mater. Joaquin Agramonte enrolled his two daughters in St. Mary's Academy in St. Augustine. Bernabé Sánchez of Camagüey placed his five children, Gabriel, María, Emilio, Julio, and Bernabé, in New York area schools. Eduardo Justo Chibás, who had obtained his engineering degree in New York, sent his son Eduardo (Eddy) to Storm King School in Cornwall-on-the-Hudson. Veterinarian Antonio Martínez de Arredondo, educated and trained in the United States, encouraged his daughter Alicia Alonso to study dance in New York. In Lizandro Chávez Alfaro's short story "El zoológico de papá" (1963), a student recalls his father's explanation of the decision to send him to study in Schenectady: "that if my grandfather had not sent him as a child to study in the United States, he would not be the man he is today."[135]

Expatriation served as a means to achieve self-knowledge and self-definition. The experience provided an occasion to take stock, to locate one's self and find one's way back. The social function of exile shaped the meaning of the experience, of course, but it was always possessed of a mixture of nostalgia and melancholia, being and becoming, a way to fall back to prepare to advance forward. Indeed, exile in the North persisted as one of the principal means by which "Cuban" was constructed. "I have had to come into exile to discover that, after all, I am Cuban," Luis Ricardo Alonso speaks through his protagonist in *Los dioses ajenos* (1971). "In Cuba it was much easier to feel American." Barnet suggests similar transformations in *La vida real*: Julián, who migrates to New York in the early 1950s, "feels very Cuban, distance notwithstanding." When asked if he is Cuban-American, he replies, "No, only Cuban."[136]

There was something of a predestination about destierro. It loomed large over the Cuban meditation. So familiar was the experience that it was incorporated as a normal part of the Cuban condition. To suggest destierro as an "inevitability" may overstate the argument. But it was often presumed, and with presumption came preparation.

History was destiny: past exiles were recounted, future ones rehearsed. In 1952 journalist Rubén Ortiz Lamadrid took his eight-year-old son on a vacation to the United States. Ortiz Lamadrid reflected on his own experience twenty years earlier, when he had emigrated to New York to escape political repression and economic depression during the 1930s, "without speaking a word of English and only $48 in my pocket." In 1952 he derived great satisfaction that his son, a student at Ruston Academy, already spoke English. Now, with this trip, Ortiz Lamadrid prepared "to open the door for him to a new world, under better circumstances than were available to me. . . . I have wanted to show him the way, familiarize him with the environment, to remove all the unknowns about this great country, to which sooner or later, for one reason or another, a great majority of we Cubans must travel at some time in our lives." He continued: "My son now knows the way. Now the politicians can, if they wish, condemn his generation the way ours was condemned to emigration, voluntary or forced. He . . . knows how to flee the debacle of his nation."[137] Years into his exile, Gustavo Pérez Firmat reflected on his childhood. Both of his parents had previously lived in the United States and become familiar with North American ways. "Already in Cuba," Pérez Firmat wrote, "my brothers and I were being trained to become American; without knowing it, our parents were grooming us for exile."[138]

It is impossible to fully appreciate the impact of the experience in the United States. It could not, of course, but have expanded the logic through which the normative assumptions of North American daily life were validated. This was the way that attitudes and attachments were shaped, that dispositions were formed and susceptibilities fashioned, and that ambitions and aspirations developed. The experience encouraged expectations and suggested choices derived largely from North American categories. It provided a way for Cubans to arrange their hierarchy of standards, to order their lives, to appraise their condition. These were complex transactions, for much in the formation of nationality and identity—indeed, the very means by which vast numbers struggled to define and defend a place for themselves inside Cuba—involved protracted negotiation to reconcile North American ideals with the circumstances of the Cuban reality. Expectations were derived from U.S. models and loomed large in strategies to make good and get ahead. If it is possible to speak of dominant paradigms in Cuba at midcentury, they must include the preparation for life via North American methods.

Throughout the twentieth century, travel north served to arrange the dominant discursive elements of nationality. The experience was very much a part of the process of becoming Cuban as a means of self-discovery and self-definition, associated with renewal and respite, with reflection and reinvention, always as much a manifestation of transition as a means of transformation. Indeed, the experience in the United States was one of the primary ways by which identity was arranged to assimilate North American normative structures as part of self-definition.

Much of this was driven by an internal logic of daily reality, decisions and strategies that were themselves indications of the assumptions on which countless families envisioned the future. The North was a place for Cubans to make something of themselves and return "made," appropriately formed by the North American experience and prepared to succeed in Cuba. The theme appears as early as 1887 in Ramón Meza's novel *Carmela*, where Joaquín sends his son north "to become a man." In the Luis Felipe Rodríguez short story "El dominador de la vida" (1938), Roberto Sandoval departs for New York, a place "judged to be appropriate to make himself into a man." In Condesa de Cardiff's novel *Mati: Una vida de antaño* (1928), Manolo is sent north to study engineering in the expectation that "his character will be better formed." F. L. Fesser Ferrer's novel *Los desorientados* (1948) depicts boys sent to a U.S. military academy to make them "strong men with solid principles." This theme reappears in Raúl Aparicio's short story "Figuras de Valle Capetillo" (1962), as Benito proclaims that youth "are wasting their time" and vows "cost whatever it may cost, the boys are going to a military academy. To the United States! At least they will learn English. And most of all, they will experience a different value system. The value system of that country! . . . There is no other way, and the sooner the better."[139]

This was a complex process, obliging a great many self-conscious outsiders to adjust to life in the North, to struggle to find ways to endure and prevail. It was not always easy, especially for the young men and women who during their most formative years were installed in foreign schools. It required learning new skills and mastering new methods. Adaptation occurred gradually over time and imperceptibly most of the time, often at considerable emotional and spiritual cost: self-esteem often broke down, later to be reassembled around the newly arranged moral hierarchies. And what should be done with the old ways? How could the new adaptations be reconciled with the old environment, especially when so much effort had been invested in the transformation? To experience the North was to be transformed and formed again. Familiarity with new customs and values was often accompanied by telltale signs of self-assurance and poise, reflections of the investment in and attachment to the very ways that people had worked so hard to attain. In Lesbia Soravilla's *El dolor de vivir* (n.d.), Julio returns to Cuba after several years in the United States, "converted into an arrogant and robust man," with "a certainty and self-possession that accompanied even the slightest of his gestures." In the short story "Una mujer" by Enrique Serpa, the protagonist ponders the development of his childhood friend, Julio Santillana: "I understood that the American education . . . had developed and brought out the essential attributes of Julio's character. The previously shy and slightly withdrawn adolescent had developed into a model man, the master of his destiny and in control, the sole master of his actions and as self-contained as it was humanly possible to be." In Ramos's *Coaybay*, Washington Mendoza for reasons of health traveled to New York, where he soon "recovered his energy and his determined resolve to find a way, a certain and substantial model by which to live his life." The narrative explains:

> He perfected his knowledge of English, he pursued university studies and read avidly, without neglecting sports, walks, sentimental adventures and all the other pleasant pastimes of the eternally youthful life of North America. Those two years . . . had transformed him. Now he returned prepared . . . by a

vast but defined system of analysis, which would serve to cut through in that body national where the old Spanish colonial ways persisted almost intact in the republic.

"It is the long-time custom of Cuban parents," Venezuelan writer T. R. Ybarra commented in language reminiscent of Spanish captain-generals nearly one hundred years earlier, "to send their children to be educated in colleges in the North. . . . As a result, an ever increasing number of Cuban youth, boys and girls, return to their homes, year after year, imbued with North American attitudes about mankind and matters of life. These youths hold North American beliefs, speak the jargon of *baseball*, and are easily impatient with the old traditions emanating from the Cuba of the past, that they do not know and with which they feel little sympathy."[140]

The experience in the North was often decisive and defining. Mastery of new methods and familiarity with new techniques and technologies, once acquired, were not easily discarded and often were accompanied by attitudes that only emphasized the deficiencies of home. In *El pantano en la cima* (1971), Arturo Alfonso Roselló depicts with poignant detail how an ordinary chore could provide the occasion for a larger meditation. Juan Manuel has difficulty in changing the ribbon on a Cuban-made typewriter—"This garbage typewriter! Look how I've smeared my fingers with ink!" The narrator observes: "He began to curse the manufacturer of the machine for the difficulty encountered in this simple task, something so easy on North American typewriters. He admired the *yanquis* and praised everything about them: their customs, their dances, their food, their women, and their way of being." Juan Manuel reflects: "I should have been born in the North. I cannot accustom myself to our ways. Our defects are in the blood. That's the origin. We inherited nothing good from the Spanish, only the bad."[141]

Many returned home transformed and experienced hardship in reconciling the old ways with those acquired in the United States. Adjustments were often difficult, sometimes impossible. "Cuba was not a particularly pleasant place after Dartmouth," recalled Benito Vilá. "Few, if any, people my age seemed to know what I was talking about." José Rodríguez Feo had a similar experience after returning from Harvard. "I am as lonely as ever and yet quite happy in my isolation," he wrote Wallace Stevens. Concepción Freyre de Andrade related some of her father's regrets about having studied at Cornell: "He said that, when you're away for so long, you always feel in some way a stranger in your own country when you return." In the novel *La roca de Patmos* (1932) by Alberto Lamar Schweyer, Marcelo Pimentel is "fearful of being among his own people, having become accustomed to the anonymity of the big cities, to the cold life of hotels, to the small apartment near Broadway. . . . It would require a great deal of effort to adjust himself to life in his city." Many could not conceal their impatience or exasperation with conditions that did not measure up to the standards they had adopted as their own. Herminio Portell Vilá recounted conversations with Cubans on completing their studies in the North, "arriving full of ideas, initiatives, and projects to stimulate progress and learning in our country." He reflected ruefully: "In general, the local reality has given them an immediate and disagreeable blow." In Sergio la Villa's 1923 short story, "Impresiones de muchos 'dandies' ante su propio origen," the protagonist visits his aunt after living eight years in the United States, expecting "to find her more refined, more civilized, in keeping with the customs of the time":

> In reality, I was grief-stricken. . . . Her dress was with the same printed flowers, a blouse and skirt adorned with pleats and lace trims. . . . Her hair still done in thick braids coiled about her head. Always with long sleeves and a high collar, always with jet black ear rings. . . . For me it was sad to contemplate that everything in her was irremediable, fatally common and antiquated. Only her hair, whiter, and her skin, drier, were different . . . since I last saw her before I left for the North to acquire my true education.[142]

Tens of thousands of Cubans experienced life in the United States and were immediately and thereafter implicated in alternative value systems. Many returned home with a penchant for North American practices and products; imbued with new values, they reacted with disquiet to all the ways in which their country failed to measure up to the new standards they now held dear. *El Mundo* editor Luis Botifoll, wrote his biographer, had acquired "a new perspective on how democracy ought to function" and "an abhorrence for the excesses that were becoming commonplace in Cuba." The same biographer described *Carteles* publisher Alfredo Quílez in similar terms: "Because he has lived so many years in the United States, he has been able to appreciate what is needed here, all the shortcomings and all the inadequacies. And he contemplates all this with pain. He wants the Cuban to be the most honest, the most creative, and the most civilized of the world. He has seen the North American up close and has taken stock of many virtues that his countrymen do not have. He wishes them for his own people, so that they can create a civilized environment as felicitous and productive as in the land of the North." In the Servando Tellería short story "La cobija" (1925), Narciso works and travels in the United States for several years, visiting farms at every opportunity: "He was astonished. His great desire was to buy a *finca* in the country where he was born and work it with the modern methods he had seen in California and other places, to demonstrate to all Cuban farmers that there was no land on earth capable of producing more, if done properly."[143]

Cubans educated in the United States were permanently marked by the experience. They developed similar mannerisms and assumed all the characteristics of a type. "At twenty years of age," observed José Antonio Ramos, "and in Cuba during vacation time, there is hardly a young man or a young woman who does not miss the Yankee college, the Yankee city, Yankee liberty." In Masdeu's *La raza triste*, Miguel returns "completely transformed . . . dressed almost elegantly." Rolando Masferrer developed a partiality for country and western music, Stetson hats, and cowboy shirts with pseudopearl buttons during adolescent vacations in San Antonio, Texas. In the partly autobiographical novel *El caserón del Cerro* (1961), Marcelo Pogolotti chronicles the social transformations of the republic, changes that "begin on the surface and later penetrate deeply." Teresa possesses "grace and ease in her movements, the product of her American education." The protagonist Raúl Castroverde studied engineering in the United States—a country he considered "the focal point of modern civilization." The experience was transforming. "All who had visited the United States had returned with a number of new ideas, . . . especially among the young men, who had even adopted *yanqui* names like Bill, Chuck, Bud. In the social clubs, the styles, the dances, and even the demeanor were already American." Raúl returned as a changed man, the "archetype of the Cuban transformed into the North American university athlete. . . . The natural stridency of the Cuban is amplified under *yanqui* influence." This was the power of the North: "Residence in the United States restores a new vitality to the body enfeebled by the tropics, filling the body with energy as if it were a matter of a used electrical battery that has been recharged. He had learned a doctrine of action whose fundamental precept was to overcome everything that he encountered in his way, which creates men who give an impressionable spectacle of strength." A study of the bourgeoisie in prerevolutionary Santiago de Cuba determined that a "large percentage of the descendants of these families received their higher education in the United States, and in fact were named Billy, Joe, Bob; they spoke English as their mother tongue, were familiar with North American witticisms, and in general came to form a sub-product of U.S. society." In Chávez Alfaro's "El zoológico de papá" (1963), a student, on returning home by steamship after a year in the United States, reflects "because the sea is . . . *exciting*," and he realizes: "I don't remember how to say it in Spanish." Eladio Secades wrote movingly of the young women who studied in the North, "who upon returning wish that El Prado were Broadway, that Guanabacoa were Philadelphia, and Jesús del Monte *downtown*, that by magic the Chinese restaurant would become a *quick-lunch.* . . . They are bothered by a little of everything of our ways." The return was often painful, Secades understood. "It is when she discovers that we do not speak or dress the way she would like. She is nostalgic for her college friends." Secades continued:

> It is not clear how the Cuban girl who goes to the North forgets in one *college* course everything she has learned over the years in Cuba. It is decubanization (*descubanización*) with the first snowfall. . . . One fine day she returns, interjecting English words into the Spanish language that she has almost forgotten. The sweater imprinted with logos of colleges (*coliches*). The capital

"C" for Cornell. Dreams of *glamour-girl*. . . . We are losing our nationality. Nancy, Loly, Sassy, Betty. *Wedding Cake, Buffetsupper*, Piscina-*party*,
Canasta-*party*.[144]

But it was not just that Cubans returned changed. In fact, many had departed
for the North in the first place because conditions were changing on the island;
in other words, the travel abroad was itself evidence of change. The experience
in the United States served to reinforce the predisposition for change. Cubans
traveled north after having acquired a familiarity with North Americans at
home. Roberto Fernández Retamar reminisced:

> My personal relationship with the United States, began when, at the awkward
> age of seventeen, I set off to spend an important part of my adolescence in
> New York. But I didn't need this experience to form close ties with the United
> States, for these had been formed long ago. . . . So it was hardly strange that at
> the age of twelve or thirteen I would have emulated the lefty first-baseman
> Lou Gehrig . . . or that my poetry would have become permanently influ-
> enced by Whitman.

Years later Marcelo Pogolotti recalled his departure for Rensselaer in 1918 to
study engineering: "My whole family considered [engineering] as fundamental.
For them it was the driving force and foundation of modern civilization. . . .
Scientific truths—positivism was as its apogee—possessed an absolute, definitive, and incontrovertible value, and its creative achievements benefitted humanity. Without scientific knowledge there would be no progress and we would
be living in the stone age. As an engineering student, all this made me feel
important."[145]

Change was not always discernible, but even when it was, its meaning was not
always decipherable. North American methods and modalities had become the
dominant structures around which the familiar formed. They were everywhere.
"About this time," Gustavo Pittaluga wrote, "the influence over customs, over
Cuban ways of thinking and living had become apparent. And when . . . the
interchanges not of merchandise but of people began—group travel, the education of young people in the United States, the boarding of girls in North American colleges, the press and movie theaters of Havana—the great features of a
civilization and culture different from ours were recognized as having taken root
in our midst."[146]

Travel north was an occasion for revelation and reflection, an opportunity to
behold in the most advanced form the material order on which much of life in
Cuba was now based. Which is to say, travel provided an opportunity for intensely personal meditation on the Cuban condition; it was a time to take stock
of the ways that Cuba measured up—or failed to measure up—to standards that
many Cubans had appropriated as their own model for living and being in
Cuba. This made them even more susceptible to the ever-widening reach of

North American conventions, even more disposed to conform to lifestyles and maintain standards that had become theirs.

The authenticity of the experience in the North could be neither denied nor dismissed. Under certain circumstances it could undermine self-esteem and weaken national affinity. To travel north was to cross a threshold, to encounter an environment of technology and modernity, of remarkable wealth and development, of achievement at the highest level in all the spheres that Cubans had learned to consider valuable or important. They employed normative narratives of the North as the text by which to render their reality, which meant, too, that it became difficult for many to interpret their own circumstances on any terms other than North American ones. They had adopted values of the North as the means by which to negotiate the transactions of daily life. It was not always possible for Cubans, especially young people, to look about them without feelings of awe and a sense of diminished status. In Ramos's *Tembladera*, Isolina insists that only "fully mature youth" should travel north, "men already made in Cuba and capable of assimilating advantageously North American civilization without being dazzled by it and repudiate their country, not because they miss *yanqui* culture and civility in their country, but because in their country they do not see skyscrapers, or Coney Island, or Fifth Avenue." No doubt this is what Mario Parajón had in mind when he wrote that Cuba "asphyxiates those under thirty-five years of age in such a manner as to force them to leave and to return some years later to make a new Cuba." Parajón had himself lived two years abroad and acknowledged that he had "been completely changed by the experience."[147]

North American ways insinuated themselves deeply into Cuban sensibilities but had an even greater impact on Cuban susceptibilities. Conditions in the North revealed themselves above all as a mode of living and a state of mind—a manner of being, in fact: a combination of posture and position, confidence and conviction, self-assurance and self-reliance. This was heady stuff, all the more so for its association with success and status, and, quite naturally, something to aspire to.

The proposition of progress and comfort as a derivative of the connection with the North occupied a place of prominence in the discourse on nationality. The interior monologue of the U.S.-educated protagonist in Luis Adrián Betancourt's short story "Triángulo en el hoyo ocho" (1983) offers insight into the character of the Cuban meditation:

> My name is Richard, Richard Alamilla. But everyone knows me as Dick. That's the way I have been called since I was little, my parents, my friends, my first girl friends. That has been my name since the school days at LaSalle School through Villanueva. I am an architect. But not any kind of architect. I specialize in interiors. . . . I brought to Cuba an integral vision of modern comfort and I put it into the hands of whoever has sufficient sensibility to need it.[148]

Stylishness was associated with ways of the North. Self-esteem was often invested deeply in the notion of contemporary, another way to act out the discourse on modernity: to be identified with what was in vogue. Things North American seemed always "in" simply for being from the North. Cubans were conscious of appearance, sensitive about seeming behind the times and out of fashion, of appearing as anything other than modern and contemporary. These themes are rich and recurrent as narratives of self-representation, of ways of adapting to "fit in."

Travel north was decisive, for it provided an opportunity to experience new ways firsthand. It involved a complex internal dialogue of cognizance, of contrasts, of differences. To travel north was to confront one's insularity and come face-to-face with the concept of one as the Other. This condition was a powerful agency for change, to reinvent oneself through adaptation so as to not stand out. In *Memorias de un machadista* (1937), José de la Campa González's protagonist takes up drinking whiskey because it was "very American to drink whiskey." Renée Méndez Capote recalled her self-conscious first day in Philadelphia in 1919, wearing a long black skirt, an oversized blouse, and long braided hair, realizing immediately how different she looked. "On the next day, as soon as I went out into the street," she recalled, "I transformed myself: I raised my skirt, I cut my hair, and I put on heels." She never went back to the way she used to be. In Nicolás Dorr's play *Confesión en el barrio chino* (1984), Violeta recounts her visit to the United States: "I went with my hair black—yes I wore my hair black. But when I arrived to the North, I changed. I became a blond." In Douglas's *The Cubans*, Pedro, on arriving in New York, enjoins his daughter: "Now, young lady, go put on your hat, because we are going to go out on the streets and I mean to do a little shopping. These are very civilized people we are going to see and I do not want us to look like a pair of ignoramuses."[149]

Individual hopes and dreams were fashioned in this environment, with values appropriated and incorporated into the Cuban cosmology, often without awareness that their origins were anything other than Cuban. Fernández wrote poignantly of these circumstances in *Los niños se despiden*. "They are painting his house and he wants it to be another color," the narrator explains. "He could not make up his mind what color he would like it to be, he doesn't know, he doesn't remember—blue? green? white?—with the veranda like the one that the Americans' houses have, all covered with screens and striped awnings, where they read the newspapers and drink Scotch and soda, Coca-Cola, and beer while they play cards, listen to music or converse among themselves, served by English West Indians, as if nothing was happening, as if nothing was going on in the world."[150]

Cubans inscribed themselves deeply on a cast of thought largely formed and informed by North American values, which, in turn, served as the means by which they took measure of their condition. The very notion of Cuba as modern was based on a material order and moral hierarchies derived from the North. The encounter acted as an entrée to North American structures no less than as a way to introduce and institutionalize those structures inside Cuba. But this process could also create dissonance and dysfunction. The experience often revealed disparities to which Cubans were particularly vulnerable. Under certain circumstances the experience could expose deficiencies of home and be a source of discontent. This explains the apparent contradiction of Cuban dissatisfaction with living conditions otherwise judged far superior to those in other Latin American countries.

The circumstances could only invite invidious comparison; they could only provide an occasion to contemplate the meaning of differences and distinctions and inevitably cast doubt on the concepts of modernity and progress, which were at the heart of the meaning of "Cuban." And, indeed, by what other standards could the measure of Cuban conditions be taken except by those norms that had given meaning to daily life on the island? Decades of close and constant contact had established a moral order from which much in everyday life had been formed. Comparison could not help but produce confrontation with the self. In Arturo Ramírez's short story "El hijo" (1932), the narrator tells of a son returned from the United States "to show contempt for our ways, a lack of *criollismo*, and an unbridled admiration for the North." Sydney Clark wrote of a Cuban friend who had studied at Boston College and "returned to Cuba with an enduring love for Americans and things American." Accounts such as these appear with such frequency that they must be considered an important source for any rendering of Cuban. " 'What a great country!' " Eduardo Abril Amores overheard Cuban travelers proclaim on returning from the United States. " 'What a wonderful government!' 'What order!' " Abril Amores continued: "Cuba is their country, but our poor education, our excesses, our lack of schools, our lack of parks, our lack of roads for rapid and easy automobile transportation, our lack of water, our different hygiene, our lack of firmness with our delinquents, in short, everything that is wrong in Cuba became intolerable. The United States becomes an obsession: 'This is done in this way in the United States' or 'This would not happen in the United States.' In everything they look to compare with the United States." In *The Cubans*, Alfredo completes his education in North America and returns to work in the family sugar mill, "hating it, talking always of Los Estados Unidos; in Los Estados Unidos they did this, in Los Estados Unidos they said that."[151]

The encounter with the North was experienced in many forms: by way of motion pictures and television programs, often as advertisements of U.S. products. Department store catalogs—from Macy's, B. Altman and Company, Franklin Simon and Company, Montgomery Ward, John Wanamaker, Bonwit Teller, and Sears—were widely distributed on the island. The combination of image and text that served to reveal the existence of a vast array of consumer goods was compelling. The Sears catalog, one economist observed, was "one of the most read books in Cuba." Mail-order catalogs, many of them published in Spanish, provided the opportunity to compare dissimilar realities. "I had subscribed to about ten magazines," Sergio recalls in *Memorias de subdesarrollo*, "received catalogues from publishers, and traveled every year to the United States. . . . Every new product that appears in the North American market made me conscious of our scientific, technical, and industrial backwardness." The power of these forms, Sergio realizes only after the revolution, was that they provided a point of view, a way to see the world, and he laments: "Now I do not have a frame of reference for anything by which to judge things, no information; books and products from capitalist countries no longer arrive." The suggestion by Stuart Ewen and Elizabeth Ewen that mail-order catalogs expanded markets among immigrants has direct relevance for Cuba. "The catalogue was a perfect vehicle for 'Americanization,'" they argue persuasively; "the pictorial images spoke an easily understood, universal language, demonstrating what an American appearance was all about; actual transactions could be performed in one's language of origin."[152]

The encounter with the North often revealed enormous differences: discrepancies, in fact, that registered and rankled precisely because so much of what served as the measure of the Cuban condition was derived from U.S. sources. The frame of reference centered on North American structures, and inevitably conditions that failed to meet those standards could only lead to disappointment.

These circumstances assumed the proportions of a malaise. The use of U.S. modalities to assess the Cuban condition resulted in disillusion, as comparisons could not be avoided, conclusions could not be denied.

Journalist Ernesto Ardura was one of the many thousands who had crossed this threshold and could reflect on the experience. "Here everything is unstable, insecure, provisional," he wrote from Havana in 1957. "Not even life itself is secure. In the United States the Cuban finds a social order that allows him to live with decorum, freedom, and work. . . . He finds what he wishes for his own country: a life eminently civilized." Obstacles and difficulties presented themselves in the United States, of course, for the process of adaptation was never easy. But the "sacrifice of several years was preferable in order to enjoy a better life." The ensuing change of consciousness was nothing short of remarkable. "When Cubans . . . return," Ardura wrote, "they have confessed to me that they feel out of place and they cannot stand the noise, the disorganization, the excessive authority, and the absence of real order. Cubans are never as lucid about the conditions of our island as when they are abroad, when they have perspective . . . on the profound source of our failures, of our permanent crisis." In Fesser Ferrer's *Los desorientados*, Raquel contemplates New York, "the orderliness of the traffic and pedestrians, directed by automatic lights, and [she] does not understand why so much disorder exists in her country." Washington Mendoza, the protagonist in Ramos's *Coaybay*, returns from the United States "completely transformed," disillusioned by conditions in Cuba, "praising the progress and the advances in all spheres of the great Republic of the North." In Carlos Loveira's *La última lección* (1922), Gustavo Aguirre travels from Key West to Boston by train and notes "the order, the cleanliness, the facilities, the organization, all the advances in the United States."[153]

Frequently new conventions were adopted in unremarkable fashion, introduced as often by Cubans as by North Americans, usually in good faith and with the best of intentions, always with the certainty that they were better than what had previously existed. Those most directly associated with North American ways accepted in varying degrees the moral superiority of the system in which they functioned. They came to prize efficiency and technical skills—in short, "know-how"—and looked askance at persons and circumstances that failed to meet their standards. These values could be diffused in many ways, of course, and they often were. Nor was there anything particularly insidious about this process, although under some circumstances changes had insidious outcomes. But mostly ordinary people were seeking ordinary ways to make ordinary life saner and safer, more logical and rational, more convenient and efficient—all values, of course, that had the capacity to rearrange the physiognomy of everyday life in profound and permanent ways. Simply owning a car created a material environment out of which naturally flowed a large number of diverse demands: the need for gasoline and oil, parts and parking, traffic lights and good road conditions. Automobile owners thus became a constituency whose larger interests were very much implicated in the modern condition. The line between their needs and politics was straight and direct. It is significant that among the first objects destroyed in Havana within hours of the flight of Batista on January 1, 1959, were parking meters.

That the notion of Cuban well-being had evolved largely around North American standards suggests a complex search for a usable narrative to make explicit the discursive terms of nationality. North American images served as an important source of Cuban metaphors, a way to represent modernity and progress and at the same time locate Cuba on the scale of civilization. The use of these forms as a model of the ideal shaped a hierarchy of values and set into place the framework by which to assess the Cuban condition. In Casuso's *Los ausentes*, the protagonist visits colleges, museums, and libraries in New York and reflects: "It made me think of my country, . . . of the wealthy of my country, who never donate anything to educational institutions. Who do not know, like these rich Americans, how to be generous with culture, do not know how to leave behind a single foundation to serve their country, . . . while our museums become moldy in old buildings, where not even light is available, ignored by the public, in a silence of absolute inactivity." Similar thoughts occurred to Guillermo Cabrera Leiva when he visited the University of Miami in 1951. "What are the wealthy of my country doing by not allocating some of their riches in the service of knowledge or supporting national culture with their resources? We see so many generous wealthy people here in Anglo-America that we are surprised by the indifference of our wealthy people in the sphere of philanthropy. The majority of North American colleges and universities are backed by wealthy patrons, groups of contributors who provide economic guarantees to those educational centers without returns whatsoever. . . . We are struck by the lack of generosity among our wealthy." Miguel de Zarraga wrote of "the North American millionaires who know how to be rich"—Rockefeller, Ford, Carnegie, Schwab, Morgan—who contributed to libraries, museums, hospitals, and universities. "And our rich? Where are the permanent, systematic, and productive works?" *Carteles* editorialized against Cuba's "indigent rich," who accumulated vast fortunes and passed their wealth on to their families to squander: "Cuba needs men like Vanderbilt, Ford, Morgan, and Carnegie, to support universities, orphanages, museums, hospitals, and foundations."[154]

The North loomed large over Cuban sensibilities in all spheres. It was while visiting New York that Arturo de Carricarte became aware of the backwardness of the library system in Cuba. "There are 113 *municipios* in Cuba," he complained, "and only five have public libraries supported by the state or the municipality. There are less than ten libraries maintained in private centers. There is not a single children's library in the entire country." Pedro Martínez Inclán made a similar observation: "The traveler will not find in Havana those neighborhood libraries that one sees in North America, where by giving your name and your work or home address they lend books for a certain number of days. In this, unfortunately, we still have not imitated our North American friends." José María Marcos, the municipal librarian of Cienfuegos, urged the University of Havana to establish a library degree program, "similar to the one at Columbia University in New York," and thereby "create the possibilities for a library career such as those that exist in the most advanced democratic countries." Herminio Portell Vilá drew painful comparisons. "Jacksonville, with a third of the population of Havana," he wrote in 1956, "has a public library with nearly one-half million books . . . that are read by a million people each year. The city—not the country—spends $200,000 annually in support of the Jacksonville library, while here in Havana the municipal library is found in dire need." A year later Oscar Pino Santos calculated that in the United States one public library existed for every 25,000 inhabitants, whereas in Cuba there was one library for every 200,000 inhabitants.[155]

Cubans took note of public parks in the United States, which is to say they noticed their absence in Cuba. The parks in New York City made Marcelo Pogolotti think about the lack of parks in Havana, and he asked "Why?" *Bohemia* columnist "Suzanne" pointed to New York's Central Park, the Boston Commons, and the Philadelphia Municipal Park as examples for the municipal authorities of Havana to emulate. Vicente Cubillas was enchanted with the Boston Public Garden, declaring: "If only we had one of these large parks in Havana!" Octavio Jordán called for the creation of a national park, "such as those found in all civilized countries in the world."[156]

At almost every turn, the encounter with the United States called attention to Cuba's deficiencies. Dentist Herminia Pérez Ruiz, after studying in Rochester and New York City, returned to Cuba in 1950 very troubled: "My experience in these places allows me to affirm that the Cuban government has much to do. In these American scientific centers where I worked I was able to see how mobile units functioned, . . . examining the needs of children to visit the dentist, which can be done in Cuba." José Comallonga visited the Seabrook Farm in New Jersey and was impressed with its efficiency and productivity, whereas "here in Cuba, almost all the wealthy . . . used their farms ostentatiously as a palatial residence."[157]

The most ordinary facets of Cuban life came under new scrutiny in the encounter with the North. Antonio Iraizoz told of his pleasure in shopping for ties, handkerchiefs, and shirts at 11:00 P.M. on Broadway and criticized Havana merchants for not having late evening hours. In Arcocha's *Los muertos andan solos*, Sylvia complains about the "stench of restrooms": "That's one of the things that really bothers me about Cuba. In the North, wherever one goes one can enter any restroom confident that it will be clean and well-kept. Here, from the moment one leaves Havana, you have to hold it in, even if you burst."[158]

Residents of Havana were especially given to invidious comparisons. Attorney Armando Calvo suggested the adoption of the system he saw in Cleveland, where the major streets became one-way during the rush hour. Octavio Jordán marveled at the synchronized traffic lights on "all the principal avenues in the most important cities of the United States that permit one to travel 25 to 30 blocks consecutively on green lights." The fact that this system was in use only increased Jordán's annoyance with traffic conditions in Havana. He added: "But among us, on the three small blocks of the Prado—Neptuno, San Jose, and Dragones—where there are three traffic lights, the signals never coincide, and it is necessary to stop at each one. Is it too much trouble to get them synchronized?" On another occasion Jordán insisted that if the main streets were distinguished from secondary roads—"the way Miami and other cities in the United States have done"—it would not be necessary to abuse the horn. He took note of the use of "loading zones" in New York and urged their creation in Havana. He referred to North American infrastructure as "the true wonders of the most modern engineering"—the George Washington Bridge, the Lincoln Tunnel, the highways and parkways—and asked: "Why can't the same achievements be produced in Cuba?" Ernesto Ardura called for the installation of more traffic lights to improve traffic flow. "As long as Havana lacks an adequate organization of traffic," he insisted, ". . . it can not have pretensions to be a great capital. Even the smallest city in the United States is more advanced than San Cristobal de La

Habana in this regard." Rubén Ortiz Lamadrid proposed the installation of pedestrian-controlled traffic lights, especially on Twenty-third Street, but was certain that this system, "which is found even in the most insignificant towns in the United States, is probably too much to ask of Cuban officials." Returning from a vacation in Florida, Ortiz could hardly contain his impatience with driving conditions in Cuba: "I spent a large part of my time behind the wheel, travelling through different cities and highways of Florida, and the difference between our system and theirs is as great as night and day." North American traffic flowed like clockwork, without the presence of police, "simply because there was no need, due to the fact that on each street corner of each city and town the driver is confronted with a stop light . . . and on the highways he is assisted constantly with signs providing directions and instructions."[159]

Much of day-to-day life in Cuba was rendered comprehensible and assigned meaning or value through metaphor and analogy to things North American. Comparisons provided the representations by which to translate the Cuban reality into a comprehensible narrative. The readiness with which Cubans invoked the United States as their frame of reference must itself be seen as a projection of nationality. Imagery passed into the vernacular as both structure of dialogue and source of validation. Octavio Jordán likened Twenty-third Street with its speeding automobiles in downtown Havana to "the runway of Indianapolis." When druggist Orlando Requeijo sought to characterize his economic good times, he referred to himself as "un Rockefeller en pequeño" (a Rockefeller in miniature). Convicted racketeer José Manuel Castillo became known as "the Al Capone of Cuba."[160]

Comparison also served as a measure of merit, a way to corroborate Cuban achievement by the standard that mattered most. When the Almendares River tunnel opened in 1953, Octavio Jordán proclaimed that "the project is without any doubt of first-rate quality. There is no reason to envy the famous Holland and Lincoln tunnels of New York City." The completion of "el Country Club Park" was said to be for "Habaneros what the famous Lenox Park, Tuxedo Park and other residential parks are for North American *high-life*." The Playa de Marianao was characterized as "our Newport." The Palantino amusement park was advertised as "el Coney Island de La Habana." Twenty-third Street in Havana was described as a "tropical Broadway" and likened to Massachusetts Avenue in Washington, D.C. Don Gual was downright euphoric in his comparisons: "Nothing in Hollywood, or New York, or Miami Beach comes close to the Tropicana," he exulted. "Have you heard anyone talk about a theater as large as the Blanquita? Is there a yacht club in the world as large and well equipped like the Havana Yacht Club? . . . The Centro Gallego and the Centro Asturiano make the New York Athletic Club look puny by comparison. The famous Newport Harbor Yacht Club of Los Angeles . . . has only three employees. . . . This Country Club of Havana, the Havana Yacht Club, the Vedado Tennis Club have more than 100 employees."[161]

Identification with North American forms acquired a logic of its own. Cubans adapted to ways and things North American and through pressures both sustained and subtle accepted the superiority of these ways as an article of faith, if, perhaps, without being conscious of an act of conversion. The power of these forms was in their capacity to implicate Cubans in the presumption of universality. These were complex transformations, rarely without ambiguity and ambivalence. Much in the tension of nationality was related to this duality, especially attempts to accommodate new affinities with old attachments. This dichotomy developed early and was at the heart of the discourse on nationality, for the development of the narrative of Cuban was very much transacted through the North American value system.

These circumstances had profound implications for the cognitive categories from which self-definitions were constructed. The notion of a "Cuban-American" identity, which is associated with the community of exiles in the United States after 1959, appears to have actually originated as a condition of Cuban self-definition long before the triumph of the revolution. "I've been pro-American all my life," Alfredo Barrera Lordi admitted to Oscar Lewis; "I even feel a bit American myself." Columbia University graduate Pablo Desvernine expressed a similar sentiment: "My friendship and admiration for the United States are known; I am an American, too much one, my friends say." This, no doubt, is what Alberto Candero of the National Bank of Cuba meant in 1958 when he declared: "Even though we are proud of our old Spanish traditions, we think and act as modern Americans." Benito Vilá wrote of his parents' "odd North American inclination," explaining: "My parents were ardent fans of this country; there had been talk, I was told later, of flying my mother to Miami so I could enjoy U.S. citizenship from birth." Maximiliano Pons reminisced about his decision to attend Yale: "I wanted to be an American very badly. I became an American aspirant. The United States had just emerged victorious from World War II. I was away at Yale then. Four years later I returned to Cuba, went to work for a leading American company, bought a house in the Marianao suburbs—the whole thing." Years later Ofelia Schutte would reflect on the formation of her "Cuban-American identity," recalling her childhood in Havana during the troubled times of the late 1950s, of gun battles in the streets, bombings, and body searches on entering movie theaters:

And occasionally my family would travel to Miami. . . . In Miami Beach I saw tall, good-looking courteous policemen who were nice to tourists and were kind to the children of tourists. There I went to as many movies as I liked without going through a bodily search or fearing that a bomb might explode as I watched the show. Seeing everything bright and rosy in the tourist zones of Miami Beach, I quickly reached the conclusion that the United States was the land of democracy, freedom and personal opportunity and that no other place in the world was the equal of it. English became my favorite language and the United States my favorite country. Before the revolution, my identity was already split.[162]

MIAMI MEDITATIONS

Schutte's allusion to Miami was noteworthy. Miami loomed large in Cuban narratives on nation and nationality. Miami was metaphor, so near that it could not help but serve as measure and model, a means by which to contemplate the Cuban condition. A structural relationship developed early between Miami and Havana. Both cities were shaped by similar forces, at about the same time, and acted on each other in ways that were at once defining and definitive. They became representations of one another, establishing a complex association that was both complementary and competitive and that assumed the characteristics of a border culture, much like reciprocal interactions of cities located along both sides of the U.S.-Mexican border.

Miami was a product of the North American infatuation with Cuba in the 1920s and bore distinctive markings of its origins. Coral Gables was conceived as a reproduction of a Latin American colonial city. Developer George Merrick chose the "Spanish style," noted one historian of Miami, after "having observed in trips through the West Indies and Cuba that this type had been evolved for all-year residence in tropical countries." Miami developer C. C. Lowe frequently traveled to Havana in search of ideas for new architectural designs. "I did not realize," Lowe explained during a visit in 1925, "the value of the ideas I could get in building from studying this architecture down here. It is a known fact that Havana to a very great extent influenced the Coral Gables people in building what you might call a Spanish City."[163]

The vogue of Havana insinuated itself into the vision of Miami: foreign, tropical, exotic, as ambience and circumstance through Spanish-language usage and Royal Palms landscaping. New subdivisions were named in Spanish: Alto del Mar in Miami Beach, the Naranja Nook and del Rio in Miami, Buena Vista in Coral Gables, El Retiro on Belle Isle. There were intimations of Cuba in street names (Ponce de Leon Boulevard and DeSoto Drive in Miami; Antilla, Baracoa, Bayamo, Madruga, Matanzas, El Prado, and Yumuri in Coral Gables) and in the names of hotels (the Casa Loma Hotel, the Ponce de Leon). An advertisement for the Hotel Pancoast emphasized its "atmosphere of Old Spain": waitresses were dressed as Spanish peasants, and an inner court aviary was stocked with tropical birds. Developer N. B. T. Roney created Española Way, two blocks of residential and commercial buildings built to resemble an old Spanish town. To complete the effect, Roney hired dark-eyed women to stroll about with shawls and fans.[164]

Construction materials were imported from Havana. This was nothing less than instant antiquity as weathered and worn building materials were incorporated into the new construction. Miami architects paid top prices for old clay barrel roof tiles, floor tiles, hardwood doors, cabinets, and hewn stone from Cuba. Havana landlords razed entire buildings for construction materials to sell to Florida contractors. Havana became modern, Miami became colonial. "Cuban landlords," the *Havana Post* reported in 1928, "have a chance to reap a nice harvest of profit by knocking the old Spanish tile from the roofs of their houses and putting new windows and door frames in substitution of the antiquated hard or cabinet wood ones, for Miami architects have revived their plans and efforts to erect Spanish colonial type homes in that city." The *Miami Daily News* building of 1925 was decorated with tile obtained in Havana. Villa Vizcaya, the Derring mansion on Biscayne Bay, utilized Cuban sandstone. In 1925–26, during the height of the Florida building boom, Miami developers imported more than two million tiles from Cuba.[165]

Miami's architectural trend created a demand for Cuban artisans and manufacturers. In 1925 José Escarra, Enrique Valdés, and Pedro Meliá opened a factory in Coral Gables to produce mosaic tiles for floors, walls, and ceilings and barrel tiles for roofs. Employing Cuban workers and importing Cuban limestone, the tile factory reproduced designs used in Cuba.

The local tourist economy developed around the notion of Miami as "foreign." Nightclubs and cabarets hired Cuban orchestras and *rumba* dancers—all part of the tropical ambience that gave Miami its "Latin" appearance. Club rooms of Miami Beach hotels were modeled on Havana cabarets and usually engaged "Latin" acts: the Burgundy Room at the Sands Hotel proclaimed itself "the rumba one spot"; the Ritz Plaza sponsored Monday-night rumba contests; the Roney Plaza advertised the Siboney Sextet, "the Celebrated Cuban Rhumba Orchestra"; the Atlantis Hotel booked Monchito and his Eight-Piece Orchestra; the Sapphire Room at the Belmar Hotel engaged the Juanito Sanabria Orchestra. The Starlight Patio at the Caribbean featured Tony Negrett and "His Authentic Cubans." A *jai alai* fronton opened in Hialeah in 1924. Havana itself was appropriated as a Miami tourist attraction, as local travel agents organized day trips to Cuba from Florida. As early as 1920, the Havana-American Steamship Corporation inaugurated direct service between Miami and Havana. "We recognize that Havana now is definitely a part of our tourist appeal," affirmed the *Miami Herald* in 1934. Miami convention director Joe Powers agreed: "We have never considered Cuba a competitor for our tourist trade, but have always held out a Cuban side trip as bait for our convention bids."[166]

The Cuban presence in Miami expanded slowly. A small Cuban community formed in the 1920s, consisting mainly of workers, musicians, and entertainers whose presence contributed to local "color" in the rendering of Miami as tropical. The Cuban presence increased steadily during the late 1920s and early 1930s, consisting largely of political exiles, first as opponents of the Gerardo Machado government and subsequently as members of the fallen Machado government. Hundreds of former public officials—among them, President Machado himself,

Sebastián Planazos, Alberto Barreras, Manuel Villapol, Ernesto Sarrá, José Izquierdo, Carlos Miguel de Céspedes, Alberto Herrera, Rafael Guas Inclán, and Orestes Ferrara—took up permanent residence in Miami. By the late 1930s, about six thousand Cubans lived in Miami.[167]

Miami entered the Cuban consciousness as a place of refuge and residence: it was readily accessible, the cost of living was reasonable, and most of all it was vaguely familiar. A city conceived by North American developers as a version of Havana could not fail to be congenial to Cubans.

In the years that followed, Miami teemed with Cubans who had fallen from power and out of grace, including former and future officeholders. Each change of government, whether by ballot or by way of the barracks, produced a succession of dismissals, retirements, and resignations and inevitably a new cycle of migration to Miami: throughout the 1930s, after the elections of 1940, 1944, and 1948, and especially during the years following Batista's military coup in 1952.

After World War II Cubans increasingly went to Miami as tourists, on short holidays and long vacations, on day trips and weekend excursions, as sightseers and honeymooners. The twenty-two-year-old Fidel Castro and his bride Mirta Díaz Balart were among the many thousands of Cuban newlyweds to honeymoon in Miami.

Cuban travel was both cause and effect of changes overtaking the Florida tourist industry. Postwar Miami was becoming a year-round vacation site, extending the traditional "high" winter season into a "low" summer one. Many more hotels and vacation apartments remained open, offering attractive summer rates. The fact that a summer vacation in Florida could be considered at all was in large measure made possible by the advent of air conditioning, providing agreeable respite from the blistering heat of southern Florida.

Summer was also the traditional vacation season in Cuba, and Florida had much to offer Cuban travelers. Florida had far more public beaches than Cuba, where many of the best beaches had been withdrawn from the public by hotels and private resorts. Certainly, too, budget summer rates placed Miami vacations within reach of growing numbers of families, often at far less cost than comparable facilities in Cuba. Air conditioning was also a factor. "Say what you want," wrote Berta Arocena in 1949, "the summer is far more pleasant on the beaches of Miami than on those of Cuba. . . . There they use lavish air conditioning, what is for me the modern version of the Ivory Tower of a pure poet. With air conditioning, not only do we find relief from the heat, but we find respite too from our worries and physical and moral aches." Miami was a place of "refuge to enjoy a comfortable temperature, without having gusts or blasts of wind [of fans] mess up our hairdos." Arocena concluded: "A fifty-five minute flight away the delight of a cool respite awaits us."[168]

Transportation improved as well. Service increased, costs decreased. Steamship service expanded, and by the early 1950s the cost of round-trip travel was less than $40. Automobile ferry service between Key West and Havana also increased. But it was the remarkable expansion of air services that consolidated the link between Miami and Havana. The Miami-Havana route quickly developed into one of the busiest international connections in the world. In the 1940s and 1950s Pan American Airlines scheduled an average of twenty-eight flights daily and during peak periods often had departures every twenty minutes. National Airlines provided ten flights daily. Other Miami-Havana carriers included Cubana Aviación, Eastern Airlines, and Chicago and Southern Airlines. Air travel was not only convenient—forty minutes between Havana and Miami—but it was also economical. The standard round-trip fare in the 1950s was $30. Special tour packages reduced costs even further. In 1952, for example, National Airlines offered a week in Miami for $52 including flight, hotel, and tours.

Cubans arrived by the hundreds of thousands: 40,000 annually in the 1940s and an average of 50,000 in the 1950s. In one four-month period, May-August 1948, 40,000 Cubans visited Miami. One weekend in August 1948 was especially heavy. "Cubans returning home from summer vacations in the United States almost caused a traffic jam at Miami International Airport over the weekend," according to a Pan American Airway press release. "On Saturday six extra flights were needed . . . and on Sunday . . . clippers were shuttling back and forth across the Florida Straits like buses during rush hour." The Cuban tourist business in 1948 was sufficiently brisk to keep 225 of the total 338 Miami Beach hotels open all year. "In the summer planes from Havana wing in," Newsweek reported in 1949, "bringing Cubans by the thousands: rich Cubans, poor Cubans, clerks, professional men, skilled workers, even domestic servants. . . . The Cubans are leaving their mark on Florida. . . . Last summer it sounded as if as much Spanish as English was being spoken on Miami streets. Shops hired Spanish-speaking clerks and the city broke out with a rash of signs reading 'Se habla español.'" By 1957 one observer concluded that "Spanish is fast supplanting English in Florida."[169]

Miami tourist promoters specifically targeted Cuba as the principal market of summer travel. During the spring and summer the travel sections of Cuban newspapers and magazines were filled with advertisements for Miami hotels, motels, and vacation apartments, restaurants, cabarets and nightclubs, airline carriers, steamship companies, bus lines, and automobile rental agencies. Miami promoted itself as an extension of Cuba, similar and familiar, where no effort was spared to accommodate Cuban needs. The Blackstone, the Clyde, the Saxony, the Columbus, the Sands Commodore, and Versailles were among the many hotels to advertise "Se habla español." The Miami Beach Sands Hotel publicized the availability of "Spanish speaking personnel." Hotel Whitehart also employed staff who spoke Spanish but offered "free English lessons." Morris Fleischman, owner of the Hotel Roberts, announced plans to hire a bilingual manager—"preferably Cuban"—and invest $60,000 in air conditioning. The Terrace Apartments Hotel emphasized its "proximity to the Catholic Church."

The Ocean Reef Apartments, operated by "Cuban owner Sr. Zayas," noted its "proximity to the beach, shops, restaurants and theaters." The Seacomber offered a "paradise for young vacationers," and the Henry "specialized in the Cuban clientele."[170]

Almost all sectors of the tourist economy adopted Cuban as a salient commercial motif. This had always been part of Miami's self-representation, of course, but during the 1940s and 1950s it became increasingly conspicuous. Restaurants publicized their Cuban specialties. Radio City Restaurant advertised "typical Cuban dishes." The Barclay Plaza Hotel offered "authentic Cuban cuisine under the supervision of the master culinarians Genaro C. Barrios and Antonio García." The Betsy Ross Hotel proudly announced the opening of its "Cuban restaurant under Elena Rosales, the Latin manager," and the Del Prado presented "exquisite dinners prepared by our Cuban chef." "Cuba" became the motif of cabarets and nightclubs. El Toreador cabaret advertised itself as "the only Hispanic nightclub and restaurant in Miami: a corner of Spain and a piece of Havana." The Clover Club booked "A Night in Havana Revue," described by the *Variety* magazine critic as "fast, furious and colorfully authentic cubano dance and song." The Olympia engaged a twenty-member ensemble of musicians and dancers for a "Holiday in Havana," and the "Havana Mardi Gras Revue" opened at Lucerne. The Fontainebleau presented the Carlos Ramírez Orchestra from Havana; the Hotel Delmonico room, a "Latin American Orchestra"; the Miami Beach Blue Sail, the Orquesta Sacasa; and the Hotel Belmar, Rafael y sus Rumberos.[171]

In time, Miami became Cuban in more than atmosphere and ambience. Indeed, the postwar economy of southern Florida was stimulated in large part by Cuban investments. As early as 1950, the International Bank for Reconstruction and Development reported large cash flows entering Miami saving accounts and safe deposit boxes. "Very large amounts have been used in the Miami area and other parts of the United States to acquire real estate and other investments paid for on a cash basis." According to the bank: "A spot check of the number of large-denomination dollar bills returned to New York from Florida disclosed that a startling amount of such notes has been received there in recent years, mostly originating in Cuba."[172]

Much of this cash flow was generated by the rampant corruption and official malfeasance that dominated Cuban political life during the 1940s and 1950s. Public officials at all levels of government, from presidents and cabinet ministers, senators, congressmen, and judges to army officers and police officials, lived off bribery, payoffs, and fixes. *Time* recounted the last day in office of Minister of Education José Manuel Alemán and his aides in 1948: "[They] drove four Ministry of Education trucks into the Treasury Building. All climbed out carrying suitcases. 'What are you going to do? Rob the Treasury?' joshed a guard. 'Quien Sabe?' replied . . . Alemán. Forthwith his men scooped pesos, francs, escudos, lire, rubles, pounds sterling and about 19 million dollars in U.S. currency into the suitcases. The trucks made straight for the airfield where a chartered DC-9 stood waiting." Miami was "the Mecca of Cuban thieves," proclaimed *Carteles* in 1949, a view shared by Manuel Bisbé, who described Miami as "the beachhead of Cuban corruption."[173]

Cuban investments reached into all sectors, especially real estate. More than $100 million was invested in southern Florida, mainly in apartment houses, hotels, and office buildings. Former minister of education Alemán subsequently headed La Ansana Corporation, representing almost $3 million in real estate investments, including hotels and apartment houses on Miami Beach. Former president Ramón Grau San Martín acquired a $450,000 home in Miami. The International Bank in 1950 reported that "Cuban investing syndicates" had acquired more than $8 million worth of income property and other "numerous individual investors whose purchases range from 50 thousand dollars up." As early as 1948 correspondent Miguel de Marcos commented: "Cuba has conquered Miami without firing a shot."[174]

The growing Cuban presence created other opportunities. Numerous small Cuban-owned businesses of all types, including retail shops, restaurants, and tourist-related services, expanded throughout the 1950s. Alberto Gómez operated the Restaurant Hispano-Americano, which specialized in *comidas cubanas*. By 1950 a Liceo Cubano de Miami was in existence.

Havana was integrated into the Miami economy in other ways. The two cities closed in on one another, shaping and being shaped by each other in constant interplay. Miami retailers and department stores routinely advertised in Havana newspapers: Miami Appliance Company offered "special prices" for washing machines, refrigerators, and electric dishwashers; the Biltmore Galleria promoted lamps and furniture; Paul's Carpet Company offered its "lowest prices" during the summer months; Bryon's Department Store provided "courteous translators" for prospective Cuban customers. The University of Miami announced special English-language summer classes. Bankers, real estate agents, and developers energetically pursued clients in Cuba. The Miami Beach Federal Savings and Loan Association advertised 2.5 percent interest on federally insured savings accounts. Real estate agents promoted houses, condominiums, commercial property, and land. "Buy a piece of Florida for 12¢ a *vara* [33 inches]," advertised Florida Homesite, Inc. The Atlantic Realty Investment Corporation offered Cubans "excellent opportunities for remunerative investments in Palm Beach County: hotels, businesses, urban shops, lots, houses and residences and buildings." Brown and Pearson in Miami publicized a four-unit apartment building in Coral Way. The Vero Beach Land Corporation offered real estate in the "most rapidly developing region of the United States" for $10 down and $5 a month. Realtors Dennis A. Gray and Associates of Coral Gables advertised "a magnificent investment in Miami," guaranteeing a 12 percent return on money invested in "eight of the most modern apartments."[175]

Local and state agencies also promoted Florida in Cuba. Miami proclaimed July 11 "Cuba Day," a one-day commemoration preceded by weeklong festivities that included dinners and dances, parades and parties, visits by Cuban dignitaries, a courtesy call by a Cuban naval vessel, and a baseball game between the Miami and Havana teams of the Florida International League. Daytona Beach designated March 24 as "Batista Day" and declared the Cuban president an honorary citizen. The Miami city government advertised an "invitation to our Cuban neighbors: visit Miami soon and often. You are only minutes away. Bring your family. Your children will enjoy their recreation. And a visit to the United States will be educational." The Miami Department of Information struck a similar note in a 1953 announcement: "In Miami you will feel as if you are in your own home. Spanish is spoken in the hotels, restaurants, shops and theaters. The great department stores and specialty shops of Miami offer summer sales in all types of merchandise, especially in sports clothes and accessories designed for comfort in the tropics." In June 1958 the Miami Publicity Department launched a "visit Miami" campaign in Cuban newspapers: "Whatever you desire in your vacation, you will find here: a mild climate, a picturesque landscape, thousands of accommodations in hotels, motels, and apartments. And when one talks about shopping, Miami offers you the latest and most select variety in whatever you seek, be it sports clothing, eveningwear, furniture or jewelry, electrical accessories or general garden utensils or tableware."[176]

The allusion to shops was both product and promotion of what had become one of the principal attractions of travel north: shopping. "Florida has the solution to all your shopping needs," the Florida Development Commission advertised in 1957. "Whether you are a businessman buying specialized equipment or a housewife in search of famous wardrobe articles made in Florida or an entire family in search of a marvelous vacation. Florida is the closest place where you can obtain products and services of the U.S.A. And 'Se habla español' almost everywhere." When Chicago and Southern Airlines announced direct service from Havana to New Orleans, it invoked "love, romance, history, ambience. And something more for the woman: shops and styles from Paris."[177]

Shopping in Miami represented savings. Merchandise in Cuba was uniformly more expensive than the same goods in the United States. A 4 percent customs duty, as well as a variety of sales taxes and consular fees, together with added transportation costs and local distribution markups, raised costs to exorbitant levels. Shopping in the North developed into almost a national pastime. Indeed, in the 1950s Cuban visitors to Florida spent an estimated $70 million annually. "Beside the vacation," *Newsweek* observed in 1949, "the whole family can be outfitted with new wardrobes at half the cost of clothing in Havana. Electrical household appliances can be bought at prices that astonish the Cubans. . . . They stagger under the weight of packages of all sizes and descriptions." In Enrique Serpa's novel *La trampa* (1956), the protagonist shops in the North, "where many things, especially radios, refrigerators, electric irons, washing machines and things like that are much cheaper." In *Our House in the Last World* (1983) by Oscar Hijuelos, Alejo dreams of returning to his town of San Pedro "with gifts of fine clothing, electrical appliances, watches, and jewelry for everyone." Gustavo Pérez Firmat recalled his annual family travels north: "Always the best part of these trips was getting a chance to load up on war toys of various vintages, which my brother and I bought up by the dozens at the five-and-ten."[178]

Miami captured the Cuban imagination. In Miami, noted an *El Mundo* correspondent, Cubans found the "most famous shops in the world . . . in which to obtain the most exclusive items, the most elegant styles, and a million knick-knacks at prices within reach of all pockets." Eladio Secades commented perceptively on the Miami phenomenon. "All we Cubans have gone to Miami by now," he observed in 1957. "Miami is the city of hotels and store windows. . . . The sign is visible in numerous establishments: 'SE HABLA ESPAÑOL.' Spanish is spoken everywhere in Miami: in restaurants, in the shops, in the hotels, on the streets. There are moments in which the foreigner could think that what is not spoken in Miami is English." Secades continued: "Miami is the *Ten-Cent* of the United States. It gives the impression of many shops in one large store. It is subject to a tourism which instead of going to see cathedrals and museums goes to window shop. . . . Cuban women go to Miami to shop and to meet the requests of relatives: from an electric mixer to an Elvis Presley pullover." "It is curious to note," remarked an observer in July 1950, "that among the list of passengers . . . women predominate, who travel not only to enjoy vacations that they could more or less have in Cuba, but who go with the expressed purpose to do their shopping, especially shoes, perfumes and clothing in the elegant and air conditioned stores of Miami." "My mother used to shop in Miami all the time," María Sánchez said. "She would leave on the 7 A.M. flight on Saturday, call in the afternoon to make sure we had eaten our lunch, and return on the 7 P.M. flight. Air travel was relatively inexpensive, and would in any case be more than offset by the savings made in merchandise and purchases. Shoes that cost $10 in Havana were purchased for $2 in Miami. She bought shoes for herself, my brothers and sisters and me, as well as towels, sheets, pajamas, and food." Shopping loomed large in the distant Miami memories of José García Pedrosa. "One morning Pepito and I visited one of the large department stores," he remembered. "After filling two sacks with different toys and knickknacks, he saw on display a magnificent bicycle that he wanted. Some papers had to be completed because it was to be an export item. . . . When we returned to the hotel with the sacks full, María also wanted two sacks of toys, and her mother took her out the next day."[179]

Retailers in Havana did not mistake the meaning of travel to Miami. The spectacle of Cuban shopping sprees in Miami caused deepening consternation among Havana merchants. In August 1948 the U.S. commercial attaché wrote of the "adverse effect on retail sales" occasioned by "the unprecedented Cuban tourist migration to the United States," adding: "Such travelers normally return from the United States laden with consumer goods for personal use, families and friends. Miami hotels and stores, fully cognizant of the potentialities of the summer Cuban tourist trade, have been conducting advertising campaigns in Cuba by means of both press and radio and the very high costs at most Cuban vacation resorts have facilitated Florida's efforts to lure Cubans to its shores."[180]

Merchants in Havana responded with annual sales timed to coincide with peak summer travel months and designed to compete with Miami. A summer clothing sale at Lency Modas on Galiano announced "a great sale at prices cheaper than Miami." Indeed, "at Miami prices" became the refrain of sales organized by Cuban retailers.[181]

Merchants also appealed for government intervention, calling for legislation to restrict Cuban purchases abroad. The Chamber of Commerce in Havana complained about the "strong competition of our retail trade within a one-hour flight of Havana." Merchants' organizations threatened Havana newspapers with a boycott if they accepted advertisements from Florida department stores. The U.S. commercial attaché reported in 1952 the growing annoyance of retailers "over the persistent inclination of Cuban tourists to window shop in Havana and then opt for better bargains encountered in Florida." When Cuban authorities finally acquiesced to merchant pressure in 1953 and increased duties, the Miami Beach Chamber of Commerce issued a formal protest to the U.S. State Department, asserting that such charges threatened to "reduce Cuban travel to Miami by 50 percent to 80 percent."[182]

The annual visits of tens of thousands of Cubans to Miami assumed the proportions of ritual and were incorporated into the experience of being Cuban. Miami occupied a large place in the Cuban imagination, a place to take measure of everyday life in the most personal terms. Without being entirely conscious of the larger implications of the experience, vast numbers engaged in a complex meditation on the Cuban condition, setting into motion forces that would extend into the next century. Miami became a familiar world, a representation of things Cuban at their best and appropriated directly as the model of Cuban. Miami was an "extension" of Havana, commented one observer, with "the same blue sky and the Royal Palm." Cubans often quipped that "Biscayne Boulevard [was] merely an extension of Havana's Prado."[183] In some ways it was.

Miami entered the Cuban consciousness as a condition, a state of being, and insinuated itself into daily life as local news. What happened in Miami seemed to matter in Havana. Newspapers and magazines routinely included news stories and feature articles about Miami. Manuel Arrebola wrote a weekly column, "Noticias de Miami," in *El Mundo*, and *Diario de la Marina* published a section "Información de Miami." Miami was characterized as the ideal of the Cuban condition—style, comfort, and convenience—and inevitably subject to appropriation. The circumstances were reminiscent of the Cuban connection to Key West and Tampa in the nineteenth century. "To go to Miami is so common, as if to go to a city in Cuba itself," affirmed José Montó Sotolongo. "Sometimes even more so, and in comfort, hygiene, ambience—everything—it is so pleasant and familiar for us. . . . To speak here of Flagler Street, Biscayne Boulevard, Lincoln Road, Miami Beach, the Seminoles, the pools, and the area of Coral Gables, for example, is to talk about our own places." In 1955 another observer commented: "Miami is not simply close to us in kilometers but it is close by way of identification, which everyday becomes more palpable. . . . At this time there are no *Habaneros* in the beautiful Florida city who do not feel as if we are in our own capital. The names of the stores, streets, restaurants, avenues, and bus lines are as well known to the Cuban as those of the capital, or those of the city where one resides."[184] Mario Parajón declared that "Miami has slowly taken possession of us. Its odes have intoxicated us." He continued:

> Its shops, the bauble and trinkets sold in its stores, have transformed us into children. [Miami] is the "Pandora's box" of Cubans of modest means (*cubanitos modestos*) who wish to travel. It is the temptation of the girls who work in the office and dream of a little escape (*escapadita*) in a cheap excursion during their two week vacation. . . . Miami entices us the way the sirens enticed the ancient mariner. It can overpower us because everyone who visits Miami forgets about the conflicts and the dramas. And to forget the conflicts and dramas is our obsession, it is "our conflict and drama." In Miami one enjoys in life a vacation of a lifetime. And because we go to Miami to rest, it appears to us that Miamians live in perpetual rest and that they never work or toil.[185]

Miami was as much an invention of Cuban needs as Havana was a creation of North American ones. "Miami, in a word, for us Cubans," Rubén Ortiz Lamadrid asserted, "is the anteroom of the home, . . . a cradle of repose for the body and soul." José Montó Sotolongo compared Miami to a "comfortable apartment of a near-by relative where we can visit frequently and easily because it is only a block from our house." "For us," Montó Sotolongo affirmed in language reminiscent of North American tourists in Cuba during the 1920s, "the most important element is that Miami allows us the luxury of leaving the country and remaining close to it at the same time." He added:

> Miami is ideal for tourism: skyscrapers and colonial houses, very modern shops, flashing colors in bathing suits and shorts, air conditioning everywhere, and during the summer season more Cubans than North Americans. At every turn in Miami and Miami Beach, the loud voices of Cubans are heard. The political discussions of our country are heard everywhere, our newspapers are read . . . as if we were on our own soil but with the advantage . . . that we are on vacation.[186]

Miami was escape and pleasure. "In Miami," Berta Arocena insisted, "the most important thing is to free yourself of your woes and enjoy the few days of freedom with the innocence of a small child."[187]

Miami entered the Cuban consciousness as fulfillment of the Cuban ideal, a representation of what Havana could become. It occupied an anomalous place in the Cuban sensibility: a city so near, so similar, but different in the ways that often mattered most. It summoned more invidious comparisons and, as so often in the past, served as a source of disquiet and disappointment. "On Miami streets, hotels, restaurants, and public places, the tourist is free of hustlers and other peddlers," noted a visitor. "One is not detained on the sidewalks, or in the entrance to stores, or getting in or out of automobiles, or at the table where one eats." The difference could not help but invite comparison: "In Havana this condition is so onerous that it produces irritation and anger. In Miami there are no beggars who stop the pedestrian with hand extended. . . . Here one is not confronted with the sight of a family thrown out on the street, with children sleeping on the pavement and young women revealing the desolation of their misery."[188]

Things were so different in Miami. The city offered public access to magnificent beaches. On this subject, Antonio Iraizoz gave poignance to the Cuban meditation: "The beach: that clean and expansive beach that appears to us as symbol of a functional democracy. Everyone can bathe on the beach. . . . The beach belongs to everyone and it is for all." At almost every turn, something invited contrasts and comparisons. "Everything is clean, everything is cared for," Cleto writes to a friend from Miami in Antonio Patiño's novel *Ritmo de la juventud* (1957). "There are no beggars or guides who force themselves on one, or hustlers who make the life of foreigners miserable." Antonio Iraizoz wrote in 1950 of the annual summer "migration to Miami" to escape "our unruliness, our disorder, our official torpor, our uncivilized life, our noise, the lack of beaches, the absence of water, the lack of shame of the men who rule in the country that could be the best and provide everything that Miami has—and more!" In Ramón Ferreira's 1958 play *El hombre inmaculado*, Ana María explains to her fiancé that she wants "to be far away . . . at least in Miami," a preference that no doubt reflected the disquiet of daily life in Havana that year. Ana María continues: "It's near-by . . . but I don't have to listen to talk about politics, or about terrorists, that I shouldn't go to the stores because I could be killed; I want to go shopping and walk the streets at any time with you and without being afraid of anything." After visiting Miami, Mario Guiral Moreno drew the comparison explicitly:

In Miami . . . the pavement of all the streets are in perfect condition, without the potholes and crevices that are found in Havana. Nor does one find there, like we do here, those huge holes . . . where water gathers and sits after rain. . . . Nor does one see in the lovely Florida city, or any other important city in the United States, those horrible construction sites that we find on almost all avenues of Havana. . . . It is likewise true that the sidewalks of all the public streets in Miami are always found clean, because they are scrupulously swept daily, in contrast to what happens in our capital, where the streets— even the principal ones—are seen constantly dirty.[189]

Havana and Miami were reciprocal formulations, always seeming to reproduce each other, relentlessly; Miami was a place where Havana saw its image reflected in imaginings of what Havana could have become. More than any other city in the United States, precisely because of its familiarity, Miami loomed as the dominant ideal. *Carteles* used Miami as the standard against which to measure the state of the nation. "Cuba, we have proclaimed many times," the magazine editorialized as early as 1941, "with minimum effort could be the most prosperous and pleasant place in the universe." But "indolence, apathy, and lack of will" had sapped morale nationwide. In Miami, on the other hand, a city "that until a few years ago was hardly more than an inhospitable sand pit," visitors were astonished to discover the beauty created by a dedicated citizenry. "In Cuba, things are different: there is no public spirit, no civic pride."[190]

The dominant discursive structure of the Havana-Miami narrative was contrast. Perhaps it could not have been any other way, for to be in Miami was like being in Havana but more so: the recognition of similarities could not occur without the realization of differences. A columnist using the pen name "El Curioso Parlanchín" told of friends who, after vacationing in Miami, "upon returning to our capital were rudely shocked by the violent and disagreeable impression, due to the contrast observed in the order, tranquility, the good education, the mutual respect among residents, and the cleanliness of Miami, with the disorder, the insufferable noise, the misconduct, and the individual egoism of Havana." Gabino Delgado experienced Miami as a revelation of Havana. "Fifty minutes from Havana," he wrote in 1949, "one finds a different world, a life dramatically opposed to ours, and possessed with the means to contrast our ways." Delgado continued:

Accustomed to a lack of respect, to scandal, to political chicanery, abuse, insult, and to a range of irregularities that are today common in our daily life, the Cuban likes to find himself in Miami, because there he functions with a discreet, serious, respectful and moral standard that is characteristic of North American life. He is taken aback by the courtesy and consideration he receives in the bus, in the hotel, in the restaurants and shops. . . . When he lives the North American life, when he observes how public officials work in behalf of the citizens, promote their maximum well-being, are attentive to their needs, he has to think: And why do my government officials not treat me in the same manner?

Delgado concluded: "Our politicians have not learned anything, for they have failed to establish here anything they have seen there. But the people, who have been travelling to Miami by the thousands, are slowly seeing the light. And the object lesson that they are learning will someday lead to their reclaiming the benefits to which they are entitled."[191]

Miami was itself a city in transition, in large part driven by the logic of the Cuban experience and the power of Cuban needs. After 1959 this transformation assumed dramatic dimensions. It is not certain, of course, that the changes would have proceeded as quickly or as extensively had there not been a huge emigration in the wake of the Cuban revolution. However, the changes that occurred during the fifteen years between the time Eladio Secades observed that nearly every store in Miami advertised "Se habla español" and the year that Edward Linehan visited the city on assignment for *National Geographic* and noted "signs in some shop windows read 'English spoken here'" more than adequately prepared the way for the post-1959 migration.[192]

Miami was transformed by the Cuban presence. From its very beginnings the city had appropriated Cuban as pretension and panache: it fashioned itself as "Latin," trading on mild winter weather, Royal Palms, Spanish colonial architecture, Spanish street names, and nightclubs with exotic names booking tropical acts. Certainly this held strong appeal for North American tourists. But Cubans traveled to Miami for many of the same reasons and found Miami sufficiently recognizable, whereupon they proceeded to make it more familiar, more authentic, more their own. Powerful economic and cultural forces had set in place the basic structures that would facilitate and, indeed, foster the gigantic migration after 1959. The more Miami became familiar, the more it became Cuban. Hundreds of thousands of Cubans had experienced Miami as an extension of home, like *El Mundo* editor Luis Botifoll, who had vacationed annually in Miami for years and for whom, his biographer affirmed, "living in Miami . . . was a natural choice . . . when he left his native island." Writer David Rief dined with Raúl and Ninón Rodríguez, the "most glamorous couple in Cuban Miami," and learned that "as children, the Rodríguezes had come regularly to Miami." In short, "It was scarcely a foreign place." Ofelia Schutte recalled learning when her family was "thinking of leaving Cuba for good": "Miami looked like the only legitimate destination, and my parents decisively took it."[193]

7

ILLUSIVE EXPECTATIONS

The habit of consuming American products, or better, perhaps, the necessity of consuming them, the basis of our commercial relations with the United States, is very pronounced in Cuba. This necessity has been created not only by that facility of being in contact with the great commercial centers of the world, but also the development of primary, secondary, and superior education and of the habits of hygiene and civilized life in all classes of society. The Cuban, even the peasant from the most remote localities, is familiar with the thousands upon thousands of articles which industry of man has created to satisfy the natural desire for a more healthful, pleasant, and comfortable life.
—Guillermo Patterson y Jaureguí, Cuban Ambassador to the United States, 1936

Before the Revolution, everything here was from the United States. Whatever they had, we wanted too. We lived as if we were a city of the United States.
—Inocencia Acosta Felipe, in Oscar Lewis, Ruth M. Lewis, and Susan M. Rigdon, *Four Women*, 1977

The destiny of Cuba cannot be to sell sugar in order to buy automobiles.
—Hilda Perera, *Mañana es 26*, 1960

Years ago . . . if a family fell upon hard times, the first thing that would be said was: "They have just lost their automobile."
—*El Mundo*, November 18, 1954

Why do we have to live down here when others live up there? Why can't we become rich? What can I do? I don't know what I'm living for. To be starving to death all my life! We live worse than dogs! Better to die than live like this! . . . Ay, to be poor is such a humiliation!
—Tita Mina, in Nicolás Dorr, *La puerta de tablitas*, 1977

The Castro regime seems to have sprung from a deep and widespread dissatisfaction with social and economic conditions as they have been heretofore in Cuba and to respond to an overwhelming demand for change and reform.
—U.S. Ambassador Philip W. Bonsal, August 1959

The 1950s were difficult years in Cuba for almost everyone. Political corruption and public malfeasance certainly contributed to these conditions. So, too, did economic uncertainty. But the crisis of the 1950s had more to do with the way these circumstances combined to undermine some of the most fundamental assumptions around which the proposition of "Cuban" had assumed definitive form.

Some of this was related to the military coup of March 10, 1952. It was not simply that General Fulgencio Batista had overturned a democratically elected government and subsequently suspended constitutional guarantees and abrogated civil liberties. These were not small misdeeds, of course. Cubans had taken considerable pride in the Constitution of 1940. Its promulgation announced the end of one age and the onset of another. The new constitution established a model liberal democracy, affirming civil liberties, economic freedom, and social justice. It had been hailed as a triumph of civilization, variously described as "one of the world's most advanced," a "progressive model for all of Latin America," "modern and advanced." "One of the most progressive on the continent—in some respects ahead of its time," affirmed Néstor Carbonell. Fernando Alvarez Tabío proclaimed that Cuba's place among "modern constitutional democracies" was secure.[1]

THE REALITY OF EXPERIENCE

The military coup had undone more than a decade of constitutional development in ways that were direct and immediate. But the decisive blow occurred at another level entirely. Cubans celebrated their success in the development of democratic government, ratified by the 1940 Constitution and confirmed by three successive national elections. Only months before the military coup, Ernesto Ardura had written joyfully about the prospects of democracy in Cuba. "We have been able to strengthen our democracy," he argued, "eliminate tyrants and develop the Republic by ways of progress. . . . The Constitution of 1940 has been the historic solution. All ignominy has gradually disappeared and the Cuban Republic has been developing by way of true democratic sustenance."[2]

The larger implications of the coup, and certainly its deeper significance, were to be found at the point where it shattered collective self-esteem and undermined some of the most cherished assumptions of self-representation. The celebrated Constitution of 1940 had been unceremoniously shunted aside by a common barracks revolt, forcing Cubans to confront a reality that most would have thought unimaginable only months earlier. Cuba was different from other Latin American countries, Cubans were wont to insist. It had registered notable progress and could rightfully claim its place alongside the select group of modern liberal constitutional democracies of the world. Constitutional legality, free elections, freedom of speech, and a free press were attributes of advanced civilized nations by virtue of which Cubans claimed membership. This was the proposition of constitutionality and the rule of law as a condition of civilization, encoded into the larger narrative of nationality and modernity. Ernesto Ardura had asked only two years previously, "Are we civilized?" Answering in the affirmative, he asserted: "We have even established a permanent climate of freedom and an exercise of liberties and an exercise of democracy in which the will of the people determines results."[3]

The military coup changed everything. The tenor of public discourse was henceforth openly characterized by embarrassment and humiliation, doubt and diminished confidence. "We had pride that the 1940 Constitution was one of the most advanced of our time," lamented Jorge Mañach. Auténtico Party candidate for the presidency in 1952, Carlos Hevia wrote to the State Department describing "the humiliation of [Cubans] losing their right to elect their Government." The U.S. economic affairs counsel, Harold Randall, reported the feeling of "most people . . . of resentment, if not shame, at the fact that Cuba does not have a constitutional government." Ambassador Arthur Gardner later observed that the coup had "wounded the pride of many Cubans." John Dorshner and Roberto Fabricio described Cubans who joined the opposition "out of a sense of embarrassment, a feeling that while they could boast of their air conditioners and TV sets that seemed to put them almost on a par with Americans, they had as government a shabby military dictatorship that seemed more worthy of an old banana republic than a country aspiring to join the modern world."[4]

Things were never quite the same after March 10, 1952. The military coup reached deeply into the sources of self-representation and self-confidence, from whence the most widely shared and deeply held formulations of nationality and identity originated. Cuba's claim to civilization and membership in the community of modern countries was called into question. After March 10, Andrés Felipe Labrador later wrote, "Cuba ceased to belong to the world." Hernández Travieso could not help wonder if the coup revealed that "we are incapable of exercising democracy and, as a result, spiritually we have gone back to the colonial era, where our grandparents lived reconciled to law being the caprice of a Captain General." "Control of the country was taken in such an illegal manner," journalism professor Arnaldo Ramos Yaniz lamented, "as if Cuba were a country where the laws of the jungle prevailed." The violation of the 1940 Constitution, Herminio Portell Vilá reflected, "makes one wonder if perhaps it would be preferable not to have laws that will be violated, even though by not having them we would find ourselves in regard to civilization below the savage tribes of New Guinea and the Amazon. . . . The foreign visitor departs from our country thinking that the gloss of civilization has not penetrated very deeply."[5]

The moral was only hinted at, by insinuation and innuendo, but it was on many people's minds. Perhaps Cuba was not so different from other Latin American countries after all. "We Cubans moved about the democratic world with our heads held high," Portell Vilá commented, "proud that after so many years of turbulence beyond the reach of a constitution, we had ten years of guaranteed political rights and personal liberties. . . . Travelers from Central America, South America, and the West Indies . . . considered Cuba, and with good reason, an oasis of liberties." Carlos Hevia linked the absence of "elements essential to free men" directly to the inability "to advance along the road of material improvement." He continued: "That is the sad picture of Cuba today, of a Cuba that had presented itself proudly before the world, and especially before its sister republics in the Americas, for having been able to overcome the sordid era of military coups." Ernesto Ardura stated bluntly what many were suggesting indirectly: "At the moment we believed that Cuba had consolidated its democratic institutions and that it had reached a political maturity that could serve as an example in the continent, a de facto regime has come to wake us up to reality and has brought us to the common level of the Latin American countries."[6]

Throughout the 1950s, men and women of goodwill observed firsthand and from afar the exercise of democracy in the United States and drew comparisons that were both invidious and inevitable. The military coup took a large toll on national morale. The U.S. presidential elections in November 1952 only deepened Cuban anguish. "These North American elections," political commentator Manuel Bisbé observed, "make us think with sadness about the ones we could not complete on June 1." Leví Marrero, who was in the United States during the 1954 congressional elections, wrote on his return of "the vote freely given and honestly counted," where "the people, without violence and scandal, can truly decide with the bloc of their votes." This process, Marrero added, "necessarily consolidates our faith in democracy as a system, although here we are still far from reaching . . . a similar position that will someday make us respectable among free people."[7]

The military coup also opened a deep divide between Cubans and North Americans. The apparent indifference with which the U.S. government reacted to the abrogation of civil liberties in Cuba shocked and appalled many on the island. Cubans were unabashed admirers of North American democratic institutions and enormously susceptible to their appeal. Their shared institutions had created an affinity and important linkages between the two countries. North Americans had made much of the virtues of democratic institutions, a discourse that had contributed to the shaping of Cuban civic sensibilities. Dartmouth alumnus Benito Vilá would later write about "the guarantees I was brought up with," which included "freedom of speech, due process, a jury trial, the right to confront one's accusers." Eliseo Riera Gómez, a naturalized U.S. citizen, could hardly contain his indignation at Washington's acceptance of the Batista government. "The fact that Cuba . . . deprived of its public freedoms and under the sway of a military dictatorship," Riera Gómez protested, "has to arouse in the democratic public opinion in the United States . . . a desire to condemn such a situation. Never was the present time more right, since the United States is constantly calling the free world to oppose and resist the aggression of Soviet totalitarianism, and little could be said of these preachings if some of the peoples appeared to suffer, in their internal life, an oppression and indignity of a nature similar to that which they are requested to fight."[8]

The estrangement deepened as resistance to the Batista government expanded and repression increased. To the incredulity and mounting indignation of the opposition, the United States openly supported Batista. Ambassador Gardner often heaped lavish praise on the dictator. *New York Times* correspondent Ruby Hart Phillips was not alone in believing that "at times [Gardner] even embarrassed President Batista with his support."[9] The use of U.S. arms and ammunition, airplanes and artillery, tanks, bombs, and equipment against the opposition intensified public ire. Almost all the officers and technical support staff of Batista's armed forces received training under the U.S. Military Assistance Program (MAP). Nearly 75 percent of the pilots, 90 percent of the air force technicians, and almost all the naval officers were U.S.-trained. Almost 90 percent of the officers of the First Infantry Battalion dispatched to the Sierra Maestra were trained by U.S. personnel; half of its equipment had been obtained through MAP.

The 1952 military coup plunged the island's political system into disarray. Political repression and armed resistance increasingly became the principal civic transaction between the government and the governed from which there seemed neither respite over time nor immediate remedy. But it was no less certain that the sources of the people's discontent were far more complex and elusive. The Cuban economy was in the throes of profound adjustments to structural changes, the primary effect of which was to reveal that many of the fundamental assumptions of daily life were flawed or worse: in many instances, they were shown to be false.

The realization had been slow in coming. The surge of economic growth occasioned first by World War II and later the Korean War had obscured the structural weaknesses of the export economy. World sugar prices increased and Cuban production expanded. Imports rose nearly 25 percent, from $515 million in 1950 to $640 million in 1951. "Havana port warehouses," reported the U.S. embassy in language recalling the situation in 1920, "are filled to capacity due to a tremendous influx of imports by local merchants. . . . Ships arriving in Havana cannot be certain that dock facilities will be available for the discharge of cargo." A month later the State Department received further news: "In-bound Havana harbor ship congestion was more of a problem in October. . . . Some boats have had to wait a week for a berth. Goods piled on dock waiting delivery are probably greater than even before." Private construction of homes and business establishments reached new levels. Building permits issued in Havana in 1950 had represented a value 50 percent higher than in 1949, an estimated $46.4 million for 3,342 buildings. Total receipts for first-run films increased 17 percent, from $2.6 million to $3.1 million. Retail sales rose. Imports of consumer durables soared. "The widespread prosperity and higher payrolls," the U.S. commercial attaché reported in 1952, "had reflection in the more active retailing prosperity of consumer goods, which reached a peak in the weeks before Christmas and which was notable in autos and household equipment, including refrigerators, washing machines and TV sets."[10]

Under the circumstances, it may have been difficult to realize that Cuba was nearing a crisis. Prosperity and plenty were everywhere in evidence, it seemed, and the good life for many remained unaffected. In fact, however, the limits of economic growth had been reached decades earlier. By the early 1950s Cuba had no place to go but down. Hard times arrived after 1953. The "conditions of real depression," the U.S. commercial attaché commented tersely, ". . . had not been escaped; they have been merely postponed."[11]

Sugar was losing its capacity to sustain economic growth. The last sugar mill had been built in 1925; indeed, Cuba could not increase the world supply of sugar without risking a reduction in prices. In 1922, with a population of nearly 3 million people, Cuba had exported 5 million tons of sugar, 3.9 million tons of it to the United States. In 1956 Cuba still exported 5.1 million tons of sugar, 2.6 million tons of which reached the United States, but the population had more than doubled to 6.5 million people. World markets, moreover, were increasingly quota-controlled and tariff-protected, further limiting prospects of expanded sugar exports. In the early 1920s Cuba had produced 20 percent of the world's supply of sugar, but by the mid-1950s the Cuban share had declined to 10 percent. Cuba existed in a world, the National Bank of Cuba warned somberly in 1956, that "does not offer sufficient markets to absorb all that the country can produce today and tomorrow." Between 1952 and 1954 the decline in the international sugar market precipitated the first of a series of recessions. Per capita income fell by 18 percent, neutralizing the gains of postwar prosperity. In 1956 the National Bank estimated that the gross national product had increased sufficiently between 1948 and 1954 to permit the maintenance of the 1947 living standard in only five of the seven years; in only two years (1951 and 1952) was it sufficient to permit a 2 percent increase over the 1947 level. At this rate, the National Bank predicted grimly, the sugar harvest of 1965 would have to reach 9.3 million tons and obtain a value of almost $800 million to guarantee the population in 1965 the same living standard that it had enjoyed in 1947.[12]

In fact, Cubans had been living in the past, and only in the 1950s did they arrive at the realization that the future was uncertain indeed. The data were bleak and the consensus was chilling. Real income was increasing slowly and sometimes not at all. The purchasing power of exports between 1952 and 1956 remained at approximately the same levels as thirty years earlier. In other words, Cubans were worse off in the 1950s than they had been in the 1920s. "The increment in net per capita income registered in the last 25 years," reported the United Nations Economic Commission in 1955, "and particularly during the post-war period, constitutes, in large measure, a mere return to the income levels already attained in Cuba in the past." The International Bank for Reconstruction and Development arrived at similar conclusions. "The present per capita income of about $300 is only slightly above that of the early 1920s," commented the bank in 1951, adding: "Cuba's present standard of living . . . depends mainly on an industry which stopped growing many years ago." It also observed that "Cuba is living in—and on—the past and weakened by events beyond her control." The U.S. Department of Commerce also warned of "the extent of the problem confronting Cuba in its efforts to maintain, let alone increase, the standard of living of its people." Per capita income during the 1950s was in flux, moving irrevocably if irregularly downward. Between 1957 and 1958 per capita income declined again, this time by nearly 10 percent, from $370 to $335.[13]

Unemployment and underemployment added further uncertainty and insecurity in households across the island. Precise data are difficult to obtain, but contemporary commentators agreed that about 600,000 to 800,000 men and women, approximately one-third of the total labor force, languished permanently in conditions between unemployment and underemployment. "Unemployment continues to be a major problem," observed economic affairs counsel C. A. Boonstra in 1955, "especially in the provinces, and is particularly severe during the summer and early fall months in rhythm with the seasonal slump in the economy."[14]

Many Cubans were at a loss to make sense of their times. They had prepared for a world that did not exist, trained to function within structures that were incapable of serving their needs adequately, if at all, struggling to get by—and failing. The implications of a stalled economy were set in dramatic relief by the steady population growth. An estimated 40,000 men and women annually reached working age in an economy unable to generate sufficient employment opportunities. Between 1955 and 1958 approximately 8,000 new jobs were created in industry during a period in which about 160,000 young Cubans joined the labor force. "In the cafés of the towns," noted Agustín Tamargo in 1956, "in the grocery stores of the sugar towns or on the porches of the houses in the mill, one sees large numbers of youths who have nothing to do. They are not ill or disabled. They are simply the latest shipment that upon arriving to working age find everything occupied and nothing remaining for them."[15]

Nor were unemployment hardships limited to the working class. Cubans of all classes, including and especially the middle class, men and women with education and preparation, faced diminishing prospects. The economy could not absorb the 1,200 young men and women graduating every year from the University of Havana. "How many of them will pass on to enlarge the long columns of the unemployed that make up the majority of our work-age men?"

Leví Marrero asked in 1955. Legions of surplus lawyers could not find work for which they were trained and accepted low-paying jobs as clerks and secretaries. The University of Havana was graduating annually an average of 200 physicians for whom there was no employment. By 1955 there were about 3,000 unemployed doctors, many of whom were obliged to work as orderlies and pharmacists. It was to these sectors of the middle class that Fidel Castro addressed his comments in *History Will Absolve Me* in 1953, "the 10,000 . . . doctors, engineers, lawyers, veterinarians, school teachers, dentists, pharmacists, newspapermen, painters, sculptors, etc., who come forth from school with their degrees, anxious to work and full of hope, only to find themselves at a dead end with all doors closed and where no one hears their clamor or supplication."[16]

By the 1950s Cubans were publicly discussing the "crisis of the professions," specifically the growing number of university graduates unable to find employment. "Rather than create many universities to train physicians, lawyers, and architects," Andrés Valdespino suggested, "and thereby making the professional crisis daily more acute, technical schools appropriate for . . . our geographic and economic environment should be built."[17]

But graduates of technical schools were not faring much better. A group of students at the Industrial Technical School in Ranchos Boyeros wrote to *Bohemia* to complain that after years of training they faced few prospects of employment. In fact, insisted *Bohemia*, the lack of opportunity was aggravated by "the lack of factories and shops in sufficient numbers to absorb those Cuban technicians upon graduation."[18]

Employment possibilities were deteriorating, moreover, at the precise moment that difficult economic times were forcing more women, especially middle-class women, into the labor force as a strategy to arrest and reverse declining living standards. All through the mid-1950s increasing numbers of women were obliged to seek work outside the home. "Without doubt we have lost the home," affirmed Filomena García Betancourt, a teacher at the Instituto Nacional Cubano teacher, in 1955, "and from that perspective we cannot but lament that women have found themselves obliged to work out on the street." She concluded: "I myself am an example of this. If I had my way, I would be at home, dedicated exclusively to my children, my husband, my home. But the necessities created by modern life, impose on me the obligation to contribute to the support of the house. . . . Imagine a home with children, in which the earnings of the man are not adequate to cover all expenses."[19]

The cost of living cast a dark shadow over households of all social classes: among salaried professionals and wage workers, homemakers and students, in the city and in the countryside. The cost of basic foodstuffs was rising, in some regions by as much as 40 percent. Price increases in Havana between 1956 and 1957 affected almost every staple of the daily diet. "Cost of food has risen considerably during the month," reported first secretary R. M. Connell, "and the scarcity of certain staple items may force the working man's expenditures for food to an even higher level." From 1956 to 1957 the price of animal products increased 4.1 percent; vegetable products rose by 9.2 percent. In some instances the rise for specific products was dramatic: potatoes (37 percent), black beans (31 percent), and rice (28 percent). In early 1958 prices increased again: potatoes (52 percent), black beans (88 percent), and rice (30 percent).[20]

The full toll of Cuban integration into the North American market structures was becoming apparent. Cuban consumption of U.S. imports came at prices higher than consumers paid in the United States. While salaries and wages remained comparatively fixed through the 1950s, the value of foreign imports increased from $515 million in 1950 to $649 million in 1956 to $777 million in 1958. The International Bank estimated that the average ratio of Cuban imports to national income ranked among the highest in the world, averaging more than 26 percent for the years 1945–49. The increased spending on imports as income increased was estimated to be even higher. Between 1903 and 1940 fifty cents of each additional dollar of national income was spent on imports. "The Cuban people," Antonio Riccordi maintained as early as 1948, "and especially the popular classes, can not live off what they earn, simply because everything becomes daily more expensive. Cuba is largely an importer country and almost everything that it needs and consumes must come from abroad for which we must pay whatever is demanded." Rufo López Fresquet agreed: "We have become accustomed to import products, acquired over centuries of waiting for ships to satisfy the larger part of our needs. . . . We like to consume in ways varied and large." At a time of mounting economic difficulties, Cubans paid U.S. prices plus the cost of transportation and handling, insurance fees, tariffs and taxes, and the obligatory markups charged by local wholesalers and retailers. The result was often prices twice and sometimes three times U.S. retail costs. A television costing $160 in the United States sold for as much as $550 in Cuba. A hi-fi console with radio and phonograph priced at $170 cost $695. Charges for farm equipment were about 35 percent higher, with repair parts costing 40 percent more. New car prices were similarly higher: a Chrysler costing $2,350 in the United States sold for $4,000 in Cuba; a Pontiac priced at $1,800 was marked up to $3,000. Even where the wages of Havana industries compared favorably to those in the United States, commented the U.S. commercial attaché, "living costs generally were almost twice those of Washington."[21]

The most compelling confirmation of mounting living costs was provided by reasonably well-paid U.S. government personnel assigned to Cuba. North American officials struggled to make ends meet. Naval attaché Lieutenant A. J. Powers advised "women and children accompanying naval personnel to Cuba, to bring sufficient clothing to meet requirements for a period of one year. Clothing for both women and children may be obtained in Cuba but at a considerably higher cost than in the United States. . . . Generally speaking clothing for women and children may be purchased in Cuba for approximately 80 percent to 100 percent higher cost than in the United States. Foodstuffs purchased in the local markets are very expensive. . . . Almost all items to be found in American grocery stores can be found in Havana, but are priced at from 100 to 200 percent higher than in the principal cities in the United States." First secretary R. M. Connell reported that "automobile repair and operating costs are 50 to 100 percent more than those in the United States. Expenditures for clothing and medical and dental treatment vary with individual necessity but are higher than they are in the United States. Entertainment is expensive, and luncheons, cocktail parties or dinners generally cost at least twice as much as they do in the United States." Chargé Daniel Braddock agreed:

> With certain exceptions, both men's and ladies' clothing of United States manufacture or quality is available in Cuba, but at prices well above those in the United States. American-made shoes are also available but at a considerable price mark-up. . . . It would cost a man or a woman nearly double the cost in the United States to maintain an American standard of dress in Cuba. . . . Articles of personal and household use such as cosmetics, toothpaste, shaving supplies, gasoline, tobacco, cigarettes, household tools, etc., are readily available although at higher prices than those in the United States. . . . Generally speaking it is estimated that it costs about 40 percent more to live in Havana (according to American standards) than it does in Washington, D.C. . . . All types of pharmaceuticals, drugs and medicines are available in Cuba but at prices considerably higher than the United States. . . . All standard U.S. medical products can be obtained in Cuba at about 30 percent over the going U.S. prices.[22]

Cuban families in both the capital and the provinces grimly faced downward mobility, with no relief, with no respite. A 1953 survey of leading merchants in the provinces concluded ominously that the "buying power of their clientele is drying up rapidly." Land in Vedado selling for $12 a meter in 1941 cost $200 a meter in 1957. The prospects of home ownership were diminishing for increasing numbers of the middle class. At the same time rents were rising even as the supply of affordable housing decreased. "Adequate houses and apartments are almost impossible to obtain at rental prices less than exorbitant," reported one U.S. embassy official. A sure sign of the times was an advertisement by car dealership J. Ulloa and Company: "The era of the large, high-powered, and high-priced car is passing. The present times demand in Cuba small cars that can move efficiently through congestion and park in small spaces. Cars whose low prices and efficient use of gas and oil reduce the out-flow of foreign exchange and protect the Cuban economy. . . . These difficult demands can best be met in the sensational German automobile, the Volkswagen."[23]

The buying power of tens of thousands of families was in decline. Many deferred purchases. "I've been trying to buy my wife a refrigerator for two years," a worker explained to Agustín Tamargo, "but the money I earn is hardly enough for shoes for the kids. The good times here are over."[24] Many plunged deeper into debt. Households across the island struggling to stave off insolvency and hold indebtedness at bay failed on both counts.

Perhaps no other concern preoccupied as many Cubans as the cost of living. Labor unionists in all sectors—longshoremen, machinists, shoe workers, commercial workers, miners, bakers, bus drivers, pharmaceutical employees, petroleum workers, railway workers, telephone company employees—repeatedly called for wage increases of 15 to 30 percent. Restaurant workers demanded a 60 percent reduction in rents. Textile workers called on the government to "carry on an effective campaign against the high cost of living." A survey conducted by *El Mundo* as early as 1951 revealed widespread public anxiety about rising living costs. The discrepancy between income and what people needed to buy was most vividly expressed in a deepening disquiet. "Money is not worth anything," protested Fidelina Quintana. "Lard, rice, the cost of everything, has risen a great deal. In sum, what I was able to do earlier with 3 pesos I cannot now with 6." "One can't live this way," complained Amalia Díaz, and Olivia Montalvo despaired that she was "going crazy" trying to cope with food prices that were "going through the clouds." A survey five years later suggested that concerns were mounting. "We are living in a fictitious world if one considers how expensive life is in our country," observed transportation worker Juan Núñez. "We apparently believe that this can be tolerable, but upon second look we see that we work to eat." Sales clerk Ada García indicated that the cost of living was so high "that one can hardly earn enough to buy bread every day. And on top of that," she added, "one has to pay for the education of the children. What then remains for one who earns a modest salary?" Student Hiram Sánchez Valle commented that the high cost of living was "especially difficult for a large family like mine. Most of the primary necessities are beyond the reach of the citizenry for lack of means."[25]

The 1950s were years of deepening crisis, of disquiet and despair, of disappointment and disillusionment. A pall of uncertainty settled over Cuban households. Many people had reached adulthood in the 1940s and 1950s; with families of their own, they had been sustained by expectations of a bright future only to find the future had arrived and there was nothing. Worse still, there was no more future. Héctor Quintero's play *Contigo pan y cebolla* (1962), set in Havana during the late 1950s, captures the tenor of the times. "All my life waiting, waiting, waiting," Lala despairs, "filled with hopes, with ambitions, making plans for the future, and now at 38 years of age, only 38 years, I am tired. . . . And what have I achieved? Only hopes. Hopes for the future. And when will that future arrive?" Families could no longer summon visions of the future with reasonable confidence. "There is a profound and painful sensation of frustration among the majority of our people," Joaquín Martínez Sáenz lamented in 1956. Ernesto Ardura agreed: "Whoever lends an ear to public opinion, can appreciate the state of uncertainty and confusion in which the Cuban people live. There is something of a sensation of shipwreck. That psychological state of desperation can be observed in all social classes: among workers, industrialists, and merchants, in the suffering middle class. The common psychological denominator of the national moment is lassitude and profound disillusionment. . . . There is no enthusiasm, there are no great plans with an eye to the future, for the future is a huge cloud and offers security to no one." Andrés Valdespino struck a similar note, suggesting that there was "no reason to be surprised that many young people, at an age noted for great hopes and pure ideals, are disappointed, cynics, pessimists and skeptics. Prematurely old. And it is by that means that the very roots of nationality are destroyed." José Lezama Lima despaired privately. "We are now in the chaos resulting from the disintegration, confusion, and inferiority of Cuban life of the last thirty years," he confided to his diary in September 1957. "On one hand, fear, bewilderment, confusion. On the other, desperation."[26]

Tens of thousands of young men and women faced a future with few prospects and almost no choices. "In Cuba," wrote Armando Soto in 1955, "economic well-being is a pure game of chance for limited prizes. We live in a country where employment is scarce and where it is possible to spend a lifetime waiting for a good opportunity to arrive." He concluded, "Our youth do not know what to do or how to do it," adding: "They are young men and women spiritually overwhelmed by the reality they contemplate. Their greatest wretchedness is the lack of confidence in themselves, expressed in feelings of inferiority and insecurity. What is clear is that young people have the possibilities of success limited by economic imperatives that currently cannot be overcome." One year later Agustín Tamargo wrote about the same youth, an estimated 240,000 young men and women who had entered the job market since the military coup of 1952 and could not find work. "These young people," he affirmed, "who make up the desperate population, the most recently produced in Cuba, are the ones who identify with the heroic tendency of Fidel Castro, who take actions on the street. . . . They are found in all parts and everywhere speak the language: the language of rage and revulsion."[27]

Much of what had served as the basis on which to form reasonable expectations of personal fulfillment and measure individual success had its origins in U.S. market structures. What was particularly remarkable about these developments was the degree to which North American modalities had taken hold, independently of concrete economic conditions. Cubans had embraced standards and developed expectations that were perhaps as unrealistic as they were unattainable. It was simply impossible to sustain consumption levels of such magnitude within dependent capitalist structures of a sugar export economy.

Cubans were losing the capacity to maintain the living standards to which they had become accustomed. Few could sustain—or at least sustain for very long—the standards around which vital notions of well-being, status, and security had been derived and defined. The Cuban per capita income of $370 could not support a living standard developed for the United States, where the per capita income was over $2,000; even in Mississippi, the poorest state in the union, it exceeded $1,000. This was an environment in which status and well-being had been largely defined by consumption. It was not merely that living standards were objectively in decline, but also that the world from which vast numbers had derived bearing and meaning was in turmoil and transition. What made these conditions particularly difficult was that much of what mattered most as sources of status and security was invested in the possession of these goods. The meaning of consumption had registered with far greater resonance in its social function than its economic form, especially in the degree to which consumption and display of products had implied stability and security. A lifestyle adopted by countless Cubans as their own, and with which identity was constant and complete, was becoming increasingly elusive and moving out of reach.

Nothing seems to have changed during the 1950s, of course, except that it was becoming impossible for more and more Cubans to participate in these transactions even as they inhabited an environment filled with representations of abundance and affluence, as depicted in motion pictures and on television, in automobile showrooms and store window displays, mail order catalogs, and advertisements in newspapers and magazines. Reyita Castillo recalled the 1950s as "a time of plenty in Cuba, [when] the shops were filled with all the things that one could possibly want. The only thing lacking was the money to buy them."[28]

At least as important as the level of well-being that Cubans had achieved was the level to which they aspired. The problem was not simply, or perhaps even mainly, the performance of the economy, but the assumption that Cubans were promised—and therefore entitled to—something better than what they had. The appeal of the "American way of life" had resonated in Cuba, except that expectations had surpassed possibilities. Cubans were surrounded by the artifacts of a way of life to which increasing numbers could no longer reasonably aspire. It was precisely from this widening gap between aspiration and achievement, between experience and expectation, that many structural tensions and social strains of the 1950s originated.

The pressure to sustain living standards weighed heavily on households across the island. Informed observers were not slow to recognize the symptoms even if they did not always identify the sources. For decades Cuban needs had been stimulated—and satisfied—by commodities. It was not always necessary for commodities to mediate Cuban needs immediately, or even easily, as long as the possibility of that fulfillment remained reasonably available to most. By the mid-1950s, even the pretense of illusion was difficult to sustain. "The North

Americans have passed so much time," observed Rubén Ortiz Lamadrid in 1956, "nearly half a century, pounding into the public mind that 'anyone can be a Henry Ford if he has the resolve,' that the average man in the United States, and by extension in the countries in its orbit, is not content with anything less. The press, the motion pictures, radio, and now television have contributed . . . to instilling in the popular spirit the postulates of that philosophy." Cuba was no exception, Ortiz Lamadrid insisted:

> On the contrary, our case is aggravated due to all the bad examples. . . . The man on the street, if he does not reach those exceptional summits of wealth and power, considers himself a failure. And as long as he has one bit of life, he persists in the absurdity of projecting his ambitions totally outside his possibilities. . . . It is often good that a society tries to improve itself, that one of its members undertakes a major personal effort toward that end. But when such a concept serves to disorient, when that man does not receive compensation in obtaining and enjoying the riches . . . proportional to his antecedents, capacity, and social medium, something is basically wrong, and the methods of education and knowledge must be rectified, considering them fallacious and demoralizing. A new way of living must be learned.[29]

Some of the most fundamental premises around which public life and private hopes had formed were under severe strain. Increasingly the realization took hold that the assumptions on which much of Cuban life had been based were unusable. The inability to sustain purchasing power suggested that consumption could no longer serve as an integrative national force. Consumer culture was losing its institutional base. Goods, associated with uplift and upward looking, had always possessed subversive potential, making possible imaginative transport across the threshold of everyday life to unbounded expectations. U.S. market forces could arouse expectations, and once turned loose, these hopes could serve as a powerful source of self-actualization. But to be denied those goods once access had been presumed could be no less subversive.

The original North American intent had been successful: it did produce the desire to consume. The only problem was that the power of its appeal assumed all-encompassing dimensions and attracted Cubans of all social classes to its possibilities. Vast numbers had been formed by the imperative of U.S. market structures, into which they were integrated and from which they derived their bearings. They were conversant with the vernacular of the market and familiar, too, with its requirements. They had invested themselves in these relationships. Consumption of North American commodities was self-implicating and served as a source of self-definition. Commodity and self converged and by the mid-twentieth century had emerged as one of the salient characteristics of nationality. Through commodities Cubans had become deeply invested in the market system and, inevitably, dependent on their ability to sustain access to the supply of goods and services. Nationality incorporated an ideal of identity by embracing certain modes of perception and certain idioms of representation. Whether all people participated all the time—which they did not—mattered less than the ideal that inspired plausible expectations of access.

At the heart of the deepening crisis in the 1950s was the collapse of the central formulations by which a people had come to define themselves. This was far more complex than a political conflict. It was a crisis of individual identity and inevitably a crisis of nationality. These assumptions had insinuated themselves into every facet of the narrative on nationality, so that doubt as to their relevance or denial of their usefulness inevitably called into question some of the most fundamental concepts of nationality. These assumptions were embedded deeply in the meaning of Cuban, and to challenge them necessarily implied changing the meaning of Cuban.

Tastes and preferences had been variously influenced by U.S. motion pictures and television, travel and education, and the dictates of changing styles. It was virtually impossible to distinguish the Cuban market from its counterpart in the North, for in almost every sense the former was an extension of the latter. Mass-produced consumer goods, processed foods, and clothing lines were distributed through extensive wholesale networks and highly efficient retail chains and department stores. Woolworth and Sears were as much a presence in Cuba as they were in the United States. North American products dominated the Cuban market. In 1946 Woolworth's sales approached $4 million annually. Arid deodorant generated $150,000 in sales revenue in 1953. Cubans shaved with Gillette, took pictures with Kodak, shampooed with Lustre-Creme, smoked Camel cigarettes, and enjoyed JELL-O for dessert.[30]

Consumption patterns were replicated and acquired similar meanings, which meant that economic transactions implied deeper social and psychological significance. Items of consumption were not only, or even principally, valued for their utility but rather for their power to signify. Personal identity had become thoroughly implicated in the North American market through commodities and merchandise linking personal well-being to consumption. For Reyita Castillo, the purchase of a Firestone radio with her own earnings was a momentous occasion. She reminisced to her daughter:

> That was what produced in me a tremendous transformation: a great change had occurred in my life. My independence! I could now do things without relying on my husband; I had broken with the tradition of submission to the man of the house. To such a point that once your father sat down to listen to another program at the time of the *novela*, and I told him, "Hey, listen, let me listen to my *novela*!" And he responded, "Stop your foolishness." That really irked me, for he listened to the radio as if it were his. And I responded, "No, this is *my* radio! The radio that *I* bought!" I grabbed it, took it to the kitchen, and put on the *novela*.[31]

Identity with North American market structures was so complete that the demise of Cuban participation signified a national crisis of far-reaching proportions. Such identification was central to the way vast numbers of Cubans defined themselves as a nation. Now circumstances were changing, and the capacity to take part in what passed for ordinary life to meet commonplace needs was diminishing at every turn. It was a matter of grave concern that these possibilities seemed threatened. Because consumption had become a means of collective expression and personal identity, it was difficult to contemplate the consequences of change that would restrict or otherwise reduce the ability of Cubans to act out the attributes central to the dominant formulations of nationality. "Our people have a high propensity to consume," observed Alberto León Riva, "and since almost 60 percent of the national treasury is dedicated to salaries and wages among employees and workers, in periods of decline any economic policy worthy of such a name should base itself principally on stimulating private investment to expand production."[32]

The meaning of "Cuban" had long derived resonance from a material condition linked to the notions of modernity and civilization. In fact, much of national identity had been invested in a condition that could no longer be plausibly sustained. Hopes were fading, moving beyond the reach of growing numbers. Expectations had assumed a logic of their own, embedded in what had come to mean "Cuban." This condition was subject neither to negotiation nor compromise, for it reached deeply into the sources of nationality. Leví Marrero early understood the implications of these developments and placed matters in perspective. Marrero studied national per capita income against the standard that mattered most—that of the United States—and determined that the figure for Cuba was about $300, "five times less that the United States"; he asked rhetorically: "Why this Cuban poverty?" The newspaper Revolución posed a similar question in 1959: "Why is the standard of living of the Cuban people incomparably inferior to the standard of living of the North American people?" The notion of "poverty" as a Cuban condition, as a function of structural relationships, was sobering. Antonio Llano Montes arrived at a similar view: "Although one hears daily of the prosperity that Cuba is now experiencing, the fact is that workers and the middle class find it more difficult each day to subsist owing to the scarcity of articles of basic necessity."[33]

It is not always clear what contemporary commentators had in mind when they lamented the loss of "articles of basic necessity." These goods had different meanings for different households. On the other hand, it may be unnecessary to seek a better definition, for clearly the challenge to existing living standards affected everyone, albeit differently. What mattered was that most Cubans experienced dislocation of some type, and if not to the same degree certainly with comparable effects.

Available evidence suggests that the collective capacity to sustain consensus around market-based norms was under extraordinary pressure. Decades of participation in North American market structures had fostered a great many hopes. Middle- and working-class families alike could reasonably expect to possess an automobile; radio and television sets were commonly perceived within reach of almost everyone. Many could plausibly aspire to own an air conditioner, and refrigerators and gas ranges were all but universally deemed to be "articles of basic necessity." The discourse of commodities could sustain fanciful hopes—up to a point. Certainly these expectations took hold of the popular imagination. Of course, they would: they were irresistible. And if there was any doubt, clever advertisers did all they could to reshape the dominant notions of the necessities of life. "More than pleasure: a necessity!" affirmed a Cuban Electric Company advertisement for fans. In another ad, the company made the case for a Ruud water heater: "The ideal condition is to have hot water always waiting for you to turn on. In cold weather this is not a luxury—*it is a necessity!*" Westinghouse proclaimed its radio and TV products to be "a necessity of the country . . . [to] bring views of the world into the home." Remington insisted that "all modern women today need an electric shaver."[34]

Few could fully understand what was happening to them. They could only regard their inexorable downward slide with incomprehension and incredulity. These were years of stagnant wages and rising prices. Slow growth made it impossible for some and difficult for all to secure the goods and services around which meaning in daily life had formed. Many sought second jobs as a way to maintain their living standards. Others saved less and borrowed more and still fell behind, descending hopelessly into personal debt, with no way up or out.

The pursuit of commodities had larger social implications. The desire for social and material betterment had kept working men and women striving for goods as means and marker of rising standards of living. They had taken their expectations seriously, for these were precisely what gave the future purpose. The material elements that could ensure well-being seemed available to all, and therein lay the power of their appeal. Antonio Martínez Bello commented perceptively on the power of market culture and its larger implications. "People of modest social origins dress in a manner that is hardly distinguished from people of the upper class," he observed. "The matter assumes dramatic characteristics, especially in the middle class, inasmuch as the head of a petty bourgeois family aspires that his wife and daughters mix on an equal footing, at least in appearances, with the wives and daughters of high standing. At the same time, the Cuban people have distinguished themselves for their inclination toward progress, to the acceptance of technical innovations and the adoption of various means that serve to improve their standard of living."[35]

The appeal of the market had begun to wane, not because it had lost its capacity to excite the imagination, but rather because it was defaulting on the expectations it had created and on which its endurance depended. As long as

U.S. methods retained the ability to facilitate Cuba's integration into the dominant market structures, they served a socially useful role in mediating daily encounters with the prevailing order. By the mid-1950s, however, these ways no longer seemed capable of advancing Cuban interests. The economy had contracted and opportunities had diminished. North American ways seemed less relevant, less useful, and hence suspect and susceptible to challenge.

This is not to suggest that a national consensus had formed around the need to repudiate market structures. Nothing of the sort happened. But doubt and skepticism did increase. These were small changes in attitudes and assessments, to be sure, but changes that under certain circumstances could allow for the contemplation of alternative possibilities, just at the moment when Cubans realized that the beliefs and practices they had inherited were fetters on their own development and self-understanding. A consumption norm had taken hold by the 1950s, something akin to a standard from which well-being had been derived and against which it was measured. That more and more Cubans were having difficulty meeting this standard had far-reaching implications. Many lost confidence that the prevailing order could deliver a secure, comfortable life for those who were prepared to work hard and play by the rules. Assumptions that had sustained Cuban faith in the promise of the market revealed themselves to be illusory and untenable. Increasingly demand was politicized and transferred from the market to the government. These conditions served to channel the powerful forces that surfaced in 1959. In 1951 the International Bank had been prophetic: "War prosperity has created new standards of living for many of Cuba's people. If her economy cannot maintain these—at least in some reasonable degree—in less prosperous times, it will be subject to great political strains. If leaders have neglected to prepare Cuba for this, they will be held to blame by the people. And, if that should happen, control may well pass into subversive but specious hands."[36]

Much of the tension in the 1950s reflected a complex, continuing encounter between old and new. North American conventions had seized hold among Cubans, most of whom earnestly subscribed to the proposition that mastery of these methods held the promise of success. There was an abiding faith in education and preparation, in the triumph of training and talent, strategies shaped by a belief in an open, democratic system. Many had accepted the assumptions of this order, on which they could presume to form reasonable expectations of fulfillment, confident that they controlled their own destiny. This was a moral system that seemed as comprehensible as it was compelling, where the relationship between preparation and hard work, on one hand, and success and self-fulfillment, on the other, was deemed definitive and demonstrable. They worked hard, they made sacrifices in the interest of self-discipline, they studied and mastered the techniques and technologies of the North in the belief that advancement came by merit. They had accepted the promise of North American methods in the expectation that these were the means to success. They subscribed to these propositions, made them their own, and indeed became defenders of the North American way to success. "To throw the foreigner out by force," a Cuban had written in 1936, "and thrust in his place a native without preparation does not produce the desired results." He continued:

> I am young, but I have had a position in a foreign industry for many years, a position previously held by a foreigner. I have been moving up for a long time, doing everything possible to deserve the confidence of my supervisors, as much in my work as in my integrity. I have several acquaintances who are in the same conditions. . . . If we were capable of filling these positions, would they be occupied from the outside? I think not, for nobody could compete with us because of the advantages we would have. Therefore I believe that the only and lasting solution would be to educate and inculcate into the people work habits, discipline, and integrity, and then all work, high and low, would be in the hands of Cubans.[37]

But these assumptions became increasingly untenable. Many had given themselves entirely to this moral order and come up a long way away from where they had hoped to be through no fault of their own. The success of the consumption ethic as a means of social control was limited specifically by its capacity to deliver what it had promised and to fulfill the expectations it had created. The contradictions of daily life were acutely experienced. It was not always clear whether these circumstances served more to discredit the social system for failing to live up to the ideal or to invalidate the ideal for being irrelevant to the social system, or both. In either case, faith was shaken and confidence was undermined.

Old ways were slow to change, and sometimes they did not change at all. Increasingly hope was found to be misplaced if not ill-founded. Both the work ethic of preparation and discipline and the belief in education and training to which they had entrusted their future were increasingly offended by the open and flagrant violation of the standards by which they were formed. Much in the character of public life was shaped by official abuse and corruption, by graft and malfeasance, where employment and advancement were often related at least as much to cronyism and patronage as to qualifications. Miguel F. Márquez y de la Cerra suggested insights into this system in his novel *El gallo cantó* (1972): "We lived well," Tony reminisced about prerevolutionary Cuba, "everything was fixed among Cubans, nothing was difficult. If you didn't have a political friend, you had a sister working in some Ministry or you were the friend of a cousin of the mistress of the Sub-Secretary."[38]

This was precisely what drove many people to despair. In a poignant exchange in César Leante's novel *Padres e hijos* (1967), set in the 1950s, Rubén announces his decision to emigrate to the United States, concluding that it was impossible to find a good job in Cuba: "For that one needs to have influence, connections. In this pig-sty of a country if you don't have a god-father you don't get baptized. Everything here is by way of favoritism. Even to find a job as a porter you need recommendations and I don't have them. What's more, I'm fed up with Cuba, the island of shit where everything is rotten." When told that life in the United States was no better and the only job he would find was washing dishes, Rubén replies: "Whatever! But at least I don't have to go see someone to intercede in my behalf. I will wash dishes for a while, but I will in the end succeed in making a way for myself. I know. I feel crushed." This was the point that Manuel de J. Zamora made in 1957 when discussing the plight of "youth without a future." He referred specifically to the case of Roberto, a nineteen-year-old mechanic, who had worked by day and studied at night and on graduation from the Escuela de Artes y Oficios could not find employment. "I will have to remain at the shop, where I earn barely enough to live on," lamented Roberto. "I have only knowledge; I lack influence."[39]

This was true in both public administration and private enterprise: under-qualified and overpaid in the former, overqualified and underpaid in the latter. "This country is a barrel of shit," Enrique protests in Alcides Iznaga's novel *Las cercas caminaban* (1970). "Preparation is not worth anything: look, in the *ten cents* [Woolworth's] there are university graduates as clerks and the office super-visor of the 'Clavero' sugar mill is an attorney, and what he earns there is a pitiful salary, and if he doesn't do it he will die of hunger. On the other hand, any wretch, if he has friends, is 'made' immediately." Enrique concludes: "For me the only country where ability is not worth a damn is Cuba. What makes things work here is cronyism (*amiguismo*)."[40]

The deepening tension between Cubans and North Americans was in large measure due to the degree to which Cubans adopted North American conven-tions, for which they expected full recognition and fair recompense. Teresa Casuso wrote with pride of Cuban "high work standards" in terms entirely recognizable to North Americans: "Care, precision, and skill, whether in the construction of houses, the making of clothes and shoes, or mechanical labor, are a point of national pride. We do not tolerate bad work, dawdling, careless-ness, slovenliness, or dirt." The moral of the paradigm seemed straightforward: success would come through hard work, discipline, and preparation. And, in-deed, the message resonated in Cuba: to be responsible for oneself, to make and remake oneself according to ability and ambition. These propositions were easily accommodated within the Cuban understanding of the universe and deemed worthy of respect. But Cubans expected, too, that mastery of these conventions would earn them respect—and more: that it would bring them at least parity with North Americans. Hard work was a noble pursuit to be recog-nized and respected in others, but it was also expected to command the respect and recognition of others, including and especially North Americans. "We don't think we're better than anybody," Carlos García explained to Lynn Geldof, "but definitely we're not worse than anybody. We demand equality with anybody. In any way and in every respect. That's why we do the sacrifices." The International Bank for Reconstruction and Development made a similar observation: "The Cuban has an unusually developed sense of respect for the dignity and self-esteem of those around him, and naturally expects the same in return."[41]

Much of the discontent of the 1950s can be attributed to the growing realization that mastery of North American ways had, in the end, failed to modify power relationships between Cubans and North Americans, that subordination was due not to a failure to grasp North American ways, but to the failure of North Americans themselves to live up to the standards they propounded. The estimated 150,000 Cubans working for U.S. companies held a special place in this environment; the managers, attorneys, accountants, engineers, technicians, clerks, and secretaries, among many others, were privileged by local standards. They typically received higher salaries or wages and enjoyed greater benefits. But they also occupied a unique vantage point from which to observe the practices of the North and often discovered that these methods did not always work, at least not for them. Perhaps more than any other group in Cuba, they were the most likely to be disenchanted, for they had the most frequent contact with North Americans as colleagues and supervisors. They were most likely to encounter prejudice and unfair treatment on a day-to-day basis, to see themselves as victims of discrimination and denied the success they believed that they deserved. Often the product of U.S. education and training, they were subjected to discriminatory promotion practices and differential salary levels, areas where North Americans made a mockery of the norms and values that they themselves had offered as the standards of success and well-being.

Salary differentials were particularly frustrating, as Cubans performing the same tasks as their North American counterparts were often paid substantially less. "In the American companies," recalled Rufo López-Fresquet, "the top positions were occupied by Americans, who enjoyed salaries at U.S. levels. It was extremely difficult for them to establish a relationship with the native personnel because of the difference in income." Marcelo Pogolotti, who worked briefly for the Cuban Electric Company as a bilingual clerk, recounted "irritating discrimination" when "North American clerks, who knew only English, and often with poor handwriting and performing inferior work, earned much more than the Cubans." In Juan Arcocha's partly autobiographical novel *A Candle in the Wind* (1967), engineer Esteban Ferro remembered his years with the "Wilkinson Glass Company" in San Antonio de las Lajas (i.e., Owens-Illinois Glass Company) where "the American engineers got higher salaries," although he and a friend "carried all the weight of the work on their shoulders, but these were the rules of the game and you had to play it that way." Nor was it simply a matter of Cubans discerning salary differentials in the same company. Many were aware of salaries in the United States. Alfred Padula interviewed Carlos Martínez, an engineering graduate from the University of Havana and a former employee of the Moa Bay Mining Company. Martínez, who had earned $175 monthly, recalled his astonishment on learning that an engineer occupying a similar position in the United States earned $450–475. "This difference," observed Padula, "was always a source of agitation and frustration in the old Cuba." In *Vendaval en los cañaverales* (1937), Alberto Lamar Schweyer gives voice to Márquez, a Cuban executive of the "Goldenthal Sugar Corporation," during a labor strike against the company:

> The Americanized Cuban chewed on the end of his old pipe, thinking about what Goldenthal would say when he learned of what was happening. . . . Márquez was sufficiently intelligent not to deceive himself. This was neither communism nor revolution, rather an outburst by Cubans, his compatriots, against the repeated injustices of the foreign company. Why, he himself had resentments against the company! But to be resentful, he reasoned, was not to break relations. When Kenyon, incompetent that he was and the inexperience that he had, was appointed to be nothing less than General Director of the Antilles Division of the Goldenthal Corporation, he was aggrieved by the injustice, but he kept his own counsel. In the end, Kenyon was an American, he dined every Saturday with Goldenthal in New York, and accompanied him on his winter fishing trips to Nassau. How outrageous these Americans were! What nerve they had![42]

Unequal pay and unequal treatment galled Cubans. These issues often arose in the most unlikely places, under the most improbable circumstances. Tensions often surfaced inside the evangelical church, for instance, especially as the Cuban presence increased in the decades following independence. Inevitably Cubans called for greater authority over local affairs. "There is a great deal of restlessness among our Cuban leaders," reported Methodist Paul Kern in 1942, "and they are clamoring for a major share in the direction of their own Christian program. Cuba has been far too much dominated by the missionary. . . . We have trained very few leaders whom we are willing to trust and we have been slow to trust those whom we have trained."[43] Cubans also insisted on parity with North American missionaries. The ministry had provided one more vantage point from which Cubans could take measure of their condition and in the process served as a source for the moral authority with which to demand equality. "Their poverty was indeed actual," J. Merle Davis of the International Mission Council asserted in 1942, "but when measured by American standards it seemed abysmal." Ministers educated in U.S. seminaries were "introduced to the amenities and economic standards of American society" that were "alien to the social and economic patterns of Cuban life." Cubans had been sufficiently incorporated into North American evangelical structures to recognize their own subordination. "Frequently," Davis recognized, "the American standards have become the norm against which the Cuban pastor tends to compare his own salary, living conditions, and cultural amenities." He continued:

> The American missionary's salary and household equipment, modest as these are, considerably exceed the Cuban standards. . . . This often makes the Cuban dissatisfied with the limitations of a small income and sets goals for his family and for himself which are impracticable, burden him with debt, and are apt to give him a sense of injustice and chronic economic struggle. The educated Cuban pastor is in danger of being ground between the millstones of foreign social and economic standards and the low wage level and supporting power of the membership of the Evangelical church.[44]

At least as important as the disparities between the Cuban and U.S. ministries were the differences within the pastorate. North Americans routinely received higher salaries than their Cuban counterparts. Cubans often did not earn even the minimum salaries established for members of the ministry. As early as 1907, Reverend Luis Albaladejo of Santiago de las Vegas forwarded a formal complaint over salary inequities and discriminatory appointment practices to the Methodist bishop in Atlanta. Two years later, Antero Suárez, José Mauricio Hernández, and Aurelio Alonso took their grievances directly to the U.S. Board of Missions. The "frequent injustices which all the Cuban preachers have been victims of have really become intolerable," they protested, adding: "The American ministers live in comfortable houses in good sanitary conditions, the Cuban ministers in almost every instance are compelled to live in houses that afford no conveniences and no sanitary facilities." They also complained about preferential treatment accorded to North Americans, singling out the newly arrived Reverend Benjamin Hill, who, "without experience, without practice in the work, without knowledge of the language or the character of the people," was appointed to Cárdenas, "while other men of larger experience, more years of practice in the work and full knowledge of the language are relegated to little country villages off the main lines of communication."[45] The Cuban protest was dismissed as "mischief," the product of "a small number of agitators." "Raise their salaries," warned Reverend E. E. Clements in Matanzas, "and there will be nothing to call for any sacrifice on their part. This would be unhealthy for the ministry." The petitioners were dismissed.[46]

A great many Cubans had been formed by values and norms derived from U.S. models. North Americans conjured up an order that was both rational and reasonable, of material well-being and moral merit based on propositions of equality and fair play. But their actions conveyed something quite different: privilege and preference, a tolerance for inequity and indifference to inequality. The process was profound, for it possessed the capacity to discredit dominant normative systems. Discriminatory barriers to advancement were all the more offensive because they were being raised inside Cuba. José García Pedrosa had resented the fact that a North American construction firm, "following the example of other companies of similar nationality, contracted thousands of Cuban workers who were paid lower salaries than North American personnel doing the same type work."[47]

There was perhaps no more dramatic expression of the deepening crisis than emigration. Cubans were once more traveling north in vast numbers. The lines outside the U.S. embassy stretched for city blocks as many thousands of applicants sought visas for permanent residence in the United States. "In those days of extreme poverty," Reinaldo Arenas recalled, "the dream of all who were down-and-out in Cuba was to go 'north' to work." Agustín Tamargo described the "lines of young Cubans in front of the American Embassy, youth without a future and without hope in a rich and promising country, youth who ask for jobs as dish washers in the very skyscrapers along the very Malecón which have been constructed with funds stolen from the people."[48]

Well-informed observers knew that conditions were actually worse than they appeared. Population projections forecast a growth of 200,000 inhabitants annually. At that rate, the population would nearly double between 1956 and 1980, from 6 million to 11 million. The implications were chilling. Philip Bonsal learned in 1955 from "knowledgeable Cubans in the National Bank" that "the situation of Cuba in the face of rising population and more or less stagnant living standards was truly desperate." Leví Marrero did not conceal his disquiet. "What will be the fate of Cuba if we double our population . . . without changing our economic structure?" Marrero could contemplate only one possibility: a vast emigration, perhaps as many as 2.5 million Cubans, approximately one-quarter of the population migrating to the United States.[49] Massive emigration seems to have been destined to be Cuba's fate after 1960—even without revolution.

Newspapers and magazines were filled with letters from despairing readers, many of whom saw emigration as their only salvation. "I am now studying typing, stenography, and English," wrote one young woman, "and . . . I am obliged to consider leaving for the United States, where there is a better future for young people." A young man wrote of a monthly deficit of $250 in the household budget and announced his intention to emigrate with his wife and two children. Another reader denounced those who planned to emigrate but in the process provided insight into the Cuban condition:

> I live decently and honorably on a [small] salary. . . . My daughter does not attend a private school. She is enrolled in a Cuban school . . . more in the spirit of Martí, more Cuban, more of the people. . . . When one cannot go to the movies, to the theater or cabarets, or to the beaches or make expensive trips, one simply stays home. Unable to afford gasoline or tires? Walk or take the bus. . . . Adjust your expenditures to your earnings. That is the great tragedy of many Cuban families: spending much more than they earn. In

conclusion, you mention the lines of Cubans outside the American Embassy. . . . This demonstrates nothing less than that we want to live the soft life, that we want to live in luxury.[50]

LENGTHENING SHADOWS

Thoughtful men and women could not have looked about them without dismay and distress at what they saw: indigence in the countryside and mendicancy in the cities, the homeless and the jobless, abandoned children and displaced families. The down-and-out filled Havana streets in such numbers as to prompt one observer to write of an "invasion" of beggars. Others noted rising incidents of suicide, increased street crime and juvenile delinquency, climbing divorce rates, drugs and alcoholism, gambling and prostitution, graft and corruption, the loss of public morality.[51]

Many people could not conceal their disquiet and despair over what Cuba was becoming and what it was becoming known as: a place of license and loose morality, of prostitutes, pimps, and pornography, of bars and brothels, casinos and cabarets, gambling and drugs, gangsters, mobsters, and racketeers, politicians on the take and policemen on the make. Daily life had developed into a relentless degradation, with the complicity of political leaders and public officials who operated at the behest of U.S. interests. The reputation of Cuba as the "red light district of the Caribbean," the "Las Vegas of Latin America," the "brothel of the New World" offended Cuban sensibilities. "We can not help but notice," Eladio Secades commented, "that the city is filling with bars. We are creating a capital of bars." Luis Conte Agüero was despondent about the "invasion" of "gangsters and sinister figures" and the "plague of gambling." "What has to be asked," he insisted, "is whether it is worth paying the high price of imported gangsterism, the demoralization of our customs, and the disrepute of the name of Cuba, already known as the country of *rumba* and rum." "It is no secret," Andrés Valdespino lamented in 1958, "that the capital of the republic is acquiring the sad reputation until recently held by Las Vegas as a center of gambling of the Americas." Valdespino continued:

> The most prominent representatives of the . . . North American underworld, owners and managers of gambling establishments in the universally known "city of vice," have transferred their operations to Havana. Daily figures known to Cubans only by their underworld activities arrive to our shores. . . . An economic argument is used to justify these activities. It is said that this will promote tourism. . . . Is this objective worth staining the national panorama even more, converting Cuba into a center of major scandals?

Juan Giró Rodés denounced the "marijuana bars," and Mario Parajón called for the "suppression of pornographic magazines." Baptist minister Nemesio Garcia Iglesias invoked biblical imagery: "If we continue like this . . . I believe that it will not be long that we will become worse than Sodom and Gomorrah and all the rottenness the world has ever had."[52]

The image of Cuba as casino and brothel was particularly troublesome because it reached deeply into the sources of national representation. It was even more disturbing when such topics became the subject of sensational news stories in the United States. Havana was depicted as the sin capital of the Western Hemisphere, a thriving entrepôt of commercialized vice and refuge of sinister underworld mobsters that threatened North American moral well-being. The *Saturday Evening Post* denounced Cuba for the gambling casinos that routinely victimized unsuspecting tourists. *Time* criticized Cuba for allowing drugs and prostitution.[53]

In the end, Cubans understood, these were not conditions of their making. The Cuba that North Americans condemned was of their creation, summoned into existence for their pleasure and amusement, an extensive economy of commercialized vice that could not have existed under any other circumstances. The proposition of Havana as a U.S. "invention" received powerful resonance in the film *Havana* (1990). An outraged Meyer Lansky (Mark Rydell) learns that Santa Clara has fallen to anti-Batista rebels and orders his casino manager Joe Volpi (Alan Arkin) to carry a message to Cuban officials:

> You're going to tell them they better get off their asses and start fighting pretty soon, or they're going back to being a bunch of fuckin' banana eaters like they used to be. You're going to remind them that the only reason there's civilized plumbing in their country is because the Americans came here in '98 and beat the shit out of Spain. Batista's own palace had a fuckin' outdoor crapper before we put one inside. The only reason he's got an army is because we gave him one. Well, he'd better start using it or he's going to wind up on some street corner selling beans like he started. *We* invented Havana, and can goddamn well move it someplace else if he can't control it.

The reinvention of Cuba by the United States appears and reappears as a central theme of the North American narrative on Cuba. "When the Americans came to the island," the *Havana Post* affirmed in 1924, "they found the natives living like and with their domestic animals. Today those same people are trying to live like the Americans." Several years later, travel writer Henry Wack offered a similar judgment: "But for the liberation of our Cuban neighbors by the U.S. . . . Havana would still be the dump it was in the last century."[54]

U.S. perceptions challenged some of the most vital assumptions of Cuban self-representation, for it portrayed the island in exactly those terms Cubans had so resolutely resisted: backward and undeveloped, primitive and primal, exotic and tropical. North American efforts to come to terms with this world and its people succeeded only in underscoring more sharply the otherness of the Other. Where Cubans saw similarities, North Americans stressed differences, where Cubans celebrated modernity, North Americans proclaimed primitive.

Cubans were sensitive to representations that could deny or otherwise dispute their claim to modern. A people who had located themselves in the forefront of enlightened civilization were, from March 1952 until January 1959, in the grip of a corrupt military dictatorship as well as a far-flung economy of commercialized vice operated by gangsters. Embarrassment was expressed in public and in private, with a mixture of frustration and impotence in the face of powerlessness to control the meaning of Cuban. These circumstances increasingly gave nationality an edge of defensiveness, the obverse side of which would find expression easily enough as defiant nationalism.

New narratives on nationality were taking form. The dominant cultural motif of the 1950s addressed matters of representation, a process that necessarily involved the affirmation of Cuban as distinct from and independent of things North American at a time of deepening economic dislocation and political crisis.

Cubans reacted to U.S. characterizations with incredulity and indignation. That North Americans would censure Cuba for conditions for which they themselves were largely responsible was incomprehensible. "They believe that we are a backward country," Isabel Monal protested, "not worthy of attention, . . . not fit for democracy, and hence justifying the way they act toward us." Andrés Valdespino was indignant at North American representations: "We are not a country of drunkards, although we produce rum and like beer. Neither are we a country of sexual perversions and excesses." "Who taught us to bet at the horse track?" Mario Sorondo y Tolón asked rhetorically. He continued:

Who introduced roulette and poker? The Americans.
Who are the worst drunkards—Cubans or *yanquis*? The *yanquis*!
Who introduced among us black jack, the worst card game? The Americans!
And the bars installed in Cuba, most of them: to whom do they belong? The Americans.
And for what do the majority of American tourists come to Cuba? To get drunk, to gamble, to be obnoxious and trample the law.

Hernández Traviesa smarted at the image of "allowing all who arrive in Cuba to think that Cuban women are waiting for them on the beaches, filled with the *glamour* that they only see in the movies, disposed to convert themselves into their slaves in all facets of life." The Cuban media was also drawn into a polemic with the North American press. "All Cubans should feel indignant," *Bohemia* railed against New York newspapers in 1957, "at the dirty propaganda that presents Havana as the brothel of the Caribbean." José Montó Sotolongo denounced North American images of Cuba as a place of "prostitutes and easy women." "Cuba is a nation of decent women," he insisted, "young women cared for by their parents and who know well how to take care of themselves." *Bohemia* could not resist publishing a studio publicity photograph of Jayne Mansfield—

"in one of her characteristic poses"—and drew the obvious moral as caption: "If the hapless Cuban girls who are so often the object of sensational North American magazines were to appear one day in this manner outside the doors of their homes, foreign journalists who seem to have no other obsession than to monitor their customs, would yell from atop the skyscrapers and demand that Uncle Sam wipe out its 'obscene backyard' with atomic bombs."[55]

The depiction of Havana as a city of bars and brothels in the film *Guys and Dolls*, in particular, provoked angry reaction. "The film . . . ," complained Ulises Carbó, "portrays Havana as a Mecca for vice. It even goes to the extreme of presenting an honest missionary who, influenced by what she sees here, gets drunk and passes out on a strange potion from a coconut shell in the midst of an atmosphere of scandal and prostitution." Agustín Tamargo protested that "we Cubans are portrayed as backward types, whose customs, habits, and attire are associated with the lowest level, when everybody knows this is not true." *Bohemia* denounced the film's depiction of a Cuban nightclub as "a sordid place, filled with men sporting mustaches and sideburns, and carrying knives in their belt."[56]

By the mid-1950s, the representation of Cuba projected by Ricky Ricardo (Desi Arnaz) on *I Love Lucy* was subject to increasing attack. Havana television producer Joaquín Condall denounced Arnaz as an "enemy of all Cubans" and a source of "humiliation for Cuba." Condall added: "His television role of 'Ricky Ricardo' represents a coarse and cunning type that the North Americans imagine us Cubans to be. . . . All of us who have lived in New York have felt humiliated watching this program."[57]

Enormous effort, spanning nearly one hundred years, had gone into emulation and replication, only to result in rejection and ridicule. Much of the idea of nation and nationality, no less than its symbols and sources of representation, had originated from North American sources. That so much was adaptation involved complex, continuing discourse on national identity and resulted in an abiding ambivalence toward the North. The comparison between the model and the copy was permanent. At the core of national identity thus defined, if only implicitly—and sometimes explicitly—was the need to obtain U.S. recognition of parity, with all the respect and regard that parity implied. Again and again, eager to demonstrate national achievements, Cubans set out to confront North Americans on their terms, using their forms and formulations through which to affirm accomplishment and just as often, inevitably, falling short. These were the larger meanings associated with travel north, where Cubans beheld the model and intuitively understood the shortcomings of the copy.

The deficiencies of the Cuban condition were thus made conspicuous and often led to self-doubt, embarrassment, and humiliation. This was the meaning of Jorge Mañach's allusion to the Cuban "inferiority complex" and "pessimism" as a result of Cuba's proximity to the United States. Juan Marinello wrote about the "old politics" that employed an "inferiority complex" as a means of survival.

For a different reason but with similar language, the U.S. State Department observed that actions of the Cuban people were "sometimes influenced by a sense of inferiority, which promotes exaggerated nationalism."[58]

By the 1950s national identity had developed into contested terrain, a complex process by which Cubans sought to establish control over the terms of representation. The process signified affirmation, distant from an explicit political arena but, of course, possessed of far-reaching political implications. It produced reflections on nationality reminiscent of the discourses of the nineteenth century. The affirmation of Cuban took many forms, almost all of which necessarily implied confrontation with things and ways North American as a means of differentiation and distinction. North American forms had insinuated themselves deeply into the commonplace, so much so that they could easily appear to be Cuban. To challenge these forms inevitably meant, too, the need to confront the meaning of Cuban at some of its most fundamental sources. Attention was given specifically to defining the means of self-representation. *El Mundo* editorialized against "rampant immorality" induced by tourists. "We complain from time to time," the newspaper affirmed, "that certain North American publications dedicate their pages to articles in which Havana is portrayed as a city where virtue does not exist and our civic associations protest against certain Hollywood movies that use Havana to signify a frankly immoral setting." To counter these images, *El Mundo* insisted, it was necessary to "clean up" the capital.[59] To "clean up" Havana had sweeping implications; few, indeed, could have foreseen the full reach of this project.

Culture became the site of contest, the place at which to seek recovery precisely because it was everyday and everywhere. In the 1950s Cuban politics and culture increasingly converged; the affirmation of one thing could not be achieved without the negation of something else. The growing political crisis gave new urgency to the reconfiguration of cultural forms and in the process created possibilities for radical political change. At a time of widening political repression, culture became a substitute for politics, a way to pose imaginary solutions to real problems. This was the point at which imagination and moral life intersected to produce a national dialogue in which narratives often appeared distant from the issues at hand but whose subtext went to the very heart of the national crisis. Cultural forms served as a surrogate for politics, a way to try out values permissible in the ordinary facets of everyday life but proscribed as explicit political articulations. Cultural change thus served as a way to create space for a new vision of politics. A radical prospect was no longer unthinkable, for it had already been summoned in the popular imagination.

The exaltation of Cuban assumed a new resonance. Defense of *patria* promised to release the forces of uplift and advance. These were points of differentiation, in their own way decisive and defining, a means of redemption, and at the same time creating distance and disengagement. José Pardo Llada denounced the "vicious deformation of nationality," which included the "facil disposition of the Cuban to adopt foreign ways (*extranjerizarse*)." Pardo Llada condemned the gangster, detective, and cowboy comic books read by children. Architecture had lost all national character, Pardo declared, giving "all apartment houses constructed in the last ten years the appearance of North American skyscrapers. Even the old top floors are now called '*pent-houses.*'" He singled out the "adulteration of our language," the insidious "invasion of foreignisms" into the popular vernacular: "Already, in effect, the *bodegas* are called 'grocerys,' the *salones de belleza* are known as 'beauty-parlor,' the *sociedades* are named 'clubs.' . . . The social chronicle is plagued with 'cocktail partys,' 'teen-ager' and 'five o'clock.'"[60] In Bodeguita del Medio restaurant singer Carlos Puebla performed his song "Influencia," lamenting that "nobody here remembers how to speak Spanish":

> The *bodega* here is called the *grocery*
> The *barbería* today is called *barber shop*
> The *entresuelo* is called *mezzanine*
> And the *azotea* is converted to *penthouse*
> Even the *fonda* is called *restaurant*
> *Pollo frito* is called today *baked chicken*
> And the *salchicha* with bread is called *hot dog.*[61]

Calls to buy national products and protect home industries were issued with increased frequency. Cubans were exhorted to vacation at home before going abroad. Leví Marrero urged Cubans to discover their own country, to appreciate its beauty and natural resources. The popular song "Conozca a Cuba" exhorted Cuban tourists "to see Cuba first, and foreign countries later" and "as a Cuban visit first the charms that are found here." Artist María Luisa Ríos criticized the reproduction of northern scenes as the representation of Christmas. "We Cuban painters do not have need to seek inspiration in foreign motifs to create nativity scenes," asserted Ríos. "In Cuba there exists untapped motifs waiting for the magic of lines and color to shape them on the canvas." Nereyda de Muxo opposed the use of styles and fabrics of North American furniture, "those immense sofa-chairs of heavy tapestry into which we Cubans literally sink and proceed to perspire profusely." Moreover, de Muxo added: "It is ridiculous and illogical to see ourselves dressed in linen seated in sofa chairs designed for a cold winter night in the country of its origin." She called for the use of rattan, bamboo, wicker, and iron, for "light and breezy furniture appropriate for our climate," but most of all for a domestic furniture industry to meet national needs. Fashion writer Angela Velarde urged women to patronize the domestic cosmetics industry and use products designed to meet needs peculiar to Cuban latitudes, not the climate of New York or Paris. Designer Raúl Hernández exhorted women to patronize local fashion designers, who were committed to developing styles appropriate for "our latitudes and climate." Another designer,

An advertisement for "modern" furniture, 1957. (Author's collection)

Lily del Barrio, struck a similar note, insisting that "we already have in Cuba sufficient numbers of designers with talent and technical skills to produce our own styles." Del Barrio told an interviewer from *Vanidades* magazine:

> It is absurd that we continue to allow ourselves to be governed by the fashion canons of the French and Americans, inspired by a figure diametrically op-

posed to ours. The curvilinear shape is the dominant figure in our country. Tell the women readers of *Vanidades* that our designers are desirous of creating for them. . . . Our climate, moreover, demands a radical change. Styles should be made with light fabrics. . . . Colors should also be chosen carefully. It is not necessary to be restricted to the tyranny of foreign styles to appear attractive. Cuba *can* and *should* have its own styles and colors that accentuate the unrivaled beauty of the Cuban woman.[62]

Increasingly, too, the ubiquity of North American cultural forms passed under critical scrutiny. Fernando G. Compoamor wrote that he had indeed obeyed the exhortation "to see Cuba first" and took his vacation at Varadero Beach. "If you need a hair cut you should find the *barber shop* (your wife will go to the *beauty shop*); to cope with the temperatures by way of an *helado* of native fruits, have an *ice cream*, and to choose black beans the *grocery* awaits you. . . . As we contemplate the meaning of these developments, on the highway, we are beset at all turns by the billboards of Goodrich and U.S. Royal, and the gas station signs of Shell, Sinclair and Esso . . . and every kilometer and every cross roads the unending signs of Coca-Cola."[63]

The pervasiveness of the English language also became a source of controversy and contention. Mario Guiral Moreno criticized hotels with such names as Belmont, Blackstone, Park View, and Hollywood and movie theaters called Duplex, Majestic, Strand, Ambassador, and Roxy. At about the same time, the Cuban Congress debated a bill to prohibit the use of all foreign language in words, titles, stamps, and letterheads manufactured in Cuba and on public and private buildings and all other establishments. "There is not a shop that does not call itself 'Miami Store' or 'Fifth Avenue Store,' " protested *Bohemia* in 1957; "there is not a snack joint with pretensions that does not call its sausages (*salchichas*) 'hot dogs' and its fried meat (*fritas*) 'hamburger.' " Accordingly, "We must begin to Cubanize Havana." The pursuit of Cuban insinuated itself into the most ordinary usages. When Ñico responds to his parents' request with an "Okay" in a José Antonio Mases short story, "the parents look at each other. Once again that word. The father felt ashamed." This dialogue follows: "Don't say that word, my son. It is not ours. I can teach you many other words. Your mother also doesn't want you to use those words. 'Those words? Words like *okay*.' Exactly. They may be perfectly fine, I don't doubt it, but they are not ours."[64]

These were some of the ways Cuban forms moved toward ascendancy during the 1950s, even as the armed struggle against Batista expanded. The extent to which these forms qualified as "Cuban" was not always clear, for their origins were often as diverse as they were dissimilar. Nor perhaps was it necessary to identify these distinctions. What mattered most was the degree to which these forms could promote Cuban interests. Baseball could be appropriated as the "national pastime" precisely because it fostered community and favored national identity, and hence was accorded a place of prominence. On the eve of revolution, Cuba was in the throes of far-reaching cultural transformations that would both encourage and facilitate radical political change.

REVOLUTION

It may never be possible to fully comprehend the range of emotions released in the days and weeks after January 1, 1959: spontaneous joy and prolonged jubilation, exuberance and exhilaration. "Incredible euphoria," recalled Fichu Menocal, "such complete happiness." The revolution was redemption and resonated Cuban, obtaining its most compelling representation in the larger metaphysics of *pueblo* and *patria*. Not since the end of the nineteenth century had the proposition of patria assumed such purpose and promise. It was a powerful formulation, raising to exalted heights the meaning of Cuban and possessed of a widespread capacity for popular mobilization and national cohesion. The remarkable triumph of arms and spirit against the U.S.-backed Batista government had conferred on the insurgent people a heightened sense of empowerment. Cubans had seized their history, claiming the power of self-determination and self-definition. In overthrowing the dictatorship, unassisted and at great human cost, they had also defeated the United States; in the process, they had now won the right to determine their own future. Antonio Ortega wrote reverently about the triumph of the *barbudos* (bearded guerrillas), who had "a sense of liberty and a sense of *patria*. They had a sense of human dignity. That's why they won. And how they won! These bands . . . defeated face to face one of the best equipped armies of Latin America." Andrés Valdespino saw the revolution as a victory of all Cubans:

> A people has given to the world a glorious example of an indomitable will. . . .
> A *pueblo*, above all, that has arisen . . . with faith in its own destiny. This has been, perhaps, among the greatest of all the achievements of the Revolution: of having restored faith to Cubans. . . . For the first time a Revolution has triumphed without compromise and mediation, . . . a revolution that overthrew a regime supported by great capitalist interests and the American embassy. A revolution that achieves power without foreign intervention that divests it of its nationalist sentiments and without a military coup that threatens its democratic inclination.

Jorge Mañach also stressed the power of the revolution to restore faith. "We are living in Cuba a brilliant moment of profound renovation," Mañach asserted in March 1959. "Renovation . . . of the spirit of our people, of hopes and of will; most of all, of faith in ourselves. . . . What has been reborn in Cuba is not as much faith as the confidence of Cubans in themselves." Mario Llerena arrived at a similar conclusion: "Never before in the history of Latin America has power been achieved with as much freedom from compromise and conditions. . . . The obstacles that have traditionally limited or counteracted the exercise of popular sovereignty—the armed forces, North American embassy, capital, and reactionary groups—have been destroyed." Presbyterian minister Rafael Cepeda agreed. "We are now free," he wrote in the *Heraldo Cristiano* in May 1959. "Perhaps for the first time in the history of Cuba we are politically and economically free. Liberty has brought with it a restoration of truth. We have needed liberty in order to know that we are capable of overcoming the habitual practice of deceiving ourselves. Whether we want it or not, our destiny is defined and sealed."[65]

The revolution had become at one and the same time the means and a mandate for change. It facilitated change by creating the possibility of change; casting Cubans as agents of change made change all but inevitable, for there was so much that Cubans wanted changed. The direction and the velocity of change in 1959 were determined by a great force that had welled up from the people and imposed their urgency on public life. Demands long deferred or otherwise denied found outlet in a highly charged environment, much of which had to do with living conditions, with wages and salaries, with the cost of living. This was the time for demands, and few failed to appreciate the importance of timing: a newly established provisional government, seeking ways to consolidate its authority, could not long sustain its mandate to rule without responding to the call of an aroused citizenry. Across the island men and women mobilized: they prepared petitions and drafted demands, they marched and demonstrated, they organized work stoppages and strikes, and they called for higher wages and lower living costs. In January the Frente Obrero Nacional Unido (FONU) issued a twelve-point proclamation calling for a 20 percent increase in salaries, wages, and pensions; the creation of unemployment insurance; and lower costs for life's necessities, including clothing, shoes, medicine, rent, transportation, telephone service, and electricity. A month later, the Juventud Obrera Católica (JOC) organized a mass rally in the plaza of the Cathedral and called on the government to improve living standards. The National Congress of Sugar Workers demanded a 30 percent reduction in the cost of living. Almost all unions insisted on the renegotiation of old contracts. Employees of Burrus Mills called for a 35 percent raise; office workers at Goodyear de Cuba, a 30 percent raise; and workers of the Nickel Processing Company, an 80 percent increase. Motion picture workers demanded a 20 percent increase in wages. So did workers at Coca-Cola, First National City Bank, and Sherwin Williams. Workers closed the Nestle's plant over a wage dispute. A strike by sugar workers in February halted production in twenty-one mills. A labor slowdown halted operations at the Cuban Electric Company. The 3,000 workers at Moa Bay Mining Company returned to work only after obtaining a 17 percent wage increase.[66]

The presentiment of change was palpable. Demands dominated the public discourse, and what everyone seemed to be demanding most was change. Certainly many had viewed the armed struggle as a defense of democracy and freedom. But "democracy" and "freedom" meant different things to different people; the terms had long been associated with a material condition, implying convenience, comfort, and contentment. "We saw no future for our children," explained attorney Alejandro Suero in 1959. The revolution had been conceived principally by lawyers, engineers, physicians, accountants, and university professors, "men with a great sense of pride." Suero complained of the high prices of refrigerators—"more than twice its American prices"—as well as the cost of televisions, automobiles, and bathroom fixtures. "We Cubans would like to buy many more things that in our country are synonymous of democracy, independence of life and healthy living, but we cannot afford them, we like them, we would like to have them."[67]

The promise of nation and the meaning of Cuban were deeply vested in the proposition of material well-being comparable to that of other modern countries. Fidel Castro defended reforms by comparing himself to Franklin Roosevelt, who, he noted, was also criticized for seeking to raise living standards. Cuba could indeed aspire to the living standards of the United States, Castro proclaimed. "We are equal and we have the same rights." In fact, the revolution, he predicted, would bring to Cuba a higher standard of living than that enjoyed in the United States and the Soviet Union. "We want to raise the standard of living of the people so that the peasant can live with all the comforts and benefits to which a man working in such a rich country as this one has a right."[68]

Reforms began immediately and gained momentum. In January 1959 the provisional government reduced pharmaceutical prices by 15–20 percent. Postal rates were lowered. The Cuban Telephone Company was intervened and its rates reduced. Cuban Electricity Company rates were lowered by 30 percent. The Urban Reform Law decreed a 50 percent reduction in rents of $100 or less, a 40 percent reduction in those between $100 and $200, and a 30 percent reduction in those exceeding $200 per month. Minimum wages were increased in agriculture, industry, and commerce. Tax codes were rewritten. More than two hundred taxes were reduced, particularly those falling directly on middle- and working-class households. New laws targeted wealthy tax evaders. Of the 30,000 members of Havana's exclusive social clubs, only 5,000 appeared as registered taxpayers. "We are headed toward a true fiscal justice," Minister of the Treasury Rufo López-Fresquet announced, "whereby taxes are to be paid by those with greater economic capacity, by those who can afford to consume luxury articles and who receive income from non-economic activity or an activity not conducive to the development of the country."[69]

Early measures were designed to deliver immediate relief. "Not only will we lower the cost of rent," Fidel Castro predicted in March 1959, "but that money can be allocated to consumption articles at a lower price. Not only will we increase income but we will where possible lower prices on goods, at least they will not go up." Castro also vowed to end the "usurious rates of interest charged to people in installment purchases." López-Fresquet later wrote that rent savings alone "greatly increased" the "purchasing power of the public." The additional income resulting from the reduction and the increased minimum wages of state employees totaled $140 million annually, money placed "in the hands of low-income sectors of the population with a high marginal propensity for consumption."[70]

New policies also sought to control the consumption of foreign imports, especially consumer durables and luxury items, including typewriters, televisions, automobiles, motorcycles, refrigerators, washers and air driers, yachts, and jewelry. An ad valorem surcharge of 30 to 100 percent was levied on luxury and semiluxury items. These measures were necessary, explained National Bank president Felipe Pazos, to protect Cuba's balance-of-payments position and to reduce the annual outflow of foreign exchange by an estimated $200 million. The age of the Cadillac in Cuba was coming to an end. Policies sought specifically to promote the purchase of cheaper, small, and fuel-efficient automobiles, almost all of which were European. A new fee schedule revised the taxes on automobile plates. The amount for tags on cars valued at less than $2,000 was set at $50; the fee for automobiles worth more than $3,000 was fixed at $5,000. "How much have we spent in gasoline riding around in cars?" Fidel Castro asked rhetorically. "It is one thing if they had been small cars, but Cadillacs consume a gallon of gasoline per kilometer. That is why we say: buy small cars because they cost less, they get more kilometers per gallon of gas, and they take less [parking] space." As early as April 1959, the U.S. commercial attaché described a "badly depressed" market for U.S. automobiles and a corresponding rise in European auto imports.[71]

In fact, the Cadillac served as a metaphor for the malaise. "How could we import rice and buy Cadillacs?" an aroused Fidel Castro asked in July 1959. "That is what we did before. Is that not madness? The act of a disoriented country, where a small handful of people live here beyond all limits without in the slightest concerning themselves for the well-being of the nation." He continued:

> Why were we buying Cadillacs when what we needed were tractors? We need tractors, not Cadillacs! The Cadillac costs thousands of dollars of our foreign exchange. The Cadillac does not plough, the Cadillac does not cultivate, the Cadillac does not produce. What the Cadillac does do is to waste 12 gallons per kilometer—do you understand?—and spend more foreign exchange in gasoline. . . . The Cadillac does not provide jobs for anyone. The Cadillac does not increase the wealth of the country, it diminishes it.[72]

Reforms assumed a logic of their own. Pressure from below provided impetus for change from above, which in turn served to garner wider support from below. Policies designed to improve living standards had necessitated a redistribution of wealth on a scale previously unimaginable. The reduction of rents served to increase the amount of disposable income among many lower-middle-

and working-class families, and consumption did indeed increase. Woolworth's sales reached record levels. "We saw the material benefits of the Revolution beginning to take shape," Gracia Rivera Herrera recalled of the first year. "Everything that Fidel had promised was like a wonderful dream coming true. I could see it with my own eyes. . . . at the end of 1959 we were quite prosperous."[73]

At the same time, however, the consumption of many middle- and upper-middle-class families declined. Upward mobility for some signified downward mobility for others. New taxes reduced the purchasing power of the wealthy. Investors in urban real estate experienced a drastic loss of revenue.

Reforms reached deeply into the realms of middle-class sensibilities. These were bewildering times, and meanings were not always clear or consistent. Old patterns of daily life had been disrupted and new ones had not yet taken hold. Changes affected the material renderings of nationality and inevitably raised larger questions about the character of "civilization" in Cuba. Luis Sanjenis insisted that the new leaders were addressing problems central to the integrity of the republic. "All they are trying to do," he explained, "is provide the basic needs of a civilized people which happen to occupy a piece of real estate located just 90 miles away from the country with the highest standard of living in the world." *Diario de la Marina* editor José Ignacio Rivero warned that import controls threatened to ruin the middle class and, by implication, destroy "civilization" as it had been known. Certainly all Cubans should consume national products, Rivero conceded, but Cuba did not "produce cars, calculators and typewriters, diesel engines, cameras, washing machines, refrigerators, air conditioners, radios, and televisions." Although it was true that it was "not necessary to write with a typewriter nor to ride in automobiles or have a refrigerator," Rivero countered:

> But the fact is that our people have become accustomed to the use of these conveniences which are appropriate to a highly civilized country as Cuba undoubtedly is. The level of civilization of a human community is not measured solely by the satisfaction of prime necessities . . . but also by the use and enjoyment of certain technical advances that, if you wish, can be classified as luxurious, but that indicate a high level of individual and collective well-being of a nation.[74]

Fidel Castro immediately offered alternative determinants of the "level of civilization":

> And if we measure the level of civilization of a country by the number of unemployed? And if we measure the level of civilization of a country by the number of cases of tuberculosis? And if we measure the level of civilization of a country by the number of children afflicted with parasites? And if we measure the real level by the rate of illiteracy and the rate of infant mortality in the country? What would the illustrious *Diario de la Marina* tell me? Well,

it would have to say that we are a barbaric country, an uncivilized country, for any country that is thinking of the luxury of radios, refrigerators, televisions, etc., with thousands of children affected with tuberculosis, in a nation with unpaved streets, with cities lacking water supplies, with a high rate of parasitism, anemia, and unemployment is a barbaric country.

Payments for imported "comforts and conveniences," Castro insisted, were bankrupting the country. "One cannot measure the level of civilization by the standard of small groups who lived well." How was it possible, he asked, that Cuba with a per capita income one-sixth that of the United States could claim higher per capita owners of Cadillacs? And more to the point, how was it possible that some could "drive around in Cadillacs while in Manzanillo 150 children died annually of gastroenteritis due to a lack of an aqueduct and . . . vast numbers of citizens cannot earn enough to live daily"?[75]

The dominant paradigm of "civilization" was in transition. The power of the revolution was in its capacity to rearrange in usable form the standards by which to measure civilization and in the process summon a vision of an alternative moral order. The proposition of patria took on new meaning as an all-inclusive community through which to find a sense of purpose and a source of identity. The notion of patria, free and sovereign, was reinvented around instrumental functions in which an egalitarian project served as the necessary condition of civilization. This implied patria as a means of mobility and the guarantor of well-being. "The reality is," Fidel Castro argued, "that the man who does not own even an inch of land can not speak of *patria*. *Patria* is where he experiences hunger, where his family goes hungry, where his children go hungry. He does not have a house, he has nothing. He wants to work but he cannot find a job. He is dying of hunger. Can that citizen say: 'I have a *patria*'? Ah! The owner of 6,660 acres can speak of *patria*. Well, we are going to do something: we are going to speak about a *patria* for everyone, but we are all going to have the right to speak of *patria*, and we are going to see to it that the *patria* belongs to everyone, the way Martí wanted." Patria hence implied the promise of well-being for all citizens. "It is necessary," Castro proclaimed on the passage of the Agrarian Reform Act in May 1959, "to write once and for all on our pure solitary star the formula of the Apostle that the *patria* belongs to all and for the good of all." Six months later, he announced: "For the first time in Cuba that of which Martí spoke, that the *patria* belongs to all and for the good of all, is being observed."[76]

The character of "Cuban" had become contested terrain, and the contest itself served as a force of change. Never before had the narrative on nationality so fully engaged the public imagination. Much of this had to do with the affirmation of Cuban, of a Cuba for Cubans. "We have been calling for the love of that which is ours, of our *Patria*, of our things," Fidel Castro exhorted in April 1959. "We have been Cubanizing Cuba, because although it may appear paradoxical, Cuba was not Cubanized, and we ourselves lived imbued with that type of complex of doubt, of resignation and where we undervalued the interest of our nationality before things foreign. We lived with the sensation that everything here was bad."[77]

The proposition of Cuban resonated across the island. Once more consumption became a way to affirm nationality, but now the products were Cuban-made. Advertisers stressed the virtues of locally produced merchandise. Vitamin supplement Transfusán B-12 was identified as "Cuban and better!" The advertisement concluded: "When you buy Transfusán B-12 you fulfill the call to consume Cuban products." In October 1959 the Agricultural and Industrial Development Bank of Cuba (BANFAIC) sponsored an "Exposition of Cuban Toys," designed "to exhort the public to buy toys produced in Cuba." The organizers affirmed: "In addition, the social function of the toy must be stressed, for from the most distant past to the present this has been one of the principal means to promote in the child knowledge of the civilization in which he develops." In November, the Ministry of Education decreed regulatory powers over all education in Cuba, effectively ending the private school system.[78]

Cuban became the dominant fashion motif, and cotton replaced dacron as the fabric of choice. In May 1959 designer Melly López exhibited her new line of summer wear at a fashion show luncheon at the Club Parisién in the Hotel Nacional. The new styles, observed one reviewer, "all bore a 'Made in Cuba' stamp, all designed to be worn for the hot summer. . . . Discarded is the wide-skirted American model, and in their stead is a simple line designed to emphasize the waist."[79]

The demand for Cuban spread in all directions. Architects called for a national building style. "Operación discos cubanos" announced a campaign to organize a national record company. The National Ballet was established in June 1959. A national film company, the Cuban Institute of Cinematographic Art and Industry (ICAIC), was organized in March 1959. Cuban musicians and entertainers began to work the nightclub and cabaret venues. For the first time since its opening in 1957, the Copa Room at the Hotel Riviera staged an all-Cuban production. The Club Parisién announced its *revista criolla* called *Te quiero Cuba*. The Casino de Capri (Hotel Capri) presented a new revue dedicated to consumption of Cuban products: *Consumiendo Productos Cubanos*. In the early 1960s *el filin* became a proscribed musical genre. Lisandro Otero would recount how the National Council of Culture concluded that the "sentimental melodies had been adopted by lumpen elements and counter-revolutionaries; everyone who liked *el filin* was called sickly (*enfermito*)."[80]

In small, countless ways, adjustments and adaptations to the times were made, mostly to become more Cuban, less North American. Naty Revuelta, who had studied at Ruston Academy and attended school in Philadelphia, in 1959 changed the spelling of her first name "Natty" by dropping a "t"—"to make it less *snob*, less North American." All sorts of mannerisms assumed new meanings. A billboard sign along the highway to Pinar del Río proclaimed: "Chewing Gum, No! Malanga, Si!"[81] By the early 1960s sports jackets and suits, as well as dress shirts and ties, so long the dominant fashion for men, were all but discredited and replaced with the *guayabera* (shirt jacket). Indeed, to wear a tie and dress shirt was to invite scorn and raised suspicion about one's dedication to the revolution, which then became, of course, a way to register disaffection with the new order.

Facets of everyday life were subject to scrutiny. One reader wrote to *Bohemia* that "in the same manner that Fidel reduced completely the cost of rents, he should order the removal of those store names in English, in French, and even in Italian that have transformed the capital of the Pearl of the Antilles into a city with an ambiguous nationality."[82] Andrés Valdespino, formerly president of Juventud Católica and undersecretary of the Treasury in 1959, who would later break with the Castro government, was eloquent about the task at hand. "We Cubans have felt until now dominated by a type of historical, geographic, and economic determinism that has taken us, consciously and unconsciously, to a position of mental dependency with respect to our neighbor of the North." He continued:

> And it has not simply translated itself into an object submission of previous governments to the *yanqui* command but also in the diffuse tendency of the "Americanization" of our customs. It would not be objectionable if that influence were limited to technical and scientific advances, but it is objectionable when the pedant arrives among us to name our commercial establishments in English, names to attract customers, or in the lamentable instance of some exclusive private schools where great effort is made to teach English at all hours and students graduate without knowing even how to write in Spanish.

Drama critic Rine Leal complained of the "invasion of foreign words," of "idioms brought principally from the United States, of terms that express another mental reality that have served to wreak havoc on our language and on our manner of expression." According to Leal:

> Language is nothing more than the means by which our cultural consciousness is revealed. It is well known that the cultural consciousness of the Cuban is far from having attained artistic form. If we add to this the high percentage of illiterates and semi-literates, the lack of libraries, the poor taste of our television and radio programs, the poorly written newspapers and magazines, and the poverty of the cultural projects of previous governments, it is not strange to see why the Cuban cannot engage in excellent literary dialogue, because in reality . . . the Cuban even at the cultural level has seen himself dislodged by outside influences, manipulated by way of film, news agencies, and foreign sensibilities.[83]

And, indeed, language became another contested sphere. Spanish affirmed jurisdiction and fixed the terms of transaction, all the while advancing the primacy of Cuban. In November 1959 the Ministry of Commerce mandated the use of Spanish words on all foodstuff packages, wrappers, and labels "in order to guarantee the consumer the best and proper knowledge of the nature, quantity, and other characteristics of the merchandise they purchase."[84] Even baseball was not spared, as authorities attempted—unsuccessfully, in the end—to replace English with Spanish usage: "pitcher" became *lanzador*; "catcher," *receptor*; "outfielder," *jardinero*; "jonrón," *cuatro bases*; and "inning," *espacio*.

Holidays were transformed. The celebration of Thanksgiving was suspended. Christmas changed. New emphasis was given to the celebration of a "Cuban Christmas," which signified the revival of Spanish traditions and the consumption of Cuban products. Fifty years earlier, the means of expressing Cuban involved replacing Spanish customs with North American ones. In 1959 the affirmation of Cuban implied rejection of North American practices for Spanish ones. Merchants, retailers, and advertisers were exhorted to emphasize Kings Day (January 6) as more consistent with Cuban customs. "The idea that we celebrate Christmas in accordance with our old traditions," affirmed Alejo Carpentier, "is absolutely reasonable. More than reasonable, it is legitimate." Carpentier called for the rejection of Santa Claus and the Christmas tree as practices "alien to our traditions." Roberto Fernández Retamar agreed, longing "to celebrate Christmas the way we always use to, . . . the way we remember in our childhood." The time had come to banish Santa Claus—"difficult to pronounce"—from the "Cuban Christmas" and restore the three wise men. Santa Claus had become something of a persona non grata and seemed to have been unceremoniously removed from public view. "Not a single shop along Galiano displays the merry St. Nicholas," a longtime resident of Havana observed in December 1959. Contrary to persistent rumors, columnist Milton Guss assured his readers, Santa Claus had not "taken asylum in the American Embassy." Speaking through his protagonist in *Arbol de la vida* (1990), Lisandro Otero recalled the displacement of Santa Claus:

In the newspaper a new personality appeared: Don Feliciano, who came to substitute *Sinter Claes* or Santa Claus o Santiclós o San Nicolás in the spirit of the season. It seemed reasonable to me that a Revolution achieved to change social organization would also involve itself in customs. What were Germanic legends, Protestant myths, snow-covered pine trees, and sleighs doing in a tropical, underdeveloped Country? The department stores, the importers of North American articles, and the advertising agencies had promoted the assimilation of Nordic myths that had absolutely nothing to do with our Hispanic, Catholic, Latin, and African traditions, much less than with the new styles that were to be created within a new rationality.

On the occasions where Santa Claus did appear, his beard was often colored black to resemble a *barbudo*. The Ministry of Commerce discouraged merchants from importing Christmas trees, Christmas decorations, candies, and other merchandise associated with "traditions foreign to the nation." The only exception to the ban on foreign imports was the Spanish candy *turrón*, which was permitted, as it formed part of the "true Spanish-Cuban tradition."[85]

It is not at all clear that U.S. officials understood the sources and subtleties of Cuban transformations. Nor is it reasonable to have expected them to. Many Cubans did not comprehend the vertiginous swirl in which they were caught up. More than any other single factor, the inability of official Washington to "reach" Cuban authorities and impose some restraint and a moderating influence, the failure to persuade Cubans to provide even the slightest assurance that U.S. interests would be protected, aroused suspicion almost immediately.

Reform policies affected North American interests directly. U.S. imports declined. International Telephone and Telegraph protested the reduction of its rates. So did the Cuban Electric Company. U.S. sugar companies opposed the agrarian reforms and U.S. employers inveighed against increased wages. Washington complained, both publicly and privately. But the Cubans proceeded undaunted and undeterred. As early as March 1959, Ambassador Philip Bonsal reported a "noticeable trend" in the public pronouncements of Fidel Castro "toward greater extremism, particularly in his economic thinking" in which he "repeatedly draws pictures of an egalitarian paradise in Cuba where the rich will be lowered and the poor raised to the same social and economic level." By November, first secretary John Topping had determined that the "long continuation of the Castro Government as now constituted and following the policies it now follows, is not something which would be in our best interests." Topping expressed hope for "a change in the reasonably near future" and urged that nothing be done to "delay that change." On the contrary, "our efforts should be aimed at smoothing the road, and possibly at accelerating the time table." Two weeks later, the State Department concluded that it was "unrealistic" to assume that the United States "shall ever be able to do business with the Castro Government on a basis which could be termed even reasonably satisfactory."[86]

Mounting criticism from the United States was received in Cuba with incredulity and indignation, provoking an already aroused public. These were heady times, when the Cuban people, flush with their recent triumph over a U.S.-supported dictatorship and the promise of a better future, were filled with euphoric self-confidence that expressed itself easily enough as a mixture of bravado and brashness. The early months were filled with a sense of urgency, in large measure driven by the initiative seized on the overthrow of Batista. An impatience filled the air, as if it were necessary to make up for lost time, to get on with the task at hand: reconstructing life on entirely new terms. Signs in government offices reflected the spirit of the times: "Hemos perdido 50 años—hay que recobrarlos—sea breve." More than 1,500 laws decrees and edicts were enacted in the first nine months of 1959. Fidel Castro seemed everywhere—in the capital and in the provinces—exhorting and expounding, pleading and pronouncing, delivering spellbinding speeches for hours at a time in dense and animated rhetoric with extraordinary vitality, sometimes reaching three hundred words per minute.

That the United States would publicly criticize a popular leader after having remained silent about an unpopular dictator was incomprehensible. The breach between Cuba and the United States widened. Support of Batista had cost the United States dearly, for it had forfeited the moral authority to render credible judgments about Cuban affairs. Certainly, this was the official response in Havana, and it was employed with great effect. Fidel Castro articulated these sentiments early and often, in a fashion that surely resonated across the island. "I believe," he asserted, "that this nation has the same right of other nations to govern itself, to chart its own destiny, freely, and to do things better and more democratically than what others do, who spoke of democracy and sent Sherman tanks to Batista."[87]

What is perhaps most remarkable about the growing dispute in 1959 was that so many reforms were devised and implemented not by radicals, but by liberals, Protestants, and graduates of U.S. schools, who, in fact, carried the moral of North American value systems to their logical conclusion. The ranks of the insurrection had been filled with Protestants of all denominations. Frank País, Oscar Lucero, and Marcelo Salado were only some of the most prominent Baptists killed in the revolution. Huber Matos rose to the rank of *comandante* in the Rebel Army, and Faustino Pérez directed the Civic Resistance in Havana. Presbyterians were also active. Reverend Cecilio Arrastía, a graduate of Princeton Theological Seminary, raised funds for antigovernment activities, and Mario Llerena, another graduate of the Princeton seminary, represented the 26 July Movement in the United States. Presbyterian minister Raúl Fernández Ceballos later affirmed that "99 percent of our members opposed the Batista regime during the armed struggle." Almost all of the teachers and administrators of La Progresiva in Cárdenas were active in the 26 July Movement, including Director Emilio Rodríguez and Subdirector Blanca Ojeda Díaz. Students at the Methodist Agricultural and Industrial School in Guaro aided guerrillas of the Second Front. At the other end of the island, Neill Macaulay later wrote, a "contingent of Methodists" joined the guerrilla column in Pinar del Río. He observed: "There were more Protestants in our group than practicing Catholics."[88]

Protestants proceeded to fill numerous positions in the new government. Faustino Pérez served as minister for the recovery of property. Among the Presbyterians, José A. Naranjo became minister of the interior, Manuel Ray was appointed minister of public works, Emilio Rodríguez Busto participated in the literacy program, the Reverend Raúl Fernández Ceballos headed the literacy campaign, and the Reverend Daniel Alvarez served in the Ministry of Social Welfare. Methodist pastor Manuel Salarría was in charge of a juvenile center. So was Baptist minister Carlos Herrera. Undersecretary of labor Carlos Varona had attended the Episcopal Mission School in Camagüey. La Progresiva had more than twelve graduates in the Ministries of Treasury and Education. The Methodist Agricultural and Industrial School at Guaro had eleven graduates in the Ministry of Agriculture and five graduates in the Ministry of Social Welfare. Richard Milk, director of the Agricultural and Industrial School, drew connections between government policies and Protestant education. "Many are increasingly aware," he wrote in March 1960, "that the highest ideal of the new government originated from the ideals of the Protestant Church."[89]

Liberals of all types joined the new administration, many of whom were educated in North American schools. Almost all of them would resign by the end of the first eighteen months, as radicals took over the government. But the point here is that the U.S. dispute with Cuba in 1959 was, ironically, largely with the policies and programs enacted by men and women most closely identified with North American practices. Minister of Communication Enrique Oltuski was an engineering graduate of the University of Miami. Minister of Public Works Manuel Ray was educated at the University of Utah. President of the National Bank Felipe Pazos attended Columbia University. Minister of the Treasury Rufo López-Fresquet, formerly an employee of Chase National Bank and a member of the American Club, completed graduate courses at Columbia. López-Fresquet—described by U.S. chargé d'affaires Daniel Braddock as "the most pro-American member of the cabinet"—played a strategic role in the reform policies of 1959. Minister of the Economy Regino Boti received an M.A. degree from Harvard. *Comandante* Manuel Piñeiro had studied economics at Columbia University. Vilma Espín had attended the Massachusetts Institute of Technology. Minister of Social Welfare Elena Mederos was raised by North American governess Addie Burke, who, Mederos's biographer maintained, was "one of the great and beneficial influences that contributed to forming Elena's personality." Mederos, who had attended Candler College, was characterized by chargé Braddock, at the time she was named to the new cabinet, as having "basically pro–United States orientations."[90]

U.S. opposition to the reforms of 1959 contributed to the undermining of the internal position of liberals. Men and women trained in North American methods of problem solving, and imbued with many of the same expectations, brought those experiences to bear in behalf of a better Cuba. They had been prominent participants in the formulation of reforms, thereby lending credibility and providing momentum to the proposed changes. In the end, they added legitimacy and respectability to Cuban demands as an expression of national sentiment. They gave their considerable expertise and prestige to the cause of national renovation and fully expected U.S. acquiescence to reforms that, within the logic of the Cuban reality, were not only reasonable but also necessary. They justified the changes, and indeed made appeals on their behalf, in terms calculated to resonate within a U.S. frame of reference. Nicolás Rivero, a member of the *Diario de la Marina* Rivero family, defended the attempt to reform the "unbalanced economy, which even in time of prosperity could not provide year-round employment for more than 75 percent of its economically active population—a higher rate of unemployment than that of the United States in its worst period of depression." Even from exile in 1961, Felipe Pazos continued to insist on the importance of precisely the reforms that the United States had opposed. "Cuba needed to break up large land holdings and to create a substantially larger number of land owners who cultivate their land," Pazos insisted; "to establish new industries to occupy the unemployed (seasonal, cyclical and structural); to step up its rate of economic growth; to tax more heavily high incomes and to collect taxes effectively; . . . to improve services for the people, especially education, health and housing."[91]

Liberals understood the nature of the market forces confronting Cuba; they also appreciated the limitations of market mechanisms in an export economy. What was especially striking about many of the reforms of 1959 was the degree to which the liberals chose to engage the North American presence in Cuba on its own terms, with its own rhetoric and rationale. They could not have known in advance that the United States would oppose their efforts, placing them in a position of extreme vulnerability, between U.S. opposition to reform and Cuban demand for revolution.

For those schooled in U.S. ways who participated in or were otherwise party to the reform project of 1959, the opposition of the United States was as incomprehensible as it was indefensible. They were dedicated to North American methods; indeed, they often defended reforms with reasoning derived explicitly from North American paradigms. They understood, too, that the ground was giving way under them and that the definition of "Cuban" was in transition. U.S. opposition and veiled threats against Cuba contributed to discrediting these representatives of North American ways. Cubans could not counter North American opposition without also calling into question some of the most fundamental assumptions on which their daily life had been based.

The result of U.S. opposition was to contribute to a profound crisis that transformed the proposition of revolution. The United States assumed the role of adversary, and henceforth the conventions that had insinuated themselves into almost every facet of Cuban life were subject to repudiation. It thus became increasingly difficult to hold on to North American affiliations without inviting scorn and arousing suspicion.

Politics and culture inexorably closed in on each other and assumed a larger logic. The revolution could not have proceeded along the course it pursued had it not been for the confrontation inside Cuba over formulations of national identity. The discourse assumed the proportions of a narrative on self-definition that could only accelerate the speed and expand the scope of change. The affirmation of Cuban now seemed to require new forms, free of U.S. traces and tendencies. Thirty years earlier philosopher Alberto Lamar Schweyer had reflected on the sources of *cubanidad* late in the nineteenth century. "To be Cuban and to be a patriot was to be anti-Spanish," he affirmed, "and in that unanimity was to be found the driving force of *cubanidad*."[92] After 1959, to be Cuban implied increasingly to be anti-American.

North Americans had operated from the presumption of familiarity, out of which was derived the notion that something "special" linked Cuba to the United States. Familiarity in this instance did indeed breed its own form of contempt. North Americans could presume sufficient familiarity with Cuba and Cubans to obtain images for their music, their films, their fiction, and then proceed to make a totality of that fragment of the Cuban reality that they themselves had created. They insisted on dealing only with the image of their creation. Cuba was not to be taken seriously. It was exotic and very tropical, a place for fun, adventure, and abandon. It was a background for honeymoons, a playground for vacations, a brothel, a casino, a cabaret, a good liberty port—a place for flings, sprees, and binges.

North Americans were neither prepared to accept nor willing to acknowledge the depth of Cuban grievances. They manifestly refused to consider the possibility that reality could exist in any form other than the one they had constructed. North Americans refused to address Cuban concerns with the respect and decorum Cubans demanded. "I talked to him like a Dutch uncle," Vice President Richard M. Nixon later recounted of his meeting with Fidel Castro in April 1959. (Robert Stevenson, Nixon's interpreter during the meeting, wrote that the vice president "had talked to Dr. Castro just like a father.") Senator Allen J. Ellender believed that Cubans regarded North Americans as "big brothers." Cubans were represented as children incapable of understanding their best interests. Acting secretary of state Christian Herter described Fidel Castro as "very much like a child in many ways, quite immature regarding problems of the government." At a February 1959 National Security Council meeting on Cuba, Central Intelligence Agency (CIA) director Allen Dulles expressed the view that "the new Cuban officials had to be treated more or less like children," they "had to be led rather than rebuffed" for if they were rebuffed, "like children, they were capable of doing almost anything."[93]

The failure to take Cuba seriously, indeed—given the structures and relationships through which North Americans had derived their perceptions of Cubans—perhaps the inability to take Cuba seriously, had profound consequences. Cubans meant to be taken seriously in 1959, and the victory over the U.S.-backed Batista government heightened their self-esteem and self-confidence. The terms of Cuban-U.S. relations were henceforth to be different. During a high-level meeting at the U.S. embassy in February 1959, minister of the economy and Harvard graduate Regino Boti informed North American officials "that while Cuba wanted friendly relations with the United States, from now on the [United States] would find the Cubans tougher to bargain with."[94]

The affirmation of national sovereignty and self-determination and the demand for control—control over their resources, control over their lives, control of their future, much of which had been derived from U.S. sources—were simply not accepted at face value in the United States. Ambassador Philip Bonsal characterized this determination as a product of "extreme sensitivity over Cuba's position as a small brother," which led "frequently to exaggerated reactions intended to assert complete independence and equality."[95] These were moments of euphoric self-discovery, inspired above all by hope for change never before experienced with such intensity or wide appeal. This demand for parity, this insistence on equal opportunity, this appeal to fair play—very much formulated in North American terms—was in the United States implausible coming from Cubans.

By the late 1950s Cubans had come to question the assumptions and the everyday reality of their world. Even while enjoying its benefits, they had become uneasy, even shamefaced, and they despaired, ever more predisposed to break with this order. The point is that even the most ardent and faithful defenders of North America were susceptible to occasional appeals of anti-American sentiment—if for no other reason than to protest the exclusivity of their patrons. That Cuban elites were the beneficiary of U.S. hegemony did not mean that they were entirely reconciled to and untroubled by their dependent status. Under the proper circumstances, they, too, could get caught up in a "nationalist moment" as a function of social uncertainty and economic insecurity.

Privilege in Cuba came at a cost. One cost that had become increasingly difficult to bear was continued acquiescence to the primacy of U.S. interests. What made this particularly onerous in the 1950s was that the economy was contracting, unemployment was rampant, the cost of living was soaring, and the standard of living was plummeting.

From the beginning of the century, the United States had set out to "Americanize" Cuba but had never considered the consequences of success: a First World frame of reference within Third World structures and no way within the latter to fulfill the former. North Americans taught generations of Cubans important truths about history, science, political economy, technology, and culture. Out of that experience vast numbers of Cubans grasped the fundamentals of modern life yet were never quite able to free themselves from the constraints imposed by North American structures.

Cubans had in fact become more or less "Americanized," but in ways that the North Americans could never have foreseen. They had acquired sufficiently the values, methods, and expectations to allow them to identify and articulate the malaise of dependent capitalism in ways that directly challenged the premises of U.S. hegemony in Cuba: on its own terms.

In growing numbers Cubans were arriving at the realization that emulation could not produce authenticity, that North Americans could not deal with them on any terms other than instrumental ones—without a past, without a future: only as a means, and that the meaning of Cuban had come to imply submission and subservience. They were learning that "Cuban" was defined simply as the North Americans' exotic and tropical Other.

Cubans of all classes, in varying degrees, had grievances against the status quo, and many of those grievances were a function of ties—historic and actual— with the United States. For one critical moment in 1959, all Cubans—men and women of all classes and ages, black and white—participated in a joyful nationalist celebration, unaware that the exaltation of things Cuban had profoundly different origins and radically different objectives. The revolution contained many diverse and divergent tendencies, central to which was the expectation that nationalism offered everyone a means of upward mobility.

The policies of the revolution reached across the social layers of Cuba. Wealth was redistributed, social hierarchies were rearranged. It is arguable, and indeed there is ample evidence to suggest, that the measures of the first twelve months obtained concurrence from almost all Cubans, even those adversely affected by reforms. This is not to suggest that they were pleased about the loss of property and income. They were not, of course, and some immediately opposed the new policies. But the larger point was that many Cubans at whose expense social justice was obtained could reconcile themselves to the requirements of the moment. The revolution released powerful forces, many of which had to do with the need to find new belief systems, to seek immersion in new experiences of community, in which to be Cuban acquired new meaning and assumed the capacity to provide redemption.

Identification with ways and things North American was unabashed and unambiguous, but it was not untroubled, not without its anomalies. It would be facile to suggest that these were positions without conflict or contradiction. Cubans had linked both worlds sufficiently to cross between each with frequency and familiarity. But frequent and familiar crossings inevitably invited invidious comparisons, and Cubans came up short at almost every turn. They had created a world of borrowed forms, improvised in large measure as a strategy for mobility and security and requiring, in the end, a redefinition along the lines of North American models. This was an illusory world sustained principally by dissimulation and self-deception. Enormous effort and energy had gone into an endeavor that proved to be unrealistic and thus unattainable.

And therein lay the source of the Cuban angst. A great many people had mastered the vernacular of the dominant paradigms and typically conducted themselves according to their practical dictates. But the more they were forced to comply with the terms of U.S. transactions, the more they came to discern and invoke the distinction between North American and Cuban. The contradictions between the world idealized in the North American moral order and the world experienced daily as the Cuban reality were becoming ever more acute. Cubans had fashioned a version of the North in the tropics, one that created high expectations but had no capacity to deliver. They went forth into a world for which their training had prepared them, only to find no such world in Cuba. Prerevolutionary Cuba had reached the limits of economic growth and social advance within a context of dependent capitalist structures sustained by sugar exports. Large numbers of Cubans, middle class and working class alike, those seeking individual advance and those committed to collective mobility, despaired of solutions within existing institutional structures, many of which were derived from and integrated into North American ones. These institutions could not resolve the mounting tension, driven largely by the demand for the primacy of Cuban interests—the one eventuality that such institutions were designed to prevent.

An uncertainty existed and was growing, the primary element of which was the loss of confidence in the future. In large part, this loss was itself derived from familiarity with the United States, as many Cubans came to realize that they could not keep up with the standard that they had established as the measure of their own well-being and more: that nation and national identity had assumed the form of commodity. In *Dreaming in Cuban* (1992), Cristina García has Delia writing plaintively to Gustavo in 1954: "Cuba has become the joke of the Caribbean, a place where everything and everyone is for sale. How did we allow this to happen?" Looking back on this time poet Heberto Padilla arrived at substantially the same conclusion: "Cuba was a country for sale, a parody of a country." This was precisely the same imagery used by the 26 July Movement with effect in its "Program-Manifesto" of 1956: "The Republic is a sorrowful caricature, through the fault of Cubans."[96]

Cuba had become a parody of a nation, as increasingly Cubans lost control of the means to define themselves, on their own terms, in their own forms, and underwent repeated transfiguration until all that remained was the caricature. It is in this sense that *I Love Lucy* serves as metaphor, but as more: tens of millions of Americans in the 1950s arrived at their construction of Cuban through Ricky Ricardo, the archetypical representation of Cuban adaptation: acculturated imperfectly and oblivious to the imperfections, one who mispronounced English and used idioms incorrectly, mangled syntax and routinely employed bad grammar, all of which were easy targets of Lucy's ridicule and mimicry and the enduring source of audience laughter. Ricky could hold his own only by reverting to Spanish: a defense of self-esteem expressed in forms beyond the understanding of Lucy and the viewing audience, but at considerable cost—he is wholly incomprehensible and hence ineffective. "Whenever Ricky became frustrated beyond words—usually by his yankee wife," wrote the series historian, "he regressed into his native tongue." Ricky is an outsider once more. Acting secretary of state Herter described a meeting with Fidel Castro in strikingly similar terms: "In English he spoke with restraint and considerable personal appeal. In Spanish, however, he became voluble, excited, and somewhat 'wild.'"[97]

No other attribute characterized Cuban sensibilities more than identification with the United States. Emulation did not, however, bring acceptance. On the contrary, imitation was suspect and ridiculed and resulted largely in an indulgence that was both patronizing and mocking. North Americans demanded emulation and adaptation but rejected the finished product as unauthentic. In its final form, emulation represented total submission—something North Americans understood and Cubans could only suspect. No amount of acquired customs or adaptive behaviors could offset factors of race and ethnicity. The willingness with which Cubans sought integration with North American capitalist structures, adopted U.S. cultural forms, and assimilated elements of the normative system from which they were derived could not, in the end, deliver to them control of those forces that most directly governed their lives. The harder they tried and the more complete their adaptation, the more difficult it became for Cubans to preserve the integrity of their nation, of their culture, and of themselves.

These circumstances produced among Cubans their own version of familiarity with North Americans and resulted in a love-hate relationship with a people that they were having difficulty living with but would have greater difficulty living without. That many ultimately chose to live without must be understood as a purge that reached deep into the very sources of nation and, perhaps more than any other single development, set Cubans against one another—a conflict between those who stayed and those who left.

It is important to stress that Cubans criticized North Americans with the presumption of familiarity, as insiders, possessing privileged insights accumulated over decades. This was the conventional wisdom, that Cubans knew North Americans better than any other people in Latin America—"better than Cubans knew even Spaniards," declared José de la Campa González. The chief of the State Department Bureau of Caribbean Affairs, Henry Holt, agreed: "The Cubans have probably a better understanding of our way of life than any other Latin American people." José Martí used his vantage point of having lived "inside the monster" to "know its entrails." In *En el año de enero* (1963), José Soler Puig speaks through his protagonist Felipe Montemayor also to locate Cubans "inside" the United States: "We are inside them, we live in their throat."[98]

Cubans did know North Americans well. They had come to learn their behaviors, attitudes, and customs, from which they could devise generalizations and opinions. Familiarity came in many ways—through personal contact and motion pictures and television programs, from afar and up close. Cubans could conjure up North Americans with their eyes closed, by scents. In *Los niños se despiden* (1968), Pablo Armando Fernández could write of a Havana nightclub as "smelling of American marines," a mixture of "U.S. cigarettes, whiskey, chiclets, Mennen aftershave lotion, Lifebuoy soap, khaki and U.S. Keds sneakers." Fernández described a "New York smell" of "French fries, hamburgers and hot dogs, pizzas and spaghetti," whereas Mario Parajón could conjure up a "characteristic Miami smell" of "cafeteria, sausage, bacon and eggs, [and] skin toasting in the sun covered with ample sun tan lotion." In Edmundo Desnoes's *Memorias de subdesarrollo* (1965), Elena speaks of "the peculiar American smell," a combination of "the smell of nylon, toothpaste, deodorant, and things like that."[99]

Cubans had failed to resolve the contradictions created by their relationship with the United States. In fact, these contradictions could not be resolved—not, at least, without challenging existing social and economic relationships within Cuba, which in turn required challenging existing relationships between Cuba and the United States. The revolution's demand for the primacy of Cuban interests as the principal consideration of national policy struck a responsive chord from all classes. But it implied more than a simple adjustment of domestic programs. So profoundly institutional, so intrinsically structural were the sources of U.S. hegemony that Cuban determination to advance national interests over foreign ones could not fail to produce a confrontation with the United States.

The affirmation of patria implied the primacy of Cuban. Men and women of all classes—factory workers and farmers, professionals and merchants—gave evidence of a heightened sense of empowerment associated with being Cuban. The character of relations between Cubans and North Americans was transformed in ordinary ways everywhere on the island. Anti-Americanism was expanding, chargé Braddock observed as early as February 1959. "It is concentrated almost entirely among the educated civilians who participated in revolutionary activities." North Americans in Cuba reported encounters unlike anything they had experienced before. Fights in private schools between Cuban and North American students increased. Many workers had performed their tasks daily for years, often in quiet and mounting resentment. It is probable that little would have come of this discontent had it not been for the triumph of the revolution in 1959. That the revolution took some of the turns that it did can be explained by the backlog of grievances that suddenly found an opportunity for release and revelation. One of the striking and recurring accounts of 1959 is the surprise of North Americans on discovering the depth and breadth of Cuban anger and frustration. These North Americans were startled or even astonished to see people they previously believed to be friends and colleagues suddenly turn against them. It was a painful personal experience.

Many thousands of men and women had done exactly what they were told they should do to become successful and, by implication, to obtain parity. For most of them, it had never happened. Everywhere Cubans began to redefine the terms of their relationship with North Americans. Cuban Protestant pastors broke with their U.S. colleagues. Formerly compliant Cuban employees defied their North American supervisors. The United Fruit manager of Preston, reported U.S. consul Park Wollam after the passage of the Agrarian Reform Law in 1959, was bitter about his Cuban staff: "The manager felt that some Cuban employees, some of them with many years of service, had 'turned against the Company.'" Wollam also noted that United Fruit administrators were "disturbed about rumors that their company houses were already marked for distribution by the Cubans." Not far away at Guaro, Richard Milk observed a similar phenomenon: "Needless to say, the foreigners feel a cultural isolation, shock at past and impending changes." *New York Times* correspondent Ruby Hart Phillips reported in September 1959 incidents where "American school children here, who speak Spanish as well as they do English, don't talk [in] English on the buses any more for fear of being insulted." A month later the U.S. embassy disclosed "a few cases of molestations and taunts of Americans." According to USIS officer William Lenderking, North American property owners, merchants, and residents in Las Villas, Camagüey, and Oriente had expressed concern for their property and personal safety. All of them cited "isolated incidents, such as insults, anonymous telephone calls, etc." Longtime Havana resident John Snook had another kind of experience. "I was quite shocked the other day," he wrote in November 1959, "when in a government building I was awaiting service and a government employee, who I must assume felt I didn't understand Spanish, said to another 'deja el Americano esperar hasta el último.' Bluntly it was 'leave the American waiting till the last.' I did too. As a matter of fact I waited two hours for a very simple matter." Snook added as an afterthought: "If anyone had ever said to me this would happen in Cuba, I would have laughed in his face." Jerome Cohen, a Havana resident for seventeen years, on returning to Cuba in October 1959 after a six-month absence, was shocked to see "the hatred among the Cubans for all of us Americans and this from a people who always loved and respected us." Milton Guss recounted his experience of seeing a longtime friend in an anti-U.S. demonstration carrying a placard reading "Yanqui Go Home." "I was in disbelief," Guss wrote, "I . . . inquired, 'Pepe, what is this, a joke or something?' But my erstwhile buddy just pointed a finger at me and shouted: 'Latifundista! Yankee Imperialista! Wall Street Capitalist!'"[100]

One result of the changed circumstances was seen in the solicitous treatment of Cuban employees by North American management. Cubans in U.S. companies received promotions and salary increases. But there were consequences. Efforts to give "more attention to Cuban officers and personnel" in the Nicaro Nickel Company, reported consul Wollam, had produced resentment among U.S. employees.[101]

The first year of the revolution ended in accelerated tension and uncertainty. Fidel Castro became increasingly strident in his attacks against the United States before millions of Cubans, many of whom did not know how to react to the spectacle unfolding before their eyes. Some publicly approved but were privately appalled. At the beginning almost everyone went along, for there were many truths that had to be told, and if Fidel was willing to tell them, that was good. It was, after all, a moment of celebratory euphoria, intoxicating and dizzying, a perfect occasion for catharsis and excess, even to be a little irresponsible and let lose with inflammatory rhetoric. Almost everyone believed that sobriety would soon return and life would get back to normal.

But it did not. Inflammatory rhetoric inflamed the public mood and provided the condition for more inflammatory rhetoric. Many Cubans shuddered, not knowing what to think or do. Surely the United States would react, surely the United States would not remain a passive object of attack. Juan Arcocha, in *Los muertos andan solos* (1962), captured these moments in poignant detail: "Carmen delighted to the orations of Fidel Castro. So young and so intelligent, and he said such magnificent things." Carmen was among those who believed that this state of affairs "would last only a few days and that later life would return to normal and be like it was before, when Batista had not yet taken power and everyone could live and be happy without problems. But instead of things calming down, matters became more intense." For Esperanza, too, the early days were a joy. "At first, when Fidel had put it to the Americans," the narrator comments, "she had liked that, because finally there was in Cuba a man of integrity who would stand up boldly and speak sternly to the Americans. Later Fidel had gone too far, his insults became more frequent and his tone had become more aggressive, and this was going to come to no good." Gloria González recalled her husband's certainty, "like so many others, [that] it was just a matter of time before things returned to 'normal.'"[102]

The prospects for those Cubans most closely identified with North America were also becoming increasingly problematical. For the tens of thousands of Cuban employees of U.S. enterprises, the conflict between Cuba and the United States had far-ranging implications. Among the first Cubans to emigrate were U.S. employees whose departures were arranged as company transfers. "I came to the United States in 1960," Maximiliano Pons recounted, "after Fidel nationalized the American company I was working for, I decided to leave. My family left with me. The company's U.S. base offered me a job in New Orleans. I took it." Coca-Cola transferred Roberto Goizueta to its Nassau plant in 1961. Pablo Medina remembered arriving in 1960 to a two-bedroom apartment in New York, "which we would not have been able to afford were it not for the graces of the company my father worked for."[103]

Distributive policies were not necessarily the determining factors of emigration. Rather, it had more to do with the reconfiguration of the proposition of Cuban, specifically the rapid and radical transformation of the normative context in which Cuban had been defined. Behaviors previously associated with promise were condemned; attitudes previously associated with success and security were now a source of scorn and suspicion. In ways perhaps too many and too complex to fully appreciate, from professional standards to personal style, from disposition and demeanor to customs and conduct, including attitudes, gestures, manners, and habits, all of the things that Cubans had become—in short, so much of what had signified national identity—were now denounced and despised.

The full dimensions of the mental strain and psychological stress experienced in many thousands of households may never be known. These must be seen as deeply personal and traumatic confrontations for vast numbers who slowly and painfully arrived at the realization that the norms of their everyday lives, the values and the moral codes that had served as the basis of their being, were under assault. "As the revolution became more radical," recalled Nicolás Rivero, "it alienated the upper classes in Cuba and created in me personally a psychological conflict between my ideological identification with the aims of the revolution and my family ties." The ground had shifted under families like the Riveros, and they now discovered themselves on unfamiliar terrain. The moral universe was transformed into something unrecognizable and unnegotiable. They were becoming outsiders in a place they had called home, strangers in their own land. In *Los muertos andan solos* Esperanza felt "as if the world was collapsing, without knowing what was coming next."[104]

As ties to the United States weakened, as attachment to ways North American no longer served as a means of security but rather as a source of suspicion, numerous Cubans found themselves increasingly unable to retain a grip on those elements by which they had previously negotiated the terms of everyday life. It was not only that the new hierarchies of Cuban could not accommodate the continued presence of North American forms, but also that in the new order these forms no longer served as a way to advance. The world had turned upside down; many people who had previously done the "right" things to make a place for themselves in Cuba found that the rules had changed and they no longer "fit in." Throughout the film *Memorias de subdesarrollo*, Sergio struggles to understand the changes occurring all around him and fails. "I keep my mind clear. It is a disagreeable clarity, an emptiness," he reflects. At another point, he asks: "What does this all mean? You remember many things, you remember too much. Where is your family, your work, your wife? You are nothing, you are dead." And later: "In another time, I would have been able to understand what was going on here. Now, I can't." In Otero's *Arbol de la vida*, the protagonist thinks about Cuba as he had previously known it: "And now all that was disappearing and the knowledge that the pillars of society as we knew them would cease to exist left me with a strange emptiness. . . . An unknown world opened before me, without the values that were familiar to me." He continued:

I learned to live with insecurity. One woke up every morning with the impression that at the end of the day life would be over; no one could possibly know what complexities, what changes, reforms, and transfigurations would transpire in the course of a day. Everything was in transition: the earth could open and swallow us up in a flash and the Revolution go up in smoke and nothing would remain, not even a sentimental memory of our passing through this world. Millennia and seconds fused, permanence and ephemera began and ended in an eternal daily routine. Where was life and where was death?[105]

The protagonist's voice vaguely reflects Otero's personal experience. Years later, he wrote: "I felt torn between the world I had grown up in and the one in which I now lived," adding:

The economic well-being my family enjoyed had accustomed me to the gleaming surface of a system that had been eradicated. For me, that vanished universe had been positive and pleasant. The world of consumer goods and good taste, of our carefully maintained heritage, of cleanliness and abundant lighting, of beautiful things was all part of my natural place. As a result, I found slovenliness, shabby gentility, neglect, inefficiency, ugliness—everything associated with the revolutionary changes that had elevated the humblest sectors to positions of authority—unbearable. I had no craving for opulence, having always been indifferent to that, but I needed the same standard of living available to any intellectual in the first world.[106]

The creative power of the revolution consisted in its capacity to challenge old ways even while promoting values that were antithetical to existing moral hierarchies. The new order was clearly influenced by the one to which it reacted, and in this sense many old values persisted, if in new forms. But it was no less true that the new terms of national identity were made possible by the displacement of social groups previously in positions of influence and power. The nation was defined more inclusively, even if the position of the old bourgeoisie in the new order was anomalous.

The normative hierarchies by which much in prerevolutionary Cuba had derived value were in transition. Change was most directly experienced at a personal level, as the ways vast numbers defined themselves in the most basic and intimate facets of their daily life were under assault. "I noticed that something fundamental had changed," comments Adriana in Freddy Artiles' play *Adriana en dos tiempos* (1972). "I did not fully understand what, but I sense that it was something new and above all something different. Even the people seemed different. The outside world entered into the home and into one's self."[107] There was no space, no escape, for the new moral order was all-encompassing, daily and directly. This was a bewildering experience, as inconceivable as it was incomprehensible, for it attacked the very assumptions by which the Cuban people had come to understand the world and their place in it.

Exile was the obvious option. But the fact that it was obvious does not mean that it was easy. It was not. Nor does the fact that almost all of the early emigration represented self-imposed exile mean that departure was without heartache. The most susceptible to emigration were the people who had been most effectively integrated into North American structures and whose belief system prevented them from fully comprehending the implications of the changes they were experiencing. Fichu Menocal recalled the departure of her family and friends. "They had never been politically persecuted," she insisted. "The great emigration was simply because Cubans did not accept a real change in their life, their way of life."[108] Salvador Díaz-Versón remembered "the comfortable home in Arroyo Arenas, the garden, the library, the luxury of long evenings together, the friends, the accomplishments," the loss of which "was a blow to the very centers of our being." Díaz-Versón stated: "Thousands upon thousands of Cubans have sought refuge in Miami. Doctors, engineers, newspapermen, writers, businessmen—in short, the people who together form the backbone of any civilized nation—were uprooted and transported to Florida. . . . People once able achievers thanks to study, hard work and sacrifices became in their bewilderment a frightened legion of the dispossessed."[109]

For many the decision to emigrate was made slightly more bearable in the belief that the United States would eventually lose patience with the new order in Cuba and, as so often in the past, intervene to set things right. Their ties to North American ways, their understanding of U.S. behaviors past and present, persuaded them to believe that Washington would rid Cuba of Fidel Castro. Soler Puig captured these moments effectively in *En el año de enero. Hacendado* Felipe Montemayor affirms confidently: "Almost all of Cuba is American—the land, the sugar mills. Do you think that anything can be done here without consulting them? Don't be stupid! . . . They will not allow this fool to introduce communism here. . . . They will not permit it. Forget it! They'll knock it down as if it were a rotten palm tree." In Raoul Fowler's novel *En las garras de la paloma* (1967), Pepe, whose sugar mill was nationalized, resigns himself to wait: "I am convinced that this will not last much time. Do you think the United States is going to tolerate the seizure of a billion dollars of its properties? No, my friend, absolutely not. The Americans passively endure insults, but when the offense involves property. . . ."[110]

Most Cubans who left early expected to return shortly, after the United States had stepped in to return things to the way they used to be. "We arrived in the United States in 1960," Marifeli Pérez-Stable recalled three decades later, "certain that our stay would be temporary." Pablo Medina remembered his arrival in exactly the same terms: "We expected to return in a few months." Similar expectations filled the Pérez Firmat household in Miami: "Soon enough either Cubans would get fed up with the Revolution and overthrow Castro, or the Marines would show up on the Malecón and wrest the government from him. Then we and the thousands of other exiles could return. My father would go back to his *almacén*, my mother would go back to the house and the rounds of baptisms and birthday parties, the children would go back to our schools and our *tatas* (nannies), and we would all pick up where we had left off." Arcocha's *Candle in the Wind* captured these moments through his protagonist Vicente: "What happened was a kind of hysteria. Everyone said the Americans were going to invade and it would be the end of the world. Besides, they calculated that their exile would be short. The Americans would come and topple Fidel and they could return as heroes who opposed communism." In Desnoes's *El cataclismo*, Cristobal assures Cristina on the eve of their departure that "this won't last even six months. It will be nothing more than a trip abroad." In any case, Cristina says, she owned "enough clothing for a couple of years—until the Americans return." In the Machado play *Once Removed*, Olga imagines "exile" as "an aristocratic city where kings and princesses went, till the hard times were over, before they went back home."[111]

What many Cubans could not have appreciated, of course, was that North American hegemony in Cuba had depended on their presence inside Cuba, those who shared U.S. values and identified with U.S. ways, and who, in defense of their own interests, could be relied on to defend U.S. interests. Emigration guaranteed the internal success of the revolution.

Emigration presumed familiarity with North American ways, and this, too, encouraged exile. Certainly knowledge of English, to a lesser or a greater extent, reduced doubts about moving to North America. "For me and my brothers," Gustavo Pérez Firmat wrote, "as for other Cuban exiles, English may have been foreign, but it wasn't strange."[112] Cubans could expect to move about confidently in the United States, for this was a place with which they were familiar. That many subsequently succeeded in exile was in large part due to prior experience with the North American market culture.

For vast numbers the most familiar place outside Cuba was Miami, and indeed such familiarity was central to the process of emigration. The Cuban presence in Miami had expanded markedly during the 1940s and 1950s. Cubans owned and operated shops and restaurants, apartment houses and hotels, restaurants and retail shops, movie theaters, and nightclubs. As many as 20,000 Cubans resided in Miami prior to the revolution. Many times that number had visited frequently, as shoppers and travelers, to work and play, to invest and sightsee. Arcocha's protagonist in *Los muertos andan solos* captured the appeal of Miami after the revolution: "At times Carmen also felt the desire to leave for Miami. It was such a pleasant place. She had been there many times on her vacation and always took advantage of the trip to buy clothing at low prices. She was fascinated by the easy life of the tourists, the acquaintances that were made

A Miami storefront, "Cuba in Miami," assuring prospective customers that English was spoken in Miami, n.d. (Courtesy of the Library of Congress, Washington, D.C.)

on the beach and in the hotel with people one never saw again. The Americans certainly knew how to live well."[113]

Cubans waited to return. Months turned into years and years into decades. Miami was transformed into a Cuba-in-exile. Miami began as an imitation of Havana in the 1920s and 1930s, then was imitated by Havana during the 1940s and 1950s; in the 1960s it was a copy of a copy that was copied. There was, in the end, nothing whimsical about María Cristina García's choice of title for her book, *Havana USA*—it was a perfect fit. In the years that followed many Cubans prospered as bankers, industrialists, real estate developers, sugar planters, merchants, and shop owners. They revitalized southern Florida. By the early 1970s they owned and operated nearly 20,000 businesses, including banks, car dealerships, movie theaters, radio and television stations, supermarkets, travel agencies, and retail stores. Spanish was the requisite language of employment. Cuban Rotary and Lions clubs were reestablished in Miami. The penchant for private education found renewed vitality in exile, as the old schools of Havana were reorganized in Miami, but no longer to advance familiarity with things North American but to preserve Cuban ways: among them, LaSalle, Baldor, Lincoln, La Progresiva, Edison, and Colegio La Luz. And as in Havana in the past, a curious mixture of English and Spanish names of retail shops and business establishments appeared: Yeyo's Loans, El Caney Grocery, Blanquita Supermarket, La Caridad Hardware, La Cubana Bus Line, Pepito's Flowers, La Esperanza Junk, Conchita Beauty Salon, Virgen Milagrosa Supermarket, Mongo's Travel. During the 1950s Miami was the stuff of local news in Havana; after the 1960s Havana was the stuff of local news in Miami. Eladio Secades captured Cuba-in-exile with perspicacity and affection:

> Exile in Miami feels less like exile. It has intimate compensations that the Cuban does not find elsewhere. The émigré who goes north will have to adapt. Those who have stayed in Miami have formed here a miniature Cuba, marvelous and new. The pain of the lost country is much reduced by the sensation that one lives in a city conquered peacefully. And for the same reason, almost as if it belonged to us. There are so many Cubans in Miami and the manner of living has assumed a tone and flavor so *criollo* that at times we even reach the point of thinking that the North American is a foreigner. We suddenly hear English spoken on 8th Street and we believe that it is an unfortunate tourist who has lost his way.[114]

Remembrances of Cuba were thus preserved and passed on, and the nostalgia of parents became the memories of children, as if these had been lived as their own experiences. More than a place was lost: being was lost, and more. The source of self-definition was lost, for what had made the North American part of self-definition "work" was the Cuban part. Becoming Cuban in the United States began all over again.

On April 13, 1961, El Encanto department store was destroyed by fire: a suspicious fire, to be sure. Some suspected arson by the Central Intelligence Agency. It probably does not really matter, although if it was the CIA, it suggests a remarkably nuanced understanding of Cuban sensibilities. Cubans could point to El Encanto with pride, an institution, actually, that served to validate the Cuban claim to cosmopolitan. El Encanto was the premier department store of the republic. It was synonymous with chic and elegance, the newest fashions and latest styles. The months after January 1959 were difficult ones for El Encanto. The window displays had been sharply reduced and display counters contained little of the merchandise for which it had long been famous. The fire destroyed a store that was older than the republic and one that had given form to Cuban longings.

The timing was also striking. Three days later, Fidel Castro proclaimed the revolution as socialist. The Bay of Pigs invasion began the next day.

Change assumed explicitly ideological formulations, and the revolution had become something else. The emigration of tens of thousands of middle-class families identified with ways and things North American began in earnest. Their departure facilitated the changes that followed. The fact that the revolution was able to consolidate itself on the terms that it did, as easily as it did, was in no small way made possible by the absence of sustained opposition from within. Cuba was now reinventing itself. Edmundo Desnoes was among the first to discern the change. Havana had not been the same since El Encanto burned down, the narrator reflects in *Memorias de subdesarrollo*. "It looks like a city of the interior, Pinar del Río, Artemisa or Matanzas. It no longer looks like the Paris of the Caribbean, as the tourists and whores used to say. Now it looks like a Central American capital, one of those dead and underdeveloped cities, like Tegucigalpa or San Salvador or Managua. It's not just because they destroyed El Encanto and there are few good things left in the store, few consumer goods of quality. It's the people too; now all the people one sees on the streets are humble, dressed poorly, they buy everything they see even those that don't need it." In the film version, Pablo carries the point one step further: "These people say they are making the first socialist revolution in America. So what? They are going to return to the jungle. They are going to go hungry, just like the Haitians. They toppled Napoleon and so what?"[115] Once again the Cuban discourse on self found expression in allusions to civilization.

As years passed, many Cubans could only react to the reality of Eastern European socialism with disbelief and dismay. Their tastes and sensibilities had been formed in a market environment of abundance, of products that were a part of the normal landscape of daily life. The initial contacts with socialist bloc countries were sobering indeed. The narrator in *Arbol de la vida* recounts the impression of an early visit by a Cuban delegation to Budapest:

> They called us early from the lobby. Our guide was waiting to take us to a supermarket; they wanted us to see the high standard of living they had achieved. We walked along the rows of shelves in a frenetic inspection. There were cans with outrageously colored labels, jams in thick and dark glass, musty merchandise. The clothing section was a disaster area: ridiculous shirts, common dresses, coarse and out of style suits, crude shoes that seemed made for field work. I remembered the dazzling display cases and counters at El Encanto.

The narrator concludes: "What they promised us could not compare to what we already had: we were accustomed to the efficient products manufactured by North American industry, to the aesthetic standards of Western Europe, and this coarse and crude merchandise could not be a substitute for the well-being we knew. . . . If we were going to persevere on the road of the revolutionaries, it would be for ideological reasons, for the desire for equality."[116]

Cuba had indeed been transformed, and yet much of what was Cuban persisted unchanged. The grip of North American forms may have loosened after 1961, but it never let go entirely. Cubans continued to prefer North American motion pictures, they still looked to U.S. musical forms—especially popular music and jazz—for creative possibilities, and vice versa. Baseball persisted as the national pastime. Protestant churches, almost all of which traced their origins to North American denominations, remained among the principal mainstays of the revolution, a development of significant irony.

The power of North American conventions is suggested by their resilience. Under the circumstances, it must be presumed that a basis for reconciliation has always been there.

APPENDIX

TABLE 1.1. *U.S. Merchant Houses in Cuba, 1850–1895*

Havana
James C. Burnham Company
G. Lawton Childs and Company
Edwin F. Churchill Company
DeConnick, Spalding and Company
Gardner and Dean Company
McQuaker Basoth Company
Perkins and Burlin Company
Oliver Pollock
Robertson and Company
Vernon Brothers
R. L. Ward

Matanzas
George Bartlett and Company
James Bayley Company
George W. Brinkerhoff Company
Joseph Jarris and Company
Latting and Glen Company
Moses Taylor and Company
Charles Tying and Company

Caibarién
Bishop and Company

Santiago de Cuba
Wright, Shelton and Company

Cárdenas
John F. Cahill Company
George Harris and Company
Howland Brothers and Company
Charles Madden Company
Cornelius O'Callaghan Company
William F. Safford and Company
Dudley Senden and Company
Samuel Trask Company
Henry Treat Company

Sagua la Grande
M. H. Morris Company
J. P. C. Thompson and Company

Trinidad
Charles Edmonstone Company
Frederick Freeman and Company
Tate and Company

Cienfuegos
Martin Knight and Company
Augustus L. Richardson and Company

TABLE 1.2. *The Emigré Press, 1850–1898*

New York
La Verdad (1848–69)
La Crónica (1851)
El Filibustero (1853)
El Eco de Cuba (1855–56)
Cuba y Puerto Rico (1868–69)
Boletín de la Revolución (1869)
El Libertador (1869)
El Revolucionario (1869–71)
El Demócrata (1870)
Diario Cubano (1870)
Diario de Nueva York (1870)
La Estrella de Cuba (1870)
La Voz de la Patria (1870–72)
La República de Cuba (1871)
La Revolución de Cuba (1871–73)
El Mundo Nuevo (1872–74)
La Independencia (1873–80)
El Tribuno Cubano (1875–76)

El Pueblo (1875–78)
La Verdad (1876–78)
El Ciudadano (1880)
La República (1880–89)
La Juventud (1889)
El Avisador Cubano (1890)
El Cubano (1890)
El Porvenir (1890–98)
El Independiente (1890, 1898)
La América (1892)
Patria (1892–98)
Las Novedades (1893)
El Radical (1893)
Guáimaro (1895)
La Doctrina de Martí (1896–98)
Cuba y América (1897–98)
Cuba (1898)

Washington
Cuba Libre (1898)

New Orleans
El Faro de Cuba (1852)
El Independiente (1853)
La Verdad (1854)
Las Dos Repúblicas (1869)

La Libertad (1869)
El Machete (1869)
La Patria (1870–71)
El Emigrado (N/A)

Key West
La Republicano (1869–76)
La Igualdad (1874)
La Libertad (1876–77)
El Yara (1878–98)
La Voz de Hatuey (1884)
El Obrero Cubano (1886)
El Ecuador (1887)

La Ilustración (1890)
El Vigía (1897)
El Eco Popular (1897–98)
El Intransigente (1897–98)
Revista de Cayo Hueso (1897–98)
La Propaganda (N/A)
El Rifle (N/A)

Tampa
Revista de la Florida (1886–87)
El Crítico de Ybor City (1890)
El Patriota (1890)
La Revista de Cuba Libre (1892)
Cuba (1893–98)
El Eco de Martí (1896)
El Expedicionario (1896–97)

El Mosquito (1896)
La Opinión (1896)
El Oriente (1897)
La Libertad (1897)
La Contienda (1897–98)
La Nueva República (1897–98)
El Emigrado Cubano (1898)

TABLE 2.1. *Agricultural Property Losses, 1862 and 1877*

	1862	1877	% Decrease
Sugar mills (*ingenios*)	1,521	1,191	22
Tobacco *vegas*	11,550	4,511	61
Coffee estates	782	194	75
Ranches	6,175	3,172	49
Miscellaneous farms (*estancias* and *sitios*)	34,546	17,074	51

Source: Diana Abad, María del Carmen Barcia, and Oscar Loyola, *Historia de Cuba: La Guerra de los Diez Años* (Havana, 1989), pp. 99–102.

TABLE 2.2. *Net Taxable Profits, 1862, 1877, and 1883*

Year	Agriculture	Urban Real Estate	Industry, Commerce, and Professions	Total Income
1862	$38,032,502	$17,040,043	$77,384,649	$132,457,194
1877	26,183,581	13,473,136	17,388,125	57,044,842
1883	22,700,951	13,685,737	12,075,465	48,562,153

Sources: U.S. Consulate, Havana, "Havana Weekly Report," August 23, 1884, Dispatches/Havana; *Boletín Comercial*, April 10, 1890.

TABLE 2.3. *U.S. Land Development and Colonization Companies in Cuba,*
1898–1912

Name	Site of Incorporation	Site of Holdings
Almacigos Springs Land Company	N/A	Matanzas
American Colony Lands Company	Buffalo	Consolación del Sur
American Cuban Development Company	St. Louis	Las Villas
Bahía Honda Land Company	N/A	Pinar del Río
Carlos Investment Company	Los Angeles	Oriente
Cauto Produce Company	Norwalk	Oriente
Cuba Colonial Company	Chicago	Matanzas
Cuba Colony Company	Battle Creek, Mich.	Pinar del Río
Cuba Land Company	Rockford, Ill.	Camagüey
Cuba Polish Company	Toledo	Oriente
Cuban Agricultural and Development Company	Pittsburgh	Oriente
Cuban American Land and Fruit Company	New York	Camagüey
Cuban Colonization Company	Cleveland	Oriente
Cuban Development Company	Detroit	Oriente
Cuban Land and Developing Company	Cleveland	Pinar del Río
Cuban Land and Mortgage Company	New York	Las Villas
Cuban Land and Steamship Company	New York	Camagüey
Cuban Products Company	N/A	Oriente
Development Company of Cuba	New York	Camagüey
Eastern Cuba Plantation Company	N/A	Oriente
Eastern Cuban Development Company	Chicago	Oriente
Havana Land and Mortgage Company	New York	Las Villas
Herradura Land Company	South Dakota	Pinar del Río
Illinois Cuban Land Company	Hoopeston, Ill.	Oriente
Isle of Pines Company	New Jersey	Isle of Pines
Isle of Pines Land and Development Company	Iowa	Isle of Pines
Las Tunas Realty Company	Youngstown, Ohio	Oriente
Las Uvas Land Syndicate	N/A	Pinar del Río
McKinley Colony Company	N/A	Isle of Pines
Pine Island Land and Lumber Company	Spencer, Iowa	Isle of Pines
Pittsburgh Development Company	Pittsburgh	Isle of Pines
Potosi Land and Sugar Company	Cincinnati	Oriente
San Claudio Land Company	New York	Pinar del Río
San José Company	N/A	Pinar del Río
Sancti-Spíritus Land Company	N/A	Sancti-Spíritus
Santa Clara Commercial Company	Cleveland	Las Villas
Santa Fe Land Company	Iowa	Isle of Pines
Swedish Land and Colonization Company	Minneapolis	Oriente
Taco Bay Commercial Company	Boston	Oriente
Tropical Land Company	Detroit	Sancti-Spíritus
United States Real Estate Company	N/A	Las Villas
Youngstown Cattle Company	Youngstown	Oriente

TABLE 2.4. *North American Newspapers and Magazines in Cuba, 1898–1909*

Newspaper/Magazine	Year Founded
American Supplement (Fénix)	1898
Cárdenas Herald	1898
Havana Advertiser and Weekly Gazette	1898
Santiago Enterprise	1898
Commercial and Financial Review	1899
Cuba Opportunities	1899
Daily American	1899
Havana Citizen	1899
Havana Daily Advertiser	1899
Havana Journal	1899
Cuban Tourist and Settler	1900
Havana Herald	1900
Havana Police Gazette	1900
Havana Post	1900
Havana Star	1900
Havana Evening Telegram	1901
Havana Sun	1901
Cuba Review and Bulletin	1902
Morning Sun	1902
La Gloria Cuban-American	1904
Daily Telegraph	1905
Cuban Interpreter	1907
Modern Cuba	1909
Cuba Magazine	N/A
Isle of Pines Appeal	N/A

TABLE 3.1. *Songs of Cuba, 1910s–1950s*

Title	Composer	Year
Havana	E. R. Goetz, J. Kendis, and H. Paley	1910
Down on Old Havana Bay	E. Madden and A. Fred Phillips	1911
Havana Anna Ann	H. Atteridge and M. Gideon	1911
Havana Rose	Harold B. Freeman	1911
There's a Girl in Havana	A. Baldwin and E. R. Goetz	1911
Havanola	Hugo Frey	1912
My Cuban Dream	S. D. Mitchell and F. Washauer	1916
Cuban Dreams	N/A	1919
Cuban Moon	Norman Spencer and Joe McKiernan	1920
Havana	John L. McManus	1920
Havana	John Meown and Teddy Lauxman	1920
I'll See You in C-U-B-A	Irving Berlin	1920
In Gay Havana	Gus Kahn and Walter Blaufuss	1920
It Will Never Be Dry in Havana	Wm. Tracey and Halsey K. Mohr	1920
Let's Go to Cuba	Jack Darrell	1920
Sweet Cuban Love	Sam A. Perry and J. Fred Coots	1920
Cubana	H. L. Cort, G. E. Stoddard, and O. Motzan	1921
Cuban Eyes	I. Caesar, Jack and Nat Shilkert	1921
Havana Moon	Walter Smith	1921
Havana Rose	Arnold and Brown	1922
My Cuban Pearl	Harry Waxman and V. Dattilo	1922
Cubanita	J. Huarte	1923
Havana	Abe Lyman, M. and J. Schonberger	1923
A Cuban Nocturne	William and Margaret Lester	1924
Sunny Havana	Horatio Nicholls	1925
A Toast to Cuba	Tito Schipa and Laurence Lipton	1925
Havana	Richard Rodgers and Lorenz Hart	1926
Havana	Vincent Rose and Raymond B. Egan	1927
Down in Old Havana Town	Irving Caesar and Cliff Friend	1928
One Night in Havana	Hoagy Carmichael	1929
Cubanita	William Kernell	1930
Cubalero	L. Banker, J. Young, and J. Siras	1931
Cuban Holiday	M. Parish, F. Washaver, and S. Sprigato	1931
Cuban Love Song	H. Stothart, J. McHugh, and D. Fields	1931
She Went Havana	G. Whiting, A. von Tilzer, and G. Boyce	1931
Under a Cuban Moon	N/A	1931
Under a Cuban Sky	N/A	1931
The Cuban Iceman	Jack Meskill and Joseph Meyer	1932
Cuban Serenade	Moisés Simons and Marjorie Harper	1932
In Havana	Harry Revel and Mack Gordon	1932
Cuban Belle	Marion Sunshine and Moisés Simons	1933
Cuban Cabaret	E. Heyman, B. Kaplan, and R. Childs	1933
In a Hut in Old Havana	Al Neiburg, Marty Symes, and J. Myrow	1934
Sidewalks of Cuba	B. Oakland, M. Parish, and I. Mills	1934

TABLE 3.1. *Continued*

Title	Composer	Year
Havana Heaven	H. Johnson, E. G. Nelson, and N. Dostal	1935
There's a Riot in Havana	Sigmund Rombert and Oscar Hammerstein	1935
The Cuban Cabby	N. Simon, J. Cavana, and J. Redmond	1936
Cuban Pete	Norman Henderson	1936
Havana	Moe Jaffe and Clay Boland	1936
Two Hearts in Cuba	N/A	1936
At a Cuban Cabaret	Abner Silver and Alex Hyde	1937
The Cuban in Me	Marion Sunshine	1937
Havana's Calling Me	Eliseo Grenet and Marion Sunshine	1937
José O'Neill—The Cuban Heel	H. Warren, A. Dubin, M. Jerome, and J. Scholl	1937
The Moon over Cuba Was High and So Was I	N/A	1937
By the Light of a Cuban Moon	Xavier Cugat, S. Walter, and T. Sarli	1938
Cuba-Duba-Doo	I. Caesar, A. Bryan, and G. Marks	1939
Havana for a Night	Oscar Hammerstein and Gonzalo Curiel	1939
A Cabana in Havana	Tom Seymour and Mabel Wayne	1940
Cuban Gondolier	Marion Sunshine and Alejandro Rodríguez	1940
Episode in Havana	N/A	1940
Cuba Libre	Xavier Cugat and Eddie Asherman	1941
Cubalita	Albert Rizzo and Harry Sims	1941
Cuban Barbeque	D. Mario, F. Bausa, and V. Ayala	1941
A Weekend in Havana	Mack Gordon and Harry Warren	1941
Episode in Havana	N/A	1942
Cuban Blues	Marion Sunshine	1944
Cuban Moon	Elsie Grable and Clarence Mayer	1944
Cuba	A. D. Z. and Eduardo Sánchez de Fuentes	1947
Holiday in Havana	Desi Arnaz	1949
Anna from Havana	N/A	1950
Cuban Cutie	Ethel Smith and Billy Taylor	1950
Cuba	Paul Hastings	1951
Cuban Nightingale	Don George and Rogelio Martínez	1952
Havana Heaven	Nico Dostal, Howard Johnson, and Ed Nelson	1952
My Cuban Sombrero	Antar Daly and Marion Sunshine	1956
Cuban Moonlight	Eddie Duchin	n.d.
Cuban Sugar Mill	Freddie Stack	n.d.
Havana	Charles Adler and Jack London	n.d.
Yankee in Havana	Will Hudson	n.d.

TABLE 5.1. *Motion Picture Theaters and Their Seating Capacity, 1955*

Location	Number of Theaters	Total Seating Capacity
Havana and suburbs	138	136,000
Oriente	104	63,000
Las Villas	100	59,000
Camagüey	58	37,049
Havana Province	55	28,000
Matanzas	52	27,000
Pinar del Río	42	20,446
Total	549	370,495

Source: *Anuario cinematográfico y radial cubano, 1955* (Havana, 1956).

TABLE 5.2. *Columns and Features on Hollywood, 1940–1958*

Cables de Cine	Hoy en Hollywood
Cables de Hollywood	La Voz de Hollywood
Cables de la Meca de Cine	Notas de Cine
De la Tierra del Celuloide	Notas de Estudio
Desde Hollywood	Notas de Hollywood
Desde la Meca del Celuloide	Noticias de Hollywood
Ecos de Hollywood	Noticias de Pantalla
Escareos de la Pantalla	Noticias de Peliculandia
Hollywood Observa	Secretos de Hollywood
Hollywood por Dentro	

Sources: *El Mundo, Social, Carteles, Grafos, Bohemia*, and *Vanidades*.

TABLE 6.1. *U.S. Syndicated Columns in Cuban Press, 1945–1958*

Advice to Women
Vivian Brown, "Entre muchachas"
Cynthia Lawry, "Entre mujeres"

Beauty Tips
Joan Beck, "Seamos hermosas"
Betty Clarke, "Belleza"
Arlene Dahl, "Seamos hermosas"
Ida Jean Kain, "Mantenga la línea"
Edith Thornton McLeod, "Como ser bella
    después de los 40"

Child Rearing
David Taylor Marke, "Su hijo, hoy"
Sylvia, "Con los pequeños"
Edith Thomas Wallace, "Consejo a los padres"

Diet and Nutrition
June Owen, "Nutrición"

Entertainment
Cecil Brownstone, "Parties infantiles"

Etiquette and Manners
Elinor Ames, "Lo correcto"
W. P. Warren, "Consejos prácticos"

Fashion and Style
Eileen Calhahan, "Modas"
Helen Chandler, "Sugerencias"
Anne Yates Clark, "Elegancias"
Dorothy Roe, "Modas del momento"

Household
Theodore Bailey, "Decoración interior"
Elizabeth Hyller, "La mujer y el hogar"
Jane Nickerson, "Auxiliares de Cocina"
Betty Pepis, "Decoración"

Sources: El Mundo, Diario de la Marina, Bohemia, Carteles, and *Vanidades.*

NOTES

ABBREVIATIONS

AHPM	Archivo Histórico Provincial de Matanzas, Matanzas
AN	Archivo Nacional, Havana
BBC	Braga Brothers Collection, University of Florida Library, Gainesville
BIA	Bureau of Insular Affairs, Record Group 350, NA
Dispatches/ Cienfuegos	Dispatches from U.S. Consuls in Cienfuegos, U.S. Department of State, General Records, 1876–1906, Record Group 59, NA
Dispatches/ Cuba	Dispatches from U.S. Ministers to Cuba, U.S. Department of State, General Records, 1902–6, Record Group 59, NA
Dispatches/ Havana	Dispatches from U.S. Consuls in Havana, U.S. Department of State, General Records, 1783–1906, Record Group 59, NA
Dispatches/ Matanzas	Dispatches from U.S. Consuls in Matanzas, U.S. Department of State, General Records, 1820–99, Record Group 59, NA
FHC	Friends Historical Collection, Guilford College, Greensboro, N.C.
FRUS	U.S. Department of State, *Foreign Relations of the United States, 1958–1960: Cuba* (Washington, D.C., 1991)
GLD	George Leland Dyer Papers, J. Y. Joyner Library, East Carolina University, Greenville, N.C.
GMA	General Board of Global Ministries Archives, New York, N.Y.
IA/1945–49	Confidential Central Files, Cuba, Internal Affairs, U.S. Department of State, General Records, 1945–49, Record Group 59, NA
IA/1950–54	Confidential Central Files, Cuba, Internal Affairs, U.S. Department of State, General Records, 1950–54, Record Group 59, NA
IA/1955–58	Confidential Central Files, Cuba, Internal Affairs, U.S. Department of State, General Records, 1955–58, Record Group 59, NA
IA/1959–60	Confidential Central Files, Cuba, Internal Affairs, U.S. Department of State, General Records, 1959–60, Record Group 59, NA
IAC	Internal Affairs of Cuba, U.S. Department of State, General Records, 1910–29, Record Group 59, NA
LC	Manuscript Division, Library of Congress, Washington, D.C.
MGC	Military Government of Cuba, Record Group 140, NA
NA	National Archives, Washington, D.C.
N-YHS	Manuscript Department, New-York Historical Society, New York, N.Y.
SFW	Shirley F. Woodell Correspondence, J. Walter Thompson Papers, Perkins Library, Duke University, Durham, N.C.
WL-EU	Special Collections Department, Robert W. Woodruff Library, Emory University, Atlanta, Ga.

1. See Roland T. Ely, *Cuando reinaba su majestad el azúcar* (Buenos Aires, 1963), pp. 515–16.

2. José García de Arboleya, *Manual de la isla de Cuba*, 2d ed. (Havana, 1859), pp. 215–16; J. Isern, "Cuba: Primer país de la América Latina que utilizó el barco de vapor," *Carteles*, March 16, 1952, pp. 30–31; A Physician, *Notes on Cuba* (Boston, 1844), p. 247.

3. A. de las Casas, *Cartas al pueblo americano* (Buenos Aires, 1897), p. 104.

4. García de Arboleya, *Manual de la isla de Cuba*, pp. 226–27. For details on the development of the cable to Cuba, see Canter Brown Jr., "The International Ocean Telegraph," *Florida Historical Quarterly* 68 (October 1989): 135–59. See also *New York Times*, August 18, 1867, p. 1.

5. William Cullen Bryant, *Letters of a Traveler* (New York, 1850), p. 373. The early Cuban railroads were constructed under the supervision of Alfred Cruger, Benjamin H. Wright, Simon Wright, and Ezra K. Dodd. See Duvon C. Corbitt, "El primer ferrocarril construido en Cuba," *Revista Cubana* 12 (April–June 1938): 179–95; Gert J. Oostindie, "La burguesía cubana y sus caminos de hierro, 1830–1868," *Boletín de Estudios Latinoamericanos y del Caribe* 37 (December 1984): 99–115; and Oscar Zanetti Lecuona and Alejandro García Alvarez, *Caminos para el azúcar* (Havana, 1987), pp. 113–29.

6. Charles J. Helm to Lewis Cass, June 14, 1859, May 5, 1860, Dispatches/Havana; "Estado que manifiesta los maquinistas extranjeros que residen en esta jurisdicción," June 11, 1854, and "Relación de los maquinistas existentes en estos cuartones," February 27, 1855, Fondo Gobierno Provisional, file 6, no. 99, AHPM.

7. Maturin M. Ballou, *History of Cuba; or, Notes of a Traveler in the Tropics* (Boston, 1854), pp. 145–46; Richard Henry Dana Jr., *To Cuba and Back: A Vacation Voyage* (1859; reprint, Carbondale, Ill., 1966), p. 60.

8. George W. Williams, *Sketches of Travel in the Old and New World* (Charleston, S.C., 1871), p. 8.

9. These included the Matahambre copper mines in Pinar del Río (American Metal Co.), the nickel mines near Daiquirí (Pennsylvania Steel Co.), the iron mines in El Caney (Sigua Iron Co.), and the manganese and iron mines in Santiago de Cuba (Bethlehem Steel Corp.).

10. Richard R. Madden, *The Island of Cuba: Its Resources, Progress, and Prospects* (London, 1849), pp. 83–84.

11. M. A. DeWolfe Howe, *The Articulate Sisters: Passages from Journals and Letters of the Daughters of President Josiah Quincy of Harvard University* (Cambridge, 1946), p. 107; U.S. Congress, Senate, "Report of the Secretary of the Treasury," June 25, 1864, 38th Cong., 1st sess., S. Doc. 55 (Washington, D.C., 1864), pp. 22–23; Dana, *To Cuba and Back*, p. 7.

12. Cuba, Centro de Estadística, *Noticias estadísticas de la Isla de Cuba, en 1862* (Havana, 1864), n.p.

13. Williams, *Sketches of Travel*, p. 8; John Glenville Taylor, *The United States and Cuba: Eight Years of Change and Travel* (London, 1851), p. 165; Madden, *The Island of Cuba*, p. 83; R. W. Gibbes, *Cuba for Invalids* (New York, 1860), p. 109; Joseph Judson Dimock, "Trip to Cuba and Back, 1859," Diary, Dimock Family Papers, WL-EU.

14. José Ahumada y Centurión, *Memoria histórico-política de la isla de Cuba* (Havana, 1874), pp. 268–70; Miguel Tacón to Ministro de Gobernación, January 1, 1838, *Boletín del Archivo Nacional* 10 (January–February 1911): 17–18; Herminio Portell Vilá, *La decadencia de Cárdenas: Estudio económico* (Havana, 1929), pp. 34–36; José G. de la Concha to Ministro de Gobernación, July 2, 1851, *Boletín del Archivo Nacional* 16 (January–February 1917): 394–96; Valentín Cañedo, "Memoria," August 24, 1852, in Sedano y Cruzat, *Cuba desde 1850 a 1873* (Madrid, 1873), p. 166.

15. Richard S. McCulloh, "Report of Scientific Investigation Relative to the Chemical Nature of Saccarine Substances and the Art of Manufacturing Sugar," 29th Congress, 2d sess., S. Doc. 209 (Washington, D.C., 1847), p. 209; Julia Ward Howe, *A Trip to Cuba* (Boston, 1860), p. 111.

16. Clair M. Badaricco, "Sophia Peabody Hawthorne's Cuba Journal: Volume Three, 31 October 1834–15 March 1835," *Essex Institute Historical Collections* (October 1982): 291.

17. Charles Rosenberg, *Jenny Lind in America* (New York, 1851), p. 130; Fredrika Bremer, *The Homes of the New World* (New York, 1853), pp. 291, 353; Amelia N. Murray, *Letters from the United States, Cuba and Canada* (New York, 1856), p. 243; Williams, *Sketches of Travel*, pp. 5–19; Edward N. Tailer Diary, N-YHS; Eliza McHatton-Ripley, *From Flag to Flag* (New York, 1889), p. 125; Silvia Sunshine, *Petals Plucked from Sunny Climes* (Nashville, 1880), p. 407; John S. Abbott, *South and North* (New York, 1860), p. 52.

18. Charles J. Helm to Lewis Cass, May 5, 1860, Dispatches/Havana; Félix Erenchún, *Anales de la isla de Cuba, Año de 1855*, 4 vols. (Havana, 1856), 3:1910–14.

19. Ramon O. Williams to William F. Wharton, June 24, 1890, Dispatches/Havana.

20. Dimock, "Trip to Cuba and Back, 1859."

21. Charles G. Helm to Lewis Cass, May 5, 1860, Dispatches/Havana; Paul Lewis, *Queen of the Plaza: A Biography of Adah Isaacs Menken* (New York, 1964), p. 46. "Havana seems to be a favorite place for American women . . . dedicated to the life of sin," commented a traveler in 1867. "It must be confessed that the number of American courtesans has largely increased of late years." *New York Times*, August 18, 1867, p. 1.

22. William T. Minor to William Seward, February 19, 1866, Dispatches/Havana; McHatton-Ripley, *From Flag to Flag*, pp. 132, 149–269; Emeterio S. Santovenia, "Fugitivos de la guerra de Lincoln en Cuba," *Carteles*, October 31, 1948, pp. 26–27.

23. Edward Robert Sullivan, *Rambles and Scrambles in North and South America* (London, 1852), p. 247; James Anthony Froude, *The English in the West Indies* (London, 1906), pp. 297, 309.

24. U.S. physicians in Havana included Joseph Bechtenger, Daniel M. Burgess, Joseph W. Eddy, James Warner, Arthur Gross, and Philip Hartman. Among those in provincial towns were John B. Dod (Remedios) and A. J. Simmons (Santiago de Cuba). North American dentists included Erastus Wilson, Joseph A. Ansley, Joseph F. Down, Joseph E. Salles, David L. Whitmarsh, Samuel G. Wheeler, and David Wood.

25. A. K. Blythe to Lewis Cass, July 20, 1857, Dispatches/Havana.

26. Manuel Moreno Fraginals, *El ingenio: Complejo económico social cubano del azúcar*, 3 vols. (Havana, 1978), 1:72–73. William Henry Hulbert, *Gan-Eden; or, Pictures of Cuba* (Boston, 1854), p. 165.

27. Enrique José Varona, "Cuba contra España: Manifiesto del Partido Revolucionario Cubano a los pueblos hispanoamericanos," October 23, 1895, in Varona, *De la colonia a la república* (Havana, 1919), p. 51.

28. J. S. Thrasher, "Preliminary Essay," in Alexander von Humboldt, *The Island of Cuba* (New York, 1856), pp. 77–78.

29. Ricardo Núñez de Villavicencio, *Aventuras emocionantes de un emigrado revolucionario cubano* (Havana, 1929), p. 8. José María and Nicolás de Cárdenas of Havana obtained positions with Moses Taylor in New York. Lorenzo Jiménez was employed as a clerk by Robertson and Company in Havana and subsequently was transferred to New Orleans. Eduardo Cabrera worked for the William G. Stewart agency in New York as translator of Latin American correspondence. Sebastián Romagosa left Cienfuegos in 1888

to practice law in New York. Hilario Cisneros joined John Townsend's law practice in 1871. See the Cabrera-Steward correspondence, William G. Stewart Papers, N-YHS, and Eduardo Codina to José Ignacio Rodríguez, June 18, 1888, Rodríguez Papers, LC.

30. Moses Taylor Papers, Rare Books and Manuscripts Division, New York Public Library; William G. Stewart Papers and Lynch and Aymar Co. Papers, N-YHS; Conde de Mirasol, "Memoria," March 9, 1850, in Sedano y Cruzat, *Cuba desde 1850 a 1873*, p. 141.

31. Luis A. Baralt, "Carta de Saratoga," *La Habana Elegante*, September 15, 1889, pp. 6–7; Eugenio Coffigny to Emilio Buch, June 9, 1863, Miguel and Emilio Buch Papers, N-YHS.

32. See Ely, *Cuando reinaba su majestad el azúcar*, pp. 355, 404–8, and Portell Vilá, *La decadencia de Cárdenas*, p. 35.

33. Among the most successful Cuban manufacturers in the United States were Cayetano Soria, Manuel Barranco, Enrique Canales, Eduardo and Gabriel Hidalgo Gato, Francisco Marrero, Martín Herrera, Romualdo Pérez, Cecilio Henríquez, José Angulo, Antonio del Pino, Blas Trujillo, and José Alejandro Huau.

34. U.S. Congress, Senate, *Proceedings of the Cuba and Florida Immigration*, 52d Cong., 2d sess., Rept. 1263 (Washington, D.C., 1893), p. 66.

35. *Key West Daily Equator-Democrat* (trade ed.), March 1889; *Tampa Morning Tribune*, May 21, 1896; José Rivero Muñiz, "Los cubanos en Tampa," *Revista Bimestre Cubana* 79 (First Semester, 1958): 5–140; Louis A. Pérez Jr., "Cubans in Tampa: From Exiles to Immigrants, 1892–1901," *Florida Historical Quarterly* 56 (October 1978): 129–40; Gerald E. Poyo, *"With All, and for the Good of All"* (Durham, 1989), pp. 52–69; U.S. Congress, Senate, *Proceedings of the Cuba and Florida Immigration*, pp. 3, 5.

36. Manuel Valdés Rodríguez, *La educación popular en Cuba* (Havana, 1891), p. 33.

37. Varona, "Cuba contra España," p. 61; Arturo Rosell, "Una aspiración de la juventud cubana," *Revista Cubana* 19 (1894): 396–403.

38. Thrasher, "Preliminary Essay," p. 78.

39. Undergraduates included Ramón Ignacio Arnao (Girard College), Rafael Montoro (St. Francis), Carlos Sedano Cruz (University of St. Louis), Carlos and Teodoro Zaldo (Fordham), Leonardo Sorzano Jorrín (Georgetown), Raimundo de Castro (Columbia), Eugenio Sánchez Agramonte (Fordham), José Agustín Quintero (Howard), Leandro Vicente Lombido (Hampton College), Arístides Mestre (Penn), and Luis Marino Pérez (Michigan). Writer Carlos María de Rojas studied poetry at Harvard under Henry Wadsworth Longfellow. Business college graduates included José Miguel Tarafa and Alcides Betancourt (New York Business College), Eduardo Lores y Llorens (Eastman Business College), and Alfredo P. Lacazette (Poughkeepsie Academy of Commerce). Among the graduates of professional schools were physicians Joaquín Castillo Duany, Leopoldo Dulzaides, Pedro Calvo Castellanos, Eduardo Francisco Rodríguez, Arístides Agramonte, Pedro Betancourt, Emilio Martínez, Leonicio del Junco Despau, Luis A. Baralt Peoli, Carlos J. Finlay, and Juan Guiteras; engineers Emilio Aymerich Auler, Francisco Javier Cisneros, Carlos Morales Calvo, José Celedonio del Castillo, Aniceto Menocal, Juan Miguel Portuondo Tamayo, Fernando Figueredo Socarrás, Sotero E. Escarza, and José Ramón Villalón; dentists Emilio Núñez, Eladio Aguilera Rojas, Raimundo Portuondo Barceló, Ricardo Ruiz, and Pedro Calvo Castellanos; attorneys Gonzalo de Quesada, Gustavo Pino, José Agustín Quintero, Federico García Ramis, José Manuel Mestre, and Pablo Desvernine; and at least one veterinarian, Honoré F. Lainé.

40. Nicolás Tanco Armero, *Viaje de Nueva Granada a China* (Paris, 1861), p. 27; Gerald Lee Gutek, *An Historical Introduction to American Education* (New York, 1970), pp. 49–51;

S. Alexander Rippa, *Education in a Free Society: An American History*, 4th ed. (New York, 1980), pp. 166–71.

41. Grover Flint, *Marching with Gomez* (Boston, 1898), p. 84.

42. Gaspar Betancourt Cisneros to José Antonio Saco, August 7, 1849, in Saco, *Contra la anexión*, 2 vols. (Havana, 1928), 2:54.

43. Nicolás Heredia, *Leonela* (1893; reprint, Havana, 1972), pp. 73, 107–8.

44. Ahumada y Centurión, *Memoria histórico-política*, pp. 262–64; José G. de la Concha to Ministro de Gobernación, July 2, 1851, *Boletín del Archivo Nacional* 16 (January–February 1917): 394–95, and to Ministro de Gracia y Justicia, January 9, 1851, *Boletín del Archivo Nacional* 3 (November–December 1904): 47–48; de la Concha, *Memorias sobre el estado político: Gobierno y administrativo de la isla de Cuba* (Madrid, 1853), pp. 64, 341–42, 348–49.

45. Fernando Portuondo del Prado estimates that a total of 100,000 persons emigrated between 1868 and 1898, whereas Spanish historian Justo D. Zaragosa insists that 100,000 Cubans emigrated just during the first twelve months of the Ten Years War. In the early 1890s U.S. immigration authorities estimated that 50,000 to 100,000 Cubans traveled annually between the island and the United States. See Fernando Portuondo del Prado, *Historia de Cuba*, 6th ed. (Havana, 1957), p. 438, and Justo D. Zaragosa, *Las insurrecciones en Cuba: Apuntes para la historia política de esta en el presente siglo*, 2 vols. (Madrid, 1872–73), 2:374; U.S. Congress, Senate, *Proceedings of the Cuba and Florida Immigration*, pp. 1, 61.

46. Carlos M. Trelles, "A Tampa," *Cuba y América*, July 1, 1897, p. 4.

47. Henry C. Hall to E. B. Washburn, March 11, 1869, and Hall to John Hay, March 2, 1880, Dispatches/Havana. See also Granda, *Memoria revolucionaria*, pp. 199–201.

48. Diana Abad, "Las emigraciones cubanas en la Guerra de los Diez Años," *Santiago* 53 (March 1984): 173–74; Adam Badeau to John Davis, December 19, 1882, and Henry C. Hall to John Hay, April 13, 1881, Dispatches/Havana; William W. Cross to Department of State, October 2, 1878, Dispatches/Cienfuegos.

49. Francisco de Frías, "Colonización e inmigración," *Revista Cubana* 7 (February 1880): 128–29.

50. *Daily Equator-Democrat*, March 26, 1889, p. 3.

51. In New York, these included the Hotel Central owned by Gervasio Pérez, Nuevo Boarding Cubano of Alfredo Du-Bouchet, Leopoldo Ortiz's Hotel Habana, Hotel Fénix owned and operated by F. Ferrer, Hotel América owned by Bernardo Pérez, Gran Boarding Cubano, Troncoso House, and Casa de Huéspedes Cubana. In Saratoga, Pedro M. Suárez owned the Everett House, offering "special arrangements for families," and Luis Baralt operated the Congress Park House—advertised as "a Cuban family hotel located at the best site in Saratoga." In Tampa, Miguel Montejo was proprietor of the Hotel Victoria, and the Hotel de La Habana passed through several ownerships before burning down in the early 1900s; in Key West, Martín Herrera owned the Hotel Monroe.

52. *Patria*, October 22, 1892, p. 4.

53. See Michael Schudson, *Discovering the News: A Social History of American Newspapers* (New York, 1978), pp. 31–42; Robert A. Rutland, *The Newsmongers: Journalism in the Life of the Nation, 1690–1972* (New York, 1973), pp. 240–62; and Sidney Kobre, *Foundations of American Journalism*, 2d ed. (Westport, Conn., 1970), pp. 300–307.

54. Raimundo Cabrera, *Sombras que pasan* (1916; reprint, Havana, 1984), p. 109.

55. Gustavo Robreño, *La acera del Louvre* (Havana, 1925), p. 245.

56. José Martí, "El Partido Revolucionario Cubano," April 3, 1892, in Martí, *Obras completas*, ed. Jorge Quintana, 5 vols. (Caracas, 1964), 1, pt. 2:303–7, and "La proclamación del Partido Revolucionario Cubano, el 10 de Abril," ibid., 1, pt. 2:307–13.

57. Wenceslao Gálvez, "Nicotina," *Revista Bimestre Cubana* 29 (May–June 1932): 409–10.

58. The juntas and clubs included: in New York, Liga de las Hijas de Cuba, Club Mercedes de Varona; in Tampa, Club Estrella Solitaria, Discípulas de Martí, Club Gonzalo de Quesada, Club Justo Carrillo; in Key West, Club Hospitalarias Cubanas, Grupo Alegórico del Cayo, Protectoras de la Patria, Club A. Díaz-Marcano, Club Mariana Grajales de Maceo, Hijas de la Libertad, and Hermanas de Ruis Rivera. For the activities of women's clubs in Key West, see Raoul Alpízar Poyo, *Cayo Hueso y José Dolores Poyo* (Havana, 1947), pp. 26, 43–44; *Revista de Cayo Hueso*, May 19, 1897, pp. 1–2; and K. Lynn Stoner, *From House to Streets: The Cuban Woman's Movement for Legal Reform, 1898–1940* (Durham, 1991), p. 24.

59. José Mayner y Ros, *Cuba y sus partidos políticos* (Kingston, Jamaica, 1890), p. 78; María Collado, "La evolución femenina en Cuba," *Bohemia*, December 11, 1927, p. 58.

60. Francisco Díaz Vólero, *Amor, patria y deber* (Havana, 1921), p. 87; Juan Pérez Rolo, *Mis recuerdos* (Key West, 1928), pp. 6–9.

61. Juan Manuel Planas, *La corriente del golfo* (Havana, 1920); U.S. Congress, House of Representatives, *Tenth Annual Report of the Commissioner of Labor, 1894*, 54th Cong., 1st sess., H. Doc. 339, 2 vols. (Washington, D.C., 1896), 1:138–49.

62. Alvaro de la Iglesia, *Cosas de antaño* (Havana, 1917), p. 180; A Physician, *Notes on Cuba*, p. 42.

63. Aurelia Castillo de González, *Un paseo por América: Cartas de Méjico y de Chicago* (Havana, 1895), pp. 63–64.

64. Eusebio Guiteras, *Un invierno en Nueva York* (Barcelona, 188?), pp. 134–40; Carlos Loveira, *Generales y doctores* (Havana, 1920), pp. 189–200.

65. Guiteras, *Un invierno en Nueva York*, p. 88; Castillo de González, *Un paseo por América*, p. 64, and "Cartas de Aurelia Castillo," *Revista Cubana* 21 (April 1895): 307–29.

66. *Revista de Cayo Hueso*, March 27, 1898, p. 7; "Farmacia cubana en Nueva York," *Carteles*, September 18, 1955, p. 117; *El Fígaro*, March 3, 1895, p. 117; Ana Núñez Machín, *La otra María* (Havana, 1975), pp. 24–110.

67. Samuel Hazard, *Cuba with Pen and Pencil* (Hartford, Conn., 1871), pp. 84–85.

68. Valentín Cañedo, "Memoria," August 24, 1852, in Sedano y Cruzat, *Cuba desde 1850 a 1873*, p. 166.

69. Heredia, *Leonela*, p. 60; Miguel de Carrión, *Las honradas*, 2d ed. (Havana, 1919), p. 61; José Antonio Ramos, *Las impurezas de la realidad* (1929; reprint, Havana, 1979), pp. 49–50.

70. Loveira, *Generales y doctores*, pp. 190–91, 197; Mary Peabody Mann, *Juanita: A Romance of Real Life in Cuba Fifty Years Ago* (Boston, 1887), pp. 183–85.

71. Máximo Gómez to Francisco Carrillo, July 27, 1888, in Hortensia Pichardo, ed., *Máximo Gómez: Cartas a Francisco Carrillo* (Havana, 1986), p. 93.

72. Heredia, *Leonela*, p. 63.

73. See E. P. Herrick, "Our Cuban Work in Florida and Cuba," *Home Missionary* 72 (October 1899): 85–87; Harold Edward Greer, "History of Southern Baptist Mission Work in Cuba, 1886–1916" (Ph.D. dissertation, University of Alabama, 1965), pp. 53–54; *Tampa Tribune*, September 16, 1896, p. 1.

74. Raimundo Cabrera, *Cuba and the Cubans* (Philadelphia, 1896), p. 256; John M. Kirk, *José Martí: Mentor of the Cuban Nation* (Gainesville, 1982), p. 119. See also Luis Toledo Sande, "Anticlericalismo, idealismo, religiosidad y práctica en José Martí," *Anuario del Centro de Estudios Martianos* 1 (1978): 79–131.

75. Salvador Díaz-Versón, *One Man, One Battle*, trans. Elena Díaz-Versón (New York, 1980), p. 2.

76. Gerardo Castellanos García, *Misión a Cuba: Cayo Hueso y Martí* (Havana, 1944), pp. 44–45.

77. See *The Christian Index*, November 22, 1888, p. 9; A. Pereira Alves, *Prominentes evangélicos de Cuba* (El Paso, 1936), p. 23; Rafael Cepeda, *Apuntes para una historia del presbiterianismo en Cuba* (Havana, 1986), p. 15; Una Roberts Lawrence, *Cuba for Christ* (Richmond, Va., 1926), pp. 156–60; Marcos Antonio Ramos, *Panorama del protestantismo en Cuba* (San José, 1986), pp. 91–131.

78. See Alfredo V. Díaz to Ramon O. Williams, July 6, 1888, Dispatches/Havana; I. S. Tichenor, "Another Visit to Cuba," *Our Home Field*, March 1889, pp. 5–6; *El País*, June 26, 1890, p. 1.

79. Manuel Deulofeu, *Historical and Biographical Notes of the Cuban Mission* (Tampa, 1899), p. 41.

80. George Lester, *In Sunny Isles* (London, 1897), p. 97; Deulofeu, *Historical and Biographical Notes*, p. 3.

81. Deulofeu, *Historical and Biographical Notes*, pp. 4–5.

82. Juan Bautista las Casas to Civil Governor, Matanzas, August 18, 1890, Fondo Religión, file 2, no. 62, AHPM.

83. Francisco Calcagno, *En busca del eslabón* (1888; reprint, Havana, 1983), pp. 200–201.

84. Eusebio Guiteras, *Un invierno en Nueva York*, pp. 110–33; Carlos M. Trelles, "Un poeta cubano en Chicago," *Revista Cubana* 19 (April 1894): 303–4; *El Progreso*, February 1, 1890, p. 81; Raimundo Cabrera, "Los Estados Unidos de América," *Revista Cubana* 9 (February 1889): 125–126; Manuel S. Pichardo, *La ciudad blanca: Crónicas de la exposición colombina de Chicago* (Havana, 1894), pp. 22–23.

85. Enrique Hernández Miyares, "New York—Primeras impresiones," *La Habana Elegante*, June 24, 1894, p. 7.

86. "Nuestras escuelas públicas y las de Nueva York," *La Fraternidad* (Sancti-Spíritus), November 27, 1892, p. 3.

87. Carlos de la Torre, "Impresiones de viaje," *El Fígaro*, July 9, 1893, p. 278; Raimundo Cabrera, *Ideales* (1918; reprint, Havana, 1984), pp. 232–33; Wenceslao Gálvez, *Tampa: Impresiones de emigrado* (Ibor City, Fla. 1897), p. 26.

88. "Cartas de José María Heredia," *Revista Cubana* 5 (February 1879): 102; Ramón Meza, "Un parque a Colón," *Revista Cubana* 14 (August 1891): 250–51; Carlos Trelles, "Recuerdos de viaje," *Cuba y América*, December 1900, p. 123; José Silverio Jorrín, "Dos bibliotecas norteamericanas," *El Fígaro*, April 22, 1894, p. 166; Domingo del Monte, *Humanismo y humanitarismo: Ensayos críticos y literarios* (Havana, 1960), pp. 79–80.

89. Domingo del Monte to Salustiano Olózaga, March 1846, in Domingo del Monte, *Escritos de Domingo del Monte*, 2 vols. (Havana, 1929), 1:219–21.

90. Thorstein Veblen, *The Theory of the Leisure Class* (1899; reprint, New York, 1934), pp. 25–32.

91. *El Cronista*, *El Avisador Comercial*, *Cuba y América*, and *Patria*, 1890s.

92. Veblen, *Theory of the Leisure Class*, p. 25.

93. U.S. Congress, Senate, *Proceedings of the Cuba and Florida Immigration*, p. 67; Enrique Hernández Miyares, "De vuelta a Cuba," *La Habana Elegante*, August 5, 1894, p. 7.

94. Dolores María de Ximeno y Cruz, "Aquellos tiempos: Memoria de Lola María," *Revista Bimestre Cubana* 24 (January–February 1929): 97–131, and *Memorias de Lola Maria* (Havana, 1983), p. 185; Castillo de González, *Un paseo por América*, pp. 60–133; Pichardo, *La ciudad blanca*, pp. 33, 50.

95. Raimundo Cabrera, "Chicago," *Revista Cubana* 18 (November 1893): 397–495; Castillo de González, *Un paseo por América*, p. 64. See also "Exposición universal colombina de Chicago," *La Habana Elegante*, March 26, 1893, pp. 8–9, and "La mujer en la exposición de Chicago," *El Eco de las Damas*, March 5, 1893, p. 3.

96. Pichardo, *La ciudad blanca*, p. 122; "La Exposición Columbina de Chicago," *El Base-Ball*, May 7, 1893, p. 3. See also Eva Canel, "Crónicas de la Exposición de Chicago," *Boletín de la Cámara Oficial de Comercio, Industria y Navegación de La Habana* 5 (July 3, 1893): 101–88.

97. Guiteras, *Un invierno en Nueva York*, pp. 134–35.

98. *La Habana Elegante*, November 24, 1889, p. 9; B. May and Co., *Mercantil para el año bisiesto 1868* (Havana, 1867), pp. 264–73; William P. Pierce to William F. Wharton, January 14, 1890, Dispatches/Matanzas. See also George W. Roosevelt to John Hay, January 31, 1881, Dispatches/Matanzas.

99. Robert P. Porter, *Industrial Cuba* (New York, 1899), pp. 275–76; James McQuade, *The Cruise of the Montauk to Bermuda, the West Indies and Florida* (New York, 1885), p. 369.

100. "La historia de 'La Barata,'" *El Hogar*, October 14, 1894, p. 7; Bryant, *Letters of a Traveler*, p. 373; Cirilo Villaverde, *Dos amores* (1887; reprint, Havana, 1930), p. 22.

101. Dimock, "Trip to Cuba and Back, 1859."

102. Ramon O. Williams to James D. Porter, June 25, 1886, Dispatches/Havana.

103. Francisco J. Ponte Domínguez, *Matanzas: Biografía de una provincia* (Havana, 1959), pp. 113–14; Antonio Miguel Alcover, *Historia de Sagua y su jurisdicción* (Sagua la Grande, 1906), p. 132.

104. Vicente Menéndez Roque, *Otros días* (Havana, 1962), pp. 35–36.

105. Ramón de Sagra, *Historia física, económica-política, intelectual y moral de la Isla de Cuba*, rev. ed. (Paris, 1861), p. 151.

106. Eduardo Rosell y Malpica, *Diario del teniente coronel Eduardo Rosell y Malpica, 1895–1897*, 2 vols. (Havana, 1949), 2:47; Jorge Calderón González, *Amparo: Millo y azucenas* (Havana, 1970), p. 47; Victor S. Clark, "Labor Conditions in Cuba," *Bulletin of the Department of Labor* 41 (July 1902): 713.

107. William Drysdale, *In Sunny Lands* (New York, 1889), p. 58; Daniel M. Mullen to John Davis, September 25, 1884, Consular Dispatches from Sagua la Grande, U.S. Department of State, General Records, 1878–1900, Record Group 59, NA; Dimock, "Trip to Cuba and Back, 1859."

108. Tesifonte Gallego García, *Cuba por fuera* (Havana, 1890), pp. 120–25; Heredia, *Leonela*, pp. 216–17.

109. I am indebted to architectural historian Lohania Aruca of the Comisión Nacional de Historia in Havana for this information.

110. M. T. McGovern, "La electricidad en Cuba," *Revista Bimestre Cubana* 12 (November–December 1927): 835–40.

111. Carlos Hellberg, *Historia estadística de Cárdenas* (Cárdenas, 1957), p. 144; Raimundo Cabrera, *Cuba and the Cubans* (Philadelphia, 1896), p. 40; Elliott Durand, *A Week in Cuba* (Chicago, 1891), p. 24.

112. Rafael Otero, *Cecilia la matancera* (Matanzas, 1861), p. 79; Heredia, *Leonela*, pp. 156–57.

113. *Diario de la Marina*, August 22, 1893, p. 4; *La Gimnástica*, November 13, 1894, p. 3. These clubs are featured in the magazines *El Sport*, January 14, 1886 (p. 3), June 24, 1886 (p. 1); *El Fígaro*, February 2, 1888, p. 6; and *El Ciclista*, August 15, 1895, p. 3.

114. José Martí to Editor, *La Nación*, July 2, 1886, in José Martí, *Obras completas*, 27 vols. (Havana, 1975), 11:15; Martí to Editor, *La Nación*, June 7, 1884, ibid., 10:60.

115. F. A. Poyo, "El base ball en Key West," in Ramón S. Mendoza, José María Herrero, and Manuel F. Calcines, eds., *El base ball en Cuba y América* (Havana, 1908), pp. 101–4; Alpízar Poyo, *Cayo Hueso y José Dolores Poyo*, pp. 25–26; Lester, *In Sunny Isles*, p. 66; "Ybor City Description" (manuscript), p. 10, in Federal Writers' Project Collection, Special Collections, Library, University of South Florida, Tampa.

116. See Aurelio Gravados, "Como empezó el base-ball en Cuba," in Raúl Díez Muro, ed., *El baseball en La Habana, Matanzas y Cárdenas* (Havana, 1907), p. 26; J. F. Prieto, "Historia del club 'Almendares'" (pp. 554–55), and Enrique Morejón, "El 'Habana B.B.C.'" (pp. 558–59), *El Fígaro*, December 9, 1900; "¿Cual fué el inicio del béisbol en Cuba?," *Carteles*, November 27, 1955, p. 87; and René Molina, "Evocando el pasado," *Bohemia*, December 24, 1950, p. 91.

117. "El baseball y la raza de color," in Mendoza, Herrero, and Calcines, *El base ball en Cuba y América*, p. 77.

118. *Revista Villaclareña*, December 11, 1892, p. 6; *El Sport*, September 16, 1886 (p. 3), February 2, 1888 (p. 4); Wenceslao Gálvez y Delmonte, *El base-ball en Cuba* (Havana, 1889), pp. 15, 82; *El Base-Ball*, April 9, 1893, p. 3.

119. See *Revista Villaclareña*, December 11, 1892, p. 6.

120. *El Sport*, February 25, 1886, p. 2; *El Fígaro*, March 24, 1888, p. 6.

121. "Los términos de base-ball," *El Base-Ball*, October 30, 1881, p. 1; Manuel Márquez Sterling, "Vocabulario del beisbol," *El Fígaro*, December 9, 1900, p. 556.

122. "Expediente relativo a la Sociedad 'Base Ball Club Mascota' de Matanzas," August 6–September 1, 1886, Fondo Asociaciones, file 5, no. 155, AHPM; *El Base-Ball*, April 9, 1893, p. 4.

123. Quoted in Richard Butler Gray, *José Martí: Cuban Patriot* (Gainesville, 1962), p. 116.

124. Enrique José Varona, "Una afición epidémica: Los toros," *Revista Cubana* 6 (February 1887): 180–84; Enrique José Varona, "El base ball en La Habana," *Revista Cubana* 6 (January 1887): 85–86; Rafael M. Merchán, *Free Cuba* (New York, 1896), p. 112; Gálvez y Delmonte, *El base-ball en Cuba*, p. 15; *El Pitcher*, February 12, 1888, pp. 1–2; Antonio Prieto, "Ni gallos, ni toros, ni pugilato," *El Base-Ball*, March 12, 1882, p. 1; Loveira, *Generales y doctores*, pp. 36–37. See also José Rivero Muñiz, "Las corridas de toros en Cuba," *Etnología y Folklore* 5 (January–June 1968): 59–108.

125. Richard Henry Dana, while visiting Cuba in 1859, was horrified at the "meanness and cruelty" of a bullfight in Havana; as he looked around, he was comforted by one realization: "Thankful I am, and creditable it is, that there were no women." See Dana, *To Cuba and Back*, p. 98. Only a year later R. W. Gibbes attended a Havana bullfight at which he estimated 1,000 persons present, and "not over a half dozen ladies, and a few little girls in the crowd." See Gibbes, *Cuba for Invalids*, p. 15.

126. *El Base-Ball*, June 18, 1882 (p. 1), July 23, 1882 (p. 2). For the organization of the *directiva de honor* of the Unión Baseball Club of Cárdenas, see "Reglamento del 'Unión B.B.C.,'" June 1894, "Expediente relativo a la Sociedad 'Unión Base Ball Club de Cárdenas,'" Fondo Asociaciones, file 5, no. 172, AHPM.

127. Writing generally about the relationship between sports and nationalism, E. J. Hobsbawm observed that the "individual, even the one who only cheers, becomes a symbol of his nation himself"—and presumably a symbol of her nation herself. Hobsbawm, *Nations and Nationalism since 1780* (Cambridge, England, 1990), p. 143.

128. Gálvez y Delmonte, *El base-ball en Cuba*, p. 66.

129. Benjamín de Céspedes to Wenceslao Gálvez y Delmonte, August 1, 1889, in ibid., p. 8.

130. Aurelio Miranda, "Mi recuerdo y mi opinión," in Mendoza, Herrero, and Calcines,

El base ball en Cuba y América, pp. 27–29. See also "El sport y nuestro carácter," *El Score*, October 21, 1888, n.p.

131. "Expediente relativo a la Sociedad de Base-Ball 'Club Yara' de Matanzas," September 1, 1888–April 27, 1931, Fondo Asociaciones, file 5, no. 158, AHPM; Abel Du-Breuil, "Cincuenta años," *La Lucha*, February 1, 1929, p. 8; Varona, "El base ball en La Habana," pp. 86–87; Gálvez y Delmonte, *En base-ball en Cuba*, pp. 89, 95; "El base ball en Cárdenas," in Mendoza, Herrero and Calcines, *El base ball en Cuba y América*, p. 39.

132. Gálvez y Delmonte, *El base-ball en Cuba*, p. 15.

133. Lorenzo Youngman, "Tópicos," *La Habana Elegante*, February 15, 1890, p. 9; Manuel Curros Enríquez, "Introducción," in Mendoza, Herrero and Calcines, *El base ball en Cuba y América*, pp. 3–5.

134. "Cuaderno por rebelión contra Emilio Sabourín de Villar," December 18, 1896, file 91, no. 38, Fondo de Asuntos Políticos, AN.

135. Varona, "Cuba contra España," pp. 64–65; Loveira, *Generales y doctores*, pp. 187–88.

136. José de la Campa González, *Memorias de un machadista* (Tampa, 1937), p. 26.

137. Wenceslao Gálvez, "Luz eléctrica," *El Pelotero*, February 17, 1889, p. 6; Cirilio Villaverde, *Cecilia Valdés*, 2 vols. (1882; reprint, Havana, 1982), 2:48; Heredia, *Leonela*, p. 225; Francisco Faura, "Nuestro siglo," *Sagua Elegante*, July 1, 1894, p. 4; José A. Asencio, "Villaclara," *Revista Villaclareña*, July 15, 1894, p. 2.

138. Enrique José Varona, "Cuba y sus jueces," *Revista Cubana* 6 (September 1887): 276.

139. Antonio Gonzalo Pérez, "Cuba for Cubans," *Contemporary Review* 74 (November 1898): 694.

140. Manuel Villanova, "Españoles y cubanos," *Revista Cubana* 10 (January 1889): 85–86; Alfredo Virgilio Ledón, "La inferioridad de la raza española," *Revista Cubana* 11 (March 1890): 193–208; Manuel Linares, "La Voz de Cuba," January 15, 1882, in Linares, *Un libro mas: Fragmentos* (Havana, 1906), p. 29.

141. Gaspar Betancourt Cisneros to José Antonio Saco, October 19, 1848, in Betancourt Cisneros, *Cartas del Lugareño*, ed. Federico de Córdova (Havana, 1957), p. 308; Justo González, *Cubagua: Historia de un pueblo* (Havana, 1941), p. 67.

142. Domingo del Monte to Conde Montalvo, January 5, 1849, in del Monte, *Escritos*, 1:238–39; Cabrera, *Cuba and the Cubans*, pp. 59–60; Loveira, *Generales y doctores*, p. 199.

143. Castillo de González, *Un paseo por América*, p. 85; María Antonia Reyes de Herrera, "Como debe educarse la mujer," *El Hogar*, February 23, 1890, p. 95.

144. Anselmo Suárez Romero, "Incompleta educación de las cubanas," in Suárez Romero, *Colección de artículos* (Havana, 1860), pp. 110–18; Carlos Saladrigas, "La educación de la mujer," *Revista Cubana* 13 (April 1883): 289–303.

145. Enrique José Varona, "El fracaso colonial de España," December 3, 1896, in Varona, *De la colonia a la república*, p. 129; Varona, "Cuba contra España," pp. 64–65.

146. Cabrera, *Cuba and the Cubans*, p. 23; Fidel G. Pierra, *Cuba* (New York, 1896), pp. 35–36.

147. Mayner y Ros, *Cuba y sus partidos políticos*, p. 179.

148. Diego Vicente Tejera, "La indolencia cubana," *Cuba Contemporánea* 28 (March 1922): 172.

149. Sergio Aguirre, "Nacionalidad a nación en Cuba," *Universidad de La Habana* 196 (February–March 1972): 36; Saco, *Papeles sobre Cuba*, 3:46.

150. Poyo, *"With All, and for the Good of All,"* p. 106.

151. José Martí, *La cuestión racial*, rev. ed. (Havana, 1959), pp. 25–40.

152. Manuel Sanguily, "Los negros y su emancipación," March 31, 1893, in Sanguily, *Frente a la dominación española* (Havana, 1979), p. 174. Italics in original.

153. Rafael María Merchán, *Cuba: Justificación de sus guerras de independencia*, 2d ed. (Havana, 1961), pp. 41–42; Un Cubano Sin Odio [Manuel de la Cruz], *La revolución cubana y la raza de color: Apuntes y datos* (Key West, 1895), pp. 16–17.

154. Raimundo Menocal, *Tres ensayos sobre la realidad cubana* (Havana, 1935), p. 78.

155. Martín Morúa Delgado, *La familia Unzúazu* (1896; reprint, Havana, 1975), pp. 137–38.

156. Tomás Justiz y del Valle, *El suicida* (Havana, 1912), p. 198; González, *Cubagua*, pp. 238–39.

157. Immanuel Wallerstein, "The Construction of Peoplehood: Racism, Nationalism, Ethnicity," in Etienne Balibar and Wallerstein, eds., *Race, Nation, Class: Ambiguous Identities* (London, 1991), p. 78.

158. Ramiro Guerra y Sánchez, *Guerra de los Diez Años*, 2 vols. (Havana, 1986), 2:341–42.

CHAPTER TWO

1. Domingo Dulce, "Decreto," February 12, 1869, in Cuba, Gobierno Superior Político, *Datos y noticias oficiales referentes a los bienes mandados embargar en la Isla de Cuba* (Havana, 1870), p. 14.

2. See *Gaceta Oficial*, August 6, 1869 (p. 1), November 8, 1870 (p. 2); *Diario de la Marina*, November 9, 1870, p. 1; Joaquín Llaverías, *El Consejo Administrativo de Bienes Embargados* (Havana, 1941); Inocencio Casanova to Thomas Biddle, February 24, 1871, Dispatches/Havana; and Leopoldo Horrego Estuch, "Emilia Casanova," *Carteles*, October 16, 1949, pp. 34–35.

3. Cuba, Gobierno Superior Político, *Datos y noticias oficiales*, pp. 21–27, 162–214. For specific cases, see "Consulta sobre declarar si debe o no rendirse cuenta de los productos de los bienes secuestrados a los insurrectos de Cuentos de Reino," 1870, file 28, no. 2946, Consejo de Administración, AN.

4. Rolando Alvarez Estévez, *La emigración cubana en Estados Unidos, 1868–1878* (Havana, 1986), p. 4. The subject of punitive expropriations is well treated in Alfonso W. Quiroz, "Loyalist Overkill: The Socioeconomic Cost of 'Repressing' the Separatist Insurrection in Cuba, 1868–1878," *Hispanic American Historical Review* 78 (May 1998): 271–84.

5. Adam Badeau, "Report on the Present Condition of Cuba," February 7, 1884, Dispatches/Havana.

6. *Diario de la Marina*, November 24, 1888, p. 1.

7. David Vickers to John Davis, July 2, 1884, Dispatches/Matanzas.

8. Javier de Acevedo, "La sociedad habanera en 1888–1894 de mis recuerdos," *Social*, April 1929, pp. 19, 70.

9. A. C. Crowe to Foreign Office, May 4, 1888, PO 277, no. 57, Embassy and Consular Archives, Cuba, 1870 Onwards, Public Records Office, Kew, London, England.

10. U.S. Tariff Commission, *Effects of the Cuban Reciprocity Treaty* (Washington, D.C., 1929), p. 167; José R. Alvarez Díaz et al., *A Study on Cuba* (Coral Gables, Fla., 1965), pp. 96–97; Francisco López Segrera, *Sociología de la colonia y neocolonia cubana, 1510–1959* (Havana, 1989), p. 73; George B. Rea, "The Destruction of Sugar Estates in Cuba," *Harper's Weekly*, October 16, 1897, pp. 10–34; Jorge Quintana, "Lo que costo a Cuba la guerra de 1895," *Bohemia*, September 11, 1960, pp. 4–6, 107–8.

11. *Washington Evening Star*, September 24, 1898, p. 21; *The State*, November 5, 1898, p. 5.

12. Fitzhugh Lee, "Special Report of Brigadier General Fitzhugh Lee, U.S.V., Commanding Department of Province of Havana and Pinar del Río," September 19, 1899, in John R. Brooke, *Civil Report of Major-General John R. Brooke, U.S. Army, Military Governor, Island of Cuba* (Washington, D.C., 1900), p. 342.

13. Robert P. Porter, *Report on the Commercial and Industrial Condition of Cuba* (Washington, D.C., 1899), p. 5; Ramiro Guerra y Sánchez, *Un cuarto de siglo de evolución cubana* (Havana, 1924), p. 16. For a thoughtful treatment of the effects of the war, see Fe Iglesias García, "El costo demográfico de la Guerra de Independencia," *Debates Americanos* 4 (July–December 1997): 67–76.

14. See José Miguel Gómez to Francisco Carrillo, August 31, 1898, Fondo Donativos y Remisiones, file 180, no. 196, AN; Manuel Piedra Martel, *Mis primeros treinta años: Memorias* (Havana, 1944), p. 496; Enrique J. Conill, *Enrique J. Conill: Soldado de la patria* (Havana, 1956), p. 21; Francisco Díaz Silveira to Gualterio García, August 31, 1898, in Gonzalo de Quesada, *Documentos históricos* (Havana, 1965), p. 486; Rodolfo Bergés Tabares, *Cuba y Santo Domingo: Apuntes de la guerra de Cuba de mi diario de campaña, 1895–1898* (Havana, 1905), p. 167.

15. Pulaski Hyatt to William W. Rockhill, May 12, 1897, Dispatches from U.S. Consuls in Santiago de Cuba, U.S. Department of State, General Records, 1799–1906, Record Group 59, NA; *Diario de la Marina*, December 10, 1899, p. 2.

16. Raimundo Cabrera, *Sombras eternas* (Havana, 1919), p. 95.

17. Salvador Quesada Torres, "El silencio," in Quesada Torres, *El silencio* (Havana, 1923), pp. 18–19.

18. Alejandro Rodríguez to Gonzalo de Quesada, June 13, 1899, in Quesada, *Archivo de Gonzalo de Quesada*, 2 vols. (Havana, 1948–51), 2:179–80.

19. Captain Carlos Muecke to G. Creighton Webb, September 3, 1898, Webb Papers, N-YHS.

20. Raimundo Cabrera, *Ideales* (1918; reprint, Havana, 1984), pp. 78–79.

21. Arturo Montori, *El tormento de vivir* (Havana, 1923), pp. 20–21.

22. Seeking to disband units of the Liberation Army after the war, many of whose soldiers were facing starvation, U.S. officials refused to distribute relief supplies until Cuban troops surrendered their weapons. In Santiago de Cuba, Leonard Wood proclaimed: "No Cuban bearing arms should have work or food." Quoted in Hermann Hagedorn, *Leonard Wood: A Biography*, 2 vols. (New York, 1931), 2:255. See also General H. S. Lawton to General Agustín Cebreco, September 5, 1898, file 186, Santiago de Cuba, Records of the U.S. Army Overseas Operations and Commands, 1898–1942, Record Group 395, NA.

23. Brooke, *Civil Report*, pp. 13–14.

24. Porter, *Report on the Commercial and Industrial Condition of Cuba*, p. 411.

25. "Recapitulation of the Statistical and Fiscal Condition of the Province of Havana," in Brooke, *Civil Report*, p. 149; U.S. War Department, *Informe sobre el censo de Cuba, 1899* (Washington, 1900), p. 554.

26. *Cuba Bulletin* 1 (June 1903): 4; Albert G. Robinson, "Industrial and Commercial Conditions in Cuba," *Review of Reviews* 26 (August 1902): 199; Patricio Ponce de León to Herbert G. Squires, December 8, 1904, Dispatches/Cuba.

27. *Diario de la Marina*, July 20, 1899 (p. 1), September 28, 1899 (p. 1); Pulaski F. Hyatt and John T. Hyatt, *Cuba: Its Resources and Opportunities* (New York, 1898), p. 95; Francis M. J. Craft to General O'Beirne, January 30, 1900, Craft Papers, N-YHS.

28. Leonard Wood, *Report by Brigadier General Leonard Wood on Civic Conditions in*

Department of Santiago and Puerto Principe (Cristo, 1899), pp. 5–6; Edward Marshall, "A Talk with General Wood," *Outlook*, July 20, 1901, p. 670.

29. U.S. Department of Commerce, *Historical Statistics of the United States: Colonial Times to 1970* (Washington, D.C., 1979), p. 135. See also Charles Hoffman, *The Depression of the Nineties: An Economic History* (Westport, Conn., 1970), pp. 47–96.

30. *New York Journal*, November 6, 1898, p. 26.

31. *Havana Post*, July 13, 1900, p. 2.

32. Franklin Matthews, *The New-Born Cuba* (New York, 1899), pp. 8, 203–6; James Gould Cozzens, *The Son of Perdition* (New York, 1929), pp. 225–26; Charles M. Pepper, *To-Morrow in Cuba* (New York, 1899), pp. 338–40; Trumbell White, *Our New Possessions* (Philadelphia, 1898), p. 591.

33. "Real Estate Notes in Cuba," *Commercial and Financial World*, April 7, 1906, p. 12; *Havana Post*, June 19, 1900, p. 4. Other agencies followed in quick order: the Island of Cuba Real Estate Co. (Havana), D. E. Kerr Real Estate (Camagüey), L. G. Weeks and Co. (Santiago de Cuba), H. Weston Real Estate (Havana), J. A. Miller and Co. (Isle of Pines), Cuban Realty (Santiago de Cuba), American Real Estate Co. (Camagüey), R. G. Ward and Co. (Havana), Hughes Real Estate (Havana), Oscar S. Durfee Realty (Camagüey), and U.S. Land and Investment Co. (Havana).

34. Frank G. Carpenter, "Cuba in 1905," *Cuba Review* 3 (November 1905): 11.

35. Irene Wright, *Cuba* (New York, 1910), p. 322.

36. *New York Times*, May 7, 1900, p. 7.

37. *Havana Post*, September 21, 1900, p. 3.

38. A. González Curquejo, "Los carros eléctricos de La Habana," *Cuba y América*, December 1901, pp. 91–97; *Havana Post*, April 10, 1901, p. 1.

39. Leonard Wood, *Civil Report of Brigadier General Leonard Wood, Military Governor of Cuba, from the Period from December 20, 1899 to December 31, 1900*, 12 vols. (Washington, D.C., 1900), 5:3–196; J. F. Pellón, "Las obras públicas y la intervención," *Cuba y América*, February 1902, pp. 324–26; James H. Hitchman, "Unfinished Business: Public Works in Cuba, 1898–1902," *The Americas* 31 (January 1975): 335–59.

40. *Havana Post*, November 24, 1900, p. 1.

41. Ibid., October 14, 1900, p. 3.

42. Oscar Zanetti Lecuona and Alejandro García Alvarez, *Caminos para el azúcar* (Havana, 1987), pp. 209–32; U.S. Tariff Commission, *Effects of the Cuban Reciprocity Treaty*, p. 169.

43. Carlos Venegas Fornias, "Havana between Two Centuries," *Journal of Decorative and Propaganda Arts* 22 (1996): 18.

44. George Leland Dyer to Susan Dyer, June 30, 1900, GLD; Victor S. Clark, "Labor Conditions in Cuba," *Bulletin of the Department of Labor* 41 (July 1902): 711. On the Cuba Company, see Cuba Co. Papers, especially boxes 1–3 for correspondence, and reports of construction projects, Archives and Manuscripts Department, McKeldin Library, University of Maryland, College Park.

45. *Havana Post*, February 6, 1900 (p. 3), May 11, 1901 (p. 2).

46. Ibid., December 8, 1900, p. 4; *Diario de la Marina*, September 12, 1899, p. 1.

47. *Havana Post*, May 1, 1900 (p. 2), March 26, 1901 (p. 5), January 14, 1906 (p. 5); *Havana Sun*, January–February 1902; *El Correo de la Juventud*, April–May 1899.

48. Cristóbal Díaz Ayala, *Música cubana: Del Areyto a la Nueva Trova* (San Juan, 1981), p. 118 (American Café). See *Diario de la Marina*, November 20, 1899 (p. 1), October 31, 1899 (p. 2), November 18, 1899 (p. 1).

49. *Havana Post*, 1901–20; Alejo Carpentier, "Sobre La Habana, 1912–1930," in Carpentier, *Obras completas de Alejo Carpentier*, 16 vols. (Mexico, 1983–94), 14:91.

50. *Havana Post*, 1900–1902.

51. Ibid., 1908–16.

52. *New York Journal*, September 7, 1898, p. 7.

53. Herbert G. Squiers to John Hay, September 17, 1904, Dispatches/Cuba; Thomas Rees, *Spain's Lost Jewels: Cuba and Mexico* (Springfield, Ill., 1906), p. 44.

54. *El Hogar*, 1900; *Diario de la Marina*, 1901; *Havana Post*, 1900–1901; *La Lucha*, 1901.

55. *El Libro Azul de Cuba* (Havana, 1917).

56. *La Lucha*, *La Discusión*, and the *Havana Post*, 1900–1910.

57. *New York Journal*, September 11, 1898, p. 50.

58. Matthews, *The New-Born Cuba*, p. 21.

59. *Havana Post*, November 25, 1900, p. 1.

60. Ibid., October 7, 1900, p. 3.

61. Llilian Llanes, *1898–1921: La transformación de La Habana a través de la arquitectura* (Havana, 1993), pp. 175–93.

62. Venegas Fornias, "Havana between Two Centuries," p. 23.

63. *Havana Post*, November 16, 1924, p. 4.

64. Ibid., November 29, 1900, p. 1; *La Lucha*, September 19, 1903, p. 1.

65. Harry A. Franck, *Roaming through the West Indies* (New York, 1920), p. 37. See also José A. Gelabert-Navia, "American Architects in Cuba: 1900–1930," *Journal of Decorative and Propaganda Arts* 22 (1996): 133–49.

66. Herbert G. Squiers to John Hay, September 17, 1906, Dispatches/Cuba.

67. Horace J. Dickenson, "Supplementary Information on the Mining Industry in the Antilla Consular District," April 30, 1927, 837.63/66, IAC.

68. Sydney A. Clark, *Cuban Tapestry* (New York, 1936), pp. 146–48.

69. Luis Felipe Rodríguez, "El despojo," in Salvador Bueno, ed., *Antología del cuento en Cuba, 1902–1952* (Havana, 1953), p. 77.

70. Ariel James, *Banes: Imperialismo y nación en una plantación azucarera* (Havana, 1976), pp. 121–22.

71. Cabrera, *Sombras eternas*, pp. 155–56; José Antonio Ramos, *Teatro*, ed. Francisco Garzón Céspedes (Havana, 1989), p. 157.

72. *Havana Post*, November 10, 1900, p. 1.

73. Ibid., October 16, 1900, p. 3.

74. *La Lucha*, April 29, 1902, p. 1.

75. Orestes Ferrara, *Una mirada sobre tres siglos: Memorias* (Madrid, 1975), pp. 141–42; Alejandro García, *La gran burguesía comercial en Cuba, 1899–1920* (Havana, 1990), pp. 70–71.

76. "Memorandum Dealing with the History of the Practice of Public Accountancy in Cuba and the Present Situation Thereof," January 17, 1945, 837.9212/1-2245, IA/1945–49.

77. Thomas F. O'Brien, "The Revolutionary Mission: American Enterprise in Cuba," *American Historical Review* 98 (June 1993): 778.

78. Robert B. Davies, *Peacefully Working to Conquer the World: Singer Sewing Machines in Foreign Markets, 1854–1920* (New York, 1976), p. 135; *El Mundo*, November 1, 1953, p. A-1.

79. Germán Alvarez Fuentes, "Recuerdos del Camagüey del ayer," in Alvarez Fuentes, *Ficciones y realidades* (Oviedo, 1970), p. 263.

80. John R. Stanley to Max J. Baer, October 24, 1902, Dispatches/Cienfuegos.

81. Francisco Díaz Vólero, *Amor, patria y deber* (Havana, 1921), p. 172.

82. U.S. War Department, *Informe sobre el censo de Cuba*, p. 215.

83. Wen Gálvez, "Cocas," *El Fígaro*, February 4, 1900, p. 53.

84. Loló de la Torriente, *Testimonio desde dentro* (Havana, 1985), p. 297; Carlos Loveira, *Los inmorales* (Havana, 1919), p. 12.

85. Julio Villoldo, "Nuevas orientaciones de la juventud cubana," *Cuba Contemporánea* 15 (September 1917): 11–14; Carpentier, "Sobre La Habana, 1912–1930," 14:114.

86. "De la vida comercial," *El Fígaro*, February 1–8, 1920, pp. 106–7; "Un joven de grandes esperanzas: Bernardo Barria Ortega," *El Fígaro*, January 4–18, 1920, p. 59. See also Andrés Segura Cabrera, "La juventud cubana se abre paso," *El Fígaro*, November 23–30, 1919, p. 12.

87. Armando Maribona, "Estrenos," *Grafos*, September 1935, p. 45.

88. Jesús Castellanos, *Colección póstuma*, 3 vols. (Havana, 1914), 1:124.

89. J. A. Schweinfurth, "Cuba as a Vacation Trip," *American Architect and Building News* 92 (December 28, 1907): 217.

90. *El Fígaro*, May 13, 1900, p. 213.

91. *Diario de la Marina*, February 19, 1907, p. 3; Eduardo Anillo Rodríguez, *Cuarto siglos de vida* (Havana, 1919), pp. 13, 101–2; Miguel de Carrión, *La última voluntad* (Havana, 1903), p. 50; Leonardo Morales, "Arquitectura republicana," *El Arquitecto* 1 (April 1926): 4; Alejo Carpentier, *El recurso del método* (Mexico, 1974), p. 149.

92. Francisco X. del Castillo Márquez, *Bajo otros cielos* (Valencia, 1905), pp. 113–14; Rubén Darío, *Obras completas*, 15 vols. (Madrid, 1917), 12:40.

93. George Leland Dyer to Susan Dyer, December 3, 1900, GLD.

94. Alberto Díaz to I. T. Tichenor, December 22, 1887, *The Christian Index*, January 19, 1888, p. 2.

95. Renée Méndez Capote, *Memorias de una cubanita que nació con el siglo* (Havana, 1964), p. 186.

96. José de la Campa González, *Memorias de un machadista* (Tampa, 1937), p. 214.

97. *La Lucha*, January 12, 1901, p. 2.

98. *Diario de la Marina*, June 19, 1901, p. 2; Juan Antonio Barinaga to Editor, September 20, 1900, *Havana Post*, September 21, 1900, p. 4.

99. *New York Times*, October 2, 1898, p. 3.

100. Walter B. Booker to William R. Day, May 24, 1899, Day Papers, LC; Fred E. Bach to James H. Wilson, September 10, 1901, Wilson Papers, LC; Major John A. Logan to General John C. Bates, January 22, 1899, file 294/4, BIA.

101. George W. Davis to A. R. Chaffee, January 29, 1899, file 482, MGC; William Ludlow to Chief of Staff, May 11, 1899, file 3066, MGC; "Report of Brigadier General William Ludlow, Commanding Department of Havana," August 1, 1899, in U.S. War Department, *Annual Report of War Department, 1899*, 3 vols. (Washington, D.C., 1899), 1, pt. 1:227–29; L. H. Carpenter to Adjutant General, March 1, 1899, file 1903, MGC; Leonard Wood to Elihu Root, June 21, 1900, Root Papers, LC; James H. Wilson, "Supplemental Report—Confidential," September 7, 1899, file 995/48, BIA; U.S. Congress, Senate, Committee on Relations with Cuba, *Conditions in Cuba* (Washington, D.C., 1900), p. 4.

102. *Havana Post*, October 21, 1900, p. 1.

103. Many former residents of the United States also obtained appointments, including Nestor Ponce de León (director of archives), José Eliseo Cartaya (Havana customs), Manuel Trelles (treasurer, Matanzas province), Federico García Ramis (chief clerk, Supreme Court), Nicolás Heredia y Mota (director, Public Instruction), and Juan Antonio Lliteras (chief,

Notary Division). Joaquín Quílez, appointed governor of Pinar del Río in 1901, had lived in the United States between 1878 and 1898. Scores of mayors were U.S. citizens, including Leandro Rodríguez Colina (Güines), Rafael Gutiérrez Marín (Cabañas), Saturnino Sánchez Iznaga (Trinidad), Leopoldo Dulzaides (Unión de los Reyes), Domingo García Loyola (Caibarién), and José Vidal (Camajuaní).

104. *New York Times*, December 31, 1898, p. 2.

105. José Soler Puig, *Un mundo de cosas* (Jalapa, 1989), p. 176.

106. *Havana Post*, 1900–1901.

107. Ibid., November 4, 1906, p. 4.

108. *Diario de la Marina*, March 4, 1900, p. 4; *Havana Post*, May 9, 1900 (p. 3), May 22, 1901 (p. 3).

109. *Havana Post*, November 18, 1901, p. 5; *Diario de la Marina*, November 26, 1899 (p. 12), January 1, 1901 (p. 5).

110. Concepción Baloña de Sierra, *La mujer en Cuba* (Havana, 1899) p. 21; *La Lucha*, May 14, 1905, p. 2.

111. *Havana Post*, October 15, 1915, p. 4.

112. Loveira, *Los inmorales*, pp. 10–11.

113. Gualterio García to Gonzalo de Quesada, August 15, 1898, in Quesada, *Archivo de Gonzalo de Quesada*, 1:190; *Havana Post*, June 5, 1901, p. 3.

114. Francisco García, *Tiempo muerto: Memorias de un trabajador azucarero* (Havana, 1969), pp. 33–34; Luis Conte Agüero, *Eduardo Chibás: El adalid de Cuba* (Mexico, 1955), p. 59.

115. I am indebted to Olga Cabrera for this information.

116. Havana Post, 1904–14; Méndez Capote, *Memorias de una cubanita que nació con el siglo*, pp. 29, 78, 81–82.

117. José Raúl Capablanca, *My Chess Career* (New York, 1966), p. 13; *Diario de la Marina*, October 3, 1900, p. 1; José García Pedrosa, *Memorias de un desmemoriado* (Miami, 1979), p. 85.

118. Pepper, *To-Morrow in Cuba*, p. 335; *La Lucha*, March 3, 1905, p. 4.

119. *Diario de la Marina*, January 12, 1905 (p. 6), November 23, 1901; *La Lucha*, October 2, 1902 (p. 2), May 18, 1903 (p. 3).

120. *Havana Post*, April 3, 1900 (p. 4), September 11, 1901 (p. 4).

121. *Diario de la Marina*, June 21, 1900, p. 4, March 21, 1900; *Havana Post*, June 26, 1900, p. 3; W. W. Barnes, "Baptist Education in Cuba," *Our Home Field*, September 1911, pp. 3–5; Miguel J. Casado, "From the Life of a Lad," Memory Books of Sylvester and May Mather Jones, FHC; Una Roberts Lawrence, *Cuba for Christ* (Richmond, Va., 1926), pp. 226–27; Albion Knight to Charles Magoon, January 23, 1907, Confidential Correspondence, 1906–9, file 56, Records of the Provisional Government of Cuba, Record Group 199, NA.

122. *Havana Post*, June 6, 1900, p. 3.

123. "The 'Oliver' Typewriter," *Commercial and Financial World*, April 7, 1906, p. 13.

124. Frank A. Guiral, "Emilia de Córdoba: La primera oficinista cubana," *Carteles*, January 21, 1945, pp. 54–55; Frederic M. Noa, "The Condition of Women in Cuba," *Outlook Magazine*, March 16, 1905, p. 643.

125. *La Lucha*, 1903–6; *Havana Post*, 1910–16.

126. U.S. War Department, *Informe sobre el censo de Cuba*, p. 480; Cuba, *Census of the Republic of Cuba, 1919* (Havana, 1919), pp. 666–67.

127. Charles Berchón, *A través de Cuba: Relato geográfico descriptivo y económico* (Sceaux, 1910), p. 44.

128. U.S. War Department, *Informe sobre el censo de Cuba*, pp. 152–53.

129. *Diario de la Marina*, January 1, 1901 (pp. 1, 5), July 13, 1901 (p. 3), January 4, 1907 (p. 1), January 12, 1901 (p. 6).

130. Oliver Otis Howard, *Fighting for Humanity* (New York, 1898), p. 201; Leonard Wood to William McKinley, April 12, 1900, Wood Papers, LC.

131. Elihu Root to Charles W. Eliot, May 4, 1900, Root Papers, LC.

132. *Havana Post*, November 30, 1900, p. 1 (Wilby); Howard B. Grose, *Advance in the Antilles* (New York, 1910), p. 130.

133. *La Lucha*, February 19, 1903, p. 1.

134. Leonard Wood to William McKinley, April 12, 1900, Wood Papers, LC.

135. Alexis E. Frye, *Manual para maestros* (Havana, 1900), pp. 80–86, 135–36. See also Matthew E. Hanna, "Report of 1st Lieutenant Matthew E. Hanna, Commissioner of Public Schools of Cuba, for the Period of September 1, 1901 to May 20, 1902," in U.S. War Department, *Civil Report of Brigadier General Leonard Wood, Military Governor of Cuba, for the Period from January 1 to May 20, 1902*, 6 vols. (Washington, D.C., 1902), 1:503; Oscar F. Rego, "Cuba 1899: La educación también fué intervenida," *Bohemia*, February 3, 1976, pp. 89–90.

136. Leonard Wood, "The Military Government in Cuba," *Annals of the American Academy of Political and Social Science* 21 (March 1903): 13.

137. "Charter of the City Schools," April 1, 1901, in U.S. War Department, *Civil Report of Brigadier General Leonard Wood, Military Governor of Cuba, for the Period from December 20, 1899 to December 31, 1900*, 12 vols. (Washington, D.C., 1900), 8:28–30.

138. Elihu Root, *The Military and Colonial Policy of the United States*, ed. Robert Bacon and James Brown Scott (Cambridge, Mass., 1916), pp. 197–98; Wood, "Report of Brigadier General Leonard Wood," July 5, 1902, in U.S. War Department, *Civil Report of Brigadier General Leonard Wood . . . 1902*, pp. 17–18; *Washington Evening Star*, June 20, 1899, p. 11.

139. Elihu Root to Charles W. Eliot, May 4, 1900, Personal Correspondence, Root Papers.

140. *Havana Post*, July 24, 1900, p. 2.

141. Wood, "Report," July 5, 1902, 1:18.

142. Former teachers included Arturo Díaz, who became the first superintendent of schools. Emilio Planos later became a Methodist pastor in Matanzas. Justo Falco ended his career as a Havana judge. Fernando de Zayas served as magistrate of the *audiencia* of Havana. Nicolás Pérez Raventós and Francisco Henares joined the faculty of the University of Havana. Alberto Barreras would be elected a Liberal Party senator from Havana. Historian Ramiro Guerra served as superintendent of schools and as secretary to President Gerardo Machado; he subsequently became editor of *Diario de la Marina*.

143. *New York Herald*, May 24, 1897, p. 8.

144. *Havana Post*, August 19, 1921 (p. 1), September 4, 1921 (p. 5).

145. Alberto Lamar Schweyer, *Vendaval en los cañaverales* (Havana, 1937), pp. 245–46.

146. Ramón Gómez de Rosas to Editor, *Havana Post*, May 6, 1921, p. 4; Raimundo Cabrera, "La enseñanza del inglés en Cuba," *Cuba y América*, December 1915, p. 92.

CHAPTER THREE

1. *Havana Post*, August 7, 1914, p. 2.

2. Cuba, Secretaria de Hacienda, Sección de Estadística, *Inmigración y movimiento de pasajeros en el año. . . .* [1914–30] (Havana, 1915–31); Susan Schroeder, *Cuba: A Handbook of Historical Statistics* (Boston, 1982), p. 462.

3. Hart Crane to William Slater Brown and Susan Jenkins Brown, May 7, 1926, in Brown,

ed., *Robber Rocks: Letters and Memories of Hart Crane, 1923–1932* (Middletown, Conn., 1969), p. 54.

4. *Havana Post*, January 29, 1920 (p. 10), November 1, 1924 (p. 8), February 12, 1924 (p. 6), February 15, 1924 (p. 6).

5. Carlton Bailey Hurst, *Arms above the Door* (New York, 1932), p. 307.

6. Edward L. Reed to Secretary of State, September 7, 1929, 837.00 General Conditions/22, IAC; "Iniciativa fecunda: La 'Cuba Cervercera, S.A.,'" *El Fígaro*, April 4–11, 1920, pp. 182–84.

7. *Havana Post*, November 30, 1924, n.p.

8. Ibid., 1915–24.

9. Ibid., 1918–25; *The Key to Havana* (Havana, n.d.), p. 186.

10. *Havana Post*, 1922–25.

11. Ibid., 1920–30.

12. Ibid., November 13, 1924 (p. 4), August 7, 1928 (p. 5), January 6, 1925 (p. 4), February 15, 1925 (p. 4), October 27, 1924 (p. 4); Novel Richardson, *My Diplomatic Education* (New York, 1923), p. 33.

13. *Havana Post*, January 13, 1915, p. 2 (first quotation); Henry W. Wack, "Cuba and West Indies Charm," *Arts and Decoration* 34 (February 1931): 52; René Martínez, "Golf: Un juego antiguo en época moderna," *Grafos*, March 1935, p. 41.

14. Jess Losada, "30 años de deporte profesional," *Carteles*, May 24, 1936, pp. 117, 129.

15. "Comentarios," *Gráfico*, March 13, 1915, p. 7; Randy Roberts, *Papa Jack: Johnson and the Era of the White Hopes* (New York, 1983), pp. 199, 201–2.

16. *La Lucha*, April 7, 1915, p. 1; *Havana Post*, April 7, 1915, p. 3.

17. Jorge Alonso, *Puños dorados: Apuntes para la historia del boxeo en Cuba* (Santiago de Cuba, 1988), pp. 27–34.

18. Elio Menéndez and Víctor Joaquín Ortega, *El boxeo soy yo: Kid Chocolate* (Havana, 1990), pp. 109–17, 165–66.

19. Jess Losada, "Golfito," *Social*, August 1931, p. 84.

20. Hurst, *Arms above the Door*, pp. 305–6.

21. Joseph Hergesheimer, *San Cristobal de La Habana* (New York, 1920), p. 144; Sydney A. Clark, *Cuban Tapestry* (New York, 1936), p. 231.

22. Wack, "Cuba and West Indies Charm," p. 52.

23. Olive G. Gibson, *The Isle of a Hundred Harbors* (Boston, 1940), p. 17; *Havana Post*, May 20, 1925, p. 8; Anaïs Nin, *The Early Diary of Anaïs Nin, 1920–1923* (New York, 1982), p. 495; Hart Crane to Clarence Arthur Crane, May 20, 1926, in Thomas S. W. Lewis, ed., *Letters of Hart Crane and His Family* (New York, 1974), p. 493; *Havana Post*, January 6, 1924, p. 8; Alcyone Hart Barltrop, interview by author, Tampa, October 26, 1991.

24. Tourist postcard, n.d. (in author's possession); Hurst, *Arms above the Door*, p. 276.

25. *Havana Post*, November 25, 1928, p. 26.

26. J. J. Van Raalte, "El cubano y su amor por los deportes," *Carteles*, February–March 1921, pp. 28–29; *Havana Post*, November 19, 1920, p. 2; Basil Woon, *When It's Cocktail Time in Cuba* (New York, 1928), pp. 4–6; Isabel Stone, "Cuban Freedom Is Keynote of Tropical City," *Havana Post*, December 14, 1930, p. 5.

27. Wack, "Cuba and the West Indies," p. 53; "Portrait of a City: Havana, Booming Playground," *Latin American Report* (New Orleans) 1 (September 1956): 14; *Havana Post*, December 23, 1928, p. 6; Philip Sanford Marden, *Sailing South* (Boston, 1921), p. 42; Cecil Roberts, *Havana Bound* (New York, 1930), p. 120; Clark, *Cuban Tapestry*, p. 98; Bruce Bliven,

"And Cuba for the Winter," *New Republic*, February 29, 1928, p. 61; Wallace Stevens to Elsie Stevens, February 4, 1923, in *Letters of Wallace Stevens*, ed. Holly Stevens (New York, 1966), p. 235; Karl K. Kitchen, "Mr. Manhattan," *New York Evening World*, March 10, 1928, p. 5.

28. *Anuario Azucarero, 1942* (Havana, 1943), p. 149.

29. Francisco González Díaz, *Un canario en Cuba* (Havana, 1916), p. 100.

30. *Havana Post*, December 15, 1928, p. 6; tourist postcards dated 1928, 1947 (in author's possession); Marion Sunshine and Eliseo Grenet, "Havana's Calling Me," Edward B. Marks Music Corp., New York, 1937; *Havana Post*, January 7, 1930, p. 5; Woon, *When It's Cocktail Time in Cuba*, pp. 3–4; W. Adolphe Roberts, *Havana: The Portrait of a City* (New York, 1953), p. 263.

31. *Havana Post*, July 8, 1916 (p. 4), December 5, 1915 (p. 4).

32. Burnham Carter, "Journey by Moonlight," in *Post Stories of 1940* (Boston, 1941), p. 323; Hart Crane to William Slater Brown and Susan Jenkins Brown, May 7, 1926, in Brown, *Robber Rocks*, p. 54; *Havana Post*, November 30, 1929, n.p.

33. Edward Heyman, Bert Kaplan, and Reggie Childs, "Cuban Cabaret," Harms, Inc., New York, 1933; Elsie Graber and Clarence Mayer, "Cuban Moon," Clarence Mayer, Lansdowne, Pa., 1944; Ben Oakland, Mitchell Parish, and Irving Mills, "Sidewalks of Cuba," Mills Music, Inc., New York, 1934.

34. Hergesheimer, *San Cristobal de La Habana*, pp. 196–97; A. Hyatt Verrill, *Cuba Past and Present* (New York, 1920), p. 11; "America's Favorite Offshore Resorts," *House and Garden*, May 1956, p. 93; Helen Lawrenson, "The Sexiest City in the World—Havana I, 1955," reprinted in Lawrenson, *Latins Are Still Lousy Lovers* (New York, 1968), pp. 80–82.

35. Consuelo Hermer and Marjorie May, *Havana Mañana: A Guide to Cuba and the Cubans* (New York, 1941), pp. 3–4; Milton Guss, "Smoke Signals," *Times of Havana*, March 14, 1957, p. 9; Lawrenson, "The Sexiest City in the World," p. 82; Georgie Anne Geyer, *Guerrilla Prince* (New York, 1991), p. 46; Andrei Codrescu, "Picking the Flowers of the Revolution," *New York Times Magazine*, February 1, 1998, p. 35.

36. William McFee, *Sailors of Fortune* (Garden City, 1935), p. 101; Joseph Hergesheimer, *Cytherea* (New York, 1922), p. 214; Waldo Frank, "Habana of the Cubans," *New Republic*, June 23, 1926, p. 140; Edmund S. Whitman, *Those Wild West Indies* (New York, 1938), p. 101; Sydney A. Clark, *Cuban Tapestry* (New York, 1936), p. 231; E. L. Stafford, "The Inspiration," *Social*, June 1921, p. 29.

37. Irving Berlin, "I'll See You in C-U-B-A," Irving Berlin, Inc., New York, 1920; Harry Waxman and V. Dattilo, "My Cuban Pearl," Ansonia Music Co., New York, 1922; Tom Seymour and Mabel Wayne, "A Cabana in Havana," Mayfair Music Corp., New York, 1940; Moe Jafe and Clay Boland, "Havana," Irving Berlin, Inc., New York, 1936; Irving Caesar and Cliff Friend, "Down in Old Havana Town," n.p., New York, 1928; Edward Heyman, Bert Kaplan, and Reggie Childs, "Cuban Cabaret," Harms, Inc., New York, 1933; Marion Sunshine and Moisés Simons, "Cuban Belle," Edward B. Marks Music Corp., New York, 1933.

38. "Portrait of a City: Havana, Booming Playground," p. 17; Woon, *When It's Cocktail Time in Cuba*, p. 51; Sydney A. Clark, *All the Best in Cuba* (New York, 1954), pp. 99–100; Warren Miller, *Flush Times* (Boston, 1962), p. 43; Graham Greene, *Our Man in Havana* (1958; reprint, New York, 1969), p. 108.

39. Keith Reddin, *Rum and Coke* (New York, 1986), p. 43; Jay Robert Nash and Stanley Ralph Ross, *The Motion Picture Guide*, 12 vols. (Chicago, 1983–92), 3:1137; Ernest Hemingway, *Islands in the Stream* (New York, 1970), pp. 266, 269.

40. Horace Sutton, *Travelers: The American Tourist from Stagecoach to Space Shuttle*

(New York, 1980), p. 133; Barbara Dubivsky, "A Working Girl's Debut in Shipboard Society," *New York Times*, December 16, 1951, sec. 2, p. 28.

41. *Havana Post*, June 28, 1925, p. 4; Johnny Mercer and Bernie Hanighen, "The Week-End of a Private Secretary," Renick Music Corp., New York, 1937; Juan Arcocha, *Los muertos andan solos* (Havana, 1962), p. 55; Charlie Barnet, *Those Swinging Years: The Autobiography of Charlie Barnet* (Baton Rouge, 1984), pp. 67–68; Helen Lawrenson, "Latins Are Lousy Lovers," reprinted in Lawrenson, *Latins Are Still Lousy Lovers*, pp. 24–28, and "The Sexiest City in the World," p. 84.

42. Graham Greene, *Ways of Escape* (New York, 1980), p. 248; Lester Velie, "Suckers in Paradise," *Saturday Evening Post*, March 28, 1953, pp. 32–33; *Time*, April 21, 1952, p. 38; *Variety*, July 23, 1952, p. 52.

43. G. L. Morill, *Rotten Republics* (Chicago, 1916), p. 279.

44. *Havana Post*, January 24, 1930, p. 16; *La Lucha*, May 1, 1912, p. 1; Raymond Leslie Buell, *Problems of the New Cuba* (New York, 1935), p. 87; Hugh Thomas, *Cuba: The Pursuit of Freedom* (New York, 1971), p. 1097.

45. W. Adolphe Roberts, *Havana*, pp. 105, 222–23; T. Philip Terry, *Terry's Guide to Cuba* (Boston, 1929), pp. 200–201; Clark, *All the Best in Cuba*, pp. 159–60.

46. Tom Miller, *Trading with the Enemy* (New York, 1992), p. 168; Tennessee Williams, *Memoirs* (Garden City, 1975), p. 67; Ava Gardner, *My Story* (New York, 1990), p. 161; Hoagy Carmichael, *The Stardust Road* (New York, 1946), pp. 113–14; Greene, *Ways of Escape*, pp. 248–49; Neill Macaulay, *A Rebel in Cuba* (Chicago, 1970), pp. 25–26; John Sayles, *Los Gusanos* (New York, 1991), p. 73; Arthur Gardner to Henry F. Holland, January 13, 1956, lot file 570295, IA/1955–58.

47. *Variety*, March 4, 1953, p. 56.

48. *Miami Herald*, January 12, 1958, p. 1.

49. Ibid., pp. 1, 12; Hank Messick, *Lansky* (New York, 1971), p. 89; Dennis Eisenberg, Uri Dan, and Eli Landau, *Meyer Lansky: Mogul of the Mob* (New York, 1979), pp. 173–75, 226–34, 253–60; Robert Lacey, *Little Man: Meyer Lansky and the Gangster Life* (Boston, 1991), pp. 223–37, 246–59; Ernest Havermann, "Mobsters Move in on Troubled Havana and Split Rich Gambling Profits with Batista," *Life*, March 10, 1958, p. 34; *Havana Post*, January 19, 1956, p. 2; Harry J. Anslinger and Will Ousler, *The Murderers* (New York, 1961), p. 106.

50. Velie, "Suckers in Paradise," p. 33; *Miami Herald*, January 8, 1958, pp. 1–2; *Newsweek*, January 20, 1958, pp. 22–23; Milton Guss, "Smoke Signals," *Times of Havana*, January 16, 1958, p. 9; Manuel Antonio de Varona to Estes Kefauver, February 4, 1958, Kefauver Papers, University of Tennessee Library, Knoxville.

51. Edward B. Marks, *They All Sang* (New York, 1934), p. 162.

52. León Primelles, *Crónica cubana, 1919–1922* (Havana, 1957), p. 137; Samuel Feijóo, *El son cubano: Poesía general* (Havana, 1986), pp. 40–41.

53. Cristóbal Díaz Ayala, *Música cubana: Del Areyto a la Nueva Trova* (San Juan, 1981), p. 115. For an informative discussion of the *son*, see Robin D. Moore, *Nationalizing Blackness: Afrocubanismo and Artistic Revolution in Havana, 1920–1940* (Pittsburgh, 1997), pp. 87–113.

54. Clark, *All the Best in Cuba*, p. 156. For an excellent treatment of the rumba, see Yvonne Daniel, *Rumba* (Bloomington, 1995), and Earl Leaf, *Isles of Rhythm* (New York, 1948), p. 22.

55. Edith P. Pitts, *Cuba* (New York, 1976), p. 23; Clark, *Cuban Tapestry*, p. 33; Boaz Long to Secretary of State, October 8, 1920, 837.00/1802, IAC.

56. Edmund S. Whitman, *Those Wild West Indies* (New York, 1938), p. 108; "Our Trip to

Cuba," February 1930 (anonymous diary, original manuscript in author's possession); Ted Shawn, "Havana Nights," *Havana*, January 26, 1929, pp. 7–8.

57. Hergesheimer, *San Cristobal de La Habana*, pp. 147–48; Herbert C. Lanks, *Highway across the West Indies* (New York, 1948), p. 26.

58. Harold Adamson and Jimmy McHugh, "Blame It on the Rhumba," Universal Music Corp., New York, 1936; Wyngard, Weitzner, and DeKarlo, "The Last of the Rumbas," Edward B. Marks Music Corp., New York, 1936; Carol Raven and Pedro Via, "In the Madness of the Rumba," Edward B. Marks Corp., New York, 1934.

59. *Variety*, January 1, 1940, p. 1.

60. Maurice C. Zolotow, "South of the Border—On Broadway," *New York Times Magazine*, February 18, 1940, p. 11.

61. *Havana Post*, February 24, 1932, p. 6.

62. *La Lucha*, December 31, 1920, p. 4.

63. Cristóbal Díaz Ayala, *Cuba canta y baila: Discografía de la música cubana, 1898–1925* (San Juan, 1994).

64. Díaz Ayala, *Música cubana*, p. 121. Liner notes of "Antonio Machín, 'El Manisero': Early recordings, 1929–1930," Tumbao Compact Disc 026, 1993.

65. *Variety*, January 21, 1931, p. 65.

66. Leaf, *Isle of Rhythm*, p. 40; Winthrop Sargeant, "Cuba's Tin Pan Alley," *Life*, October 6, 1947, pp. 145–57; *Variety*, February 26, 1941, p. 41.

67. Xavier Cugat, "The Flair for Latin-American Music," *Etude* 62 (July 1944): 386; *Time*, July 29, 1946, p. 43; Xavier Cugat, "Conga Uninhibits Americans," *Variety*, October 1, 1941, p. 57.

68. Desi Arnaz, *A Book* (New York, 1976), p. 62; Mary M. Spaulding, "Nuestro Desi Arnaz," *Carteles*, December 22, 1940, pp. 8–9.

69. José Norman, "Cuban Pete," J. Norris Music Publishing Co., New York, 1936, 1946.

70. Edward Jablonski, *Gershwin: A Biography* (New York, 1987), p. 13; Charley Gerard and Marty Sheller, *Salsa! The Rhythm of Latin Music* (Crown Point, Ind., 1989), p. 77.

71. John Tasker Howard, *Our Contemporary Composers* (New York, 1941), p. 180.

72. Johnny Sipel, "Prado's Enthusiastic Crew Sells Newest Band Sound since Dizzy," *Billboard*, June 9, 1951, p. 3.

73. *Down Beat*, September 21, 1951 (p. 1), October 5, 1951 (p. 15).

74. Bill Simon, "Mambo for All," *Saturday Review*, September 25, 1954, p. 63; *Newsweek*, August 16, 1954, p. 54; Walter Waldman, "Mambo: The Afro-Cuban Dance Craze," *American Mercury*, January 1952, p. 15; *Variety*, September 29, 1954 (p. 45), June 16, 1954 (p. 1).

75. *Down Beat*, October 6, 1954, p. 29; *Variety*, August 4, 1954 (p. 43), July 7, 1953 (p. 1).

76. *Billboard*, July 17, 1954, p. 12; *Variety*, October 20, 1954, p. 121.

77. *Down Beat*, October 6, 1954, p. 29.

78. See Helio Orovio, *Diccionario de la música cubana* (Havana, 1981), pp. 110–12.

79. John Wilson, "Ga-ga over Cha Cha," *New York Times Magazine*, March 15, 1959, p. 57; John Storm Roberts, *The Latin Tinge* (New York, 1979), p. 132.

80. *Variety*, September 25, 1940 (p. 50), October 30, 1940 (p. 50); Martin Gottfried, *All His Jazz: The Life and Death of Bob Fosse* (New York, 1990), p. 36.

81. *Variety*, August 3, 1938 (p. 46), June 15, 1938 (p. 46), November 29, 1939 (p. 35).

82. Ibid., February 3, 1956, p. 55.

83. Myrna Katz Frommer and Harvey Frommer, *It Happened in the Catskills* (New York, 1991), p. 133; Stanley Dance, *The World of Swing* (New York, 1974), pp. 315–17.

84. Frommer and Frommer, *It Happened in the Catskills*, pp. 139–41; Joey Adams and Henry Tobias, *The Borscht Belt* (New York, 1959), p. 11.

85. *Variety*, July 7, 1954 (p. 48), September 23, 1953 (p. 47).

86. Ibid., July 1, 1942, p. 49.

87. Bill Coleman, *Trumpet Story* (Boston, 1981), pp. 170–71.

88. Zolotow, "South of the Border—On Broadway," p. 11; *Variety*, February 26, 1941 (p. 41), February 5, 1941 (p. 54).

89. See José Antonio Cabrera, "Cubanos sin empleo en Nueva York," *Bohemia*, June 29, 1958, pp. 48–49.

90. Benito Rivadulla Pascual "Problemas cubanos," *La Lucha*, January 28, 1928, p. 12.

91. *San Francisco Progress*, March 22–23, 1945, p. 5; Xavier Cugat, *Rumba Is My Life* (New York, 1948), pp. 122–23.

92. Bart Andrews, *Lucy and Ricky and Fred and Ethel: The Story of "I Love Lucy"* (New York, 1976), p. 5.

93. Donald F. Glut and Jon Harmon, *The Great Television Heroes* (Garden City, 1975), p. 118.

94. Michael McClay, *"I Love Lucy"* (New York, 1995), p. 41; Andrews, *Lucy and Ricky and Fred and Ethel*, p. 207.

95. Andrews, *Lucy and Ricky and Fred and Ethel*, pp. 189, 243.

96. Ramiro Sarteur, "Cugat en La Habana," *Carteles*, April 15, 1951, p. 44.

97. Eladio Secades, *Las mejores estampas de Secades* (Miami, 1983), p. 33; Tibor Mende, *América Latina entre en escena* (Santiago de Chile, 1953), pp. 262–63.

CHAPTER FOUR

1. Leland Jenks, *Our Cuban Colony* (New York, 1928), pp. 132, 284; León Primelles, *Crónica cubana, 1915–1918* (Havana, 1955), p. 183.

2. *Havana Post*, July 21, 1925, p. 4; Richard A. Smith, letter to author, December 29, 1991; George A. Braga, "A Bundle of Relations," p. 201 (manuscript, n.d.; copy in author's possession); "Los grandes centrales," *Bohemia*, June 10, 1923, pp. 13–15, 17–24; Carlos Martí, *Films cubanos: Oriente y Occidente* (Barcelona, 1915), pp. 106–8; Eva Canel, *Lo que vi en Cuba: A través de la isla* (Havana, 1916), pp. 286–87.

3. William McFee, *Sailors of Fortune* (Garden City, 1935), p. 232; Warren Miller, *90 Miles from Home* (New York, 1961), pp. 169, 172; Irene A. Wright, "The Nipe Bay Country—Cuba," *Bulletin of the Pan American Union* 32 (June 1911): 992; "El Central 'Palma,'" *Bohemia*, January 18, 1920, pp. 23, 75; Harry A. Franck, *Roaming through the West Indies* (New York, 1920), p. 80.

4. T. Philip Terry, *Terry's Guide to Cuba*, rev. ed. (Boston, 1929), pp. 344–45; Charles E. Chapman, *A History of the Cuban Republic* (New York, 1927), p. 14.

5. Herbert C. Lanks, *Highway across the West Indies* (New York, 1948), p. 40.

6. Terry, *Terry's Guide to Cuba*, p. 382; Sydney Clark, *Cuban Tapestry* (New York, 1936), pp. 242–43.

7. *La Lucha*, April 11, 1920, p. 4; Rafael Estenger, *El pulpo de oro* (Mexico, 1954), p. 60; Walfredo Rodríguez Blanca, "República cubana con territorios extranjeros," *Carteles*, September 1, 1929, p. 12.

8. Katherine Ponvert, *Cuban Chronicle* (Fredericksburg, Va., 1961), p. 60; Luis Felipe Rodríguez, "Ensayo sobre rutas cubanas," *Bohemia*, July 5, 1936, pp. 12–13.

9. Armando Leyva, *La provincia, las aldeas* (Santiago de Cuba, n.d.), p. 76; Erna Fergusson, *Cuba* (New York, 1946), pp. 238–39.

10. Alberto Quadreny, "Un viaje a Imías, Baracoa," *Carteles*, June 12, 1938, pp. 34–35; Rafael Rojas Domínguez to Editor, *Carteles*, July 24, 1938, p. 6.

11. Carlos E. Forment, "En Banes se polarizan dos civilizaciones," *Bohemia*, November 6, 1938, pp. 40–41, 43.

12. Carlos Martí, *Films cubanos*, pp. 106–8.

13. Ibid., pp. 106–8, 207–8; Juan Carlos Santamarina, "The Cuba Company and Cuban Development, 1900–1959" (Ph.D. dissertation, Rutgers University, 1995), pp. 254–55; *La Lucha*, April 13, 1928, p. 9; Leví Marrero, *Geografía de Cuba* (Havana, 1951), pp. 634–35; Commanding Officer, USS *Petrel*, to Secretary of the Navy, July 17, 1912, 837.00/908, IAC; Víctor Amat Osorio, *Banes, 1513–1958: Estampas de mi tierra y de mi sol* (Miami, 1981).

14. James Gould Cozzens, *Cock Pit* (New York, 1928), pp. 191–93; Carlos Martí, *Films cubanos*, p. 107.

15. Eduardo de Ulzurrún to Manuel Rionda, December 16, 1916, ser. 1, BBC; Braga, "A Bundle of Relations," p. 103; Wright, "The Nipe Bay Country—Cuba," p. 992; Ariel James, *Banes: Imperialismo y nación en una plantación azucarera* (Havana, 1976), pp. 115–16; *La Prensa*, June 23, 1925, p. 2.

16. Dora Alonso, *Tierra inerme* (Havana, 1961), p. 34; Ponvert, *Cuban Chronicle*, p. 40; Gonzalo Mazas Garbayo, "Mi Señorita," in Pablo de la Torriente Brau and Gonzalo Mazas Garbayo, *Batey* (Havana, 1930), p. 17.

17. Forment, "En Banes se polarizan dos civilizaciones," p. 43.

18. Ayuntamiento of Sancti-Spíritus to Manuel Rionda, April 19, 1927, Tuinicú-Ricardo Bianchi File, ser. 10, BBC.

19. Ponvert, *Cuban Chronicle*, p. 54.

20. Alberto Lamar Schweyer, *Vendaval en los cañaverales* (Havana, 1937), p. 177.

21. Hiram H. Hilty, *Friends in Cuba* (Richmond, Ind., n.d.), pp. 21–22, 58–60; Amat Osorio, *Banes, 1513–1958*, pp. 206–8.

22. Wright, "The Nipe Bay Country—Cuba," p. 989; Edgar G. Nesman, interview by author, Tampa, October 27, 1988.

23. Zenas L. Martin to Susie Martin, May 10, 1902, Martin and Haworth Family Papers, FHC.

24. Paul J. Acker to J. F. Dulles, March 5, 1955, 611.37/3-555, DS/RG 59; Richard G. Milk to James E. Ellis, March 8, 1959, United Methodist Church, Missionary Correspondence, 1956–61, GMA; Edgar G. Nesman, interview by author, Tampa, July 9, October 14, 1991.

25. Hilty, *Friends in Cuba*, pp. 82–83; Sergio la Villa, "Un pueblo del interior," *Carteles*, September 7, 1924, p. 8.

26. "Cantidades solicitadas para sueldos," September 5, 1940, Tuinicú: Salaries and Wages, ser. 10, BBC.

27. Fernando Berenguer, *La riqueza de Cuba* (Havana, 1917), pp. 232–33; Lamar Schweyer, *Vendaval en los cañaverales*, p. 124; Luis Felipe Rodríguez, "Los subalternos," *Carteles*, November 25, 1928, pp. 14, 57.

28. Lamar Schweyer, *Vendaval en los cañaverales*, p. 24.

29. Ana Núñez Machín, ed., *Memoria amarga del azúcar* (Havana, 1981), p. 84; Rodríguez, "Los subalternos," p. 14.

30. Pablo Armando Fernández, *Los niños se despiden* (Havana, 1968), p. 128.

31. Librado Reina, *Solares* (Manzanillo, 1927), pp. 77–78.

32. Núñez Machín, *Memoria amarga del azúcar*, p. 85.

33. Leyva, *La provincia, las aldeas*, p. 76.

34. Estenger, *El pulpo de oro*, pp. 122–31; Justo González, *Cubagua: Historia de un pueblo* (Havana, 1941), p. 144; James Gould Cozzens, *The Son of Perdition* (New York, 1929), pp. 9, 27–28.

35. Spruille Braden, "Conditions in Cuba and Our Policies in Respect Thereto," July 22, 1944, Braden Papers, Butler Library, Columbia University, New York, N.Y.

36. J. M. Buck to Secretary of State, November 22, 1919, 837.6551/2, IAC; Oscar Zanetti and Alejandro García, *United Fruit Company: Un caso del dominio imperialista en Cuba* (Havana, 1976), p. 117.

37. James, *Banes*, p. 147; Santiago García Cañizares to Manuel Rionda, August 1, 1924, Tuinicú: Applications for Employment, and Alfonso Fanjul to Gabino Gálvez, January 22, 1936, Tuinicú: Fanjul File, BBC; González, *Cubagua*, p. 144.

38. *Havana Post*, August 21, 1915, p. 4; El Curioso Parlanchín, "Parias en su propia patria," *Carteles*, January 2, 1930, p. 12; Inocencio Lego, "Una cruzada en favor del maltratado guajiro," *Bohemia*, September 6, 1936, p. 30.

39. Raimundo Cabrera, *Sombras eternas* (Havana, 1919), p. 273.

40. Carlos Forment, "Extrangulación económica," *Bohemia*, September 11, 1938, pp. 10–11, 51; José Comallonga, "La tierra," *Carteles*, June 7, 1931, pp. 20, 49.

41. Noel Navarro, *Marcial Ponce: De central en central* (Havana, 1977), p. 57; Lamar Schweyer, *Vendaval en los cañaverales*, pp. 96–192, 245–46; Cozzens, *Son of Perdition*, p. 264; Estenger, *El pulpo de oro*, p. 109; Virginia Schofield, telephone interview by author, October 7, 1991; Edgar G. Nesman, interview by author, Tampa, October 14, 1991.

42. Sergio la Villa, "Un pueblo del interior," *Carteles*, September 7, 1924, p. 8; Walfredo Rodríguez Blanca, "República cubana con territorios extranjeros," *Carteles*, September 1, 1929, p. 12, and "Aquí hace falta un pueblo," *Carteles*, December 29, 1929, p. 12.

43. *La Lucha*, November 8, 1926, p. 9; "Guantánamo: La cloaca de Cuba," *Bohemia*, March 20, 1938, p. 45.

44. *Havana Post*, October 28, 1928, p. 12.

45. Gervasio G. Ruiz, "Guantánamo, Caimanera y la base naval norteamericana," *Carteles*, May 7, 1950, p. 40; Rigoberto Cruz Díaz, *Guantánamo Bay* (Santiago de Cuba, 1977), p. 105; *La Lucha*, November 8, 1905, p. 7.

46. *Times of Havana*, January 13, 1958, p. 12.

47. "Guantánamo: La cloaca de Cuba," p. 40; George B. Wally, *Vivan los cubanos* (Havana, 1946), n.p.

48. H. M. Wolcott to Secretary of State, June 7, 1917, 837.1241/—, IAC; Ira E. Sherman to James E. Ellis, July 22, 1952, United Methodist Church, Missionary Correspondence, 1950–55, GMA.

49. Cruz Díaz, *Guantánamo Bay*, p. 102; *Havana Post*, September 16, 1928, p. 6; Ira E. Sherman to John Branscomb, March 23, 1952, United Methodist Church, Missionary Correspondence, 1950–55, GMA; Ira E. Sherman, letter to author, December 3, 1991.

50. James C. Manning, "Swans of Cong" (manuscript, 1968), p. 18. The author acknowledges with gratitude Mr. Manning's generosity in making available a copy of his unpublished novel.

51. "Guantánamo: La cloaca de Cuba," pp. 40, 45.

52. Herminio Portell Vilá, "Vergüenza nacional," *Bohemia*, August 29, 1954, pp. 27, 110.

53. Richard Aumerle Maher, "Protestantism in Cuba," *Catholic World*, November 1914, p. 207; David W. Carter to Warren A. Candler, March 24, 1904, Candler Papers, WL-EU.

54. *La Lucha*, July 23, 1903, p. 1; General N. MacDonald, "General Statistics of Protestant Missions on the Island of Cuba," March 4, 1902, Warren A. Candler Papers, WL-EU.

55. Albion Knight to Charles Magoon, January 23, 1907, Confidential Correspondence, 1906–9, file 56, Records of the Provisional Government of Cuba, Record Group 199, NA.

56. Albion W. Knight, *Lending a Hand in Cuba* (Hartford, 1916), p. 121; "By-products of Christian Missions in Cuba," *Missionary Review of the World* 35 (January 1912): 66; May Mather Jones, Journal, February 1901, Sylvester and May Mather Jones Papers, FHC; E. P Herrick, "Our Cuban Work in Florida and Cuba," *Home Missionary* 72 (October 1899): 86; Howard B. Grose, *Advance in the Antilles* (New York, 1910), pp. 71, 86.

57. Henry L. Morehouse, *Ten Years in Eastern Cuba* (New York, 1910), p. 38; May Mather Jones, Journal, February 1901, Sylvester and May Mather Jones Papers, FHC; Grose, *Advance in the Antilles*, p. 130.

58. Cozzens, *Cock Pit*, pp. 58–59.

59. J. Milton Greene, "What Americans Have Done in Cuba," *Missionary Review of the World* 30 (August 1907): 597; J. Merle Davis, *The Cuban Church in a Sugar Economy* (New York, 1942), p. 123.

60. Grose, *Advance in the Antilles*, p. 123; Greene, "What Americans Have Done in Cuba," pp. 595, 597; Benjamin F. Trueblood, "Cuba's Need of Gospel," *American Friend* 6 (December 29, 1899): 1242; Morehouse, *Ten Years in Eastern Cuba*, p. 25; Richard G. Milk to A. Wassons, March 31, 1950, David White to Friends, April 18, 1953, and Edgar G. Nesman to Friends, December 25, 1954, United Methodist Church, Missionary Correspondence, 1950–55, GMA.

61. Edgar G. Nesman, "Education for Technological Change in Rural Cuba" (M.S. thesis, Michigan State University, College of Agriculture and Applied Sciences, 1960), pp. 40–42; Carroll English to Friends, April 1955, United Methodist Church, Missionary Correspondence, 1950–55, GMA.

62. González, *Cubagua*, p. 189; Arthur R. Gray, *The New World* (New York, n.d.), p. 148; Richard W. Milk to James E. Ellis, March 21, 1958, United Methodist Church, Missionary Correspondence, 1956–61, GMA; Davis, *The Cuban Church in a Sugar Economy*, pp. 53, 74.

63. M. N. McCall, *A Baptist Generation in Cuba* (Atlanta, 1942), pp. 118–19; Albion W. Knight, "The Episcopal Church Mission in Cuba," *Missionary Review of the World* 37 (March 1914): 199; Una Roberts Lawrence, *Cuba for Christ* (Richmond, Va., 1926), pp. 91–92.

64. *Havana Post*, November 24, 1930, p. 6; Edgar G. Nesman, interview by author, Tampa, July 29, 1991; Nesman, "Education for Technological Change in Rural Cuba," pp. 6–7.

65. Margaret E. Crahan, "Religious Penetration and Nationalism in Cuba: U.S. Methodist Activities, 1898–1958," *Revista/Review Interamericana* 8 (Summer 1978): 208; Marcos A. Ramos, *Protestantism and Revolution in Cuba* (Miami, 1989), pp. 34–36; C. Alton Robertson, "The Political Role of the Protestants in Cuba—1959 to 1962," *Occasional Bulletin from the Missionary Research Library* 18 (January 1967): 1.

66. Marcos A. Ramos, *Panorama del Protestantismo en Cuba* (San José, 1986), p. 420; Davis, *The Cuban Church in a Sugar Economy*, p. 56.

67. See Davis, *The Cuban Church in a Sugar Economy*, pp. 101–2.

68. *Havana Post*, March 23, 1901, p. 2.

69. Vedado Tennis Club, *Libro de oro, 1902–1952* (Havana, 1952), pp. 11–97.

70. Zenas L. Martin to Susie and Eva Martin, February 12, 1901, Martin and Haworth Family Papers, FHC; *Havana Post*, July 24, 1900, p. 3.

71. *Diario de la Marina*, January 4, 1901, p. 2; *La Lucha*, January 29, 1910, p. 7.

72. H. R. Moseley, "The Sunday-schools in Santiago and Suburbs, Cuba," *Home Missionary Monthly* 22 (October 1901): 281; Ralph C. Estep, *El Toro: A Motor Car Story of Interior Cuba* (Detroit, 1909), p. 59; Lawrence, *Cuba for Christ*, pp. 115–16.

73. Byron White, *Azúcar amargo: Un estudio de la economía cubana* (Havana, 1954), p. 103.

74. Ponvert, *Cuban Chronicle*, pp. 22–23.

75. See Juan Esposito to Manuel Rionda, October 8, 1925, Elia—Baseball Club File, BBC; Manuel Rionda to Gerard Smith, October 27, 1919, ibid.; Salvador Rionda to Manuel Rionda, April 11, 1928, Manatí File, ibid.; James M. Sullivan to William Jennings Bryan, November 1, 1913, 839.00/962, IAC.

76. See Tuinicú—Baseball Team File, BBC.

77. In Paula J. Pettavino and Gerolyn Pye, *Sport in Cuba* (Pittsburgh, 1994), p. 63.

78. Michael M. Oleksak and Mary Adams Oleksak, *Beisbol: Latin Americans and the Grand Old Game* (Grand Rapids, 1991), pp. 55–56; Orestes "Minnie" Miñoso, *Extra Innings: My Life in Baseball* (Chicago, 1983), p. 19; Jess Losada, "La Habana se convirtió en plaza de Liga Grande," *Carteles*, November 3, 1946, pp. 52–53; Juan Arcocha, *Los muertos andan solos* (Havana, 1962), pp. 53–54.

79. Tommy Lasorda with David Fisher, *The Artful Dodger* (New York, 1985), p. 74.

80. W. O. McGeehan, "McGraw Maulers Baffled by Tuero, Cuban Pitcher," *New York Tribune*, May 25, 1919, p. 2-S; *Sporting News*, January 23, 1952, p. 1.

81. Roy Campanella, *It's Good to Be Alive* (Boston, 1959), p. 191; Jess Losada, "Amorós, heroe del año," *Carteles*, October 16, 1955, pp. 82–84; *Bohemia*, October 9, 1955, pp. 73, 91.

82. Mariblanca Sabas Alomá, "Irresponsabilidad," *Carteles*, October 9, 1932, p. 40.

83. *Times of Havana*, October 12, 1958, p. 3.

84. Manuel F. de la Reguera, "Sports," *Grafos*, April 1936, p. 57.

85. This subject is well treated in Lisa Brock and Bijan Bayne, "Not Just Black: African-Americans, Cubans, and Baseball," in Brock and Digna Castañeda Fuertes, eds., *Between Race and Empire: African-Americans and Cubans before the Cuban Revolution* (Philadelphia, 1998), pp. 168–204.

86. *New York Age*, September 28, 1911, p. 6.

87. David Q. Voigt, *America through Baseball* (Chicago, 1977), p. 111; Howard Senzel, *Baseball and the Cold War* (New York, 1977), p. 257; Janet Bruce, *The Kansas City Monarchs* (Lawrence, 1985), p. 9; Donn Rogosin, *Invisible Men: Life in Baseball's Negro Leagues* (New York, 1983), pp. 158–59; Jules Tygiel, *Baseball's Great Experiment* (New York, 1983), pp. 11–12.

88. Bruce, *The Kansas City Monarchs*, p. 6; Jerry Malloy, ed., *Sol White's History of Colored Baseball, with Other Documents on the Early Black Game, 1886–1936* (Lincoln, Nebr., 1995), pp. lix–lx.

89. Brock and Bayne, "Not Just Black," p. 175; William Brashler, *The Bingo Long Traveling All-Stars and Motor Kings* (New York, 1973).

90. Adolfo Fonts, "Los Cubanos son triunfos," *Bohemia*, April 12, 1936, p. 16.

91. John B. Holway, *Black Diamonds: Life in the Negro Leagues from the Men Who Lived It* (Westport, Conn., 1989), p. 127.

92. *The Call*, January 25, 1929, p. 6. For the series batting averages, see *New York Age*, December 29, 1910, p. 6, and *The Call*, January 25, 1929, p. 6.

93. Holway, *Black Diamonds*, pp. 127–28, 136.

94. Ibid., p. 128; Rogosin, *Invisible Men*, pp. 162–63.

95. Campanella, *It's Good to Be Alive*, pp. 95, 130–31; Tygiel, *Baseball's Great Experiment*, pp. 164–65.

96. Raúl Gutiérrez, "Los fanáticos cubanos no quieren managers extranjeros," *Bohemia*, September 20, 1953, pp. 74–75; Mario Vidal, "Furia de pelota," *Carteles*, December 15, 1946, p. 57; *Bohemia*, October 19, 1952, p. 81; Herminio Portell Vilá, "Deportes," *El Mundo*, December 1, 1949, p. 10; Gustavo Robreño, *La acera del Louvre* (Havana, 1925), p. 78.

97. Tom Meany, "Play Ball, Amigos," *Collier's*, January 20, 1957, 35; *Bohemia*, October 25, 1936, p. 36.

98. Jacob Canter to Department of State, May 19, 1950, 837.4533/5-1950, IA/1950–54; Walter M. Bastian Jr., to Department of State, March 11, 1953, 837.4533/7-353, ibid.; Rafael H. Reyna to Albert Chandler, February 11, 1957, 837.40634/2-1747, IA/1955–58; Reyna to Chandler, December 10, 1947, 837.40634/3-1847, IA/1945–49.

99. Guillermo Pi, "Sports," *Bohemia*, October 24, 1920, p. 12; Adolfo Font, "Resurge el baseball profesional," *Bohemia*, November 3, 1935, p. 27.

100. Rodríguez, "Los subalternos," pp. 14, 57.

101. José Sixto de Sola, "El deporte como factor patriótico y sociológico," *Cuba Contemporánea* 5 (June 1914): 121–29.

102. Ibid., p. 128; José Soler Puig, *En el año de enero* (Havana, 1963), p. 98; Jess Losada, "Efectos de la serie St. Louis–Cuba," *Carteles*, March 22, 1936, pp. 46–47; José Agustín Martínez, "Record," *El Mundo*, August 6, 1955, p. A-6; Mario Guiral Moreno, "Sentido patriótico del deporte," *El Mundo*, August 10, 1955, p. A-6.

103. Interview with José Antonio López del Valle, *Carteles*, February 3, 1935, p. 38; Hernández Travieso, "El deporte," *El Mundo*, October 15, 1955, p. A-6.

104. Armando Villegas, "Los Cubanitos: Institución ejemplar," *El Mundo Ilustrado*, June 30, 1957, pp. 4–5.

105. Losada, "Efectos de la serie St. Louis–Cuba," pp. 46–47.

106. *El Mundo*, May 16, 1953, p. A-1, and 1952–55 generally; *La Correspondencia*, December 29, 1925, p. 10.

107. J. Saiz de la Mora, "El lenguaje de los 'sports,'" *Revista Habanera* 3 (March 20, 1915): 296–97.

108. I am indebted to Francisco Pérez Guzmán and Oscar Zanetti for information on some of these expressions. See also José Sánchez-Boudy, *Diccionario de cubanismos mas usuales*, 3 vols. (Miami, 1978–86); Espina Pérez, *Diccionario de cubanismos* (Barcelona, 1972); Luis Pérez López, *Asi hablaba Cuba* (Miami, 1968); and Argelio Santiesteban, *El habla popular cubano de hoy* (Havana, 1982).

109. Jess Losada, "Lo que vi en Holguín y en Manzanillo," *Carteles*, December 5, 1937, p. 8; "Compariencia en el canal 2," *Obra Revolucionaria* 7 (June 11, 1960): 10; Robreño, *La acera del Louvre*, p. 78.

110. Tirso A. Valdez, *Notas acerca del béisbol dominicano del pasado y del presente* (Ciudad Trujillo, 1958), p. 11; Gilbert M. Joseph, "Documenting a Regional Pastime: Baseball in Yucatán," in Robert M. Levine, ed., *Windows on Latin America: Understanding Society through Photography* (Coral Gables, Fla., 1987), pp. 79–81; Gilbert M. Joseph, "Forging the Regional Pastime: Baseball and Class in Yucatán," in Joseph Arbena, ed., *Sport and Society in Latin America* (Westport, Conn., 1988), pp. 30–31.

CHAPTER FIVE

1. Cuba, *Census of the Republic of Cuba, 1919* (Havana, 1921), pp. 632–34.
2. Teresa Casuso, *Cuba and Castro*, trans. Elmer Grossberg (New York, 1961), pp. 9–10.

3. Franklin D. Roosevelt Diary: Trip to Cuba, January 21–25, 1917, Roosevelt Papers, Hyde Park, N.Y.; *Facts about Sugar*, August 19, 1916, p. 101; *Havana Post*, November 5, 1916, p. 4; "Property in Cuba," *Scientific American*, July 1918, p. 66; William Joseph Showalter, "Cuba—The Sugar Mill of the Antilles," *National Geographic*, July 1920, pp. 1, 6.

4. *La Prensa* (New York), March 8, 1920, p. 7; Carlton Baily Hurst, *The Arms above the Door* (New York, 1932), p. 278.

5. J. M. Hopgood to Norman H. Davis, September 1, 1920, 837.1561/73, IAC; E. L. Bogart to Secretary of State, August 18, 1920, 837.1561/55, IAC.

6. Harry A. Franck, *Roaming through the West Indies* (New York, 1920), p. 50.

7. E. F. Sweet to Secretary of State, January 30, 1919, 837.75/6, DS/RG 59.

8. Marcelo Pogolotti, *Del barro y las voces* (Havana, 1982), p. 83; Loló de la Torriente, *Testimonio desde dentro* (Havana, 1985), p. 93.

9. Raúl Rodríguez, *El cine silente en Cuba* (Havana, 1992), pp. 103–4, 122; *Havana Post*, August 22, 1916, p. 2.

10. *La Lucha*, January 16, 1929 (p. 5), February 2, 1929 (p. 6); Pogolotti, *Del barro y las voces*, pp. 39, 177.

11. Alejo Carpentier, "Sobre La Habana, 1912–1930," in Carpentier, *Obras completas de Alejo Carpentier*, 16 vols. (Mexico, 1983–94), 14:113; Joseph Hergesheimer, *San Cristobal de La Habana* (Havana, 1920), p. 145; *Havana Post*, October 31, 1921, p. 4; Michael Chanan, *The Cuban Image* (London, 1985), p. 52.

12. "Teatro 'Trianón,'" *El Fígaro*, April 4–11, 1920, pp. 182–84.

13. Héctor García Mesa, María Eulalia Douglas, and Raúl González, "El cine mudo en Cuba, 1897–1993," in Miguel Angel García, ed., *Cine latinoamericano, 1896–1930* (Caracas, 1992), pp. 151–57; "Expediente sobre relación de cines y espectáculos públicos de la provincia de Matanzas," 1925, Fonda Miscelánea de Expedientes (Cultura), file 2, no. 8, AHPM.

14. *La Lucha*, April 1, 1920, p. 9; León Primelles, *Crónica cubana, 1915–1918* (Havana, 1955), p. 100; Chanan, *The Cuban Image*, pp. 47–48; Esteban Palacios Hoyas, *Memorias de un pueblito cubano* (Miami, 1985), p. 39; Rigoberto Cruz Díaz, *Guantánamo Bay* (Santiago de Cuba, 1977), p. 102; Idaless Westly, "What I Found in Cuba," *Havana Post*, August 29, 1921, p. 4.

15. Nevio López Pellón, "Los millones que gastamos en ir al cine," *Bohemia*, March 27, 1955, pp. 32–33, 120; Katherine Ponvert, *Cuban Chronicle: The Story of Central Hormiguero in the Province of Las Villas, Cuba* (Fredericksburg, Va., 1961), p. 33.

16. "Nuestros cines elegantes," *Carteles*, January 1924, p. 22; René Jordán, "¡Aquí está Cinerama!," *Bohemia*, February 16, 1958, pp. 38–39.

17. *La Lucha*, April 4, 1920, p. 9.

18. José Manuel Carballido Rey, *El tiempo en un centinela insobornable* (Havana, 1983), p. 10; Lisandro Otero, *Arbol de la vida* (Mexico, 1990), p. 279; Guillermo Arrebola, *Historia de Nuevitas, 1492–1943* (Camagüey, 1943), p. 47; Ernesto T. Brivio, *Cuba: Isla de las maravillas* (Havana, 1949), p. 70.

19. *New York Post*, January 24, 1920, sec. 5, p. 15; Marta Vignier, "Los adolescentes cubanos de hoy: ¿Qué hacen? ¿Qué piensan? ¿Qué les preocupan?," *Carteles*, September 16, 1956, pp. 48–51; Oscar Lewis, Ruth M. Lewis, and Susan M. Rigdon, *Four Women: Living the Revolution* (Urbana, Ill., 1977), p. 361.

20. Néstor Almendros, *A Man with a Camera*, trans. Rachel Phillips (New York, 1984), pp. 27–28; Guillermo Martínez Márquez, "El poema eterno del amor que nace," *Social*, February 1926, pp. 38–39; Hortensia de Varela, *Cuentos* (Havana, 1932), pp. 200–201; Luis Adrián Betancourt, *Expediente almirante* (Havana, 1977), p. 18.

21. Samuel Feijóo, *Diario abierto* (Havana, 1959), p. 69; Reinaldo Arenas, *Before Night Fall*, trans. Delores M. Koch (New York, 1993), p. 34.

22. Pogolotti, *Del barro y las voces*, p. 94; José Pardo Llada, *Yo me recuerdo* (Miami, 1993), p. 66; Joaquín G. Santana, *Recuerdos de la calle Magnolia* (Havana, 1980), pp. 76–77.

23. *La Lucha*, March 21, 1920 (p. 1), April 11, 1920 (p. 9).

24. *Bohemia*, *Carteles*, and *Social*, 1926–35.

25. *Vanidades*, June 15, 1958 (pp. 24–25), November 15, 1958 (pp. 26–27); Olga André, "Gregory Peck opina sobre la mujer ideal," *Vanidades*, October 1, 1954, p. 122; "Yvonne de Carlo describe al hombre ideal," *Carteles*, July 28, 1946, pp. 14–17; "El beso de amor y el de Hollywood," *El Mundo*, June 25, 1948, p. 23.

26. Among the stars who appeared on the cover of these magazines were Jane Wyman, Shirley Temple, Myrna Loy, Hedy Lamarr, Vivian Blaine, Robert Sterling, Joan Fontaine, Glenn Ford, Eleanor Parker, Cornell Wilde, Gloria Swanson, Roscoe "Fatty" Arbuckle, Jean Harlow, Rudolph Valentino, Carole Lombard, Joan Crawford, and Douglas Fairbanks.

27. Armando Couto, *La triste historia de mi vida oscura* (Miami, 1978), p. 26; Wenceslao Gálvez, *Costumbres, satiras, observaciones* (Havana, 1932), pp. 121–22.

28. Pico Iyer, *Cuba and the Night* (New York, 1995), p. 23.

29. G. Cain, "Los 'Oscares' de 1953," *Carteles*, April 4, 1954, pp. 42–43; J. M. Valdés-Rodríguez, "Especulación en torno a los 'Oscares' 1956," *El Mundo*, March 2, 1957, p. B-11; *Bohemia*, August 5, 1934, p. 45.

30. Mary M. Spaulding, "Después de 32 años Tom Mix nos visita," *Carteles*, February 23, 1930, pp. 24, 64–65; "Charlando con Norma Talmadge," *Bohemia*, February 8, 1920, p. 15; G. Cain, "Marlon Brando, un amigo," *Carteles*, March 4, 1956, pp. 42–44, 48; Ramiro Sarteur, "John Wayne en La Habana," *Carteles*, May 20, 1951, p. 51.

31. Ofelia Rodríguez Acosta, *En la noche del mundo* (Havana, 1940), p. 54.

32. *Revista Habanera* 2 (September 30, 1914): 107; *La Prensa*, March 8, 1920, p. 7; Rita Guibert, *Seven Voices* (New York, 1972), p. 400; *Havana Post*, July 22, 1936, p. 2; Marcelo Pogolotti, *El caserón del Cerro* (1940; reprint, Havana, 1961), p. 148; *La Lucha*, July 4, 1920, p. 2; J. A. Morales, "El peligro de los cines," *Gráfico*, January 27, 1917, p. 21.

33. José Antonio Mases, *Los padres nuestros y el fusil* (Barcelona, 1973), p. 167.

34. Enrique Serpa, *Felisa y yo* (Havana, 1937), p. 99; Miguel de Marcos, *Papaíto Mayarí* (1947; reprint, Havana, 1977), p. 20; Luis Ricardo Alonso, *Los dioses ajenos* (Barcelona, 1971), p. 171; Nicolás Dorr, *La chacota* (Havana, 1989), pp. 177, 185; Luis Santeiro, *The Lady from Havana* (New York, 1991), p. 42; Pablo Armando Fernández, *Los niños se despiden* (Havana, 1968), p. 306; Edmundo Desnoes, *Memorias de subdesarrollo* (1965; reprint, Mexico, 1975), p. 83; Guillermo Cabrera Infante, *Tres tristes tigres* (1965; reprint, Barcelona, 1970), pp. 62, 204, 149, 155, 157, 166, and *Infante's Inferno* (New York, 1979), pp. 61, 121, 221, 278; Matías Montes Huidobro, "Su cara mitad," in Moisés Pérez Coterillo, ed., *Teatro cubano contemporáneo: Antología* (Mexico, 1992), p. 663.

35. *Bohemia*, February 19, 1939, pp. 16–17; Juan Marinello, *Cuba: Cultura* (Havana, 1989), p. 336; Raúl Roa to Pablo de la Torriente, June 5, 1936, in Pablo de la Torriente, *Cartas cruzadas*, ed. Víctor Causáus (Havana, 1981), p. 582; Luis Rolando Cabrera, "En Quivicán, cinco guajiritos quisieron jugar a los bandidos," *Bohemia*, October 31, 1954, p. 83; Oscar Lewis, Ruth M. Lewis, and Susan M. Rigdon, *Neighbors: Living the Revolution* (Urbana, Ill., 1978), p. 245; Alberto Quadreny, "Un viaje a Imías, Baracoa," *Carteles*, June 12, 1938, p. 34; Antonio Iraizoz, "No me voy a Morón," *El Mundo*, February 14, 1956, p. A-8; Max Lesnik, "Violencia, inmoralidad y reelección," *Bohemia*, April 29, 1956, p. 51; *Granma*, June 8, 1996, p. 3.

36. Alvaro Prendes, *Piloto de guerra: Crónicas de un aviador* (Havana, 1981), p. 124; *Bohemia*, February 23, 1958, supp. 6; Betancourt, *Expediente almirante*, p. 203.

37. R. Suárez Solis, "La vida en el cine," *Social*, June 1929, p. 59; Ofelia Rodríguez Acosta, *Sonata interrumpida* (Mexico, 1943), pp. 12–13; Gálvez, *Costumbres, satiras, observaciones*, p. 122.

38. Enrique Serpa, *Contrabando* (1938; reprint, Miami, 1973), p. 85; Guillermo Cabrera Infante, *Mea Cuba* (New York, 1994), p. 150.

39. Diary of Joseph J. Dimock, Dimock Family Papers, WL-EU; Maturin M. Ballou, *History of Cuba; or, Notes of a Traveller in the Tropics* (Boston, 1854), p. 78; James W. Steele, *Cuban Sketches* (New York, 1881), p. 59; Carolina L. Wallace, *Santiago de Cuba before the War* (New York, 1899), p. 36; Benjamín de Céspedes, "Las mujeres flacas," *La Habana Elegante*, March 30, 1890, p. 7.

40. *Social*, January 1924, p. 48; "Las delgadas están de moda," *Bohemia*, June 3, 1928, p. 36; "Consultorio de belleza," *Social*, October 1924, p. 54; Marisabel Sáenz, "¿Es realmente bella la mujer Cubana?," *Carteles*, July 29, 1934, pp. 14, 55.

41. Lesbia Soravilla, *El dolor de vivir* (Havana, n.d.), pp. 185–86.

42. Don Galaor, "Miss Cuba," *Bohemia*, July 20, 1930, p. 48; Jaime Deristel, "Sex-Appeal," *Bohemia*, June 5, 1932, pp. 11–12.

43. Ofelia Rodríguez Acosta, "El derecho de amar," *Bohemia*, May 22, 1932, p. 13.

44. *Grafos*, January–March 1935; Jean Harlow, "Mis secretos de belleza," *Bohemia*, December 1, 1935, p. 58; *Vanidades*, June 15, 1955 (p. 126), July 1, 1956 (p. 16), November 15, 1956 (p. 122), August 15, 1958 (p. 108), October 1, 1932 (p. 32); Cyd Charisse, "Cuidando la línea," *Vanidades*, August 15, 1955, p. 108; Joan Crawford, "Joan Crawford nos explica como se seduce a un hombre," *Vanidades*, August 15, 1940, p. 51; "Como manicurarse las uñas como lo hacen las estrellas de cine," *Bohemia*, April 11, 1937, p. 31; Sara Hamilton, "Lo que comen las estrellas de Hollywood," *Bohemia*, October 9, 1932, p. 23; *Carteles*, February 16, 1947, p. 11; Mary M. Spaulding, "¿Mujeres bonitas?," *Carteles*, February 24, 1935, pp. 42–51, and "Narices estelares," *Carteles*, November 28, 1937, pp. 42–43; *Vanidades*, July 1, 1955 (p. 35), July 15, 1956 (pp. 24–25); María Julia de Lara, "Salud y belleza," *Carteles*, November 24, 1935 (pp. 48–49), December 29, 1935 (pp. 48–49), May 27, 1934 (pp. 58–59), May 6, 1934 (pp. 52–53), April 29, 1934 (pp. 52–53), May 19, 1935 (pp. 48–49).

45. *Carteles*, August 1, 1926, p. 35; *El Mundo*, August 7, 1949 (p. 10), 1948–54.

46. Juan de la Habana, "Las Shirley Temple cubanas," *Carteles*, March 29, 1936, pp. 38–39; "Shirley Temple y sus vestidos," *Vanidades*, February 1937, back cover; Berta A. de Martínez Márquez, "Las navidades de Shirley Temple," *Grafos*, December 1935, p. 73; Rigoberto Cruz Díaz, *Muy buenas noches, señoras y señores . . .* (Santiago de Cuba, 1972), p. 39.

47. Isabel Margarita Ordext, "Las norteamericanas," *Gráfico*, November 4, 1916, p. 10; Cabrera Infante, *Infante's Inferno*, p. 207; María Julia de Lara, "Salud y belleza," *Carteles*, January 21, 1954, p. 56; *El Mundo*, May 26, 1954, p. B-9; *Vanidades*, December 15, 1936 (p. 36), March 1, 1948 (p. 23); Soravilla, *El dolor de vivir*, p. 190; Eduardo Muñoz, "En busca de la mujer ideal," *Carteles*, April 6, 1958, pp. 37–39.

48. Mary M. Spaulding, "Narices estelares," *Carteles*, November 28, 1937, pp. 42–43; Maida Soto, "Una nariz puede cambiar un destino," *Vanidades*, March 15, 1959, pp. 22–23.

49. *Carteles*, October 27, 1929, pp. 50, 58; *Social*, August 1921, p. 6; *Bohemia*, November 2, 1952 (p. 89), August 1, 1954 (p. 83), February 23, 1958 (p. 117), July 27, 1958 (p. 99).

50. Jess Losada, "Idolos de la juventud," *Vanidades*, March 1, 1940, p. 51; Rodolfo Arango, *Cuentos despampanantes* (Havana, n.d.), pp. 139–40; Pepita Riera, *Tú vida y la mía* (Havana, 1949), p. 55; Luis M. Sáez, *El iniciado* (Havana, 1967), p. 27.

51. José Juan Tablada, "Nueva York de día y de noche," *Bohemia*, March 24, 1929, p. 21.

52. Lesbia Soravilla, "Las diez mujeres mejor vestidas de La Habana," *Vanidades*, June 1, 1956, pp. 12–13, 142; Algernón, "Para el hombre," *Carteles*, February 6, 1944, p. 56.

53. Sara Hernández, "Los caballeros las prefieran rubias," *Vanidades*, November 15, 1958, pp. 16–17; Eva Fábregas, "Sus veinte años y nuestros veinte años," *Vanidades*, March 15, 1957, p. 12.

54. Desnoes, *Memorias de subdesarrollo*, p. 50; Pablo Medina, *Exiled Memories: A Cuban Childhood* (Austin, 1990), pp. 41–41; Warren Miller, *90 Miles from Home* (New York, 1961), pp. 221–22.

55. Pablo de la Torriente, "Una aventura de Salgari," *Carteles*, July 22, 1956, p. 66; Otero, *Arbol de la vida*, p. 199; Medina, *Exiled Memories*, p. 59.

56. Gustavo Pérez Firmat, *Next Year in Cuba* (New York, 1995), pp. 212, 217.

57. Marcia del Mar, *A Cuban Story* (Winston-Salem, N.C., 1979), p. 5; Raúl González de Cascorro, *Arboles sin raíces* (Havana, 1959), p. 195; Oscar Zanetti, "American History: A View from Cuba," *Journal of American History* 79 (September 1992): 530.

58. Antonio V. Menéndez Alarcón, *Power and Television in Latin America: The Dominican Case* (Westport, Conn., 1992), p. 79.

59. Jorge Delano, "Hollywood and South America," in Writers' Congress, *The Proceedings of the Conference Held in October 1943 under the Sponsorship of the Hollywood Writers Mobilization and the University of California* (Berkeley, 1943), p. 50.

60. Leonard H. Price to Department of State, November 8, 1955, 837.321/10-3155, IA/1955–58; J. Bruce Swigert, letter to author, May 3, 1992. Estimates of advertising space were made by USIS analysis of the Cuban press. See Earl T. Crain to Department of State, October 21, 1953, 937.61/11-553, IA/1950–54.

61. *Bohemia*, August 1, 1927, p. 44; *Carteles*, August 18, 1940, p. 76; *Bohemia*, May 19, 1957, p. 136.

62. Frank Presbrey, *The History and Development of Advertising* (Garden City, N.Y., 1929), pp. 608, 610, 613.

63. J. Bruce Swigert, letter to author, May 3, 1992.

64. Eduardo Machado, *The Floating Island Plays* (New York, 1991), p. 28; Pérez Firmat, *Next Year in Cuba*, p. 27.

65. J. Bruce Swigert, letter to author, June 11, 1992.

66. *Social*, *Carteles*, *Bohemia*, *Vanidades*, and *El Mundo*, 1922–48.

67. *Bohemia*, December 18, 1957, p. 29; María Subira, "Consultas y opiniones," *Bohemia*, May 18, 1923, p. 27; *La Lucha*, December 11, 1920, p. 4; *Social*, October 1927, p. 2; *Bohemia*, 1923–28.

68. *Social*, *Carteles*, and *Bohemia*, 1920–50.

69. *Vanidades*, 1946–48.

70. U.S. War Department, *Report of the Census of Cuba, 1899* (Washington, D.C., 1900), p. 385; Cuba, *Census of the Republic of Cuba, 1919* (Havana, 1921), p. 606; K. Lynn Stoner, *From the House to the Streets: The Cuban Woman's Movement for Legal Reform, 1898–1940* (Durham, 1991), p. 134.

71. *Vanidades*, July 15, 1957, p. 131; Isabel Margarita Ordext, "La mujer que trabaja: Hacia la más rápida preparación," *Vanidades*, March 1937, p. 70; Marcelo Pogolotti, *El caserón del Cerro* (1940; reprint, Havana, 1961), p. 186.

72. *La Prensa*, March 8, 1920, p. 7; Anaïs Nin, *The Early Diary of Anaïs Nin, 1920–1923* (New York, 1982), p. 505; Federico de Ibarzabal, "Un escándalo social," *Social*, May 1926, pp. 20–21, 85.

73. *La Lucha*, November 30, 1929, p. 4.

74. Ibid., February 2, 1926, p. 6; Arango, *Cuentos despampanantes*, p. 139.

75. Alfonso Hernández Catá, *El placer de sufrir* (Madrid, 1921), p. 30.

76. Florisa de Neveres, "Evolución femenista," *Bohemia*, September 12, 1926, p. 7; Ofelia Domínguez, "Voto y libertad," *Carteles*, February 10, 1929, pp. 20, 45.

77. Isabel Margarita Ordext, "Las modas de 1915," *Gráfico*, January 2, 1915, p. 21.

78. *Havana Post*, August 22, 1920, p. 10.

79. Ana María Borrero, "New York vs. Paris," *Carteles*, August 30, 1936, pp. 41–42.

80. El Curioso Parlanchín, "Tribulaciones de los 'papis' criollos," *Carteles*, November 23, 1941, p. 74.

81. Luis Felipe Rodríguez, *La ilusión de la vida* (Valencia, 1910), pp. 131–32; Loló de la Torriente, *Mi casa en la tierra* (Havana, 1956), p. 126; Lewis, Lewis, and Rigdon, *Neighbors*, p. 236.

82. Stuart Ewen and Elizabeth Ewen, *Channels of Desire* (New York, 1982), p. 215.

83. Loló de la Torriente, *Testimonio desde dentro* (Havana, 1985), p. 94; Pogolotti, *El caserón del Cerro*, p. 88; Rodríguez Acosta, *Sonata interrumpida*, p. 77; Isabel Margarita Ordext, "La mujer moderna y el automóvil," *Carteles*, August 1919, p. 37.

84. Graziella Garbalosa, *El relicario* (Havana, 1923), pp. 69–70.

85. Miguel de Marcos, *Fotuto* (1948; reprint, Havana, 1976), p. 24.

86. Paula S. Fass, *The Damned and the Beautiful American Youth in the 1920s* (New York, 1977), pp. 280–81.

87. "Consultorio de belleza," *Social*, July 1924, p. 60.

88. Eva Fabregas, "Sus veinte años y nuestro veinte años," *Vanidades*, March 15, 1957, pp. 12–13; Nin, *Early Diary*, p. 72; *La Lucha*, July 3, 1926, p. 3.

89. *Havana Post*, June 27, 1924, p. 7; Carolina Adela Alió, "Melenas triunfadoras," *El Fígaro*, March 8, 1925, p. 69.

90. Emilio Roig de Leuchsenring, "Los novios de ventana," *Carteles*, October 1923, p. 23; Rodríguez Acosta, *Sonata interrumpida*, pp. 111–12.

91. Roger de Lauria, "Los sendos de Beocacia," *Bohemia*, February 27, 1927, p. 21.

92. Emilio Roig de Leuchsenring, "Once soluciones a un triángulo amoroso," *Social*, June 1927, pp. 27, 69; Bartolomé Galíndez, "Infidelidad," *La Lucha* (Sunday ed.), February 17, 1929, p. 17; José A. Giralt, "Lo irremediable," *Bohemia*, November 17, 1929, pp. 61–62; Rodríguez Acosta, *Sonata interrumpida*, p. 111.

93. *Carteles*, September 4, 1927, p. 2; *Havana Post*, January 17, 1930, p. 11.

94. José Antonio Losada, "El Instituto Nacional de Cultura Física," *Carteles*, October 7, 1928, p. 34; Gerardo del Valle, "La mujer y los deportes," *La Lucha*, September 4, 1929, p. 1; Adolfo Font, "La mujer cubana y los deportes," *Bohemia*, August 28, 1932, pp. 46–47.

95. Captain Dwight Aultman, "Project for Combining the Cuerpo de Artilleria with the Rural Guard," January 25, 1902, file 2, MGC; Frank R. McCoy to Hugh L. Scott, July–December 1901 Folio, McCoy Papers, LC; Elihu Root to Leonard Wood, April 14, 1900, file 1327-3, BIA; Root to Wood, June 20, 1900, Correspondence Between General Leonard Wood and Secretary of War, 1899–1902, BIA.

96. *Diario de la Marina*, August 15, 1901, p. 1.

97. Aline Helg, *Our Rightful Share: The Afro-Cuban Struggle for Equality, 1886–1912* (Chapel Hill, 1995), pp. 93–101; Arthur A. Schomburg, "General Evaristo Estenoz," *Crisis*, July 1912, pp. 143–44.

98. *Havana Sun*, February 27, 1902, p. 2.

99. *Havana Post*, March 1, 1915 (p. 3), December 15, 1921 (p. 7), January 16, 1916 (p. 5), October 19, 1914.

100. Ibid., April 25, 1925, p. 6; *El Mundo*, July 22, 1953, p. C-4; José Luis Massó, "Ha caído una gran barrera racial," *Bohemia*, December 9, 1951, pp. 48–49, 111.

101. *Havana Post*, December 7, 1928 (p. 6), December 4, 1924 (p. 6); Arnold Rampersad, *The Life of Langston Hughes*, 2 vols. (New York, 1986–88), 1:203; Langston Hughes, *Something in Common and Other Stories* (New York, 1963), pp. 28–29; *The Call*, January 25, 1929, p. 6.

102. Juan Arcocha, *Los muertos andan solos* (Havana, 1962), p. 125.

103. Juan Giró Rodés, "Ni Changó ni Yemayá," *El Mundo*, July 16, 1955, p. B-4; Mario Sorondo y Tolón, *De la vida tranquila* (Havana, 1925), p. 85; José Montó Sotolongo, "Esa no es Cuba," *El Mundo*, September 8, 1955, p. A-6.

104. Carolina Amram, "The Assimilation of Immigrants in Cuban Society during the 1920s and 1930s" (M.A. thesis, University of Miami, Coral Gables, 1983), p. 16.

105. Susan Schroeder, *Cuba: A Handbook of Historical Statistics* (Boston, 1982), p. 433.

106. Graziella Garbalosa, *La gozadora del dolor* (Havana, 1922), pp. 86–87.

107. José Antonio Ramos, *Las impurezas de la realidad* (1929; reprint, Havana, 1979), pp. 82–83.

108. *Havana Post*, September 2, 1921, p. 8; Primelles, *Crónica cubana, 1915–1918*, p. 190; Gerardo del Valle, "Alma de La Habana: El teléfono," *Bohemia*, November 20, 1927, p. 7; *El Arquitecto* 2 (April–May 1927): 56.

109. "Los teléfonos de servicio público en 1924," *Revista Bimestre Cubana* 21 (September–October 1926): 759; José A. Alvarez Díaz et al., *A Study on Cuba* (Coral Gables, Fla., 1965), p. 274; Schroeder, *Handbook of Historical Statistics*, p. 335; U.S. Department of Commerce, *Investment in Cuba* (Washington, D.C., 1956), p. 115.

110. *La Lucha*, April 17, 1929, p. 8; M. T. McGovern, "La electricidad en Cuba," *Revista Bimestre Cubana* 12 (November–December 1927): 835–40; Edward J. Bash to Department of State, August 29, 1956, 837.2614/8-2956, IA/1955–58; Cuba, Tribunal Superior Electoral, *Censos de población, viviendas y electoral: Informe general, 1953* (Havana, 1955), pp. 208–9.

111. "An Interview with Mr. Charles E. Mitchell, President of the National City Bank of New York on Economic Conditions in Cuba," April 24, 1924, 837.50/34, IAC.

112. Domingo A. Galdós to William Van Horne, June 1, 1915, Cuba Co. Records, box 15, Archives and Manuscript Department, McKeldin Library, University of Maryland, College Park.

113. See Thomas F. O'Brien, "The Revolutionary Mission: American Enterprise in Cuba," *American Historical Review* 98 (June 1993): 774.

114. *Social*, April 1926, p. 79.

115. Robert Butler to Secretary of State, July 30, 1948, 837.50/7-3034, IA/1945–49; Jorge Quintana, "La Independent Electric es una empresa cubana al servicio de la nación," *Bohemia*, March 4, 1951, pp. 39–40, 126.

116. Graziella Garbalosa, *Mas arriba está el sol* (Havana, 1931), p. 180; "Asombroso progreso de la electricidad industrial en Cuba," *Social*, July 1931, p. 2.

117. Enrique C. Betancourt, *Apuntes para la historia: Radio, televisión y farándula de la Cuba de ayer* (San Juan, 1986), p. 50; Oscar Luis López, *La radio en Cuba* (Havana, 1981), p. 91.

118. Rodríguez Acosta, *Sonata interrumpida*, p. 139.

119. José Baró Pujol, "Radio y electricidad," *La Lucha*, January 3, 1929, p. 5.

120. James Schwoch, *The American Radio Industry and Its Latin American Activities*,

1900–1939 (Urbana, Ill., 1990), pp. 107–8; Raymond Leslie Buell, *Problems of the New Cuba* (New York, 1935), pp. 418–19; Alvarez Díaz, *A Study on Cuba*, p. 583; Michael B. Solwen, *Radio and Television in Cuba* (Ames, Iowa, 1994), pp. 19–33.

121. Juan de la Habana, "El radio y la cultura," *Carteles*, April 29, 1935, p. 32; Gerardo del Valle, "El radio instrumento social," *Bohemia*, April 10, 1932, p. 13.

122. Schwoch, *American Radio Industry*, p. 141.

123. Reynaldo González, *Llorar es un placer* (Havana, 1988), pp. 110–11.

124. Richard C. Salvatierra to Department of State, October 25, 1950, 937.40/10-2550, IA/1950–54.

125. *Bohemia*, July 21, 1946, p. 36; Betancourt, *Apuntes para la historia*, p. 46; Juan de la Habana, "El radio y la cultura," p. 32; Samuel Feijóo, "Decadencia del canto guajiro," *Bohemia*, September 30, 1951, pp. 20–22, 103.

126. *Variety*, April 23, 1952, p. 33.

127. "Contrabando," *Bohemia*, January 8, 1956, p. 69; Raymond L. Harrell to Department of State, May 7, 1952, 937.44/5-752, IA/1950–54; Emma Pérez, "Cuba en el 9° lugar de la TV mundial," *Bohemia*, April 14, 1957, pp. 42–44, 119, and "¿Qué va allevar la televisión a los lugares mas apartados y atrasados del país?," *Bohemia*, February 19, 1956, pp. 48–49.

128. Shirley F. Woodell to David, February 14, 1951, SFW.

129. Eladio Secades, "La televisión," *Bohemia*, October 13, 1957, pp. 50, 117.

130. *El Mundo*, March 25, 1955, p. B-8; Pérez Firmat, *Next Year in Cuba*, p. 39.

131. Rolando R. Pérez, "El Programa de los $64,000," *Carteles*, June 9, 1957, pp. 30–31.

132. Emma Pérez, "¿Cree usted que la televisión perjudica a los niños?," *Bohemia*, April 7, 1957, p. 42.

133. Shirley F. Woodell to Miss Beck, January 23, 1947, SFW.

134. Inter-American Affairs, "Office Memorandum: Reduction of Advertising in Cuban Communist Newspaper Hoy," August 8, 1950, 937.61/8-250, IA/1950–54; Henry A. Holt to Department of State, June 28, 1950, 937.61/7-2850, IA/1950–54; William B. Connett, "Memorandum of Conversation: Communist Infiltration on U.S. Rubber's Television Program in Cuba," February 25, 1955, 737.001/2-2555, IA/1955–58; Carlos C. Hall to Department of State, April 26, 1955, 937.50/4-2655, IA/1955–58.

135. *Havana Post*, October 17, 1900, p. 3; "El automóvil en La Habana," *El Fígaro*, December 15, 1901, pp. 542–43.

136. Fernándo López Ortiz, "Cincuenta años de automovilismo en Cuba," *El Mundo*, April 11, 1951, p. 6. Other dealerships included the Imperial Automobile Co. (Chrysler Imperial), E. Morales de los Ríos Co. (Westcott), International Motor Co. (Chalmers), Brouer and Co. (Dodge), Ortega y Fernández (DeSoto), Hermanos Fumagalli (Haines), Gómez y Martínez (Singer), F. Rodríguez and Co. (Chevrolet), J. M. Dueñas (Chalmers), Manuel J. Carreño Co. (White), Tolksdorff y Ulloa (Studebaker and Packard), Guillermo Petriocione (Buick and Cadillac), Frank White Co. (Chevrolet and Marmon), Edwin W. Miles (Paige and Scripps-Booth), and McVan Lindsay (Maxwell and Metz).

137. Zenas L. Martin to Eva and Samuel Haworth, September 27, 1915, Martin and Haworth Family Papers, FHC.

138. *Havana Post*, July 15, 1915, p. 2; *Carteles*, November 1, 1926 (p. 3), December 6, 1926 (p. 3).

139. Félix Soloni, *Merse* (Havana, 1926), p. 43; Rodríguez Acosta, *Sonata interrumpida*, p. 30; Wallace Stevens, *Letters of Wallace Stevens* (New York, 1966), p. 235; Pedro Martínez Inclán, *La Habana actual* (Havana, 1925), pp. 22, 46; "Comentarios," *Gráfico*, May 8, 1915, p. 7.

140. England, Department of Overseas Trade, *Report on the Economic Conditions in Cuba* (London, 1923), pp. 13–14.

141. *El Mundo*, November 15, 1955, p. A-1; Desnoes, *Memorias de subdesarrollo*, p. 35.

142. *El Mundo*, July 5, 1953, p. C-6; David S. Green to Department of State, March 16, 1953, 937.51/3-1653, IA/1950–54; Leonard H. Price to Department of State, March 31, 1958, 937.71/3-3158, IA/1955–58; Jorge Vega, "Económicos autos de Liliput y gigantescos carros de enueno por las vías de Cuba," *Carteles*, January 27, 1957, pp. 38–39.

143. Ludwig Bemelmans, "The Best Way to See Cuba," *Holiday*, December 1957, p. 66; Tana de Gámez and Arthur R. Pastore, *Mexico and Cuba on Your Own* (New York, 1954), p. 84.

144. *El Mundo*, February 5, 1950, p. 32; H. T. Andersen, "Annual Economic Review—Cuba," April 15, 1952, 837.00/4-522, IA/1950–54.

145. José Gutiérrez Cordovi, "Contrabando de autos," *El Mundo*, June 10, 1956, p. A-15; Thomas Mann to Undersecretary of State, July 17, 1953, 611.379/7-1753, IA/1950–54; C. R. Durden, National Automobile Theft Bureau, to Representative James C. Davis, January 15, 1959, 611.379/1-2159, IA/1959–60.

146. George Clarke Musgrave, *Cuba: Land of Opportunity* (London, 1919), p. 56; *La Lucha*, May 23, 1920, p. 2; "Carreteras y automóbiles en América Latina," *Revista Bimestre Cubana* 24 (July–August 1929): 616; *La Lucha*, March 15, 1926, p. 1.

147. International Bank for Reconstruction and Development, *Report on Cuba* (Washington, D.C., 1951), p. 264.

148. Octavio Jordán, "Extraordinario auge del automovilismo en los últimos 10 años," *El Mundo*, April 12, 1955, p. C-16.

149. *Havana Post*, June 12, 1924, p. 4; Adrián del Valle, *La mulata Soledad* (Barcelona, n.d.), p. 106.

150. *New York Evening Post*, October 16, 1920, p. 6; "An Englishwoman's Impressions of Havana," *Havana Post*, July 15, 1921, p. 4.

151. Gustavo Robreño, "El automóvil nos reivindica," *Gráfico*, November 27, 1915, p. 11.

152. Rafael Pérez Lobo, "Las pobrecitas guaguas," *Bohemia*, March 17, 1929, pp. 11–12.

153. "El automóvil como medio indispensable de locomoción y como artículo de lujo," *Bohemia*, February 27, 1927, p. 45.

154. Pablo Medina, *The Marks of Birth* (New York, 1994), p. 13.

155. "'Ases' de la industria automovilista," *El Fígaro*, May 8, 1921, p. 160; *El Mundo*, November 13, 1955, p. C-6; Angel G. Feijóo, "Medio siglo de automovilismo en Cuba," *Carteles*, May 18, 1952, p. 137; Rubén Ortiz Lamadrid, "El auto ya no es cosa de ricos," *El Mundo*, April 2, 1955, p. A-6; Mario Parajón, "El automóvil es una necesidad," *El Mundo*, November 18, 1954, supp. D, p. 2.

156. Octavio Jordán, "Con el tanque lleno," *El Mundo*, March 16, 1951, p. 6; R. M. Connell, "Annual Automotive Report for 1950," June 1, 1951, 937.51/6-151, IA/1950–54.

157. *La Lucha*, January 20, 1929, p. 16; *Havana Post*, February 1921, p. 3; *Social*, April 1926 (p. 2), April 1923 (p. 67).

158. John T. Fishburn, "Notes on Cuban Labor," July 28, 1953, 837.06/7-2853, IA/1950–54; U.S. Department of Commerce, *Investment in Cuba*, p. 24; Juan de Zengotita, "Cuba's Manpower Resources," June 15, 1955, 837.06/6-1555, IA/1955–58.

159. Fernández, *Los niños se despiden*, pp. 250–51; Mary Cruz del Pino, *Camagüey: Biografía de una provincia* (Havana, 1955), p. 251; Lewis, Lewis, and Rigdon, *Neighbors*, p. 227.

160. José Sixto de Sola, "El pesimismo cubano," *Cuba Contemporánea* 3 (December 1913): 283; Carlos Loveira, *La última lección* (Havana, 1924), p. 1; Alfonso Hernández Catá, "El

rascacielo y la accesoria," *Social*, April 1930, pp. 11–12; José Manuel Poveda, *Prosa*, ed. Alberto Rocasolano, 2 vols. (Havana, 1981), 2:31; "Automóbiles," *Social*, June 1916, p. 27; Pedro Martínez Inclán, *La Habana actual* (Havana, 1925), pp. 40–41; José Pla, "Carta de Cuba," *Bohemia*, December 19, 1954, pp. 36–38.

161. Guillermo Cabrera Infante, *Tres tristes tigres*, p. 188; Eladio Secades, "Juan Tenario," *Bohemia*, November 4, 1951, p. 45.

162. Antonio Ricardi, "La comodidad no es un lujo, sino prueba del progreso," *El Mundo*, November 27, 1955, p. D-1; "El Mundo del aire acondicionado: Es una necesidad en nuestro clima," *El Mundo*, June 12, 1955, sec. C; Adrián, "La ciencia está creando una nueva era para el hogar," *Magazine Semanal (El Mundo)*, November 15, 1953, p. 2; Antonio Hernández Travieso, "Aire acondicionado," *El Mundo*, June 18, 1955, p. A-6.

163. Tomás Justiz y del Valle, *Ultima esperanza* (Havana, 1910), p. 31; Constantino Suárez, *Emigrantes* (Havana, 1915), p. 134; James Weldon Johnson, *Along This Way* (New York, 1933), p. 234; Juan Bosch, *Cuba: La isla fascinante* (Santiago de Chile, 1955), p. 182.

164. Charlie Seigle, "Progreso de la televisión cubana," *El Mundo*, April 12, 1955, p. C-15; Jorge Quintana, "Cuba se coloca a la cabeza en la producción de detergentes sintéticos en la América Latina," *Bohemia*, December 23, 1951, pp. 80–82.

165. H. S. Tewell to Secretary of State, September 30, 1948, 837.50/9-3048, IA/1945–49; Harold M. Randall to Department of State, January 13, 1955, 837.00/1-1355, IA/1955–58; Banco Nacional de Cuba, "El crédito a plazos en Cuba," *Carta Semanal*, August 25, 1958, p. 1.

166. Daisy Rubiera Castillo, *Reyita, sencillamente: Testimonio de una negra nonagenaria* (Havana, 1996), pp. 138–41; Eladio Secades, "Vivimos a plazos," *Bohemia*, June 28, 1953, p. 13.

167. Pérez, "Cuba en el 9 lugar de la TV mundial," pp. 42–44; Lewis, Lewis, and Rigdon, *Four Women*, pp. 155, 171; Rubiera Castillo, *Reyita, sencillamente*, p. 136.

168. Mariblanca Sabas Alomá, "¡Cuanto miseria!" *Carteles*, December 6, 1931, pp. 48, 58; Jorge Mañach, *Pasado vigente* (Havana, 1939), pp. 226–27.

169. "La mendicidad," *El Mundo*, September 7, 1949, p. 10; América Ana Cuervo, "Mejoramiento de la vivienda campesina," *Bohemia*, June 21, 1936, pp. 24–25; Mario Llerena, "Los dos caminos: Política y educación," *Carteles*, April 22, 1956, pp. 14–15, 102; Jorge Quintana, "Cuba no es un país civilizado a juzgar por su mortalidad infantil," *Bohemia*, April 27, 1952, p. 68; Pepín Rivero, *El pensamiento de un gran orientador* (Havana, 1964), p. 177; T. García Triana, "El bohío," *Bohemia*, June 24, 1934, pp. 18, 64; Octavio Jordán, "Con el tanque lleno," *El Mundo*, February 13, 1952, p. 4.

170. Herminio Portell Vilá, "Hablemos de Guantánamo," *Bohemia*, April 26, 1959, pp. 60–61, 113; Herminio Portell Vilá, "Descrédito," *El Mundo*, July 16, 1950, p. 32.

171. *El Mundo*, May 31, 1956, p. B-2; Juan Arcocha, *Los muertos andan solos* (Havana, 1962), p. 53; Carlos Garate, "Una mentira," *Bohemia*, November 27, 1921, p. 8.

CHAPTER SIX

1. Loló de la Torriente, *Testimonio desde dentro* (Havana, 1985), p. 93; José Antonio Ramos, *Coaybay* (1926; reprint, Havana, 1975), p. 77.

2. "De cubita bella," *Social*, September 1922, p. 20; Roger de Lauria, "Las sendas de Beocia," *Bohemia*, February 27, 1927, p. 21.

3. Francisco González Díaz, *Un canario en Cuba* (Havana, 1916), p. 44; Rafael Santa Coloma, "Charlas del domingo," *Bohemia*, December 24, 1922, p. 22.

4. T. R. Ybarra, "La influencia norteamericana en Cuba," *Carteles*, March 26, 1939, pp.

40–41; José Antonio Ramos, "Páginas salvadas: Fragmentos de las memorias," *Nueva Revista Cubana* 1 (October–December 1959): 153; Benito Vilá, "Learning Capitalist Culture II: The Schooling in Bourgeois Self-Consciousness of a Cuban-American Immigrant," p. 34 (manuscript, 1994; copy in author's possession).

5. Rafael Hernández, conversation with author, Havana, July 27, 1991; *Gaceta Oficial*, November 27, 1952, p. 1.

6. *Havana Post*, December 9, 1928, p. 2; Sixto Figueras, "La invasión de Santa Claus," *Carteles*, December 19, 1954, p. 10; John M. Snook, "The Way I See It," *Times of Havana*, December 25, 1957, p. 35; Agustín Tamargo, "Cuatro postales de navidad," *Bohemia*, December 30, 1956, p. 72.

7. *Havana Post*, January 25, 1930 (p. 2), April 11, 1920 (p. 2).

8. Antonio Barba, *Cuba, el país que fué: Unos recuerdos* (Barcelona, 1964), pp. 106–7.

9. John Dorschner and Roberto Fabricio, *The Winds of December* (New York, 1980), p. 89; Orlando Requeijo, interview by author, Havana, July 23, 1992; Katherine Ponvert, *Cuban Chronicle* (Fredericksburg, Va., 1961), p. 81.

10. *Times of Havana*, July 8, 1957, p. 13; Richard C. Salvatierra to Department of State, May 29, 1951, 737.001/d-2951, IA/1950–54.

11. See Vivian Brown, "Disfrutando un baño," *El Mundo*, April 10, 1954, p. B-7; Dorothy Malone, "Paquetes de Navidad," *Vanidades*, December 1, 1956, p. 113; Lawrence K. Frank, "Carreras propias para los jóvenes," *El Mundo*, March 6, 1949, p. 27; Donald A. Laird, "El secreto de los sueños," *Carteles*, May 19, 1940, p. 69.

12. "Decoración interior: Telas estampadas como factor decorativo," *Vanidades*, April 1, 1950, p. 34; "Nuevas tendencias en decoración interior," *El Mundo*, September 21, 1952 (p. C-4), July 5, 1952 (p. C-5), June 29, 1959 (p. C-5), September 14, 1952 (p. C-7).

13. Cynthia Lowry, "Entre mujeres," *El Mundo*, October 30, 1952, p. B-2.

14. *Vanidades*, March 1, 1946 (pp. 52–53), July 1, 1946 (pp. 68–69); Nereyda M. de Muxo, "Tu casa y mi casa: Decorado con estilo," *Vanidades*, February 15, 1956, p. 38; Leonor Barraqué, "La nursery," *Carteles*, August 14, 1932, p. 7; M. Millares Vázquez, "El secreto del éxito," *El Mundo*, August 5, 1952, p. A-6.

15. See Elena Otero de Armas, *El juego de sala en la Cuba republicana* (Havana, 1985), pp. 10–67.

16. Teodoro Espinosa, *Usos de la razón* (Havana, 1989), p. 33.

17. See in *Vanidades*: C. R. Adams, "¿Cual es la mejor edad para casarse?" (February 1, 1956, p. 128), "La seguridad en el matrimonio" (January 15, 1956, p. 130), and "¿Sabe su marido que usted lo quiere?" (January 1, 1956, p. 119); Priscilla Wayne, "¿Sigue siendo usted la novia de su marido?" (February 1, 1947, p. 9); Evelyn A. Whitman, "¿Eres emocionalmente apta para el matrimonio?" (February 1, 1946, p. 15); Paul Popenoe, "¿Le da usted a su esposo el apoyo emocional que necesita?" (December 1, 1946, pp. 62–63); and Marjorie Anderson, "¿Carrera o matrimonio?" (September 15, 1944, p. 22).

18. *El Mundo*, June 1952; Edith M. Sterne, "Criaturas privilegiadas," *El Mundo*, March 24, 1954, p. B-7; Robert Clark, "Como ser un buen padre," *Bohemia*, April 13, 1937, pp. 22–23; Hortensia Lamar, "Cuida la adolescencia de tú hija," *Carteles*, January 13, 1935, p. 8; Hortensia Lamar, "Obedencia," *Carteles*, April 16, 1933, p. 4; Sylvia, "Con los pequeños," *El Mundo*, January 10, 1948 (p. 6), January 14, 1948 (p. 6); David Taylor Marke, "Al niño se la puede eseñar a ser responsable," *El Mundo*, July 10, 1952, p. B-2.

19. *Bohemia*, December 8, 1935, p. 24; *El Mundo*, January 14, 1948, p. 6; David Taylor Marke, "Como escoger el juguete adecuado" (May 18, 1952, p. 32) and "No crie hijos pegados a su saya" (December 21, 1952, p. C-6), *El Mundo*.

20. Martín Rosales, "Lo que gasta La Habana en juguetes para sus niños," *Carteles*, January 5, 1941, pp. 42–43.

21. *Carteles*, November 1919, p. 50.

22. Gerardo del Valle, "La locura del yo-yo," *Bohemia*, March 23, 1930, pp. 8, 57. See *El Mundo*, January 29, 1950 (p. 40), February 4, 1950 (p. 3).

23. *El Mundo*, 1950–57 (advertisements); Osvaldo Valdés de la Paz, "Juguetes para 1950," *Carteles*, January 1, 1950, pp. 30–31.

24. *El Mundo*, 1955–56.

25. Ibid., January 28, 1955, p. B-9; J. Lamar, "Las amas de casas, accionistas de los Minimax," *Bohemia*, September 30, 1956, pp. 80–81.

26. *El Mundo*, July 2, 1954 (p. A-6), December 19, 1954 (p. A-6); Luis Rolando Cabrera, "La bodega deja el lugar al grocery," *El Mundo*, Sunday supp., August 6, 1950, pp. 8–9.

27. Roberto Pérez de Acevedo, "¿Deriva el cubano hacia mantenerse en una sola comida?," *Carteles*, December 7, 1947, pp. 42–43.

28. *El Mundo*, January 6, 1952, p. 6. See also *Bohemia*, January, February, March 1956.

29. "La mujer y la cocina," *La Lucha*, January 20, 1929, p. 16; María Subira, "Consultas y opiniones," *Bohemia*, May 11, 1924, p. 23; *Carteles*, May 3, 1931, p. 60; *Vanidades*, March 15, 1956, p. 125; *Bohemia*, July 15, 1934, p. 52.

30. *El Mundo*, September 5, 1954, p. A-7; *Bohemia*, October 21, 1956, p. 100.

31. Virgilio Piñera, "El caramelo," in José Rodríguez Feo, ed., *Aquí once cuentos cubanos* (Montevideo, 1967), p. 55; Lisandro Otero, *En ciudad semejante* (Havana, 1970), p. 150; Calvert Casey, "Mi tía Leocadia, el amor y el paleolítico inferior," in Casey, *El regreso: Cuentos* (Havana, 1962), p. 37.

32. Ruby Hart Phillips, *Cuba: Island of Paradox* (New York, 1954), pp. 357–58; Sydney Clark, *All the Best in Cuba* (New York, 1954), pp. 97–98; Juan Arcocha, *Los muertos andan solos* (Havana, 1962), p. 52.

33. Shirley F. Woodall to David, February 14, 1951, SFW.

34. Felicia Rosshandler, *Passing through Havana* (New York, 1975), p. 60; Guy L. Bush to Department of State, March 12, 1951, 837.2331/3-125, IA/1950–54.

35. Vedado Tennis Club, *Libro de oro, 1902–1952* (Havana, 1952), p. 406.

36. *El Mundo*, March 31, 1957, p. B-10; Gabino Delgado, "La moda del boleo en Camagüey," *Vanidades*, June 15, 1949, pp. 88–89; Nivio López Pellón, "Escuelas de 'Rin-Tin-Tines' en Cuba," *Bohemia*, April 6, 1958, pp. 42–43.

37. Federico de Ibarzabal, *La charca* (Havana, 1938), p. 65; Carlos Loveira, *La última lección* (Havana, 1924), pp. 14, 16; Otero, *En ciudad semejante*, p. 307; Rogelio Llopis, *El fabulista* (Havana, 1963), p. 17; Luis Ricardo Alonso, *El palacio y la furia* (Barcelona, 1976), p. 132; Juan Esteban Estevanell, *Santiago: 39 grados sobre o* (Havana, 1980), p. 82; Lisandro Otero, *Arbol de la vida* (Mexico, 1990), pp. 125, 219, 251, 308; Luis Agüero, *La vida en dos* (Havana, 1967), p. 27; Rogelio Llopis, "Un hombre infame," in *Nuevos cuentos cubanos* (Havana, 1964), p. 200; Luis Andrián Betancourt, "Triángulo en el hoyo ocho," in Agenor Martí, ed., *Cuentos policiales cubanos* (Havana, 1983), p. 78; Eladio Secades, *Estampas de la época* (Havana, 1958), p. 32; Edmundo Desnoes, *El cataclismo* (Havana, 1965), p. 107; Hilda Perera, *Los Robledal* (Mexico, 1987), p. 206; Loló de la Torriente, *Los caballeros de la marea roja* (Havana, 1984), p. 188; Abel E. Prieto, *Noche de sábado* (Havana, 1989), p. 60; Jean Stubbs, "When the Fizz Goes Out of the Soda Pop," *Cuba Update*, April 1990, p. 28.

38. Argelio Santiesteban, *El habla popular cubana de hoy* (Havana, 1982); Fernando Ortiz, "Un catauro de cubanismos," *Revista Bimestre Cubana* 16 (May–June 1921): 129–57; José Sánchez Boudy, *Diccionario de cubanismos más usuales*, 3 vols. (Miami, 1978–86).

39. Darío Espina Pérez, *Diccionario de cubanismos* (Barcelona, 1972), p. 130; *El Mundo*, April 13, 1948, p. 29; Antonio Llano Montes, "Tras la noticia," *Carteles*, December 11, 1955, p. 40; Otero, *En ciudad semejante*, p. 44; Leonel López-Nussa, *Tabaco* (Havana, 1963), p. 256.

40. *El Mundo* and *Diario de la Marina*, 1948–58.

41. Samuel Feijóo, "Presente criollo," *Bohemia*, June 27, 1954, p. 50; Sergio Chaple, *La otro mejilla* (Havana, 1978), p. 18; Matías Montes Huidobro, *Segar a los muertos* (Barcelona, 1978), p. 24.

42. Marcelo Salinas, *Un aprendiz de revolucionario* (Havana, 1937), p. 172; Arturo Alfonso Roselló, *El pantano el la cima* (Barcelona, 1972), p. 111; Reynaldo Castillo, "Clave 26," in Martí, *Cuentos policiales cubanos*, p. 145; Armando Couto, *La triste historia de mi vida oscura* (Miami, 1978), p. 62; Raúl González de Cascorro, *Traición en Villa Feliz* (Havana, 1978), p. 176; Abelardo Piñero, *El descanso* (Havana, 1962), p. 93; *Bohemia*, July 28, 1957, p. 60; Miguel de Marcos, *Papaíto Mayarí* (1947; reprint, Havana, 1977), p. 68.

43. Luis Baez, *Secretos de generales* (Havana, 1996), p. 241; Llopis, *El fabulista*, p. 20; Enrique Serpa, "Burócratas," in Enrique Serpa, *Aletas de tiburón* (Havana, 1976), p. 87; Alonso, *El palacio y la furia*, pp. 85, 87; Desnoes, *El cataclismo*, p. 21.

44. *Vanidades*, 1952–54; *Bohemia*, 1954–57; *El Mundo*, 1952–54.

45. Vedado Tennis Club, *Libro de oro*, p. 454.

46. The long list of social clubs includes Vista Alegre Tennis Club (Santiago de Cuba), Ciudamar Yacht Club (Santiago de Cuba), Diágoras Sports Club (Pinar del Río), Cojímar Beach Club, Limones Country Club, el Caney Country Club, Cienfuegos Yacht Club, Jagüey Sporting Club, Caibarién Yacht Club, Ranchuelo Tennis Club, Matanzas Tennis Club, and Matanzas Yacht Club.

47. José Soler Puig, *Bertillón 166* (Havana, 1960), p. 51.

48. Marcelo Pogolotti, *Del barro y las voces* (Havana, 1982), p. 129; Ybarra, "La influencia norteamericana en Cuba," pp. 40–41; Phillips, *Island of Paradox*, p. 358; Peter Ustinov, *Dear Me* (Boston, 1977), p. 275.

49. El Duende de la Luz, "La Habana: ¿Gran capital o pequeña aldea?," *Carteles*, September 25, 1949, pp. 34–35; Feijóo, "Presente criollo," pp. 48–50, 99.

50. Ponvert, *Cuban Chronicle*, p. 82; Noel Navarro, *Los días de nuestra angustia* (Havana), 1962.

51. U.S. Department of Commerce, *Investment in Cuba* (Washington, 1956), p. 184.

52. E. Ralph Estep, *El Toro: A Motor Car Story of Interior Cuba* (Detroit, 1909), p. 59; George Miller Stabler, "Bejucal: Social Values and Changes in Agricultural Practices in a Cuban Rurban [sic] Community" (Ph.D. thesis, Michigan State University, 1958), pp. 21–23.

53. D. Abascal y Moré, "El jinete criollo," *Bohemia*, February 24, 1929, p. 21; Marcelo Salinas, "Crónicas sinceras," p. 9; Feijóo, "Presente criollo," *Bohemia*, June 27, 1954, pp. 48–50, 99; Herbert C. Lanks, *Highway across the West Indies* (New York, 1948), p. 31; "Lo que piensan los jóvenes," *Carteles*, July 27, 1930, p. 30; Armando Leyva, *La provincia, las aldeas* (Santiago de Cuba, n.d.), p. 53.

54. See Aurelio Capote Carballo, "La mujer cubana," *Social*, January 1918, p. 23.

55. For newspapers, see *El Mundo* and *Diario de la Marina*, 1945–55. Representative yearbooks include Buena Vista/Candler College, *Year Book, 1957*, and Colegio de las Ursulinas, *Memoria Anual: Curso Escolar, 1951–1952*.

56. Miguel Barnet, *La vida real* (Madrid, 1984), pp. 172–73; Victor Amat Osorio, *Banes, 1513–1958: Estampas de mi tierra y de mi sol* (Miami, 1981); José Manuel Fernández, *Todo angel es terrible* (Havana, 1964). I am indebted to Marel García and Ana Ibarra for much of this information.

57. Julio de Céspedes, ed., *Registro social de La Habana* (Havana, 1959); Pablo Alvarez de Cañas and Joaquín de Posada, eds., *Libro de oro de la sociedad habanera* (Havana, 1956).

58. Cañas and Posada, *Libro de oro*.

59. Leonor Barraqué, "Un cuadro de hoy," *Carteles*, September 2, 1934, p. 5; Gonzalo de Quesada y Miranda, "Por amor y arte," *Carteles*, November 29, 1929, p. 36; Luis Ricardo Alonso, *Los dioses ajenos* (Barcelona, 1971), p. 101; Miguel de Marcos, *Fábula de la vida apacible* (Havana, 1943), p. 305; Andrés L. de Linares, "Dos señoritas de vanguardia," *Bohemia*, January 27, 1929, pp. 76–79; José de la Campa González, *Memorias de un machadista: Novela histórico social* (Tampa, 1937), p. 27.

60. José García Pedrosa, *Memorias de un desmemoriado* (Miami, 1979), p. 152; Antonio Benítez Rojo, *El escudo de hojas secas* (Buenos Aires, 1972), p. 24; Cristina García, *Dreaming in Cuban* (New York, 1992), p. 94.

61. Pablo Medina, *Exiled Memories* (Austin, 1990), p. 54; Oscar Hijuelos, *Mambo Kings Play Songs of Love* (New York, 1989), p. 38; Gustavo Pérez Firmat, *Next Year in Cuba* (New York, 1995), p. 52.

62. Phillips, *Island of Paradox*, p. 358; Eladio Secades, "La cubana que estuvo en el Norte," *Bohemia*, July 8, 1956, p. 65.

63. Eduardo Machado, *Once Removed* (New York, 1986), p. 69; Marcelo Pogolotti, *Segundo remanso* (Havana, 1948), p. 65; Carmela Nieto, *Como se va el amor* (Havana, 1926), pp. 90–91.

64. José Antonio Mases, *Los padrenuestros y el fusil* (Barcelona, 1973), p. 24; *Carteles*, June 16, 1929 (p. 46), August 3, 1929 (p. 46); *Bohemia*, May 24, 1930 (p. 65), June 15, 1930 (p. 53), July 28, 1934 (p. 59).

65. Pérez Firmat, *Next Year in Cuba*, pp. 51–52; Gilberto Seguí, "Los olores de la calle," in Jacobo Machover, ed., *La Habana, 1952–1961* (Madrid, 1995), p. 34.

66. *Bohemia*, September 23, 1956, p. 137; *El Mundo*, August 22, 1954, p. C-2; *Carteles*, January 27, 1935, p. 68.

67. López-Nussa, *Tabaco*, p. 41; Héctor Quintero, *Contigo pan y cebolla* (Havana, 1965), pp. 61–62; *El Mundo*, November 23, 1953, p. A-6; Gonzalo Mazas Garbayo to Pablo de la Torriente, May 28, 1936, in Víctor Casáus, *Cartas cruzadas: Pablo de la Torriente* (Havana, 1981), p. 578.

68. Fergusson, *Cuba*, pp. 66–68, 104; *Times of Havana*, February 4, 1957, p. 6.

69. *Times of Havana*, February 21, 1957, p. 5; *El Mundo*, February 28, 1952, p. 16; *Havana Post*, February 17, 1915, p. 2.

70. See *El Mundo*, May 18, 1952, p. 29; *Times of Havana*, March 7, 1957.

71. R. M. Connell to Department of State, January 15, 1951, 837.392/1-1551, IA/1950–54.

72. Lanks, *Highway across the West Indies*, p. 16.

73. *El Mundo*, February 4, 1951 (p. 16), May 15, 1950 (p. 16).

74. *Carteles*, 1938–42; Raúl Aparicio, *Frutos del azote* (Buenos Aires, 1961), pp. 27–28.

75. Fergusson, *Cuba*, p. 104; Consuelo Hermer and Marjorie May, *Havana Mañana: A Guide to Cuba and the Cubans* (New York, 1941), pp. 44–45.

76. *El Mundo*, November 25, 1951 (p. 25), December 2, 1951 (p. 19); *Vanidades*, December 1, 1946, p. 10.

77. *Billboard*, June 24, 1950, p. 13; *Havana Post*, April 6, 1930, p. 6; Paul Bowles, "In the Tropics: Page from a Journal," *Modern Music* 22 (January 1946): 16; Guillermo Cabrera Infante, *Infante's Inferno*, trans. Suzanne Jill Levine (New York, 1979), pp. 45–46.

78. *Havana Post*, January 14, 1915, p. 2; "El paso del gato," *Bohemia*, June 19, 1921, p. 16;

José B. Fernández, *Los abuelos: Historia oral cubana* (Miami, 1987), p. 43; *La Prensa*, February 12, 1920, p. 3; Eduardo Zamora Pons, "Música cubana," *La Lucha*, September 20, 1929, p. 5.

79. Harold B. Quarton, "Cuban Protest against American Musicians," December 18, 1929, 837.4038, IAC; Juan Pastrana, "Los músicos desamparados," *Bohemia*, October 13, 1929, pp. 23, 64; Rafael Piñeiro del Villar, "Los músicos cubanos," *Bohemia*, November 22, 1931, p. 59.

80. Ariel T. Napolés, "La música popular cubana," *Bohemia*, August 18, 1957, pp. 78–79; Andrew Salkey, *Havana Journal* (Baltimore, 1971), pp. 40–41; Liner notes by Cristóbal Díaz Ayala, in "El Original Cuarteto D'Aída," RCA Victor, 1957, reissued as CD 3393-2-RL, 1992; *Billboard*, June 24, 1950, p. 13; Sergio Chaple, *La otra mejilla* (Havana, 1978), p. 16; Arcocha, *Los muertos andan solos*, pp. 62–63, 68.

81. Cristóbal Díaz Ayala, *Música cubana: Del Areyto a la Nueva Trova* (San Juan, 1981), pp. 257–59.

82. Rine R. Leal, "El rock 'n' roll en Cuba: Debe y haber," *Bohemia*, February 10, 1957, p. 32.

83. Enrique Alvarez Jané, *Macuta La Habana* (Havana, 1981), p. 141; *El Mundo*, April 28, 1957, p. C-7; Braulio Robet, "En el Dia del Idioma: 'Do you Speak English?,'" *Carteles*, April 27, 1958), p. 21; Leal, "El rock 'n' roll en Cuba," p. 33.

84. William H. Dorsey, letter to author, December 12, 1991; Office of Commercial Attaché, "Companies or Corporations in Cuba Wholly Owned by United States Companies or Corporations," October 28, 1952, 837.05137/10-2852, IA/1950–54.

85. J. Bruce Swigert, letter to author, November 25, 1991.

86. Eladio Secades, "Los matrimonios salen a divertirse," *Bohemia*, February 9, 1958, p. 48; García, *Dreaming in Cuban*, p. 6; Arturo Suárez, "Post Profiles," *Havana Post*, February 4, 1936, p. 4.

87. *Times of Havana*, March 4, 1957, p. 7.

88. *La Lucha*, August 17, 1907, p. 7; *Havana Post*, September 24, 1924, p. 10; "Los 'boy-scouts' y el futuro de Cuba," *Carteles*, January 16, 1944, 19.

89. *Havana Post*, November 9, 1915, p. 2.

90. The subject of Rotary Clubs is generally developed in Emily S. Rosenberg, *Spreading the American Dream* (New York, 1982), pp. 111–12.

91. The charter members included A. L. Hoffman (National City Bank), C. R. Ricker (Havana Electric Railway), Urbano González (Hotel Sevilla), Angel del Valle (Castañeda and Co.), W. Harry Smith (Ward Line), Manuel A. Suárez (planter), Lelend Rogers (Maryland Casualty Co.), and Ramón Argüelles (Romeo and Juliet Cigar Co.). In 1920 U.S.-educated Julio Blanco Herrera, owner of La Tropical beer, was elected president of the Havana Rotary Club.

92. Noble Brandon Judah, "Diary of My Stay in Cuba," Judah Papers, LC.

93. The Havana Lions included such prominent Cubans as Jorge Mañach, Gonzalo de Quesada, Emeterio Santovenia, Fermín Peraza, and Néstor Carbonell.

94. Members included J. Herbert Sawyer (Esso), Henry L. Brandon (Union Oil), Jorge Faz Vega (Atlantic Refining Co.), Emilio Arango de Núñez (Cuban Standard Oil Co.), and Fernando Freyre de Andrade (Freyre Andrade y Montalvo).

95. Ann Hutchison, letter to author, July 9, 1991; Rufo López-Fresquet, *My 14 Months with Castro* (Cleveland, 1966), p. 27.

96. Víctor Muñoz, *Junto el Capitolio* (Havana, 1919), pp. 253–57.

97. Hermer and May, *Havana Mañana*, p. 71.

98. See Emilio Roig de Leuchsenring, "El desastre de nuestra segunda enseñanza," *Car-*

teles, July 4, 1926, p. 12, and Mario Guiral Moreno, "La escuela privada en Cuba," *El Mundo*, April 30, 1954, p. A-6.

99. *Havana Post*, November 16, 1926, p. 1; *El Mundo*, February 7, 1954, pp. A-1, A-10; Susan Schroeder, *Cuba: A Handbook of Historical Statistics* (Boston, 1982), p. 133; *El Mundo*, February 9, 1954, p. A-6; República de Cuba, Tribunal Superior Electoral, *Censos de población, viviendas y electoral* (Havana, 1953), p. 99.

100. Ernesto Martínez, "Cuesta un ojo de la cara educar a un niño," *Bohemia*, November 13, 1955, pp. 76–79.

101. *Havana Post*, September 25, 1915, p. 2; Jesús Masdeu, *La raza triste* (Havana, 1924), p. 40; International Bank for Reconstruction and Development, *Report on Cuba* (Washington, D.C., 1951), p. 414; *Bohemia*, September 9, 1956, pp. 56–57.

102. *El Mundo*, 1950–54; *Bohemia*, 1953–56; *Carteles*, 1952–54.

103. *El Mundo*, 1953–56.

104. *El Mundo* and *Bohemia*, 1954–56.

105. Rosshandler, *Passing through Havana*, pp. 76–79; *Carteles*, August 5, 1934, p. 50.

106. I am grateful to Marta Morales de Zanetti for making available to me her copies of *Columns* for the years 1957–60.

107. Jacob Canter to Department of State, June 17, 1952 (837.43/6-1672), July 19, 1952 (837.43/7-1852), and March 26, 1953 (837.43/2-2653), IA/1950–54.

108. Arturo Montori, "Reglamentación de las escuelas privadas," *Cuba Contemporánea* 14 (July 1917): 215–16; *El Mundo*, November 29, 1949, p. 10.

109. Arturo Ramírez, "La vida," *Carteles*, June 17, 1934, p. 17; "Lo que piensan los jóvenes," *Carteles*, July 1930, p. 34.

110. Medina, *Exiled Memories*, pp. 54–58; Miguel Barnet, "Intervención especial 'La historia como identidad,'" in *Cuba: Cultura e identidad nacional* (Havana, 1995), p. 214.

111. Robert L. Packard, *Education in the Philippines, Cuba, Puerto Rico, Hawaii and Samoa* (Washington, D.C., 1901), p. 164.

112. Gilbert K. Harroun, "The Cuban Educational Association of the United States," *Review of Reviews* 20 (September 1899): 334–35.

113. Gilbert K. Harroun to F. P. Machado, September 16, 1899, General Correspondence, Cuban Educational Association Papers, LC.

114. Gilbert K. Harroun to John Van R. Hoff, March 22, 1900, ibid.

115. *Washington Post*, January 1, 1899, p. 24. The project also obtained the support of the annexationist Cuban-American League. Free college education for Cubans, league vice president Francisco Figueras wrote, "would prove of such value to us that I do not doubt that all obstacles in our way would vanish and adhesion and converts to the cause of union with the United States would flock in hundreds of thousands." Figueras predicted that the program would "surround us immediately with universal good-will and sympathy"—something indispensable to "install American sentiment among the Cubans and, at the same time, the desire for annexation." Figueras to William D. McDowell, January 13, 1899, General Correspondence, Cuban Educational Association Papers, LC.

116. José Comallonga, *Algunas instituciones americanas* (Havana, 1922); *El Mundo*, June 1, 1952, p. 29.

117. *Diario de la Marina*, October 3, 1900, p. 1; Luis Báez, *Los que se quedaron* (Havana, 1993), p. 289.

118. *Havana Post*, December 10, 1916, p. 8; Institute of International Education, *Education for One World: Annual Census of Foreign Students in the United States, 1951–1952* (New York,

1952), pp. 26, 45, and *A Report on International Exchange: Open Doors, 1958* (New York, 1958), pp. 34–43.

119. Institute of International Education, *Report on International Exchange*, pp. 42–43.

120. The bishop of Pinar del Río was educated at Catholic University. Alfonso Ulloa attended the Sacred Heart Training College in Las Vegas, N.Mex. Among the Protestant ministers to complete seminary programs in the United States were Sergio Arce, Mario Llerena, and Manuel Salabarria (Princeton Theological Seminary); Rafael Cepeda and Bartolomé Lavastida (McCormick Seminary); Ondina Maristany (Southwestern Baptist Theological Seminary); and Gabriel Jiménez (Baptist Missionary Training School of Chicago).

121. Air Force colonel Felipe A. de la Catasús graduated from the Georgia Institute of Technology and completed his training at Moody Air Force Base. Lieutenant Pedro A. Barrera received artillery training at the Ordinance School of Aberdeen Proving Grounds. René Bustamante, Miguel Raúl Cabeza, and R. R. Bustillo Ascencio were only some of the pilots trained in the North. General José Ramón Fernández, one of the principal Cuban commanders at the Bay of Pigs, studied artillery in the United States between 1953 and 1954.

122. Daniel M. Braddock to Department of State, February 19, 1958, 611.37/2-1958, IA/1955–58; Earl E. T. Smith to Department of State, October 28, 1958, 611.37/10-2258, ibid. USIS grant recipients included teachers (Ursula Beltrán Costa, Ruth Robés, Pedro Méndez, Umbelina G. de Landera) and journalists (Ernesto Ardura Pardal, José Ignacio Rivero, José Sánchez Rubín, Armando Machado Pérez, Humberto Medrano, Jorge Zayas Menéndez).

123. Francis J. Donohue to Department of State, May 22, 1956 (937.6211/5-2256), and June 13, 1957 (937.6211/6-1356), IA/1955–58.

124. Institute of International Education, *Report on International Exchange*, pp. 42–43.

125. Other businessmen included banker José Ignacio Cámara (Packard Business School), hoteliers Antonio Larrea (Yale) and J. E. Muriss (Fordham), industrialists Andrés Carrillo (Lehigh) and Carlos Portela (Georgia Tech), and Cuban Electric Co. president Antonio Rosado (Massachusetts Institute of Technology).

126. See Manuel Porfirio Arca, "Influence of Cubans in the Present Expansion of the Sugar Industry in the Central Florida Area around Lake Okeechobee" (MBA thesis, University of Miami, Coral Gables, Fla., 1962). Among the most prominent architects and engineers were Juan Prieto, Ramiro Irabién, and Orlando A. Rodríguez (Georgia Institute of Technology); Primitivo Portal Vera, Eduardo Montoulieu, and Raúl Otero (Harvard); Miguel Chinchilla Varona and Frank Casablanca (Cornell); Pedro Martinez (Auburn), Manuel Ray (University of Utah); M. A. González del Valle (University of Illinois); and Mario Ulibarri (Florida). Among the planters who studied in the North were Julio Lobo (Columbia and Louisiana State University), Gustavo de los Reyes (Georgetown), Tomás Puyans (Packard Business College), Manuel Arca (Rensselaer), Manuel Aspuru (Pennington College), Julio Tarafa (Cornell), José M. Casanova Jr. (Culver Military Academy), and Fernando de la Riva (Yale).

127. Fernando Tarafa completed a B.S. degree in electrical engineering at Rensselaer and subsequently worked for McFarlane Foundry, American Bond and Share Co., Babcock and Wilcox, and the Moa Bay Co. Jorge Tarafa (Rensselaer) returned to Cuba as a factory representative of sugar mill equipment for the Nash Engineering Co., Riley Stoker Corp., and Jeffrey Manufacturing Co. Enrique Tonarely (Louisiana State) was employed by Gulf Atlantic, José M. Coussé (Pierce Business College) worked for the Cuba Mail Steamship Co., and José Enrique Pedro (Virginia Military Institute) secured a position with Chase National Bank in Havana. After completing his studies at Louisiana State, Alberto M. Larrieu got a job with the Goodyear Tire Co. in Cuba.

128. Marcelo Pogolotti, *Del barro y las voces* (Havana, 1982), pp. 86–87; Marjorie Moore and Adrienne Hunter, *Seven Women and the Cuban Revolution* (Toronto, 1996), p. 127.

129. Teresa Casuso, *Los ausentes* (Mexico, 1944), p. 27; *Carteles*, March 20, 1932, p. 11; Oscar Pino Santos, "¿Por que muchos cubanos están abandonando a su patria?," *Carteles*, October 23, 1955, pp. 46–50; Angel Reaud, "La crisis del profesionalismo y las nuevas vías de trabajo para la juventud," *Nueva Revista Cubana* 1 (April–June 1959): 124–25; Carlos Castañeda, " '¡Me voy porque no encuentro que comer!,' " *Bohemia*, January 22, 1956, pp. 20–21, 92.

130. Orestes "Minnie" Miñoso, *Extra Innings: My Life in Baseball* (Chicago, 1983), pp. 11–13; Arturo Ramírez, "Charla con Miguelito Valdés," *Carteles*, April 11, 1943, p. 28; Arturo Alfonso Roselló, "En charla con el ilusionista Gil," *Carteles*, April 10, 1932, pp. 24–25; Xavier Cugat, *Rumba Is My Life* (New York, 1948), p. 49.

131. *Bohemia*, July 11, 1954, p. 64; Don Galaor, "Miss Cuba," *Bohemia*, July 20, 1930, pp. 48, 63; Eladio Secades, "Futuras estrellas de cine," *Bohemia*, March 31, 1957, p. 32.

132. Carlos Felipe, *Teatro* (Boulder, 1988), p. 209; María Domínguez Roldán, *Entre amor y música* (Havana, 1954), pp. 177–78; Jaime Sarusky, *La búsqueda* (Havana, 1961), p. 13; José Antonio Ramos, *Teatro*, ed. Francisco Garzón Céspedes (Havana 1976), p. 209; Piñeiro, *El descanso*, p. 57; Leante, *Padres e hijos*, p. 118.

133. Arturo Alfonso Roselló, "De La Habana a New York," *Carteles*, July 7, 1935, p. 54; José Antonio Ramos, *Las impurezas de la realidad* (1929; reprint, Havana, 1979), pp. 191, 239–40; Edmundo Desnoes, *Memorias de subdesarrollo* (1965; reprint, Mexico, 1975), p. 94; Manuel Douglas, *The Cubans* (New York, 1981), p. 525; Ricardo Porro, "Una arquitectura romántica," in Machover, *La Habana, 1952–1961*, p. 48; Moore and Hunter, *Seven Women and the Cuban Revolution*, pp. 4, 107; Pablo Armando Fernández, *Los niños se despiden* (Havana, 1968), pp. 294–95, 298–300.

134. Desnoes, *Memorias de subdesarrollo*, p. 90; Reinaldo Arenas, *Before Night Falls*, trans. Dolores M. Koch (New York, 1993), pp. 31–32; Barnet, *Vida real*, p. 174.

135. Lizandro Chávez Alfaro, *Los monos de San Telmo* (Havana, 1963), pp. 114–15.

136. Luis Ricardo Alonso, *Los dioses ajenos*, p. 201; Barnet, *La vida real*, p. 185.

137. Rubén Ortiz Lamadrid, "Veinte años después," *El Mundo*, October 3, 1952, p. A-6.

138. Pérez Firmat, *Next Year in Cuba*, p. 52.

139. Ramón Meza, *Carmela* (1887; reprint, Havana, 1978), p. 128; Luis Felipe Rodríguez, "El denominador de la vida," *Carteles*, October 9, 1938, pp. 34–35; Condesa de Cardiff (Concepción de Macedo de Sánchez), *Mati: Una vida de antaño* (Havana, 1928), p. 104; F. L. Fesser Ferrer, *Los desorientados: Novela de la revolución cubana* (Havana, 1948), p. 227; Raúl Aparicio, *Hijos del tiempo* (Havana, 1964), p. 102.

140. Lesbia Soravilla, *El dolor de vivir* (Havana, n.d.), p. 17; Enrique Serpa, "Una mujer," in Enrique Serpa, *Aletas de tiburón* (Havana, 1976), p. 303; Ramos, *Coaybay*, pp. 38–39, 126, 152–53; Ybarra, "La influencia norteamericana en Cuba," pp. 40–41.

141. Arturo Alfonso Roselló, *El pantano en la cima* (Barcelona, 1971), p. 93.

142. Benito Vilá, "Learning Capitalist Culture II," p. 10; José Rodríguez Feo to Wallace Stevens, November 30, 1946, in Beverly Coyle and Alan Filreis, eds., *Secretaries of the Moon: The Letters of Wallace Stevens and José Rodríguez Feo* (Durham, 1986), p. 90; Moore and Hunter, *Seven Women and the Cuban Revolution*, p. 124; Alberto Lamar Schweyer, *La roca de Patmos* (Havana, 1932), pp. 18–19; Herminio Portell Vilá, "Temor al saber," *El Mundo*, July 18, 1951, p. 6; Sergio la Villa, "Impresiones de muchos 'dandies' ante su propio origen," *Social*, November 1923, p. 17.

143. Octavio R. Costa, *Luis J. Botifoll: An Exemplary Cuban* (Coral Gales, Fla., 1992), p. 25,

and *Hombres y destinos* (Havana, 1954) p. 234; Servando Tellería, "La cobija," *Bohemia*, December 6, 1925, pp. 9, 26.

144. José Antonio Ramos, *Manual del perfecto fulanista* (Havana, 1916), pp. 121–22; Masdeu, *La raza triste*, p. 217; Marcelo Pogolotti, *El caserón del Cerro*, pp. 97–99, 104; Chávez Alfaro, *Los monos de San Telmo*, p. 115; Rafael Duharte and Radamés de los Reyes, *La burguesía santiaguera, 1940–1950* (Santiago de Cuba, 1983), pp. 18–19; Eladio Secades, "La cubana que estuvo en el Norte," *Bohemia*, July 8, 1956, pp. 65, 86.

145. Roberto Fernández Retamar, "Cuba Defended: Countering Another Black Legend," *South Atlantic Quarterly* 96 (Winter 1997): 110; Pogolotti, *Del barro y las voces*, pp. 110–11.

146. Gustavo Pittaluga, *Diálogos sobre el destino* (Havana, 1954), p. 191.

147. Ramos, *Teatro*, p. 209; Mario Parajón, "A los que van a estar fuera," *El Mundo*, June 6, 1957, p. A-6.

148. Betancourt, "Triángulo en el hoyo ocho," pp. 49–50.

149. Campa González, *Memorias de un machadista*, p. 28; Renée Méndez Capote, *Hace muchos años, una joven viajera . . .* (Havana, 1990), pp. 21–22; Nicolás Dorr, *La chacota* (Havana, 1989), p. 185; Douglas, *The Cubans*, p. 528.

150. Fernández, *Los niños se despiden*, pp. 251–52.

151. Arturo Ramírez, "El hijo," *Carteles*, October 9, 1932, p. 36; Sydney A. Clark, *Cuban Tapestry* (New York, 1936), p. 16; Eduardo Abril Amores, *Bajo la garra* (Santiago de Cuba, 1922), pp. 67–68; Douglas, *The Cubans*, p. 186.

152. Byron White, *Azúcar amargo: Un estudio de la economía cubana* (Havana, 1954), p. 170; Desnoes, *Memorias de subdesarrollo*, p. 65; Stuart Ewen and Elizabeth Ewen, *Channels of Desire* (New York, 1982), pp. 64–65.

153. Ernesto Ardura, "¿Por qué emigra el cubano?," *El Mundo*, May 5, 1957, p. A-6; Fesser Ferrer, *Los desorientados*, p. 213; Ramos, *Coaybay*, p. 125; Carlos Loveira, *La última lección* (Havana, 1924), p. 204.

154. Casuso, *Los ausentes*, pp. 77–78; Guillermo Cabrera Leiva, "Un aporte indispensable," *El Mundo*, March 9, 1951, p. 4; Miguel de Zarraga, "Crónicas de New York," *Bohemia*, January 29, 1928, p. 72; "Los ricos indigentes," *Carteles*, September 12, 1937, pp. 17, 51.

155. Arturo R. de Carricarte, "Las bibliotecas públicas," *Bohemia*, August 15, 1920, pp. 10–11; Pedro Martínez Inclán, *La Habana actual* (Havana, 1925), p. 96; "Organización y régimen de bibliotecas," *Carteles*, June 1, 1941, pp. 46–47; Herminio Portell Vilá, "Comparación de progresos," *Bohemia*, January 8, 1956, p. 27; Oscar Pino Santos, "El cubano, lector que no lee," *Carteles*, July 21, 1957, p. 38.

156. Marcelo Pagolotti, "Los totíes del Paseo," *El Mundo*, September 6, 1952, p. A-6; Suzanne, "Parques y bosques," *Bohemia*, December 1, 1935, p. 24; Vicente Cubillas Jr., "Sitio ideal para el turista por su bellezas y por sus lugares históricos," *El Mundo*, September 4, 1955, p. B-10; Octavio Jordán, "Con el tanque lleno," *El Mundo*, August 12, 1950, p. 7.

157. "Piden gabinetes dentales y aterial quirújico los dentistas cubanos," *Vanidades*, June 1, 1950, pp. 84–85; José Comallonga, "Las grandes fincas," *Carteles*, September 25, 1932, p. 44.

158. Antonio Iraizoz, "La vagancia del verano," *El Mundo*, April 13, 1990, p. 12; Arcocha, *Los muertos andan solos*, pp. 117–18.

159. *El Mundo*, August 5, 1950 (p. 7), May 11, 1950 (p. 7), May 24, 1950 (p. 7), March 1, 1953 (p. A-6), October 5, 1954 (p. A-4), September 25, 1955 (C-2), September 8, 1955 (p. A-6).

160. *El Mundo*, February 10, 1951, p. 7; Requeijo, interview.

161. Octavio Jordán, "Con el tanque lleno," *El Mundo*, April 28, 1953, p. A-4; *Social*, February 1918 (p. 4), July 1918 (p. 40); *Diario de la Marina*, January 20, 1907, p. 3; Ernesto

Ardura, "La calle 23 y su rampa," *El Mundo*, June 18, 1950, p. 12; Don Gual, "En esta Habana nuestra," *El Mundo*, February 17, 1954, p. B-4.

162. Oscar Lewis, Ruth M. Lewis, and Susan M. Rigdon, *Four Men: Living the Revolution* (Urbana, Ill., 1970), p. 211; William Gonzales to William Jennings Bryan, May 22, 1914, 837.152 H11/295, IAC; Alberto Candero, "Speech," October 23, 1958, 837.14/10-1458, IA/1955–58; Benito Vilá, "Learning Capitalist Culture II," p. 6; José Llanes, *Cuban-Americans: Masters of Survival* (Cambridge, Mass., 1982), pp. 54–55; Ofelia Schutte, "Reflections on Cuban-American Identity" (Panel presentation, Ethnic Diversity in the Americas Colloquium, University of Florida, Gainesville, October 1992).

163. Kenneth Ballinger, *Miami Millions* (Miami, 1936), p. 22; *Havana Post*, February 5, 1925, p. 4.

164. Ann Armbruster, *The Life and Times of Miami Beach* (New York, 1995), pp. 38–41.

165. *Havana Post*, November 6, 1928, p. 1; Miguel A. Bretos, *Cuba and Florida: Exploration of an Historic Connection, 1539–1991* (Miami, 1991), pp. 111, 113; *Havana Post*, December 31, 1932, p. 4.

166. Armbruster, *Life and Times of Miami Beach*, p. 121; *Miami Herald*, February 3, 1934 (p. 6), May 10, 1945 (p. B-1).

167. Jess Losada, "La contrarrevolución de cerca," *Carteles*, January 14, 1936, p. 36.

168. Berta Arocena, "Abanicos en Miami," *El Mundo*, September 9, 1949, p. 8.

169. Pan American Airways, Miami, box 357, Cuba Folder, University of Miami Library, Coral Gables—I am grateful to Catherine M. Skwiot for bringing this material to my attention; *Time*, November 29, 1948, p. 43; *Newsweek*, July 4, 1949, p. 36; *Times of Havana*, July 11, 1957, p. 9.

170. *El Mundo*, *Diario de la Marina*, and *Bohemia*, 1951–57.

171. *El Mundo* and *Bohemia*, 1952–56; *Variety*, July 2, 1952, p. 52.

172. International Bank for Reconstruction and Development, *Report on Cuba*, pp. 518–19.

173. *Time*, November 29, 1948, p. 43; Fernando Alloza, *Noventa entrevistas políticas* (Havana, 1953), p. 37; *Carteles*, May 15, 1949, p. 21.

174. International Bank for Reconstruction and Development, *Report on Cuba*, p. 519; *Miami Herald*, September 18, 1949, p. 1; *Time*, November 29, 1948, p. 42.

175. *El Mundo*, 1949–53; *Vanidades*, 1956–57; *Diario de la Marina*, 1952–54.

176. *El Mundo*, May 18, 1952 (p. 30), July 12, 1953 (p. C-2); *Bohemia*, June 1, 1958, p. 100.

177. *Bohemia*, May 19, 1957, supp. 10; *El Mundo*, April 24, 1948, p. 5.

178. *El Mundo*, March 9, 1949, p. 1; *Times of Havana*, July 8, 1957, p. 13; *Newsweek*, July 4, 1949, p. 36; Enrique Serpa, *La trampa* (1956; reprint, Havana, 1980), p. 250; Oscar Hijuelos, *Our House in the Last World* (New York, 1983), p. 33; Pérez Firmat, *Next Year in Cuba*, p. 18.

179. *El Mundo*, July 1, 1951, p. 31; Eladio Secades, "Ir a Miami," *Bohemia*, June 12, 1957, pp. 151, 160; *El Mundo*, July 16, 1950, p. 32; María Sánchez, interview by author, Havana, January 23, 1992; García Pedroso, *Memorias de un desmemoriado*, pp. 158–59.

180. Robert Butler to Secretary of State, August 30, 1948, 837.50/8-3048, IA/1945–49.

181. *El Mundo*, July 19, 1953, p. B-7.

182. David S. Green to Department of State, August 1, 1952, 737.00(w)/8-152, IA/1950–54; Ben H. Brown Jr. to George Smathers, January 30, 1953, 837.11/1.2353, ibid.

183. *Bohemia*, February 4, 1934, pp. 24–25; *Time*, November 29, 1948, p. 40.

184. José Montó Sotolongo, "Por los Estados Unidos," *El Mundo*, July 8, 1956, p. C-10; "Miami, la cercana," *El Mundo*, September 25, 1955, p. C-2.

185. Mario Parajón, "Amistad cubano-miamense," *El Mundo*, June 26, 1955, p. A-8.

186. Rubén Ortiz Lamadrid, "Miami," *El Mundo*, January 12, 1952, p. 6; José Montó Sotolongo, "Tópicos de viaje," *El Mundo*, June 29, 1952, p. C-1.

187. Berta Arocena, "Collins Memorial," *El Mundo*, September 18, 1949, p. 13.

188. "Panorama de los exilados cubanos en Miami," *Bohemia*, February 4, 1934, pp. 24–25, 44.

189. Antonio Iraizoz, "En Miami está el amor," *El Mundo*, May 5, 1950, p. 12, and "Fuga hacia Miami," *El Mundo*, May 2, 1950, p. 12; Antonio Patiño, *Ritmo de la juventud* (Havana, 1957), p. 158; Ramón Ferreira, *Teatro* (Miami, 1993), p. 125; Mario Guiral Moreno, "Contraste entre Miami y La Habana," *El Mundo*, April 19, 1950, p. 12.

190. "Antitesis criolla," *Carteles*, February 2, 1941, p. 21.

191. El Curioso Parlanchín, "Por el ornato limpieza y embellecimiento de La Habana," *Carteles*, April 28, 1940, 72; Gabino Delgado, "Miami: Lección objetiva para los cubanos," *Carteles*, May 1, 1949, pp. 50–51.

192. Edward J. Linehan, "Cuba's Exiles Bring New Life to Miami," *National Geographic*, July 1973, p. 68.

193. Octavio R. Costa, *Octavio R. Costa: An Exemplary Cuban* (Coral Gables, Fla., 1992), p. 117; David Rief, *Going to Miami* (New York, 1987), p. 228; Schutte, "Reflections on Cuban-American Identity."

CHAPTER SEVEN

1. Néstor T. Carbonell, *And the Russians Stayed* (New York, 1989), p. 93; Fernando Alvarez Tabío, *Teoría general de la constitución cubana* (Havana, 1946), pp. 12–14.

2. Ernesto Ardura, "La suerte del cubano," *El Mundo*, June 17, 1951, p. 8.

3. Ernesto Ardura, "¿Somos civilizados?," *El Mundo*, February 12, 1950, p. 12.

4. Jorge Mañach, "El golpe del 10 marzo," *Bohemia*, June 8, 1952, pp. 52–53; Carlos Hevia to Jack M. Cabot, July 31, 1953, 737.00/7-3153, IA/1950–54; Harold M. Randall to Department of State, April 2, 1953, 737.00/4-253, IA 1950–54; Arthur Gardner to Department of State, February 21, 1955, 837.2351/2-2155, IA/1955–58; John Dorshner and Roberto Fabricio, *The Winds of December* (New York, 1980), p. 132.

5. Hernández Travieso, "La lección del martes," *El Mundo*, November 10, 1956, p. A-8; *El Mundo*, March 29, 1952, p. 6; Andrés Felipe Labrador, "Soberanía del espíritu," *Revolución*, September 12, 1959, p. 2; Herminio Portell Vilá, "Futilidad de la ley," *El Mundo*, June 20, 1952, p. A-6.

6. Herminio Portell Vilá, "Suma y sigue," *El Mundo*, March 12, 1952, p. 6; *El Mundo*, March 25, 1952, p. 7; Ernesto Ardura, "Un año de decadencia," *El Mundo*, January 4, 1953, p. A-6.

7. Manuel Bisbé, "Jubilo que entristece," *El Mundo*, November 9, 1952, p. A-6; Leví Marrero, "Recursos y política," *El Mundo*, November 14, 1954, p. A-6.

8. Benito Vilá, "Learning Capitalist Culture II: The Schooling in Bourgeois Self-Consciousness of a Cuban-American Immigrant," p. 14 (manuscript, 1994; copy in author's possession); Eliseo Riera Gómez to Attorney General, January 20, 1953, 737.00/2-453, IA/1950–54.

9. Ruby Hart Phillips, *Cuba: Island of Paradox* (New York, 1959), p. 311.

10. C. Burke Elbrick to Department of State, October 13, 1950, 737.00 (W)/10-1350, IA/1950–54; F. D. Leatherman to Department of State, November 2, 1950, 837.00/11-250,

ibid.; R. M. Connell, "Annual Economic Review, 1950," March 31, 1950, 837.00/6-1951, ibid.; H. T. Andersen, "Annual Economic Review—Cuba," April 15, 1952, 837.00/4-1552, ibid.

11. David S. Green to Department of State, April 12, 1953, 837.00/4-1053, ibid.

12. Banco Nacional de Cuba, "Temas sobre cuestiones económicas generales: El desarrollo económico de Cuba," *Revista* 3 (March 1956): 273, 276; Oscar Pino Santos, "El nivel de vida del pueblo cubano es hoy peor que a principios de la república," *Carteles*, November 6, 1955, pp. 46–49, 111; United Nations, Department of Economic and Social Affairs, *Economic Survey of Latin America for 1954* (New York, 1955), p. 161.

13. United Nations Economic Commission for Latin America, "Some Aspects of the Recent Evolution of Cuba's Economy," *Economic Review of Latin America* (New York, 1955), p. 48; International Bank for Reconstruction and Development, *Report on Cuba* (Washington, D.C., 1951), pp. 6–8; U.S. Department of Commerce, *Investment in Cuba* (Washington, D.C., 1956), p. 7; E. A. Gilmore, "Cuban National Income and Products Accounts," July 29, 1959, 837.10/72959, IA/1959–60; Pino Santos, "El nivel de vida del pueblo cubano," pp. 46–49, 111.

14. Cuba, Tribunal Superior Electoral, *Censos de población, viviendas y electoral* (Havana, 1953), p. 176; Carlos M. Castañeda, "¡665,000 cubanos sin trabajo!," *Bohemia*, February 16, 1958, supp. 16–17; C. A. Boonstra to Department of State, October 17, 1955, 837.00/10-1755, IA/1955–58.

15. Luis Rolando Cabrera, "Está aumentando día y día la desocupación en el país," *El Mundo*, March 28, 1954, p. A-12; Agustín Tamargo, "Sobre el campo mojado, hambre, hambre y más hambre," *Bohemia*, October 21, 1956, pp. 60–61.

16. Jorge Ibarra, *Cuba, 1898–1958: Estructura y procesos sociales* (Havana, 1995), pp. 176–78; Leví Marrero, "Graduación—¿Luego que?," *El Mundo*, June 22, 1955, p. A-6; Mario Greitín, "300 nuevos médicos se suman a los 2,500 desempleados que hay en la profesión," *Carteles*, October 30, 1955, pp. 15–16, 112; Fidel Castro, *History Will Absolve Me* (Havana, 1967), p. 42.

17. Andrés Valdespino, "La carta de un padre," *Bohemia*, June 16, 1957, pp. 55, 114.

18. "Estudiar en Cuba . . . ¿Para que?," *Bohemia*, November 25, 1956, p. 63.

19. Gervasio R. Ruiz, "Mujeres que trabajan," *Bohemia*, October 16, 1955, p. 118.

20. R. M. Connell to Department of State, March 30, 1951, 837.00/3-3051, IA/1950–54; Leonard H. Price, "Wholesale Price Index, Second Quarter of 1957," August 7, 1957, 837.01/8-757, IA/1955–58; E. A. Gilmore Jr., "Wholesale Price Index, First Quarter of 1958," July 14, 1958, 837.01/7-1458, IA/1955–58.

21. International Bank for Reconstruction and Development, *Report on Cuba*, pp. 99, 726; Antonio Riccardi, "¿Por qué encarece más cada día el costo de la vida en Cuba?," *Carteles*, August 1, 1948, p. 46; Rufo López Fresquet, "El mercado cubano," *El Mundo*, July 19, 1953, p. A-11; Waldo Medina, "Enriquecimiento sin causa," *El Mundo*, January 19, 1952, p. 6; R. M. Connell to Department of State, November 10, 1950, 937.40/11-1050, IA/1950–54; *El Mundo*, February 5, 1950, p. 32; D. S. Green to Department of State, October 6, 1952, 837.00/10-6252, IA/1950–54.

22. A. J. Powers, "Report on Living Conditions in Havana, Cuba," July 2, 1945, 837.5017/6-2945, IA/1945–49; R. M. Connell, "Living and Office Operating Costs in Cuba," April 17, 1950, 837.01/4-1750, IA/1950–54; Daniel Braddock, "Living Conditions in Cuba," August 26, 1958, 837.01/8-2658, IA/1955–58.

23. David S. Green, "Economic and Financial Review—Second Quarter of 1953," July 9, 1953, 837.00/7-953, IA/1950–54; A. J. Cope to Secretary of State, November 18, 1948, 837.5017/11-1848, IA/1945–49; *El Mundo*, January 7, 1954, p. A-6.

24. Tamargo, "Sobre el campo mojado," pp. 60–61.

25. *El Mundo*, May 2, 1951 (pp. 1, 7), March 12, 1951 (p. 4), January 17, 1956 (p. A-8).

26. Héctor Quintero, *Teatro* (Havana, 1983), p. 56; Ernesto Ardura, "Raíces de la crisis cubana," *El Mundo*, January 11, 1953, p. A-6; Joaquín Martínez Sáenz, "Cuba libre e independiente," *Bohemia*, May 19, 1956, pp. 40–41; Andrés Valdespino, "¿Quienes son los que han hecho daño a Cuba?," *Bohemia*, March 17, 1957, p. 61; José Lezama Lima, *Diarios*, ed. Ciro Bianchi Ross (Mexico, 1994), pp. 107–8.

27. Armando Soto, "Mensaje a la juventud cubana," *Bohemia*, September 18, 1955, pp. 3, 134; Agustín Tamargo, "¿Somos un país cangrejo?," *Bohemia*, July 1, 1956, pp. 52–53.

28. Daisy Rubiera Castillo, *Reyita, sencillamente: Testimonio de una negra cubana nonagenaria* (Havana, 1997), p. 104.

29. Rubén Ortiz Lamadrid, "Vida moderna," *El Mundo*, April 12, 1956, p. A-8.

30. "Conflictos en los Ten Cents," *Bohemia*, July 14, 1946, p. 49; Shirley F. Woodell to Carroll, February 23, 1953, and to Miss Moran, February 16, 1957, SFW.

31. Rubiera Castillo, *Reyita, sencillamente*, pp. 136–37.

32. Alberto León Riva, "Precios y salarios," *El Mundo*, March 12, 1954, p. A-10.

33. *Revolución*, September 2, 1959, p. 16; Leví Marrero, "¿Por que somos pobre?," *El Mundo*, March 7, 1954, p. A-8; Antonio Llano Montes, "Tras las noticias," *Carteles*, March 24, 1957, p. 57.

34. *Havana Post*, November 17, 1932, p. 2; *Bohemia*, August 25, 1935, p. 12; *El Mundo*, November 10, 1954, p. B-3; *Vanidades*, February 12, 1957, p. 12.

35. Antonio Martínez Bello, "Menos importación y más capital," *El Mundo*, July 30, 1954, p. A-6.

36. International Bank for Reconstruction and Development, *Report on Cuba*, p. 13.

37. Un Obrero Nativo to Editor, *Carteles*, December 6, 1936, p. 8.

38. Miguel F. Márquez y de la Cerra, *El gallo cantó* (Río Piedras, Puerto Rico, 1972), p. 33.

39. César Leante, *Padres e hijos* (Havana, 1967), p. 84; Manuel de J. Zamora, "Juventud sin futuro," *El Mundo Ilustrado*, April 21, 1957, p. 2.

40. Alcides Iznaga, *Las cercas caminaban* (Havana, 1970), pp. 96–97.

41. Teresa Casuso, *Cuba and Castro*, trans. Elmer Grossberg (New York, 1961), p. 13; Lynn Geldof, *Cubans* (London, 1991), p. 190; International Bank for Reconstruction and Development, *Report on Cuba*, p. 138.

42. Rufo López-Fresquet, *My 14 Months with Castro* (Cleveland, 1966), p. 25; Marcelo Pogolotti, *Del barro y las voces* (Havana, 1982), pp. 213–14; Juan Arcocha, *A Candle in the Wind* (New York, 1967), p. 35; Alfred L. Padula Jr., "The Fall of the Bourgeoisie: Cuba, 1959–1961" (Ph.D. dissertation, University of New Mexico, 1974), p. 304; Alberto Lamar Schweyer, *Vendaval en los cañaverales* (Havana, 1937), pp. 156–57.

43. Paul B. Kern to Elizabeth Lee, December 27, 1942, Paul B. Kern Correspondence, General File Correspondence, 1917–55, United Methodist Church, GMA.

44. J. Merle Davis, *The Cuban Church in a Sugar Economy* (New York, 1942), pp. 77–79.

45. Sterling A. Neblett to Warren A. Candler, November 20, 1907, Candler Papers, WL-EU; Antero Suárez, José Mauricio Hernández, and Aurelio Alonso to Secretary of the Board of Missions, October 2, 1909, ibid.

46. Sterling A. Neblett, *Methodism's First Fifty Years in Cuba* (Wilmore, Ky., 1976), p. 72; Euston E. Clements to Warren A. Candler, October 9, 1909, and Hubert W. Baker to Candler, October 7, 1907, Candler Papers, WL-EU.

47. José García Pedrosa, *Memorias de un desmemoriado* (Miami, 1979), pp. 174–75.

48. Reinaldo Arenas, *Before Night Falls*, trans. Dolores M. Koch (New York, 1993), p. 31; Agustín Tamargo, "¿Por que lucha actualmente el pueblo de Cuba?," *Bohemia*, July 28, 1957, pp. 64–65.

49. Philip W. Bonsal, *Cuba, Castro, and the United States* (Pittsburgh, 1971), p. 271; Leví Marrero, "Cuba: 11 million dentro de 25 años," *El Mundo*, November 14, 1956, p. A-6.

50. *El Mundo*, November 22, 1956 (p. B-4), November 29, 1956 (p. B-2).

51. Miguel Agustín Gacel, "Aumentada notablemente la mendicidad en los últimos meses," *El Mundo*, November 14, 1954, p. E-1; Mario Guiral Moreno, "La juventud delin-cuente," *El Mundo*, March 14, 1956, p. A-8; Regino Martín, "La delincuencia juvenil en Cuba," *Carteles*, November 7, 1954, pp. 46–48; Rubén Ortiz Lamadrid, "El juego en Cuba," *El Mundo*, March 8, 1956, p. A-6; Antonio Llano Montes, "Tras la noticia," *Carteles*, May 5, 1957, p. 32.

52. Eladio Secades, "La Habana se ha llenado de bares," *Bohemia*, November 18, 1955, p. 71; Luis Conte Agüero, "¡Atrás el hampa!," *Bohemia*, February 23, 1958, supp. 17–18; Andrés Valdespino, "Cuba se nos llena de hampones y tahures," *Bohemia*, February 16, 1958, pp. 63, 100; Juan Giró Rodés, "Confidencialmente," *El Mundo*, March 15, 1956, p. B-2; Mario Parajón, "Divagación sobre la decencia," *El Mundo*, July 18, p. A-6; *El Mundo*, March 16, 1955, p. B-6.

53. *Saturday Evening Post*, March 28, 1953, pp. 32–33; *Time*, April 21, 1952, p. 38.

54. *Havana Post*, May 11, 1924, p. 9; Henry W. Wack, "Cuba and West Indies Winter Charm," *Arts and Decoration* 34 (February 1931): 53.

55. "Arrecia en los Estados Unidos la campaña de descrédito contra Cuba," *Bohemia*, January 13, 1957, pp. 70–72; Valdespino, "Cuba se nos llena de hampones y tahures," p. 63; Mario Sorondo y Tolón, *De la vida tranquila* (Havana, 1925), pp. 85–86; Hernández Tra-viesa, "Lo que se dice de Cuba," *El Mundo*, November 12, 1955, p. A-6; José Montó Soto-longo, "Esa no es Cuba," *El Mundo*, September 8, 1955, p. A-6; "La prensa amarilla de New York sigue cebandose en la reputación de Cuba," *Bohemia*, May 26, 1957, p. 65; *Bohemia*, June 16, 1957, p. 37.

56. *Time*, December 5, 1955, p. 34; Agustín Tamargo, "Quien injuria a Martí y a Maceo no puede ser amigo de Cuba," *Bohemia*, August 26, 1956, pp. 49–50; " 'Ellos y Ellas,' otra ofensa de Hollywood a los cubanos," *Bohemia*, November 18, 1956, pp. 12–13, 120.

57. Bernardo Viera, "¡Desi Arnaz es enemigo de todos los cubanos!," *Bohemia*, April 25, 1954, pp. 28–29, 128.

58. Jorge Mañach, *Pasado vigente* (Havana, 1939), pp. 222–23; Juan Marinello, "Sobre la inquietud cubana," *Avance* 3 (December 15, 1929): 357; Office of Middle American Affairs (MID), "Cuba—A Summary of Situations, Interests, and Policies Affecting the United States," February 20, 1953, 737.0012-2453, IA/1950–54.

59. *El Mundo*, March 23, 1956, p. A-8.

60. José Pardo Llada, "¿Es Cuba de los cubanos?," *Bohemia*, April 22, 1956, pp. 61–62, 92.

61. "Influencia" was recorded live in March 1957 and rereleased as a compact disc, entitled "La Bodeguita del Medio," featuring Carlos Puebla, Santiago Martínez, and Pedro Sosa, Riverside/Milestone World Music, MCD 9209-2.

62. Leví Marrero, "La base indispensable," *El Mundo*, May 22, 1955, p. A-8; Mercedes Alemán, "La navidad debe ser nuestra navidad," *Vanidades*, December 1, 1958, p. 16; Nereyda M. de Muxo, "Muebles adecuados a nuestro clima," *Vanidades*, May 1, 1955, p. 34; Angela Velarde, "Nuestra clima demanda determinadas consejos de belleza," *Vanidades*, October 15, 1955, p. 41; Marta Vignier, "Raúl Hernández: Quiere hacer de La Habana un pequeño Paris,"

Vanidades, April 15, 1954, pp. 24–25; Marta Vignier, "Orientaciones de nuestros especialistas en el arte del bien lucir," *Vanidades*, May 15, 1955, p. 36; Hada Rosete, "Lily del Barrio: Decana de los diseñadores cubanos," *Vanidades*, August 15, 1954, pp. 22–25. The original recording of "Conozca a Cuba" by Ramón Veloz was reissued in the collection *De Cuba: Su música*, vol. 2, Egrem CD 0016, 1992.

63. Fernando G. Campoamor, "Varadero Beach," *El Mundo*, July 14, 1954, p. A-6.

64. Mario Guiral Moreno, "La ley del idioma," *El Mundo*, April 20, 1951, p. 6; "A La Habana hay que cubanizarla," *Bohemia*, June 23, 1957, p. 61; José Antonio Mases, *Los padrenuestros y el fusil* (Barcelona, 1973), p. 130.

65. Antonio Ortega, "Los barbudos," *Bohemia*, January 11, 1959, p. 73; Andrés Valdespino, "La batalla que aun falta," *Bohemia*, January 18–25, 1959, p. 13; Jorge Mañach, "La revitalización de la fe en Cuba," *Bohemia*, March 15, 1959, pp. 26–27; Mario Llerena, "El paraíso de los intereses creados," *Bohemia*, March 8, 1959, pp. 64–65; Rafael Cepeda, *Apuntes para una historia del presbiterianismo en Cuba* (Havana, 1986), p. 243.

66. *Revolución*, January–March 1959; Leonard H. Price, "Survey of Cuban Labor Demands," April 22, 1959, 837.062/4-2259, IA/1959–60.

67. Alejandro Suero, "Open Letter to the American People," *Times of Havana*, January 30, 1959, p. 15.

68. Fidel Castro, *El pensamiento de Fidel Castro*, 2 vols. (Havana, 1983), 2:10, 198–99.

69. López-Fresquet, *My 14 Months with Castro*, p. 85.

70. Castro, *El pensamiento*, 1:297; López-Fresquet, *My 14 Months with Castro*, p. 97.

71. *Revolución*, September 19, 1959, p. 12; Leonard H. Price to Department of State, April 20, 1959, 837.00/4-2059, DS/RG 59.

72. *Revolución*, July 7, 1959, p. 20.

73. Oscar Lewis, Ruth M. Lewis, and Susan M. Rigdon, *Four Women: Living the Revolution* (Urbana, Ill., 1977), p. 171.

74. *Times of Havana*, October 12, 1959, p. 9; *Diario de la Marina*, September 26, 1959, p. 1.

75. *Revolución*, September 19, 1959 (p. 12), September 30, 1959 (p. 8).

76. Castro, *El pensamiento*, 1:190, 308.

77. *Revolución*, April 6, 1959, p. 9.

78. Ibid., May 17, 1959, pp. 1, 3.

79. *Bohemia*, April 12, 1959, p. 19.

80. Nicolas Quintana, "Arquitectura cubana. . . . Una búsqueda de la verdad," *Arquitectura* 27 (April–March 1959): 166–72; *Revolución*, October 15, 1959 (pp. 1, 6), July 20, 1959 (p. 22); Lisandro Otero, *Llover sobre mojado: Una reflexión personal sobre la historia* (Havana, 1997), p. 83.

81. Naty Revuelta, interview by author, Havana, June 7, 1996; Warren Miller, *90 Miles from Home* (New York, 1961), p. 81.

82. *Bohemia*, April 12, 1959, p. 106.

83. Andrés Valdespino, "Las trompetas de Josué," *Bohemia*, April 12, 1959, pp. 53, 137; Rine R. Leal, "Actuales corrientes en el teatro cubano," *Nueva Revista Cubana* 1 (April–June 1959): 165.

84. *Gaceta Oficial*, November 25, 1959, p. 1.

85. Alejo Carpentier, "Navidades cubanas," *Revolución*, October 12, 1959, p. 18; Roberto Fernández Retamar, "Navidades cubanas: La tradición como revolución," *Revolución*, October 17, 1959, p. 2; *Times of Havana*, December 12, 1959 (p. 8), December 24, 1959 (p. 7); E. A. Gilmore to Department of State, October 6, 1959, 837.00/10-659, IA/1959–60; Lisandro Otero, *Arbol de la vida* (Mexico, 1990), p. 113.

86. Philip W. Bonsal to Department of State, March 17, 1959, 737.00(W)/3-1759, IA/1959–60; John L. Topping to Richard B. Owen, November 6, 1959, 737.00/11-659, ibid.; Roy R. Rubottom to Bonsal, November 20, 1959, Philip W. Bonsal Papers, LC.

87. Castro, *El pensamiento*, 1:5.

88. Vicente Cubillas, "El aporte de la iglesia evangélica a la causa redentora," *Bohemia*, February 1, 1959, p. 108; Brunelda Oves and Juan Ojeda, former teachers of La Progresiva, interview by author, Cárdenas, July 26, 1991; Neill Macaulay, *A Rebel in Cuba: An American's Memoir* (Chicago, 1970), p. 82. Among the teachers at La Progresiva most active in MR 26-7 clandestine operations were Manuel del Cueto, Esteban Hernández Alfonso, and René Castellanos.

89. Richard G. Milk to "Dear Friends," March 25, 1960, United Methodist Church Missionary Correspondence, 1956–61, GMA.

90. Daniel M. Braddock to Department of State, January 28, 1959 (737.13/1-2859) and January 19, 1959 (737.13/1-1959), IA/1959–60; María Luisa Guerrero, *Elena Mederos: Una mujer con perfil para la historia* (Miami, 1991), pp. 22–23.

91. Nicolás Rivero, *Castro's Cuba* (Washington, D.C., 1962), pp. vii–viii; Felipe Pazos to Herbert Matthews, October 19, 1961, Philip W. Bonsal Papers, LC.

92. Alberto Lamar Schweyer, *La crisis del patriotismo* (Havana, 1929), p. 88.

93. Thomas G. Paterson, *Contesting Castro* (New York, 1994), p. 257; Robert A. Stevenson to Philip W. Bonsal, April 22, 1959, Bonsal Papers, LC; "Diary Entry by Senator Allen J. Ellender," December 14, 1958, *FRUS*, p. 676; "Memorandum of a Conference between the President and the Acting Secretary of State," April 18, 1959, *FRUS*, p. 475; "Memorandum of Discussion of the 396th Meeting of the National Security Council," February 12, 1959, *FRUS*, p. 398.

94. "Memorandum of Conversation," February 12, 1959, 737.00/2-1359, IA/1959–60.

95. Philip W. Bonsal to Department of State, November 27, 1959, 611.37/11-1759, ibid.

96. Cristina García, *Dreaming in Cuban* (New York, 1992), p. 164; Heberto Padilla, *Self-Portrait of the Other*, trans. Alexander Coleman (New York, 1990), p. 17; "Manifiesto-Programa del Movimiento 26 de Julio," November 1956, *Humanismo 7* (November–December 1958): 15.

97. Michael McClay, *"I Love Lucy"* (New York, 1995), p. 43; "Memorandum of a Conference between the President and the Acting Secretary of State," April 18, 1959, *FRUS*, p. 475.

98. José de la Campa González, *Memorias de un machadista: Novela histórico-social* (Tampa, 1937), p. 530; Henry A. Holt to Marshall T. Rice, December 3, 1954, 611.37/11-2254, IA/1950–54; José Martí to Manuel Mercado, May 15, 1895, in Martí, *Obras completes*, ed. Jorge Quintana, 5 vols. (Caracas, 1964), 1:271; José Soler Puig, *En el año de enero* (Havana, 1963), p. 162.

99. Pablo Armando Fernández, *Los niños se despiden* (Havana, 1968), pp. 229, 349; Mario Parajón, "Amistad cubano-miamense," *El Mundo*, June 26, 1955, p. A-8; Edmundo Desnoes, *Memorias de subdesarrollo* (1965; reprint, Mexico, 1973), pp. 50–51.

100. Daniel M. Braddock to Secretary of State, February 16, 1959, 737.00/2-1659, IA/1959–60; Richard Milk to James E. Ellis, February 13, 1960, United Methodist Church, Missionary Correspondence, 1956–61, GMA; Park F. Wollam to Department of State, July 29, 1959, 737.00/7-2959, IA/1959–60; Ruby Hart Phillips Interview, Oral History Collection, Cuba-Foreign Observers, Robert Alexander Papers, Rutgers University Library, New Brunswick, N.J.; Philip W. Bonsal to Department of State, October 30, 1959, *FRUS*, p. 649; William R.

Lenderking, "Impressions of a Recent Trip," December 8, 1959, 737.00/12-859, IA/1959–60; John Snook, "The Way I See It," *Times of the Americas*, November 12, 1959, p. 9; Jerome D. Cohen to Christian Herter, November 9, 1959, 611.37/11-959, IA/1959–60; Milton Guss, "Smoke Signals," *Times of Havana*, July 16, 1959, p. 9.

101. Park F. Wollam to Department of State, July 29, 1959, 737.00/7-2959, IA/1959–60.

102. Juan Arcocha, *Los muertos andan solos* (Havana, 1962), pp. 109–10, 135; Marjorie Moore and Adrienne Hunter, *Seven Women and the Cuban Revolution* (Toronto, 1996), p. 64.

103. José Llanes, *Cuban-Americans: Masters of Survival* (Cambridge, Mass., 1982), pp. 53–54; Gene Griessman, "Giant Steps: An Interview with Roberto Goizueta," *Atlanta* (November 1982), p. 80; Pablo Medina, *Exile Memories: A Cuban Childhood* (Austin, 1990), p. 3.

104. Rivero, *Castro's Cuba*, p. vii; Arcocha, *Los muertos andan solos*, p. 111.

105. Lisandro Otero, *Arbol de la vida* (Mexico, 1990), pp. 128–29.

106. Lisandro Otero, "Utopia Revisited," *South Atlantic Quarterly* 96 (Winter 1997): 27–28.

107. Freddy Artiles, *Adriana en dos tiempos* (Havana, 1972), p. 150.

108. Geldof, *Cubans*, p. 14.

109. Salvador Díaz-Versón, *One Man, One Battle* (New York, 1980), p. 123.

110. Soler Puig, *En el año de enero*, pp. 159, 162; Raoul Fowler, *En las garras de la paloma* (Havana, 1967), p. 54.

111. Marifeli Pérez-Stable, *The Cuban Revolution: Origins, Course, and Legacy* (New York, 1993), p. vi; Medina, *Exile Memories*, p. 113; Gustavo Pérez Firmat, *Next Year in Cuba* (New York, 1995), p. 20; Edmundo Desnoes, *El cataclismo* (Havana, 1969), pp. 57, 165; Eduardo Machado, *Once Removed* (New York, 1986), p. 2.

112. Pérez Firmat, *Next Year in Cuba*, p. 51.

113. Thomas D. Boswell and James R. Curtis, *The Cuban-American Experience* (Totowa, N.J., 1984), p. 74; Arcocha, *Los muertos andan solos*, p. 136.

114. María Cristina García, *Havana USA* (Berkeley, 1996); Eladio Secades, *Las mejores estampas de Secades* (Miami, 1983), p. 37.

115. Desnoes, *Memorias del subdesarrollo*, p. 15.

116. Otero, *Arbol de la vida*, pp. 244–45.

INDEX

Bay of Pigs, 503
Benítez, Manuel, 413
Betancourt, Luis Adrián, 287, 423
Betancourt, Pedro, 44
Betancourt Cisneros, Gaspar, 34, 38, 86; on U.S. education of Cubans, 35
Bicycle clubs, 75
Bolet, Jorge, 413
Botifoll, Luis, 420, 444
Boxing, 175–77, 413; and use of English language, 381
Braga, George, 222, 228
Bremer, Fredrika, 22
Brooke, John R., 106, 155
Bryant, William Cullen, 19, 70
Bullfighting, 78–79
Byrne, Bonifacio, 39

Cabrera, Raimundo, 39, 103, 137, 237, 416; and Ten Years War (1868–1878), 45–46; and Catholic Church, 56; on United States, 61–62, 63; on Chicago Columbian Exposition, 67; on Cuban character, 87, 89; and English language, 164; and U.S. sugar mill, 237
Cabrera Infante, Guillermo, 347; and U.S. movies, 29 3, 295, 297, 301
Cabrera Leiva, Guillermo, 427–28
Caimanera, 352; and U.S. naval station, 239–42; prostitution in, 240
Calcagno, Francisco, 61
Calderón González, Jorge, 72
Calejo, Miguel M., 56
Campa de Grillo, Adela, 51
Campa González, José de la, 84–85, 424, 494
Cañedo, Valentín, 21–22; on Cubans educated in United States, 53
Capablanca, Raúl, 153, 413
Carmichael, Hoagy, 194
Carpentier, Alejo, 144; and Havana, 144, 146; on U.S. films, 284; and Christmas, 485
Carricarte, Arturo de, 428
Carrillo, Francisco, 43
Carrión, Miguel de, 39; and Havana, 146
Casanova, Emilia, 48

Casanova, Ignacio, 97
Casanova, J. M., 30
Casey, Calvert, 411
Casino Nacional, 179
Castellanos, Jesús, 145
Castellanos García, Gerardo, 56
Castillo Duany, Demetrio, 29, 43
Castillo de González, Aurelia, 35; on women in United States, 50, 51, 87; on life in United States, 67; and Chicago Columbian Exposition, 67–68
Castillo Márquez, Francisco del, 146
Castro, Fidel, 452, 480, 486, 487, 496–97; and baseball, 265–66, 277; and provisional revolutionary government, 479; on need for reform, 481–83; in United States, 490; declares revolution socialist in character, 503
Casuso, Teresa, 412, 427, 464
Catholic Church, 55–56; and Protestant missionaries in nineteenth-century Cuba, 59–60
Cepeda, Rafael, 478
Cervantes, Ignacio, 43
Céspedes, Benjamín de, 81
Céspedes, Carlos Manuel de, 41
Cha-cha-chá, 208–10, 212–14; influence on U.S. popular music, 210
Chalía, Rosalía, 43
Chibás, Eduardo, 153
Chicago Columbian Exposition (1893), 67–68
Chongo, María, 58
Christmas, 147–48, 364, 398; and U.S. sugar mills, 228; in republic, 357–58; and revolution, 485
Cigar manufacturing, 30–32
Cleveland, Grover, 22
Cobb, Ty, 260
Coffigny, Eugenio, 29
Collazo, Evaristo, 57
Concha, José G. de la, 21–22; and Cubans educated in the United States, 36–37
Conga, 205, 214, 218
Córdoba, Emilia de, 155
Cova, José Victoriano de la, 57, 58
Cozzens, James Gould, 228, 235, 237–38

Cruz, Manuel de la, 92
Cruz del Pino, Mary, 346, 411
Cuban-American Sugar Company, 229
Cuban Education Association, 406
Cuban Revolutionary Party (PRC), 44, 162; and participation of women, 48–49
Cuéllar, Miguel (Mike), 259
Cugat, Xavier, 203, 204, 215, 217, 412; as popularizer of Cuban music, 204–5, 217
Curros Enríquez, Manuel, 83

Dana, Richard, 19, 20
Dance, 204–5, 355; and popular music, 198–204; rumba, 203–4, 214, 218, 469; conga, 205, 214, 218; and Katherine Dunham, 206; mambo, 206–8, 212, 216; cha-cha-chá, 208–10, 212–14
Darío, Rubén, 147
Delgado, Gabino, 443–44
Del Monte, Domingo, 64, 87
Del Monte, Leonardo, 38
Del Monte, Ricardo, 34
Desnoes, Edmundo, 411, 495, 504; on automobiles, 338
Deulofeu, Manuel, 56
Diago, Fernando, 29
Diago, Pedro, 29
Díaz, Alberto J., 58, 147
Díaz, Eladio, 56
Díaz, Mercedes, 58
Díaz, Miguel, 137
Díaz de Herrera, Rosalía, 43
Díaz-Versón, Salvador, 56, 500
Díaz Vólero, Francisco, 141
Dimock, Joseph, 23, 71; on U.S. presence during nineteenth century, 21, 72
Domínguez, Ofelia, 314
Domínguez Roldán, Guillermo, 137
Domínguez Roldán, María, 413
Dorr, Nicolás, 424
Drake, Carlos, 29
Duarte, Pedro, 57
Dumois, Hipólito, 137
Dunau, Rita, 54
Dunham, Katherine, 206
Durand, Elliott, 74

Economic development: and war for independence (1895–1898), 97–99; and postwar conditions, 100–104, 106–40; and U.S. military intervention (1898–1902), 104–39; and U.S. investments, 151–52; and unemployment, 450–52; and cost of living, 452–55; and standard of living, 457–59
Education: of Cubans in United States during nineteenth century, 32–36, 43, 44; as "Americanization," 34, 159–60; and Spanish colonial government, 35, 36–37; and women, 35, 51, 88; Cuban-owned schools in United States, 43; Cuban teachers in United States, 43; and Protestant missionaries during nineteenth century, 57; and race relations, 92; in early republic, 153–55; during U.S. military occupation (1898–1902), 159–61; and Protestant missionaries during twentieth century, 246–48, 250, 252; and English-language training, 386–87, 501; private schooling, 399–405; of Cubans in United States during twentieth century, 406–11, 422
Electricity, 119, 122–23; in nineteenth century, 74; and retail trade, 329–31
Elks Club, 397
Enríquez, Carlos, 413
Episcopal Church, 230, 243, 246, 255, 395; in nineteenth century, 56, 57, 60; and education, 155, 247; and social services, 246, 254
Espín, Vilma, 488
Estenger, Rafael, 224, 235
Estrada, Dionisia, 51
Estrada Palma, Tomás, 43, 44

Fajardo, José, 208
Fashion, 361; and "Americanization," 316; and U.S. influence, 388–90
Feijóo, Samuel, 287–88, 380
Fergusson, Erna, 225–26, 387
Fernández, Pablo Armando, 411, 424, 495; on sugar mill, 234; on New York, 414
Fernández de Velasco, Rafael, 38
Fernández Retamar, Roberto, 411, 422, 485

Menken, Adah Isaacs, 23

Menocal, Mario G., 232–33, 397, 407; and U.S. education, 44; and U.S. sugar mills, 236; and sports, 256

Menocal, Raimundo, 92–93

Merchán, Rafael M., 78; and race relations, 92

Methodist Church, 56, 230, 231, 238, 243, 252, 255, 395; and United Fruit Company, 232; and social services, 246, 254; and education, 247, 252

Meza, Ramón, 63, 417–18

Miami, 431; early development of, 432–33; and Cuban emigration, 433–34; and Cuban tourism, 434–36, 438–40; Cuban investment in, 436–37; as frame of reference for living conditions, 440–44; and post-1959 emigration, 501–3

Miller, Warren, 191; on Nicaro, 222

Mining, 220, 257; and U.S. interests during nineteenth century, 21

Miñoso, Orestes (Minnie), 259, 272, 412

Miranda, Aurelio, 81

Miranda, Luis Rodolfo, 44

Miyares, Carmen, 48

Montaner, Rita, 212, 413

Monteagudo, José de Jesús, 407

Montori, Arturo, 104, 404

Montó Sotolongo, José, 441

Mora, José María, 38

Morales, María, 58

Morales Lemus, José, 43, 97

Moreno de Soría, Amalia, 58

Moreno Fraginals, Manuel, 25

Morúa Delgado, Martín, 43; on race relations, 93

Moya, María Josefa de, 48

Muecke, Carlos, 103

Muñoz, Víctor, 39

Muñoz de Monte, Luis E., 33

Murray, Amelia, 22

Music, 381; Cuban musicians in the United States during nineteenth century, 43; about Cuba, 182–83, 188–89, 190–91, 205–6, 512–13; and tourism, 198–202; and dance, 198–204; *son*, 199, 205; rumba, 199–204, 214, 218, 469; conga, 205, 214, 218; mambo, 206–8, 212, 216, 218; cha-cha-chá, 208–10, 212–14; and U.S. performers, 212–15; rock 'n' roll, 387, 392–93; and U.S. influence, 390–92; "el filin," 392, 483

Navarro, Noel, 379

Newspapers: Cuban émigré, 44–45, 508; U.S., in Cuba, 125, 511

Nieto de Herrera, Carmela, 39

Nixon, Richard, 490

Núñez, Emilio, 28, 44

O'Farrill, Juan, 18

Ordext, Isabel Margarita, 313, 314

Ortega, José María, 38

Ortiz, Benigno, 35

Otero, Ana, 51

Otero, Lisandro, 286, 368, 498, 504; and Christmas, 485; on revolution, 499

Otero, Rafael, 74

Padilla, Heberto, 411, 493

Palma, Joaquín de, 56

Panic of 1893, 107

Pardo Llada, José, 473–74

Partido Femenista de Cuba, 51

Partido Sufragista Cubano, 51

Pascual, Camilo, 272

Patiño, Antonio, 442

Pazos, Felipe, 480

Pedrosa, Paulina, 48

Peláez, Amelia, 413

Peña, José, 57

Pérez, Antanasio (Tony), 259

Pérez, Antonio Gonzalo, 86

Pérez, Emma, 349

Pérez Bueno, Francisco, 56

Pérez Prado, Dámaso, 206, 212

Pérez Rolo, Juan, 49

Pérez-Stable, Marifeli, 500

Phillips, Ruby Hart, 368, 384

Phonograph, 127, 390; in nineteenth century, 75; recordings, 203, 210–13

Pichardo, Manuel, 62; and Chicago Columbian Exposition, 68

Pierra, Fidel, 89

Piñeiro, Ignacio, 205
Piñera, Virgilio, 368
Piñeyro, Enrique, 39
Pittaluga, Gustavo, 422
Pla, Eduardo, 43
Platt Amendment, 110
Pogolotti, Marcelo, 293, 313, 421, 428, 465; and U.S. films, 288; education of, 411
Ponce, Marcial, 237
Ponce de León, Néstor, 43, 97
Ponce de León, Patricio, 106
Ponce de León, Ricardo, 33
Ponte Domínguez, Francisco, 71
Ponvert, Katherine, 224, 229, 230
Portell Vilá, Herminio, 428; on baseball, 271; and Caimanera, 352; on Cubans in United States, 420
Porter, Robert, 101, 106
Portuondo, María Dolores, 28
Portuondo Tamayo, Juan Miguel, 44
Poveda, José Manuel, 346
Presbyterian Church, 60, 230, 243, 246, 255, 395, 396; and education, 247, 252; and revolution, 477, 487–88
Press. See Newspapers
Prieto, Antonio, 79
Prieto, Isabel, 58
Progreso Artistic and Literary Society (Sancti-Spíritus), 63
Prohibition (Volstead Act), 167–69, 183–86
Protestant missionaries, 136, 242–55, 466–67; Methodists, 21, 56, 230, 231, 238, 243, 246, 247, 252, 254, 255, 395; and Cuban émigrés in United States, 55–60; and education, 57, 155, 246–48, 250, 252; in nineteenth century, 57–58; and Spanish colonialism, 57–60; and women, 58; Presbyterians, 60, 230, 243, 246, 255, 395, 396; Quakers, 155, 230, 232, 244, 246, 247, 248, 252, 255; Episcopalians, 155, 230, 243, 246, 247, 254–55, 395, 477; and U.S. sugar corporations, 230–31; Baptists, 244, 246, 247, 253–55, 257; and social services, 246; sources of appeal, 253–54; and Cuban ministers, 255; and Cuban revolution, 487–88
Prostitution, 285; in nineteenth century, 23;

and tourism, 193–94; and U.S. naval station, 239–42; during 1950s, 469–70

Quakers, 230, 231, 232, 244, 246, 248, 255–56; and education, 155, 247, 252
Quesada, Flora, 51
Quesada, Gonzalo de, 44
Quesada, Leopoldina, 51
Quesada Torres, Salvador, 103
Quílez, Alfredo, 420
Quincy, Margaret Morton, 20
Quintero, Héctor, 455

Race relations: within separatist coalition, 89–95; and formation of nationality, 90–95; and education, 92
Radio, 331–33, 346, 347
Railroad, 72, 107, 140, 282; in nineteenth century, 18, 19; operated by U.S. crews, 19; and U.S. manufactures, 19; and distribution of U.S. imports, 72–73; during U.S. military occupation (1898–1902), 117–18, 220–21; in early republic, 123; and tourism, 166
Ramírez, Arturo, 405, 425
Ramos, José Antonio, 137, 328, 356–57, 420–21, 423, 427; and U.S. influence, 53; and English language, 418
Recio, Carlos, 29
Reciprocity Treaty (1903), 110, 129
Reconcentration policy, 99–100
Recreational forms, 320, 390; and U.S. influence, 364, 369, 399
Retail trade, 367–68, 459; in colony, 70–71; in postcolonial period, 130–32; and credit purchases, 349–50; and supermarkets, 365–66; and catalog, 425–26
Revuelta, Naty, 483
Reyes, Rafael E. de los, 30
Reyes de Herrera, María Antonio, 87
Riera Gómez, Eliseo, 448–49
Rivero, José Ignacio, 481
Robreño, Gustavo, 46, 271, 340–41
Rodríguez, Adelaida, 155
Rodríguez, Alejandro, 103
Rodríguez, Arsenio, 206
Rodríguez, Carolina, 48

H. EUGENE AND LILLIAN YOUNGS LEHMAN SERIES

Lamar Cecil, *Wilhelm II: Prince and Emperor, 1859–1900* (1989).

Carolyn Merchant, *Ecological Revolutions: Nature, Gender, and Science in New England* (1989).

Gladys Engel Lang and Kurt Lang, *Etched in Memory: The Building and Survival of Artistic Reputation* (1990).

Howard Jones, *Union in Peril: The Crisis over British Intervention in the Civil War* (1992).

Robert L. Dorman, *Revolt of the Provinces: The Regionalist Movement in America* (1993).

Peter N. Stearns, *Meaning Over Memory: Recasting the Teaching of Culture and History* (1993).

Thomas Wolfe, *The Good Child's River,* edited with an introduction by Suzanne Stutman (1994).

Warren A. Nord, *Religion and American Education: Rethinking a National Dilemma* (1995).

David E. Whisnant, *Rascally Signs in Sacred Places: The Politics of Culture in Nicaragua* (1995).

Lamar Cecil, *Wilhelm II: Emperor and Exile, 1900–1941* (1996).

Jonathan Hartlyn, *The Struggle for Democratic Politics in the Dominican Republic* (1998).

Louis A. Pérez Jr., *On Becoming Cuban: Identity, Nationality, and Culture* (1999).